W9-AEM-063

LOUISIANA STATE UNIVERSITY AND A.&M. COLLEGE
LOUISIANA STATE
UNIVERSITY OF MISSISSIPPI
OXFORD
MISSISSIPPI

MISSISSIPPI STATE COLLEGE
RESEARCH LEARNING INDUSTRY
1878
MISS. STATE

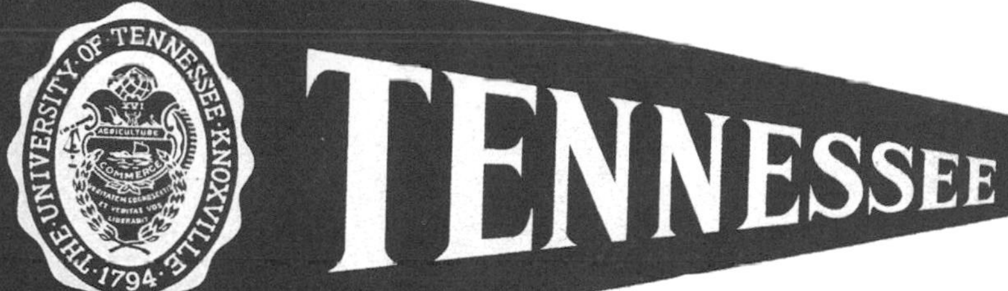
THE UNIVERSITY OF TENNESSEE KNOXVILLE
1794
TENNESSEE

SIGILLUM UNIVERSITATIS VANDERBILTAE
MDCCCLXXIII
VANDERBILT

The SEC

ALSO BY
BERT RANDOLPH SUGAR

Where Were You When the Lights Went Out? with Jackie Kannon
Race Riots
". . . Sting Like a Bee" with Jose Torres
Inside Boxing with Floyd Patterson
The Sports Collectors Bible
Houdini: His Life and Art
The Assassination Chain with Sybil Leek
The Horseplayers Guide to Winning Systems with Alec MacKenzie
"Who Was Harry Steinfeldt?" and Other Baseball Trivia Questions
Classic Baseball Cards
Great Baseball Players of the Past
Hall of Fame Baseball Cards
The Book of Sports Quotes
The World Series Book
The Nostalgia Collectors Bible
"The Thrill of Victory"
Hit the Sign and Win a Free Suit of Clothes from Harry Finklestein

The SEC

A Pictorial History of Southeastern Conference Football

Edited by

Bert Randolph Sugar

Foreword by Keith Jackson

THE BOBBS-MERRILL COMPANY, INC.
Indianapolis • New York

The following supplied pictures for THE SEC and deserve a special "Thanks": Kirk McNair, University of Alabama; Buddy Davidson, Auburn University; Norm Carlson, University of Florida; David Storey and Perry McIntyre, University of Georgia; Russell Rice, University of Kentucky; Paul Manasseh, LSU; "Bobo" Champion and Ralph Carpenter, University of Mississippi; Bob Hartley, Mississippi State University; Haywood Harris, University of Tennessee; Lew Harris, Vanderbilt University; and Joe Horrigan, Pro-Football Hall of Fame.

Published by The Bobbs-Merrill Company, Inc.
Indianapolis New York

Designed by M. E. Reed
Manufactured in the United States of America

First printing

Library of Congress Cataloging in Publication Data

Main entry under title:

The SEC: a pictorial history of Southeastern Conference football

1. Southeastern Conference—History. 2. Football—Southern States—Records. I. Sugar, Bert Randolph.
GV958.5.S59S18 796.33′263′0973 79-11591
ISBN 0-672-52517-8

This book is dedicated to those hundreds of thousands of fans
who have made SEC football number one in the nation
and in their hearts

Contents

Foreword

It has long been my feeling that the game of college football reflects the fabric of our society more than any other game we play and/or watch. Virtually all the elements of life can be found in sixty minutes of football except possibly childbirth; and if social change continues at the heady pace of the seventies through the eighties, even that might happen.

There are few instances of alleged entertainment and relaxation that can match a college football game in stirring the deepest flames of partisanship and outright (overt) provincialism. And down South you can color that partisanship passionate!

As a lad living on a west Georgia farm and getting acquainted with life, I can remember breaking a lot of Grannie's needles trying to keep an old football sewn together so I could throw it through a tire swinging from a hickory tree behind the barn. And I can still remember the furious conversation between an uncle and a nephew over which school the young man would play his football at. The uncle insisted emphatically that if the nephew went beyond the Plains of Auburn he would not be welcome at the uncle's hearth. The nephew did have a daring spirit, I'm happy to tell. He went as far as Tennessee. Lord only knows what might have happened if he had chosen Michigan!

Regional loyalty has obviously diminished everywhere over the years because of communications and transportation. But it still thrives with fervor in the South—and it's difficult to really find anything wrong with that. The old argument that young people should try to go to school where they want to live and grow still has great meaning.

Long before the Southeastern Conference was formed in 1933, Southerners' philosophy for college football and their appetite for the game were well established. Probably helped somewhat, too, by the fact that professional football didn't move into the region until after the Second World War and really didn't get a foothold until the late sixties. And probably only then because of an increasingly transient society.

I became a transient myself, taking my collegiate schoolwork at Washington State University—which is on the opposite corner of the nation from the bottomland where I was born and raised. But I have never lost the taste for college football the way it is played, coveted, argued about and fought over in the South.

It is not always easy to separate history and legend in sport, because so much of the history has been tempered and tampered with as the years passed. But I reckon there oughta be a few things in life that a person should be allowed to lie a little about, especially in sport, where no real damage can be done. Unless of course the Teller is from 'Bama and the Listener is from Tennessee . . . that might get a little touchy.

As you read this history of the Southeastern Conference, you should become more familiar with a long-running Yankee plaint: "Those ole boys may talk funny, but they sure don't think funny." And that has long since been proven in all venues well beyond the playing fields.

As we leave the seventies, there is only one member of the Southeastern Conference that is not a land grant college or a state university. That would be Vanderbilt. But in the football history of the SEC, Vandy is very prominent; and a lot of Commodore victories went a long way toward establishing the quality of Southern football in the early years. I can remember being told that you had to have a lot of walking-around money if you wanted to go to school at Vanderbilt. But when in later years I learned more about alumni salesmanship, I accepted that argument for what it was.

After better than a quarter century of traveling through the Southeast, broadcasting and televising college football, I still enjoy looking out across the stadium wall on a clear night and calling that yellow ball "a possum moon." I relish grits with my eggs in Birmingham, pee-can pie in Athens, salty ham, cornbread and buttermilk in Knoxville, key lime pie in Baton Rouge, and—if you know the right fella—a little touch of scuppernong wine just outside Phenix City on your way to Auburn. And it's hard not to spin around when you see a pretty little lady wearing ROLL TIDE in bold print across the seat of her britches.

You can't help but be impressed by the bottom line of all this weekend football fervor: that it is merchandising of the first order for the schools, the cities, the states and the region. Maintaining loyalty is a very important factor within any society. And it has been and is being done with stunning success in the Southeastern Conference.

The Sports Information Directors chronicled their respective team histories for this book; a gentleman whose name is Southern enough, Bert Randolph Sugar, put it together; and on its pages are names and successes and failures that are truly legendary in college football history.

You may well notice that *all* the current coaches of these SEC teams played and learned in the South. Though they traveled to many places to enrich their craft, all of them came home to practice it. That should tell us all something.

Keith M. Jackson
ABC Sports
January 1979

Preface

The Southeastern Conference is at once a patch of ground and a state of emotion. To some it is also a state of mind. Viewed dispassionately, it is ten teams in seven contiguous states playing that national institution, college football, every Saturday during the fall. But few in the Southeast view the game of football dispassionately.

To them, SEC football is to Southern life what fried chicken is to Southern cuisine: the main course *and* something special. They follow it secure in their knowledge that it is the best brand of football in America. Period. For they have seen more top ten teams, more All-Americans and more bowl champions than those produced by any other conference. And more heroics, hoopla and hyperbole as well.

While the rest of the country undergoes a quiet change in the colors of their regional foliage, the ten teams that make up the SEC provide their own autumnal coloration in the form of banners, floats, cheerleaders and brightly attired players—not to mention fans—all collaborating to make Southern football something more than a mere game. For in that special region of the country on a special day, college football is no longer an institution. It is, instead, an obsession, coloring the sights, sounds and smells of the fall season as nothing else can anywhere else in the country.

The color that is SEC football manifests itself in many ways: in the uniforms worn by each team—from the burnt orange and navy blue of Auburn to the orange and blue of Florida, from the old gold and black of Vanderbilt to the purple and gold of LSU and the red and black of Georgia, and from the blue and white of Kentucky to the cardinal red and navy blue of Ole Miss; in the nicknames of a number of its teams—from the Crimson Tide of Alabama to the Maroons of Mississippi State and Tennessee's Big Orange; and in the colorful names of some of those who have performed on the gridiron—including names like Red Lutz, Pinky Rohm and, of course, the doubly blessed Blondy Black.

But more importantly, the color of SEC football is a color that transcends the mere colors of the rainbow. It is also the color of the South. For where else but in the SEC could you find Dixie Howell, Cotton Clark and Showboat Boykin? Where else but in the SEC could you find each and every one of the ten member-schools involved in a traditional rivalry? Sometimes two? And where else could you find the citizens of an entire state rooting for *their* team, whether or not they attended the school? Only in the SEC, that's where!

The Southeastern Conference jumped full-grown out of the brow of the old Southern Conference, forming a thirteen-team amalgam from those teams in the old conference that were west and south of the Appalachians.

As sportswriter O. B. Keeler wrote in the 1933 *Illustrated Football Annual:* "Since the conclusion of the last football season there has been secession in Dixie. Rebellion, no less. One bright and sparkling day in December the old Southern Conference blew up with a detonation that shocked the natives as much as would the explosion of an under-nourished and water-logged firecracker.

"The old conference was too big and the geographical range too great for unity of thought and purpose. It stretched from the terrapin-infested shores of the Chesapeake and the bonded-bourbon depositories of Kentucky to the moss-hung oaks of Florida and Louisiana, and included twenty-three institutions of widely different scholastic and athletic standards. It was too unwieldy, everybody admitted.

"But the division took a funny turn. Thirteen colleges, which happened to include the half-dozen or so which usually have first-class football teams, seceded. They were Tulane, Alabama, Vanderbilt, Tennessee, Georgia Tech, Georgia, Auburn, Kentucky, Louisiana State, Florida, Sewanee, Mississippi and Mississippi State."

Since that day forty-six years ago, the basic makeup of the SEC has stayed remarkably stable, with only three teams dropping out along the way. But unlike Agatha Christie's ten little Indians, the ten that have remained have prospered during the intervening years. However, while some schools have developed traditional rivalries, both intrastate and across borders, others have remained like kissin' cousins once removed: close to each other but not in contact, like Alabama and Auburn, which went forty-one years without meeting each other. Still the SEC schedule is one of the strongest in the country, both within the Conference and outside. And the teams it has developed are, on the whole, unsurpassed by those of any other conference in the country. In fact, it has become a Southeastern way of life to count the fall season not so much by months as by wins; and the success of the season by a postprandial bowl bid.

The SEC: A Pictorial History of Southeastern Conference Football is a record, in words and pictures, of the many men and teams that have colored the SEC what it is today—the best in college football. But it is more, much more. For this book is also a celebration of the Conference itself, its glamorous forty-six-year history, its glorious present and its great future.

And for their hand in helping make this celebration possible and the book take form and flight, I wish to thank my own first team for helping a damnyankee—albeit one from up Virginia way—bring off what can only be described—as it has been by Roger Stanton, publisher of *The Football News*—as "The classic by which football books will be judged from now on." Those men who gave not only of themselves but of their knowledge and their picture files are Kirk McNair, University of Alabama; Buddy Davidson, Auburn University; Norm Carlson, University of Florida; David Storey and Dr. John Stegeman, University of Georgia; Russell Rice, University of Kentucky; Paul Manasseh, Louisiana State University; James "Bobo" Champion and Ralph Carpenter, University of Mississippi; Bob Hartley, Mississippi State; Haywood Harris, University of Tennessee; and Lew Harris and John Tischler, Vanderbilt University. Added to these representatives from the ten member schools are Mark Womack and Elmore "Scoop" Hudgins of the SEC office. To these "11" I can only say thank you all. Or, to be more idiomatically correct, "Thank y'all!"

Bert Randolph Sugar
June 1979

University of Alabama

by Kirk McNair

The Million Dollar Band spells out its favorite four-letter word.

The formation of the Southeastern Conference prior to the 1933 football season was not a factor in establishing the University of Alabama as a well-known football school. The Crimson Tide had already been in the football business for thirty-nine years and was recognized as one of the nation's football powerhouses, primarily because of its successful participation in the most prestigious of all games, the Rose Bowl.

Kirk McNair, sports information director for the University of Alabama, joined the Alabama staff in 1970 after serving as Assistant Sports Editor of the Birmingham Post-Herald.

Going into the 1933 season, Alabama boasted a 200–79–19 record and a winning percentage of better than .700. One of 'Bama's major accomplishments in those early years was a twenty-game winning streak put together under the coaching of the great Wallace Wade. The streak, which is still the longest in Alabama history, began with the last game of the 1924 season and carried through the ninth game of 1926. In addition, the Tide had forged winning records against all its traditional opponents save one, Georgia Tech, and although the All-American teams had been limited to Eastern players for almost half of 'Bama's first thirty-nine years of competition, by 1933 seven Alabama players had been honored with All-America recognition: tackle W. T. "Bully" Van De Graaff in 1915, quarterback A. T. S. "Pooley" Hubert in 1925, end Hoyt "Wu" Winslett in 1926, fullback Tony Holm in 1929, halfback John Suther and tackle Fred Sington in 1930, and fullback Johnny Cain in 1931.

The first of Alabama's many All-Americans—Tackle W. T. "Bully" Van De Graaff (1915).

Two games during that early period established both Alabama and Southern football as important football entities. In 1922 Alabama accomplished what few other teams from the South had been able to up until that time: the Tide defeated Pennsylvania, for one of the South's few wins against the East. The game was played in Philadelphia, with 'Bama coming out on top 9–7. Shorty Propst gave 'Bama a 2–0 lead when he blocked a punt for safety, but then Penn rallied to take the lead 7–2. In the fourth quarter, 'Bama's Charles Bartlett went twenty-nine yards to the Penn 6, and three plays later Allen Graham McCartee went in for the winning score. The win touched off the biggest victory celebration in Tuscaloosa history.

Football historians still speak of the 1926 Rose Bowl game as the most exciting in the annals of the Pasadena game. Washington, featuring the great halfback George Wilson, was widely regarded as the nation's finest team. Alabama, though undefeated and scored on only once (in a 50–7 win), was expected to be little trouble for Washington. The experts scoffed at 'Bama because its record had been forged against the likes of Union College, Birmingham Southern, LSU, Sewanee, Georgia Tech, Mississippi State, Kentucky, Florida and Georgia.

Washington made it look easy in the first half, rolling to a 12–0 lead. As Damon Runyon wrote in his Universal Service story:

"You wouldn't have given a nickel for Alabama's chances as the second half opened. The Crimson Tide of Southern football was on the ebb. Two touchdowns behind and badly outplayed by the champions of the Pacific Coast all throughout the first half—that was the situation. And 45,000 spectators . . . were wondering just what excuse the Alabamans had for coming here other than a desire to see the country. Then, suddenly, Alabama unleashed a species of human wildcat named Pooley Hubert, quarterback of the Alabama team. . . . and before the Washington lads fully realized what was happening this Pooley Hubert was all over them, kicking and scratching and throwing forward passes. . . . He was responsible more than any one man for Alabama's defeat of Washington by a score of 20–19."

'Bama struck for three touchdowns in less than seven minutes, the last two on passes from Hubert to Johnny Mack Brown, who later went to Hollywood to become a cowboy movie star.

Game referee Walter Eckersall wrote later:

"Washington is a mighty fine team and deserving of a lot of credit for its great game. But the lion's share of the honors belong to the team from Tuscaloosa, Alabama, a town now placed on the map by

The team that first brought Southern football to national prominence—the 1926 Rose Bowl champs.

The stars of 'Bama's first great football triumph—Johnny Mack Brown and Pooley Hubert.

a band of players who placed the Southern brand of football on a par at least with that played in other sections of the country. . . ."

The 1925 season was one of Alabama's five pre-SEC undefeated seasons, the others coming in 1897, 1906, 1926 and 1930. 'Bama returned to the Rose Bowl in 1927 to gain a 7–7 tie with Stanford, and again in 1931 to humble Washington State 31–0. After entering the SEC, 'Bama made three more trips to the Rose Bowl and compiled a sparkling 4–1–1 record in the granddaddy of bowl games before Pasadena shut off Southern entry.

In some respects, Alabama remains a football school of national rather than Conference stature. In the first year of Southeastern Conference competition, 'Bama's goal was not to win the league championship but to go to the Rose Bowl, because in those days the winner of the Rose Bowl was regarded as the closest thing to a national champion. As the Southeastern Conference nears its fiftieth anniversary, the goal at Alabama remains the national championship rather than the SEC title.

"We figure that if we're in contention for the national championship at the end of the season, the SEC championship will have taken care of itself," says Alabama head coach Paul "Bear" Bryant. "We want everyone involved with Alabama football setting their goals high."

This high-minded attitude has paid off, for unquestionably Alabama has not only dominated the Southeastern Conference, but remained in the forefront of the national football scene. At the conclusion of Coach Bryant's twenty-first season as head coach at 'Bama and the Tide's eighty-fourth year of collegiate football competition, Alabama boasts a record of 554–195–41, for a phenomenal winning percentage of .714—an average of less than three losses per season.

Alabama's 1978 SEC championship marked the Crimson Tide's sixteenth—the Tide has won thirteen championships outright and tied for three others. Thus, by shorthand calculation, 'Bama has won every third championship. No other school has been involved in more than eight championships. 'Bama has won seven of the nine championships during the 1970s, and eleven times during Coach Bryant's twenty-one-year reign the SEC title has gone to Tuscaloosa.

Since the formation of the SEC, the Tide's intra-Conference record of 212–79–19, for a winning percentage of .714, is far and away the best. Tennessee is a distant second with a 162–92–16 mark, for a winning percentage of .630. Somewhat surprisingly, Alabama has been the SEC runner-up five times and has had only five losing records and only eight second-division finishes in its forty-five years of SEC competition.

Among 'Bama's SEC lodge brothers, only Tennessee has a respectable record against the Tide in league play. Tennessee trails by only 22–17–6 in a series that has attained national prominence. Alabama's great "winning tradition" includes the winning of twenty-one of thirty-one games against Auburn and Georgia, nine of eleven against Florida, fifteen of sixteen (with one tie) against Kentucky, seventeen of twenty-six (with two ties) against LSU, nine of fourteen (with one tie) against Ole Miss, and thirty of forty-three (with four ties) against Vanderbilt.

'Bama's most thoroughly dominated opponent is the one who is closest geographically. It's only ninety miles from Tuscaloosa to Starkville, but over the years the football distance between 'Bama and Mississippi State has grown far greater. Although the teams meet each year, most of the players on the two teams were not even born the last time Alabama lost—in 1957. Twenty-one straight Tide wins have pushed the Tide's record against State to 35–6–1. As for former SEC opponents, Alabama's record is 3–0 against Sewanee, 17–9–1 against Georgia Tech, and 14–7–2 against Tulane.

Since SEC play began in 1933, Alabama has had four head football coaches. Frank Thomas was the Tide's head coach when the SEC was formed, having taken over the coaching reins from the great Wallace Wade in 1931. Thomas's fifteen-year record of 115–24–7 included thirteen years of SEC competition, during which he amassed a league record of 59–16–6 and four Conference championships. Harold "Red" Drew took over the 'Bama fortunes in 1947 and compiled an eight-year record of 54–29–7, including a 33–21–7 mark in SEC play and one SEC title. J. B. Whitworth was at the helm during the three bleak years from 1955 through 1957. During that time the Tide was the league's doormat, compiling an overall record of only 4–24–2 and a league mark of 3–18–1—including three of 'Bama's five losing seasons. The Tide's fortunes *had* to improve.

Hall of Fame coach Wallace Wade, whose 'Bama teams from 1923 through 1930 won sixty-one, lost thirteen, and tied two.

But no one could have imagined how much they were to improve when Paul "Bear" Bryant was called by his alma mater in 1958. A sophomore letterman on 'Bama's first SEC team in 1933, Coach Bryant had gone on to serve as head coach at Maryland, Kentucky, and Texas A & M, and earned a national reputation as a winner. He had rebuilt both the Kentucky and the Texas A & M programs and then coached the teams through their greatest eras, compiling an overall record of 91–39–8. In his twenty-one years at Alabama, he has compiled a 193–38–8 record, for a winning percentage of .824, and his teams have dominated the SEC with a record of 117–24–5, including eleven Conference titles.

But it is the race for the national championship that consumes Alabama players, coaches and followers. When the Associated Press began its national football poll in 1936, Alabama finished fourth, posting an 8–0–1 record (5–0–1 in SEC play). Surprisingly, LSU finished second, ahead of Alabama for the SEC title. 'Bama was rated fourth again in 1937, winning the SEC championship for the third time. Alabama has played forty-two seasons of football since that first year of AP polling and has finished in the nation's top ten more than half of those years. United Press International joined the polling business in 1950, and since then the Tide has made the UPI top ten a total of sixteen times.

In some years the polls were made prior to bowl games, and in some years they were made following bowl games. 'Bama has both benefited and suffered as a result of the timing of national polls. AP national championships were awarded to 'Bama's 1961 and 1964 teams before the bowl games. Alabama's 1961 team won its bowl game, but the 1964 team lost. As a result, in 1965 the AP decided that its national champion would be determined after the bowl games. What a stroke of luck for 'Bama, ranked only fourth in the nation with an 8–1–1 record! A series of upsets set up the Orange Bowl as the national championship game, and the Tide's 39–28 victory over Nebraska gave 'Bama its second straight national title.

UPI concurred with AP in 1961 and 1964, but awarded its 1965 championship prior to the bowl games. 'Bama fans had to appreciate UPI's pre-bowl selection process in 1973, however, when the Tide reaped the crown, only to lose its hold on first place (and the consensus national championship) by losing to Notre Dame in the Sugar Bowl. That 24–23 Irish win ranks with the greatest bowl games of all time and accounts for one of four times that Notre Dame has denied the national crown to Alabama.

And then there was 1978. 'Bama followers felt that they had been robbed in 1977; still, even the most hard-bitten could at least understand—if not appreciate—the logic of a team jumping from fifth to first by virtue of a win over the previously undefeated and number one–ranked team, Notre Dame's route to the title. But apparently what was to work for one was not allowed to work again, as the Tide, ranked number two in both polls prior to the bowls, dropped undefeated and number one–ranked Penn State 14–7 in the 1979 Sugar Bowl, and was bypassed by UPI, who selected Southern Cal, the winners in the Rose Bowl and winners over 'Bama during the year. However, AP delivered the only verdict possible when on January 3 they voted Alabama number one in the country for 1978!

By the time the first football season in Southeastern Conference history had begun, Frank Thomas had already thrown off the mantle of Wallace Wade and established himself as a brilliant football strategist and staunch disciplinarian. A former player at Notre Dame under Knute Rockne (and roommate of the legendary George Gipp), Thomas employed the Notre Dame box as his primary offense. In his first two seasons he compiled a 17–1 record. But there was concern in the Crimson Tide camp: John "Hurry" Cain, an All-American back in 1931 and later a member of the National Football Hall of Fame, had graduated; Tom Hupke, All-Southern guard as a junior in 1932, had been injured in an automobile

Frank Thomas, the first Notre Dame graduate to coach at a Southern school. In fifteen years, his team won 108 games.

accident; and the two men who had alternated at center in 1932 had both graduated.

Alabama opened its 1933 season with an easy 34–0 victory over Oglethorpe. The newcomers showed promise—notably left halfback Millard "Dixie" Howell. Oglethorpe Coach Harry Robertson predicted after the game that 'Bama could go undefeated using either its first or its second team. His prediction, however, proved false, as the following week a lightly regarded Ole Miss team battled 'Bama to a scoreless tie in Birmingham. The Rebels nearly turned their moral victory into an actual one, just missing on two late field-goal attempts. And so Alabama's chances of winning the first SEC title had been practically wiped out in its first-ever Conference game.

As had been the case in most seasons, Mississippi State proved easy fare for 'Bama, succumbing in an 18–0 victory. But then it was on to Knoxville to face Coach Robert Neyland's Tennessee, the Tide's most bitter rival—even at that time. Tennessee had posted a classic victory over the Crimson Tide in 1932 and had suffered only three losses in eight years—none in Knoxville—since the great Neyland had become head coach.

Dixie Howell, who would gain All-American honors and be named to the National Football Hall of Fame as well as to the all-time Rose Bowl team, was the star of the day against Tennessee. Howell had a great day punting (including an 89-yard effort that is still the longest in 'Bama history), returning punts, rushing and passing. He scored on a 4-yard run in the fourth quarter to give the Tide a 12–6 win.

Millard F. "Dixie" Howell, the throwing end of the famed "Howell-to-Hutson" passing duo.

The old Southern Conference, composed of twenty-three teams stretching from Virginia to Louisiana, had made it difficult to keep up with a championship race. Now, with thirteen teams in the Southeastern Conference, it was easier to determine contenders. With its victory over Tennessee, 'Bama was back in the race.

A loss to Fordham in New York the following week by a 2–0 score was 'Bama's last setback for the first year of SEC play. 'Bama rolled to a 20–0 victory over Kentucky and a 27–0 win over non-Conference foe Virginia Tech. Then the Crimson Tide went to Atlanta to meet Georgia Tech. The Engineers were not having a good season, but by all accounts they had been a team of bad luck. Again it was Dixie Howell who led 'Bama to a 12–9 win, scoring on runs of 8 and 11 yards. Now there were only two undefeated teams in the SEC—Alabama, which had a tie, and LSU.

Alabama met Vanderbilt on Thanksgiving Day, November 30, and the Friday morning newspapers would declare Alabama the first champion of the Southeastern Conference. Again it was the superlative play of Dixie Howell that carried the day; on fourth down from the Vanderbilt 3, he went over left end, stumbled just before reaching the goal line, and then carried the ball in. 'Bama's 7–0 victory, coupled with LSU's tie with Tulane, clinched the championship for the Tide.

At the conclusion of the 1933 season, 'Bama had hopes of a trip to Pasadena for the Rose Bowl. Stanford was the West Coast representative, and the 1927 game between Stanford and Alabama, which had ended in a 7–7 tie, was considered a classic, a game worthy of a rematch. But the call never came to Tuscaloosa, and 'Bama began readying itself to defend its SEC championship by commencing spring training soon after the conclusion of the 1933 season.

Alabama and Tulane have met on the football field relatively few times, and they did not play each other during the 1934 season. As a result, in its second year of play, the Southeastern Conference had its first tie for a championship—Tulane finishing with an 8–0 league record and Alabama with a 7–0 mark. However, to Alabama went the spoils, the coveted Rose Bowl invitation.

Prior to the 1934 season, the football in general use at that time was redesigned. The ball, which had looked like a pregnant goat's bladder, was slimmed down in the middle, allowing for greater control. According to Coach Thomas, the innovation was instrumental in the development of one of college football's all-time-great passing combinations, "Dixie" Howell to Don Hutson.

The 1934 season was an interesting one for Howell. Because he had been injured the previous spring, he was moved to right halfback (wingback) during early fall drills. However, Coach Thomas soon realized that he needed Dixie at the left halfback (tailback) position, so Howell was moved back to that crucial position. During the season Howell spent only thirteen minutes practicing at full speed; he spent most of each workout with a scrub center and a receiver, away from contact work. In 'Bama's 41–0 victory over Mississippi State, Coach Thomas did not even play Howell or his backup Joe Riley.

Alabama went into its final game of the 1934 season with the knowledge that a victory over Vanderbilt would bring a Rose Bowl invitation. Vandy also had an incentive—the game would be the last one for Coach Dan McGurgin, retiring after thirty-one years of coaching the Commodores. A tough, close contest was expected, one of national importance. NBC broadcast the game to the nation over its radio hookup—it was one of the first Southeastern Conference games to be carried on the network. However, 'Bama made a shambles of McGurgin's valedictory, beating Vandy 34–0. The game was the climax of a 10–0 season in which the Tide rolled up the nation's high of 287 points, giving up only 32, none in its final three games. The very next day the Tide accepted an invitation to the Rose Bowl.

Famed sportswriter Grantland Rice described Alabama's convincing 29–13 victory over Stanford in the twenty-first Rose Bowl thusly: "Dixie Howell, the human howitzer from Hartford, Alabama, blasted the Rose Bowl dreams of Stanford today with one of the greatest all-round exhibitions football has ever known."

Alabama had electrified the 1935 Rose Bowl crowd with a 22-point second quarter that put the game away. Howell passed for 96 yards during that frantic quarter, completing four passes to Hutson and three to 'Bama's now-famous "other end," Bear Bryant; he ran for another 96 yards, including a sensational 67-yard touchdown sprint.

Following the conclusion of the 1934 season, Howell, Hutson and tackle Bill Lee, the 'Bama captain, were voted All-American honors, and guard Charlie Marr joined them on the All-SEC team. Also given All-SEC mention were Bryant, center "Kay" Francis, and quarterback Riley Smith. In 1969 the famed combination of Howell and Hutson was honored by being chosen the subject for one of four paintings commemorating the first one hundred years of college football.

Alabama's 1935 season got off on the wrong foot with a 7–7 tie with little Howard College of Birmingham. On a Tide touchdown play that would have won the game, 'Bama's end Paul Bryant was detected off side, and he said later that he would never forget the game as long as he lived. Following the tie, 'Bama went on to six victories and two defeats, posting a mediocre 4–2 league record. The losses were to Mississippi State (20–7 in Tuscaloosa) and then to Vanderbilt (14–6 in Nashville) in the season finale. In the Tide's loss to Mississippi State, Bryant suffered a broken leg, but the next week he tore off the cast and played against Tennessee.

In 1936 the Tide narrowly missed winning its third SEC championship, finishing with an overall record of 8–0–1 and a league mark of 5–0–1. 'Bama came within a yard of tying for the title. In its game against Tennessee, played in terrible weather and featuring outstanding punting and defense, 'Bama's Joe Riley was brought down 3 feet short of the goal line.

The 1936 season saw 'Bama turn in five shutouts and give up more than one touchdown in only one game, a 20–16 victory over Georgia Tech in Atlanta. Alabama was not highly regarded at the beginning of the season, but by the season's end the Tide was one of the nation's candidates for a Rose Bowl berth. 'Bama closed out the season with impressive wins over Tulane (34–7), Georgia Tech (20–16), and Vanderbilt (14–6). The Sugar Bowl was now in its second year, and in the early going it preferred to host one of the Louisiana teams, Tulane or LSU, so 'Bama did not get a bowl bid.

About 1930, Alabama picked up the nickname the Red Elephants because of the huge size of its players. It was, however, a streamlined Crimson Tide that marched through the 1937 campaign, with no starter weighing more than 200 pounds. Twenty years later Bear Bryant's teams would feature the same type of light, fast, hard-hitting players.

The 1937 Alabama team regained the SEC crown and received a Rose Bowl bid. Pre-season newspapers predicted a successful season, and Alabama lived up to expectations by rolling to a perfect 9–0 regular season record, turning in six shutouts. In regular season play 'Bama piled up 225 points to just 20 for the opposition. The Tide finished the season as the nation's only major undefeated and untied team, thanks to Sandy Sanford's last-minute heroics against Vanderbilt when he kicked a 22-yard field goal from a severe angle with only three minutes to play.

Alabama's appearance on New Year's Day resulted in the Crimson Tide's only loss in Rose Bowl play. California demonstrated too much power and speed,

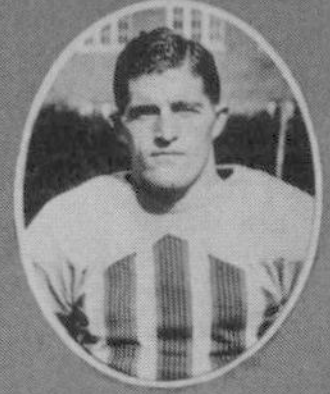

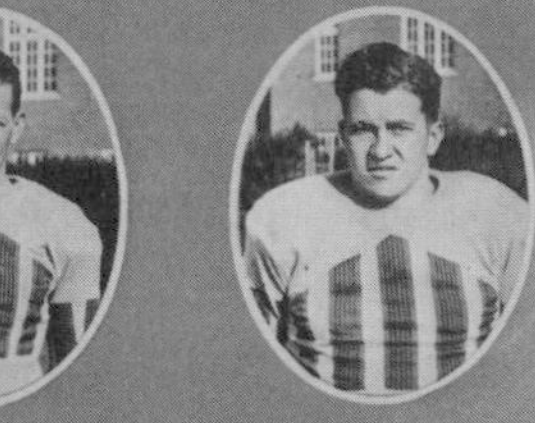

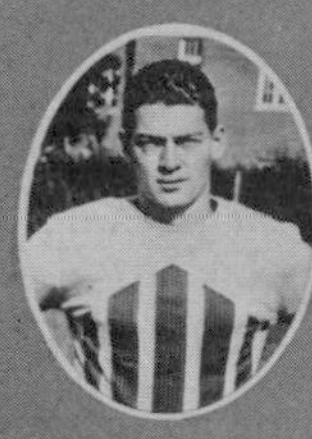

The 1934 national champions, victors over Stanford in the 1935 Rose Bowl.

"The Other End" on the 1934 team—Paul William "Bear" Bryant.

better balance, and some exceptionally skilled and rugged players. And 'Bama was plagued by its own mistakes, giving up the ball eight times on four fumbles and four interceptions. One of the fumbles came at the California 1, another at the 6. Although 'Bama was stung by the loss, the then incredible payoff of over $100,000 (today the Rose Bowl pays over $1½ million to each team), as well as a hero's welcome when the club returned home, lightened the burden of the loss.

Following the 1937 season 'Bama fans had just cause to be proud of their team, the owners of the nation's best record over the previous five years, 40–5–3, an auspicious start in the SEC. However, for the next three years the SEC crown would go to 'Bama's most troublesome rival, Tennessee. During that three-year period, 'Bama would not defeat the Volunteers—and to this day Alabama has never won an SEC championship while losing to Tennessee, just as Tennessee has never won the title while losing to Alabama. The third Saturday in October, more often than any other weekend, has determined the league's champion.

Alabama opened the 1938 season with a trip to the West Coast and a major victory over Southern Cal, 19–7. Shutout victories over Howard and North Carolina State added to the luster of a team that West Coast critics acclaimed as better than the 1937 squad. Alabama and Minnesota were recognized as the nation's two finest teams, and Alabama Governor Bibb Graves earnestly proposed that the two teams meet in a charity game in New York or Chicago to raise $1 million for Red Cross relief for the storm-ravaged Northeast.

Nothing came of the proposal, however, and ten days later, when Tennessee thrashed 'Bama in Birmingham 13–0, the proposal was forgotten, as were 'Bama's chances for the SEC championship. The Tide never threatened against the smaller—but faster—Vols. With five shutouts and a tie against Georgia Tech, Alabama went on to a respectable 7–1–1 season. The Tide's record was good enough for a tie with Tulane for a second-place finish in the SEC, but still was a disappointment for 'Bama's fans, who had entered the season with much higher hopes.

Frank Thomas experienced his first poor season in 1939 as the Tide struggled to a 5–3–1 record after winning its first three games. In an all-or-nothing scenario, 'Bama shut out four opponents, and in turn was shut out by three of its opponents—including Tennessee 21–0, as the Vols went through the regular season undefeated, untied and unscored-upon and finished eighth in the thirteen-team Conference.

Alabama started the 1940 season with only ten lettermen and the aftereffects of Thomas's first mediocre campaign the previous year—a season that saw the Tide struggle to a 5–3–1 record and an eighth-place finish in the thirteen-team SEC. And yet, despite all the less-than-encouraging signs, 'Bama followers still possessed great expectations for a standout season.

It was obvious to all that the season would turn on the Tennessee game, when 'Bama would play the team that had beaten them the previous two years. No team had ever defeated Alabama three seasons in a row. And so, the reasoning went, when the two teams met on October 19, Alabama would have its chance not only for retribution, but hopefully for a national crown as well.

By the time of the game the two rivals were still unbeaten, and Tennessee unscored upon. The game attracted national attention as a "shoot-out" between two of the nation's finest teams, a showdown for Conference and national honors. The Tide's Jimmy

Jimmy Nelson, All-SEC halfback 1940 and 1941, who set a 'Bama record with three touchdown catches in one game.

Nelson was outstanding—but in defeat. For Johnny Butler, filling in for Tennessee's great tailback Bob Foxx, who was injured, ruined 'Bama for the second straight year with long runs and pinpoint passes. Tennessee's 27–12 victory marked one of only two games in which the Vols would give up points on the way to a 10–0 record for regular-season play. And it was one of only two losses for Alabama, who finished third in the Conference, behind Tennessee and Mississippi State.

Alabama finally broke the Tennessee spell in 1941 and ended the season with a respectable 9–2 record. However, both losses came during Conference play—to Mississippi State and Vanderbilt—and State won its sole SEC title that year. An Alabama win over State would have given the title to 'Bama regardless of the outcome of the Vanderbilt game, while a win by Tennessee over the Tide would have given the Vols their fourth straight championship. But State's

Ball crooked in the arm of Holt Rast, All-American end, marks the end of the three-year domination of the Tide by Tennessee (1941).

convincing win blunted 'Bama's chances. When 'Bama met Vanderbilt in the Tide's final game, it was rumored that the winner would receive a bowl bid, either to the Sugar Bowl or to the Orange Bowl, although Vandy's invitation would depend on the Commodores' also beating Tennessee the following week. Vandy gained a 7–0 victory over Alabama but lost the following week's game to Tennessee. Alabama's bowl hopes were considered dashed as the team headed for its final game against Miami. State sentiment was high for Alabama and Auburn, who had not met since athletic relations had been broken off following a riot in 1907, to play a post-season game. However, plans for the game were canceled when on December 1 the Tide was invited to play in the Cotton Bowl in Dallas against Texas A & M.

'Bama's first bowl trip other than to Pasadena was clouded by World War II, but the game against Texas A & M was one of the most bizarre in the history of Crimson Tide football. The Tide made only 1 first down to 13 for Texas A & M. Alabama picked up only 75 yards total offense to 309 for the Aggies. The Tiders clicked on just 1 pass while A & M completed 13. And 'Bama ran 32 plays while Texas A & M ran 79. Yet the Tide led 29–7 midway in the fourth quarter, held off an Aggie rush at the end, and finished with a 29–21 victory. Significantly, Alabama had 7 pass interceptions and 5 fumble recoveries. 'Bama scored on a long punt return by Jimmy Nelson and a pass interception runback by Holt Rast. All other scores resulted from short drives, the result of Texas A & M turnovers.

Joe Domnanovich, All-American center and captain of 'Bama's 1943 Orange Bowl team.

By the 1942 season, the war was beginning to take its toll on college football. Some schools, for instance, did not even field teams that season, and Alabama's schedule included games with Pensacola Naval Air Station and Georgia Pre-Flight. Before the season Coach Thomas predicated that 'Bama would have a good team. Halfway through the schedule he was proving an accurate prophet, as the Tide had given up only one touchdown, that in a 21–6 "revenge" against Mississippi State. 'Bama defeated Tennessee and thereby was practically conceded the League championship. However, Alabama had three games left with teams from the state of Georgia—the University of Georgia, Georgia Tech and Georgia Pre-Flight—and the Tide came up the losers against all three, finishing the season with a 7–3 record and a fifth-place Conference finish. Nevertheless, by this time Alabama was the number one name in post-season bowl play, and the Orange Bowl came calling. The opponent was a Mike Holovak–led Boston College team. The Easterners stung 'Bama with two first-quarter touchdowns, but 'Bama had forged into a 22–21 lead by halftime, and went on to a 37–21 victory.

There was no football team at Alabama in 1943, as the war came first. Coach Thomas spent most of his time heading war bond drives, but he did not forget football. He was actively recruiting, particularly a skinny little halfback in Birmingham who wasn't interested in going to college despite nationwide attention. His name was Harry Gilmer, and he planned to get a job and get married upon graduation from high school. But Coach Thomas hired Gilmer's high school coach, Malcolm Laney, and Gilmer followed. Gilmer played football in 1944, and thirty-five years after his arrival at the University he is still considered by many to have been Alabama's greatest player.

The 1944 team was a band of teenagers, sprinkled with a few men who were ineligible for the military draft. The squad tied LSU 27–27 in its first game, a game the 150-pound Gilmer said would be "just like a high school game" as far as he was concerned. 'Bama went on to a 5–1–2 regular-season record, including a shocking 19–0 victory over the Shorty McWilliams–led Mississippi State team, then unde-

All-SEC guard Don Whitmire (1942).

Harry Gilmer, who holds the 'Bama record for longest touchdown run—95 yards—takes off on another gallop.

feated. When bowl invitations were announced, no one was more surprised than Frank Thomas when Alabama received a bid from the Sugar Bowl to meet a great Duke team made up of veteran Navy trainees. There was some sentiment that 'Bama should not go to the game, because the freshmen would obviously be no match for the Blue Devils. But Thomas, who said later that the "war babies" were his favorite team, took them to New Orleans nevertheless.

The trip to the Sugar Bowl made Alabama the first team to attend all four major bowls—Rose, Cotton, Orange and Sugar. And the 1945 Sugar Bowl is still considered one of the greatest of all bowl games. The lead changed hands four times, and the outcome was uncertain until the final play. Most of the 72,000 in attendance were on their feet for the entire game. Duke won the game 29–26, but Alabama won the hearts of America's football fans. Grantland Rice watched Gilmer complete eight of eight passes and in his game story called him "the greatest college passer I ever saw." Rice concluded his report: "I've never seen a more thrilling game."

Alabama's 1945 team could have been its greatest. The Tide rolled up 430 points—averaging over 50 points in five games, including a 71–0 victory over Vanderbilt—and gave up only 80, the closest score being its 28–14 victory over Georgia. As the SEC champion and second-ranking team in the country, behind the mighty Army team of Davis and Blanchard, 'Bama was selected as the East's representative to the Rose Bowl, an invitation that shocked Army Coach Earl Blaik.

When asked which team he would prefer for an opponent, Gilmer did not hesitate. "Southern Cal," he said, "because they've never been beaten in the Rose Bowl." Alabama fans could be justly proud of their team's 3–1–1 mark in previous Rose Bowl games, but the record paled when compared to Southern Cal's perfect mark of eight wins in eight appearances.

Former All-American center Vaughn Mancha, who returned to Alabama in 1945 in the position of athletic director.

The game itself belied Southern Cal's invincibility. It was no contest—'Bama won 34–14, rolling up 351 yards in total offense to the Trojans' 41 (with only 6 rushing). The score was 27–0 before Southern Cal had a first down. Gilmer, of course, was the star, passing for one touchdown and rushing for 116 yards on 16 carries. West Coast writers said afterwards that the score might easily have been 50–0 had Thomas not pulled out his starters early in the game.

The 1946 team was Coach Thomas's last. He had begun to lose energy early in the 1945 season and in the spring of 1946 was warned of high blood pressure. In 1946 he coached from an elevated trailer, using a loudspeaker because of his weakness. 'Bama won its first four games and was preparing to meet Tennessee when the University president, Dr. Raymond Paty, suggested that Thomas resign as head coach for his own good. Thomas refused. 'Bama had eight starters returning from its great 1945 team, including the starting backfield. Seven of the eight had also started in 1944. But the 1946 team won only seven games and lost four. Tennessee, Georgia, LSU and Boston College were all victors over 'Bama in road games. Co-champions Tennessee and Georgia both scored shutout victories over 'Bama. At the end of the season, Coach Thomas resigned as head football coach, retaining his title of director of athletics, and Alabama's second great era of football had ended.

Harold "Red" Drew had been as much a fixture at Alabama as Frank Thomas. Drew had originally been with Thomas at Chattanooga and had replaced him there as head coach in 1928 when Thomas left. He joined Thomas at Alabama as end coach in 1931 and stayed with him through 1942, when he joined the Navy. Drew returned in 1945, only to depart again in 1946, to become head coach at Ole Miss. But when the head slot opened up at Alabama, Drew was released from the last two years of his three-year contract to take over the fortunes of the Crimson Tide.

Coach Drew's first Alabama team, the 1947 crew, had twenty-one lettermen returning, including many of the war babies, who were now seniors. Harry

Head coach H. D. "Red" Drew, who led the Tide to a 54–28–7 record in eight years.

Gilmer was featured as one of the nation's outstanding players. He had finished in the top seven in Heisman trophy balloting his sophomore and junior years, and would finish fifth for the second time as a senior. While Coach Drew worried publicly about the most difficult schedule in the Tide's history, the Alabama legislature tried to make 'Bama's task all the more difficult by insisting that Alabama restore relations with Auburn. Athletic Director Thomas had been fighting such a move, believing that resumption of relations could help only Auburn, whose athletic kitty had not prospered as well as Alabama's. But the legislature won the battle by threatening to cut off funds to both schools if a game was not played by 1949.

'Bama's 1947 season started on a less than promising note, as the Tide lost back-to-back games to Tulane (20–21) and Vanderbilt (7–14) in the second and third games of the campaign. Then 'Bama straightened itself out and came back to win the remaining seven games on its schedule—including a 13–0 victory over a favored Kentucky team coached by young Bear Bryant, Bryant's second loss at the hands of his alma mater and the last time he was to coach against them—and a bid to the Sugar Bowl.

The 1948 game was 'Bama's second trip to the Sugar Bowl and its second loss, this time to Texas, 27–7. For Harry Gilmer, who had enjoyed such an outstanding game three years before as a freshman, it was a disappointing "declincher" to his collegiate career. In what by his own admission was "the worst day of my career," Gilmer completed only 3 of 11 passes and ran for only 5 yards. The star of the game was his opposite number on the Texas team, quarterback Bobby Layne.

In 1948 'Bama lost four games for the second time in three seasons, beginning with its opener in New Orleans against Tulane down through a 35–0 lambasting at the hands of Conference champion Georgia, the worst shellacking an Alabama team had suffered since 1910.

But despite its 6–4–1 record, the Tide did manage to salvage much of the season in one game: the finale against Auburn that marked the renewal of their intrastate rivalry after a forty-one-year interruption. Although Alabama had lost the battle of the Auburn question, they did not lose the game.

In a game that had been arranged with all the subtlety of a shotgun wedding, Alabama, led by Eddie Salem, a sophomore who had just begun to hit his stride late in the season, was made a two-touchdown favorite over Auburn, led by Travis Tidwell. The game was more than a game—it was the mating of two natural opponents after almost two score years. And the excited football fans in the state greeted the renewal of their rivalry with over 130,000 requests for tickets.

Eddie Salem, responsible for eighteen 'Bama touchdowns in 1950.

But if it was more than a game, it was also no game at all, as the Tidal Wave piled up over 400 yards total offense, while Auburn managed only 3 yards rushing and 45 passing. The final score of 55–0 included 1 run and 3 passes for touchdowns by Salem—who completed 8 out of 10 passes for 159 yards—and a blocked punt that was turned into a Tide touchdown. (But the blocked punt was not remembered nearly as well as later blocked punts in this famed series.)

Pre-season predictions in 1949 had Alabama finishing no better than eighth in the SEC. As it turned out, the season was not that disastrous; as the Tide compiled a 6–3–1 record, earning sixth place in the standings. The Tide started out with losses to Tulane and Vanderbilt before rolling over Duquesne in the home opener. General Bob Neyland's Vols were headed for another good season when Tennessee met Alabama in Birmingham. Neither team was a championship contender, but the game they played on October 15, a 7–7 tie, was one of the finest ever seen in the long series. Alabama linebacker Pat O'Sullivan, who had been instrumental in the Tide's 10–0 defeat of Tennessee in 1947, was again the 'Bama star, making tackles all over the field, recovering two fumbles, and intercepting a pass. 'Bama then rolled up five straight victories before taking on Auburn. The Tide was a three-touchdown favorite, but one of the few upsets in this series occurred in 1949. Auburn had won only one game going in, but the Tigers came away with a 14–13 victory that was no fluke. Alabama, still playing from the old Notre Dame box as well as from the new T-formation, had a chance to salvage a tie with just over a minute to play, but Salem, who had hit seven extra points in a row in the 1948 romp, was far to the left on the tying try.

With more than half of the 1949 team returning, Alabama and its followers greeted the opening of the 1950 season with renewed optimism. The Tide was not a big team, particularly on the line, but Salem and Butch Avinger were joined by outstanding performers in the persons of Bobby Marlow, guard Mike Mizerany, and end Al Larry. Returning lettermen included linebacker Pat O'Sullivan and a senior tackle whose family would ultimately become an Alabama tradition, Herb Hannah. The 1950 season also saw Alabama join the modern football era, as it began using the split-T formation more and more—and, reluctantly, platoon football.

It did not take long for the Tide's train to begin running off the tracks. By the halfway mark 'Bama had lost two games: Bill Wade threw three touchdown passes as Vanderbilt upset 'Bama; and then there was the Tide's traditional nemesis, Tennessee. When the Tide and Tennessee met in Knoxville, it was generally conceded that the winner's stock in national ratings would skyrocket, while the loser would drop among the also-rans. Tennessee scored a touchdown in the final minutes, and one of Alabama's finest efforts went unrewarded. Despite an Alabama ground game that produced 314 yards, the Vols were 14–9 winners. After the Tennessee setback, Alabama got its game together and closed out the season with six straight victories, outscoring its final half-dozen foes by a 210 to 46 margin. Bobby Marlow had his first of three great games against Auburn, as he led the Tide to a 34–0 victory with 113 yards on 23 carries, 3 of them for touchdowns.

Alabama had never lost more than four games in any one season and had not suffered a losing season since the infancy of Crimson Tide football—a 3–4 mark in 1903. But 1951 was to change all of that, as 'Bama posted a 5–6 season and an eighth-place finish in the SEC standings. The season had started brightly enough with an 89–0 trouncing of Delta State. But four straight losses followed. Then, just when it appeared that the Tide might be able to pull out a winning season after all, back-to-back losses to Georgia Tech and Florida sealed the Tide's fate for the season. However, 'Bama did salvage state bragging rights with a 25–7 victory over Auburn, as Bobby Marlow rushed for 233 yards—still an Alabama one-game record—and caught 3 touchdown passes, setting a Conference record with 12 touchdown catches for the year.

Red Drew's contract had not been renewed for the 1953 season, and a recurrent question throughout

Bobby Marlow, who rushed for an average of 6.4 yards per carry in three games against Auburn, gaining more than 100 yards per game—including the 'Bama single-game record, 233 yards (1951).

the 1952 season was whether he was fighting for his job. If he was worried about it, he did not let it affect his discipline. Three players were married prior to the season, knowing that this meant loss of scholarship, but Drew did not relent. Pre-season predictions varied as to whether 'Bama would be strong in 1952, but few predicted the 10–2 season the Tide was to have. A 20–0 shutout at the hands of Tennessee in Knoxville and a 7–3 loss to Georgia Tech in Atlanta dropped 'Bama to fourth place in the SEC. But a closing win over highly regarded Maryland and another shutout over Auburn (Marlow gained 132 yards on 28 carries and set a Tide record with 950 yards for the season, 2560 for his career) gave 'Bama its first bowl bid in five years. The Tide was to meet Syracuse in the Orange Bowl. But Drew still did not have his contract, and word was out that if it was allowed to run out at midnight on December 31, hours before the Orange Bowl game, Drew and his staff and many players would not show for the game. However, that confrontation was sidestepped when Drew, who had just been named SEC Coach of the Year, was awarded a new two-year contract.

It was estimated that fewer than half of the 66,208 who attended the 1954 Orange Bowl stayed around for the end. It was the first time that all four major bowl games were televised, and the TV directors begged Orange Bowl officials to cut the final quarter short since the game was approaching three hours. The reason? Alabama was drubbing Syracuse 61–6, breaking fifteen Orange Bowl records. Coach Drew tried to keep the scoring down by playing everyone, but as tackle Van Marcus said, "We didn't want to leave any records still standing," and the parade continued. Among those who took part in the scoring was a freshman quarterback who had one outstanding run, hit 8 of 12 passes, and threw a late touchdown pass. He was future NFL great Bart Starr.

Alabama entered the 1953 season as a consensus choice to be among the nation's top ten teams. Grantland Rice went so far as to pick the Tide number one. Drew knew better; too many top players had been lost to graduation, and early fall practices had not gone well. It did not take long to convince the rest of the football world that the Tide was in trouble. In its first game, 'Bama was embarrassed by Southern Mississippi 25–19, losing a 19–6 halftime advantage. Alabama would tie three times, but lose only once more (a shutout at the hands of Maryland), and the 4–0–3 Conference record was good for a Cotton Bowl berth against Rice which would provide one of football's most memorable moments. 'Bama clinched the title when Bobby Luna kicked a fourth-quarter field goal to beat Auburn 10–7.

A young Bart Starr, who would go on to greatness in the NFL.

The Cotton Bowl play for all time came with Rice leading 7–6 midway in the second quarter, en route to a 28–6 victory. Rice halfback Dickie Moegel, who had a day all runners dream about (265 yards rushing on 11 carries), took off around right end, apparently headed for a touchdown. But Tommy Lewis, who was sitting on the 'Bama bench, suddenly ran onto the

Fullback Tommy Lewis, "Too full of Alabama" in the 1954 Cotton Bowl.

field and threw his body into Moegel's legs. Rice was awarded a touchdown, and Lewis gained football immortality. "I'm just too full of Alabama," said Lewis, whose apologies spoke eloquently for the feeling of all Crimson Tide followers everywhere.

In his first seven seasons Red Drew had a winning record (49–21–5), defeated Auburn five times, and went to three major bowl games. However, when in 1954 the team's record fell to below .500 for the second time during his reign (a 4–5–2 mark that included a shutout loss at the hands of Auburn), Drew was forced to step down as coach.

Alabama dipped into the ranks of its alumni for its next coach, Jennings Bryan "Ears" Whitworth, a guard on the 1929–31 teams. Whitworth's first season was a disaster, one of only three (the others were in the 1890s, the era of four-game seasons) in which 'Bama failed to win a game. In 1955 the record was 0–10. No opponent failed to score at least twenty points, while Alabama was shut out four times and had a high-game output of only fourteen points. And to cap a "perfect season," Auburn scored its second straight shutout victory over 'Bama.

Jennings Bryan "Ears" Whitworth, Alabama coach before the coming of Bryant.

Alabama improved slightly in 1956, but the quality of play still was not up to 'Bama's high standards. A 2–7–1 mark included wins over Mississippi State and Tulane and a tie with Southern Mississippi. Auburn again drubbed Alabama, 34–7, while Tennessee and Georgia Tech shut out the Tide. 'Bama alumni were restless. A Committee for Better Football at Alabama within the alumni association came within a vote of calling for Whitworth's resignation. The Tide coach was hanged in effigy several times on the Tide campus. But Alabama players expressed their support for Whitworth, and in early January 1957 it was announced he would be retained.

The 1957 season, however, was Whitworth's last. The season produced another 2–7–1 record, including shutout losses and an eleventh-place finish in the SEC. A tie with Vanderbilt and a one-point win over Georgia were the only high points in an otherwise dismal season.

By midseason the rumors that Alabama would have a new football coach in 1958 had been substantiated. Before the year was out, sentiment was almost a hundred percent in favor of having ex–Tide end Bear Bryant take over the coaching chores. Bryant did not commit himself immediately when his alma mater

Paul "Bear" Bryant, head football coach at the University of Alabama from 1958 to the present.

called, but eventually he secured his release from his contract at Texas A & M—where he had rebuilt his third college team in as many tries, after stints at Maryland and Kentucky—and he signed a ten-year contract as head football coach and director of athletics at Alabama.

Bryant's first Alabama game was something Tide fans would not have to live with too often—a loss. LSU took the measure of the Tide with a 13–3 victory, but a victory for 'Bama would have been an upset of momentous proportions, as the Billy Cannon–led Bengals were en route to the 1958 national championship. A scoreless tie with Vanderbilt followed, and then Paul William Bryant coached his first victory for the Crimson Tide, a 29–6 victory over Furman in Tuscaloosa. As the season progressed, the size of Coach Bryant's first squad dwindled. There were forty-two returning lettermen when fall drills began. Before the first game, the number was down to less than twenty-five, the overall squad numbering less than fifty. The squad was small in another way: the biggest men on it weighed in at under 215.

When asked to describe Bear Bryant's first Alabama team, Vanderbilt coach Art Guepe commented, "It's sort of a faceless team. There isn't any one man to watch. Or two or three. It's just a bunch of players who hit you like a ton of bricks. They play hard, fierce football and won't give up a foot without a fight."

That observation by one of Bryant's fraternity brothers was to serve as the hallmark of Bryant teams, as they played "hard, fierce football" right from the start, compiling a 5–4–1 season record in Bear's first campaign—'Bama's first winning record in five years.

Coach Bryant's first year was capped with an invitation to something called the Blue Grass Bowl to be held late in 1958 in Lexington, Kentucky. Bryant turned it down. But bowls would come, and come, and come. . . .

Many thought that perhaps Bryant's first team had done too well, and that the team could not expect to improve on its 1958 record. Alabama took it on the chin from the Fran Tarkenton–led Georgia Bulldogs, but it would be 'Bama's only loss of the 1959 season. Ties with Vanderbilt and Tennessee were upsets; victories over Georgia Tech and Auburn were even greater upsets. After the Tide's 9–7 win over Tech, the name Alabama again surfaced in bowl circles. For the first time in years, Alabama was back among the nation's top-ranked teams. After its 10–0 victory over Auburn (with Tommy Brooker kicking a field goal and Bobby Skelton hitting five-foot-six, 148-pound Marlin Dyess on a 39-yard touchdown play), 'Bama announced that it would once again "pass" on a bowl bid.

However, there was a new bowl game following the 1959 season, the Liberty Bowl in Philadelphia, and when the invitation to play Penn State arrived, the 'Bama players asked Coach Bryant to accept. He did, and Alabama, once king of the bowls, was back in post-season play.

In many respects Alabama's first bowl appearance in six years was less than rewarding. At the outset of the game the weather was perfect, but strong winds soon blew up, causing the temperature to drop dramatically. "I had to get volunteers to go out for the second half," Coach Bryant said later.

The final score was 7–0, the Penn State touchdown coming as the first half ended. It was set up by a 4-yard 'Bama punt into the wind and came off a fake field-goal attempt. The score could have been much worse, with Penn State dominating the play—and the score. But it was important to 'Bama to get back into bowl competition.

Placekicker Tommy Brooker, whose only two field goals in 1960 gave 'Bama its only points in a 3–0 win over Auburn and a 3–3 tie with Texas in the Bluebonnet Bowl.

'at Trammell, the first of a long line of great Tide quarter-
acks developed by Bryant.

The year 1960 saw further improvement. 'Bama vent 8-1-1 in regular-season play, the tie coming gainst Tulane and the loss to Tennessee in Knox-ille. The wins included one of the most exciting in labama history, a 16-15 come-from-behind effort ver Georgia Tech in Atlanta.

Tech had been favored and ran up a 15-0 lead vhile holding 'Bama to only one first down. Three imes during a final desperation drive 'Bama went for first down on fourth down and made it, the last ime on a Bobby Skelton pass to a surrounded Butch Vilson at the Tech 6. With the clock running out, the 'ide lined up for a field goal by end Richard O'Dell, ho had never kicked one before. The 24-yard effort vasn't picture perfect, but, nevertheless, it was good. 'he game ended, and 'Bama had what would be oted the Comeback of the Year. 'Bama then chieved its second straight shutout victory over uburn 3-0, when Tommy Brooker kicked a 23-yard ield goal into the wind in the second quarter.

The Tide went bowling again, this time to the Bluebonnet Bowl against Texas. Brooker, whose only field goal of 1960 had been the game winner against Auburn, kicked a 30-yarder in the third quarter. Texas later matched it, tying the game. And that was the way the game ended, despite Texas's try on the last play of the game for a 35-yard field goal, set up by a controversial pass interference call. The kick was short and wide, and the score went down as a 3-3 deadlock. A young Alabama center-linebacker, Lee Roy Jordan, was named Outstanding Lineman of the game.

The 1960 season witnessed various bowls announcing their all-time teams, and predictably Alabama, which had appeared in fourteen bowl games, was well represented: halfbacks Johnny Mack Brown (1925) and Dixie Howell (1935) made the Rose Bowl squad: center Joe Domnanovich (1943) and tackle Don Whitmire (1943) were selected by the Orange Bowl; center Vaughn Mancha (1945), guard Ray Richeson (1945), and halfback Harry Gilmer (1945) the Sugar Bowl team; and end Holt Rast (1942), tackle Don Whitmire (1942), and halfback Jimmy Nelson (1942) were elected to the Cotton Bowl honor team.

Alabama did not ambush anyone in 1961. The Tide was almost a unanimous choice to win the SEC championship, and pre-season polls put Alabama as high as number two in the nation. Alabama immediately illustrated that the predictions were well based, as they romped over Georgia, 32-6. The Tide had a close call against Tulane, then began rolling. But others were rolling too, and after a midseason victory over Tennessee (34-3), 'Bama was ranked only fifth in the nation.

In early November the Tide had moved to its eighth straight win, but were still ranked only fourth in the nation. Then Dame Fortune stepped in—as a few upsets of higher-ranked teams moved 'Bama into second place, behind a Texas team that had three seemingly easy games remaining on its schedule. Although the outlook was not bright for the 'Bama eleven in its quest for the national championship, things were looking up on other fronts: it was generally assumed that the Tide would have its choice of bowls, including the Rose Bowl, as sentiment on the West Coast favored inviting Alabama rather than the Big Ten champion to Pasadena. However, after shutting out Georgia Tech—their fifth shutout of the year and fourth straight—the Tide learned that the Rose Bowl committee would not change its policy, and 'Bama voted instead to accept a Sugar Bowl bid to play ninth-ranked Arkansas.

Joe Willie Namath, suspended by Bryant in 1963 in one of the nation's most famous disciplinary cases, came back in 1964 to lead 'Bama to the SEC championship.

But the big stories that followed in the wake of the Tide's victory over Tech did not concern bowl invitations. One had to do with 'Bama's alleged "dirty play" in the Tech win—a furor grew over Alabama linebacker Darwin Holt's elbowing of Tech back Chick Graning. The other concerned Texas's upset loss to lowly TCU, an upset that left Alabama as the nation's only unbeaten and untied team and as the rankings' king of the mountain, with only Auburn still to play.

Alabama ended its all-winning season with a 34–0 whitewash of rival Auburn. The win gave the team a 10–0 record, 287 points to but 22 for their opponents, the SEC championship, and, most importantly, the national championship.

'Bama capped its most successful season in sixteen years by meeting—and beating—Arkansas in the Sugar Bowl. But barely. The game produced a slim 10–3 victory, with Pat Trammell running 12 yards for a touchdown and Tim Davis adding a 32-yard field goal. Late in the game, with a chance to tie or even win, standout Razorback halfback Lance Alworth lost a potential touchdown pass that just trickled off his fingertips. Alabama had its perfect season, and its national championship. And the freshmen who had come to Alabama with Coach Bryant had achieved their four-year goal.

Bryant was understandably proud of his 1961 Alabama team. "I said early in the season they were the nicest, even the sissiest bunch I'd ever had. I think they read it, because later on they got unfriendly."

Going into the ninth game of the 1962 season against Georgia Tech, Alabama had a twenty-six-game unbeaten streak. With a sophomore quarterback named Joe Namath leading the way, the Tide held on to the number one ranking. 'Bama had given up no more than one touchdown to any foe all year. But even such excellent defense was not enough. Tech took a 7–0 lead, but the Tide got a touchdown with just over five minutes to play. In an all or nothing gamble, the Tide went for two points but came up just short, trailing 7–6. 'Bama had one final chance after it recovered an on-side kick, but an interception inside the Tech 20 killed Alabama's final hopes.

Alabama closed out the season with its fourth straight shutout of Auburn, 38–0, then went to the Orange Bowl against Bud Wilkinson's Oklahoma team. With such standouts as quarterback Joe Namath and linebacker Lee Roy Jordan, who made tackles from sideline to sideline, 'Bama beat Oklahoma 17–0 and ended up fifth in the nation with an overall 10–1 record.

Alabama began the 1963 season ranked among the nation's top half-dozen teams and cruised to easy victories in its first three games. On October 12 in Tuscaloosa's Denny Stadium, the Tide was upset by Florida 10–6, Bear Bryant's only defeat on campus in twenty years of coaching at Alabama. For Florida, which has never won an SEC championship, it was one of the greatest victories in the school's history and one the Gators certainly deserved, as they outplayed Alabama in every phase of the game. 'Bama rebounded from that loss in their next home game, surviving a tremendous scare at the hands of Mississippi State, 29–19. The Tide went into the season's regularly scheduled finale against Auburn with only one loss and a chance for the SEC championship.

Auburn broke a four-year scoring drought against the Tide with a first-quarter field goal and then took advantage of an Alabama fumble—one of four 'Bama fumbles lost that day—to stretch their lead to 10–0. 'Bama got back into the game with an 80-yard Benny Nelson touchdown run, but the Tide could not pull the game out, even after a two-point conversion, and fell to the Tigers 10–8. In a game originally scheduled for November 23 but postponed in deference to the memory of President Kennedy, 'Bama got by Miami 17–12 for its eighth win of the year.

In the Sugar Bowl against Conference champion Ole Miss, Tim Davis set a bowl record by kicking four field goals, and young sophomore quarterback Steve Sloan, filling in for the suspended Namath, ran the club like a veteran as Alabama upset the Rebels 12–7. Alabama had concluded what in pre-Bryant days would have been an extremely successful season: a record of nine wins in eleven games (the other two games were lost by a total of six points) and a ranking of ninth in the national ratings.

Rumors had Bryant retiring following the 1964 season. "Only if I lose ten games," replied the coach. Hardly likely! Especially with Joe Namath back in Bear's good graces. Alabama opened its '64 season in grand style as Namath scored three touchdowns in a 31–3 rout of Georgia. Among the Alabama victories was a 21–0 win over North Carolina State, its fourth straight win. However, there was little cause for celebration. For, on a running play in which he made a quick cut, Namath went down with a twisted knee that would plague him the rest of his great career. 'Bama had moved into the top three in the nation by midseason, when Florida returned to Tuscaloosa.

One of Tim Davis's record four field goals in the 1964 Sugar Bowl game that beat Ole Miss 12–7.

The Tide got out of this one, but barely, as a Florida field-goal attempt on the last play of the game went wide and 'Bama came away with its closest call, 17–14.

The 1964 season included an incident that reinforced 'Bama fans' belief in the powers of their coach. Bryant had said he wanted a dry field for Alabama's game with LSU, but it was raining on the Saturday of the all-important confrontation between the two undefeated powers. The sky was dark and rain was falling when the cover was removed from the field. It was still raining when LSU came out to warm up. More so when Alabama came out. But when Coach Bryant appeared, the rain stopped and the sun came out. More important, Alabama came out with a 17–9 victory and moved into second place in the national polls behind Notre Dame.

By now Alabama was using Namath for precious seconds at a time, protecting his knee. And eighty of those seconds were among the most explosive in college football history. Just 1:47 remained in the first half of a scoreless game with Georgia Tech in the last meeting between the two schools when Namath was sent in with the ball at Tech's 49. In 29 seconds it was 7–0, Alabama. Namath had passed to Ray Ogden, moving the ball to the one, with Steve Bowman taking it in. An on-side kick followed, and the Tide had it again at Tech's 48. Namath to Ogden took it to the three, and seconds later it was Namath to David Ray and a 14–0 lead en route to a 24–7 victory.

Ogden would also star against Auburn, returning a kickoff from the end zone for a touchdown in a 21–14 victory that clinched an undefeated season for the Tide. When Notre Dame blew a 17-point lead to Southern Cal two days later, 'Bama had its second national championship in four years.

'Bama players could have chosen to go to the Cotton Bowl, giving Tide seniors a chance to complete the bowl circuit—Orange, Sugar and Cotton—but Namath wanted to go back to the Orange Bowl, and the Tide players agreed with him. Texas was to be their opponent—the same team that had battled Alabama to a 3–3 tie in the Bluebonnet Bowl just four years before.

During the week of practice before the game, Namath reinjured his knee, and was feared lost. But although he did not start, Namath put on a one-man show when he came in—completing 18 of 37 passes for 255 yards and 2 touchdowns—and nearly pulled out a victory over the inspired Longhorns. Texas finally won when Namath was stopped inches short of the goal line in the final quarter, one official signaling touchdown before another ruled Namath had gone down just before crossing the last hash mark. Alabama fans who witnessed the unbelievable scene have always maintained that the official made the sign of the Longhorns and proclaimed, "He's this short!" But the fact remains that Texas beat Alabama 21–17. At least in the *official* record books.

The year 1965 would find Alabama at the top of the rankings again. But this time the path was more circuitous and, for the fans and followers of the Tide, even tortuous. For in its very first game 'Bama got off on the wrong foot, losing 18–17 to Georgia in Athens on a controversial lateral off a pass that accounted for a last-second Bulldog touchdown. Then, after notching its first win, the Tide came up against an inspired Ole Miss team. Mississippi led 16–7 going into the last quarter, and 16–10 with just over five minutes to play. With Alabama looking defeat squarely in the face, Steve Sloan directed an 89-yard march, taking the winning touchdown in himself. 'Bama next beat Vanderbilt, and then was forced to settle for a tie with Tennessee when, on fourth down

All-SEC quarterback Steve Sloan, one of thirty-eight disciples of Bryant who have gone on to become head coaches.

at the Vols' 4-yard line, quarterback Ken Stabler intentionally—and inexplicably—threw away the ball to stop the clock. Any hopes for a national crown seemed doomed only five games into the season.

But the Tide closed out the schedule with five straight regular-season victories, including a surprisingly easy 30–3 victory over a strong Auburn team, a victory that deprived the Plainsmen of the SEC title. Instead, Alabama became the SEC champion for the second year in a row, and the third time since the coming of Bryant.

But the designation of a mythical national champion would have to await the outcome of the bowl games, the first time in the history of the polls that the national crown would be decided on the basis of post-season play—a direct result of 'Bama's having lost its bowl game the previous year after being voted the nation's number one team. The ratings going into the bowls showed Michigan State number one, Arkansas number two, Nebraska number three, and Alabama number four. All four were playing in bowl games that January 1: Michigan State in the Rose, Arkansas in the Cotton, and Nebraska and Alabama in the Orange. January 1 could just as easily have been called Ratings Day as New Year's Day.

By now the Orange Bowl had become a nighttime fixture, the last of the bowl games. It was almost as if fate had staged 'Bama's scenario. First Arkansas lost the Cotton Bowl to LSU. Then Michigan State's highly regarded team went down to defeat at the hands of UCLA. And so, by game time at the Orange Bowl, both Alabama and Nebraska knew what was at stake: the national championship would go to the winner.

In a game that was not as close as the final score would indicate, to steal a Duffy Daugherty line, Alabama beat Nebraska 39–28. Although Alabama was outweighed nearly 40 pounds to the man, it wasn't avoirdupois but aerial power that won for 'Bama as Steve Sloan completed 20 passes for 296 yards and the Tide rolled to a new bowl record of 518 yards in total offense. Alabama was number one in the nation again.

The 1966 team was a memorable one; in fact, several believe it to have been Alabama's greatest ever. The defending national champion was a clear-cut choice to win the SEC championship, although some thought that if 'Bama had a weakness it was at quarterback, where Steve Sloan's graduation had left a gaping void.

The man who took Sloan's place, Ken "Snake" Stabler, would prove to be every bit as worthy as his predecessor. Alabama tuned up for its title defense by shutting out little Louisiana Tech 34–0 before a sold-out Legion Field crowd of 65,000. The Tide showed little in that game, but showed plenty the next week in dropping Ole Miss 17–7, with Stabler completing 16 of 19 passes. 'Bama would have only one more tough game, but it would be as tough as they come. Playing against Tennessee in the rain, the Tide quickly fell behind 10–0. Going into the fourth quarter, that was still the score. Stabler, who had not completed a pass in the first half, suddenly got hot, hitting 7 of 9 in the second and taking it in for a touchdown himself early in the final quarter. He then hit on a two-point conversion pass to make it 10–8. Steve Davis, brother of 1964 Sugar Bowl hero Tim, kicked a field goal with just over three minutes to play, and 'Bama finally breathed a sigh of relief when Tennessee missed on a 20-yard field-goal attempt with just sixteen seconds left.

Kenny "Snake" Stabler, holder of 'Bama season and career records for highest percentage of passes completed.

At the end of the season, Notre Dame, who had played Michigan State to a tie earlier in the year, was ranked number one in the nation, Michigan State was number two, and Alabama—the nation's only major undefeated-untied team and the team that had been the pre-season number one selection in the Associated Press poll—was ranked third. The polls had reverted to the time-honored practice of naming their national champion before the bowl games. The decision by the wire services to conclude their balloting before the bowl games was a bad blow for 'Bama, especially so because Notre Dame, who did not accept bowl bids in those days, would not have to prove itself and Alabama was about to conclude its all-winning season by playing one of its greatest games.

The bowl game that was meaningless as far as the poll-watchers were concerned, but meaningful to Tide-watchers everywhere, was a rematch with Nebraska, 'Bama's opponent in the 1966 Orange Bowl "shoot-out." This time 'Bama was to meet the sixth-ranked Cornhuskers in the Sugar Bowl. The game not only produced one of the most perfect offensive football games ever played—with Stabler completing 12 of 17 passes for 218 yards and rushing for 40 more as he scored one touchdown and passed for another in a 34–7 rout—but also served to reinforce Alabama fans' absolute faith in Coach Bryant. One of the faithful was overheard to say: "Coach Bryant don't walk on water, but he sure do know where the stumps are."

The team that had given up only 37 points in regular-season play in 1966 got off on the wrong foot in 1967, giving up 37 points to Florida State in its home opener in Birmingham. Fortunately, the Tide also scored 37 points, making it the highest scoring tie game in the history of major college football. Ken Stabler, who was in Coach Bryant's doghouse, did not start the game for 'Bama; he had to earn his way back into a starting job. Alabama got back on a winning track with three straight wins, but gave up three touchdowns to Vanderbilt in a 35–21 win. Then Tennessee clipped 'Bama's wings in what was to be the first of four straight wins for the Vols in the historic series. Alabama struggled through the remainder of the season with a three-point win over Clemson, a one-point win over LSU, and a four-point win over archrival Auburn, losing its stranglehold on the SEC crown with a second-place finish.

Nevertheless, the Tide was still top bowl material, and the Cotton Bowl invited 'Bama to play against the school that Coach Bryant had coached ten years earlier, Texas A & M. Former Bryant assistant Gene Stallings—one of thirty-eight former Bryant players and assistants who have gone on to become head coaches in college or professional football—led the Aggies to a 20–16 upset. Time and again 'Bama threatened, but five Crimson Tide turnovers sealed Alabama's fate. It was the first of eight straight bowl games from which 'Bama was to come away without a win.

Alabama started the 1968 season with a win, an improvement over the 1967 start, but the win was not particularly impressive—the Tide got by Virginia Tech in Birmingham 14–7. The following week 'Bama pulled out a win over Southern Mississippi. Then the Tide tangled with a power, Ole Miss, and the Rebels broke a fifty-eight-year dry spell against 'Bama with a 10–8 victory. Both 'Bama and Ole Miss had sophomore quarterbacks, Scott Hunter for Alabama and Archie Manning for Ole Miss. Hunter missed the game with an injury, just as he would miss their senior confrontation. 'Bama had one more close loss, 10–9 to Tennessee in Knoxville. Alabama could have tied the game when it pushed across a late touchdown, but it went for the two-point conversion try and came up short. Alabama had lost two SEC games in the same season for the first time in ten years. Alabama would win its next five games, but none by more than nine points. When Alabama met Auburn in the regular season finale, a special sideline guest of Coach Bryant was Pat Trammell. Three days later the momentary elation over 'Bama's 24–16 win was replaced by sorrow at the tragic news that Pat Trammell had lost his bout with cancer at the age of twenty-nine. The entire state mourned his death.

Alabama had been invited to one of the four major bowl games for seven straight years, but following the 1968 season the Tide dropped down a notch and met Missouri in the Gator Bowl. The game was close for three quarters, but in the fourth period, which Alabama had always considered its strongest, the Tigers were too powerful. Missouri pushed across three touchdowns and destroyed Alabama 35–10. In the worst drubbing a Bryant-coached team ever suffered, Alabama finished with just 23 yards total offense, minus 45 on the ground.

'Bama opened the 1969 season with a tough win over Virginia Tech, followed by an easy win over Southern Miss. Now Scott Hunter was ready to duel Archie Manning. National television was primed to show the game from Birmingham. The Rebels decided to wait until game day to come into town, the first team to try that maneuver on 'Bama since Florida State in 1967, the year of the 37–37 tie.

The Tide and the Rebels played what might be called "a doozy of a game," with Alabama finally pulling it out 33–32, as Hunter and Manning put on one of football's all-time great shows. Manning rushed 15 times for 104 yards and 3 touchdowns, and hit 33 of 52 passes for 436 yards and 2 touchdowns. His counterpart, Hunter, hit 22 of 29 passes, including one for the clinching touchdown with less than four minutes to play. The seesaw game had Alabama take a 21–14

Scott Hunter, holder of game, season and career records for most passes completed and most yards gained in a season (2157).

lead in the third quarter, with Ole Miss closing the gap to one point just before the fourth quarter but missing on a two-point conversion try. There were four touchdowns and four tries for two-point conversions in the fourth quarter; none of the extra-point tries were good. Ole Miss forged ahead 26–21, then 'Bama came back to make it 27–26. Ole Miss then went ahead 32–27. And finally, on a fourth-down play from the Ole Miss 15, Hunter hit George Ranager near the goal line for the winning score.

But it did not take 'Bama long to come down off its winning high. With sophomore running back Johnny Musso left behind in Tuscaloosa to recuperate from injuries, the Tide was upset by Vanderbilt in Nashville 14–10. Against highly ranked Tennessee, 'Bama suffered its second straight loss, 41–14, the most points scored against an Alabama team since 1907, when Sewanee scored a 54–4 victory over the Tide. Alabama was headed for an eighth-place finish in the ten-team SEC and a 6–5 overall record. Auburn destroyed 'Bama 49–26, breaking a five-year losing streak against the Tide. Nevertheless, 'Bama was again invited to a bowl game, the Liberty Bowl. Bowl officials probably desired an offensive show and felt that the Tide and Colorado could deliver one. They were not disappointed. Unfortunately for 'Bama, Colorado took a 47–33 decision, although the Tide led 33–31 going into the final period.

So although the 1960s ended on a "downer," the Tide and Coach Bryant had been the winningest team of the decade, posting a 90–16–4 record. Coach Bryant's achievements were recognized by his peers, who voted him Coach of the Decade.

Alabama fans were invited to vote for a Super Sixties team. The results of that voting placed the following players on the decade's all-star team: tight end, Bill Battle; split end, Ray Perkins; flanker,

Bear Bryant in his traditional skinny-brimmed plaid hat.

Dennis Homan; tackles, Billy Neighbors and Cecil Dowdy; guards, Alvin Samples and Jimmy Sharpe; center, Paul Crane; quarterback, Joe Namath; running backs, Mike Fracchia and Steve Bowman. The defense: ends, Mike Ford and Creed Gilmer; tackles, Billy Neighbors and Dan Kearley; noseguard, Alvin Samples; linebackers, Lee Roy Jordan, Mike Hall and Darwin Holt; defensive backs, Bobby Johns, Donnie Sutton and Cotton Clark. The punter was Steve Davis, while brother Tim Davis was the placekicker. Jordan, who was named on over ninety-six percent of the ballots, was chosen the Player of the Sixties.

Linebacker Lee Roy Jordan, member of the Quarter-Century All-SEC team and 'Bama's "Player of the Sixties."

Prior to the 1970 season, the NCAA passed a rule that allowed teams to schedule an eleventh game. 'Bama jumped in with both feet, scheduling Southern Cal to open the 1970 and 1971 seasons.

"Has Bear gone crazy?" asked Auburn Coach Shug Jordan when told of the move.

Anyone watching 'Bama's 1970 opener might have thought so. Bryant's good friend John McKay called off the horses, but the Trojans still rolled to a 42–21 victory in Birmingham.

It was another miserable year for the Tide; they suffered a shutout loss at the hands of Tennessee; Ole Miss rolled over a Tide team without Scott Hunter; LSU gained its second straight victory over 'Bama; and Auburn came from behind to win 33–28 after Alabama had taken a quick lead. One high point of the season was a come-from-behind 30–21 victory over highly ranked Houston in the Astrodome, an upset that would propel 'Bama back to Houston's fabulous football house for the Astro-Bluebonnet Bowl.

Oklahoma, another storied name from the past that had fallen on hard times and was rebuilding with young players, was the Crimson Tide's foe. In the contest against 'Bama, the Sooners went ahead 21–7, but 'Bama battled back to go up 24–21. With just under a minute to play, the Sooners went for the tie, kicking a field goal from the 32. 'Bama marched back quickly, and with five seconds left the Tide had a shot at victory with a 34-yard field goal. The try was far off the mark, but at least 'Bama had broken its three-year bowl losing streak.

In 1971 'Bama unveiled its wishbone offense in Los Angeles against USC, and the result was perhaps the biggest win in recent Crimson Tide history, a 17–10 upset over the team that was a consensus choice for number one. The celebration that followed in Tuscaloosa lasted until daylight, and an estimated 50,000 fans turned up at the Birmingham airport the next night to greet the returning Tiders. 'Bama football was back, led by quick-footed quarterback Terry Davis and all-time great Tide running back Johnny

Terry Davis, All-SEC quarterback (1972).

Musso. 'Bama rolled over its next ten opponents with only one real fight, a 14–7 victory over LSU in Baton Rouge. The last regular-season game was the most highly publicized Alabama-Auburn game in history. Both teams were undefeated, as were Nebraska and Oklahoma. Alabama was already scheduled to play Nebraska in the Orange Bowl, and Auburn was set to meet Oklahoma in the Sugar Bowl.

Alabama went into the game not knowing whether Musso would be able to play. He had suffered a badly sprained toe in the game against LSU and could not walk without the aid of crutches a week before the Auburn meeting. Alabama trainer Jim Goostree devised a special pad, and the Tide senior jogged a bit two days before the game. When Coach Bryant was calling out the starting lineup prior to the Auburn game, he inserted Musso's backup man at left halfback. No 'Bama assistant coach had ever questioned Bryant's starting lineup, but back coach John David Crow—winner of the Heisman trophy at Texas A & M under Bryant in 1957—said, "Coach, when you've got a stud horse, you ride him. Start Johnny."

Musso started and had a terrific day, rushing 33 times for 167 yards and allowing Alabama to monopolize the football and keep it away from such outstanding talents as Heisman trophy winner Pat Sullivan and split end Terry Beasley. Sullivan had his worst day ever, and 'Bama had a 31–7 victory, the SEC championship, and a number two national ranking—with a chance to become number one by beating Nebraska, who had defeated Oklahoma to set up the Orange Bowl showdown.

"The Italian Stallion," Johnny Musso, holder of most of 'Bama's rushing records.

But 'Bama was never in the game, losing 38–6, as a result of three fumbles that led to quick Nebraska scores. For the first time in the season, the Tide had to play catch-up ball, the outstanding weakness of its new wishbone formation. As a result of its win, Nebraska claimed the national championship.

Alabama was the only SEC team with eight Conference games scheduled in 1972, and it turned out that the extra game gave 'Bama the league championship. The season included two incredible comebacks, one favorable and one unfavorable, from Alabama's viewpoint. The Tide ripped through the first half of its season with little trouble before taking on Tennessee in Knoxville. Tennessee had fallen only to Auburn, the miracle team of 1972. The Vols held a 10–3 lead over 'Bama in the closing minutes when the Tide forced a punt. Starting at Tennessee's 48, Terry Davis hit Wayne Wheeler for a 20-yard completion, and Steve Bisceglia ran 26 yards to the Tennessee 2. Wilbur Jackson scored from the 2, and a

Running back Wilbur Jackson, All-SEC (1973).

crucial decision had to be made with only 1:48 remaining. Tide linebacker coach Pat Dye advised Coach Bryant to kick the tying point, promising the head man that his defense would get the ball back in time to win. Alabama kicked the extra point, tying the score 10–10. On Tennessee's third down after the kickoff, Mike Dubose—credited with 20 tackles in the game—forced a fumble, and 'Bama recovered at the Vols' 22. On first down Davis went in for the score, and 'Bama had a comeback 17–10 victory.

Alabama had already clinched the SEC championship when the Tide met Auburn in the regular-season finale. Although Auburn had had a fine season, winning 8 of 9 games, Alabama was picked to win by most experts. With the score in the fourth quarter 16–0 in favor of Alabama, it looked as if the experts would be right. But Alabama got careless on two punts that were nearly carbon copies of each other. Auburn blocked both and ran them in for touchdowns, and the Tigers had the greatest win in the team's history, a 17–16 verdict that, unlike the outcome of most other Alabama-Auburn games, has survived more than one season of memory.

It was an unenthusiastic Alabama that went to the Cotton Bowl to meet Texas. In a battle between the nation's two most sophisticated Wishbone offenses, Texas came from behind to win 17–13. The Tide had taken a 10–0 lead on a 50-yard Greg Gantt field goal and a 31-yard touchdown run by Wilbur Jackson. However, the Longhorns battled back, and quarterback Alan Lowry's 34-yard touchdown run along the sidelines gave Texas a victory and ended what had had all the markings of a great Alabama season.

All-American guard John Hannah (1972), one of Alabama's "First Family of Football."

Alabama won UPI's national championship in 1973, but the Tide's title was tainted—coming before the bowl games, a choice that bowl results did not bear out. The Tide had three scares during the year, but kick returns ignited big 'Bama comebacks in all of them. Alabama trailed Kentucky 14–0 at the half, but when Willie Shelby broke the second-half kickoff for a 100-yard touchdown run, momentum shifted and the Tide cruised to a 28–14 victory. Two weeks later against Georgia in Tuscaloosa, the Bulldogs had 'Bama down 14–13 with time running out when Georgia punted to Shelby. He returned the kick 36 yards to the Georgia 8, and seconds later quarterback Gary Rutlege went in with the go-ahead score. The Tide went on to a 28–14 win, scoring again in the final minute of play. Alabama and Tennessee were tied 21–21 going into the fourth quarter when the Vols punted to Robin Cary. Cary was better known as a slugging 'Bama outfielder and because of his ability to judge and catch flyballs was used as a "safe" punt-return man. He took the punt at the Tide 36 and raced 64 yards up the middle untouched. Moments later Wilbur Jackson went 80 yards to sew up a 'Bama victory, 42–21.

The next week 'Bama ripped through Virginia Tech and NCAA and SEC record books with a 77–6 verdict. Alabama piled up 748 yards rushing and 833 yards total offense, both new NCAA records, and tied a national record when four Tide backs went over 100 yards rushing in the same game—Wilbur Jackson, James Taylor, Calvin Culliver and Richard Todd. Alabama closed out its undefeated 11–0 season with a 35–0 blanking of Auburn.

Then it was on to the Sugar Bowl to meet unbeaten Notre Dame, ranked third in the nation behind top-rated 'Bama. If ever a Sugar Bowl classic would outdo the Alabama-Duke effort of 1945, this was it! The meeting of the two top names in college football for the first time produced the kind of "dream" game everyone expected. But unfortunately, for Alabama, the outcome was more a nightmare than a dream. Notre Dame came from behind to defeat 'Bama 24–23. A daring pass from the Notre Dame end zone iced the victory for the Irish and gave Notre Dame the AP's national championship.

The 1974 team was another fine one—for the second year in a row and the third time in four years, Alabama went through the season undefeated. Quarterback Richard Todd's daring run from punt formation lifted 'Bama to a 21–14 victory over Maryland, and so the Tide was undefeated when it met the team with the nation's longest losing streak, Florida State. The game was nearly a disaster for the Tide, as its

Richard Todd, All-SEC quarterback (1975).

offense could do nothing with the fired-up Seminoles, who scored on their first possession. Alabama finally cut the lead to 7–3 with a third-period field goal. Then, with just under two minutes to play and backed up against its own goal line, Florida State made the strategically sound move of taking an intentional safety, narrowing the score to 7–5. Alabama returned the ensuing free kick to midfield. Sophomore quarterback Jack O'Rear then chose that moment to complete the first pass of his college career to Ozzie Newsome. When the drive stalled with half a minute to play, Bucky Berrey kicked a 36-yard field goal to give Alabama a hard-fought 8–7 win. Alabama was besieged by injuries throughout the year, particularly at the quarterback position, as Gary Rutledge was lost for the year and Richard Todd was out frequently. But the defense allowed only 7.5 points per game, the second best record in the nation, to lead the tide to an 11–0 season.

Alabama and Notre Dame were rematched on January 1, this time in the Orange Bowl. The Irish once again spoiled 'Bama's national championship hopes, as the underdogs upset the Tide 13–11. Alabama had been ranked first in one poll; in another they were second behind Oklahoma, which was on probation and ineligible for a bowl bid. Notre Dame, ranked eighth in one poll and ninth in another, was playing its last game under its highly successful coach Ara Parseghian. A 'Bama fumble gave Notre Dame an early touchdown, and an Alabama penalty—the only one of the game against the Tide—kept another drive alive as the Irish jumped out on top 13–0. 'Bama got a field goal in the second quarter. In the fourth period Todd hit Russ Schamun for a 48-yard score, then Todd passed to tight end George Pugh, to cut the lead to 13–11. Alabama drove into Notre Dame territory for one final try, but a great interception by Notre Dame's Reggie Barnett ended Tide hopes for a victory and a national crown.

Alabama had won twenty-two regular-season games in a row and forty-three of forty-four of its last regular-season games when the Tide opened the 1975 season on national television against Missouri. The Tigers, who have been among the nation's top spoilers for years, lived up to their reputation with a 20–7 upset victory. But the Tide rebounded, rolling over its next ten opponents with little trouble. A highlight of the season was the meeting with Washington, fifty years after Alabama's 1925 team met Washington in their first bowl game. However, the 1975 game did not quite mirror the titanic struggle of the 1926 Rose Bowl, as 'Bama rolled over the Huskies 52–0 in front of all the surviving members of both teams, who were guests of the university. Alabama clinched its record fifth straight SEC championship with a 28–0 victory over Auburn, Richard Todd running for two touchdowns and passing for two more.

Under a new arrangement that called for the Conference champion to serve as "host" team in the Sugar Bowl, third-ranked Alabama went to New Orleans to play eighth-ranked Penn State—'Bama's very first bowl opponent in the Bear Bryant era. This time Alabama pioneered in another first—the first Sugar Bowl game played in New Orleans's new Superdome. The game itself was primarily a defensive one, and 'Bama snapped its losing streak with a 13–6 victory over the Nittany Lions, sparked by what Penn State coach Joe Paterno called "one of the greatest performances I've seen by a quarterback in my days at Penn State." Tide quarterback Richard Todd hit on 10 of 12 passes for 210 yards, one of them setting up the winning touchdown by Mike Stock. Todd was named the game's Most Valuable Player.

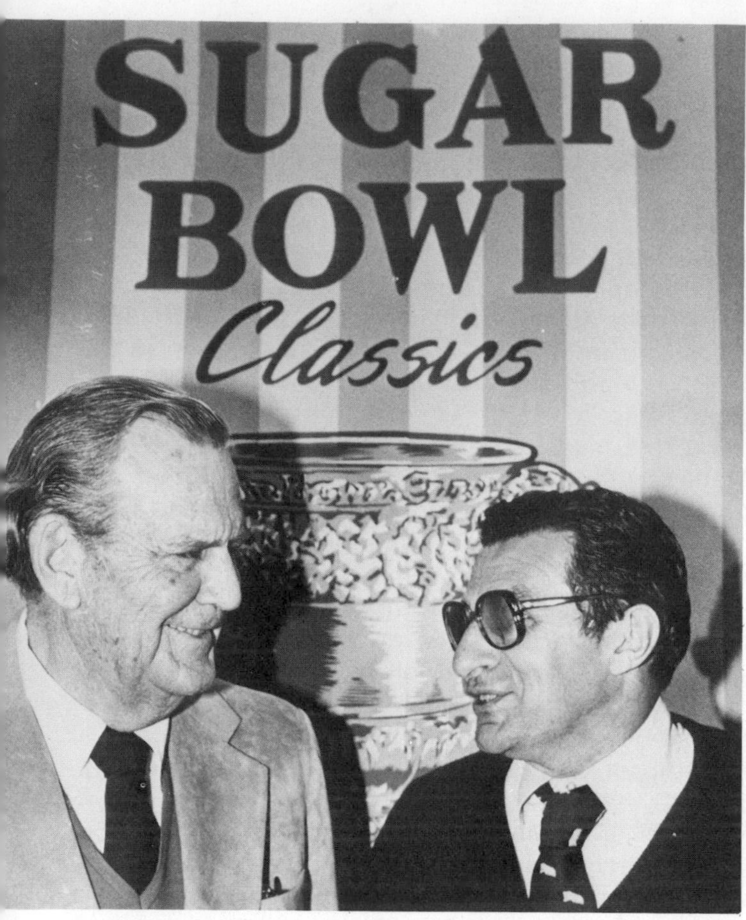

Bear Bryant and Joe Paterno, two of college football's winningest coaches, shake hands before the 1976 Sugar Bowl game—something they would repeat two years later.

All-American linebacker Barry Krauss, Alabama's leading tackler for two years and the hero of the 1979 Sugar Bowl game.

Alabama came down to earth hard in 1976, when its hold on the SEC championship was broken. The Tide dropped the opening game to Ole Miss, 10–7, in Jackson, then fell 21–0 to the eventual SEC champ, Georgia. The salt in the 1976 wound was another loss to Notre Dame, this time by three points. The win made the series 3–0 in favor of the Irish—wins by one, two and three points. However, the Tide got stronger as the year wore on and finished out with its fourth straight victory over Auburn, 38–7. Then the Tide took on UCLA in the Liberty Bowl. The Bruins had just missed going to the Rose Bowl and were heavily favored over thrice-beaten Alabama. The weather was horrible—temperature in the twenties and a strong wind blowing. Those who watched the game will long remember the ski mask that all but covered Coach Bryant's face. But what warmed him more than his mask was the performance of his Crimson Tide. 'Bama struck with blinding quickness when linebacker Barry Krauss, who would make 18 tackles, returned an intercepted pass for a 44-yard game-opening touchdown. 'Bama led 17–0 at the end of the first quarter, 24–0 at halftime, and 27–0 going into the final period, before giving up a late touchdown. The final score was 36–6, and 'Bama felt it had a hope to build a dream on for the 1977 season.

In 1977 Alabama avenged its two 1976 SEC losses with victories over Ole Miss and Georgia and reclaimed the league championship. 'Bama didn't have a set defense to start the year, and defense was often a weakness, but after a second-game loss to Nebraska (24–31) in Lincoln, the Tide began to roll. One of the nation's most difficult schedules did not help matters, but after its upset over number one–ranked Southern Cal, 21–20, in Los Angeles, the Tide was back in the national championship picture. Sophomore defensive end Wayne Hamilton made the big plays against the Trojans; an interception that set up one of two Tony Nathan touchdowns and a great rush that forced a bad pass as Southern Cal tried for the winning two-point conversion with only seconds to play. The Tide trailed only once more in the season, and that was in their final game, way after they had clinched the SEC crown with a 24–3 victory over LSU. 'Bama fell behind Auburn 7–0, but had little trouble in registering its fifth straight victory over the Tigers, 48–21.

"Touchdown" Tony Nathan scores another of his fifteen touchdowns in 1977.

It was then back to the Sugar Bowl for an historic meeting—the first confrontation between two of football's biggest names, Ohio State and Alabama. The game also pitted the nation's two winningest active coaches. Bear Bryant went into the game with 272 wins and Woody Hayes with 231, a total of 503 victories between them. Alabama was hoping that circumstances would vault them past unbeaten Texas and once-beaten Oklahoma to the national title. A 35–6 victory over Ohio State impressed the voters, but not as much as fifth-ranked Notre Dame's victory over Texas at the Cotton Bowl, played at the same time as the Sugar Bowl. It was the fourth time that Notre Dame had denied 'Bama the national championship.

Which brings us up to 1978, the proverbial "Next Year" 'Bama fans had pointed to since 1973 in their quest for an undisputed national championship. With first place in the pre-season polls virtually conceded to them, the Tide went out and scored a surprisingly easy season-opening 20–3 win over a Nebraska team which had cost them the 1977 title. Then, after another victory over still another Big Eight powerhouse, Missouri—a come-from-behind 38–20 win—'Bama faced the Southern Cal Trojans in a showdown for national honors in Birmingham. The visiting Trojans returned the Tide's favor of the previous year—when they had beaten the top-ranked Trojans 21–20 in Los Angeles—by beating 'Bama 24–10, costing them the number one position in the polls. The Tide had one more tough non-Conference game, beating Rose-Bowl-champs Washington 20–17; but they successfully met and conquered seven Conference opponents without much difficulty in landing their seventh Conference title in eight years. This was to set up what was to amount to "The Game" for the

Quarterback Jeff Rutledge, who broke Joe Namath's record for career touchdown passes with thirty.

national championship, but not without some outside factors conspiring to help.

It had appeared, going into the next-to-last weekend of the season, that Georgia—which did not play Alabama—would end in a tie with the Tide for the SEC championship. Under the SEC's agreement with the powers-that-be at the Sugar Bowl, this meant that Georgia would receive the bid to New Orleans, since 'Bama had been to the Sugar Bowl more recently than Georgia (1978 vs. 1977). It also appeared that Nebraska, which had defeated Oklahoma after its loss to Alabama and won the Big Eight championship and a bid to the Orange Bowl, would play number one–ranked Penn State in Miami. But then strange things began to happen. Georgia was held to a tie by Auburn, costing them a piece of the SEC championship. Nebraska lost to the same tough Missouri team Alabama had beaten earlier in the year. And Penn State opted to play Alabama for all the marbles in New Orleans on New Year's Day.

It was a classic confrontation, number one undefeated Penn State against number two Alabama. A record crowd of 76,824 jammed into the Superdome, paying scalpers as much as $200 a ticket, to see the national championship decided. They were not to be disappointed, as the game lived up to its billing. And then some.

In a defensive struggle, both teams played the first half conservatively, with the outstanding punting of Woody Umphrey contributing to Alabama's slight supremacy. But as the first half neared its conclusion, it looked like both teams would go into the locker rooms at halftime scoreless. Then, when it appeared that 'Bama, with the ball at its own 30 and less than a minute to go, would be nursing the ball, lightning struck. Penn State had called time on two previous plays, hoping to get the ball in good field position and give their placekicker Matt Bahr a chance for a last-second score. But on third down, against a Penn State defense that had given up only

'Bama's goal-line stand in the 1979 Sugar Bowl game.

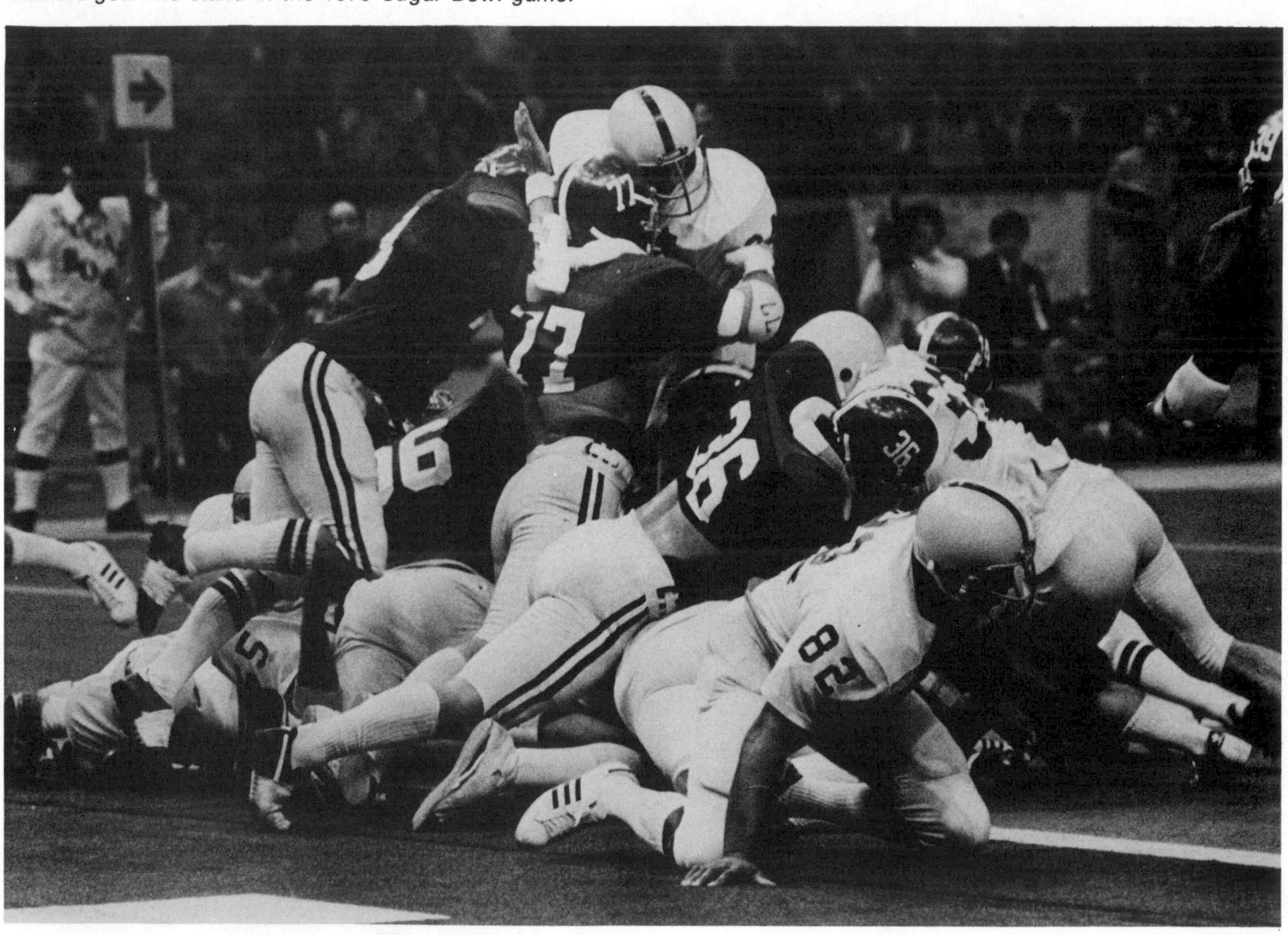

54 yards rushing per game throughout the year, Tony Nathan—who was to run for 127 yards against the Nittany Lions—shook loose for 30 yards to the Penn State 37. Now, with twenty-one seconds to go, it was Penn State's turn in the barrel as Alabama called time. Nathan added 7 more yards, and another time-out was called. And then, with fifteen seconds to go, Rutledge found Bruce Bolton open in the end zone and hit the man who had merely gone out to decoy the cornerback for the go-ahead touchdown. 'Bama led 7–0 with eight seconds to go in the half. All of a sudden that mysterious twelfth man, Mo Mentum, had taken his place on Alabama's side.

But if he had, he was to leave during the third quarter, when Penn State intercepted a pass deep in 'Bama territory and scored on a quick 17-yard Fusina-Fitzkee pass to tie the score 7–7 after three quarters. But the best was yet to come.

Alabama took command of the game again when the third-team punt returner, Lou Ikner, fielded a 50-yard Penn State punt and returned it 62 yards to the Lions' 11. On third down, Rutledge rolled out and pitched to Ogilvie, who powered in for the go-ahead touchdown. Score: Alabama 14, Penn State 7.

But it wasn't Ikner's punt return, nor Rutledge's passes or even Nathan's running that will be remembered when the 1979 Sugar Bowl game is recalled. It was a goal-line stand that will be remembered as one of the finest in the history of college football.

Midway through the fourth quarter, an Alabama fumble set up Penn State at the Tide's 19-yard line. One play gained 11 yards, making it first-and-goal

Bear Bryant is carried from the field after the Sugar Bowl win, his 284th collegiate win—just thirty fewer than the all-time leader, Amos Alonzo Stagg.

from the 8. A run gained two and set up three great 'Bama defensive plays. On the first, Chuck Fusina completed a pass to his favorite receiver, Fitzkee, who was open at the 1. 'Bama defender Don McNeal, who was in the end zone, came flying out and pushed Fitzkee out of bounds at the 1-yard line. Penn State then went with its bread-and-butter play, Matt Suhey up the middle. But power was met with power, and Suhey's charge was met by David Hannah and Rich Wingo for no gain. Penn State called time out, and Fusina came up to the ball to see how much the Lions would need on fourth down. Marty Lyons, who had come to know Fusina through their attendance at several All-American affairs, was blocking Fusina's view of the ball. "How far, Marty?" asked the Penn State quarterback. Lyons spread out his hands and said, "About ten inches. You'd better pass."

But despite the bait, Penn State didn't pass. Mike Guman got the call to go over the middle, where he was met head on by Barry Krauss. Guman was slammed down for no gain. Krauss was knocked out by the impact. And Penn State was knocked out of the number one spot.

When the AP poll became known two days later, 'Bama could celebrate its fifth national championship.

Alabama's football history is as illustrious as any school's, and it has obviously been the result of hard work on the part of many people, some of whom have been chronicled in the preceding pages, many who have not. Because Coach Bryant has vowed to remain as Alabama's head coach as long as he is contributing, with a goal of breaking Amos Alonzo Stagg's all-time record of 314 college victories, there is ample reason to believe that football will continue to be successful at Alabama.

Football is important to Alabama. University of Alabama President Dr. David Mathews told a Crimson Tide team:

"No one can help but be aware of rich tradition that is associated with this team and with this University. There are people too old now to go to the games who still remember wearing a crimson and white jersey, men for whom the University of Alabama has great meaning. There are also some young men who are still too young to be left alone in the stadium now who would like one day to wear a crimson and white jersey and to be part of the University of Alabama. That is tradition and it's something which is very, very important and very much a part of the University of Alabama.

"I'm convinced that greatness in any field has to come out of some kind of tradition. And our job is to make certain that the tradition that is the University of Alabama means as much and stands for as much for those who are yet to come, as it has for us and those who have gone before us."

Once again the cry, "We're number one!" rings out.

Auburn University

by Buddy Davidson

The story of Auburn football is the story of Ralph "Shug" Jordan, two blocked punts, John Heisman, Pat Sullivan and Terry Beasley, bowl games, and the underdog rising to the challenge. It is the story of people such as Gump Ariail, Billy Atkins, Tom Banks, Ken Bernich, Alex Bowden, Jackie Burkett, Loran Carter, Boots Chambless, Lloyd Cheatham, Joe Childress, Tim Christian, Bill Cody, Charlie Collins, Frank D'Agostino, Chaddie Davidson, Ed Dyas, Joel Eaves, Dave Edwards, Bennie Fenton, Jim Fenton, Tucker Frederickson, Bobby Freeman, Mike Fuller, Monk Gafford, Phil Gargis, three-time All-American Walter Gilbert, Lee Gross, Terry Henley, Billy Hitchcock, Auburn's first All-American Jimmy Hitchcock, Bobby Hoppe, Bobby Hunt, Ty Irby, Fob James, Gardner Jett, Lynn Johnson, Casey Kimbrall, Mike Kolen, Curtis Kuykendall, Mac Lorendo, Tommy Lorino, Dick McGowen, Leon Myers, Haygood Paterson, Jimmy Phillips, Jorge Portela, Jim Pyburn, Ken Rice, John Riley, Bo Russell, Dick Schmalz, Jimmy Sidle, Benny Sivley, Zeke Smith, Bobby Strickland, G. E. Taylor, Jack Thornton, Travis Tidwell, Tommy Traylor, Howell Tubbs, Tex Warrington, Cleve Wester, Ripper Williams, Larry Willingham, Jerry Wilson, Woody Woodall, and Gusty Yearout.

But it is more—much more. For the story of Auburn football is not only the story of people; it is also the story of the traditions, symbols and legends that have combined to give Auburn a rich and colorful history and a place on the Southern—as well as the national—football scene.

Throughout its long and storied history, Auburn University has been known by various names: East Alabama Male College, Alabama Agricultural and Mechanical College, and Alabama Polytechnic Institute.

William Max (Buddy) Davidson, director of sports information at Auburn, has been associated with the school's sports information department since his graduation from Auburn in 1964 and has served as president of the SEC Sports Information Directors Association.

It has also possessed more fanciful names, nicknames used to identify Auburn's athletic squads. One such sobriquet was Plainsmen, a name derived both from the school's geographic location and from the reference in Oliver Goldsmith's poem "The Deserted Village" to "Sweet Auburn! lovliest village of the Plain." Another of its nicknames is the more ferocious-sounding Tigers, pinned on the newly named Alabama Polytechnic Institute in 1900 following a 23–0 win over Tennessee.

And still another nickname frequently used to describe Auburn's teams is an outgrowth of the popular cheer "War Eagle!" Several theories exist as to the origin of the cheer. Legend has it that the first time the cry "War Eagle!" sounded at the Lovliest Village

War Eagle, the Auburn mascot.

was during a pep rally in Langdon Hall prior to the Auburn-Georgia game in November 1913. William L. White, a 1914 graduate, tells the story:

"Cheerleader Gus Graydon told the crowd, 'If we're going to win this game, we'll have to get out there and fight, because this means war.'

"During Graydon's speech, E. T. Enslen, dressed in his military uniform, felt something fall from his cap. He reached to the floor and picked up the metal emblem of an eagle and held it in the air. Someone asked what the object was and he replied, 'A war eagle.'"

Another version has it that during the 1914 game with the Carlisle Indians, Auburn decided to tire out Carlisle's best player, a tackle named Bald Eagle, by running all its plays in his direction. As the Auburn team assumed its formation, the quarterback, without the necessary formality of a huddle, merely yelled "Bald Eagle" to signify yet another play directed at the Carlisle tackle. As he continued to bellow "Bald Eagle," the Auburn partisans began to respond to his calls with an almost-echoing "War Eagle!"

Whatever the genesis of the cheer, it apparently worked, as Auburn beat both Georgia and Carlisle. Another decade and a half was to pass before the cheer took flight and form in the shape of War Eagle II, a live eagle captured on a farm outside of Auburn and given to the A-Club.

But unfortunately War Eagle II's upkeep was so expensive that he was soon released, and the War Eagles were eagleless for another thirty years. Then War Eagle III was captured in a cotton field where the famed Alabama International Speedway now stands, near Talladega; he first appeared at football games in 1961. He too had a short reign, for he escaped in 1964, to be replaced by War Eagle IV. Today the reigning mascot resides in a specially built cage next to Jordan-Hare Stadium and appears at all Auburn games to give support to the team and life to the cheer.

Just as the symbols and traditions of Auburn came to life, so too did its football program, brought to life in the persons of many illustrious men who toiled long and hard to bring Auburn football to its present place of eminence.

The first in that long line of illustrious men associated with Auburn football was Dr. George Petrie, who, in the fall of 1891, formed and coached the first Auburn team, becoming known as "the first football coach in the Deep South." Dr. Petrie, who was to serve as coach for only one season before "retiring" to become dean of the Graduate School for fifty-five more years, took his charges out to do battle in Auburn's inaugural year of 1892. Their very first game was played against the University of Georgia at Piedmont Park in Atlanta, kicking off the oldest continuous rivalry in the South. Auburn won that first game 10–0. And except for the war years 1917/1918 and 1943, the two Southeastern Conference rivals have met every year—82 times—with only a one-game difference in the won-lost column: Auburn 37, Georgia 38, and 7 ties.

Auburn closed out its first foray into the intercollegiate ranks with a 26–0 win over Georgia Tech, to even the first-year record at 2–2. Played every year but six since then, the Auburn-Tech series stands 38–39–4 after eighty-one games, with Tech owning a twelve point advantage in total scoring.

But while Auburn's series with Tech and Georgia are older and its rivalries with Florida and Mississippi State are longer, its series with Alabama has emerged as *The* Series.

The first game between the two SEC rivals took place in 1893, a post-season game between the two 1892 teams called the Tuskaloosa Boys and the Auburns. Searching for a way to balance the first season's budget, the members of the Auburn squad conceived the idea of playing a post-season game with Alabama. The manager of the Auburn team was deputized to go to Tuscaloosa and talk to the manager of the Alabama team to set up such a confrontation. As a result, a game was planned for Birmingham on Washington's Birthday 1893.

In the freelance world that governed football in its early years, football players were not always chosen from the student body. In fact, more often than not, former students and faculty members were pressed into duty. And so it came as no surprise when the Alabama team manager asked permission to play Eli Abbott, a faculty member and coach of the University team. Auburn, adhering to the code then in existence, graciously allowed Abbott to play.

Auburn was not without its own resourcefulness. Seeking a more experienced Easterner to prepare the team for its all-important first meeting with Alabama, the treasurer of Auburn borrowed enough money to send telegrams to the Eastern powerhouses—Harvard, Yale, Princeton and Penn—asking each school if it could recommend someone to coach Auburn for the game. And although the text of the telegram carefully explained that there would be no money to pay for this service—only a small amount to pay for the expenses incurred—surprisingly, every school responded.

From the names recommended, Auburn chose F. M. Balleit, a former University of Pennsylvania center who was famous for the "Balleit Snap," a method of throwing the ball through his legs so that it hit the ground and bounded into the arms of the runner. The Auburn team manager wrote to Balleit, who promptly accepted his offer.

The game itself turned out to be a little of Abbott and a lot of Balleit. And in the end the disciples of Balleit won over the Tuskaloosa Boys 32–22.

After the game Balleit received the team's wholehearted thanks, but, as promised, no pay for his efforts. However, after Balleit had made a little speech indicating that the experience was well worth it and that he had enjoyed his first visit to the South, Auburn's manager conferred with the team and decided to give Balleit money for a trip to New Orleans, making him Auburn's first paid coach.

Auburn and Alabama were to meet ten more times after that first game, with Auburn compiling an overall 6–4–1 edge in the series before it came to an abrupt halt after the 1907 game.

The reason for the termination of the then-burgeoning series was—despite the many rumors that arose about fights, dirty play and even shootings—a matter of $43.00. It seems that Auburn wanted a traveling squad of twenty-two men, with $3.50 allocated to each to cover train fares, hotel accommodations and meals. Alabama, however, wanted to limit the traveling squad to seventeen men, with only $2.00 in expense money for each. So for a total of $43.00—the price of four tickets to today's Auburn-Alabama game—the series was interrupted for forty-one years!

The legendary John W. Heisman, for whom the coveted Heisman trophy is named, took over as Auburn head coach in 1895. One of the great innovators of early football, Heisman brought with him some of the techniques that would make him one of the greatest coaches of all time—techniques such as the "hidden-ball" trick, the "hike" or "hep" vocal signal for starting plays, interference on end runs, the spin buck, the placement of his quarterback at safety on defense, and many more. Several of these innovations he would ultimately master during his five-year tenure at the Plains.

The legendary John Heisman, Auburn coach 1895–1899, for whom the coveted Heisman trophy is named.

Heisman also brought with him a sense of pomp and ceremony. A Shakespearean actor in the off-season, he would speak in exaggerated English, imploring his players in Macbethean terms to "thrust your projection into their cavities, grasping them about the knees and depriving them of their means of propulsion. They must come to earth, locomotion being denied them." Whether they understood the words or not, the players seemed to comprehend their import, for before Heisman left Auburn in 1900 to assume the coaching reins first at Clemson, then at Georgia Tech, Pennsylvania, Washington & Jefferson, and Rice over the next quarter-century, his Tiger teams lost only four of eighteen games.

Then, in 1904, Heisman's rather large shoes were more than adequately filled by Mike Donahue, who would ultimately join Heisman in the prestigious Hall of Fame. A son of the old sod, born in County Kerry, Ireland, Donahue had been schooled at Yale, where he had starred in football, basketball, baseball, track and cross-country.

Considering Donahue's renown and legendary athletic prowess, the people at Auburn expected a big strapping man, somewhat in the Frank Merriwell mold. So when the five-foot-four Donahue stepped off the train, he could see and feel the disappointment in the faces of the Auburn faithful who had turned out to greet him.

But that would be the one and only time he would disappoint them during his eighteen-year stay at the Plains. Starting with his first year—Auburn's first perfect season—Donahue was to lead Auburn to unprecedented heights, amassing an overall record of 89–26–4. An innovative coach who believed that the best offense was a good defense, Donahue fielded teams that shut out the opposition seventy-seven times and, in one twenty-three-game stretch, allowed only 13 points. During one period, starting with the 1913 opener and extending to the next-to-last game of the 1915 season, Donahue's Tigers won 22, lost 0 and tied 1, going through the entire 1914 season without being scored upon.

Hall of Fame coach Mike Donahue, Auburn coach for eighteen years.

But Donahue's contributions cannot be gauged by his record alone. For over and above his winning percentage of .752 was the all-important impetus he provided for the recognition of the brand of football played in the South.

For many years the term collegiate football had been used interchangeably with the phrase Eastern football. Indeed, ever since Walter Camp had begun to make up his list of the eleven greatest men on the gridiron in 1889, that "official" list had been dominated by Ivy Leaguers. In the very beginning only Harvard, Princeton and Yale appeared, to the exclusion of any other schools. In 1891 a center from the University of Pennsylvania sneaked onto Camp's team, and in 1895 a Cornell quarterback entered the *sanctum sanctorum.* But it was to remain an Ivy League monopoly until Clarence Hershberger of the University of Chicago was selected in 1898. Then, with a stunning show of begrudging ecumenicalism, Camp selected a Carlisle halfback in 1899 and two Army players in 1901. In 1904 he named two Midwesterners, but still the team had eight Ivy Leaguers and nine Easterners. It was to remain that way until 1915, when, in his twenty-seventh year of selecting teams, Camp finally added a Southern player: third-team guard G. E. Taylor of Auburn.

Coach Donahue had finally broken the geographic barrier. Now football reigned from sea to shining sea, a truly national game.

And so when Donahue left Auburn after the 1922 season to assume the head coaching position at LSU, he left behind a legacy to be remembered by all. Today he is remembered not only by his winning record, his outstanding defensive teams, and his contributions to Auburn football, but also by the very street Auburn's present stadium stands on, Donahue Drive—a fitting tribute to a man on whose small but sturdy shoulders Auburn's early fame solidly stood.

Auburn's football fortunes took a decided decline A.D.—After Donahue. In the nine years immediately following Donahue's departure, Auburn compiled a lackluster record of 28–46–8 under five head coaches. It had only three winning seasons, and two of those were marginal, at best.

But 1932 was another story. Under the leadership of Chet Wynne, a former Notre Dame fullback, the Tigers were the class of the South and the old Southern Conference. With Auburn's first consensus All-American, Jimmy Hitchcock, supplying the spark with his open field running and punting and Casey Kimbrell the firepower, the fastest running backfield in the South tore through its first nine opponents, running up a total of 255 points to only 34 for the opposition. Only a last-game tie with South Carolina sullied Auburn's otherwise perfect record as it attained a top-ten national ranking and long-awaited national prestige.

Chet Wynne, former Notre Dame fullback who brought Rockne's box formation and winning tradition to Auburn. Head coach of the unbeaten 1932 team.

Jimmy Hitchcock, Auburn's first All-American (1932).

Two-time All-SEC and All-American center Walter Gilbert with coach Jack Meagher.

However, when the Southeastern Conference began play in 1933, the Tigers reverted to form and fell to a 5–5 record, signaling Wynne's exit as head coach.

Under the aegis of new coach Jack Meagher, Auburn rebounded in 1935 to an 8–2 record and a third-place finish in the newly formed SEC. Led by center Walter Gilbert, a three-time All-American selection, the Tigers followed that in 1936 with a 7–2–1 record and their first invitation to a post-season bowl, the long-departed Rhumba Bowl in Havana, where they battled Villanova to a 7–7 tie.

The next year saw Auburn beat Tennessee, the Vols' last away loss for almost four years, and finish with a 5–2–3 record, meriting them their second bowl bid, this time to the Orange Bowl, where they held a once-beaten Michigan State team to zero first downs—still a bowl record—and beat them by a score of 6–0, to finish the season ranked fourteenth in the country.

But that was to be the Tigers' last hurrah for many years to come, as they sank from the zenith of the mid-thirties to the nadir of the late forties and early fifties, putting together only two winning seasons in fourteen years. Their low point—rock bottom, in fact—occurred during the coaching reign of Earl Brown. From 1948 through 1950, Auburn managed only three victories in twenty-nine games—including a 1950 team that went 0–10—and might have gone winless if it had not been for the exploits of a great quarterback named Travis Tidwell, who almost singlehandedly gave Brown his three wins as head coach.

One of those wins was over Alabama in 1949, the second game in the resumption of the state rivalry after a forty-one-year hiatus, and a game that has been called one of Auburn's greatest victories.

The renewal of the series between Auburn and Alabama had been a long time in coming. Following the rupture in relations over the $43.00 misunderstanding, representatives of the two schools tried mightily to resume athletic relations, but to no avail. There was an attempt in 1908, but the tentative agreement had to be abandoned because final negotiations were not concluded until after Auburn was well into its fall schedule and had no dates remaining for a game with Alabama. Again in 1911, 1923, 1932 and 1945 further attempts were mounted by both sides. However, the outcome was the same: no game.

Halfback Monk Gafford, All-American and engineer of Auburn's great victory over Georgia (1942).

Tex Warrington, All-American center (1944).

Finally, in April of 1948, the presidents of the two schools, with the not-too-subtle prodding of the state legislature, agreed to resume their rivalry. Another meeting took place in May of 1948 in Montgomery, and the presidents agreed that a game would be played on December 4, 1948, at Legion Field in Birmingham—the first game between the two natural rivals in more than forty years.

The occasion was more than just a game—it transcended that. It was the rallying point for thousands of followers of both schools, the fight for "bragging rights" to the entire state for an entire year. And, not incidentally, possession of the O.D.K. Trophy Cup, the symbol of state superiority.

In front of 46,000 fans, including Mike Donahue, who had coached Auburn the last time the two schools met, the two-touchdown-favorite Tide routed the Tigers 55–0, with Tidwell watching the game from the bench after an early-game injury.

But 1949 was different. 'Bama entered the second renewal as a three-touchdown favorite, fearing only the passing arm of Tidwell. But Tidwell and Auburn were not passing that afternoon. They threw only two the entire game, completing both. What they did best was play head to head against an Alabama team that had gone undefeated in its last seven games, and go them one better—one point better, in fact. Auburn won 14–13.

Tidwell remembers the magic of that moment:

"We had a better team than a lot of people thought by the end of the year. We didn't lose in our last four games, so we thought we had a better team than Alabama going into the game.

"The fact that they had won 55–0 the year before did not create any anger in us. We were fired up because it was Alabama, naturally. But we felt we would win.

"The statistics were about even, but it was no fluke that we won, unless you want to call it luck that they missed an extra point."

Tidwell avoided 'Bama's pass rush all afternoon, sometimes faking a pass before running the ball and sometimes dancing around in the pocket, avoiding the oncoming rush before taking off.

Travis Tidwell, hero of the 1949 Auburn-Alabama game.

Tidwell felt that the turning point came early in the game: "Alabama had us backed up deep in the first quarter, and Jim McGowen quick-kicked 84 yards into the Alabama end zone. It was not played up big at the time, but that changed things completely and to me it turned the game around."

But whatever did it, it worked. And as the Auburn players carried their hero—Travis Tidwell—off the field on their shoulders, they could look back with some satisfaction on a year that had ended 2–4–3. They had won the big one, the only one that really counted—they had beaten Alabama.

However, unbeknownst to all, that memorable victory, which had salvaged both the 1949 season and Coach Brown's job, was to be Brown's last. His 1950 edition suffered through the worst season in Auburn history, losing all ten of its games and scoring a scant thirty-one points.

And yet, from the ashes of that disastrous season would emerge a chain of events that would trigger Auburn's emergence as a national power and lead to the Golden Era of Auburn football.

The chain of events started with the dismissal of Brown, whose three-year record was a less-than-satisfactory 3–22–4. The next link in the chain was the appointment of Jeff Beard as athletic director in January 1951. Beard and a special committee were quickly invested with the solemn charge of finding a promising coach, one who could turn around the Auburn football program after seven successive nonwinning years and reverse the financial picture of the entire athletic department, which had fallen deeply in debt during that seven-year famine.

Beard decided that only one man could handle that Herculean task—Ralph "Shug" Jordan.

But at that magic moment in time, Jordan, who had applied for the Auburn head coaching position three years earlier and received little or no encouragement from the hiring committee, was head basketball coach and number one assistant to football coach Wally Butts at the University of Georgia. Remembering past slights, Jordan evinced absolutely no interest when the Auburn job opened up again in 1951.

Presuming that Jordan's lack of interest was, in reality, an indication of his interest, Beard approached his old classmate directly and requested that, as a personal favor to him, Jordan allow his name to be submitted to the committee as a candidate for the head coaching position. And although Jordan asked that he not be recommended to the committee, he nevertheless submitted a letter of application which read simply: "I hereby apply for the job of head football coach at Auburn."

With the backing of Beard and Auburn President Dr. Ralph Brown Draughon, the reluctant candidate soon became the overwhelming choice of the committee as a whole. And so, on February 26, 1951, Beard crowned his efforts and provided Auburn with

Coach Ralph "Shug" Jordan, Auburn coach for twenty-five years.

his proudest achievement—over and above his resuscitation of the dreary financial picture and the addition of 41,000-plus seats to Jordan-Hare Stadium—by announcing that James Ralph "Shug" Jordan had returned to the Plains as head coach.

Auburn's twenty-second football coach—and, fittingly enough, coach for the Golden Anniversary of organized football at the Plains—was an Auburn man through and through.

Born in Selma, Alabama, on September 25, 1910, young James Ralph Jordan began his organized athletic career in 1918, when, as a little tow-headed boy in overalls, he "drug a stalk of sugar cane in the front door of the YMCA and said, 'I want to play basketball.'" Thus Jordan is remembered by his first coach, Paul Grist.

Following Grist's maxim "Don't wait to be a great man; be a great boy," Jordan went on to participate in every sport Selma High School and the YMCA had to offer, including shot put, where he set the state record. What the young man-boy lacked in ability, he made up for with determination and desire. Even then Jordan's formula for success was taking shape, a philosophy that later evolved into his Seven D's of Success: Discipline, Desire to Excel, Determination, Dedication, Dependability, Desperation, and Damn it anyway—do something!

Jordan enrolled at Auburn—then called Alabama Polytechnic Institute—in the fall of 1928 and quickly established himself as one of Auburn's most promising all-round athletes, lettering in football, basketball and baseball. In football, he was a center whom the 1932 *Glomerata* called "as dependable a center as any team in the South could boast of." In baseball, he was a pitcher–first baseman, whose greatest moment as a player came in 1932, when he pitched Auburn to the Southern Conference championship with a 5–3 victory over Florida and hit a three-run home run to win the game. But while his skills at other sports were exceptional, Jordan was nonpareil when it came to basketball. With an outstanding two-hand set shot and a thorough knowledge of the give-and-go game, "Lefty" Jordan led the old Southern Conference in scoring in 1929 and was elected captain of the team in his junior year, a feat that the *Glomerata* noted "speaks for itself."

Jordan's athletic contribution prompted the 1932 *Glomerata* to proclaim, almost jubilantly, "Auburn is back in athletics. War Eagle is once again a national anthem."

Upon graduation, Jordan determined to make his avocation his vocation and pursue coaching as a career. But he was to learn that sometimes life can be less than the idyllic one usually pictured on the playing fields. Such was the case when he applied for his first coaching position at a small Alabama high school. When school officials noticed that Jordan's religious preference was marked "Catholic," they quickly withdrew their offer.

Jordan's football coach, Chet Wynne, heard about the unfortunate—and unfair—turn of events and offered Jordan a job as an assistant freshman football coach, with the added incentive of becoming a member of the basketball coaching staff. It was, to paraphrase Humphrey Bogart's closing remark to Claude Rains in *Casablanca,* the beginning of a beautiful relationship; one that, with the exception of two short sojourns, would last for the next forty-four years.

One of those sojourns was for something called World War II. Never one to pass up a good battle, Coach Jordan became Lieutenant Jordan and saw his share of combat in the next four years, participating in four of the war's major invasions: North Africa, Sicily, D-Day and Okinawa. When the world was once again safe for democracy, the decorated hero returned to the Plains. There he found a strange Auburn, an alien Auburn. For when he had marched off to the war, he had been assured that his job would still be open to him and that he would be welcomed back with open arms. He was wrong on both counts. The coaching regime had changed, and the new head coach wanted his own staff, not legacies from other administrations.

The thirty-five-year-old Jordan, who had given Auburn thirteen years of his life and his devotion, now faced the crossroads of his career. Jordan sought help from an old and trusted friend, Cliff Hare. Hare, a quarterback on Auburn's first football team, was dean of the School of Chemistry, chairman of the Faculty Athletic Committee, and former president of the old Southern Conference. But more than his titular positions, Hare had a rare gift for understanding and insight. Jordan came to him seeking no favors, only advice and a friendly ear. The two men spent many a Sunday afternoon together on the front porch of the Hare home on South Gay Street, discussing Auburn in general and Jordan in particular. Twenty-eight years later, in 1973, their names would be enshrined side by side on Auburn's Jordan-Hare Stadium. But at that time, captured in the stop-action of an historical freeze-frame, it was the collective opinion of these two Auburn giants that Jordan's future at the Plains looked bleak.

Auburn's first game under Jordan was against Vanderbilt, a team the Tigers had not beaten since 1925. Jordan remembers stepping out onto the field for his first time ever as head coach: "Cliff Hare Stadium held just over 20,000 then, and I remember looking up and seeing room for just over 20,000."

Auburn, sporting an inexperienced defense, expected Vanderbilt's great quarterback Bill Wade to put the ball in the air most of the time, and they were not disappointed. However, the Tigers turned three fumble recoveries and an intercepted pass by Vince Dooley into a 24–14 upset victory, and the Jordan legend was underway.

And so, in 1946, Jordan left the Plains for what appeared to be greener pastures elsewhere. His first stop was Miami and professional football. But the Miami Seahawks of the old All-American Conference were doomed to extinction almost before they began, and within the year Jordan was on his way to the University of Georgia.

At Athens, Jordan served from 1947 through 1950 as line coach for Wally Butts, as well as head basketball coach. Then came the phone call from Jeff Beard, and the rest is history.

It was to be the beginning of a glorious quarter-century that would produce 175 Auburn victories, 12 bowl appearances, 20 All-Americans, 67 All-Conference selections, a Heisman trophy winner (Pat Sullivan, 1971), an Outland trophy winner (Zeke Smith, 1958), a Jacobs award winner (Tucker Frederickson, 1964), and a national championship. And it was a period that would be proudly known as the Jordan Era.

All-American end Jim Pyburn (1954).

All-American tackle Frank D'Agostino (1955).

Jordan's first team finished at 5–5, a marked improvement over the previous year. In 1952, however, Jordan suffered a severe setback, as injuries and breaks brought the War Eagles down to earth hard, with a 2–8 record.

But if Jordan's first two seasons were disappointments, his third was a modern miracle, laying to rest all doubts about his abilities and establishing his credentials as a wonder worker. For all Jordan's 1953 team did was: finish the season with a 7–2–1 record, Auburn's first winning season in ten years and the most wins by a Tiger team since 1936; place two players—tackle Frank D'Agostino and end Jim Pyburn—on the All-SEC team, the first time two Auburn players had been selected to the All-Conference team in seventeen years; finish with more points scored than scored-against for the first time in eight years; win four Conference games for the first time in sixteen years; win the SEC Coach of the Year award for Jordan; and win an invitation to the Gator Bowl, only the third bowl bid in Auburn history.

Despite the fact that Auburn lost to Texas Tech 13–35 in the bowl game, they would have an opportunity to avenge their loss the following year. In fact,

Auburn's 1954 backfield—Fob James, Bobby Freeman, Joe Childress and Dave Middleton.

when they returned, this time with a 7–3 record, including their first win over Alabama since the 14–13 game of 1949, they beat Baylor by an almost-identical score: 33–13.

But the best was yet to come!

In 1955, with a backfield that included Joe Childress, Fob James and Howell Tubbs, the high-flying War Eagles put together an 8–1–1 record, including their second straight shutout of 'Bama, to finish second in the SEC, a half-game behind Ole Miss. For the third year in a row they won a bid to the Gator Bowl, but this time ran into an inspired Vanderbilt team, which beat them 25–13.

The year 1956 saw the Tigers "fall" to a 7–3 record, with another victory over the Tide to add to their ever-growing collection of 'Bama pelts. But the stage was set for Jordan's—and Auburn's—greatest years. And one of these was the national championship year of 1957.

The drive to the national championship had a rather inauspicious beginning. Just days before the start of fall practice, Jordan kicked his starting quarterback and fullback off the team for disciplinary reasons. He then moved a third-string, left-handed halfback to quarterback, and all Lloyd Nix did was lead Auburn to a perfect 10–0 season. The following year, Nix led the Tigers to a 9–0–1 season and became the only quarterback in Auburn history never to appear in a losing game.

All-American fullback Joe Childress (1955).

All-SEC halfback Fob James (1955).

Buck Bradberry, now the executive secretary of the Auburn Alumni Association, was the offensive coach in 1957. He recalls:

"We weren't picked very high, but we had a lot of character and dedication among our players. We felt we could win with Nix because he had the instincts to do the right thing with the ball.

"We ran a relatively simple offense. It was the straight fullhouse T-formation backfield. We relied a lot on the belly series because Nix knew just what to do with the ball. We didn't throw much."

Auburn won big with defense, allowing only 28 points all year. The Tigers led the nation in defense in all ten games and went on to set an NCAA record by leading the nation in defense for twenty-four straight weeks. Only Chattanooga, Houston, Florida State and Mississippi State managed to score seven points. And Auburn trailed only once all year, and that was to State, the only SEC team to score all year.

The season opened in Knoxville on a rainy day. Tennessee had beaten Auburn 35–7 the year before. Billy Atkins scored the only touchdown and kicked the point after, as Auburn won, 7–0. Atkins went on to score 82 points that year, an all-time Auburn record. He scored all the points in Auburn's first three SEC games: 7–0 over Tennessee, 6–0 over Kentucky, and 3–0 over Georgia Tech (the only field goal of his career).

End Jimmy Phillips, member of the Quarter-Century All-SEC football team.

Guard Tim Baker and end Jimmy Phillips were captains of the national championship team. Phillips was an outstanding two-way player who earned All-American honors that year. He caught only twelve passes, but three went for touchdowns. His reception from Nix won the Georgia game 6–0, after Auburn had held Georgia inside the Tigers' 4-yard line on eight straight plays.

The Tigers closed out the 1957 season with a 40–0 triumph over Alabama, in which sophomore linebacker Jackie Burkett intercepted a pass and returned it 64 yards for a touchdown.

"War Eagle" was once again a national anthem. Most of the 1957 team members returned in 1958, and only a 7–7 tie with Georgia Tech kept Auburn from running its string to thirty-one straight victories.

The 1958 team led the SEC in both total offense and passing, with Nix the SEC leader in completion percentage, prompting Bradberry to quip: "Even a knuckleball can be controlled."

But the offense was only half the story. Once again the Tigers' defense was superb. Led by Outland trophy awardee and All-American Zeke Smith, the War Eagles held all but one opponent to a touchdown or less; and that opponent, Mississippi State, scored fourteen points in a game in which the Auburn offense amassed its highest point total of the year, 33.

Zeke Smith, two-time All-American guard and winner of the Outland trophy as the nation's best lineman (1958).

Jackie Burkett, member of the Quarter-Century All-SEC football team.

The undefeated Tigers placed four members of their starting eleven on the first-team All-SEC, more than any other Auburn team: end Jerry Wilson, tackle Cleve Wester, guard Zeke Smith, and center Jackie Burkett, all linemen.

All-American fullback Ed Dyas (1960).

All-American quarterback Jimmy Sidle (1963).

Jordan added to his burgeoning laurels with a 7–3 record in 1959 and an 8–2 mark in 1960, bringing his five-year total to an astounding 41–8–1. But like the little girl who was all dressed up with no party to go to, Auburn was denied a bid to bowls during those five years because of an NCAA-imposed sanction.

After two mediocre years by Jordan's standards—6–4 in 1961 and 6–3–1 in 1962—the 1963 team put it all together and put Auburn back into the bowl picture. Behind the great blocking of tailback Tucker Frederickson and the running of quarterback Jimmy Sidle, the Tigers roared through their schedule winning nine of ten games, the only blemish on their record being a 13–10 loss to Mississippi State. For their efforts, Frederickson won the first of two straight Jacobs trophies, emblem of the outstanding blocker in the SEC, and Sidle, the first T-formation quarterback ever to lead the nation in rushing, was named to the All-SEC team and many All-American teams. The team was rewarded for its effort with a national ranking and an invitation to play in the Orange Bowl. And Coach Jordan was justifiably named the SEC Coach of the Year for the second time.

With the Orange Bowl bid in hand, Auburn met Alabama in the traditional season finale, the sixteenth game in the renewal of this great state rivalry. For the first time in their history, the two schools were nationally ranked in the top ten, Alabama number five and Auburn number six. And the game reflected the closeness in the two schools' standings.

Auburn scored first, when end Howard Simpson caused and then recovered a fumbled punt return deep in Tide territory. Back-up quarterback Mailon Kent came in for the injured Sidle and promptly tossed a touchdown pass to Frederickson to capitalize on the turnover. And when Woody Woodall kicked the PAT, it was 7–0 in favor of Auburn. Woodall later extended the lead to 10–0 with a field goal. Then 'Bama, which also had lost only one game all year, came roaring back as Benny Nelson ran 80 yards from scrimmage for an Alabama touchdown. The Tide went for two and made it, and the score stood at 10–8 in favor of Auburn. In the fourth quarter, with Joe Namath at the controls, Alabama mounted an effective aerial attack. With the wind at its back, 'Bama needed only a few more yards to get within range for the field goal required to win. However, when the Tide went to the air to get those precious yards, it was denied them by the flip-flop coverage Auburn right halfback George Rose put on Tide end Jimmy Dill. Rose broke up enough passes to ensure a 10–8 Auburn victory, its first victory over the Tide in five years.

All-American fullback and SEC Most Valuable Player (1964) Tucker Frederickson.

The Orange Bowl was a "declincher," with Nebraska holding off the Tigers to squeak by 13–7.

In 1964, with Sidle and Frederickson returning, Auburn was picked by the national news media to win the national championship. However, it was not to be, as Sidle injured his right shoulder in the very first game. Later moved to running back, Sidle could not hope to duplicate his 1963 feat of compiling a total of 1715 total yards on offense, and the Tigers suffered accordingly, slipping to a 6–4 record.

The following year, 1965, Auburn finished the season with a 5–4–1 record. But with strong wins in three of their last four games, the Tigers finished second in the SEC and merited a bid from the Liberty Bowl. The first Liberty Bowl game ever played in Memphis saw a record 38,607 fans brave freezing temperatures to watch the Tigers take on Ole Miss in the so-called Battle of the Chickasaw Bluff. After breaking on top 7–3 at halftime on a 44-yard run by Tom Bryan, the Tigers gallantly held off the one-touchdown-favorite Rebels until an Ole Miss pass, only one of four completed all night, went for a touchdown and a 13–7 Mississippi win.

All-American linebacker Bill Cody (1965).

Following 4–6 and 6–4 seasons in 1966 and 1967, the Tigers, behind the running of Mike Currier and the passing of Loran Carter, finished the 1968 season with another record of 6–4. But this time the 6–4 mark earned them a bid to face Arizona in the Sun Bowl, the first in a string of seven consecutive bowl appearances.

The War Eagles suffered an early setback in the Sun Bowl when Carter was injured and forced to leave the game in the opening moments. But from

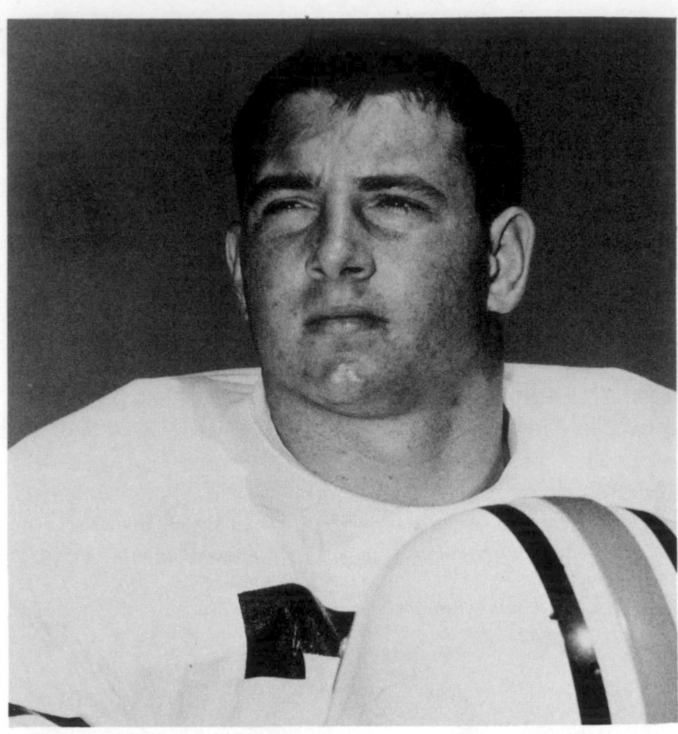

All-American tackle Jack Thornton (1965).

Freddie Hyatt, All-American end (1967).

then on, everything seemed to turn Auburn's way. One example of just how the Tigers' fortunes had changed occurred when wingback Connie Frederick, who also did the punting, had one of his kicks blocked, the ball rolling into the end zone some 30 yards away. Frederick retreated into the end zone

Buddy McClinton, All-American safety (1969).

and rolled the ball laterally 15 yards before he picked it up, avoided five Arizona Wildcats, and got off another punt. With Carter's back-up, Tommy Traylor, coming off the bench to lead the Tigers, and with All-American safety Buddy McClinton intercepting three passes for a Sun Bowl record, Auburn beat Arizona by the resounding score of 34–10, its first bowl win in fourteen years.

While the 1968 Tigers were starting a winning streak in bowl play, a pair of future All-Americans were leading the Auburn freshman team to an unbeaten season. Never before had two freshman players generated the interest quarterback Pat Sullivan and split end Terry Beasley had stirred among Auburn-watchers. Highly favored in their final game of the year, the Auburn freshmen traveled to Tuscaloosa to meet Alabama. There were more Auburn fans on hand than Alabama fans, but Alabama stunned Auburn early and ran up a 27–0 lead midway through the second quarter. At this point, Sullivan went to work. In less than five minutes he put 15 points on the board, and the Tiger Cubs trailed by only 12 at the half. Auburn then scored the first time it had the ball in the third period and closed the gap to just 6.

Faced with a fourth and 14 at his own 32, Cub punter David Beverly decided to run from punt formation and picked up 16 yards and the first down. Moments later, the Cubs went in for the score, taking the lead for the first time, 28–27. One more touchdown made the final score Auburn Frosh 36, Alabama Frosh 27.

The emergence of the tandem team of Sullivan and Beasley also signaled the reemergence of Auburn in the rivalry with Alabama. Winner of but one of the last ten games in The Series, Auburn looked forward to unleashing its dynamic duo against 'Bama in the classic the following year.

The 1969 matchup between the Tide and the Tigers was an event worth waiting for, at least from the standpoint of Auburn fans. Going into the game with a 7–2 record and a national ranking, Auburn was favored to win the game. But Alabama took an early 10–7 lead before Sullivan got cranked up. WIth just thirty-one seconds left before the half, Sullivan launched a bomb to Connie Frederick, who took the ball away from a defender at the 3. No time-outs remained as Auburn lined up with seven seconds left. Fullback Wallace Clark plunged through a big hole over Greg Robert and Jimmy Speigner and went into the end zone untouched, putting the Tigers back in the lead, 14–10.

Moving consistently on offense and making big plays on defense, Auburn built up a 42–26 lead with two minutes left to play. Auburn had fourth and 6 at its own 16 and the game safely in hand when Frederick went back to punt for Auburn. Alabama sent its great running back Johnny Musso back in single safety and put up a ten-man rush, hoping to block the punt.

The ten-man rush was just a disguise for a punt return, and Frederick was well aware of it. All week he had studied films of the 'Bama punt rush, and he knew they often sent only one end across the line of scrimmage to ensure that the punter kicked, while the other end peeled back to set up the wall. During Thanksgiving dinner two nights earlier, Frederick had told Sports Information Director Buddy Davidson, "I'm going to score against Alabama if I have to run out of punt formation on fourth down."

Davidson incredulously gulped and asked, "Are you going to do this on your own?"

"Well, if it's close to the half and the ball is around midfield and we can't get hurt if I don't make it, I'll ask permission," Frederick replied.

On several fourth downs early in the game, Davidson thought that *that* was the time Frederick was going to run. But with fourth and 6 at the 16, the

Two men who would rewrite the SEC record books: quarterback Pat Sullivan and wide receiver Terry Beasley.

thought never crossed Davidson's mind that *this* was the time.

"I made up my mind I was going to check both ends, and if one of them turned as soon as I got the snap I was going to run his way. He did, and I did," Frederick said.

Even his teammates were caught completely by surprise. With Frederick about 30 yards downfield and hearing no sound of foot meeting ball, they started looking for the ball—first up in the air, then around. All they could discern was the wild cheering of the crowd urging Frederick on as he headed up the right sideline. When he got to midfield, most of the players on both teams still had their backs to him.

Frederick, who ran like a man afraid someone *would* catch him for the first 45 yards and afraid they *wouldn't* for the last 45, was in the clear, but tiring. He evaded the single safety and lumbered the 84 yards for a touchdown, the longest run ever from scrimmage by an Auburn player in an SEC game, and, not incidentally, the longest run from scrimmage ever against the opposing head coach.

Auburn play-by-play announcer Gary Sanders caught the moment: "Back to kick is Connie Frederick, on the 1-yard line. We've just done a little figuring ourselves, remembering the Tennessee game . . . Hey, Frederick's gonna run the ball. . . . Frederick's gonna run it! He's over the 20 . . . 25 . . . 30 . . . 40 . . . midfield! He's got one man to beat at the Alabama 30. . . . He's gonna run for a touchdown! Connie Frederick has just run for a touchdown on a fake punt. Ronnie Ross made a great block for him, but it was mostly just the surprise of the moment. Holy smokes, what a run by Connie Frederick!"

In even more dramatic fashion, Auburn came from 17 points behind to win the 1970 classic. Again with a 7–2 record, Auburn had entered the game as the favorite. But Alabama had refused to read the pregame predictions, and with Scott Hunter completing his first five passes and Johnny Musso rushing for 72 yards, 'Bama built up a 17–0 lead with two minutes left in the first quarter. Undaunted, Sullivan went to work. With his record-setting sidekick Terry Beasley sitting on the bench with an injury, Sullivan called on every teammate to take up the slack. And they all responded.

Tiger defenders came alive and gave the offense the ball in excellent field position. Suddenly it was 17–7. Another pass interception halted a 'Bama drive. Beasley came back into the game just before the half and caught three straight passes from Sullivan. With seconds left on the clock, Gardner Jett kicked a field goal, cutting the margin to 7. The score at the half was 17–10.

Early in the third quarter, with Beasley as a slotback, Sullivan handed the ball to Terry, who made one of the greatest runs in Tiger history, reversing his field twice before stepping out of bounds at the Tide 7. Beasley's 43-yard run set up Sullivan's 7-yard

Connie Frederick, Auburn's punter-cum-runner.

Larry Willingham, All-American defensive back (1970).

sweep for a touchdown on the next play, making the score 17–17. Then each team added a field goal. In the fourth quarter, Auburn went ahead 27–20, only to see Alabama score on a bomb and make the two-point conversion, to take the lead 28–27.

Facing the moment of truth with less than five minutes remaining, Sullivan hit Alvin Bresler for a 19-yard completion. He then dumped off a swing pass to tailback Mickey Zofko, who raced 36 yards to the Alabama 6. Wallace Clark scored two plays later to give Auburn a 33–28 lead. With less than three minutes to play, 'Bama tried the same long pass that had put it ahead scant moments before. But this time Auburn defensive back Dave Beck, who had been victimized before, made the interception, and the Tigers ran out the clock. The game and the annual "bragging rights" were theirs: 33–28.

In the lead story in the Tuscaloosa *News* the next morning, Charles Land wrote, "Pat Sullivan, Auburn's fabulous junior quarterback, may not be able to part the Red Sea, but he certainly has a way with Crimson Tides."

Pat Sullivan, 1971 Heisman award winner.

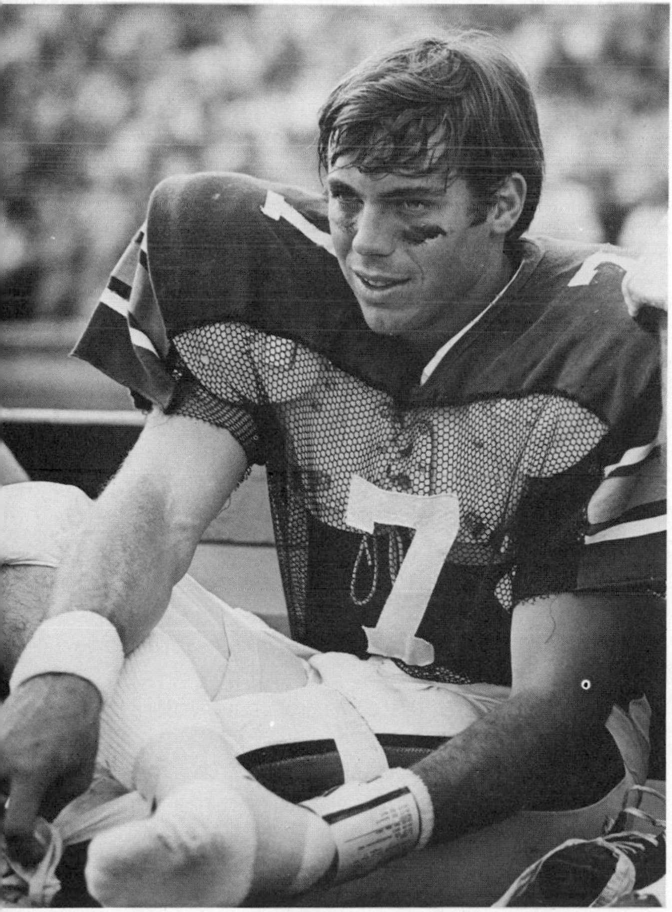

It was the third straight comeback victory Sullivan had engineered over Alabama.

To crown Auburn's greatest season in seven years, the War Eagles returned once again to the Gator Bowl, where, in a battle of quarterbacks, Sullivan and Auburn outgunned Ole Miss and Archie Manning 35–28. Sullivan not only set new records for total offense in a Gator Bowl game but was named the Outstanding Player in the contest and selected to the all-time Gator Bowl team as well.

It was but one more honor to add to the burgeoning list of incredible accomplishments this talented junior amassed. For setting the all-time NCAA record for most average yards gained per play and leading the nation in total offense, Sullivan was named to several All-American teams and selected as the Most Valuable Player in the SEC by the Nashville *Banner,* the Birmingham Quarterback Club, and the Atlanta Touchdown Club. But it was to all serve as a table-setting for his senior year.

In 1971 Sullivan lived up to expectations by becoming the first player from a school where John Heisman had coached to win the trophy that bears his name. Early in the season, Sullivan engineered a late fourth-quarter drive that produced a 10–9 victory over Tennessee. Routine victories followed, until the Tigers came to the next-to-last game of the year, the time-honored battle with the Georgia Bulldogs, waged in Athens. Never before in the history of Southern football had two unbeaten teams met so late in a season. Both schools were ranked in the top five teams in the country for the first time ever, and the SEC and national championships were at stake. All the major bowls awaited the outcome.

The Atlanta *Journal* sent writers to both campuses for the week prior to the game. Each day the writers wrote companion stories on the same subject: interviews with the head coaches' wives, the man on the street, the cooks in the dining halls. Every angle was covered, no stone left unturned. In a fishbowl all year, Sullivan knew, as did football fans everywhere, that he faced a date with destiny on November 13; if he was to win the Heisman, this was the game in which to do it.

The atmosphere in Athens was more carnival than football. Georgia students maintained a night-long pep rally outside the Auburn team headquarters, with many of them making their presence known by parading across the roof at regular intervals. Hundreds of members of the media converged on the University of Georgia that weekend, all wanting to see the national, SEC and Heisman trophy winners crowned.

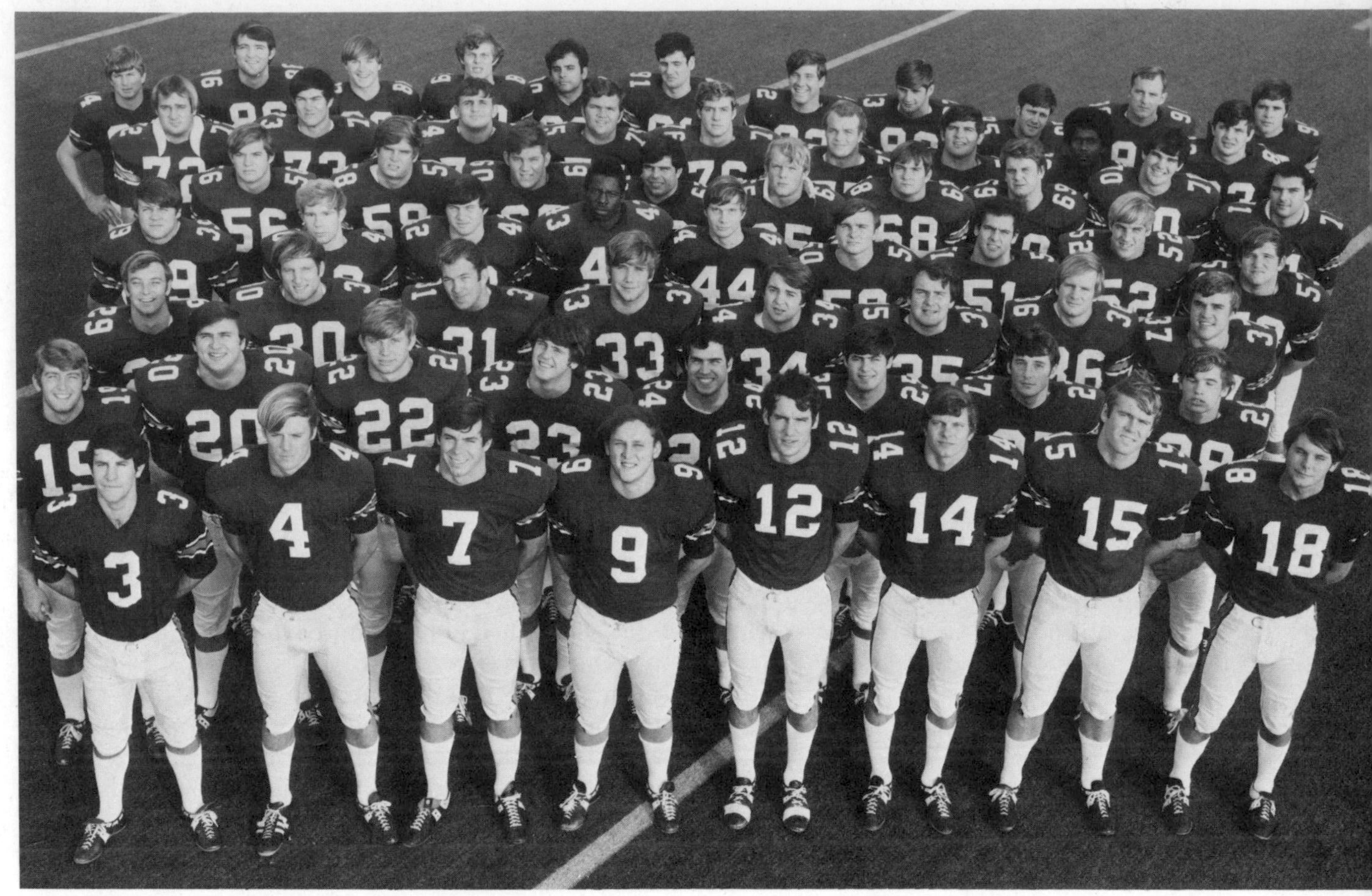

1971 team—Auburn's first and only Sugar Bowl team.

Like no other team before it, Auburn rose to challenge. Loose and confident, the team arrived at Sanford Stadium two hours prior to kickoff, only to find the stadium jammed to the rafters with hostile-sounding fans. Thousands more were perched on the railroad trestle across the street from the stadium.

Playing before the largest press corps ever to cover a game in the Southland, Sullivan etched his name indelibly among the great quarterbacks of all time, picking apart the best defensive team in the nation. He hit on 14 of 24 passes for 248 yards, an average of 8 yards gained per play, and threw 4 touchdown passes, 2 to Beasley, as the Tigers "whupped" the Bulldogs 35–20. It was a virtuoso performance by a master. Just as he had eleven times before, Sullivan had faced a top ten–ranked team and come away victorious. But this time he came away with something more: the Heisman trophy.

After you've just had a Heisman trophy winner and your first Sugar Bowl team, what do you do for an encore? Jordan was not exactly sure when the next season started, but he had an answer by the season's end.

The 1972 Tigers were supposed to start "the demise of Auburn," according to the Associated Press pre-season predictions. Looking at the schedule and the pre-season lineup, the prediction seemed more than realistic. Gone were the name players, the All-Americans, the high pre-season rankings, the slick magazine covers. Jordan could only call on a defensive secondary whose biggest member weighed all of 169 pounds. He did not have a quarterback who had ever taken a snap, and several starters were former walk-ons.

The Tigers struggled to beat Mississippi State 14–3 and Chattanooga 14–7, setting the stage for the two-touchdown favorite Tennessee Vols to put the Tigers in their place.

The game was supposed to mark the initiation of a "gentlemen's agreement" requiring the visiting team to wear white jerseys when two SEC teams played. Tennessee, the visitors to Legion Field, came out in their traditional orange jerseys, expecting some kind of furor over their brand of gamesmanship. When approached in the press box by the Tennessee media, Auburn officials merely said, "We came here to win a football game. We don't care what color jerseys the other team wears."

Auburn lost the jersey war, but won the battle 10–6. On three other occasions that season the Tigers were more than two touchdown underdogs and still won. Going into the season finale, Alabama led the nation in rushing and was ranked number two in both polls. Alabama was such an overwhelming favorite that in the poll of sports editors in the state conducted by the Associated Press, only two had picked Auburn.

At his annual appearance before the Birmingham Quarterback Club twelve days prior to the game, the Alabama head coach said, "I would rather beat the Cow College once than Texas ten times." The "Cow College" remark rankled most of Auburn's fans and all of its players, many of whom had played on teams that had beaten 'Bama two out of the preceding three years. Now they ached to make it three out of four.

But to do that the Tigers would have to keep the ball away from Alabama and control 'Bama's vaunted Wishbone offense, an offense that had scored 37-plus points per game and powered the Tide to ten straight victories and a number one national ranking. Indeed, the Tiger defense created the game's first scoring opportunity when David Langner—whose father had been the starting fullback in 1949 when Auburn upset the Tide—intercepted a 'Bama pass and returned it 10 yards to the Alabama 25. Three runs by Terry Henley netted 21 yards, and the Tigers needed just 4 more to break on top. But they could not get them, and when the snap on a fourth-down field-goal attempt was high, the Tigers came away empty.

Early in the second quarter, 'Bama scored on a sustained 71-yard drive. When little Roger Mitchell, who had almost blocked Alabama's first punt, broke through to block the extra point, the score stood 6–0, an important factor in the ultimate outcome of the game. Following the early interception by Langner, Auburn's offense had come to a dead stop, managing just 8 yards in total offense and one first down. But the Tiger defense, led by Danny Sanspree, Mike Neel, Johnny Simmons, Bill Newton, Dave Beck and Langner, played their hearts out, and limited the Tide to a 9–0 halftime lead and only 112 yards in total offense.

It was 16–0 Alabama at the end of three quarters, and the visiting dignitaries from the Gator Bowl, who had come to watch their invitees, the War Eagles, in action, decided to depart in an attempt to beat the traffic to the airport. Gator Bowl President L. C. Ringhaver, who had flown to the game in his private plane, personally acknowledged Auburn's gallant effort to the school's officials and let them know that he was looking forward to having them in Jacksonville.

At the start of the fourth quarter, Auburn finally got its offense going, driving for three straight first downs and its longest drive, from its own 34 to the 'Bama 19. On fourth and 8, Jordan sent in his field-goal unit. Both sides voiced their disapproval, 'Bama fans because a field goal would beat the 16-point spread and Auburn fans because they wanted a touchdown. As it turned out, Jordan made the right decision. Gardner Jett made the longest field goal of his life, 42 yards, and Auburn was on the scoreboard—but still down 3–16—with 9:50 to play.

The Gator Bowl contingent was just taxiing into place for takeoff. The parking-lot printers tore up their red and white 16–0 bumper stickers and reprinted them to read 16–3. The press-box photographers all left to go to the sidelines to duly record the victory celebration. Only one photographer stayed upstairs, sixteen-year-old Joe King, son of Les King, the director of Auburn Photographic Services. And little Joe recorded two of the greatest moments in college football history.

After the ensuing kickoff, 'Bama moved for three first downs before a fired-up Auburn defense stopped them at midfield. On fourth down, with a kicking situation at hand, Johnny Simmons dropped back in single safety. The rest of the Tiger eleven lined up for a ten-man rush: Mitchell on the left side, Langner on the right, and linebacker Bill Newton inside Langner on the right side.

Newton, who would be a key man in two of Auburn's key moments, was a walk-on, the twin brother of Bob Newton, one of Auburn's starting defensive tackles. A standout linebacker all year, he was to make ten individual tackles and six assists during the game. But now he was just an inside lineman who, it was thought, did not stand a chance of blocking the punt.

At the snap of the ball, Newton raced forward, expecting to be hit. No contact, so he continued his charge, stretching over the outstretched leg of the punter. He blocked the kick, and Langner, coming in from the outside, scooped up the ball on the bounce and raced into the end zone. Jett, still another former walk-on, kicked the PAT. With 5:30 left, Auburn kicked off, trailing 16–10.

Alabama promptly made three first downs before facing a third and 4 on its own 48. Anticipating that Alabama would run its best play, the Wishbone option, assistant head coach and defensive coordinator Paul Davis substituted his number two rover, Jim Sirmans, for the strong-side linebacker. Davis then directed the two outside linebackers, or rovers, to both go directly for the quarterback and force him to make a quick decision. They did, and Mike Neel, the rover on the left side, penetrated untouched and made the tackle on quarterback Terry Davis, forcing a punt.

What would have been a routine play before Auburn blocked the first punt now became a cause for concern, as both teams began maneuvering in a mental chess match that would have done justice to Fischer and Spassky.

Sirmans, already in the game, usually replaced the strong-side linebacker in punting situations. So when Paul Davis sent in a substitute, with instructions to line up in the same formation that had forced the first blocked punt, Sirmans stayed in. Auburn had too many men on the field. As Alabama lined up to punt, Davis realized there were too many orange and blue uniforms and frantically called time out.

Meanwhile, the Gator Bowl visitors made contact with Atlanta radar and asked for the college scores. Upon hearing that "their" team, Auburn, had cut the lead to 16–10 with 2:50 to play, they breathed a sigh of relief. The parking-lot print shops were busy printing red and white 16–10 bumper stickers. Joe King reloaded his camera. And Auburn President Harry M. Philpott made his way to the sidelines, where he expressed his feelings to Auburn journalism professor David Housel: "This is a highly respectable way to finish the season. We can go to the Gator Bowl with our heads held high."

The Alabama line was kneeling facing the Auburn defense, whose members were huddled with their backs to the line. Punter Gregg Gantt was the only

Bill Newton goes up to block the first 'Bama punt, and David Langner stands ready to field the ball for an Auburn touchdown.

In an instant replay of the first blocked punt, Newton and Langner combine to give the Plainsmen a memorable 17–16 win over 'Bama.

'Bama player on his feet. The rest of his teammates seemed unconcerned.

Davis finally finished chewing out Sirmans for not coming out of the game when he was supposed to. He then turned to Coach Jordan and said, "We haven't got a chance now. The time-out gave them time to get together."

The time-out did give Alabama time to get together. But almost too much time, as they began to outsmart themselves. Since Roger Mitchell had almost blocked the first punt and had blocked the first PAT from the outside, Alabama set its punt protection for an outside rush, not realizing that Newton had come from the inside.

The last thing Newton told his teammates when they broke the huddle was for one of them to block the punt because he would not "have a chance." Little did he realize that within a matter of seconds he would become the answer to an all-time sports trivia question: Who is the only player in college football history to block two consecutive Alabama punts?

Once again, at the snap of the ball, Newton burst through untouched and again got his hand on the ball. In an instant replay of the first blocked punt, Langner swooped in from the outside, picked up the ball on the bounce, and raced untouched into the end zone.

Pounded by his teammates when he got back to the bench, Langner sat on the bench breathing hard as the PAT unit lined up. Forgetting that Mitchell had blocked the first 'Bama PAT, he looked up and asked, "What is everybody so excited for? Why are we kicking an extra point? We need a two-point conversion to win, don't we?"

But the War Eagles only needed one now. And they got it when Beck fielded a bad snap and set it up on the tee just in time for Jett to drive it through the goal posts for the extra point and the 17–16 victory.

The Gator Bowl committee landed in Jacksonville, heroes for having had the foresight to bring the team that had beaten Alabama. Joe King wound up as the only photographer with photos of both blocked punts. The parking-lot printers hastily changed to orange and blue ink and sold thousands of 17–16 bumper stickers, forerunners of the best-selling bumper sticker in the state of Alabama: "Punt 'Bama Punt!" And in the dressing room following the game, Jordan hesitated, then told his 1972 team that they were his all-time favorites.

Tom Siler, the highly respected sports editor of the Knoxville *News Sentinel,* put the game into perspective this way: "Thirty years from now, when people have stopped talking about Roy Reigels's wrong way run in the Rose Bowl, they will be talking about Auburn blocking two punts and beating Alabama in 1972."

And the 1972 team did not let Jordan down in the Gator Bowl, as it beat yet another two-touchdown favorite, Colorado, 24–3.

Three years later, Ralph "Shug" Jordan retired. He had not only been Auburn's football coach for twenty-five years, he had been Auburn football for that quarter-century. A legend in his own time, Jordan was the first SEC coach to win a hundred games at his alma mater, compiling a record of 175–83–7; the third-winningest active coach in the nation when he retired; the head coach at his alma mater longer than any other coach in the history of the SEC; and the first coach to have two stadiums named for him, Jordan-Hare Stadium in Auburn and Ralph Jordan Track and Field in Selma.

Pat Sullivan and "Shug" Jordan.

But a barebones statistical recapping of Jordan's accomplishments tells only part of the story. The other part is the man himself. On Jordan's retirement after the 1976 season, David Davidson of the Atlanta *Journal* wrote: "Shug Jordan will be missed by many come the fall of 1976. Jordan offered a dignity to Southern football that will be difficult to replace. The Deep South will share Auburn's loss of the gentleman-coach."

Pat Sullivan put it another way: "Winning the Heisman trophy was the second-highest honor of my life. The first was playing for Coach Jordan."

Although Jordan's retirement left a huge void in the hearts of football fans everywhere, his place—if not his shoes—has been adequately filled by Doug Barfield, who stepped up from his position as Auburn's offensive coordinator.

Barfield, like Jordan before him, grew up in athletics. He also grew up in much the same mold as Jordan: both are true Southern gentlemen, well educated and articulate. Born in Castleberry, Alabama, Barfield was raised in the small town of Grove Hill and played his collegiate football at Southern Mississippi, where he had the unusual distinction of playing quarterback on two Southern Miss teams that beat and tied Alabama.

With the guiding philosophy of "building one brick at a time," Barfield has guided Auburn to a 16–16–1 overall record and two straight third-place finishes in his three years at the helm. And he has developed one of the best bricks to a winning team imaginable, an awesome running game and the best running back in the school's history in Joe Cribbs. As a junior in 1978, Cribbs led the SEC in four rushing categories, set six new Auburn records for season and career rushing and scoring, set the one-game rushing mark with 250 yards against Georgia, and averaged 154.1 yards for every game he started.

With such an offensive potential, Barfield may well be the logical successor to Ralph "Shug" Jordan in achievement as well as title as he seeks to restore Auburn to the championship heights it has known so well, and so frequently, in the past.

The men, traditions and legends that have come to immortalize "Sweet Auburn" have been many. But

The changing of the guard: former coach Ralph "Shug" Jordan and his successor, Doug Barfield, Auburn's twenty-first head coach.

none has symbolized the spirit of Auburn more than the Auburn Creed, written by the first Auburn coach, Dr. George Petrie, and memorized by Auburn students, players and nonplayers alike down through the years as the embodiment of all Auburn has come to mean:

"I believe that this is a practical world and that I can count on what I earn. Therefore, I believe in work, hard work.

"I believe in education, which gives me the knowledge to work wisely and trains my mind and my hands to work skillfully.

"I believe in honesty and truthfulness, without which I cannot win the respect and confidence of my fellow men.

"I believe in a sound mind, in a sound body, and a spirit that is not afraid, and in clean sports that develop these qualities.

"I believe in obedience to law because it protects the rights of all.

"I believe in the human touch, which cultivates sympathy with my fellow men and mutual helpfulness and brings happiness for all.

"I believe in my country, because it is a land of freedom and because it is my own home, and I can best serve that country by 'doing justly, loving mercy, and walking humbly with my God.' Micah 6:8.

"And because AUBURN men and women believe in these things, I believe in AUBURN and love it."

University of Florida

by Norm Carlson

Since its first season in 1906, Florida football has been characterized by a series of peaks and valleys, and this phenomenon is reflected in the Gators' fanatic, frustrated fans. Week after week they fill the stadium to capacity. In the off-season they nourish themselves on tales of past heroics, their hopes high for an upcoming winning season. And occasionally they deride their team's inability to win a Southeastern Conference championship.

They have witnessed and are eager to retell the heroics of Steve Spurrier, whose last-quarter rallies established him as a legend and earned for him the Heisman trophy. And Gator fans watched breathlessly as a sophomore tailback named Larry Smith ran 94 yards for a touchdown in the 1967 Orange Bowl. Typical of the flair of Gator football was the sight of Smith's pants falling as he neared the enemy's 10-yard line. Smith tugged and tugged at his pants, barely succeeding in keeping them up as he crossed the goal line.

"The Gators are delightfully implausible," says Orlando *Sentinel* sports editor Larry Guest.

And so when you think of Florida football, you recall big plays by superior talents, big wins at the oddest of moments, and oh-so-close brushes with that Southeastern Conference title.

After playing musical campuses in Ocala and Lake City, the University of Florida finally set up shop in Gainesville in 1906, following passage of the "Buckman Bill," which merged the state's seven institutions of higher learning into four. For all intents and purposes, this was the beginning of University of Florida football. In 1907 the alligator was adopted as the school's emblem, and it has been the Florida Gators ever since.

Those early Gator teams were powerhouses. From 1906 to 1913 they compiled a record of forty wins, thirteen losses and five ties. "Dummy" Taylor set field-goal records that remained standing until the David Posey days of the mid-1970s, and the 1913 team crushed Florida Southern 144–0, a scoring mark that still stands as the best in the school's history.

Norm Carlson joined the University of Florida staff in 1963 as sports publicity director after five years as sports information director at Auburn University. He was executive secretary of the Florida Sportswriters Association for eleven years. He is currently assistant director of athletics.

Taking the caliber of the competition into account, the finest of the early years of Gator football began in 1923, when a young ROTC officer named James A. Van Fleet took over the head coaching job. Major Van Fleet guided the Gators to a two-season record of 12–3–4, earning a pair of 7–7 ties with national power Georgia Tech, whipping Alabama 16–6, tying Texas 7–7, and playing mighty Army off its feet before bowing.

The 1923 Alabama game was the biggest victory in Florida's young history. The unbeaten Tide needed one more win to clinch the Southern championship, and the game was played in Birmingham. Using the punting of Ark Newton, the great all-round play of Edgar Jones, who scored all 16 Florida points, and the tactical genius of Coach Van Fleet, the Gators came away with a victory.

The game was played in a driving rain and ankle-deep mud. At halftime, Van Fleet ordered his regular players to exchange uniforms with the dry, clean scrubs, and the lighter, faster Gators came from a 6–0 deficit to win going away, 16–6.

Coach Van Fleet said, "Coach Wallace Wade never spoke to me again after that game."

Van Fleet went on to become one of our nation's military heroes in World War II and the Korean War. He was a graduate of West Point and had played football there—explaining why the 14–7 loss to his alma mater was the toughest defeat in his brief coaching career. In that game the Gators came close to victory, scoring two touchdowns that were disallowed.

Gator football, however, continued to prosper, and the 1928 team still ranks as perhaps the finest in school annals. Featuring blazing speed, the Charles Bachman–coached Gators led the nation in scoring with 336 points. They won eight consecutive games before falling, 13–12, in a legendary contest with Tennessee played in Knoxville for the Southern championship.

An overview of Florida Field, where 62,800 watch the Gator Band spell out their favorite initials.

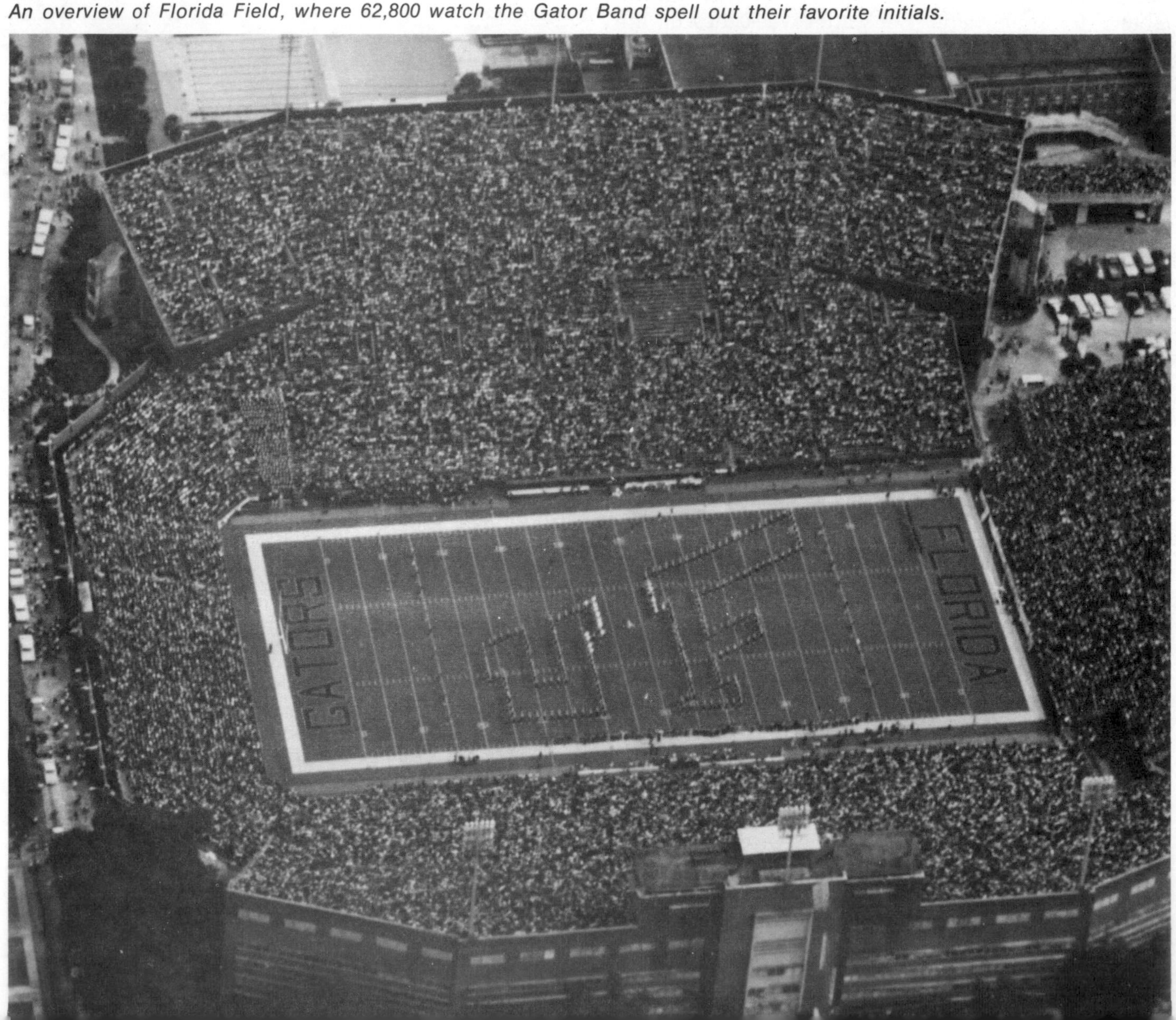

The other major Southern power that came closest to the Gators was Georgia, which lost by a 26–6 score. Auburn lost 27–0, and only lightly regarded N.C. State kept the final score close, holding Florida to a 14–7 victory.

The Gators were led by a pony backfield of quarterback Clyde "Cannonball" Crabtree, halfbacks Royce Goodbread and Carl Brumbaugh, and fullback Rainey Cawthon. This quartet averaged only 168 pounds, but their blazing speed would have delighted a track coach. The strength of the team was reflected in the quality of its reserves—most notably the team captain, Goof Bowyer, an outstanding athlete who was only the second-string quarterback, and Red Bethea, who would have started on most collegiate teams of that era, but was a reserve in the Gator backfield.

Clyde Crabtree was an extraordinary athlete possessing the ability to pass with either hand and to kick or throw on the run. To elude tacklers he used his five-foot-eight, 148-pound frame in much the same manner as an "India Rubberman." In addition to having a talented backfield that shared ball-carrying assignments with equal success, the Gators were dangerous throwing the football. Their standout receiver was end Dale Vansickle, who became the school's first All-American on the basis of his two-way performance and exceptional pass-catching ability.

Clyde Crabtree, outstanding back for the 1927–1928–1929 Gators, who won twenty-three out of twenty-nine games.

A Gainesville native, Vansickle is rated as one of the finest all-round athletes in Gator history. Those who watched his performances game after game claim that Vansickle was way ahead of his time and would have attracted pro scouts in droves, as his skills would have meshed perfectly with the pro-style passing attack.

Vansickle went on to become one of Hollywood's most famous stuntmen and president of the Hollywood Stuntmen's Association. He died in his mid-sixties as the result of an accident while attempting a stunt.

Coach Bachman said about Vansickle:

"In those days the halfbacks passed more than the quarterback, and we had an excellent passer in Brumbaugh, who went on to play quarterback for the Chicago Bears. We got the ball to Vansickle in the flat, and he caught it with great concentration and hands. Then, when the defense moved up to stop that, he would go deep with his tremendous speed and we'd get the easy long-gaining play."

End Dale Vansickle, Florida's first All-American (1928).

Despite losing Vansickle to Hollywood and Brumbaugh to professional football—where he quarterbacked the great Chicago Bear teams of the thirties, starring Red Grange and Bronko Nagurski—the Gator team was every bit as good in 1929 as it had been in 1928. Crabtree was back, and he powered the still-potent offense, winding up his career with an 81-yard punt return against national power Oregon that led Florida to a 20–6 victory and an 8–2 record. The cumulative record for 1928–29 was 16–3, the most illustrious record in the long history of Florida football, and one that included back-to-back victories over Georgia.

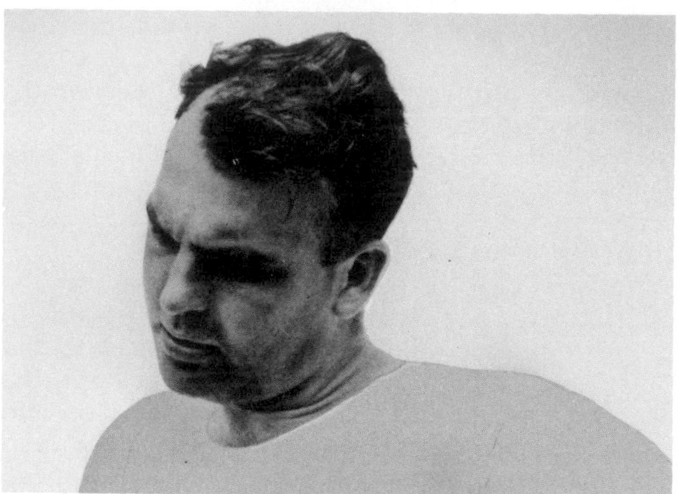

Quarterback Carl Brumbaugh, 1927–1928, who went on to pro stardom. Courtesy of Pro Football Hall of Fame.

For the next nineteen years the story of Gator football is characterized by outstanding individual performances and monumental upsets over heavily favored opponents. Florida had only three winning seasons during this period and at one point was mired in a thirteen-game losing streak.

A roll call of some of the great names of that period would include tailback Walter "Tiger" Mayberry, who became the first Florida player to earn All-Conference honors in the then young Southeastern Conference. The versatile runner-passer-punter was a genuine triple-threat player who carried teams of mediocre talent to lofty heights. Mayberry is still in the Gator record books for career total offense: 2019 yards during 1936–37–38; season total offense: 1019 yards in 1937; career rushing: 415 carries for 1306 yards in 1937; and season rushing: 164 carries for 818 yards, also in 1937.

"Tiger" went on to become a Marine pilot in World War II; he was shot down in the Pacific and died in a Japanese P.O.W. camp. War wounds also eventually claimed the life of another superstar of that era, end Forest "Fergie" Ferguson of Stuart.

Ferguson, an All-Conference player on offense and defense, finished third in the nation in pass receiving in 1941, climaxing a brilliant career in which he started every Gator game, beginning with the first game of his sophomore season, 1939. He graduated with an ROTC commission as a second lieutenant and received the nation's second-highest medal for bravery under fire during the D-Day invasion of Normandy. He also received severe wounds from which he never recovered. He died ten years after D-Day.

Another outstanding back during the 1939–41 seasons was Tommy Harrison, whose 1170 yards passing yardage went primarily to Ferguson. Harrison also ran for 963 yards, ranking him high in the Gators' all-time record charts. Harrison, now president of Blair Radio Corporation, led the 1940 Gator team to a 5–5 mark, which included first-time wins over both Georgia and Georgia Tech. Both were upsets, 16–7 over Tech and 18–13 over the Bulldogs.

The quartet of teams the Gators fielded from 1946

All-SEC back Walter "Tiger" Mayberry (1937), holder of many Gator offensive records, hits the books as well as the line.

to 1949 did not win many games, because of a distinct lack of talent, but produced several athletes who gained national reputations.

Foremost was halfback Charlie Hunsinger, one of the finest runners in Florida history. Hunsinger was a two-time All-SEC choice whose best games came against the best teams. For example, in 1948 the underdog Gators lost to a strong Alabama team 34–28, despite a tremendous effort by Hunsinger which included a 96-yard touchdown kickoff return, a 77-yard run, another score on a 5-yard pass reception, and a total of 171 yards rushing.

The game against the Crimson Tide was not Hunsinger's finest hour, however. This came a year later against nationally ranked Georgia, when he powered the Gators to an amazing upset, rushing 174 yards on 18 attempts and scoring 3 of the 4 touchdowns. He set up the fourth on a 31-yard run to the Bulldog one-yard line.

Only one other Gator, center Jimmy Kynes, earned All-Conference honors during the years 1933–49. A standout athlete from Marianna, he was captain of the 1949 Gators and All-SEC. Kynes, whose sons Jimmy and Billy performed for Florida in the 1970s, was an honor student and later became attorney general of the state of Florida.

Victories were scarce during these lean years, but some of them were shockers.

In 1939 the Gators went 5–5–1. Early that season Coach Josh Cody's team took its 1–2 record (the victory coming over Stetson) to Boston's Fenway Park to face powerful Boston College, a nationally ranked, unbeaten team with a new coach, Frank Leahy.

Leahy lost only two games in his two seasons at Boston College—one of those the fourth game of the 1939 season, a contest against the Gators. Florida scored early on a pass from Bud Walton to Leo Cahill and then hung on for a 7–0 upset win. The defense anchored around the play of Fergie Ferguson, who made six game-saving tackles inside the Florida 10-yard line.

The Gator victory over B.C. was Florida's biggest upset in the early days of the SEC. But there were others. The 1934 Gators pinned back-to-back losses on heavily favored Auburn and Georgia Tech, and the 1932 season ended in Los Angeles with a ranked UCLA team coming out on the short end of a 12–2 score.

In 1947, the least likely site for a Florida win was Raleigh, North Carolina. The Gators were facing eighteenth-ranked N.C. State and found themselves mired in a thirteen-game losing streak. N.C. State was favored by twenty-five points, and those who followed Gator football closely did not think the spread was large enough. Florida scored first on a 70-yard run by Bobby Forbes, a football-baseball star who went on to become an All-World softball player for the Clearwater Bombers. Then the Wolfpack scored, missed the extra point, and then missed a close field-goal attempt in the final quarter, after a gallant Gator stand inside the 5-yard line. The 7–6 victory spawned the nickname "Golden Era" for all those who played football at Florida from 1947 to 1949.

Florida football began to regain respectability in the early 1950s with the hiring of Bob Woodruff as head coach and athletic director. Woodruff brought stability to the entire athletic program, and his football teams were tough and defense-minded.

Woodruff's coaching staffs included names that became household words in the profession: Frank Broyles, John Sauer, Dale Hall, Hank Foldberg.

Facing a far more demanding schedule than earlier Gator teams, Woodruff's Gators carved out a 54–41–6 mark during his ten-year career, compared with an average 13–24–2 record compiled by previous Florida coaches.

Woodruff's first team, in 1950, beat Billy Wade and Vanderbilt in Nashville 31–27, topped Auburn 27–7, and nearly upset Georgia Tech, losing 16–13 on a last-minute field goal.

The groundwork had been laid for the rise of Florida's football fortunes.

Although the record in 1951, another 5–5 mark, was no improvement over that of 1950, the caliber of play was much improved, and Gator hopes for the future were high.

Tough one-point losses to Auburn (14–13) and Georgia (7–6) followed a hard-fought 14–6 loss to Bear Bryant's powerful Kentucky team. Then the Gators went to Tuscaloosa, Alabama, where, powered by a rifle-armed quarterback named Haywood Sullivan, they lambasted the Tide on Homecoming Day, 30–21. Sullivan teamed with backfield mates Buford Long, Rick Casares and J. "Poppa" Hall, all underclassmen, to give the Gators the most offensive firepower seen in any Florida backfield since 1928.

Prospects for 1952 dimmed, however, when Sullivan, who was also an outstanding catcher, signed a bonus baseball pact with the Boston Red Sox. He went on to play for the Red Sox and then to manage in the major leagues and is now executive vice-president of the team.

Casares, a 220-pound bull of an athlete from Tampa, was switched to quarterback at the start of the 1952 season, but the Gator offense did not click as expected. The Gators won one, then lost in the final seconds to Georgia Tech, 17–14, in Atlanta. Tech went on to an 11–0–0 mark, beating Ole Miss in the Sugar Bowl and allowing no other team to score twice.

Following the Tech loss, Coach Woodruff went to his defensive unit and moved Doug Dickey from safety to the quarterback spot vacated by the return of Casares to fullback.

Dickey was not an extraordinary passer or runner, but he did his job and was always at his best at the right time.

"All Doug could do was win," said his coach, Bob Woodruff.

One of the things Dickey did best was understand his own limitations. He said:

"That offense was like a powerful train. All it needed was somebody to engineer it. When you have people like Casares, Hall and Long lined up behind you, it isn't too important for the quarterback to make great runs or throws.

"The quarterback's job was to get the ball to these three people at the right times and with the correct balance in order to let each of them perform up to his potential."

Dickey did just that—and more—as he led the 1952 Gators to a 7–3 record and the school's first major bowl game, a Gator Bowl matchup against Tulsa's Golden Hurricanes. Florida, buoyed by the brilliant performance of Poppa Hall, who was named the game's Most Valuable Player, beat Tulsa in a cliffhanger, 14–13.

Coach Bob Woodruff and quarterback Haywood Sullivan (1950).

Fullback Rick Casares, sparkplug of Florida's first Bowl team. Courtesy of Pro Football Hall of Fame.

Quarterback Doug Dickey, who led the Gators to the 14–13 Gator Bowl win over Tulsa in 1952.

Florida's fate for the remainder of the 1950s was to have several seasons of just above .500 football and to come ever so close to the elusive SEC crown, only to see it slip away. While the Gators were tough, and extended national champions like Auburn (1957) and LSU (1958) before losing close games, they had a peculiar—and annoying—habit of losing to teams they should have beaten.

Florida's inability to win the championship eventually produced another change in the coaching reins. Woodruff's final season was 1959, and he left a solid program and outstanding facilities to his successor, Ray Graves. Graves, assistant head coach at Georgia Tech, took over in 1960 with a promise to play exciting, gambling football. He quickly fulfilled his pledge in a game that might have been scripted in Hollywood.

In Graves's first season, his Gators had to face his old school, Georgia Tech, and his friend of many decades, Tech head coach Bobby Dodd. The game was played in Gainesville, and the drama was heightened by the fact that Florida's quarterback was Bobby Dodd, Jr. In a bone-rattling, wide-open contest, the Yellow Jackets led 17–10 in the waning moments of the final quarter. A Florida drive, the last opportunity the Gators would have, was gaining momentum. However, the Gators suffered an 18-yard loss, and all appeared lost. At this point Dodd, Jr., fired a 32-yard pass to halfback Don Deal that led to a touchdown with scant seconds remaining. The Gators then made the two-point conversion on a Larry Libertore to Jon MacBeth pass, for a thrilling 18–17 victory.

"That game set the tone for my years at Florida," Graves said. "We became known for wide-open football, and we attracted many super skill-position players because of this reputation. They knew we would throw the football and we would gamble, and they liked that style of play."

Indeed, the Graves decade—which ran from 1960 to 1969—produced more pyrotechnics than had ever been seen before over a sustained period and had, in fact, only been hinted at in two isolated seasons, 1928 and 1952. It spawned an alumni group known as the Silver Sixties and many outstanding talents—players such as Larry Dupree, Charlie Casey, Steve Spurrier, Richard Trapp, Larry Smith, Jack Harper, Carlos Alvarez, John Reaves and countless others who made football at Florida exciting to watch.

All-American halfback Larry Dupree with coach Ray Graves (1964).

"I believe most of the kids who played for us came out of the program with a good taste in their mouths," said Graves. "We beat some folks we probably had no business beating and we lost to some we had no business losing to. But we won a lot more than we lost, and we had fun playing the game."

The Graves Decade started with a 9–2 team that won the Gator Bowl by one point. Coming full circle, it ended with a 9–1–1 team that won the Gator Bowl by one point. In between was another Gator Bowl winner, an Orange Bowl winner, and a Sugar Bowl loser. Yet this loss was one of the most dramatic games that classic has ever produced and was the springboard to Spurrier's winning the Heisman trophy the following season.

Graves's overall record was 70–31–4, a .686 average. He won more games than any other coach in Florida history. His winning percentage was the best since the Gators had entered the SEC back in 1933, and few of the old-time coaches had better marks.

Some of Graves's greatest wins, in addition to the Tech game in 1960, included a 13–10 shocker over LSU that same season in Baton Rouge; a 22–3 win over fifth-ranked, unbeaten Auburn in 1962; a 17–7 upset over heavily favored Penn State in the 1962 Gator Bowl; a 10–6 stunner over Alabama in Tuscaloosa in 1963; a 20–6 pounding of LSU's 1964 Sugar Bowl team, once again in Baton Rouge; a 28–7 beating of LSU in 1966; a classic comeback to nip Georgia 17–16 in 1967; a 59–34 slaughter of number one-ranked Houston to open the 1969 season; and the final game of Graves's career, a 14–13 win over SEC champion Tennessee in 1969.

The Graves Decade produced a dozen All-Americans and a Heisman trophy winner. Florida was securely placed on the national football map, and the home fans turned out in record numbers as the stadium capacity increased from 42,000 to 62,800. More often than not, it was filled.

Some of those great wins of the 1960s bear a more detailed—and more loving—look.

FLORIDA 18, GEORGIA TECH 17

Over 39,000 fans packed Florida Field on a humid October Saturday in 1960 to watch the underdog Gators go up against one of the nation's top football teams, Georgia Tech. The drama was there: son vs. father, head coach vs. ex-boss, ex-star quarterback vs. coach.

Bobby Dodd, Jr., was the Florida quarterback, and his dad was the legendary head coach of the Yellow Jackets, Bobby Dodd, Sr. The new Gator head coach,

Bobby Dodd, Jr., the architect of Florida's stirring 18–17 win over his father's Georgia Tech team in 1960.

Ray Graves, had come from Dodd's staff, where he had been a trusted assistant head coach. And Florida's offensive coordinator was Pepper Rodgers, formerly a star quarterback under Coach Dodd.

Tech had an experienced football team, while the Gators were a young team, loaded with sophomores. The press called the game a mismatch, at best. And so it came as a surprise to all, and a pleasant surprise to the home crowd, when the young Florida team began to push the Jackets around Florida Field in the early going. Then quarterback Stan Gann connected on seven consecutive passes to move Tech to a score in the second quarter. Florida bounced back following a fumble recovery at Tech's 23-yard line and scored on a 3-yard run by halfback Don Deal. Billy Cash's PAT tied the score at seven.

Florida's touchdown jolted the Jackets, and three straight Gann completions moved the ball within field-goal range in the closing seconds of the first half. Tommy Wells kicked a 40-yarder to put Tech ahead at halftime, 10–7.

Florida came back in the third quarter. Jon MacBeth's pass interception set the Gators up for a short drive that ended with a 42-yard field goal by Cash, to knot the score at 10–10.

The Jackets quickly regained the lead on a 72-yard drive highlighted by a 47-yard pass from Gann to Billy Williamson, who scored the touchdown on a

7-yard run. Wells's point-after made it 17–10 at the end of the third quarter.

The determined Gators got a drive going early in the final quarter, but it stalled at the Tech 7-yard line. Cash missed a field goal from pointblank range, a rarity for the talented sophomore.

With five minutes remaining in the game, the Gators got the ball at their 15, and everybody knew this was their last chance of the day. With time a precious commodity, Coach Graves sent young Dodd in at quarterback because he was a better passer than sophomore Larry Libertore. On third and long yardage, Dodd found Deal for a vital 32-yard completion to the Tech 25-yard line. It was first down, and the crowd found itself in a collective state of heart-in-the-throat.

Three running plays, two by Don Goodman and one by Bob Hoover, put the ball on the Tech 2-yard line. Ninety seconds remained when the Gators sent Goodman and Deal into the line to nudge the ball to the 6-inch line in two plays.

Dodd fumbled on third down but recovered the ball himself at the 3 as the clock ticked down to thirty-two seconds. Libertore came in at quarterback on fourth down and ran an option play to his right, flicking the ball out to fellow sophomore Lindy Infante, who squeezed past two Tech tacklers into the corner of the end zone.

Graves, in a signal that became synonymous with wide-open football in Gator Country, raised his hand with two fingers in the air. "Go for two!" was the chant, and there was no doubt that's what the Gators intended to do. Everybody, including Tech, knew it!

Coach Rodgers huddled his offensive troops, designed a play, and sent Libertore and friends back out to the field with seventeen seconds remaining. Once again Libertore rolled right, and it appeared that the designed play was the option to Infante. However, fullback MacBeth did not hold his block this time, and as tacklers converged on Libertore, MacBeth slipped into the end zone. The pass was on the mark, and the Gators had won.

FLORIDA 13, LSU 10

The sixth game of the 1960 season was played in Baton Rouge, Louisiana, in front of a typical packed Tiger Stadium crowd of rabid LSU fans. Their Tigers were ranked in the top five in the nation, and, going into the game, they led the nation in defense.

LSU kicked off, and the Gators ran the ball back out to the 34-yard line, a good starting point. Sophomore quarterback Larry Libertore took the first snap and rolled to his right. Cutting inside the defensive end, Libertore faked a linebacker and ran 66 yards for a touchdown on the first offensive play of the game. Billy Cash's PAT put the Gators in front 7–0.

The lead stood up until midway in the second quarter, when the Tigers blocked a Gator punt and took over at the Florida 21-yard line. The rugged Florida defense once again stopped LSU, and the Tigers settled for a 40-yard field goal, cutting the margin to 7–3. Late in the quarter, LSU mounted its only drive of the game, going 57 yards for a touchdown and a 10–7 lead at halftime.

Florida found yardage tough to come by in this defensive struggle, but managed to punch out enough for Cash to boot a 47-yard field goal with 9:44 remaining in the third quarter, to tie the game. He kicked yet another from 35 yards with 5:01 left in the stanza. At that point, owning a 13–10 lead, Florida's defense grabbed LSU by the throat and would not let go. Vic Miranda blocked a Tiger field-goal attempt in the waning moments of the third quarter, and a fake field goal late in the game was smothered by Nick Arfaras and Pat Patchen. That was the final bid by LSU.

The win propelled the Gators to a nine-victory season and a 13–12 Gator Bowl win over Baylor.

Sophomore quarterback Larry Libertore, whose 66-yard touchdown run on the first play from scrimmage sparked the Gators to an upset 13–10 win over LSU in 1960.

FLORIDA 22, AUBURN 3

The 1962 Gators were an up-and-down outfit going into the seventh game of the season. They had thrashed Texas A&M and Vanderbilt, edged Mississippi State, blown a twenty-one-point halftime lead to lose 28–21 to Duke, and lost convincingly to Georgia Tech and LSU.

The loss to LSU was a bitter pill for Gator fans to swallow. The Gators had come off 42–6 and 42–7 wins the previous two weeks over the Aggies and the Commodores. It was Homecoming Day, and the stadium was packed. But the Tigers dominated the contest from start to finish and won going away, beating Florida 23–0.

The loss left Florida 3–3, with powerful, unbeaten, and highly ranked Auburn coming to town. The Tigers had marched through five straight opponents, and were favored by two touchdowns.

It was obvious from the start that Florida's defensive unit had, according to that old cliché, "come to play." Auburn had difficulty making a first down in the first half, and Gator defensive backs picked off a pair of Tiger passes to set up touchdowns by Bruce Starling and Jim O'Donnell.

At halftime the score was 15–0. The Gators added a Larry Dupree touchdown jaunt of 31 yards in the third quarter and allowed Auburn only a field goal.

Florida's alert defense also recovered three fumbles that afternoon, and the Auburn Tigers crossed midfield only three times. The victory was one that propelled the Gators to an invitation to play Penn State, the nation's ninth-ranked team, in the Gator Bowl.

That game turned out to be one of the biggest wins ever recorded by a Florida football team.

FLORIDA 17, PENN STATE 7

Florida was chosen to face Penn State in the 1962 Gator Bowl game prior to the Gators' season-ending battle against archrival Miami, which they lost 17–15 on a late field goal.

Now the Gator Bowl pitted the tatterdemalion Gators, possessors of a mediocre 6–4 record, against the mighty Nittany Lions of Penn State, winners of the Lambert trophy—symbolic of the best in the East—and ranked ninth in the country with a 9–1 record. The prospect brought howls of indignation from the media and a bevy of Penn State fans to Jacksonville, all of whom believed the game would be more of a mismatch than a matchup.

Penn State was so heavily favored that it was difficult to pinpoint the exact margin. Most experts felt that the Nittany Lions would win by three touchdowns. After all, Coach Rip Engle's club had lost only one once, 9–6, to Army, in a game in which two apparent Penn State touchdowns had been called back. They had won three straight bowl games and had three consensus All-Americans in the starting lineup. Those who followed Gator football closely, however, felt that this was the perfect time for another in the long line of astounding Florida upsets.

Florida installed a new defense during the eight days of pre-game practice. The "Monster" defense was a major factor in the game, as the Gator squad, wearing the Confederate flag on their helmets, held Penn State's vaunted offense to 139 yards. State crossed midfield only twice in a game that was not nearly as close as the score indicated.

Sophomore Bob "Grubby" Lyle booted a 43-yard field goal early in the first period, staking Florida to a 3–0 lead, one they would never lose. Sophomore quarterback Tom Shannon and sophomore halfback Larry Dupree combined for a 26-yard touchdown pass to make it 10–0, but State came back with its only drive of the game, cutting the margin to 10–7 at halftime.

The second half so totally belonged to the Gators that Penn State's only penetration into Florida's half of the field came with less than three minutes left in the game. And that drive ended at the 41-yard line.

Shannon, the lefthander from Miami—voted the game's Most Valuable Player—hurled a 19-yard touchdown pass to fellow Miamian Hagood Clarke on the first play of the final period, to up the margin to the final count, 17–7, and cap one of the Gators' greatest upsets.

Quarterback Tommy Shannon, Most Valuable Player in the 1962 Gator Bowl game.

FLORIDA 10, ALABAMA 6

The scene was set for another Gator upset victory in 1963. The Gators had lost to Georgia Tech, tied Mississippi State, and struggled all afternoon to edge little Richmond 35–28. After that contest, Gator assistant coach Ottis Mooney described his team as "the New York Mets of the Southeastern Conference."

The Gators' next opponent was mighty Alabama, the nation's third-ranked team. The site for the game was Tuscaloosa; the event was Alabama's Homecoming. Not only was the 1963 Alabama team unbeaten going into its game with Florida, but Coach Paul "Bear" Bryant had never lost a game at Tuscaloosa, nor had Alabama ever lost a Homecoming Day game. All that was soon to change.

The Gators spent the entire week of practice work-

Ray Graves being carried from the field after Florida beat 'Bama 10–6 in 1963.

ing on a special kickoff formation designed to go crossfield from one hash mark to the corner of the end zone. Their kickoff coverage was heaviest on the side the ball was kicked toward.

The opening kickoff worked to perfection, and Alabama never got out of the hole. The Tide put the ball in play at their own 5-yard line, where Benny Nelson caught the kickoff and was immediately engulfed by Gators. Florida pushed the Tide back to the 1-yard line before forcing a punt that came out to the 'Bama 40. Safety Bruce Bennett, a sophomore, who two years later would earn first-team All-American honors, returned the ball to the Tide 25. The rugged Alabama defense held, and Florida settled for a 42-yard field goal by Bob Lyle.

Following a fumble recovery at the Florida 34, Alabama quarterback Joe Namath ran for 9 yards on first down. That was the Tide's deepest penetration, as Gator defenders, led by linebacker Jimmy Morgan, stopped a Namath pass attempt and then turned two running plays back to the 27-yard line.

Florida controlled the football most of the remainder of the afternoon, but failed in repeated attempts to score. The Gators had first and goal at the 2 and again at the 8, but came away empty.

Early in the fourth quarter, Florida started a drive from its own 25, Larry Dupree running for 17 on first down. Then Tommy Shannon flipped an 18-yard pass to tight end Barry Brown, who made a spectacular catch. Florida was in control at Alabama's 42-yard line when Dick Kirk, primarily a defensive back, went off right tackle, cut back, and followed a great block by end Charlie Casey, en route to a touchdown that made the score 10–0 with less than seven minutes remaining.

Namath then rallied his troops for Alabama's lone drive of the day, a 77-yard beauty that resulted in a touchdown by the Beaver Falls, Pennsylvania, great on a 2-yard plunge. The try for two was no good, and only seconds remained when an on-side kick was covered by the Gators.

Going into 1979, that loss to Florida was to remain Bryant's lone setback at home.

FLORIDA 20, LSU 6

The final game of the 1964 season was played on a bitter cold evening in Baton Rouge, Louisiana. The evening was so cold that the fluid in the press-box mimeograph machine froze, and most Florida writers covering the game wore borrowed football jerseys and parkas for protection. The Gators' opponent on that improbable night for Southeastern Conference football was Sugar Bowl–bound, sixth-ranked LSU, in a game that had been postponed from October because of a hurricane. The Gators went into the game with a 6–3 record, two weeks earlier having suffered the first defeat in their history against FSU. And so once again the Gators appeared to be involved in what was fast becoming a Florida tradition, a mismatch leading to an upset win.

However, Florida took command of the game at the start and never let up, as the packed house of 65,000 dwindled to one-third that number by the middle of the third quarter.

The Gators got on the scoreboard first with Tommy Shannon's 1-yard plunge capping a 56-yard drive. Sophomore Steve Spurrier made it 14–0 with a 34-yard scoring pass to Jack Harper. LSU then kicked a field goal, to trail 14–3 at halftime.

In the third quarter, the Gators increased the margin on a fake field goal that resulted in a 20-yard touchdown pass from Allen Trammell to Harper. Doug Moreau's second field goal of the evening for LSU cut the gap to 20–6. And that's the way the game ended, as the Gators twisted the bowl-bound Tigers' collective tail.

"Super Gator" Steve Spurrier, 1966 Heisman award winner, with coach Ray Graves.

FLORIDA 28, LSU 7

Perhaps the finest performance by the Orange Bowl–bound Gator team in 1966 came in early October against powerful LSU, also bowl-bound, in Tiger Stadium. Steve Spurrier, on his way to the coveted Heisman trophy, was to use this game as a showcase for his talents.

Tiny linebacker Jack Card recovered an LSU fumble early in the first quarter, and Spurrier quickly moved the Gators to a touchdown with three passes, the final one an 8-yarder to Larry Smith. The defensive unit held, forcing a Tiger punt, and then Spurrier directed a 71-yard drive that resulted in a 1-yard touchdown plunge by Smith, for a 14–0 advantage.

LSU fumbled the ensuing kickoff, and Bill Gaisford recovered at the Tiger 25-yard line. Once again Spurrier connected three straight times, the last a 13-yard touchdown effort to Richard Trapp. It was 21–0 in the first quarter: Tiger Stadium contained 66,000 silent observers and 2600 loud Gator followers.

LSU kicked off to start the second half, and Florida marched to a touchdown sparked by Spurrier's passes to Trapp. Graham McKeel scored from the 1. The score was now 28–0, and approximately half of the fans in Tiger Stadium began filing out.

Fullback Larry Smith, three-time All-SEC selection (1966, 1967, and 1968) and All-American selection 1968.

Gator reserves played the final quarter, and LSU got on the board late on a pass from Try Prather to Bill Masters, making the final score 28–7. But everyone there that night knew that the score could have been a lot worse.

It was Florida's sixth consecutive win and moved the Gators up to number seven in the nation.

FLORIDA 17, GEORGIA 16

A classic in gutty, comeback football was staged in the annual Georgia-Florida game in Jacksonville in 1967. The game was highlighted by an outstanding individual performance by Gator split end Richard Trapp, a performance that is described to this day by ABC-TV's Keith Jackson as the finest he's ever seen in collegiate football.

There were 69,489 fans in the stands and a nationwide ABC-TV audience that Armistice Day. They saw Georgia dominate the early going, going ahead on a 1-yard plunge by Ronnie Jenkins and a 32-yard field goal by Mike McCullough for a 9–0 lead midway in the second quarter. The Gators struck back on a 33-yard touchdown pass from Larry Rentz to Mike McCann. Wayne Barfield's PAT made it 9–7. From that point on the Florida defense took control of the game.

In the third quarter, Jake Scott stepped in front of a Rentz aerial and returned the interception 32 yards for a touchdown and a 16–7 Bulldog lead. The score stayed that way until 5:41 remained in the game, when on third and 4 at the Florida 48-yard line Rentz flipped a pass over the middle to Trapp at the Bulldog 46-yard line. Trapp caught the ball near the press box (west) side of the field and sidestepped eight Bulldogs on an unbelievable zigzagging trip across the field. He wound up on the opposite side, scoring in the northeast corner of the end zone.

Florida's defenders, who allowed only 10 first downs all afternoon, forced a quick punt, and then the Gators battled Georgia—and the clock—down the field. With seventeen seconds left in the game, the ball was on the Bulldog 14. Barfield kicked a 31-yard field goal for a dramatic 17–16 win.

The Gator passing game was 13 for 25 for 235 yards. Florida racked up 20 first downs, but it all came down to a missed Bulldog extra-point attempt, a fantastic run, and a clutch field goal.

FLORIDA 59, HOUSTON 34

Some 1969 publications picked the Houston Cougars number one in the nation in pre-season rankings. Houston came to Florida Field on September 20 to face a bunch of sophomores who were indeed a "no-name" football team in that season opener. The result is part of Florida's rich football history.

Houston kicked off, and the Gators ran two plays into the line in a preconceived set of plays designed to get Houston to commit to single coverage on sophomore Carlos Alvarez. With Florida lined up on its 30, third and 7, Alvarez beat his single defender easily as fellow sophomore John Reaves lofted a long pass down the west sideline for a 70-yard touchdown bomb. Florida led 7–0, with 13:45 remaining in the first quarter.

On the second play after the kickoff Houston fumbled, and Robbie Rebol recovered on the Cougar 34. At 10:43 of that period, Richard Franco booted a 26-yard field goal, for a 10–0 lead.

Another kickoff was followed by another Cougar fumble on second down, this one recovered by Jack Burns at Houston's 38. A five-play drive resulted in a touchdown by Garry Walker on a 1-yard pass from Reaves. The score was now 17–0, with 8:16 left in the opening quarter.

All-time Florida offensive leader, quarterback John Reaves.

In the second quarter, Reaves capped a 61-yard drive with a 21-yard touchdown pass to Alvarez, and the score was 24–0, with 10:52 left. After a 37-yard touchdown-pass interception by Jimmy Barr, the score mounted to 31–0, with 10:34 remaining. The shocked Cougar offense, one of the nation's best, drove to a touchdown, with 3:16 left in the half. Jack Youngblood blocked the PAT, and the score was 31–6, with Houston showing some signs of life.

At this point, the brash sophomores cut the Cougars off for good. Jerry Vinesett took the kickoff and returned it 51 yards to Houston's 46. On first down, Reaves found Tommy Durrance for a touchdown pass, to make the score 38–6 at halftime.

In the second half, Reaves threw his fifth touchdown pass of the game, an SEC record, this one to Durrance. Reaves finished with 18 for 30 for 342 yards and was named the nation's Back of the Week in his first collegiate game. Catching 6 passes for 182 yards and a pair of touchdowns, Alvarez headed toward consensus All-American as a sophomore, the first to be so honored since SMU's Doak Walker. And Florida had scored the second highest number of points any Gator team had scored in forty years—fifty-nine—and scored another of their patented upsets as well.

All-American defensive end Jack Youngblood (1970).

Doug Dickey took over as head football coach at Florida in 1970, following six exceptional years at Tennessee, where he had been named SEC Coach of the Year twice, had won a pair of Conference titles, had gone to five consecutive bowl games, and had seen his Vols become the only team in the nation to win eight or more games for five straight years, 1965–69. Dickey was an organizer who appeared to be everywhere on the practice field. During the first eight years of his regime, his Florida teams went to four bowl games and produced some of the brightest stars in the school's history.

Dickey's teams continued the Gator tradition of bouncing back from defeats with exceptional wins. They won 14 of 16 games against FSU and Miami from 1970 to 1977; they became the first Gator outfit ever to win at Auburn, and each season they were one of the top offensive teams in the SEC.

Dickey's 1976 team came as close to winning the elusive SEC title as any team in the school's history, leading Georgia 27–13 at halftime, before bowing to a savage inside running game that cost the Gators the championship.

Doug Dickey, head coach 1970–1978.

The 1971 injury-riddled Gators were Dickey's only losing team during this period. Many of the "Super Sophs" of 1969 were missing or hobbled as seniors, including the great "Cuban Comet," Carlos Alvarez.

Florida's best record during this period, a 9–2 regular season mark, was in 1975. That Gator team lost 13–0 in the Gator Bowl to Maryland, but the two losses in regular-season play were by a combined total of four points, 8–7 to N.C. State and 10–7 to Georgia.

A year-by-year look at the "Dickey Era" reveals the following highlights:

1970: Despite a lopsided loss to Alabama in Tuscaloosa, the Gators were 3–1 going into the FSU game in Tallahassee, a contest rated even by the state's press.

Florida, powered by the passing of quarterback John Reaves, ran up a 38–6 margin by the end of the third quarter and then played reserves the rest of the way. A Seminole sophomore, Gary Huff, threw three touchdown passes in the final quarter, to narrow the final margin to 38–27.

Florida was soundly beaten by Auburn and then came back to stop favored Georgia 24–17, coming from behind on a sensational catch and run by Alvarez, one almost identical to the run by Richard Trapp against the Bulldogs in 1967. Catching a pass from Reaves at the Georgia 45 on the west side of the field, Alvarez left both a wide "Z" and Georgia tacklers on the field and scored in the northeast corner, capping the comeback triumph.

All-American end Carlos Alvarez, the "Cuban Comet" (1969).

1971: The "Walking Wounded" of 1971 lost their first five games, four of them in the SEC, then faced unbeaten, heavily favored FSU in the sixth contest of the season. But the Seminoles could not get untracked, as defensive back Jimmy Barr plucked a fumble out of mid-air and ran 46 yards for one touchdown, Reaves hit Alvarez for another, and Richard Franco added a field goal that held up for an upset victory, 17–15.

The highlight of the season came in the Orange Bowl against Miami, a Fran Curci–coached team that was favored by ten points. It was the final bow for Reaves, Alvarez and Co., and they made the most of their last game with a dazzling display of passing, backed by a solid defensive effort against the Hurricanes' newly installed Wishbone offense. The result was a 45–16 Gator victory that placed Reaves at the top of the NCAA all-time passing statistical chart.

The joyous Gators, so excited over the win and so relieved at salvaging a splendid victory from a frustrating season, all jumped into the pool at the south end of the Orange Bowl at the conclusion of the game.

1972: This up-and-down season saw some great wins, such as a 42–13 victory over FSU in Tallahassee, a game in which the Seminoles were favored by seventeen points; 16–0 over Ole Miss at Homecoming in Oxford, Mississippi; and a 3–3 tie with nationally ranked LSU and quarterback Bert Jones.

In between, the Gators suffered tough back-to-back losses to Auburn and Georgia, 26–20 and 10–7, and lost to North Carolina 28–24 on an extremely controversial call.

The 1972 season saw an ex–junior college basketball guard named Nat Moore show up in Gainesville. His coach at Miami-Dade Junior College was Bob McAlpine, a baseball teammate of Coach Dickey at Florida. One day in the summer of 1972, McAlpine called Dickey and suggested that he take a chance on a cat-quick five-foot-eleven youngster who had spent the last two years playing basketball for Miami-Dade. Moore, it seemed, wanted to give college football a try. Dickey took McAlpine's advice, Florida had a scholarship open, and for the price of a ten-cent telephone call Nat Moore became a Gator.

Moore was so far down the proverbial totem pole when practice opened in 1972 that he was not even listed in the Gators' press guide. The school doctor thought he was too small to play and asked him if he really thought he could play on a level as competitive as Florida's.

Nat did not start the first game against SMU, but he scored Florida's first touchdown of the year on an 8-yard pass from David Bowden. He started the second game and rushed for nearly 100 yards. His next start was the following week in Tallahassee, and he tore the Seminoles apart. Moore ran 46 yards for one touchdown and 8 yards for another and had 142 yards for the day. His 8-yard run was a graphic demonstration of his unbelievably quick feet. Moore took a pitchout; as he caught the ball, a Seminole was set to make the tackle. From a distance of approximately a half-yard, the would-be tackler lunged at Moore. As the tackler, No. 42, landed on top of his head without touching Nat, the Gator wonder runner scampered into the end zone.

All-SEC running back Nat Moore (1972).

At practice the following Monday, Coach Dickey called Moore out in front of the Gator squad and presented him with an athletic supporter colored garnet and gold and labeled No. 42. "They found it laying out at the 8-yard line at Doak Campbell Stadium," Dickey said.

Moore went on to break Florida's single-season rushing record with 845 yards on 145 carries. Following a senior year filled with injuries, he wound up his abbreviated two-year career with 1180 yards and a promising future as a pro.

1973: Hopes were high with a veteran squad returning, headed by All-American Moore, sturdy fullback Vince Kendrick, quarterback David Bowden, a young lion of a runner named Jimmy DuBose, and a tested, salty defensive unit.

However, luck went against the Gators early in the year, as they were beset by injuries. Moore and Kendrick both went down in the Mississippi State game, a 33–12 shocker played in the rain in Jackson, Mississippi. With Florida's running game lost, defenses concentrated on its passing game, which proved ineffective without a substantial running attack to keep the defense "honest."

Four straight SEC losses sent the Gators to Auburn with a 2–4 record. Florida had never won at Cliff Hare Stadium, and 1973 did not appear to be the year for that elusive first victory.

Dickey switched quarterbacks, inserting sophomore Don Gaffney of Jacksonville, an option-style signal-caller. And as an injured Nat Moore watched from the sidelines, Dickey moved fullback Kendrick to tailback and played DuBose at fullback. The new-look backfield responded to the challenge, Gaffney throwing an early touchdown pass to Joel Parker, Kendrick rushing for 129 yards, and DuBose clearing the way with outstanding blocking.

Two reasons why the 1973 Gators beat all of their traditional rivals for the first time in one season: Nat Moore and Vince Kendrick.

Florida led 12–0, the defensive unit shackling the Tigers, until a last-minute fumble set up a Tiger touchdown and two-point conversion on the game's final play. The result was an astounding 12–8 win for Florida, a win that triggered an incredible comeback that saw the Gators win all their November games—with wins over Auburn, Georgia, Kentucky and Miami, and a 49–0 rout of FSU, marking the first time in Gator history that they had beaten all of those opponents in the same season. As a result, Florida earned a berth in the Tangerine Bowl, which was switched to Florida Field because of construction at T-Bowl Stadium.

On a bitter cold night with temperatures in the low twenties, Miami of Ohio knocked the Gators off 16–7, with Gaffney watching most of the game from the sidelines because of a bad back.

1974: The 1974 team was an unknown quantity. Gone were Moore, Kendrick, and many stout defenders. Gaffney returned at quarterback, DuBose was back for his junior season, and there appeared to be some exceptional upcoming freshmen.

Florida opened with a solid 21–17 win over a talented California squad led by Steve Bartkowski and Chuck Muncie. Gaffney turned in a solid winning performance, and sophomore quarterback Jimmy Fisher tossed a game-winning touchdown pass.

Next came a contest against powerful Maryland in

Quarterback Don Gaffney (8) and running back Larry Brinson (39), one half of Florida's 1975 Sugar Bowl-bound backfield.

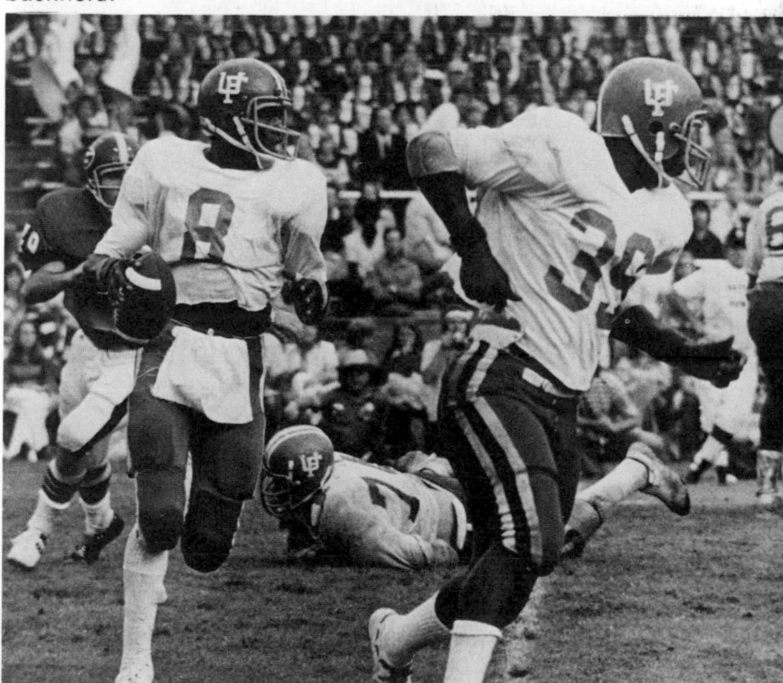

Tampa Stadium, an outstanding game in which the Gator offense consisted mainly of passes from Fisher, a Tampa native, to another Tampan, wide receiver Lee McGriff. The game winner, however, was a 74-yard touchdown run by a freshman named Tony Green, the first of many he would make on his way to breaking Nat Moore's single-season rushing record. Green wound up the 1973 season with 856 yards on 133 carries.

Powered by McGriff, DuBose, Green, Gaffney and Fisher, the Gator offense led the SEC and also led Florida to an 8–3 mark and a Sugar Bowl date with fifth-ranked Nebraska. The game was a classic, with the Gators taking a 10–0 lead on a 31-yard run by Green and a field goal by David Posey. Then Green made an apparent touchdown run, only to have it called back on a controversial call that cost the Gators the game.

Tony Green, Florida's career rushing leader.

Nebraska's physical domination eventually wore the Gators down and produced a 13–10 win for the Cornhuskers. But Gator players such as defensive end Preston Kendrick, the game's Most Valuable Player, Glenn Cameron and Ralph Ortega impressed the national television audience, and Nebraska as well, with their outstanding play.

Ortega and offensive guard Burton Lawless earned first-team All-American honors. They were joined on the All-Conference team by McGriff and defensive back Randy Talbot.

All-American linebacker Ralph Ortega (1974).

1975: The Gators opened with a 40–14 rout of SMU, then went to Raleigh, North Carolina, where they bowed, 8–7, to an N.C. State comeback touchdown and two-point conversion in the closing minutes.

With DuBose leading the way offensively and a tough defense anchored around linebacker Sammy Green, the Gators marched through five consecutive Conference foes before bowing to Georgia, 10–7.

The Gators finished 9–2 and then lost to Maryland in the Gator Bowl. DuBose finished the season with 1307 yards rushing, easily a school mark and only 5 yards short of the all-time SEC record for one season.

For his efforts "Du" was named the SEC Player of the Year. Green was a first-team All-American.

1976: The start of the season was not what a coach would draw on the blackboard. Florida went to Tampa Stadium and bowed to North Carolina 24–21, winding up at the Tar Heel 2-yard line at the end of the game. UNC went on to an outstanding season and a bowl game, as did the Gators.

Florida once again featured a big-play offense, with a fleet receiver named Wes Chandler, strong-armed Fisher at quarterback, and a corps of top run-

All-SEC running back Jimmy DuBose (1975).

Two-time All-American wide receiver Wes Chandler (1976 and 1977).

ners in Tony Green, Willie Wilder, Earl Carr, Larry Brinson and Robert Morgan.

Florida followed up the loss to North Carolina with one of the finest performances ever turned in by a Gator team. It beat another strong Houston team 49–14, and the score could have been worse. Houston was the Cotton Bowl champion that year and finished third in the nation. That night at Florida Field, however, the Cougars looked like anything but champions, as time and again they were shocked by Gator speed, the long scoring runs of Wilder and Carr, and the pass-catching of Chandler. Florida's defense, with Alvin Cowans, Charlie Williams, Scot Brantley, Darrell Carpenter, Scott Hutchinson and Melvin Flournoy leading the way, was more than Houston could handle.

Bill Kynes replaced the injured Fisher at quarterback and guided the Gators to wins over Mississippi State and LSU, combining with Chandler time after time for key aerial strikes.

With wins over FSU and Tennessee under their belts, the Gators once again headed to Auburn, where DuBose ran for 137 yards to lead Florida to its second straight win in the once-feared stadium, this one a 24–19 victory.

This win set the stage for the SEC showdown against Georgia in Jacksonville's Gator Bowl. The Gators jumped off to a halftime lead of 27–13, as Fisher tossed a pair of touchdown passes to Chandler and Georgia's fearsome offense floundered in a sea of mistakes.

The second half was a different story. The physical Bulldogs punished the Florida middle, and the "Junkyard Dogs" defense soon began to control the Gators' passing attack. The result was a comeback 41–27 Georgia win.

The following week Florida went to an ice-cold Lexington and played perhaps its worst game of the year, losing 28–9 to the Kentucky Wildcats.

But then Coach Dickey got the Gators back in the winning groove with two solid wins to wind up the season: 50–22 over Rice, and 19–10 over Miami in Orlando in a game that saw Fisher set a new school mark for total offense in one game with 366 yards.

The Gators then went to El Paso, Texas, and faced a strong Texas A & M team in the Sun Bowl. It was

Florida's fourth straight bowl appearance. But the Aggies were too much for Florida, and they won 37–14.

1977: Florida got off to a good start with an impressive 48–3 win over Rice in Houston and a televised 24–22 comeback victory in Jackson, Mississippi, over Mississippi State.

Then the bottom dropped out in Baton Rouge, the scene of so many great Gator games. LSU soundly whipped the mistake-prone Gators 36–14, limiting the Florida offense to a pair of long passes from Terry LeCount to Wes Chandler, one for an 85-yard touchdown.

Florida's first home game was against ninth-ranked Pittsburgh, and the Gator defense keyed a 17–17 tie. Florida scored when Michael DuPree shook the ball loose from a Panther runner and fellow defensive end Richard Ruth fell on it for a touchdown. Another score resulted when Tim Aydt blocked a punt and the ball rolled into the end zone, where it was covered by defensive back Chuck Hatch.

In a new offensive alignment Tony Green moved to tailback, and the change sparked a 27–17 win over Tennessee. But then the Gators were upset at Auburn.

Cris Collinsworth, one of a bevy of talented youngsters who promise to reverse Florida's football fortunes.

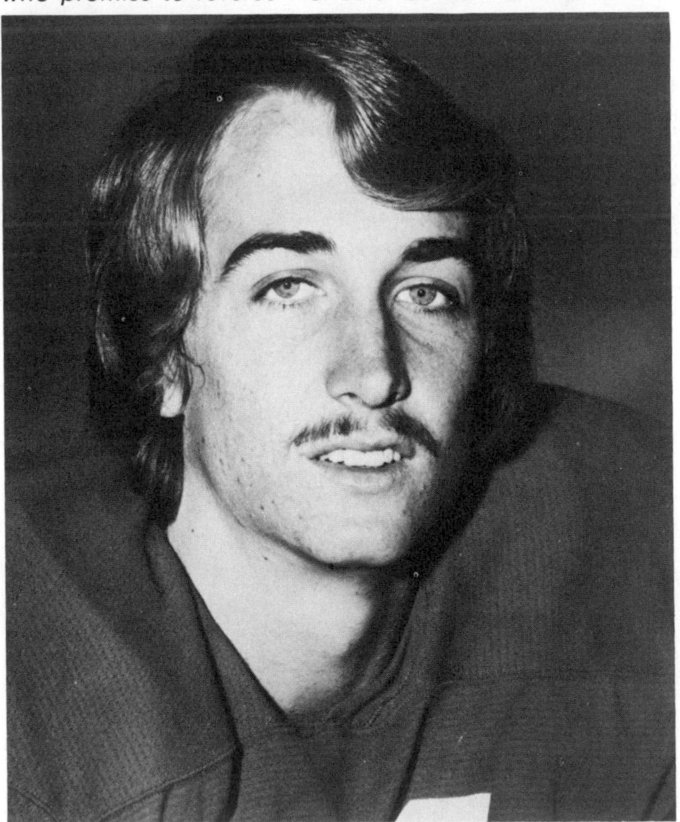

The up-and-down season continued with a comeback 22–17 win over Georgia on national television, as Chandler scored three touchdowns, one as a receiver and two as a running back. But the Gators got no chance at a comeback in their last game, a 37–9 loss to FSU, the first loss to the Seminoles since 1967.

Chandler once again earned first-team All-American honors, and a bevy of freshmen were standouts at year's end: defenders David Galloway, Dock Luckie, David Little and Derrick Burdgess and offensive player Cris Collinsworth.

1978: Despite the individual efforts of such Gator standouts as sophomore wide receiver Cris Collinsworth, linebacker Scot Brantley, and placekicker Berj Yepremian—who rewrote Florida and Conference record books for field goals and PATs—and the down-to-the-wire heroics and finishes Florida football is known for, the 1978 Gators fell to a 4–7 record, their worst overall record in seven years.

As the first step in resuscitating Florida's football fortunes, the Gators hired one of the most dynamic football coaches in the country: young Charley Pell, who had just led Clemson to two consecutive Gator Bowl berths. Pell, only the fourth Florida head coach in the last three decades, is now charged with the responsibility of taking Florida back to their rightful place as a winner. And more.

For, as young talent continues to pour into Gainesville, the Gators will continue to produce the big play and the big upset. But the quest goes on for something even bigger—their first SEC title. That is the responsibility of Coach Pell; no small chore, but one he is more than capable of.

New head coach Charley Pell.

University of Georgia

by John F. Stegeman

Tall, thin, bespectacled, and endowed with a huge black moustache, Dr. Charles Herty looked like anything but an athletic coach. And indeed he was not. But he had a football and a rule book with him, as well as memories of his recent stay at Johns Hopkins, where he had not only gained his Ph.D. in chemistry but had seen something of American rugby, or "football," the new craze of the Eastern schools.

Returning to Athens in the fall of 1891, he was determined to teach the game to the college boys of the University of Georgia, none of whom had ever seen a collegiate football game. He walked to the battered drill field beside New College, where he found the students roughhousing aimlessly. Throwing the ball into a knot of them, he challenged them to recover it. When the strongest, George Shackelford, came up with the ball, he won a place on Herty's—and the University of Georgia's—first football team. The remainder of the team was chosen in the same manner.

The first football game in the Deep South—below Raleigh, North Carolina, that is—took place on that very field, later named for Dr. Herty. It was after the Christmas break, on January 30, 1892, that a team representing Macon's Mercer College and their followers roared in on two special coaches of the Macon and Northern Railroad. All of Athens was at the playing ground—a dirt field with only a few bleachers reserved for the young ladies of Athens's finishing schools.

Dr. John F. Stegeman is the son of a former University of Georgia head coach. He is a frequent contributor to the University of Georgia literary quarterly Georgia Review *and author of* These Men She Gave, *the Civil War history of Athens, Georgia.*

The outcome of the game was not long in doubt, as "Si" Herty, the coach's nephew, broke into the clear on the first play from scrimmage and triumphantly "touched down" behind the Mercer goal. The most exciting play thereafter was when George Shackelford picked up a slim Mercer back, slung him over his shoulders, lugged him 20 yards, and deposited him behind his own goal, for a Georgia safety. The final score was 50–0, and the mismatch was soon relegated to history.

The next game, played at Atlanta's Piedmont Park on February 20, attracted attention from all over the South. Dr. Herty, through his friendship with Auburn's George Petrie, had arranged the first game

Georgia cheerleaders and mascot UGA III lead the Bulldogs onto the field.

between their respective schools. With the fans' cheers splitting the air, the rival gladiators arrived at the field in omnibuses pulled by long teams of horses. Georgia Tech students, yelling for Georgia for the first—and last—time, added their spicy songs to the occasion and drew blushes from the assembled ladies. Then it started raining, and the game was played in a quagmire. Two fumbles resulted in Auburn touchdowns—which at the time counted for 4 points and added one 2-point conversion—and Georgia went down to defeat 10–0.

In 1895 Georgia got its first bona fide coach in the person of Glenn S. "Pop" Warner, a Cornell graduate. Warner would later rank in renown alongside Stagg, Yost, Zuppke and Rockne as a great pioneer of the game. But his first year at Georgia was memorable for its adversity and incredible officiating.

The legendary Glenn "Pop" Warner.

Once Warner led his team off the field in protest in the middle of a game, which was then forfeited to Vanderbilt. It seems that a Vanderbilt player picked up the ball after a play and was handing it back to the referee when someone cried "run." He did—across the Georgia goal line—and the touchdown was allowed! Another time Warner and his players were involved in a riot that necessitated the intervention of the Atlanta police force. That occasion gave rise to football's first forward pass, thrown by a North Carolina back who was trapped in punt formation. This was some ten years before the forward pass was legalized, but the single official "didn't see it" and allowed the game's only touchdown to stand. The riot was on.

The following year, Warner's eleven won all four of its games, the only perfect season Georgia would enjoy until fifty years later. Warner left in 1897 for greener pastures, a more or less literal statement, since he once said he could easily count the blades of grass on Herty Field with the fingers of one hand.

The year 1897 was a tragic one for Georgia. A popular athlete named Vonalbade Gammon was knocked unconscious in the Virginia game and carried to the sideline, where he was soon forgotten. A doctor in the crowd, alarmed by the stricken boy's pallor, had him removed to a hospital in a horse-drawn ambulance, but Gammon died early the next morning. As a result, the Georgia legislature, in special session, voted unanimously to outlaw football in the state. But before the bill was signed, the governor received a letter from the dead boy's mother. "It would be inexpressibly sad," she wrote, "to have the cause he held so dear injured by his sacrifice. Grant me the right to request that my boy's death should not be used to defeat the most cherished object of his life."

The governor did not sign the bill.

One of the oddest spectacles in early football occurred during the Georgia–Georgia Tech game of 1904, played at Atlanta's Piedmont Park. Late in the first half, Georgia was leading 6 to 5 but was backed up to its own goal line. Since the goal posts were on the goal line, Georgia's Arthur Sullivan was behind the posts when he dropped back to punt. His back was against a wooden wall. When he kicked the ball, it struck the goal post and bounded behind him, high over the sixteen-foot wall. For several moments all the players, not knowing what to do, stood with blank looks on their faces. Since there were no end zones in those days, the referee ruled the ball still in play. The players of both teams rushed to climb the wall, made slippery by a recent rain; but no sooner would a player make his way to the top than an opponent would grab his leg and pull him back down again. Finally three men made it over the wall, a player from each team and the referee. The spectators awaited further developments. The ball was soon found on the edge of a nearby lake. The Tech player got to it first. "When [he] finally reappeared over the wall hugging the football," wrote a young *Atlanta Journal* reporter named Grantland Rice, "a storm of [Tech] cheers rolled across the battlefield." Tech was awarded the touchdown and won the game.

Georgia's football fortunes reached their lowest point in 1907, when disgruntled alumni, tired of repeated losses to Georgia Tech, hired four professional athletes from the East to join the team for the annual game against Tech. The head coach, W. S. "Bull" Whitney, was in on the conspiracy and conducted secret practices in the country. Georgia students got wind of the intrigue and bet all the money they could scrape up on their team. But on the day of the game, the Georgia team was less a team than a group of dissenting adults; the professionals had been promised a bonus for each touchdown, and all four demanded the privilege of carrying the ball across the Tech goal. Justice was served when Georgia Tech won 10–6. The plot was exposed by sportswriter Grantland Rice, and Coach Whitney was unceremoniously discharged.

Georgia's first All-American, halfback Bob McWhorter (1913).

Not until 1910 did a new day dawn for the Red and Black. Alex Cunningham, a former Vanderbilt star, was hired to lead the Bulldogs out of the doldrums. Cunningham, who had been a coach at Gordon Prep, assured himself of instant success by bringing with him a Gordon superstar named Bob McWhorter. McWhorter, an Athens native, was the son of a well-to-do railroad lawyer, Judge Hamilton McWhorter, who followed Georgia teams around the South in his own special Pullman car.

For all four years of Bob McWhorter's career, Georgia was a Southern power to be reckoned with. John Heisman's Tech team was not only beaten by the Bulldogs for the first time; it was beaten for four straight years. Stockily built and possessing powerful legs and a wide gait, McWhorter was almost impossible to bring down. He scored sixty-one career touchdowns and was the first Georgia player named to an All-American team.

Coach Cunningham not only brought McWhorter to Athens; he also brought along a bag of tricks. In a game against Sewanee played in a dense fog atop a Tennessee mountain, the coach came up with an unusual touchdown play. Quarterback George Woodruff faded back and threw his helmet far downfield toward the left sideline. As the Sewanee team chased the headgear, Woodruff slipped the ball to a fleet halfback who circled right end and crossed the goal line virtually unseen.

In a game against Alabama played at Columbus, Georgia, the Red and Black lined up for its first play on its own 20-yard line. But Alabama failed to notice that only ten Georgia players were on the field. The eleventh, a back named Alonzo Awtrey, stood on the sideline dressed in coveralls, holding a water bucket. When the ball was snapped, Awtrey dropped his bucket, ran onto the field and under a long pass, and carried the ball to the Alabama 15 before a dazed opponent dragged him down. The field became a madhouse as a full-scale riot broke out. Policemen carted a number of violent spectators to the Columbus jail. Alabama's athletic director sought out his Georgia counterpart and demanded that in the name of sportsmanship the play be called back. When the Georgian refused, his adversary flattened him—presumably in the name of sportsmanship. The play stood up, and Georgia went on to win 13–9.

In 1920, under a new coach, Herman J. Stegeman, a pupil of Alonzo Stagg at the University of Chicago, Georgia won all its games—except for a scoreless tie with Virginia. The team had little offensive strength, but its defense was nearly impregnable. No opponent managed to score a touchdown until Alabama scored

Herman J. Stegeman, Georgia coach 1920–1922.

twice in a late-season game. The Bulldogs countered with three touchdowns of their own, resulting from two blocked kicks and a recovered fumble, and won 21–14. Five members of that famous line, the original "Bulldogs," are still mentioned on Georgia's all-time team.

Georgia's biggest splash in its early years occurred in 1927, under the tutelage of George Woodruff, the former quarterback who coached the team for one dollar a year and who later became a wealthy manufacturer. Six years earlier Georgia had begun scheduling such Eastern teams as Yale, Harvard and Dartmouth, and by the 1927 season had still failed to win one of its intersectional games against those gridiron giants. In 1927, fielding its "Dream and Wonder" team, the Bulldogs had their best chance. With a fleet of small but swift backs and two great ends, Chick Shiver and Tom Nash—one or the other of whom made everybody's All-American team—Georgia had forged ahead of Yale 14–10 by halftime.

In the second half, Yale marched repeatedly to the shadow of Georgia's goal, only to be thrown back. Then late in the game a Yale end caught an apparent touchdown pass, but he was ruled out of bounds. The game over, the players rushed to congratulate Coach Woodruff, but they found him prostrate on the ground in a faint, oblivious to the fact that Georgia had gained its most important victory.

The unbeaten and untied Bulldogs had only to beat Georgia Tech to win their first Conference championship and a promised bid to the Rose Bowl. A twenty-four-hour rain, however, turned Atlanta's Grant Field into a mud hole, and Georgia's superior speed was neutralized. A powerful Tech team won 12–0, puncturing Georgia's hopes for a championship and a bowl bid.

In 1929 Yale came South for the first time to dedicate Georgia's beautiful new Sanford Stadium. On October 12, after a morning of festivities, Yale took to the field in their dark blue uniforms, with heavy jerseys and long stockings. Georgia soon proved to be too much for them, as a slender sophomore end named Vernon "Catfish" Smith recovered a blocked punt for a touchdown and kicked the extra point. Then Smith ran Yale's famed Albie Booth out of bounds for a safety, and later caught a long pass for a touchdown, thus scoring all of Georgia's points in a 15–0 victory. In 1930 and 1931, Smith led the Bulldogs to fine seasons; he concluded his career as a unanimous All-American selection.

Against Yale in 1931 Georgia took an early 6–0 lead and then kicked off to Booth. With three blockers leading the way, Booth broke into the clear. Only Austin Downes, Georgia's 140-pound safety man, stood between the Yale flier and the goal line. Downes turned his back to the Yale horde so that he could not be blocked legally and began trotting toward his own goal line. Booth began zigzagging to provide an angle for his blockers, but Downes, looking over his shoulder, merely zigzagged with him. Booth had to slow down to keep from overtaking his blockers—and Downes. And Georgia pursuers finally caught him 21 yards short of the goal line.

Georgia went on to a 26–7 victory, the third in a row against Yale, and the first time such a fate had befallen Old Eli. (The string of victories reached five before the series was called off.) After the game Adam Walsh, Yale's line coach, who had once snapped the ball to Notre Dame's Four Horsemen came to the Georgia dressing room and declared that Downes's maneuver was the smartest play he had seen in a lifetime of football.

In late season, Georgia met Tulane in Athens for the championship of the old Southern Conference and a certain Rose Bowl bid. The new stadium was packed, and 5000 fans who could not get seats crowded around the sidelines, ten deep. Tulane led 13–0 at halftime, but Georgia seized the initiative in the third period, as Homer Key threw a long touchdown pass to "Buster" Mott that set the Georgia team on fire. On Georgia's next possession, Vernon Smith slipped to the sideline on a sleeper play, well hidden by the teeming crowd. Tulane end Don Zimmerman, not seeing Smith in his usual place, pounced on the ball before it could be snapped. Zimmerman's quick reflex action, which saved a possible touchdown, cost his team only a 5-yard penalty. Georgia's adrenalin gave out in the fourth quarter, and Tulane won 20–7.

In 1933, the first year of the newly formed Southeastern Conference, Georgia swept its first seven opponents and appeared headed for the championship. But Auburn upset Georgia, ending its hopes. Nevertheless, Georgia enjoyed a successful era under Coach Harry Mehre and his assistants, Frank Thomas, Jim Crowley, Rex Enright and Ted Twomey, all former Notre Dame stars who had brought with them the famed Rockne tradition in results and tactics, including the "Rockne system," with its spectacular cadenced backfield shift.

Wallace Butts, Bulldog coach 1939–1960.

In 1938 a former high school coach, Wallace Butts, came to Athens as the Bulldogs' end coach. The following year he became head coach and welcomed to the campus the finest freshman team ever assembled by the Red and Black. Some of the players had followed Coach Butts to Athens from Male High School in Louisville, Kentucky. And two more, Frank Sinkwich and George Poschner, future All-Americans, came to Georgia as a result of a recruiting coup in Youngstown, Ohio. As upperclassmen these players led Georgia to the Orange and Rose Bowls and brought the Bulldogs their first Southeastern Conference championship. Butts's regime lasted twenty-two years and brought Georgia to the top echelon of the football world.

1942 Heisman trophy winner Frank Sinkwich.

Georgia's first bowl team was the 1941 edition, invited to Miami after a fine season featuring two great comebacks. Against Ole Miss in a night game in Athens, Georgia trailed 0–14 late in the third quarter. Suddenly Lamar "Racehorse" Davis swung around end on a reverse from his wingback position. The play started on the Rebel 45; for the first 30 yards it was a good run, but it became a great one at the 15-yard line. Davis's progress was obstructed by three Ole Miss backs who had him trapped on the sideline, but he butted and twisted his way toward the goal. Finally, battered and off-balance, with one last burst of energy he dived backward into the end zone.

In the final quarter, with Georgia now trailing by 7 points, Sinkwich passed to Poschner, who was hit by a punishing tackle at midfield. As he fell, he lateraled to Davis, who sped untouched to the Ole Miss goal. Leo Costa, Georgia's first placekicking expert—who was to go on to score in every game during his Bulldog career—split the uprights to give Georgia a 14–14 tie.

Against Auburn at Columbus, Georgia, the teams carried a scoreless deadlock into the last minute of the game. On what might have been the last play, Auburn punted out of bounds at the Georgia 36. There was no field clock, but the timekeeper signaled to both teams that three seconds remained. Sinkwich faded back and threw a "Hail Mary" pass, as high and as far as he could. "I knew Lamar Davis was down there somewhere," Sinkwich later recalled. The ball appeared to be overthrown, but Davis put on an extra burst of speed and ran under it, outlegging the anguished Plainsmen to the goal for a touchdown and a 7–0 victory.

Georgia went on to beat Texas Christian University 40–26 in the Orange Bowl. When the game ended, Sinkwich's performance was heralded as the greatest in bowl history, and its glitter has diminished very little over the years. He ran 43 yards for one touchdown, threw scoring passes of 61, 60 and 15 yards, and gained a total of 382 yards for the day. But the best was yet to come. The following year he became the first Georgia player to win the Heisman trophy.

Three teams, Georgia, Georgia Tech and Alabama, approached the end of the 1942 season with perfect records. Since each was to play the other, the championship hinged on the result of this round robin. The first encounter pitted Georgia against Alabama at Atlanta's Grant Field in early November. Sinkwich was stopped cold for three quarters, and Georgia trailed 0–10 going into the final fifteen minutes. Then he began throwing passes, 13 in all, completing 11 of them, including one to George Poschner in the left corner for a touchdown that reduced Alabama's lead to 10–7.

The Crimson Tide took the kickoff and made the fatal mistake of quick-kicking the ball to the red-hot Georgia team. Sinkwich began passing again and took his team deep into Alabama territory. Then he fired a bullet to Poschner, who was well covered in the end zone. The ball got to Poschner just as two defenders hit him simultaneously from each side, one high and one low. He turned a complete flip, landing on his head and one shoulder, but held onto the ball, and Georgia was incredibly ahead. The Bulldogs climaxed that unforgettable 21-point fourth quarter by returning a mid-air fumble for a touchdown.

Georgia Tech, also victorious over Alabama, came to Athens for the showdown—with the Rose Bowl awaiting the winner. Georgia had suffered its first loss of the season to Auburn the previous week. But the 'Dogs could still win the SEC championship by beating Tech. The contest everyone had waited for turned into no contest, as the injured Sinkwich was moved to fullback and was replaced by Charley Trippi at tailback, giving Georgia two members of its all-time team in the same backfield. The two lived up to their advance billing by devastating Tech 34–0, with Trippi contributing an 85-yard touchdown run to the rout.

The much-heralded Rose Bowl matchup between Georgia's Frank Sinkwich and UCLA's Bob Waterfield almost did not take place. Sinkwich, hobbled by two sprained ankles, spent most of the afternoon on the bench watching the 1943 classic. For three quarters the two teams sputtered and stalled, with the only offense in the game supplied by Trippi, who rolled up 115 yards in 27 carries. Finally, in the fourth quarter Trippi sparked a drive that took Georgia to the UCLA 1-yard line. But there Georgia's attack ground to a halt, and Coach Butts called for Sinkwich.

"Get in there!" yelled Butts.

"What do I do?" Sinkwich asked, as he snapped on his helmet.

"Score!" roared Butts.

And Sinkwich did just that, scoring on a straight plunge. Georgia won the game 9–0, and Trippi won both the Helms award as the outstanding player in the game and a place on the Rose Bowl's all-time team.

At the conclusion of World War II, Trippi returned to his alma mater and led Georgia to Houston's Oil Bowl, the predecessor of today's Bluebonnet Bowl. He passed 65 yards for one touchdown and returned a punt 68 yards for another, as Georgia defeated Tulsa 20–6.

In 1946, Trippi's final year of eligibility, he ran wild as Georgia won all eleven of its games, including a victory over North Carolina in the Sugar Bowl. At the end of the season the Bulldogs were the only major undefeated, untied team in the nation. The game that decided the Conference championship was played in Athens on November 2 against Alabama, the defending Rose Bowl champions, led by Harry Gilmer, rated the best passer in the land. But Gilmer went 0 for 8 against the snarling Bulldogs that afternoon. Meanwhile Trippi passed to Dan Edwards for a Bulldog touchdown and clinched the victory with one of his patented end sweeps. Starting on Alabama's 46, Trippi began circling right end, inscribing a wide arc as he raced for the sideline. He appeared to be trapped for a big loss, but then somehow, slipped tackler after tackler to break into the clear, outrunning the last frantic pursuers to score and thus clinch a 14–0 victory.

But the best example of Trippi's greatness—and All-American stature—occurred earlier in the second period, when his quick-kick was blocked and a horde of Tide linemen chased the ball as it bounded toward Georgia's goal. Trippi turned around and, in an amazing burst of speed, overtook the Tidesmen and recovered the ball at the Georgia 1. On the next play he kicked over everyone's head, ending Alabama's last scoring opportunity. Three times Trippi punted under great pressure from his own end zone, averaging 51 yards per kick.

In the Sugar Bowl against North Carolina and famed Charlie "Choo-Choo" Justice, Trippi was a marked man. In the third quarter, the Tarheels were leading 10–7 and appeared headed for a certain victory. But Trippi passed 67 yards to Dan Edwards—still a Sugar Bowl record—to give Georgia the lead. The Bulldogs went on to win 20–10.

Hall of Famer Charley Trippi, SEC Player of the Year and All-American (1946).

Johnny Rauch, SEC Most Valuable Player (1948).

Georgia repeated as SEC champion in 1948. Led by the fine quarterback and field general John Rauch, Georgia beat LSU 22–0 and Alabama 35–0, serving notice on the Conference that the Bulldogs were again a strong contender. The team just kept winning and winning. The title game came against Georgia Tech in Sanford Stadium. The Bulldogs were holding onto a precarious 14–7 lead in the fourth quarter when Ken McCall fielded a Tech punt and ran it back 56 yards for the touchdown that put the game out of reach. The final score was 21–13.

Georgia was invited to the Orange Bowl and led Texas 28–27 in the fourth quarter of a spectacular offensive show. But the Longhorns cashed in on two late opportunities to beat the Bulldogs 41–28, handing them their first bowl loss in six appearances.

After that defeat, Georgia's fortunes took a downward course. State rival Georgia Tech seized the upper hand in the recruiting war and beginning in 1949 won eight consecutive games from the Bulldogs. The ninth straight loss loomed as the 1957 Georgia team—sporting a 2–7 record—traveled to Atlanta for its season finale. But in the third quarter of a scoreless game, Bulldog linebacker Theron Sapp recovered a Tech fumble at midfield. Operating from the fullback slot, Sapp then put on one of the most remarkable one-man drives in the annals of football. He blasted through the line for a first down at the Tech 37, but then the offense bogged down until, with third down and 12 to go, Charlie Britt passed to Jimmy Orr at the Tech 26 for another first down. The ground attack was revitalized, and Sapp carried the ball six straight times through the middle of the Tech line to the 1-yard line. On third down Britt failed on a quarterback sneak. The moment that was to decide the game had arrived: the Tech line, which had not yielded a touchdown on its home field all year, braced for the final charge, knowing full well that Sapp would carry the ball. But the driving fullback thundered deep into Tech's end zone, and Georgia had the touchdown that "broke the drought," winning 7–0.

In 1959 Georgia was picked to finish ninth in the Conference, but the pollsters did not take into consideration the attributes of a junior quarterback named Francis Asbury Tarkenton, still many years away from being called just plain "Fran." Tarkenton was the son of an Athens minister who also had a practical side to him—an attribute that came in handy when he was called upon to help his son negotiate with hordes of recruiters. Tarkenton chose Georgia and almost immediately came in conflict with Coach Butts, a strict disciplinarian given to colorful oaths that offended the son of a preacher man.

As a sophomore, Tarkenton had been inserted into the opener at Texas in the fourth quarter, with the Longhorns leading 7 to 0 and Georgia going nowhere. Considering his lack of experience, Tarkenton appeared extremely confident. He proceeded to direct Georgia some 80 yards for a touchdown, then passed for a two-point conversion that put Georgia ahead 8–7. Texas scored, going ahead 13–8, but there was still time for the Bulldogs. Tarkenton readied himself to lead another attack, but instead another quarterback with more experience was sent in, and Georgia's attack never became untracked. Coach Butts was never quite forgiven by Tarkenton—or by a number of Georgia fans.

Fran Tarkenton, SEC Player of the Year (1959).

The veteran quarterback was Charley Britt, who later became the target of "boo birds" when he was given the call as starting quarterback over Tarkenton. But Britt bore his embarrassment well and later turned the tables on those who had taunted him.

In 1959 Tarkenton, now a junior, became the starting quarterback. Senior Britt, relegated to the role of safety man, won All-SEC honors at that position. But he continued to play as back-up to Tarkenton and was instrumental both offensively and defensively in sparking a number of spectacular victories.

In early November, Georgia, undefeated in Conference play, met Florida on a rainy day in Jacksonville. Britt replaced the overworked and slightly ailing Tarkenton and directed Georgia to an early touchdown. Switching to safety on defense, he anticipated a Florida quick-kick, fielded the ball over his shoulder, and raced 27 yards to the Gator 37. He followed that act with another: throwing a perfect strike to Bobby Towns for a 34-yard touchdown.

In the second period, after a 70-yard chase, Britt caught Florida's speedy Bobby Joe Green from behind to save a touchdown. But after intermission Florida drove to Georgia's 10-yard line. Then a Gator pass sailed toward the end zone. But out of nowhere a defender in a muddy red uniform appeared; it was Charley Britt. He picked the ball off at the goal line and raced the length of the field for the touchdown that put the game away, 21–10.

The Bulldogs could now clinch the championship with a victory over Auburn in Athens. But the powerful Tigers, also fighting for a share of the title, took the lead 6–0 on two early field goals. After Bobby Walden of Georgia punted out of bounds at the Auburn 3, the Plainsmen, unable to move, kicked out of their end zone. As the ball spiraled upfield, the Auburn line raced under it, ready to annihilate any man foolish enough not to call for a fair catch. But safety man Britt gave no such signal. He waited at the Auburn 45 until the last split second, then raced forward 6 yards through the first wall of Plainsmen and fielded the ball. He burst through the second wall of defenders and ran for a touchdown. Durward Pennington's placement put Georgia ahead 7–6 at the half.

In the fourth quarter, a mishap—also involving Britt—put Auburn ahead again, 13–7. As Walden stood ready to punt from deep in Georgia territory, Britt, preparing to block, backed into him. The ball struck Britt in the posterior and bounded back toward the Georgia goal. Auburn recovered at the 1 and scored on the next play.

Auburn began using up the last five minutes with a time-consuming march, but they fumbled on their own 45 and Georgia's All-American guard Pat Dye recovered for the Bulldogs.

The situation was made to order for Tarkenton. Coolly and methodically he began to pick the Auburn defense apart, sending his ends on sideline routes and passing down the middle for gain after gain. Finally, on fourth down at the Auburn 13, with twenty-five seconds showing on the clock, Tarkenton directed his left end, Bill Herron, to cut for the left sideline and look for the ball. Tarkenton took the snap, broke to his right, and trained his eyes on the right sideline. Then suddenly he stopped, turned left, and lofted the ball to Herron at the goal line. The image of Herron's touchdown catch is fixed in the minds of countless Georgia fans. Pennington's conversion gave Georgia the 14–13 victory and an undisputed Conference championship.

Georgia defeated Georgia Tech 21–14 in the regular-season finale and accepted a bid to play Dan Devine's University of Missouri team in the Orange Bowl. While the Bulldog defense held tight, Tarkenton provided most of the offense. He threw two touchdown passes to give Georgia a 14–0 victory and a happy end to a Cinderella season.

Charley Britt, one of the reasons for the 1959 SEC championship.

After Coach Butts's resignation the following year, Georgia's stock dipped until 1964, when a new athletic director and a new head coach appeared on the scene. These were, respectively, Joel Eaves, Auburn basketball coach, and Vince Dooley, who had directed Auburn's freshman football team. They were almost unknown in Athens, but their obscurity would not last long.

Coach Vince Dooley, four-time SEC Coach of the Year.

Dooley's first edition, the 1964 team, was not spectacular, but it had a definite character about it—namely, spirit and snarling effort, two traits that would become Dooley trademarks. The scores of the final four games were 14–7, 7–14, 7–0 and 7–0, which says much about the 1964 Bulldogs. The last score was a victory over Texas Tech and the great Donny Anderson in the Sun Bowl, the first of many post-season appearances for Dooley's teams.

In the opening game of 1965, Georgia faced Alabama, the defending national champion. Georgia took an early 10–0 lead on a Bob Etter field goal and a runback of an intercepted pass by tackle George Patton. But Alabama methodically forged into the lead 17–10 in the fourth quarter.

With time and hope rapidly running out, the Bulldogs were backed up to their own 20. Alabama assumed a defensive alignment that might allow a short pass, but surely not a long gainer. Georgia partisans were content to go home with a moral victory if nothing else. But just then Kirby Moore threw a harmless-looking pass over the line to Pat Hodgson. As Hodgson was falling to his knees, he flipped the ball to a trailing back, Bob Taylor, who dashed down the left sideline for a stunning, unbelievable touchdown. Although Georgia now trailed by 1 point, Etter could be counted on to tie the score and provide the Bulldogs with a great season opener. Coach Dooley, however, entertained no such thought. He sent quarterback Moore into the game with a two-point play. Moore passed to Hodgson for the winning points, and one of Georgia's greatest upsets had been posted over a team destined to repeat as national champion.

Another great upset was soon to follow. Two weeks later Georgia met mighty Michigan, Rose Bowl champions the previous year. Georgia stayed close in the first half, with Bob Etter's two field goals making the score 6–7. In the second half, instead of Michigan wearing Georgia down, Georgia wore Michigan down. Quarterback Preston Ridlehuber put Georgia in the lead with a touchdown pass to Pat Hodgson, and when Etter added his third field goal, increasing Georgia's lead to 15–7, the Wolverines were through. The Bulldogs returned home to the mightiest welcome ever accorded a Georgia team.

Three catastrophic blows then befell Georgia, ruining its hopes for a superb season. In the Florida State game, Georgia's best running back, Bob Taylor, broke his leg and was lost for the season. Against the Florida Gators, Georgia was on the verge of a 10–7 triumph when safety man Lynn Hughes fell down just as he was about to intercept a pass. Florida scored on the play to snatch away the victory. And finally, against Auburn, trailing 19–21 late in the game, the Bulldogs fumbled away the ball on the Auburn 1.

In 1966 Georgia traveled to Jacksonville to meet Florida in the most important clash of the long series. Florida, behind its "Supergator," Steve Spurrier, was undefeated and untied and on the threshold of its first Conference championship. Georgia's only blemish was a one-point loss to Miami in a non-Conference game.

Florida, the big favorite, had a 10–3 lead at halftime, but Georgia tied it 10–10 in the third quarter. Florida fans expected Spurrier's golden arm to strike again, but the tall Georgia line, led by Bill Stanfill, began penetrating the backfield, rushing the Florida quarterback unmercifully. Time after time he either was sacked or barely got his pass off. One pass was picked off by Lynn Hughes, the "goat" of the previous year, and returned 50 yards for a Georgia touchdown. Hughes was mobbed in the Florida end zone, not only by his players, but by swarms of fans who had made their way over the restraining wall. The jubilant Bulldogs, now confident of victory, added ten more points in the waning minutes to complete the rout, 27–10.

Georgia could now clinch a tie with Alabama for the Conference championship with a victory over Auburn. But the Bulldogs found themselves on the short end of a 13–0 score at the end of the half. A hard rain had turned the field to a quagmire, and chances of a comeback looked about as bright as the weather. Dooley benched his tired fullback, Ronnie Jenkins, at the beginning of the second half, and his replacement, Brad Johnson, ignoring the heavy footing, began to run wild. His touchdown narrowed the gap to 13–7, and on Georgia's next possession the Bulldogs forged ahead. The touchdown came like a bolt of lightning. From deep in his own territory, Moore tossed a short pass to Hardy King, who then headed for what looked like a short gain. Suddenly he reversed his field, swerving to his right, and outran the Auburn defenders for six points. Etter's extra point put Georgia in the lead 14–13, and Georgia eventually won 21–13.

The Bulldogs were invited to the Cotton Bowl to face the Southwest Conference Champion, Southern Methodist University. On the third play of the game, Kent Lawrence broke the game open with a 74-yard touchdown dash. Georgia went on to win 24–9, closing out a beautiful 10–1–0 season.

Two years later, Georgia was back at Auburn again, battling for the 1968 Conference championship. The Plainsmen, like Georgia, were undefeated in Conference play, and the matchup was to decide the title. Auburn recovered a Georgia fumble early in the game and got as far as the 10-yard line, where they kicked a field goal for a 3–0 lead. That was as close to victory as Auburn ever came. From that time until the fourth quarter, when the outcome was no longer in doubt, Auburn did not make another first down. Meanwhile, Georgia's defensive team staked the offense to three opportunities. Jake Scott intercepted two passes, and David McKnight caused a fumble by almost tearing an Auburn flanker in two. The Bulldogs cashed in on all three chances. Bill McCullough's field goal tied the score at 3–3, after which sophomore quarterback Mike Cavan passed for one touchdown and ran for another. Georgia won, 17–3.

Jake Scott, All-American safety (1968).

The Bulldogs had blanked Florida the week before, thus winning the two deciding games without yielding a touchdown. The championship was a fitting tribute to Erk Russell, Georgia's long-time defensive coordinator.

Andy Johnson directs the Bulldogs to a 56–25 win over Oregon State (1971).

In the regular-season finale, Georgia blasted Georgia Tech 47–8. Though tied twice, by Tennessee and Houston, the Bulldogs finished the season undefeated. But in the Sugar Bowl game against Arkansas everything suddenly fell apart. A sure touchdown was fumbled away in the end zone, and Georgia's scoring for the day was limited to a lone safety, as they went down to a 16–2 defeat.

The 1971 season produced one of the greatest comebacks in Bulldog history. The setting was Georgia Tech's Grant Field on Thanksgiving night. Georgia's only loss of the season the week before to Auburn had removed them from contention for the SEC championship. The Tech game, nationally televised, gave the Red and Black a chance to redeem some glory. But the Jackets quickly moved out to a 14–0 lead. The Bulldogs spent the rest of the night playing catch-up. Backed up in their own territory and trailing 21–24, they had their last opportunity with two minutes remaining on the clock.

Andy Johnson, Georgia's rookie quarterback, coolly put his two-minute offense into action, leading his team to one first down after another with sideline passes that stopped the clock. When he was trapped, he ran for the sideline himself, muscling his way past the first-down stake before going out of bounds. With twenty seconds to play, he hit Bob Burns with a sideline pass at the Tech 1. The clock was stopped, but there were no time-outs left. Johnson calmly gave instructions in the huddle, while screaming fans went wild. Walking slowly to the line, he barked his signal, then handed the ball off to Jimmy Poulos, who dived over defenders for the winning score.

Georgia met North Carolina, coached by Vince Dooley's brother Bill, in the Gator Bowl. The first half was a scoreless defensive struggle, but after North Carolina went ahead 3–0 on a field goal, Georgia got busy. The Bulldogs put on a spectacular 80-yard drive, with Poulos sprinting the last 25 yards, capping a 7–3 victory and a fine 11–1 season.

With Alabama dominating the Conference, Georgia did not become a contender again until 1975. But a defeat by Ole Miss at Oxford knocked them out of the Conference race. When the Bulldogs journeyed to Jacksonville to meet Florida, the Gators were undefeated in Conference play and tied for the lead. Florida's first SEC title was near at hand; but first they had to get by their old nemesis from Athens.

Florida appeared too strong, and only superb defensive play kept the Bulldogs in the game. With five minutes to play, Florida was leading 7–3 and appeared headed for a victory. Georgia was bogged down on its own 20 when Richard Appleby ran to his right on an end-around, a play he had gained good yardage with earlier in the day. The Florida secondary came up to meet him, certain that Appleby, known as a receiver not a passer, would again be running. Suddenly he stopped, planted his feet, and heaved a towering 50-yard pass. Georgia's Gene Washington had not been given coverage as he raced upfield, and now, all alone, he ran under Appleby's pass, and, with it safely ensconced under his arm, skipped and danced across Florida's goal line to score the winning touchdown.

The scene that followed was beyond description. There was pandemonium, and engineers of ABC-TV recorded the loudest and most sustained roar that had ever been heard on its network. When the roar finally died down, the SEC title had been wrenched from Florida's grasp, and Georgia was the nation's team of the hour.

Pop singer James Brown doing his song "Dooley's Junkyard Dogs" along with the Redcoat Marching Band at a 1977 halftime show.

"Junkyard Dogs," a name applied to Georgia's vicious defenders by Assistant Coach Russell, was now the rallying cry; it was put into song by James Brown. When Brown himself, in flaming red attire, stomped out his own beat and sang the words at halftime, Bulldog lovers—young and old alike—went wild. It was *their* name for *their* team and they loved it!

After beating Auburn, Georgia was rewarded with an invitation to the Cotton Bowl. But first there was the matter of the Georgia Tech game, played to a national TV audience. Football fans who wanted to see the team that had beaten Florida were not disappointed. Glynn Harrison was at his best that day and sparked Georgia to a 42–0 lead in the third quarter. A furious Tech comeback in the fourth period cut the final margin, but Georgia held on to win 42–26 for its ninth victory of 1975 and its sixth straight victory.

Against Arkansas in the Cotton Bowl, Georgia was leading 10–0 in the second quarter and seemed to have the game well in hand. Then disaster struck twice in the form of fumbles deep in Bulldog territory. The score was suddenly tied, 10–10. The second Georgia fumble came on its famous, now infamous, "shoestring play," in which the quarterback pretends to tie his shoe while the opposition supposedly relaxes. When the ball was unexpectedly snapped to a deep back in an earlier game, Georgia scored an easy touchdown. This time a more complicated maneuver was planned, but it went awry, as the ball was fumbled.

Since the costly turnover occurred just before halftime, the Bulldogs had the entire intermission to brood over it. When they returned for the second half, their confidence was obviously shaken, and they were "down." Although they held up during the third quarter, the Razorbacks ran wild in the fourth, winning 31–10.

Alabama returned to the Georgia schedule on October 2, 1976, in a big game at Athens. The Tide had been upset earlier by Ole Miss, and the Bulldogs had an opportunity to virtually eliminate the many-time

Student section of Sanford Stadium letting Alabama players know where their loyalties lie during 21–0 win (1976).

SEC champion from the Conference race and seize the upper hand themselves. Georgia responded with one of its most outstanding performances ever. The crucial play occurred in the final seconds of the first half. Georgia had the ball on the Alabama 3, with the seconds ticking off and no time-outs left. The obvious play was a quick pass that would either provide a score or at least stop the clock, leaving time for a field goal. But quarterback Matt Robinson crossed up the Tide defense and almost gave his coaches apoplexy by calling a running play. With 8 seconds remaining, he was hit hard at the line of scrimmage, but with a second effort he broke free and hurled himself over the Alabama goal. In the second half, while Georgia's defense completely smothered the Tide quarterbacks, the offense added two clinching touchdowns, to win 21–0. The shutout was one of the few Alabama had suffered since Coach Paul "Bear" Bryant had arrived on the scene—and only his second SEC shutout loss.

The Bulldogs were again upset by Ole Miss and fell a full game behind Florida in the Conference standings. When Georgia traveled to Jacksonville, the Gators were in a position to clinch the SEC title outright by beating the pesky Georgians. The Gators' past two campaigns had been ruined by the Bulldogs, and they were on special alert not to let it happen again. At the end of the half, Florida was ahead 27–13, and the Gator fans were looking forward to their first SEC title ever.

After Georgia narrowed the gap to 20–27 in the third quarter, Florida received the kickoff and prepared to put its spectacular offense in motion. Facing fourth and 1 on their own 29, the Gators

George Collins (left, All-American guard) and Joe Tereshinski carry Coach Dooley across the field after the 1976 whipping of 'Bama.

Quarterback Ray Goff throws the touchdown pass to Ulysses "Pay" Norris that ignited a second-half rally in the 1976 game with Florida. Georgia came back to win 41–27, after trailing 27–13 at the half.

confidently called a running play rather than kick the ball back to the storming Bulldogs. The play, a pitch-out, had gained big yardage all day, but this time Georgia safety man Johnny Henderson anticipated the pitch-out and slammed the ball-carrier to earth behind the line of scrimmage. Everybody in the stadium knew that this one play was the turning point in the game. The 'Dogs, with momentum building, promptly drove to the tying touchdown.

In the fourth quarter, Ray Goff, the Georgia quarterback who had already accounted for three touchdowns, assumed total control of the game. Whether he handed off to Al Pollard, pitched out to Kevin McLee, or held onto the ball himself made no difference. Florida was completely outclassed and outgunned. Goff completed the second-half rout by scoring two more touchdowns, leading his team to a 41–27 victory.

The following Saturday, while Florida was losing to Kentucky, Georgia was wrapping up its seventh SEC title by beating Auburn 28–0. Against Georgia Tech in the regular-season finale, the Bulldogs got a scare, but Allan Leavitt's 33-yard field goal with five seconds left produced a 13–10 victory.

Kevin McLee, Georgia's all-time career rushing leader, breaks loose against Auburn to gain more of his record 202 yards in the 1976 game that clinched the 1976 SEC title.

Scott Woerner, one of Georgia's greatest punt returners, takes a punt 72 yards for a go-ahead touchdown against Georgia Tech (1978).

When Georgia faced the nation's undisputed top-ranked team, Pittsburgh, in the Sugar Bowl, the national championship was on the line. A Panther win would clinch the title outright, while a Bulldog victory would throw the final selection of the number one team into the hands of the press. With a victory Georgia would have a record second to none. But the running of Tony Dorsett and the passing of Matt Cavanaugh were much too much for the Bulldogs, and Pittsburgh won, 27–3.

After being plagued by a record number of fumbles and falling to a 5–6–0 record in 1977—Dooley's only losing season—the Bulldogs were picked to finish seventh and eighth in the SEC by the two major preseason polls.

But it has always been the pattern since Vince Dooley came to Georgia that Bulldog teams, which weren't supposed to have, always had surprisingly good seasons. And 1978 was to be no exception to the pattern.

With Willie McClendon emerging as Georgia's greatest single-season ground gainer, and being named SEC Player of the Year by the Nashville *Banner*; Lindsay Scott setting rookie records for pass receptions and kickoff returns, and being named SEC Rookie of the Year; and Rex Robinson leading the SEC in points made by kicking and setting a new Georgia record, the Georgia team became known as the "Wonderdogs."

This was the team about which one writer had predicted, just prior to the opening kickoff of 1978: "There is no way Georgia can have a winning season this year. The talent just is not there and the schedule is too rough." Another added: "The Vandy game could well decide who dwells in the SEC cellar in 1978."

But the writers couldn't know that the "Wonderdogs" would be able to do more with less than any team in the history of the SEC, finishing seventh in total SEC offense, eighth in total defense, and yet second in scoring offense and scoring defense and coming from behind to cap six of their nine wins. Only a disappointing tie at Auburn cost the Bulldogs a share of the SEC crown. But still the "Wonderdogs" were rewarded with a bid to the Bluebonnet Bowl, and Coach Dooley was rewarded for his masterful job by being voted SEC Coach-of-the-Year for the fifth time in his fifteen-year career.

Dooley reflected on the "Wonderdogs'" performance: "I think what our team did was to get in so many close situations that we learned to play in them. In summing up the season, you would have to say that all the pieces in the puzzle fit, so to speak. We were a very fortunate team in that respect."

And, as a rule, the pattern is becoming evident that Georgia is becoming more and more "fortunate." The culmination of all these fortunes will be realized, however, only when the Bulldogs can capture that national title which has somehow always eluded them. But it's a day that all Bulldog fans look forward to, knowing full well that it is there—somewhere.

University of Kentucky

by Russell Rice

Tracing the origin of football at the University of Kentucky is somewhat akin to taking a multiple-choice examination. The correct answer, depending upon which football historian you elect to follow, is: (A) 1880, when the mongrelized game of football-rugby was brought to Lexington by C. L. Thurgood, a Kentucky University student who had played on a rugby football team in his hometown of Ballarat, Australia, and who introduced the game to the school at a two-hour-long contest against Centre, won by Kentucky, 13¾–0, in the first intercollegiate game played in the South and the first west of the Alleghenies; (B) 1891, when W. Durrant Berry, one of the members of Amos Alonzo Stagg's "Christian workers," came to Centre from the University of Chicago and taught students at the Danville school how to play the still-new game, a game they mastered and challenged Kentucky to play, beating them 10–0; or (C) both of the above.

Although there is a body of evidence to show that the game can be traced back to 1880, making the correct answer (A), the consensus seems to be that the 1891 game was the true beginning of football at Kentucky. For it was at that game that Kentucky University—forerunner of both Transylvania University and the Agricultural & Mechanical College, which eventually evolved into Kentucky State College, then Kentucky State University, and finally the University of Kentucky, or just plain ole UK—chose blue and light yellow as its colors, colors that would later be changed to blue and white. It was also the beginning of a rich football tradition.

The following year UK students persuaded Professor A. M. Miller, a new faculty member, to coach the team. The professor had seen the game played while a student at Princeton, and he had gained experience of a sort while attempting to coach football at a girls' school in Pennsylvania. One of his first problems was to acquire use of City Park, which at the time was serving as a pasture for UK President James K. Patterson's herd of cattle. He sold Patterson on the idea that the "cow" pasture should be enclosed,

Russell Rice, Sports Information Staff Director at the University of Kentucky, has authored The Wildcats: A Story of Kentucky Football *and* Kentucky Basketball's Big Blue Machine *and has served as president of the Southeastern Conference Publicity Directors Association.*

Professor A. M. Miller, Kentucky's first coach.

a grandstand erected on the site, and the field devoted exclusively to football. Miller then formed a stock company, with Patterson and his brother among its shareholders, to raise money to finance the project. Ten percent of the gross gate receipts was set aside for the payment of dividends.

After the 1892 team played Transylvania to a scoreless tie and then lost two games to Central before barely beating the Louisville Athletic Club, Miller stepped aside as coach and assumed the role of business manager. Jackie Thompson, who had played halfback at Purdue, was invited to come to Lexington and assist the State boys with their football. Thompson arrived in town the day before UK was to play Virginia Military Institute on the road. The UK boys played so badly that Thompson donned a sweater and played most of the game. But UK lost nevertheless, 34–0.

Many colleges in the early days of football used professional players; and UK was one of them. The practice backfired in 1894, however, when W. P. Finney, tackle and captain of the 1893 Purdue team, was hired as coach for the prime purpose of playing in a scheduled game against Centre College. Finney hobbled out on crutches for the first practice session—he had a broken leg, a memento gained while playing in a game before coming to Lexington. Centre, which had secured its own "ringer" from Yale, won, 67–0.

For the annual Thanksgiving Day battle with Transylvania in 1903, the Athletic Committee gave a free hand to a delegation that wished to raise the necessary funds to secure an outside team to play the crosstown rival. The delegation went East and secured the services of players from Columbia University and athletic clubs in and around New York. A crowd of 3500 bet $12,000 on the game, which UK lost, 17–0.

UK football in the early 1900s.

One of the most unusual situations in college football occurred in 1905, when the UK team left Lexington on Wednesday for Huntington, West Virginia, where it was scheduled to play Marshall on Thursday. The team then planned to cross the Ohio River back into Kentucky and play the Catlettsburg Athletic Association. A second game with West Virginia also was scheduled on that trip, but UK canceled it a few days before the team left Lexington. West Virginia said nothing about a forfeiture fee of $225 if the team canceled.

While the game in Huntington was in progress, the West Virginia team manager attached the gate receipts and the gear. Three officers were waiting at the hotel to confiscate UK's football gear when the players returned from the game. Realizing that otherwise money for the game just played could not be collected and that their football uniforms would be held at police headquarters, the UK players accompanied the West Virginia manager to Morgantown and lost, 45–0, to the Mountaineers.

The most one-sided loss in UK football history occurred two weeks later, when Coach F. H. Schact, with a hard game coming up against Centre, decided to conserve himself and his regulars. He asked a friend, Dr. Pryor, to accompany the team to St. Louis, assuring him that he would have a representative team. But when the team left Lexington, all the starters were missing. St. Louis won, 82–0.

The first bona fide football coach at UK was E. R. Sweetland, a graduate of Cornell and Syracuse who

Kentucky coach E. R. Sweetland, 1909.

Action during the 1909 UK-Illinois game, won by the Wildcats, 6–2.

had coached at Hamilton College, Colgate and Ohio State University. Immediately after taking over the UK team in 1909, he instituted spring practice, a training table for athletes, and class teams from which he developed material for the varsity. Kentucky's biggest victory that year or any season up to that time was a 6–2 verdict over Illinois at Champaign-Urbana. Captain Richard Barbee scored the touchdown that won. At chapel on the UK campus the following morning, Commandant Corbusier proclaimed that the State boys "fought like wildcats." The name Wildcats was officially adopted as the UK's nickname two years later.

The 1909 Kentucky team won nine games, losing only to North Carolina A & M. After the 1910 team won seven of nine games, Sweetland left to coach one year at Miami (Ohio) and then returned to coach the 1912 UK team to a 7–2 record.

A prominent name in UK football in those days was that of the Rodes family. First there was a J. Waller "Boots" Rodes, a back on the 1904 team that won nine of ten games, and his brother Pete, a halfback on the 1907 team that also won nine games while losing only to Tennessee and tying Vanderbilt. At the end of that season, Pete entered the U.S. Naval Academy, where he was to captain the 1912 Middie team.

The first of the two famous William Rodes, known as "Red Doc"—to distinguish him from his cousin "Black Doc"—was a popular halfback and defensive end on the 1909, 1910, and 1911 teams. "Black Doc," a brother to J.W. and Pete, was one of the most spectacular open-field runners and placekickers of the pre–World War I era.

William "Black Doc" Rodes leads UK to a 6–0 win over Tennessee (1915).

Another great UK athlete of that era was James Park, a four-sports star who opened the 1914 season by returning a kickoff 75 yards for a touchdown and then throwing touchdown passes of 15 and 30 yards to lead the Wildcats to an 87–0 victory over Wilmington. He threw three touchdown passes in an 80–0 romp over Maryville the following week. In that rout, William Tuttle, a fleet halfback who also starred in baseball and basketball, scored 6 touchdowns and kicked 7 extra points, a single-game scoring record that still stands.

Park thought that his best game was an 81–3 UK victory over Earlham, in which he scored 5 touchdowns rushing and completed 19 of 29 passes, with 5 going for touchdowns. As a major league pitcher with the old St. Louis Browns, Park gained fame of another sort by dishing up one of the first home-run balls to a young Boston Red Sox pitcher–pinch hitter named George Herman Ruth.

Kentucky also had a "Philadelphia Dutch" connection, which consisted of John Heber and C. C. Schrader, who were raised in the same neighborhood and attended the same high school in North Philadelphia, and F. A. Schilling, who had played football one year in Virginia and one year in Vermont and then transferred to Kentucky. After Schrader saved Schilling's life, Schrader decided to accompany him to UK. Schilling earned a varsity letter in 1912, while Schrader lettered four years and was team captain (1914) and a member of the All-Southern team. The German-born Heber worked a few years after high school graduation, played some prep school football, and then worked two more years in a mill before following Schrader to UK.

James Park, one of UK's great players (1911, 1913, 1914).

John Heber, a member of Kentucky's "Philadelphia Dutch" connection (1916–1920).

One of the big games in Heber's career was against little Centre College in 1917. Kentucky had beaten Centre 68–0 the previous year. But Centre Coach Robert "Chief" Myers, in his customary pep talk before the game, suggested that there was a power higher than that of mere humans, and that it might serve the players representing the tiny school of three hundred well if everyone bowed his head and asked for guidance from above. Centre alumnus John Y. Brown, Sr., later recalled that it was "Hunk" Mathias who, in a burst of enthusiasm, said, "Let me lead that damned prayer."

The prayer was apparently heard, as Centre, thereafter known as the "Praying Colonels," won 3–0 on a drop-kicked field goal by Bo McMillin, despite the fact that Heber, known as the "Ferret" because of his ability to unearth loose footballs, recovered no less than five fumbles and also blocked McMillin's first field-goal attempt. Heber managed to ferret out that loose football too, and had daylight ahead of him when his shoe split and he stumbled. But McMillin's second drop-kick attempt—and his last drop-kick in collegiate competition—was good, and Centre had one of its biggest victories, one that would be overshadowed only when it pulled off what sportswriters called the "Upset of the Century" in 1921, beating mighty Harvard 6–0 on McMillin's touchdown.

It was after the 1920 season that UK got its first live mascot, a Texas brindle yearling bobcat called Tom, who quickly died in captivity. Tom was succeeded the following year by TNT, who also died several months later. A tamer cat, Whiskers, died during the Georgia Tech–UK basketball game in February 1924, and was replaced by a cat obtained from New Mexico. Four years later a cat that fifteen-year-old John Hall of Rowan County, Kentucky, had traced to its den, grabbed by the nape of the neck, and brought home was presented to UK Coach Harry Gamage at halftime of the UK-Tennessee game in Lexington.

An early tragedy in UK football occurred in 1923, when Price Innes McLean, a twenty-year-old engineering junior, received a head injury in a pile-up and died the following night. The new concrete stands on Stoll Field were named in his honor the following year.

Curtis M. Sanders kicks a field goal for the first points scored in new Stoll Field Stadium (October 4, 1924).

The best fullback to play for Kentucky in those days was Curtis M. Sanders, a six-foot, 180-pound farm boy from Nicholasville, Kentucky, who averaged almost sixty minutes a game for four years, despite such handicaps as playing five games with a broken right hand in a cast, having his nose broken four times, playing with both shoulders separated and with bone chips in both ankles and damaged cartilage and vertebrae in his neck. The most notable victory in his four years of varsity ball (1921–24) was a 6–0 win over Alabama in 1922. Sanders caught a 20-yard pass and gained 9 yards in three critical plays to help set up a 7-yard scoring run by Bruce Fuller. Sanders also had 29 of UK's 53 carries and 93 of UK's 125 yards, and was recognized as the defensive star of the game.

Sanders was captain of the 1924 Wildcats and had the honor of scoring the first 16 points in a 29–0 victory over Louisville before 5000 fans in the finished half of the new stadium. He started the scoring in that dedication game by plunging through center from 1 yard out and kicking the extra point. In that same quarter, he threw a key pass to "Turkey" Hughes and kicked a 25-yard field goal. He scored 51 points that year, but the best UK could muster was a 4–5 record.

By that time Tennessee was replacing Centre as Kentucky's primary football rival. To further stimulate the rivalry, UK alumni Guy Huguelet and Rollie M. Guthrie, assuming that moonshine whisky was a common bond between the two states, started hunting for a whisky barrel as a fitting trophy to be given to the winner of each year's game. The Women's Christian Temperance Union protested, forcing the two boosters to settle for a beer keg. When the WCTU's ensuing protest was reinforced by cries from the Anti-Saloon League, the keg was rechristened the "Ice-Water Barrel." The Barrel was first carried onto Stoll Field prior to the UK-Tennessee game on Thanksgiving Day 1925, and became symbolic of the rivalry between the two schools.

Len Tracy, who later taught English at the University, scored three touchdowns, two of them on passes from Ab Kirwan, and Gayle Mohney kicked a field goal to give UK a 23–20 victory and first possession of the trophy.

The most flamboyant football player the University of Kentucky ever produced was another Kentucky farm boy: John Simms "Shipwreck" Kelly of Springfield, who later became an idolized professional player in Brooklyn; married actress Brenda Frazier, the debutante daughter of a New York millionaire; sat

John "Shipwreck" Kelly—who became a legend for his movements both on and off the field—wrecks the almost invincible Alabama line in this 1930 game.

atop flagpoles; and became part-owner and president of the old football Dodgers.

During Kelly's varsity years (1929–31), the Wildcats compiled a record of 16–6–3. Kelly's varsity debut came on October 19, 1929, when Kentucky met Maryville at Stoll Field in the first night game held in Kentucky and perhaps the first played in the South. Kelly scored UK's first three touchdowns on runs of 40, 20 and 70 yards and then caught a 20-yard touchdown pass from George Yates, as UK won, 40–0.

In other action that season, Kelly shook off four tacklers and scored on a 74-yard run for UK's final touchdown in a 20–6 victory over Washington & Lee; had a 44-yard touchdown run in a 58–0 rout of Carson-Newman; and scored a touchdown in a 33–0 win over Centre. He gained national prominence in a game against highly ranked Clemson when he took a Tiger punt, returned it 15 yards to the Clemson 47, and then on the first play from scrimmage ran to the right sideline, cut back, and raced for a touchdown. He later scored from the Clemson 47 on a similar play. Kentucky won, 44–6. UK went on to post a 6–1–1 record in 1929, losing only to Alabama in Montgomery on a trip Kelly did not make because of an illness in his family.

Kelly scored 48 points that year, mostly on long runs. He scored 46 points the following year and 30 points in 1931. In a 33–14 win over Washington & Lee in 1930, he gained more than 180 yards, including a 59-yard touchdown run and a 44-yard punt return. Despite some missing game accounts, it is known that he gained at least 2101 yards from scrimmage during a three-year career. In his senior year alone, he gained 1074 yards on 171 carries.

A teammate who eventually joined Kelly in Brooklyn was Ralph Kercheval, a Lexington native and one of the finest kickers ever to grace the collegiate and professional football scenes. In the second varsity game of his sophomore season (1931), Coach Harry Gamage sent him in to kick the ball, which rested on UK's 10-yard line. Kercheval kicked the ball 75 yards and started every game after that.

In the 9–7 loss to Alabama that year, he punted the ball 17 times, including a free kick that went for 65 yards. He rushed 161 yards in a 7–0 loss to Duke and sent his first college quick-kick 58 yards against Tennessee. He also had a 75-yard kick called back in that game because a Wildcat was offside. In his final game as a sophomore, he ran 9 yards for the touchdown that beat Florida and averaged 48 yards on 9 kicks, one traveling 66 yards.

An injury kept Kercheval out of games with Duke

Ralph Kercheval, one of the greatest punters in Southern football.

and Alabama in 1932, but he still managed to make some noteworthy contributions to UK's fortunes. His best game was against VMI, when he completed 6 of 11 passes, intercepted 3 passes, and kicked a field goal. In a 7–6 victory over Georgia Tech the following year, he had a 77-yard punt, longest in the school's history. He also kicked a 73-yard punt into the wind and averaged 45 yards on 16 kicks in that game. He kicked 101 times for 4394 yards that year, a national record that still stands.

However, the presence of such outstanding players as Kercheval and "Shipwreck" Kelly was not enough to turn the tide for Kentucky and Harry Gamage, who was fired as coach after compiling a seven-year record of 32–25. He was replaced in 1934 by Chet Wynne, who had joined with George Gipp, Frank Thomas and Johnny Marhardt to form one of the most famous backfields ever to play for Knute Rockne at Notre Dame. Wynne had coached two championship teams at Missouri College and won two more titles at Creighton. Then, in 1932, he had coached the Auburn Tigers to an undefeated season and a Conference championship. Here was the man, everyone thought, who could make the Wildcats a contender.

It was in September of Wynne's first season at Lexington that Bert "Man o' War" Johnson of UK and Bill Ellis of Washington & Lee, who had been teammates at Ashland High School, engaged in a classic kicking duel on a muddy field in Lexington. The two teams punted the ball a total of 70 times, with Ellis attempting all but one of W&L's 36 kicks and Johnson kicking 28 of UK's 34 punts. Ellis averaged 40 yards per kick, Johnson 38.5. The game's only score came in the fourth quarter, when Dick Kumm, another former Ashland player, blocked one of Johnson's punts on the UK 37, and Billy Dyer picked up the ball and advanced it to the 14. Washington & Lee scored two plays later to win 7–0. The Wildcats finished 5–5 that year.

Bob "Twenty Grand" Davis joined Johnson the following year, giving Wynne one of the finest backfield combinations in the South. In his varsity debut against Maryville, Davis scored four touchdowns, three on runs of 63, 58 and 47 yards, and another on a 38-yard pass from Johnson, who also scored two touchdowns in the 60–0 victory.

One of the biggest games played by UK in that era was played in 1935 against Ohio State before 56,696 fans at Columbus. Johnson gained 103 yards, punted brilliantly, and prevented two Buckeye touchdowns, stopping one runner on the 4-yard line and knocking down a sure touchdown pass. But even Johnson's efforts were not enough, as Ohio State won the game, 19–6. Johnson received a standing ovation when he left the game and was later named by the Buckeyes as the most outstanding player they had played against all year.

The Wildcats gave Wynne a winning season in 1935 (5–4) by defeating Tennessee 27–0, their first victory over the Vols since their capture of the original "Barrel" ten years earlier.

In the 1936 opener against Maryville, Davis carried the ball nine times for 167 yards and scored five touchdowns, mostly on long runs. The Wildcats won 54–3, and then defeated Xavier 21–0 and VMI 28–0, before losing to Georgia Tech 34–0. They then defeated Washington & Lee, lost to Florida, Alabama and Manhattan, defeated Clemson, and lost to Tennessee 7–6, for a 6–4 record.

The Men's Student Council had tried and failed to get Wynne fired in 1936, but it had more ammunition in 1937, as the Wildcats failed to score against Vanderbilt, Georgia Tech, Alabama, Boston College, Tennessee and Florida. The highlight of an otherwise dismal season (4–6) came in the fourth game, when Davis scored five touchdowns for the second time in his career. He also gained 275 yards rushing in that game, a UK total that was still in the record books in 1979. Wynne left after the 1937 season with a four-year record of twenty wins in thirty-nine games.

After Wynne failed in what was becoming known as the "graveyard of football coaches," the University hired Albert Dennis Kirwan, a scholarly Louisville high school coach who had once starred at halfback and end for the Wildcats. His 1938 team opened with impressive victories over Maryville (46–7) and Oglethorpe (66–0), but lost its remaining seven games.

The 1939 Wildcats, led by Junie Jones, Carl Combs and Ermal Allen, opened with a victory over VMI, defeated Vanderbilt for the first time in forty-three years, and then beat Oglethorpe and Georgia before tying Alabama at Birmingham. With a bowl bid in the offing, the Wildcats traveled to Atlanta and lost to Georgia Tech 13–6. They were still hopeful of a bowl bid after defeating West Virginia, but Tennessee ended that dream at Lexington, 19–0.

Kirwan's teams finished 5–3–2 in 1940, 5–4 in 1941, and 3–6–1 in 1942, the year that produced UK's first All-American, tackle Clyde Johnson. The University did not field a football team in 1943 because of the war and won only three of nine games when it returned to competition in 1944. Kirwan resigned and was replaced for one season by Bernie Shively, who had served as athletic director since the 1937 resignation of Wynne.

Shively inherited an All-Conference tackle in Wash Serini and recruited a strong-armed freshman named George Blanda, who once threw the ball the length of the football field. Basketball players Wallace Jones and Ralph Beard were also on the squad, but Beard, a halfback, would injure both shoulders and be lost early in the season. Again the team had far too few good players, and the 1945 Wildcats finished with a 2–8 record.

The president of the University at the time was Dr. Herman Lee Donovan. After the war years, he called together a group of business and civic leaders and told them that if they wanted a winning Wildcat team, they would have to either, as the old saying goes, put up or shut up. He said the University was ready to build a first-class athletic program if they were willing to supply the funds, which included $100,000 to be put in the bank as insurance against a "rainy day." A statewide campaign quickly raised the needed funds.

The University next tried to hire a "name" coach, but failed to lure such well-known mentors as Bo McMillin and Bernie Bierman. The University eventually settled on young Paul "Bear" Bryant, a former Alabama end who had coached Maryland to a successful season after his discharge from the Navy.

The changes that Bryant instituted in the UK's football program were swift, extensive and effective. He changed the color of the uniforms, the helmets, the paint on the wall, the tile on the floor, and anything else that caught his fancy. He had the ticket manager, team trainer, team manager and even some secretaries fired. He hired as his assistants men who had been associated with him in the past—all young, all willing to work practically around the clock, all adept at recruiting players, and all loyal to him.

Paul "Bear" Bryant gets a wreath and a gala welcome at Alumni Gym on his arrival at UK in 1946.

After discovering that he had inherited a nucleus of consistent losers, along with a nondescript group of pre-war players, Bryant immediately blitzed the small steel towns of western Pennsylvania and came up with a few talented freshmen, including future All-South center Harry Ulinski. He issued uniforms that spring to twenty-three holdovers from the 1945 squad, four war veterans who were members of previous squads, and eighteen newcomers. The number of candidates grew to sixty-nine the first week of practice and then fluctuated daily as a steady stream of young men tried out for the squad. He scheduled a six-week summer workout for incoming freshmen and service veterans; when the first contact work was held, he greeted a squad of one hundred. An estimated five hundred players tried out for him that year.

Bryant intently watches his first spring practice drill (1946).

Among the ninety-nine candidates invited to return that fall were discharged veterans Bill Moseley, Phil Cutchin, George Sengel, Leo Yarutis, Len Preston, Jay Rodemyre, Matt Lair, Bill Griffin, Don Phelps and Gene Meeks of the 1942 squad; Doctor Ferrell and Norman Klein of the 1944 squad; and Wash Serini, George Blanda, Dick Hensley and Wallace Jones of the 1945 squad.

Bryant's motto was "Be Good or Be Gone," and many players, succumbing to the intense drills, harassment, and long hours of practice, were soon gone. Throughout his tenure at UK, Bryant took his players to camps, on the Kentucky River and at other sites, where the training was so intense and the discipline so demanding that the highways leading out of those camps were filled with hitchhiking players. Those who survived were hardened both mentally and physically for the tough schedule ahead.

One of the returning players displeased with his lot was Blanda, who sulked when Bryant installed Ermal Allen as tailback in the Notre Dame box formation. Blanda's position was quarterback, which was really a blocking back in the Notre Dame offense. Bryant moved him to linebacker, inserting him on defense in place of Bill Chambers, who was in the starting backfield with Allen, Moseley and Phelps. Ulinski would replace Moseley on defense.

Allen led the Wildcats to victories over Mississippi and Cincinnati and was held out of a romp over Xavier while his eligibility was checked. When the Conference declared Allen ineligible, Bryant made Cutchin the team's field general. The Wildcats lost to Georgia 28–13 at Athens, defeated Vanderbilt 10–7, and then went to Montgomery, where Bryant tried to outsmart his old coach, Frank Thomas, by having the safety play up close to shut off Harry Gilmer's deadly passes. Three Alabama quick-kicks over the safety's head set up Tide touchdowns, as UK lost 21–7.

Ermal Allen, Kentucky tailback (1946).

Don "Dopey" Phelps scored seven touchdowns to lead the 1946 Wildcats to seven wins—their most since 1912.

Phelps had a fine game against highly ranked Michigan State, taking a 5-yard pass from Jim Babb early in the game and scampering the remaining 40 yards for a score. Michigan State tied the score, but Phelps caught a pass from Bill Boller and ran 61 yards to the 1, then plunged over. He scored his fourth touchdown of the day on an 11-yard pass from Cutchin. The Wildcats won, 39–14. They went on to beat Marquette at Milwaukee and then West Virginia before losing to Tennessee 7–0 at Knoxville. They finished the 1946 season with a 7–3 record; it was the first time since 1912 that a UK team had won more than six games.

Blanda carried the ball twice, threw two passes, and did not attempt a field goal during the season. His main contributions were on defense and sharing punting chores with Cutchin. The following year Bryant changed to a T-formation offense and installed Blanda at quarterback. Blanda completed only 2 passes for 4 yards, including a 4-yard touchdown to Jones, and threw 2 interceptions in a 14–7 opening loss to Mississippi. In a 20–0 win over Cincinnati, he set up a touchdown with a 35-yard pass to Phelps and kicked 2 extra points. Then he guided the Wildcats to consecutive victories over Xavier, Georgia, Vanderbilt and Michigan State.

Tennessee beat UK 13–6, but the Wildcats finished 1947 with a 7–3 record and a bid to the first and only Great Lakes Bowl. They defeated Villanova 24–14 before only 15,000 fans in Cleveland's muddy Municipal Stadium. Blanda kicked a 26-yard field goal in his first and only collegiate attempt.

One of Bryant's main concerns as the 1948 season began was the attitude of Don Phelps, whose family problems sometimes overshadowed football. Phelps opened the season by taking a lateral from Blanda and passing to Jones in the end zone. He later returned an intercepted pass 29 yards to complete a 48–7 rout of Xavier. Phelps carried 14 times for 65 yards in a 20–7 loss to Ole Miss and 7 times for 54 yards in a 35–12 loss to Georgia. After Phelps gained only 21 yards in 10 carries in a 26–7 loss to Vanderbilt, Bryant left him home while the Wildcats traveled to Milwaukee and defeated Marquette 25–0. Bryant then suspended Phelps for the season, a move that perhaps did more than anything to establish Bryant as a "no-nonsense" coach.

A young-looking Bear Bryant, right, congratulates an even younger looking George Blanda for winning the Jerome Lederer trophy, presented to the outstanding senior on the team (1948).

Phelps rejoined the squad the following year and worked his way into a backfield that included Vito "Babe" Parilli, who had tagged along to Lexington with "Skip" Doyle, a Rochester, Pennsylvania, teammate who had already signed with Ohio State but had agreed to a tryout in Lexington provided he could bring along Parilli. That visit resulted in Bryant's signing Parilli to a UK grant.

From the moment Parilli arrived in Lexington that summer of 1949, Bryant and Allen began transforming him from a single-wing fullback into a T-formation quarterback. They did the job so well that Parilli stepped onto the playing field in 1949 as one of the most polished sophomore quarterbacks of

"Sweet Kentucky Babe" Parilli, two-time All-American quarterback (1950 and 1951).

all time. Included in his supporting cast were such fine Bryant recruits as ends Ben Zaranka, Al Bruno and Nick Odlivak and backs Bill Boller, Emery Clark, "Shorty" Jamerson, Bill Leskovar, Carl Genito and Clayton Webb. The defensive unit included Bob Gain, Jerry Claiborne, Bob Pope, Jim Mackenzie, Doug Moseley, Bill Wannamaker, Gene Donaldson, Pat James, John Ignarski, Lloyd McDermott, Walt Yowarsky, Frank Fuller, Charlie Bradshaw, Charles McClendon, Dom Fucci and Charlie Bentley.

The defense was rated number one nationally that year, but Parilli was the team's premier attraction. Against Mississippi Southern in his first varsity game, "Sweet Kentucky Babe" completed 12 of 16 passes for 166 yards and 2 touchdowns, as UK won 71–7. He threw a 33-yard pass to Phelps for a touchdown the first time he got the ball against LSU and started a 47–0 stomping of favored Ole Miss with a 29-yard touchdown strike to Jim Howe. Parilli threw a 4-yard scoring pass to Dom Fucci in a 25–0 victory over

Georgia, scored 2 touchdowns in the first quarter of a 44–0 victory over The Citadel, and threw a 26-yard completion to Fucci for UK's only score in a 20–7 loss to SMU. He sparked 2 touchdown drives in the fourth quarter to beat Cincinnati 14–7, but threw 4 interceptions against Tennessee, as the Vols won 6–0 in Lexington. The 1949 Wildcats finished with a 9–2 record and accepted an invitation to play Santa Clara in the Orange Bowl.

Bryant would later admit that he took his players South too early and drove them too hard in practice. They were leading Santa Clara 7–0, with possession on the Santa Clara 2-yard line, when two rushing plays failed and time ran out in the first half. Santa Clara came back in the second half to beat the tiring Kentuckians 21–13. Despite the bowl loss, the Wildcats finished with a 9–3 record, their best record since 1929.

Bob Gain, the best lineman in the nation in 1950, started the UK season by blocking a North Texas punt, picking up the ball on the 30, and returning it to the 19 to set up a score. He repeated that feat later in the season, blocking an attempted quick-kick by Georgia Tech and recovering the ball on the Tech 13 to set up a touchdown.

Bob Gain, two-time All-American tackle and winner of the Outland trophy as the nation's outstanding lineman (1950).

Bryant flanked by two reasons for Kentucky's only outright SEC championship—Babe Parilli (left) and Bob Gain.

With Gain excelling on defense, Parilli led the Wildcats to a 25–0 victory over North Texas State, but suffered a groin injury in the process. Bryant had a special protective device devised and advised his offensive linemen that nothing had better happen to Parilli against LSU the following weekend. "The Babe" set up the first touchdown and scored another in a 14–0 UK victory over the Tigers. He then threw 4 touchdown passes against Dayton and tied a Conference record by passing for 5 touchdowns against Cincinnati. His 18 of 29 passes in that game was also a Conference record. Al Bruno caught 3 of the touchdown tosses. Parilli passed for 5 touchdowns against North Dakota, despite leaving the game with only three minutes gone in the second half. The Wildcats were undefeated and Conference champions when they traveled to Knoxville and were defeated 7–0 by rival Tennessee on a cold, snowy day.

Kentucky's greatest moment of football glory came in the 1951 Sugar Bowl, where the Wildcats met Bud Wilkinson's Oklahoma Sooners, national champions and proud possessors of a thirty-one-game winning

The Wildcats celebrate their 20–7 win over TCU in the 1952 Cotton Bowl—their last bowl appearance for twenty-five years.

streak. Bryant surprised Oklahoma by employing four tackles on defense in one pattern against the Sooners' split-T formation. The key Wildcat on defense was Yowarsky, who in essence was playing end. He set up the first score of the game—a Parilli-to-Wilbur Jamerson pass—by forcing and recovering an Oklahoma fumble on the Sooner 22 shortly after the opening touchdown plunge by Jamerson. Oklahoma scored in the second half, but Kentucky, playing conservatively, won, 13–7. Yowarsky was named the game's Most Valuable Player.

Parilli was still the nation's best passer in 1951, but the Wildcats had no runners to keep the defenses "honest." He completed 11 of 16 passes in a 72–13 victory over Tennessee Tech, but the following week he hurled a sure touchdown pass that was dropped, and the Wildcats lost to Texas 7–6 in Austin. Key fumbles cost the Wildcats a victory against Ole Miss, while excessive penalties (138 yards) were their undoing against Georgia Tech. With Bryant claiming they were now "my boys," the Wildcats put together six straight victories before playing number one–ranked Tennessee in Lexington. Parilli hit 15 of 25 passes for 179 yards, but the Vols won, 28–0.

Parilli was named Most Valuable Back in the 1952 Cotton Bowl, but the Wildcat defense deserved the major credit for the 20–7 Wildcat victory, stopping Texas Christian drives on the UK 8-, 4-, 5-, and 1-yard lines. A 31-yard pass from Parilli to Steve Meilinger was the key play in an early 53-yard scoring drive. TCU marched 50 yards in 11 plays, but Emery Clark intercepted a Mal Fowler pass on the UK 17 and returned it to the 43. Kentucky drove to another score, with Parilli hitting Clark from the 12. The Frogs finally got on the board in the third quarter, marching 80 yards in four plays, with Bobby Jack Floyd scoring on a 43-yard run. But it was too little, too late.

After Parilli graduated, the Wildcats' best player was Meilinger, who as a sophomore in 1951 ranked third in the Conference in pass receptions (38 for 515 yards) and caught 3 of Parilli's passes for 60 yards in the Cotton Bowl. Meilinger started the 1953 season at end, but his receptions were few and far between in the split-T formation that Bryant installed after Parilli left. Meilinger's punting and defensive work were outstanding, but the Wildcats needed more ammunition than that as they went 2–3–1 before traveling to Miami to meet a Hurricane team that was rated ninth best in the nation on defense.

Bryant pulled one of the big surprises of his coaching career when he inserted Meilinger at quarterback four days before going to Miami. Meilinger responded by scoring 2 touchdowns, rushing for 82 yards, catching a 9-yard touchdown pass from his old end position, and setting up another touchdown with a 49-yard pass to the 1-yard line. The Wildcats beat the Hurricanes 29–0, then defeated Tulane and Clemson and tied Tennessee before losing their season finale, 27–0, to Florida, to finish the 1952 season with a 5–4–2 record—Bryant's seventh winning season in seven years as UK coach.

Steve Meilinger, All-American end (1952 and 1953).

Bryant submitted his resignation to Dr. Donovan after the 1952 season, then relented after the UK president assured him that some changes would be made, particularly in the paramount position basketball held over football. Bryant had an impressive twelve-year contract extending from January 1, 1951, until January 1, 1962, but he grew dissatisfied after some members of Adolph Rupp's championship UK basketball teams of 1948 and 1949 became involved in a nationwide gambling scandal. The end result was an investigation by the Conference and the NCAA that turned up violations in recruiting and in other areas of the basketball and football programs.

Bryant pictured behind UK basketball coach Adolph Rupp, which was often the case during the Bear's eight years at Kentucky.

A move that many fans felt was forced on Bryant as a result of the bribery scandals occurred after UK's Cotton Bowl victory. Bryant announced a unique new recruiting policy that called for the signing of only five players from outside the commonwealth of Kentucky in a single year, with the stipulation that those out-of-state players had to seek Kentucky out and apply for scholarships. That policy eventually imposed a great burden on the UK football program.

The 1953 Wildcats lost to Texas A & M and Mississippi before Bryant moved Bob Hardy of Paducah, Kentucky, into the starting quarterback

Bob Hardy, All-SEC back (1954).

position. Hardy responded by completing 7 of 10 passes for 131 yards and 2 touchdowns against Florida; he was named SEC Back of the Week for that feat. At Baton Rouge the following Saturday, Bryant left the field early to do his radio show, thinking the Wildcats had lost 7–6. He was in the broadcast booth when he learned that LSU had also missed an extra-point attempt, leaving the final score 6–6. Hardy then led the team to victories over Rice, Houston, Vanderbilt, Memphis State and Tennessee, for a 7–2–1 record. The 27–21 victory over Tennessee was UK's first in eighteen years.

Bryant resigned after the 1953 season to become head coach and Director of Athletics at Texas A & M, leaving a 60–23–5 record that included UK's first Conference championship (1950) and appearances in one minor and four major bowls.

Bryant was succeeded by Blanton Collier, a scholarly Kentuckian from Paris who had assisted Paul Brown with the Great Lakes Naval Training Base team and then had followed Brown into the professional ranks at Cleveland.

Bryant had left Collier some fine senior players, but the new head coach took one look at the undergraduate ranks and told Donovan that the University had to resume recruiting out-of-state players. The big problem, as Collier saw it, was that the football program had lost contact with out-of-state recruiters and they had switched their allegiance to other schools.

Collier brought an entirely new concept of football to UK, one based on throwing the ball and operating the belly option system out of the old split-T. In a 20–0 loss to Maryland in the 1954 season opener, the Wildcats were in scoring position five times but threw 5 interceptions and lost 2 fumbles. They lost 28–9 to Ole Miss in a game that set an SEC record of 305 yards in total penalties (UK 16 for 123 yards; UM 15 for 182 yards). Dick Mitchell scored on a 4-yard run the following week, to give Collier his first victory, a 7–6 win over LSU. Then they beat Auburn, lost to Florida, defeated Georgia Tech, Villanova, Vanderbilt and Memphis State, and were 6–3 when Tennessee came to Lexington.

With second down and 17 to go on the UT 22, Howard Schnellenberger faked a block and was all alone when Hardy hit him in the end zone for a last-period touchdown that beat the Vols 14–13. It was the first time in modern history that a UK team had won two games in a row over the Vols. Collier was named Conference Coach of the Year for his 7–3 record.

Collier continued his mastery over Tennessee in 1955, defeating them 23–0 in Lexington, en route to a 6–3–1 season. His teams played outstanding games against Ole Miss and Rice, with Hardy earning national "Back of the Week" honors after he completed 10 of 17 passes for 125 yards, rushed 11 times for 35 yards, and scored 14 points in a 20–16 conquest of the Owls.

Coach Blanton Collier and two-time All-American tackle Lou Michaels (1956 and 1957).

One of the meanest, toughest, most dedicated and most talented football players ever to wear the blue and white was tackle Lou Michaels of Swoyersville, Pennsylvania, whose brother Walt played for the Browns under Collier. From the moment he stepped onto the playing field and personally stopped a Georgia Tech drive on the UK 1-foot line and then punted the ball 61 yards in the air out of his own end zone, until he went out in a blaze of glory against Tennessee, Michaels was the complete football player, although UK's mediocre record (14–15–1) during his varsity years does not reflect his multiple talents.

Lou Michaels, SEC Most Valuable Player (1957).

He was instrumental in UK's posting a winning record (6–4) in 1956, but even his talents could not stay the hand of fate as the Wildcats lost their first six games the following year and finished with a 3–7 record. They salvaged a "successful" season nonetheless, beating Tennessee in their last game of the 1957 season—a one-man *tour de force* by Michaels.

During the two weeks' preparation for the game against the Vols, who had defeated the Wildcats the preceding year, Collier moved Michaels to middle linebacker and gave him free rein. Michaels began his heroics in the first quarter by recovering a Vol fumble in the end zone for his first and only collegiate touchdown. Then he kicked the extra point. Less than two minutes later, he kicked the ball high to Bobby Gordon in the end zone and then tackled Gordon so hard that he fumbled the ball. Jim Urbaniak recovered for UK on the Vol 39. Bob Cravens scored from 4 yards out, and Michaels kicked the extra point. Cravens scored the final touchdown, and although Michaels missed his first kick of the season, the Wildcats—and Michaels—beat the Vols 20–6.

The Wildcats started the 1958 season with victories over Hawaii (51–0) and Georgia Tech (13–0), but lost four in a row before beating Mississippi State, tying Vanderbilt, and beating Xavier and Tennessee, for a 5–4–1 record. The victory over Tennessee was engineered by Jerry Eisaman, who stole the ball from UT fullback Carl Smith in the open field, setting up the game's lone touchdown. Tennessee scored a safety when UK's Calvin Bird was trapped in his own end zone. Bird started only four games that season, but was named SEC "Sophomore of the Year" after leading the Conference in receptions, with 21 catches for 373 yards and 4 touchdowns.

Kentucky scoring leader Calvin Bird (number 21).

The fleet mountaineer started every game for UK in 1959 and was Collier's main offensive threat, ranking third nationally in kickoff returns, eleventh in punt returns, and third in the Conference in both receiving and scoring (55 points). One of his best-remembered games that season was the one against Miami, in which the Wildcats were penalized 148 yards but still beat the Hurricanes 22–3. Although left-handed Fran Curci passed often and well, the Hurricanes were able to score only a first-quarter field goal. Meanwhile Bird returned a punt 55 yards for a touchdown early in the game and added another touchdown with a 30-yard run in the fourth quarter. He later salvaged a 4–6 season and perhaps Collier's job by scoring 19 points in a 20–0 blanking of Tennessee at Lexington, their sixth win in seven years over the Vols.

Coach Collier, left, with assistant Charlie Bradshaw.

Despite a highly touted sophomore passing combination, Jerry Woolum to Tom Hutchinson, the 1960 Wildcats lost four of their first six games. They then went on to shut out Florida State, Vanderbilt and Xavier and to tie Tennessee 10–10 on a field goal by Clarkie Mayfield in the waning minutes of the game, to salvage a 5–4–1 record. Hutchinson caught 30 passes for 455 yards and 4 touchdowns and was named All-SEC.

After the Wildcats lost to Tennessee 26–16 and finished 5–5 in 1961, the University bought up the remaining three years of Collier's contract, allowing Collier to return to the Cleveland Browns, whom he would lead to one league and five division championships.

Seeking to return to the "glory" days of Bear Bryant, the University turned to Charlie Bradshaw, a thirty-seven-year-old former Marine Corps drill instructor who had earned four letters at center and end under Bryant. He had served as an aide to Collier at UK and to Bryant at Alabama. Bradshaw brought from Tuscaloosa a tough program, reminiscent of that of Bryant's early days in Lexington. Times and attitudes had changed, however, and he met opposition on many sides, especially from the students, the academicians and the press. By the end of his first spring practice, more than fifty of the eighty-eight players he had inherited had quit the team. Those remaining formed the "Thin Thirty" squad of 1962.

Although its ranks were thin, the team did have some fine players in tackles Herschel Turner and Junior Hawthorne, center-linebacker Tommy Simpson, and halfback Darrell Cox, who in 1961 ranked fourth nationally in punt returns.

The Wildcats played a fine Florida State team to a scoreless tie, lost to Ole Miss and Auburn, and then gave Bradshaw his first victory, a 27–8 win over Detroit on the road. They lost a 7–0 decision to Bradshaw's friend and former UK teammate Charlie McClendon of LSU, tied Georgia, and wilted in the fourth quarter to George Mira and Miami, 25–17. In the next game, Turner took the ball away from Vanderbilt's Hank Lesesne, setting up a touchdown for a 7–0 UK win. Kentucky was then upset 14–9 at home by Xavier. The Wildcats ended the season on a positive note by defeating Tennessee at Knoxville, 12–10, on a 19-yard field goal by Clarkie Mayfield with sixteen seconds remaining, for a 3–5–2 record.

Bradshaw's first crop of rookies contained several outstanding players, including quarterback Rick Norton, halfback Rodger Bird, tackles Sam Ball and Doug Davis, and end Rick Kestner. They gained experience the hard way in 1963, winning three games while losing six and tying one. Bird showed promise in the season opener by returning Virginia Tech's opening kickoff 92 yards for a touchdown. He also gained 117 yards in the 33–14 victory over a VPI team coached by Jerry Claiborne, another former teammate of Bradshaw. The other UK victories were over Detroit at Lexington and over bowl-bound Baylor at Waco, where Bear quarterback Don Trull hit 17 of 30 passes for 248 yards and a touchdown, but was intercepted three times, once for a 42-yard

Coach Bradshaw with Rodger Bird (21), Rick Norton (11) and Rick Kestner (80), part of Bradshaw's first crop of rookies (1963).

touchdown return by Darrell Cox. Returning home, the Wildcats were defeated by Tennessee 19–0, as Mallon Faircloth's passing put 3 touchdowns on the board.

With Larry Seiple and Frank Antonini, two fine backs from Pennsylvania, joining the squad in 1964, UK got off to its best start in years, defeating Detroit at home and upsetting number one-ranked Ole Miss 27–21 at Jackson, where Kestner caught two touchdown passes from Norton and one from Bird to earn national "Lineman of the Week" honors. Against Auburn the following week, Bird scored two touchdowns, one on a 95-yard return of a pass thrown by Jimmy Sidle, giving the Wildcats a 20–0 victory and number seven ranking in the nation. Then they traveled to Tallahassee and were defeated 48–6 by a Florida State team that featured quarterback Steve Tensi, Fred Biletnikoff and the "Seven Magnificents."

The following day, a Sunday, Bradshaw had his players on the practice field and ran them until, as one player put it, "our tongues were hanging out and there were sick guys all over the place." Bradshaw was later called down by the University president for scheduling the Sunday scrimmage which resulted in several injuries.

The loss to Florida State was followed by three more losses before the Wildcats defeated Vanderbilt 22–21. They lost to Baylor at home and then salvaged some pride by defeating Tennessee 12–7 on a 68-yard scoring pass from Norton to Kestner, to close out a 5–5 season.

Bradshaw's senior-dominated 1965 team defeated Missouri 7–0 at Columbia, and returned home to beat Mississippi 16–7, as Seiple, back to punt on fourth and 41 in the closing minute of the game, ran 70 yards for a touchdown. The Wildcats missed two two-point conversions at Auburn and lost 23–18. Norton threw six interceptions at Baton Rouge, where they lost to LSU, 31–21. He was on target against Georgia, passing for four touchdowns in the second quarter, to spark a 28–10 UK victory. After defeating West Virginia and Vanderbilt, the Wildcats were 6–2. They received a bid to the Gator Bowl, but opted to wait for a "bigger" bid, which depended on the outcome of their game against Houston at the Astrodome.

Bradshaw's hopes for a winning football program at UK were shattered on the artificial turf in Houston. His Wildcats were ahead 21–16 at halftime, but fell 38–21 as Bo Burrus threw three Cougar touchdown passes in the second half. Norton left the game with a knee injury after hitting 19 of 23 attempts for 373 yards and 2 touchdowns.

Without their star quarterback and several other key players also injured at Houston, the Wildcats lost to Tennessee 19–3 in the season finale, to post a 6–4 record—the best in nine years.

On Thanksgiving Day 1965, Bradshaw was given a new contract of indeterminate length. Less than a month later, he broke the UK and Southeastern Conference color barriers by signing Nat Northington of Louisville to a UK grant. Greg Page, another black, signed a month later. Northington played briefly in UK's opener against Indiana in 1967 and then saw 3:17 minutes of action against Mississippi at Lexington, becoming the first black ever to play in a football game between two SEC schools.

All-SEC fullback Dicky Lyons (1967 and 1968).

The best all-round player on the UK squad during Bradshaw's last three years in Lexington was Dicky Lyons, a six-foot, 185-pound back from Louisville. In his first varsity game Lyons first set up a touchdown with a 31-yard punt return and then set up a field goal with an interception return, giving Kentucky a 10–0 win over North Carolina. Against Auburn, two games later, he blocked a Jimmy Jones field-goal attempt on the Tiger 24 and then watched from the ground as end Doug Van Meter caught the ball, headed goalward, dropped it on the 12, and then recovered it on the 15. The Wildcats scored and won the game.

Lyons had little reason to rejoice during the remainder of the season, however, as the Wildcats finished 1966 with a 3–6–1 record. They were 2–8 in 1967 and 3–7 in 1968. One of Lyons's best games came during the 1967 season, when he ran for three touchdowns against West Virginia, kicked an extra point, and made good on his first and only collegiate field-goal attempt, giving Kentucky a 22–7 win. Lyons set various school, Conference and national records for punt and kickoff returns, an indication that the teams he played on were on the receiving end of a lot of kickoffs.

When Bradshaw finally resigned to "clear the air" after the 1968 season, he was replaced by John Ray, a Notre Dame assistant who had specialized in defense during his head coaching days at John Carroll University. Described by UK basketball coach Adolph Rupp as "the guy who wrote that book about positive thinking," Ray immediately promised UK fans a Conference championship, top-ten ranking, and a bowl invitation. He preached winning and number one right up until the opening game, when a full house at Stoll Field and a regional television audience watched Harry Gonso, John Isenbarger and Jade Butcher lead Indiana to a 24–0 lead early in the game. Bernie Scruggs hit Al Godwin on a 71-yard scoring pass and later connected with Jim Grant on a fourth-down fake. Roger Gann added a touchdown on a 95-yard kickoff return, but Indiana won, 58–30, scoring the most points against a UK team in twenty-four years.

Coach John Ray, 1969–1972.

When Mississippi came to town, they scored first on a 24-yard field goal and then added six more points on a 64-yard run by Archie Manning. Dave Hunter blocked the extra point. Bobby Jones got UK on the board with a 36-yard drive that put UK ahead to stay, 10–9. The win—Ray's first—was one of the big upsets of the 1969 season.

Former UK coaches Blanton Collier, left (1954–1961), and J. J. Winn, right, are greeted by Coach Ray during a 1969 practice session.

The bubble burst the following week, when Auburn beat Kentucky 44–3. Then the Wildcats defeated Virginia Tech at Blacksburg but lost their remaining games, finishing with a 2–8 record. They were 2–9 the following year, with one of 1970's few bright spots coming in the second game of the season, when David Roller roamed the Kansas State backfield at will and sacked quarterback Lynn Dickey so many times that the K State offense only generated 3 points while Kentucky scored 16. They won only one other game all year, defeating North Carolina State 27–2.

Sophomore Doug Kotar got the 1971 season off to a good start, duplicating Rodger Bird's feat of 1963 by taking the opening kickoff against Clemson and returning it 98 yards for a touchdown. But it was downhill the rest of the season, as the Wildcats lost six in a row before beating VPI and Vanderbilt on fine plays by safety Darryl Bishop. Florida beat them 35–24, and Tennessee won 21–7, as Kentucky finished with a disappointing 3–8 record.

James "Dinky" McKay, who had guided Gulf Coast Junior College to the National Junior College championship, led the Wildcats to a 25–7 victory over Villanova in the 1972 opener, but Alabama beat them 35–0, and Indiana edged them 35–34. The Wildcats beat Mississippi State and then lost four in a row before beating Vanderbilt 14–13 and losing to Florida 14–0 and Tennessee 17–7, for another 3–8 season.

On his first varsity play, Doug Kotar returns the opening kickoff 98 yards for a touchdown against Clemson as the Wildcats win 13–10 (1971).

Ray had one year to go on his contract, but he resigned after the Board refused to grant him an extension. Although his overall record (10–33–0) was one of the worst in UK football history, he did play a vital role in molding the future. It was mostly through his efforts that a new 58,000-seat stadium was designed, ready for his successor's occupancy.

In the quest for a "big name" head coach, the University interviewed such recognized winners as Johnny Majors and Bill Dooley before hiring serious young Fran Curci, a former All-American quarterback from Miami who had rejuvenated the program at Tampa and then coached two years at Miami.

Curci came to the University fully aware that the "Graveyard of Football Coaches" had claimed a very popular victim in personable, gruff, big-hearted John Ray. But although the disadvantages of coaching the Wildcats seemed to far outweigh the advantages, Curci felt that the new Commonwealth Stadium had to help the program.

Curci did not expect the talent of UK to be spectacular, and he was not disappointed. But he did find what he called "a bunch of really dedicated young men who were tired of losing and were looking for someone to come in and show them how to win." Boosters under the Bradshaw program had waged a "This is Wildcat Country" campaign, and those associated with Ray had sponsored a "We Believe" program that also fizzled. Curci immediately let it be known that he did not believe in slogans and campaigns, just results. He instituted several changes in the physical facilities and then set out to build a winning football team.

Among the better players left over from the Ray regime were Sonny Collins, Doug Kotar and Steve Campassi, all capable backs; offensive linemen Harvey Sword, Dave Margavage and Elmore Stephens; Rick Nuzum, a second-string guard who became an All-American center; Mike Fanuzzi, who was returned to his old quarterback position after being converted to a wide receiver by Ray; linebacker Frank LeMaster, who would eventually start for the Philadelphia Eagles; tackle James McCollum; and safety Darryl Bishop.

The Wildcats, excited at playing their first game in new Commonwealth Stadium, dominated the early stages of the 1973 opener against VPI and held on to win 31–26. They were still on an emotional high when Paul "Bear" Bryant brought Alabama to Lexington for the first home game against the Tide since 1947. LeMaster was so excited that he chose the wrong end of the field after losing the flip of the coin, and the Wildcats kicked off into the wind. But Alabama failed to capitalize, and the Wildcats got two touchdowns, for a 14–0 lead at halftime. Willie Shelby fumbled UK's second-half kickoff, but he picked up the ball and returned it 100 yards for a touchdown as the Tide went on to win 28–14.

After a nightmare of fumbles and mistakes that resulted in a 17–3 loss to Indiana at Bloomington,

Head coach Fran Curci.

Curci made what he later called one of his toughest coaching decisions, moving Fanuzzi to quarterback in place of Ernie Lewis. Against Mississippi State the following Saturday, Fanuzzi had a good night and Collins exploded for 229 yards and 4 touchdowns, which earned him national "Back of the Week" honors.

The Wildcats became a better football team as the season progressed, scoring five victories, including a 12–7 decision over Georgia at Athens, where they had not won a game since 1956. They came within inches of a winning season when Ron Steele's field-goal attempt in the closing minute of the game against Tennessee passed just under the bar, giving the Vols a 16–14 win. Still, 1973's 5–6 record was the best of any Wildcat team since Bradshaw's 1965 crew finished 6–4.

Sonny Collins, SEC leading scorer (1973).

Faced with replacing seventeen starters at the beginning of the 1974 season, Curci came up with an outstanding freshman class that included Jerry Blanton, Jim Kovach, Mike Siganos, Art Still, Bob Winkel, Derrick Ramsey and Dallas Owens. He started four freshmen in the opening game against VPI and won going away, 38–7. West Virginia took advantage of the Wildcats' inexperience and beat them 16–3 at Morgantown. The Wildcats then defeated Indiana 28–22, lost to Miami (Ohio) and Auburn, defeated LSU, lost to Georgia, and defeated Tulane, Vanderbilt and Florida in succession before Tennessee beat them 24–7, for a 6–5 record, only their fourth winning season in eighteen years.

The 1975 season started off well and ended in disaster. Virginia Tech was a 27–8 victim in the first match of the season. Then the Wildcats were leading Kansas 10–7, when a tight-end reverse resulted in a fumble that Kansas recovered on the Jayhawk 41. Five plays later, after two straight pass-interference penalties, the Jayhawks were in the end zone for a 14–10 victory. Next, John Pierce kicked a 45-yard field goal with less than three minutes remaining, to tie Maryland 10–10. The Wildcats then went on to University Park, where they outplayed Penn State in most categories, but still lost 10–3. That set the stage for the game with Auburn, the game that turned the season into a full-fledged disaster. The Wildcats went ahead 9–0 on Pierce's third field goal of the game with seven minutes remaining. They seemed to have the game under control until Clyde Baumgartner, the visitors' punter and second-string quarterback, entered the game and threw a 73-yard touchdown pass to Jeff Gilligan. Collins fumbled the Auburn kickoff, and the Plainsmen took possession on the UK 23 and scored in three plays for a 15–9 win.

The demoralized Wildcats, beset by rumors of point-shaving and deflated by the come-from-behind victory by Auburn, won only one other game all season, defeating Tulane, and finished 1975 with a dismal 2–8–1 record. But the season did not end with the last game—a tough 13–17 loss to Tennessee. For immediately after the season was over, the NCAA began an investigation into recruiting violations that would ultimately result in a two-year probation for UK and sanctions for both the football and the basketball programs.

The key player in Curci's plans for the 1976 season was Derrick Ramsey, a six-foot-five, 225-pound junior who had started at quarterback in the 10–10 tie with Maryland and then been switched to tight end and finally back to quarterback for the final game of the 1975 season. Curci announced early that Ramsey was his quarterback in a backfield that also featured Chris Hill, highly touted sophomore Rod Stewart, and Greg Woods, a senior who had started on defense the year before. The best offensive lineman was Warren Bryant, who would make All-American that season. The defense, still young but hardened by experience in the trenches, was led by end Art Still, halfbacks Mike Siganos and Dallas Owens, and tackle Jerry Blanton.

Quarterback Derrick Ramsey, who led Kentucky to a 10–1 record in 1977.

The strong-running Ramsey led the Wildcats to a 38–13 victory over Oregon State, but Nolan Cromwell and the Kansas Jayhawks had too much firepower and won 37–16 at Lawrence. The Wildcats defeated West Virginia 14–10, and then pulled a major upset by defeating Penn State 22–6 in Lexington. Mississippi State was leading 14–7 at Jackson, when Jim Kovach blocked a Maroon punt deep inside MSU territory in the closing minute of the game. But David Stephens, with a clear field ahead, fell on the ball while trying to scoop it up, and the Wildcats failed to score.

The Wildcats defeated LSU 21–7, but lost to eventual Conference champion Georgia, 31–7, at Lexington. Maryland beat them 24–12 at College Park. They beat Vanderbilt and Florida before going to Knoxville and beating Tennessee 7–0, to gain possession of the Beer Barrel for the first time since 1964.

When the team accepted a bid to play in the Peach Bowl, an estimated 35,000 Kentuckians accompanied them to Atlanta. The Wildcats completely dominated a North Carolina team that was without the services of its star running back Mike Voight, who had suffered an ankle injury in practice. Rod Stewart carried 19 times for 104 yards and tied a bowl record of 3 touchdowns, as UK won 21–0. Stewart was named the game's Most Valuable Player on offense; UK linebacker Mike Martin was named the Most Valuable Player on defense.

At the end of his first four years in Lexington, Curci had posted two winning seasons, something that had not happened at UK in twenty years, and led UK to a 7–4 regular-season record, its best since 1954, and to its first post-season bowl appearance in a quarter-century. The Wildcats had tied for third place in the Conference after all the so-called experts had picked them to finish last. And, as a postscript to an already successful season, when the Executive Committee of the SEC ruled two years later that Mississippi State must forfeit all games in which an ineligible athlete participated—including the Bulldogs' 14–7 win over UK in 1976—the Wildcats were to retroactively have their record changed to 8–3 and be named as Conference co-champions.

With the return of many veteran players from the Peach Bowl squad, Curci figured to have a good team in 1977, but he was not sure what to expect of a full-house backfield that featured Ramsey, Stewart, Hill and promising sophomore Randy Brooks. He knew the defense was sound, but the kicking game had lost placekicker John Pierce and punter Pete Gemmill from the 1976 squad. The replacements were two walk-ons: Joe Bryant, who had transferred from Western Kentucky University, sat out a year of ineligibility and then kicked off for the Wildcats in 1976; and Kevin Kelly, who had spent his freshman year at Alabama and then served three years in the Navy before enrolling at UK and also sitting out a period of ineligibility.

Bryant got the 1977 season off to a good start by kicking a 22-yard field goal late in the second quarter against North Carolina. But Kelly's first punt early in the first quarter slid off his foot and sailed over the Tar Heel bench and into the crowd for a net of just 15 yards. However, the Tar Heels had been offside, and the Wildcats got a first down. Kelly kicked well the rest of the afternoon. With the Wildcats trailing 7–3 and on their own 36 late in the game, Kelly scooped up a bad snap from center and punted to Mel Collins, who tried a fair catch on the run and fumbled the ball on the NC 33. Kentucky recovered and went in for the score, to win 10–7.

Against Baylor at Waco the following Saturday, the Wildcats fumbled deep in their own territory, giving Baylor a "gift" touchdown. The Wildcat center later snapped the ball over Kelly's head, and Baylor recovered on the 14, setting up another touchdown. Then the Bears blocked one of Kelly's punts, and Mike Singletary picked it up and ran 20 yards unmolested for yet a third touchdown, "giving" Baylor a 21–6 upset win. A blustery wind in Commonwealth Stadium caused several mistakes, as UK beat West Virginia 28–13. The kicking game was still suspect when the Wildcats traveled to University Park, Pennsylvania, where Penn State went ahead in the first quarter on a field goal and furthered its lead to 10–0 on a 75-yard punt return by Jimmy Cefalo. Dallas Owens intercepted a pass and ran it in from 23 yards out for a Wildcat touchdown, and then Mike Siganos set up another touchdown with an interception, giving Kentucky a 14–10 lead. The Wildcats went on to win 24–20 against a Penn State team that was fourth-ranked in the nation.

The 1977 Wildcat team marched to its best season in twenty-seven years, defeating Mississippi State, LSU, Georgia, Virginia Tech, Vanderbilt, Florida and Tennessee in succession, for a 10–1 record. They finished sixth nationally, highest ranking ever for a UK team, and placed five players—Still, Siganos, Owens, Ramsey and offensive guard Tom Dornbrook—on the All-Conference team. Still was a consensus All-American.

The success of the 1976 and 1977 UK teams prompted many fans throughout the Commonwealth to make early hotel reservations for the 1978 Sugar Bowl game in New Orleans.

However, despite the euphoria, Curci's ranks were heavily depleted by graduation. The biggest shoes to be filled were those worn by Derrick Ramsey and Art Still. Mike Deaton, a little-used substitute who had completed a fourth quarter pass to set up the winning touchdown in the 1977 Tennessee game, earned the starting quarterback spot, but gave way to freshman Larry McCrimmon at halftime of the Ole Miss game. The Wildcats clawed back to win that game, giving them a 2–2–1 record, with an opening-game tie against South Carolina and back-to-back losses to Maryland and Penn State wrapped around a second-game victory over Baylor.

But the expected turnaround never came, and the 'Cats suffered a shutout at the hands of LSU, a last-second loss to Georgia on a field goal, a two-point loss to Florida on yet another last-second field goal, and a 29–14 loss to Tennessee, winding up with a 4–6–1 record, a far cry from the hoped-for season.

Still, the 4–6–1 record gave Curci an overall six-year record of 36–29–2 and placed him next to Bear Bryant as Kentucky's most successful football coach.

Today, with sellout crowds of 58,000 packed into Commonwealth Stadium and many Kentucky fans learning the joys of rooting for a winner, tailgating and following their team on the road, Wildcat football has come of age. And indeed it has come a long way since President Patterson used the football field as a pasture for his cattle.

Part of the sellout crowd at Commonwealth Stadium rooting their favorite team on.

SEC football is more than colorful players performing on the gridiron. Much more. On any given Saturday during the football season it also consists of the time-honored pastimes of "honey-watching," flag-waving and just plain ol' socializing—all as much a part of SEC football as the game itself. Here on the next eight pages are some of those SEC sights and sounds in color.

University of Alabama

Auburn University

University of Florida

University of Georgia

University of Kentucky

Louisiana State University

University of Mississippi

University of Mississippi

Mississippi State University

University of Tennessee

Vanderbilt University

Louisiana State University

by Paul Manasseh

The fans start drifting in as early as Thursday afternoon. From all over they come: from New Orleans and New Roads, Monroe and Mamou, Shreveport and Simmesport, Lafayette and Lutcher. And, of course, they come from Bunkie, because there is such a place, and indeed there is such a thing as college football. In this case it's college football LSU style, as it can only be played in Tiger Stadium on Saturday. And preferably at night.

Steadily the mass grows—from the die-hard tailgaters to the modern Rec vehicles—creating an instant suburb. By Saturday afternoon the immediate area around Tiger Stadium is the fourth largest city in Louisiana. There they meet new friends and chat with old ones. They speculate on the night ahead and reminisce about nights past. They eat and drink, laugh and joke. The talk is of last week's win and next week's trip to Jackson.

But mostly they wait, wait for that magic moment when the LSU Golden Band from Tigerland takes its familiar spot in the south end zone, signifying that the night is about to officially begin. There will be a brief pause, then the familiar "Daa-da-daa-da," with which over 76,000 people will join in, justifying the use of the term "Deaf Valley" (a takeoff on "Death Valley") for Tiger Stadium. The Tigers will soon appear, and with them sixty minutes of the most exciting football found anywhere. And much, much more.

Football is an institution in Louisiana now and quite a successful one, pumping $3 million into the local economy each and every year. It dominates conversations from the docks of New Orleans to the offshore drilling rigs out of Morgan City and the hills of Shreveport, and everywhere in between.

But it did not happen overnight. There had to be a Billy Cannon and a Tiger Rag. A Y. A. Tittle and a Bert Jones. Upset bowl wins and Chinese Bandits. Halloween punt returns, 1908 and "The Night the Irish Came to Tiger Stadium." Huey Long's assault on Nashville is legend, and caravans to Jackson are annual. Biff Jones and Paul Dietzel left their marks, Bernie Moore and Charlie McClendon theirs. And don't forget Steve Van Buren and Charles Alexander, national championships, and "Wait till next year. . . ."

Tiger Stadium, a/k/a "Death Valley," one of the nation's attendance leaders.

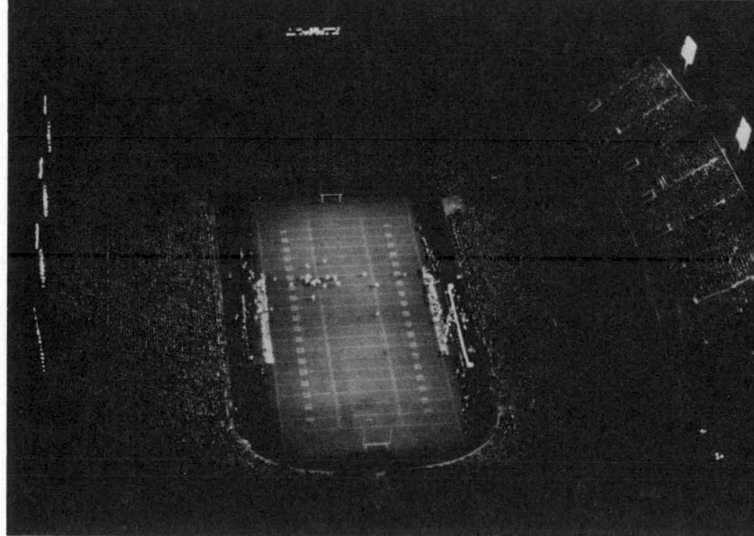

Paul Manasseh served as the original director of public relations for the Denver Broncos. He was director of press relations and general manager for the Denver Triple-A baseball team, and has been sports information director at LSU since 1971.

To trace the start of this madness, you must go all the way back to 1893, the year Professor Charles Coates decided to give the team he had organized a year earlier some incentive by scheduling a game against another school. That incentive was LSU's opponent: Tulane.

The game was set for November 25, 1893, and even way back then it was easy to tell that something far more important than just a game was in the making. The approaching game immediately caught the attention of Baton Rouge, as the *Daily Advocate* urged the State University—as it was called then—to uphold the honor of the city. Later it would be urged to uphold the honor of the entire state.

Tulane had already played one game, and the New Orleans papers gave it an advantage for that reason, although as the game neared they reported that LSU was "a great deal heavier than was first thought it would be. The backs average 154 pounds, while the rush line averages 165 pounds, and the entire team averages 160 pounds."

With this "awesome" lineup, the LSU team traveled to New Orleans, where an estimated 1500 to 2000 people witnessed the first game at Sportsman's Park. What they saw said a lot for experience over size.

Tulane scored barely two minutes into the game and added two more touchdowns before the half, for an 18–0 lead. Three more touchdowns in the second half gave the New Orleans team a 34–0 win and a 1–0 advantage in a rivalry that would become one of the most hotly contested in the nation.

But defeat in that initial game only seemed to whet the appetite of the "State University," and soon papers were reporting, "When boys study as hard as they play football, there are going to be some intellectual lights in Louisiana."

That one game constituted the entire 1893 season. And although it was anything but a success for the State University, it was the first, albeit tottering, step toward the building of one of the most fabled football programs in the country.

The next year found LSU with three games, the first of which was against the Natchez Athletic Club. The team experienced more difficulty getting to the game—its steamship ran aground some twenty miles short of the game site—than it did with its opponent, whom it beat 36–0, for the first win in LSU's history.

LSU finally played its first game in Baton Rouge later that year, against Mississippi. Another rivalry got off to a bad start, however, as the neighboring state rolled to a 26–6 win. But LSU finally chalked up its first home win shortly thereafter when it romped over Centenary 30–0.

LSU entered its third season with a cumulative record of two wins and two losses. But 1895 was to see not only the school's first victory over Tulane, 8–4, but also its first all-winning season, as it swept past its other two opponents, Centenary and Alabama, 16–6 and 12–6, respectively, but not respectfully.

1896 was a year when the schedule expanded to a half-dozen games, and once again LSU was triumphant in all of them. The season was noteworthy not only because of wins over the likes of Tulane, Ole Miss, Texas and Mississippi State, but also because of the adoption of the nickname Tigers, a lineal throwback to the name four Louisiana regiments had used during the Mexican War.

A yellow-fever epidemic delayed the 1897 season opener and telescoped the schedule down to just two games: a solid 28–6 win over the Montgomery Athletic Club and an equally solid loss to Cincinnati, 26–0. The following season the epidemic returned, as did Tulane after a year's absence. But both were conquered, the latter by a 37–0 score.

Tulane was beaten again the next year, the only bright spot in a 1–4 season that closed out the nineteenth century.

LSU football, circa 1900.

E. A. Chavanne, who had captained and coached the Tigers in 1898, took over the head coaching duties in 1900, LSU's sixth coach in its first eight years of varsity competition. His second duty began auspiciously enough with a 70–0 drubbing of Millsaps. That win, however, was followed by a 29–0 loss to Tulane and a 6–5 reversal by the same Millsaps team the Tigers had handled so handily just a few weeks before. And even though Chavanne ended the

The 1902 Louisiana State team posing with a precious trophy reflecting shutout victories over Texas and Alabama.

season with a 10–0 victory over the Alumni to even his season's record at 2–2, he found that the LSU head coaching position provided all the job security of a Storyville streetwalker; he was succeeded as head coach by W. S. Borland. Borland presided over two teams that compiled 5–1 and 6–1 records, but when his 1903 edition lost five games, all shutouts, and won only four, he too was shown the revolving door that was just outside the head coach's office.

After Dan Killan spent three years at the helm and amassed a cumulative record of 8–6–2, Edgar R. Wingard arrived on the scene from Pennsylvania to take over the head-coaching duties. He brought with him LSU's first true legend: George "Doc" Fenton, who played right end as well as Trilby to Wingard's Svengali. Together these two men turned around LSU's football fortunes.

Their first campaign met with only moderate success, as the 1907 Tigers lost two of their first three games, losing to both Texas and Texas A & M. But by the end of the year the Wingard-Fenton treatment was taking, and LSU defeated Arkansas, Mississippi State, Mississippi and finally Baylor (48–0) and Havana University (56–0), for a comeback 7–3 record.

With their first seven-win season under their belts, the Tigers entered 1908 with high hopes. The first two games immediately bore out their expectations, as they ran up 41–0 and 81–5 scores against the Young Men's Gymnastics Club of New Orleans and the Jackson Barracks team.

The next week, pitted against a Texas A & M team that had beaten them the last two years, LSU was "held" to 26 points, as they beat the respected Aggies 26–0. They followed up their string of successes by whipping Auburn, Mississippi State and Baylor, the last by a whopping 89–0, the most points ever scored by an LSU team. Within four days, the Tigers had beaten Louisiana Tech and Arkansas on the road, to wind up their first perfect season with a 10–0 record. They had scored 462 points, the most in the team's history, giving up only 11.

While Fenton was the undisputed star of the team, having been called the "greatest quarterback I ever saw on a field" by Mississippi State Coach Furman, a veteran of the tough Eastern football leagues, halfback Michael Lally and guard William Hillman—both of whom joined Fenton on the Memphis *Commercial Appeal*'s All-Southern team—made important contributions to the perfect season. The *Commercial Appeal* ranked LSU first in Southern football, LSU's first true championship.

LSU opened the 1909 season with Coach Wingard gone. But with Fenton returning, hopes were high that this was to be that "next year." Behind Fenton, LSU rolled to easy wins in its first three games, against Jackson Barracks, Ole Miss and Mississippi State. With Fenton hobbled by injuries, the Tigers then went to New Orleans to face powerful Sewanee. But even the presence of President William Howard Taft—marking the first football game ever witnessed by a U.S. President—didn't help LSU as Sewanee won 15–6, breaking a fifteen-game Tiger winning streak.

The Sewanee loss was LSU's first in sixteen starts, but criticism was heavy nevertheless, and Coach J. G. Pritchard resigned under pressure. Under their new coach, J. W. Mayhew, the Tigers bounced back for a win the next week over Louisiana Tech, but they lost again the following week to Arkansas. The season ended with wins over Transylvania and Alabama, for a 6–2 season.

The undefeated 1908 team, which outscored its ten opponents 442–11.

LSU 6, Tulane 0 (1911).

With the stars of the championship team gone, and with only one game played at home, LSU fell to a 1–5 season in 1910. A familiar scenario was repeated, and a new coach, J. K. Dwyer, hired. He led the team to wins in the first five games of the 1911 season. Then the Tigers dropped three in a row before overcoming a stubborn Tulane defense for a 6–0 win.

In Dwyer's second season, his 1912 team compiled a 4–3 record. Then in 1913 the Tigers lost one game and tied two out of nine games. The season was still considered "successful," as the Tigers smashed Tulane 40–0.

But even though Tulane had been beaten, that was all for Dwyer. E. T. McDonald took over the team in 1914 and compiled a 4–4–1 record, including the worst defeat up to that time, a 63–9 drubbing by Texas A & M, and a tie with Tulane. The Tigers' fortunes improved in 1915, as the team went 6–2, losing to only Rice and Georgia Tech, and big things were expected in 1916, as the team returned virtually intact. Four easy wins were followed by another loss to powerful Sewanee, and McDonald was sent packing.

Irving Pray, a sugar chemist scheduled to go to Cuba the following week, was called upon to take over as head coach for one game. He successfully discharged his assignment by leading the team to a win over Arkansas in Shreveport. Then for the third time in three weeks another head coach was selected. The LSU head-coaching office began to look like the stateroom scene in a Marx Brothers' movie, with all its comings and goings. This time the man selected was Dana X. Bible, who had coached at Mississippi College for three years and would go on to coach for twenty-nine more distinguished years, ending up in the Football Hall of Fame. But while Bible's stint at LSU was considerably shorter than at any of his other four coaching stopovers, his contribution to LSU was two wins and two ties in the final four games on the 1916 schedule.

Wayne Sutton became LSU's coach-for-the-year in 1917, but his 3–5 record hardly entitled him to tenure, and by the end of the year he too had joined the ever-growing army of ex–football coaches at LSU.

After a "down" year during World War I when LSU did not field a football team, LSU returned to its own football wars in 1919 under the leadership of the highly respected Pray, the Tigers' seventeenth head coach in twenty-six years. The Tigers won their first four games before losing to Mississippi State. Then, after they split the next two games, the stage was set for their traditional game against state rival Tulane. Utilizing the power running of Joe Bernstein, the Tigers swamped powerful Tulane 26–7, prompting the LSU student body to hold a public funeral for Tulane's mascot, the goat, at a pep rally the following week.

The front page of The Reveille *pictures two 1920 campus heroes, quarterback "Rabbit" Benoit and halfback "Fatty" Ives.*

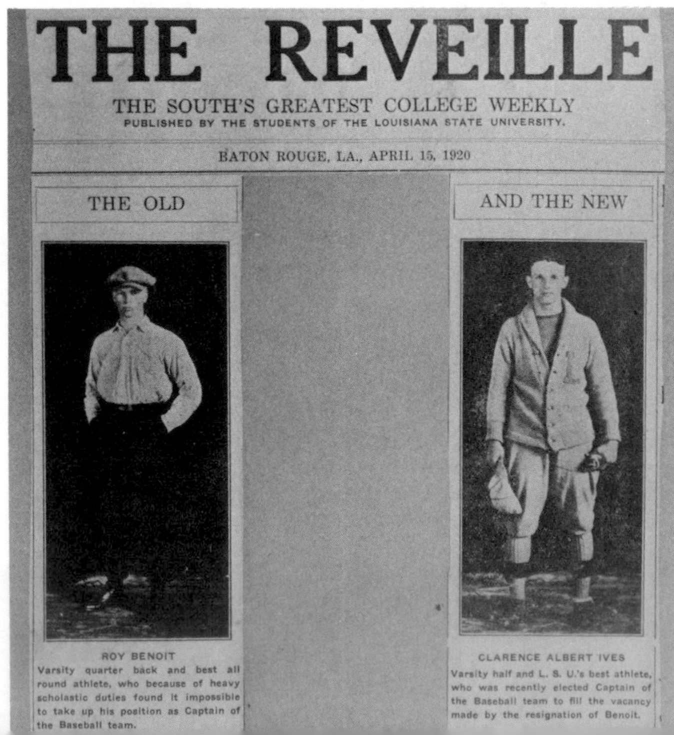

THE REVEILLE

THE SOUTH'S GREATEST COLLEGE WEEKLY

PUBLISHED BY THE STUDENTS OF THE LOUISIANA STATE UNIVERSITY.

BATON ROUGE, LA., APRIL 15, 1920

THE OLD

ROY BENOIT

Varsity quarter back and best all round athlete, who because of heavy scholastic duties found it impossible to take up his position as Captain of the Baseball team.

AND THE NEW

CLARENCE ALBERT IVES

Varsity half and L. S. U.'s best athlete, who was recently elected Captain of the Baseball team to fill the vacancy made by the resignation of Benoit.

Despite his 6–2 record, Pray left, and he was succeeded by Branch Bocock, LSU's eighteenth coach. Under Bocock the Tigers put together two winning seasons, 5–3–1 in 1920 and 6–1–1 in 1921. But two of Bocock's four losses came at the hands of Tulane, both by 21–0 scores, and he too was sent packing.

LSU lured Pray back to coach the team in 1922, but with all of his former stars gone, he could not rekindle the magic, and the team suffered through big losses: 0–51 to SMU, 0–47 to Texas A & M, 6–40 to Arkansas, and 3–47 to Alabama. The Tigers did manage to win big over Tulane, which should have saved Pray's job. But he left nevertheless.

LSU went "big time" in 1923, hiring Mike Donahue away from Auburn, where he not only had built up a solid reputation as a coach, but also had compiled a record of 94–35–5 in eighteen seasons, with three undefeated teams. But somehow the mysterious malaise continued to work at LSU, and Donahue's first Tiger team won just three of nine games, including a shutout at the hands of Tulane.

1924 saw an improvement of sorts, as LSU managed to win its first four games before dropping three of its next four. The final game against Tulane was held at the partially completed new stadium, the future scene of many great moments in LSU history. However, as 20,000 rabid Tiger fans watched, LSU closed out its 1924 season with a 13–0 loss to Tulane, hardly an auspicious beginning for an edifice that would witness so many Tiger triumphs.

There seemed to be a new day aborning in 1925. Donahue's first two years had shown a steady improvement, he had two of his great stars—halfback Norman Stevens and guard A. L. "Red" Swanson—returning, and, to add to the new outlook that pervaded Baton Rouge, classes were being held on the new campus for the first time. But after rolling up big scores against their opening two opponents—the third straight year Donahue had gotten his charges out of the gate with two straight wins—the Tigers met Rose Bowl–bound Alabama and came out the worse for wear, 42–0. The Tigers rebounded, losing only one of their next five games, and then lost 16–0 in the season finale to the one team that really counted, Tulane, to finish with a 5–3–1 record.

Donahue's fourth season started as always, with the obligatory two wins over Louisiana Tech and Southwestern Louisiana. But by midseason the slate stood 3–3, and only wins over the last three opponents—including, finally, a victory for Donahue over Tulane—enabled the season to qualify as a "success."

The 1927 season was Donahue's fifth as head coach—making him the "Iron Man" among LSU coaches—and his last. After winning the first two games, per usual, the Tigers surprised even themselves by tying an Alabama team that had not been defeated in three years. They followed up that "moral victory" with back-to-back wins over Auburn and Mississippi State and stood at the more-than-halfway

LSU 10, Arkansas 7 (1921).

mark with a 4–0–1 record. But it was all downhill for the Tigers after that, as they dropped the last four games on their schedule, ending with a 13–6 loss to Tulane and a disappointing 4–4–1 slate.

The highly respected Donahue was "euthanasically" put out to pasture; he remained at LSU for many years in various capacities, finally retiring as tennis coach in 1949. But no matter how softly he was let down, he was still another head-coaching casualty.

The fall of 1928 was the beginning of one of the most colorful eras for LSU football, indeed for the entire state of Louisiana. For it was the year Huey Long was elected governor of the Bayou State. No other governor had ever taken such an active role in the University or in its football program. The Kingfish adopted LSU in general, and LSU football in particular, as his very own, alternately serving as chief recruiter, cheerleader, sometime coach and all-round supporter. Huey decided LSU deserved a first-rate band, and, in the usual Huey Long fashion, transformed the Tiger band from a small military group into one of the finest bands in the nation.

Unfortunately for Long and the state, the quality of the band's play was not matched by that of the team. After the usual opening victories, the 1928 Tigers, now coached by Russ Cohen, lost to Alabama and Arkansas. They tied Tulane and finished with a 6–2–1 record, still their best in seven years.

The next two seasons saw the pattern repeated, as the team ran up big scores against mediocre teams early in the season and then began to falter against major competition, particularly Tulane.

1931 was memorable less for the Tigers' won-lost record than for the introduction of night football in Tiger Stadium, the beginning of a tradition that would become almost as much a part of the LSU experience as the LSU Golden Band. In what one writer referred to as a "nocturnal spectacle," LSU swamped tiny Spring Hill 35–0. But there was not much more to cheer about that season, as the Tigers went 5–4 and lost once again to Tulane, 34–7.

Russ Cohen had not beaten Tulane in his four years as head coach, a fact that did not go unnoticed by LSU fans. Or by Huey Long. And so, even though he had four winning years to his credit, Cohen was out, and LSU was faced with the prospect of hiring its twenty-second head coach.

The normal selection procedures were dispensed with. There was only one man who had the "say," and that one man was Huey Long. The man who scared away most applicants because his justly earned reputation as somewhat of a meddler had preceded him finally got the coach he wanted in Lawrence McCeney "Biff" Jones, who had just guided the U.S. Military Academy to four winning seasons and a cumulative 30–8–2 record. But the deal was made only after Jones asked for, and extracted, a promise that Long would stay out of the coaching arena.

With LSU athletics at a low ebb, the serious, hard-working Jones quickly went to work to change the overall atmosphere. And while his first-year record showed an imperceptible improvement over 1931—a rise from 5–4 to 6–3–1 in 1932—progress was obvious to all, including Long. The irrepressible governor restrained himself from interfering with Jones, confident that he had made a wise choice, and channeled his support for the team into leading parades and pep rallies and occasionally inviting the players to stay over at the governor's mansion.

In 1933 LSU became a charter member of the newly formed Southeastern Conference. Led by a pair of flashy sophomores, Jess Fatherree and Abe Mickal, the Tigers went through that inaugural SEC year without a loss. However, they were tied three times, and the title went to once-tied Alabama. LSU's first SEC game resulted in a 7–7 tie with Vanderbilt, followed by relatively easy wins over South Carolina, Ole Miss and Mississippi State. The Tulane game, which ended in another tie, produced one of the greatest plays in LSU history.

Abe Mickal, leading scorer on LSU's undefeated 1933 team.

With the score 7–0 in favor of Tulane, Mickal threw a desperation pass in the vicinity of Pete Burge in the end zone. Burge was so well covered that the ball appeared to be thrown away. But despite the omnipresent Green Wave defenders surrounding him, he leaped high into the air and made a sensational one-hand catch of the "Hail Mary" pass to tie the score and, as it turned out, the game, at 7–7.

That season saw LSU not only undefeated in SEC play, but also victorious over the champions of two other conferences, Arkansas of the Southwest and South Carolina of the Southern. This string of victories led one newspaper reporter to call the Tigers "Champs of three conferences with no crown to wear."

LSU entered the 1934 season with a promising group of players, including Mickal and Gaynell Tinsley, and the promise of another fine season. But it was not so much the on-the-field play of the team that will be remembered as the colorful off-the-field antics of Long.

End Gaynell Tinsley, LSU's first All-American (1935 and 1936).

The Tigers kicked off their season with an away tie against Rice and then prepared for the next week's home opener against SMU. However, an alternative entertainment, in the form of the Ringling Brothers' Circus, threatened LSU's opening night game. And that pleased Long about as much as a visit from Franklin Roosevelt. Long dug up an obscure law that held that no animals could enter the state without first being "dipped"—a reference obviously intended for cattle, but extended under the existing emergency to refer to other animals as well, since that suited Huey's purpose. Circus management saw the wisdom in rescheduling their show, and the SMU game went on without any further distractions.

The SMU game ended in still another tie—one of the six Jones had at LSU, giving him the rare distinction of having more games tied than lost—but then the Tigers won their next two games, setting up an all-important SEC match with undefeated Vanderbilt.

LSU's most rabid fan, Governor Huey Long.

Enter Huey Long, stage right. Deciding that we would "return the favor Andrew Jackson paid New Orleans," Long informed the railroads that they would supply special charter trains to carry the student body to Nashville and that the price of those charters would be six dollars round trip. When the railroad officials proved less than willing to go along with the ride, indicating that no such fare existed, Long merely pointed out to them that the legislature—*his* legislature—might have to consider levying a special tax on the many railroad bridges owned by the state. The officials immediately responded by granting the special charter rate. And the trip was on.

Standing, appropriately enough, in front of the Greek Theater, the histrionic Long addressed the student body, informing them of the special arrangements he had made with the railroads: there would be five trains, each composed of ten coaches and two baggage cars, all leaving Baton Rouge Friday night and returning immediately after the game.

Imploring everyone to "jump on board," he warned them that he would tolerate no "Cain-raisin'."

Then, as a postscript, the Kingfish announced that any student who could not afford the six dollars had only to see him personally to arrange for a loan—including one dollar for meal money. When a crush ensued, an impromptu loan shop was set up to handle all the requests. All a student had to do to get the seven dollars was sign his name. As the students queued up, Long emptied his wallet and then had all of his aides chip in as well. When that ready supply was exhausted, everyone repaired to Long's hotel suite, where the remaining students obtained their traveling money.

In what was to become known as "The Invasion of Nashville," the trains "chartered" by Long transported almost the entire LSU student body to the Tennessee capital for the game. Astonished city officials greeted the trains upon arrival and watched in amazement as the Tiger band and a cast of thousands paraded through the city's streets, with none other than the Kingfish in the lead.

Although it must have been anticlimactic, the game ended with the fired-up Tigers romping, 29–0.

Three more wins followed the victory over Vanderbilt—wins over Mississippi State, George Washington and Ole Miss. Then the high-flying Tigers were brought down to earth by a gambling Tulane team, 13–12, and Tennessee added still another defeat, 19–13, to the Tigers' once-glowing record.

The final game of the season brought the University of Oregon into Baton Rouge for the first time. And LSU, without the full services of its injured running back, Abe Mickal, fell behind 13–7 at halftime. Faced with the possibility of a third straight Tiger loss, Long called off all bets. He no longer considered himself duty-bound to stay out of Coach Jones's sphere of influence. Or out of the dressing room, for that matter. He insisted on giving the team a pep talk at halftime. When Jones refused to allow it, an argument ensued between the two strong-willed men. And even though Long did not fire Jones on the spot, nor coach the team in the second half, as legend has it, Jones had had enough and announced after the confrontation that he was quitting—regardless of the outcome of the game.

The Tigers came back to win the game 14–13, ending the season with a 7–2–2 record—Jones's fourth winning season in four years—but Huey was still in need of a new coach. His first choice was Frank Thomas of Alabama, but Thomas proved unavailable. Bernie Moore, the popular track coach, was the people's choice, and Long, ever the politi-

Bernie Moore, Tiger coach for thirteen years.

cian, decided to abide by the voice of the people and hired Moore.

But Long, shot down a few weeks before the start of the 1935 season, never saw a Moore-coached team. Had he lived, Moore might not have lasted past the first game, an upset 10–7 loss to Rice. The following week the Tigers bounced back on a blocked kick by Tinsley to beat Texas 18–6. And the best season since 1908 was underway.

Wins over Manhattan, Arkansas, Vanderbilt, Auburn and Mississippi State set the stage for another mass campus exodus, this time to Georgia to meet Harry Mehre's powerful Bulldog team. The students did not get quite as much of a break as before, but they witnessed a fine game, highlighted by one of the most spectacular plays in Tiger history. With the score tied 0–0, Mickal dropped back to punt from his own end zone. Instead of punting, he handed the ball behind his back to Fatherree, who took off upfield and zigzagged for an LSU touchdown. The Tigers scored again for a 13–0 win, which prompted Mehre to call LSU "the finest team that has ever played on this field."

Easy wins over Southwestern Louisiana and Tulane closed out the 1935 season with a 9–1 record, and the Tigers prepared for their very first bowl game, the Sugar Bowl against TCU and its brilliant junior quarterback, Sammy Baugh. Although Baugh is remembered mainly for his passing and, in words of the *Street & Smith Football Annual,* his ability "to throw strikes with a football at 40 yards," the man they went on to describe as "a big chunk of a football team in himself" was equally adept at punting, a fact attested to by his holding four NFL punting records, including the highest average for a career, with an incredible 45-plus yards. It was this amazing ability that allowed TCU to beat LSU 3–2 on a cold, rainy New Year's Day in New Orleans. LSU scored a safety to go ahead 2–0, but Baugh's booming free kick was fumbled, setting up a TCU field goal for a 3–2 lead that held up the rest of the way, thanks again to Baugh's punting.

Mike, the LSU mascot.

The 1936 season was a successful one for LSU, but two of the most memorable moments took place off the field. October 31, 1936, marked one of the wildest days ever on the LSU campus, for that was the day Mike the Tiger arrived. Classes were canceled as students welcomed the school's first mascot, and it was quickly agreed that the cat should be named Mike after the immensely popular athletic trainer Mike Chambers. A permanent home was built, and Mike I, as well as his three successors, became an important part of LSU football. For years the mascot made many trips to away games, particularly bowls, but this practice was finally halted after a series of near-tragic incidents, the last of which saw Mike III's rolling cage overturned on the way to an alumni meeting in Shreveport. This prompted the now famous call from a zealous fan offering to donate blood. Mike was unhurt, but further trips were canceled and now Mike makes appearances only at home games.

That year LSU added 25,000 seats to the north end zone of Tiger Stadium. Incredibly, the project was begun under the Works Progress Administration in May 1936 and was completed in time for the Tulane game the same year.

The Tigers won their game against Tulane (33–0) and all but one of their other games (a 6–6 tie with Texas, riddled with fumbles), ending with a 9–0–1 record. LSU received another Sugar Bowl bid, this time to play Santa Clara. Playing uninspired ball, the Tigers lost 21–14, remaining winless in post-season play.

Undefeated in its last nineteen regular-season games, and the SEC champion the previous two seasons, LSU looked forward to another great year in 1937. And it looked as though the Tigers were heading for it when they opened the season with four consecutive shutout wins behind the running of Pinky Rohm. Then, in their fifth game, against undefeated Vanderbilt, the Tigers lost—only the second regular-season loss during Moore's reign—when the team, as well as the spectators, lost sight of the ball.

With the addition of 25,000 seats in the north end, the seating capacity in Tiger Stadium was increased to 46,000 in 1936.

LSU beat Tulane 33–0 in the dedication game to cap a 9–0–1 season and capture the SEC championship.

The play, which gave Vanderbilt its first victory over the Bengals since 1910, was the old playground ploy, the "hidden-ball" trick. In Vanderbilt's version, the quarterback took the snap from center and placed the ball on the ground behind left guard Billy Hayes, who hovered over it, hiding it, while the quarterback swept to his left, apparently with the ball. While the LSU team pursued the quarterback en masse, Dutch Reinschmidt feigned an injury and fell to the ground next to Hayes. Then, assured that the Tigers' collective activity had taken them far enough away from the ball, he simply got up with the football and waltzed untouched toward the goal line and a touchdown. Moore protested, claiming that Reinschmidt had been in contact with the ball while his knee was on the ground. But his protest was disallowed, and Vanderbilt's score stood, for a 7–6 win.

Hall of Famer Ken Kavanaugh, the SEC's Most Valuable Player and All-American end (1939).

The Tigers recovered with wins in the final five games and made a third straight appearance in the Sugar Bowl, a rematch against Santa Clara. And for the third straight year the Tigers lost, this time 6–0.

Although the 6–4 record put together by the 1938 Tigers gave them their eleventh consecutive winning season, it was their worst overall record since 1931. But if the season left one thing to be remembered by, it was a tradition that was established after the final game, a 14–0 pasting by Tulane. Soon after the game, which had been punctuated by a number of fights between members of both schools' student bodies, the two schools brought forward a peace offering: a symbolic banner made up of the colors of both schools, to be presented to the team winning the annual game. "The Rag" belonged to Tulane that first year, but for most of the years to come it would be in LSU's possession.

In 1939 LSU became one of the first teams to travel by air, chartering two DC-3s for a trip to Boston to face Holy Cross, then a national power. Behind the play of All-American end Ken Kavanaugh, the Tigers surprised the favored Crusaders, winning 26–7. Upon arrival in Baton Rouge, the team was greeted by a wildly cheering mob. But there was little to cheer about the rest of the year, as the Tigers struggled to a 4–5 season.

The struggle continued over the next two years, with the team recording 6–4 and 4–4–2 seasons, but the Tigers did manage to take the Rag from Tulane each year, shutting out the Green Wave 14–0 and 19–0.

Steve Van Buren, 1943 SEC scoring leader with 98 points—a record that stood for twenty-six years.

1942 saw sophomore Alvin Dark lead the team to a 7–3 record. Dark, whom many believe could have been one of the all-time greats, joined the Marines the next year. But the Bengals still had one returning member of the 1942 team, Steve Van Buren. And that was enough. Van Buren, hardly noticed during his first two seasons at quarterback and blocking back, switched to tailback in 1943 and in just eight games became the SEC's all-time rushing leader with 1007 yards and all-time scoring leader with 98 points, including 14 points-after-touchdown. With the Honduras-born Van Buren providing the firepower, the Tigers finished the season with a respectable 5–3 record and capped it with an invitation to play in the Orange Bowl, their first bowl bid in six years.

Playing against Texas A & M, the Bengals, led by Van Buren, finally won their first post-season game, 19–14.

The Van Buren-less Tigers limped through a 2–5–1 year in 1944, but unveiled another future great whose exploits would become legendary in Bayou Country—Yelberton Abraham Tittle, better known as plain ol' Y.A. With Tittle at quarterback, the 1945 team bettered its mark to 7–2, and looked forward to a banner year in 1946, with the return from the wars of many favorite sons.

Yelberton Abraham Tittle, better known to LSU fans as "Y.A."

In 1946 LSU fielded a strong team that breezed through three straight opponents before being upset in Tiger Stadium by Georgia Tech. Then, behind the passing of Tittle, the Tigers rebounded with six straight wins, setting up a Cotton Bowl confrontation with Arkansas. It was a bitter cold day in Dallas, and although the Tigers completely dominated the game, they were unable to score. The game ended in a scoreless tie, the first in Cotton Bowl history.

The 1947 Tigers returned virtually intact, and high hopes for LSU's third SEC crown were bolstered by their victory over Rice in the season's opener. But the bubble burst the following week, when a fourth-quarter Georgia rally gave the Bulldogs a 35–19 come-from-behind win. After victories over Texas A & M, Boston College and Vanderbilt, the Bengals and Tittle came face to face with Ole Miss and Charley Connerly. However, it was not the aerial acrobatics of either player that turned the trick, but the running of Connerly, as he scampered for three touchdowns in a 20–18 Rebel win. The only casualty suffered by the Bengals was to Tittle's pride, as his belt broke, forcing him to pull his pants up a few times, but never, contrary to the rumors, causing him to lose them.

After beating Mississippi State, the Tigers took it on the chin again, this time from Alabama and Harry Gilmer, 41–12. They then wound up a disappointing 5–3–1 season with a 6–6 tie with Tulane that was highlighted not so much by the players as by the by-play of the students, who had secretly formed the letters LSU on the Tulane Stadium turf with rows of recently planted oats.

The Tulane tie was also Bernie Moore's last game as head coach. The man who had guided the fortunes of LSU football for a lucky thirteen years, longer than any other coach in the school's history to that time, assumed the prestigious position of commissioner of the Southeastern Conference. His achievements included a record of 83–39–6, two Conference championships, five bowl appearances, and national prominence for the Tigers. Filling his shoes would be no easy task.

The man selected to assume Moore's mantle was Gaynell Tinsley, LSU's first All-American and a member of Moore's coaching staff. Tinsley took over a squad that had been depleted by graduation. His very first game gave hints at the problems that lay ahead for the Tigers, as Texas took their measure 33–0. After victories over Rice and Texas A & M, the 1948 team lost all but one of its remaining games. A humiliating 46–0 loss to Tulane—the last time LSU would lose the Rag for twenty-five more years—closed out a 3–7 season, the worst for LSU since 1922.

LSU's malaise continued into 1949, as the team lost 19–0 to a talent-laden Kentucky team in the opener—the Wildcats numbering among their members an end named Charlie McClendon. But then the Bengals righted themselves and won two of their next three games to set the stage for the game against nationally ranked North Carolina. Here was a chance to make the entire season a successful one.

In what was to become known as the "Wet Field" game—so dubbed because the watering system had been left on, drenching Tiger Stadium, advertently or inadvertently, as the case may be—the Tigers upset North Carolina 13–7, sending the Tar Heels to their first loss in twenty regular-season games and sending the Bengals' stock soaring.

George Tarasovic, All-American center (1951).

That triumph provided the Tigers with momentum, and they rolled to easy victories the rest of the year, including a 21–0 upset of SEC champion Tulane, as the pranksters once again surfaced at Tulane Stadium, correctly predicting the score with paint on the side of the stadium.

The triumph gave the Tigers bowl-bargaining power, and an SEC rule preventing teams with less than a .750 Conference record (LSU's was .666) from playing in bowls was lifted, allowing the Tigers to meet number one–ranked Oklahoma in the Sugar Bowl. But the clock tolled twelve for the Cinderella team, as the Sooners proved too much for the Tigers, running up a 35–0 score to win.

Whatever magic the Tigers found in 1949, they quickly lost in 1950, as Tinsley and the team suffered through a 4–5–2 season. Suddenly angry alumni put pressure on Tinsley to produce a winning team.

Tinsley quieted his critics the next year, as several good recruiting years began to pay off. A routine win over Southern Mississippi opened the 1951 season. Then the squad raised some eyebrows with its win over Alabama in Mobile. The Tigers ran into trouble in midseason against strong Maryland and Vanderbilt teams, but ended the year with a win over Tulane, for a satisfying 7–3–1 season.

Fans and alumni grew critical again in 1952, when LSU did an about-face, compiling a 3–7 record. A win over Tulane probably saved Tinsley's shaky position as head coach.

Cheerleaders atop Mike's cage before Tennessee game (1952).

Sid Fournet, SEC Most Valuable lineman and All-American (1954).

The Tigers opened the 1953 season in newly enlarged Tiger Stadium, but the team continued to struggle, coming up with a 5–3–3 season. And Tinsley became a prime candidate for ex-coach.

If any more fuel was needed for the fire, it was supplied the next year, as the Bengals slipped below the .500 mark with a 5–6 record, capped by a controversy over recruiting. In a meeting before the Board, Tinsley exonerated himself of any wrongdoing, but the Board had already decided that a new head football coach was in order.

A complete housecleaning was anticipated after LSU President Troy Middleton stepped in. Two years earlier Athletic Director T. P. Heard had pushed hard for funds for the stadium expansion at a time when Middleton wanted funds allocated for a new library. The stadium won and Middleton did not forget, particularly when poor seasons failed to fill the new bowl-like addition. When the meeting was over, Middleton announced officially that he had received a request for "retirement" from Heard.

So LSU needed a new coach. And a new athletic director as well.

Several candidates were mentioned for the coaching job, but as time wore on, the name Paul Dietzel kept rising to the top of the list. Dietzel, who at the time was an assistant at Army under Red Blaik, had served under Bear Bryant at Kentucky. The personable Dietzel did his homework before coming to Baton Rouge for an interview, and after a few hours' discussion he was tendered the job as LSU's twenty-fifth football coach.

In tandem with the hiring of Dietzel, James J. Corbett was offered the position of athletic director. Corbett had first come to Louisiana on a football scholarship to Southeastern Louisiana, where he injured a knee and nearly lost his scholarship. But the resourceful Corbett talked school officials into letting him keep his scholarship in return for his working in the school's sports publicity department. Following graduation, Corbett worked with the Associated Press in New Orleans, and in 1945 he became LSU's sports publicity director. Although he had left the University at the same time as Bernie Moore, the innovative Corbett was lured back with the promise of a free hand in the running of the overall program. And he needed all the latitude he could get, inasmuch as LSU's attendance, and that accompanying intangible "spirit," had both suffered downturns in recent years.

Paul Dietzel, head coach 1955–1961, and his 1958 coaching staff.

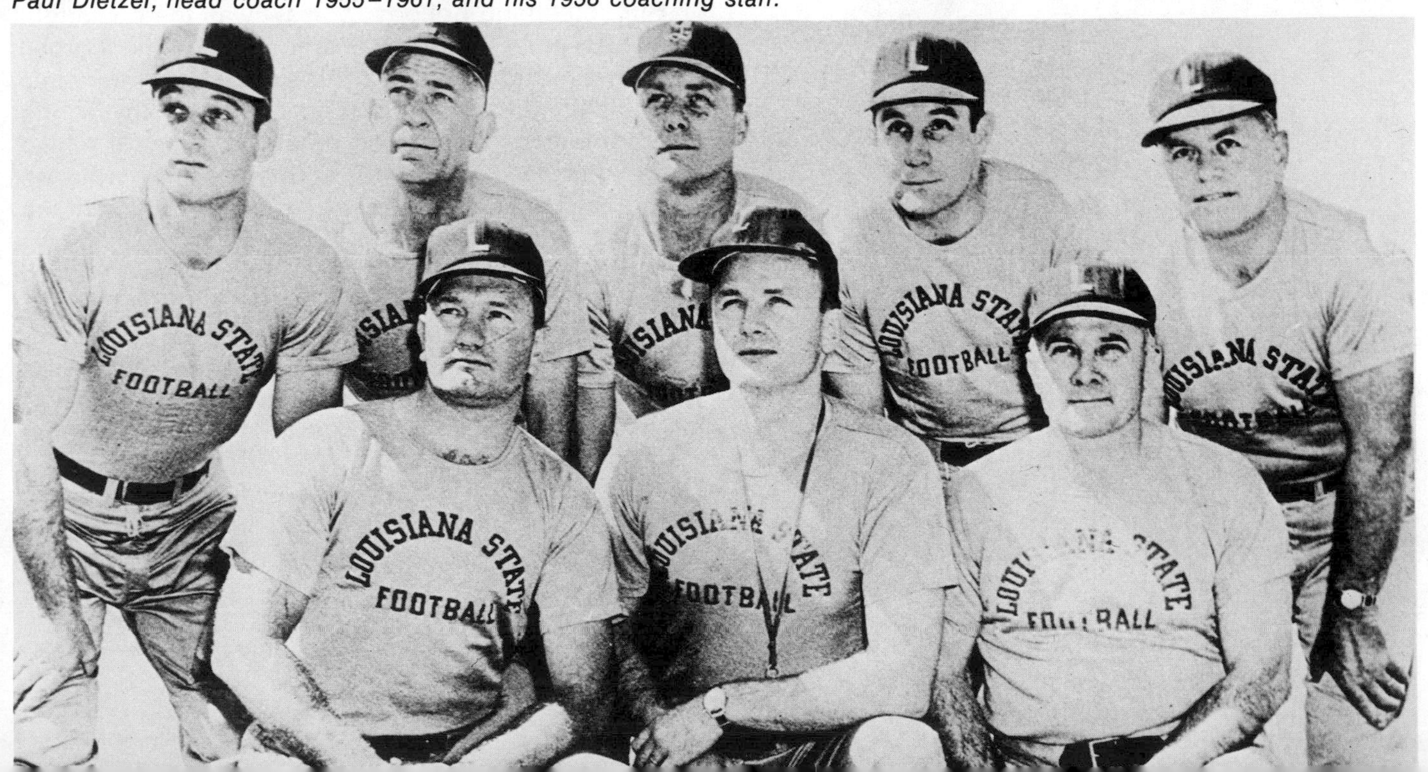

LSU fans, who had endured nineteen years without an SEC championship, were anxious for a winner. And they liked what they saw when Dietzel's first edition took the field against Kentucky. Behind the 96-yard kickoff return of Joe May, the Tigers upset the favored Wildcats 19–7. But that represented the high spot of the 1955 season; after the opening win over Kentucky, the Tigers could only manage one tie in their next six games, en route to a 3–5–2 season.

The dynamic duo of Corbett and Dietzel continued to beat the drums, calling on all followers of LSU to rally round the Bengal banner. Their efforts were partially rewarded; as the financial picture began to brighten, the team became better organized, and fans began to flock into Tiger Stadium in record numbers.

Unfortunately, their magic was not working the same wonders on the playing field, where the team was still mired in the mediocrity of previous Tiger teams. The 1956 team, despite the efforts of fullback Jimmy Taylor, suffered through a 3–7 season, even experiencing the prophetic death of Mike, the original Bengal mascot, in midseason. In the face of such a season, the usually optimistic Dietzel began to have doubts about his ability to ride home a winner. They were put to rest, however, by the enthusiastic Corbett, who had begun to notice the first promising results of Dietzel's labor.

Fullback Jimmy Taylor, All-American (1957).

One thing Corbett saw was the successful recruitment of future LSU stars like Billy Cannon, Johnny Robinson and Warren Rabb, who almost immediately began paying dividends by leading the LSU freshman team to an unbeaten season in 1957—a feat they would repeat on a varsity level two years later.

The national championship ring.

But something nobody foresaw was the onslaught of the Asian flu that hit the campus—and the football team—almost as hard as the yellow-fever epidemic had a half-century before. Led by Jimmy Taylor and his Conference-leading 86 points, the Tigers rallied back after their encounter with the flu to wind up with a 5–5 record, including a win over Tulane in the season's finale.

The year that would replace 1908 as the standard by which all LSU teams were to be judged began with the unexpected death of Mike II and with lightning striking the practice field; it ended with a perfect 11–0 record and a national championship. It was an all-or-nothing year and a tribute to the coaching genius of Dietzel.

The innovative Dietzel took advantage of the substitution rules, allowing unlimited subs to form three different teams. He used his best players on the "Go

Team." These played the bulk of the game, both on offense and defense. From the remaining players, Dietzel picked eleven players to specialize in offense. They were the "White Team." Finally there were the "Chinese Bandits," defensive specialists named after cartoon characters in "Terry and the Pirates." They became the most famous group of third-stringers ever to play college football.

Dietzel also switched to the wing-T formation, a system that better utilized the considerable talents of Cannon, Robinson & Co. A less noticed, but equally important, move saw J. W. Brodnax switched to fullback, where his blocking was essential to the successful running of Cannon and Robinson.

With Dietzel employing his three teams, thus allowing LSU to always have a fresh team on the field, LSU won the 1958 opener against Rice 26–6. Four different Tigers scored touchdowns, and while he was clearly the star of the game, Cannon gained only 53 yards.

The following week's game was against Alabama, coached for the first time by Bryant. The game was played in Mobile, and it marked the first, but certainly not the last, hurrah for the Chinese Bandits. Alabama was threatening when Dietzel inserted the Chinese Bandits, who promptly shut down the 'Bama drive, and the Tide had to settle for a field goal. An LSU legend was clearly in the making.

The second half saw the LSU offense come alive, with Rabb passing to Robinson for one score and Cannon running for another. And the Tigers had their second win of the season, 13–3.

A win over Hardin-Simmons was expected, but the following week's 41–0 bombing of a respectable Miami team was not and stirred some interest among the nation's writers, who voted the Tigers into the nation's top ten. An expected tough encounter with Kentucky quickly turned into an LSU runaway in front of a record 65,000 fans, and the Tigers were on their way. As the season reached the midway point, LSU found itself ranked third by AP, fifth by UPI.

Florida almost derailed the Tigers' express the next week, but Billy Cannon's clutch running led to a late field goal and a 10–7 win. LSU's sixth straight win moved them up to number one ranking in the AP poll, but in order to preserve that heady position and prove they belonged the Tigers would first have to get by their next opponent—unbeaten Mississippi. The Ole Miss game marked the beginning of a storied series that would affect not only the pride of neighboring states, but also the Southeastern Conference and national championship for years to come.

For the first time since the expansion of the fully enclosed 67,720-seat stadium, there was not a ticket to be had. And all ticketholders got their money's worth, as the two evenly matched teams waged a defensive struggle. LSU put up a goal-line stand early in the second quarter, and the Tigers scored on Rabb's keeper just before the half, taking a 7–0 lead into the dressing room. The teams traded touchdowns in the second half, but LSU came out ahead 14–7.

United Press International moved the Tigers up to number two ranking. Any remaining doubts were erased after the Tigers swarmed all over Duke, 50–18. UPI finally gave in—LSU was now number one in both polls.

By this time the Chinese Bandits had become famous for their spot defensive play, and fans started showing up in Tiger Stadium wearing coolie hats in their honor. Insertion of the Bandits into a game was met by the wild cheering of their fanatic followers, and the Bandits did not disappoint them—not allowing a touchdown the entire season.

Mississippi State finally scored on the Go Team the following week, but the Tigers came back with a third-period score and PAT to take a 7–6 lead that held up after the Bulldogs barely missed a last-second field goal. The all-winning season, their first since 1908, came to a close, fittingly enough, with a

The Chinese bandits form the "Great Wall of China."

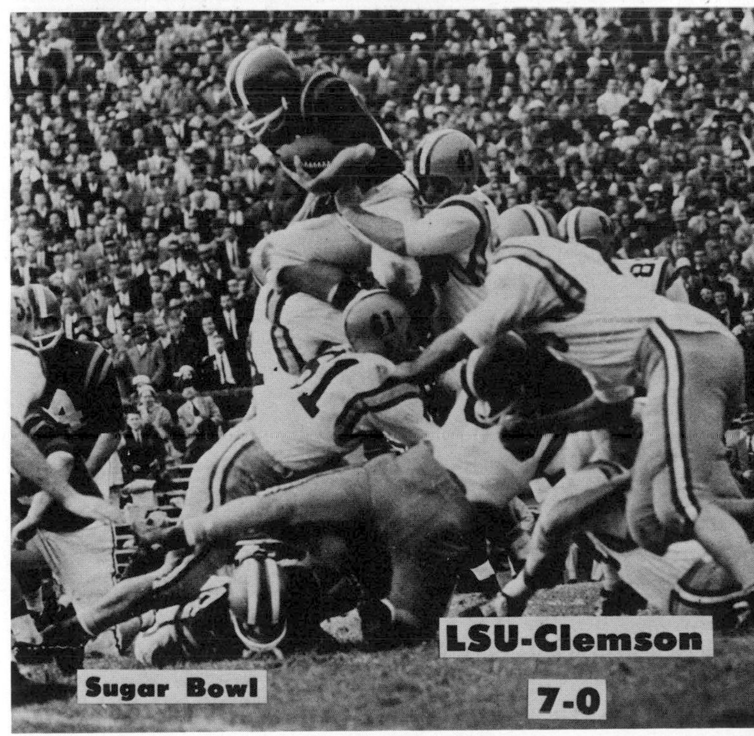

62–0 romp over Tulane, which was becoming fairly routine.

Although UPI had presented Dietzel with its version of the national championship trophy a few days after the regular season ended, and the AP followed suit the night before the Sugar Bowl, a victory over Atlantic Coast Conference champion Clemson in the Sugar Bowl was still needed for a perfect season. Billy Cannon flipped a third-quarter touchdown pass to walk-on sensation Mickey Mangham for a 7–0 lead, and Dietzel inserted the Bandits to halt a last-minute Clemson threat, preserving the Tigers' slim 7–0 lead—and their perfect season.

Awards began rolling in. The Baton Rouge trio of Cannon, Robinson and Rabb made up three-fourths of the All-SEC backfield, and Cannon was a unanimous choice for All-American, as well as runner-up for the Heisman trophy. Center Max Fugler was also named to several All-American teams.

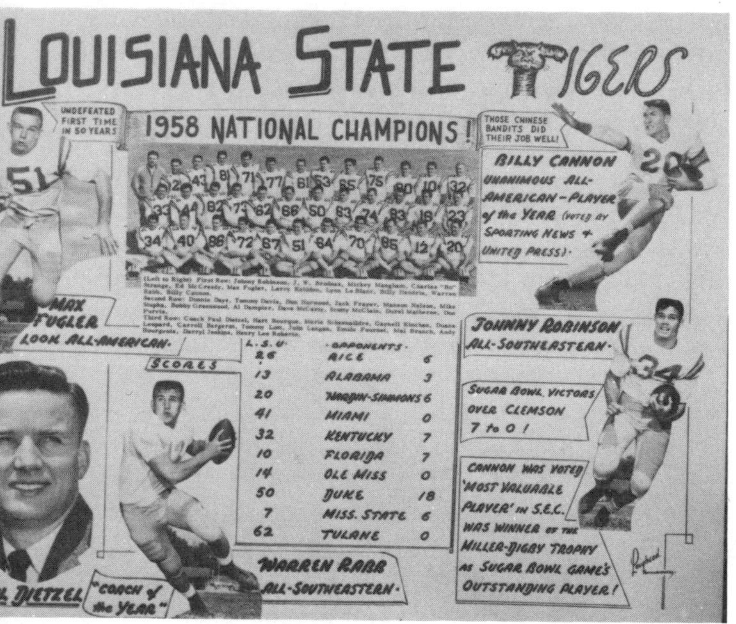

The Year That Was (1958).

LSU fans expected more of the same in 1959. After all, the last time the Tigers had won the SEC championship, it was as repeat champions in 1936. Why not now? Especially when virtually the entire championship team was returning.

There are several followers of Deep South football who consider the 1959 edition to be the finest, most exciting team LSU ever fielded. After all, playing a decidedly tougher schedule than the 1958 team, a schedule that included Tennessee and Southwest Conference champ TCU, the team allowed only three touchdowns to be scored against it all year.

In the first nationally televised game ever to originate from Tiger Stadium, the defending national champion opened its 1959 season with an unimpressive 26–3 win over Rice. A 10–0 victory over TCU, who would go on to repeat as Southwest Conference champs, followed, and a 22–0 win over Baylor came next. Miami went down the following week 27–3, setting up two successive 9–0 road wins over Florida and Kentucky stretching LSU's winning streak to eighteen straight games.

The Tigers were scarcely challenged through the first six games, yet they were often criticized for not scoring enough points, as Dietzel tended to play conservative football once his team was two or more touchdowns ahead, often punting on third down.

The next week's game against Ole Miss was probably the best game ever played in Tiger Stadium, and without a doubt it produced the greatest single play in the history of LSU football.

It is difficult to imagine two more evenly matched teams than the 1959 LSU and Ole Miss squads. Both had attained 6–0 records without really being tested. LSU had not given up a touchdown; the Rebels had allowed only one in six games! As they took the field on a foggy Halloween night, LSU was the number one–ranked team in the country, Ole Miss number three.

Neither team made much progress at first, feeling out each other's strengths. Then Cannon fumbled on the Tiger 21-yard line, and Billy Brewer recovered for Ole Miss. The Rebels managed one first down, but the drive stalled when Mickey Mangham caught Jake Gibbs for a loss at the 3-yard line, and Ole Miss had to settle for Bobby Khayat's 22-yard field goal to give the Rebels a 3–0 lead.

LSU did not move the ball in the first half, but it halted two consecutive Rebel drives. The first drive was stopped at the 20, the second, set up by Brewer's third fumble recovery of the game, ended when the clock ran out with the Rebels on the LSU 7-yard line.

In the second half, Ole Miss Coach Johnny Vaught also turned conservative, calling on his troops to punt on first down on three successive possessions. His strategy not only played havoc with LSU's complicated three-substitution game plan, but also gave the Rebels good field position on their next possession. With the ball at the Ole Miss 49-yard line, and second down, tackle Lynn LeBlanc—currently LSU's defensive line coach—caught Gibbs for a 10-yard loss. Vaught, anxious to maintain the Ole Miss momentum, ordered the Rebels to punt on third down and pin the Bengals deep in their own territory.

Gibbs's punt was taken by Cannon on the 11-yard

line, and one of the great moments in college football was underway. One witness counted twelve broken tackles as Cannon ran around, through, over and past the entire Rebel team. At midfield, only Gibbs had a chance to stop him. Cannon easily eluded Gibbs, and it was clear sailing from there to the goal line, Tiger immortality, and the Heisman trophy.

But the classic was far from over. Ten minutes remained in the game when Ole Miss, trailing 3–7, put together its last concerted effort to pull it out. Under the leadership of substitute quarterback Doug Elmore, Mississippi drove down to the Tiger 2. Then, on fourth down and 2, with but eighteen seconds remaining, and the game and the season hanging in the balance, Cannon and Rabb stopped Elmore inches short of the goal line. The ball, and the game, belonged to LSU.

LSU's winning streak ended one week later against a stubborn Tennessee team. Running back an intercepted pass for one touchdown and converting an LSU fumble into another score, the Vols scored twice in less than two minutes. They were the first touchdowns scored against the Tigers all season and gave Tennessee a 14–7 lead. LSU scored again, but a two-point conversion attempt failed and the Tigers went down to their first defeat in twenty games, 13–14.

After beating Mississippi State and Tulane to close out a 9–1 season, the Tigers accepted a bid to play in the Sugar Bowl against Ole Miss. With revenge in mind, the Rebels played inspired ball, handily beating the Tigers 21–0 in the famous rematch.

The year 1960 was a rebuilding year, and the Tigers had done well in recruiting. Sophomore Jerry Stovall was the heir-apparent to Cannon, and other sophomores, such as tackle Fred Miller and center Dennis Gaubatz, had begun to mature by the time the Ole Miss game rolled around.

The run that won the Heisman—Cannon's 89-yard punt return.

The Tigers had already lost four games but were beginning to play well by the time they traveled to Oxford for the nationally televised game. Still, no one gave the Tigers much of a chance against the powerful Rebels, who had been ranked number one until the previous week. Nevertheless, the underdog Bengals took a 6–3 lead late in the game, and it took a last-minute Rebel field goal from 41 yards to preserve a tie, the only blemish on Ole Miss's 1960 record, and one that dropped them to sixth in the national polls. But if the tie was a depressant for Ole Miss, it was therapeutic for the Tigers, who went on to sweep their final four opponents, for a 5–4–1 season.

The Tigers lost the 1961 season opener to Rice in Houston. Then, led by Earl Gros and Wendell Harris, LSU got back on the winning track with a 16–7 win over Texas A & M and a 10–0 win over Georgia Tech. Wins over South Carolina, Kentucky and Florida set up still another epic matchup with next-door neighbor Ole Miss. For the fourth consecutive year, the Rebels came into the game undefeated, this time ranked second nationally. LSU, with its one loss, was ranked seventh.

The Rebels took a 7–3 lead behind the passing of Glynn Griffing, the latest in a succession of excellent Ole Miss quarterbacks. Then Stovall turned the game around with a 57-yard run to the Ole Miss 23. The Tiger drive appeared to stall on fourth and 5, only to have Lynn Amedee complete the only pass of the day to Billy Truax for a first down. Harris scored a few plays later, and the 10–7 lead held up for an LSU victory.

LSU had beaten an undefeated Ole Miss team again, a circumstance that would lead Ole Miss Coach Johnny Vaught to remark, "They are just as good a team as they were in 1958 and 1959."

Three more wins followed, including another 62–0 win over Tulane, and the 9–1 Tigers accepted a bid to play in the Orange Bowl against Colorado. The Tigers won the game 25–7, but the fireworks were taking place off the field where it was rumored that Paul Dietzel was leaving.

Only a few weeks earlier, Dietzel had told a New Orleans alumni group that he would "never coach anywhere but LSU." It was a statement that would come back to haunt him, as events—including the dismissal of Dale Hall as Army head coach at the end of the 1961 season and the announcement by the West Point selection committee that they would not limit their search to Academy graduates—conspired to tempt him.

Dietzel, once an assistant under "Red" Blaik, had applied for the open position, and word was that it had been tendered him. Rumor approached fact when, after the Orange Bowl game, Dietzel asked the LSU Board of Supervisors to let him out of the remaining years of his contract so that he could accept the head coaching position at West Point. There was some opposition, with at least one Board member insisting that Dietzel be forced to remain. But it was finally agreed, largely because of the persuasive arguments of Jim Corbett, that no man should be forced to coach where he did not truly want to. And so Paul Dietzel, who had coached LSU for seven of its most glorious years, was off to West Point.

One era was over, but a new one began with the arrival of Charles Youmans McClendon as head coach. In point of fact, McClendon had been recognized as the genius behind the Tigers' excellent defensive units.

Paul Dietzel.

Charles Youmans McClendon, LSU's head coach since 1962.

Jerry Stovall, All-American halfback (1962).

"Coach Mac," or "Cholly Mac," as he was called by some, let it be known at his very first press conference that he was his own man: "I was McClendon yesterday and I'll be McClendon tomorrow. I can't change my personality." And so began the McClendon era, one he was to forge in his own character, not in the mold of Dietzel—or anyone else.

Mac's first season, 1962, began with a 21–0 win over Texas A & M. Then, after a second-game tie against Rice, his team reeled off four straight wins and went into the by now traditional showdown against Ole Miss with a 5–0–1 mark. The Rebels, for the fifth year in a row, were entering the game undefeated and untied. For the first time in five matchups, the Rebels emerged with their skein intact, as they finally won the classic confrontation 15–7.

But with halfback Jerry Stovall having his greatest year, the loss to Ole Miss was the first and last of McClendon's inaugural season. The new kid on the block picked up right where Dietzel had left off.

The season, however, was not over. The Tigers accepted an invitation to meet undefeated and fourth-ranked Texas in the Cotton Bowl. The Tigers put it all together against the favored Texans, the defense never letting the Longhorns near the goal line. But it was the quarterback tandem of Jimmy Field and Amedee that stole the show. Amedee kicked two field goals, one just after his touchdown pass had been nullified by a penalty, while Field ran for a score, as the Bengals beat the 'Horns 13–0, to finish the season with a 9–1–1 record and a national ranking.

McClendon's imposing task in his second year was to field a team worthy of the high standards now expected by LSU followers everywhere. Several stars of the 1962 team, including halfback Stovall, center Dennis Gaubatz, and tackle Fred Miller, were gone. Highly touted quarterback Pat Screen was injured early in the season, as were several other starters. McClendon's walking wounded began to take on the look of a cast of characters straight out of World War I trenches. But somehow he found the right spare parts to put together a football machine that not only went out to do battle, but took many of those it engaged in.

After winning two of their first three games, those patched-up Tigers of 1963 pulled out a 3–0 win over Miami. Then Billy Ezell stepped in for the injured Screen and engineered LSU wins over Kentucky and Florida, setting up still another confrontation with Ole Miss. This time, though, the fighting Tigers were no match for the unbeaten Rebels, and fell to Mississippi's well-balanced attack, 37–3. The Bengals bounced back to win two of their last three games, their only other loss coming on a missed two-point conversion against Mississippi State; they finished with a respectable 7–3 mark, respectable enough to earn them a bid to the Bluebonnet Bowl, their fifth bowl in six years.

But even though the Bengals got out of the Bluebonnet blocks first, taking a 7–0 lead over Baylor, the rest of the afternoon Baylor quarterback Don Trull passed them silly, completing 26 out of 37 attempts, to lead Baylor to a 14–7 win.

In 1964 McClendon adopted a new offense that employed Doug Moreau in the position of wide receiver, where he had shown great promise in 1963. More importantly, the new formation freed Screen from his blocking chores. Nevertheless, Pat was injured again in the third game against North Carolina. Ezell stepped in again, leading the Bengals to their fourth straight win, a 27–7 victory over Kentucky. In the fifth game, the Tigers partially broke the Tennessee jinx with a 3–3 tie. Ole Miss was next. The Rebels picked up where they had left off the previous year and jumped off to a 10–0 lead. But the Tigers steadily fought back, and when Ezell hit Billy Masters with a 19-yard touchdown pass with 3:55 left in the game, McClendon was faced with a dilemma: kick for a tie or go for two points and the lead.

Mac never hesitated; he sent in a play that called for Ezell to roll right and throw to the corner of the end zone. And that's exactly what happened. Although a Rebel defender did deflect the ball ever so slightly, Moreau grabbed the wobbly ball just before going out of the end zone, for an 11–10 win.

The next week the unbeaten Tigers met the undefeated and untied Crimson Tide, who were on their way to the national championship. The immovable object fell to the irresistible force, with 'Bama returning an intercepted pass for a touchdown and a 17–9 win. LSU followed up its loss to Alabama with wins over Mississippi State and Tulane and accepted an invitation to play Syracuse in the Sugar Bowl. After accepting the bowl bid, LSU played a makeup game with Florida that had been postponed because of Hurricane Hilda. It was an anticlimactic game for the Bengals and they played it anticlimactically, falling to a Gator team that wrought its own disaster on the Tigers, 20–6.

LSU capped its season with a victory over Syracuse in the Sugar Bowl. Its defensive unit held the running tandem of Floyd Little and Jim Nance in check all afternoon, even catching Little for a safety. Still, in spite of all its defensive heroics, LSU trailed 10–2 until Ezell connected with Moreau from 57 yards out for a touchdown and Moreau added a 28-yard field goal. Final score: LSU 13, Syracuse 10.

The 1965 season opened with games against Texas A & M and Rice; it was the tenth straight year LSU opened with one or the other of these two Southwest Conference teams. This time the outcome was the same as it had been for most of the series against the two; LSU beat them both, 10–0 and 42–14.

The real season started the following week—the season against SEC competition. And the first SEC opponent the Tigers drew was the University of Florida, sparked by "Super Gator" Steve Spurrier. But it was not Spurrier who brought down the Tigers so much as two fumbles deep in LSU territory. Florida came up with both and the game, 14–7. The Bengals rebounded with wins over Miami, Kentucky and South Carolina, setting the stage for what had become an annual event: *The Game* against Ole Miss. The game was being played in Jackson for the first time since 1934, and the Rebels responded to the magic of their capital city by dominating the Bengals—helped in no small measure by a knee injury to LSU signal-caller Nelson Stokley on the first series of downs—and winning handily, 23–0.

Stokley's knee buckled in pre-game warmups the next week against Alabama, and the Crimson Tide ran up a 31–7 score on regional television. The two crushing back-to-back losses plunged Baton Rouge into a panic, but LSU bounced back with a 37–20 win over Mississippi State, then finished the regular season with a 62–0 win over Tulane and a 7–3 record. The impressive finish quieted the irate fans and won an invitation for the Bengals to meet Arkansas in the Cotton Bowl.

The second-ranked Razorbacks were LSU's most formidable foe since Mississippi in 1959; they had not lost a game in two years, including a hard-fought battle with powerful Nebraska in the previous year's Cotton Bowl, and were anchored on both the offensive and defensive lines by such stalwarts as Glen Ray Hines and Lloyd Phillips. In short, the winners of twenty-two straight games appeared indestructible.

LSU appeared to be slated for number twenty-three in the growing list of Arkansas victims when the Razorbacks engineered an impressive 87-yard drive for an early 7–0 lead. But the Bengals bounced right back with Stokley directing a drive into Arkansas territory. When Stokley's injury forced him from the game, replacement Screen kept the drive going inside the Razorbacks' 20-yard line. From there little Joe Labruzzo followed a Dave McCormick block in for a score, and the game was tied at 7–7. Arkansas fumbled on its own 34 just before the half, and Labruzzo scored again a few plays later for a 14–7 halftime lead.

The Razorbacks threatened twice in the second half, but a missed field goal and a pass interception preserved the win for the Tigers. An Arkansas sportswriter summed up the day for the Tigers when he said, "I think if you study this game carefully, you'll find that LSU has played a perfect game against Arkansas."

The 1966 campaign saw one of the great ironies in LSU football history. Paul Dietzel had left Army to take the head coaching job at South Carolina, and his first game as South Carolina head coach was against LSU in Tiger Stadium. There was talk of little else during the summer, as resentment still ran high

Athletic Director Jim Corbett.

over Dietzel's desertion four years earlier.

The game, designated "D-Day," was one that LSU fans, the team, and most of all McClendon wanted to win badly. And they did just that, beating the Gamecocks 28–12, behind the running of a healthy Stokley and Gawain DiBetta and a recovered blocked punt by George Bevan.

After this, though, Tiger fans had little to cheer about. Steve Spurrier directed another Florida win, and Ole Miss and 'Bama both shut out the Tigers, who struggled to a 5–4–1 record.

The season ended on an even sadder note, as Jim Corbett, the man most responsible for transforming LSU football from a game into a state event, died of a heart attack on January 30, 1967. Corbett will be remembered for many things, but perhaps the best way to remember him is by his own words, which appear on the James J. Corbett Memorial Trophy, given to the outstanding college athlete in Louisiana each year: "It's nice to be important, but it's more important to be nice."

The Tigers opened the 1967 season with three wins before being upset by a stubborn Miami team, 17–15. LSU rebounded with a win over Kentucky, but kicking problems hampered the Bengals in succeeding weeks. Tennessee kicked a field goal with just over a minute to play for a 17–14 win, and the Tigers missed an extra point and fumbled the ball eight times the next week in a 13–13 tie with Ole Miss. A missed extra point again spelled doom the next week in a 7–6 loss to Alabama. But the Tigers came back for season-ending wins over Mississippi State and Tulane, and accepted a bid to meet Wyoming in the Sugar Bowl, their eighth bowl appearance in ten years.

Not an established football power, Wyoming was taken lightly by many LSU fans and by the team as well, as the undefeated Cowboys, led by All-American Jim Kiick, took a 13–0 lead at halftime.

The Tigers came roaring back in the second half behind the running of Glenn Smith and scored two touchdowns, one on a run by Smith and the second on a pass from Stokley to Tommy Morrel. The second extra point was missed, and a tie looked inevitable. But with five minutes to play, Benny Griffin intercepted a pass, and Smith, the game's Most Valuable Player, set up another Stokley-to-Morrel pass, for a 20–13 win. The win marked the third time in McClendon's six years that the Tigers had beaten an undefeated team in a bowl game.

Carl Maddox was named athletic director after the season, replacing Harry Rabenhorst, who had agreed to take the position on an interim basis after Corbett's death. An astute organizer, Maddox had been an assistant coach on the great 1958 team and had been running the massive LSU Union when he was selected for the top athletic post. Maddox would work to sustain LSU's excellence in football as well as to improve the quality of the other sports programs at LSU.

A strong LSU team took the field in 1968, scoring impressive wins in all but one of its first six games, the one loss being a 30–0 shocker at the hands of a fired-up Miami team. Then followed the annual "shoot-out" with Ole Miss, a game that would begin a series of offensive thrillers to rival the defensive struggles of the late fifties and early sixties. A sophomore Rebel quarterback named Archie Manning got his first look at Tiger Stadium, and Tiger fans got their first look at him. It was enough to give them an eyeache, as they witnessed the greatest, and most destructive, one-man performance since Samson stood eyeless at Gaza. For on that night Manning completed 24 of 40 for 345 yards, ran for 1 touchdown, and passed for 2 more—the second coming with just forty-six seconds remaining in the game, to clinch a wild 27–24 Ole Miss win.

The Tigers had trouble in Birmingham the following week, as Alabama outgunned them 16–7. The next week a Mississippi State team out for revenge for the previous year's 55–0 Tiger win gave the Tigers all they could handle before the Bengals managed a 20–16 win, aided and abetted by the officials' losing count of the downs with the Bulldogs on the LSU 12-yard line.

Tailback Allen Shorey scores winning touchdown as LSU beats Auburn 21–20 (1969).

LSU crunched Tulane 34–10, then turned its attention toward the inaugural Peach Bowl in Atlanta against Florida State. It was an offensive show, with FSU taking an early 13–0 lead. Mike Hillman's passing took LSU to a 24–13 lead, but Ron Sellers's touchdown catches put the Seminoles ahead 27–24. LSU stayed on the ground, and late in the game Maurice LeBlanc scored the winning touchdown for a 31–27 come-from-behind win in one of the most exciting bowl games LSU had ever played in.

Defense was the key in 1969, and behind the play of All-American linebackers Mike Anderson and George Bevan the Tigers allowed only 87 yards rushing in the first three games, winning by a combined score of 140–14. McClendon used more than fifty players in the win over Kentucky, and although the Wildcats were the first, and last, opponent to gain more than 100 yards rushing that season, LSU won easily. Auburn was next, and the fans in Tiger Stadium and a national television audience watched as halfback Jimmy Gilbert lofted a pass to Andy Hamilton for a touchdown on the first play of the game. Pat Sullivan then led Auburn to a 14–7 lead, only to have LSU score twice to take the lead 21–14. It took Bevan's block of an extra-point attempt to preserve a 21–20 win for the Tigers, their sixth straight.

The all-winning Tigers ran into Manning and Ole Miss again the next week. In another great individual performance, Manning ran for three touchdowns, threw for another, and added a two-point conversion, for a 26–23 lead. LSU fought back. But late in the game McClendon elected to go for the win rather than the tie, passing up a field goal on a fourth down in favor of a pass that was batted down by Rebel defenders to seal LSU's fate.

Defense dominated the next week's game against Alabama, and the Tigers held on to defeat Bear Bryant and Alabama 20–15.

After LSU demolished Mississippi State 61–6, the team waited for bowl offers that never came. LSU had expected to play in the Cotton Bowl, but Notre Dame broke a long tradition by announcing that it would play in a bowl if invited. The Cotton Bowl invited the Irish, and LSU was left out in the cold without a bid or a paddle despite a 9–1 record, a situation that thoroughly enraged LSU fans.

The lack of bowl bids was trivial compared to the tragedy that took place prior to the 1970 season. During August practice junior quarterback Butch Duhe, whom Corbett had personally recruited the night before Corbett's death, died from a ruptured blood vessel in his brain. The shock that spread through the Tiger camp was indescribable, and to this day McClendon describes Duhe's death as his worst moment in coaching.

The Tigers lost the season opener when an underdog Texas A & M team scored on a 70-yard bomb with thirteen seconds left, for a 20–18 win. They bounced back for relatively easy wins over Rice, Baylor, College of the Pacific, and Kentucky, setting up another monumental matchup with Auburn that was played in a downpour at Auburn.

LSU came out on top, 17–9, in a game that was highlighted by All-American linebacker Mike Anderson's three tackles inside the LSU 8-yard line during a drive that would have put the War Eagles in the driver's seat.

LSU beat Alabama 14–9, this time in Birmingham, then rolled over Mississippi State for another easy win before playing the team LSU fans had been waiting for all year—Notre Dame—the same team that had denied them their rightful place in a bowl the previous year. The game, played at South Bend, was one of the great defensive struggles in the history of college football. And although the Irish came away 3–0 victors after a disputed pass interference call set up a field goal late in the game, the Tigers gained the respect of the media. The Chicago *Tribune* wrote, "The unbeaten Fighting Irish of Notre Dame finally subdued Louisiana State University's clawing Tigers, 3–0, this crisp and clear afternoon in as ferocious, dramatic and uptight a game as ever has been played in this buff brick football oval dedicated here in 1930." The *Trib* went on to say, "If Notre Dame is a candidate for No. 1, LSU is surely No. 1-A."

The Tigers had arrived as a national power, but they had to win their last two games to prove it—and, more importantly, merit an invitation to meet nationally ranked Nebraska in the Orange Bowl. The win over Tulane was routine, but the win over Ole Miss, played to a national television audience, was extraordinary.

The classic confrontation with Notre Dame (1970).

Mississippi's Manning, who had beaten the Bengals almost singlehandedly the previous two seasons, had broken an arm earlier in the season. But he came back to play against the Tigers with his arm encased in a specially designed cast. Early in the game, it appeared that even a cast could not slow down the Redhead, as he picked the LSU defense apart and led the Rebels in for a score. From that point on, however, it was all LSU, as the Tigers scored practically at will, with two punt returns for touchdowns by All-American Tommy Casanova, one by Craig Burns, and All-American Ronnie Estay's sack of Manning for a safety. As the final gun went off signaling a one-sided 61–17 victory for LSU, the Tiger fans let everyone know that their team was bowl-bound by raining oranges on the field.

Unfortunately, even with LSU's late-season momentum and the enthusiasm of the student body, the team was no match for Nebraska, who subdued the determined Tigers 17–12 in the Orange Bowl—after LSU had led 12–10 in the fourth quarter—to lay claim to the national championship.

The 1971 Tigers lost the season opener to a powerful Colorado team 31–21, then put on a defensive show the next week, holding Texas A & M to just 13 yards in total offense as they routed the Aggies 37–0. The Tigers then journeyed to Madison, Wisconsin,

Quarterback Paul Lyons sets sail for the Wisconsin goal line (1971).

for the first time in their history and beat the Badgers in a high-scoring game, 38–28. Easy wins over Rice, Florida and Kentucky followed, and then came the game that would make or break the whole year, the contest against Ole Miss.

With Manning gone, the Rebels unveiled still another in a long line of fine quarterbacks in the person of Norris Weese. Weese sparked Ole Miss to a 21–0 lead, but the Bengals fought back, only to have a last-minute drive halted more by the clock than by the Rebels. LSU went down to its second defeat, 24–22.

Casanova, tabbed by at least one national magazine as the nation's finest football player that year, had been injured for most of 1971, but returned to the lineup to play Alabama the following week. In a televised game, the Tigers shut down Johnny Musso and the 'Bama Wishbone for most of the game, but still came out on the short end of a 14–7 score.

A win over Mississippi State set the stage for the long-awaited game against Notre Dame. It was to be remembered as "The Night the Irish Came to Tiger Stadium." As one Chicago writer said, "It wasn't so much a game as a year-long crusade." It was also the night a slender quarterback named Bert Jones came of age.

Paul Lyons had been the starter ever since he had directed the wild win over Wisconsin, but with McClendon's two-quarterback system, both Lyons and Jones had seen considerable action. However, when the Tigers went to the dressing room after warming up for the Irish, McClendon told Jones that he would be starting.

Tommy Casanova prepares to do what he does best —return a punt.

Jones and the Tigers shocked the powerful Irish the first time they touched the ball—Jones hitting his cousin Andy Hamilton with two 36-yard passes, the second for a touchdown. Then Notre Dame drove deep into Tiger territory, but for the first of four times, the Tigers held, this time on the 1-inch line. Warren Capone intercepted an Irish pass late in the first half, and Jones needed only one play to find Hamilton again for a 32-yard touchdown pass and a 14–0 halftime lead.

The dynamic duo—Bert Jones (kneeling) and Andy Hamilton—that accounted for eighty-four completions, 1724 yards, and fifteen touchdowns in two years of Tiger football.

The second half produced interesting individual matchups. Hamilton continually eluded Irish All-American Clarence Ellis, while Casanova stayed right in All-American Tom Gatewood's pocket.

Jones scored on a keeper late in the third quarter, and Lyons came in and hit Hamilton for another touchdown in the fourth quarter. The Irish finally scored on a pass to Gatewood, but when it was over LSU had a 28–8 win, and a jubilant mob descended onto the playing field. Many Tiger fans consider the win over Notre Dame the greatest in the history of LSU football. And Coach McClendon summed it up after the game, telling reporters, "I just wish everyone could have been in our dressing room to see what happiness really is."

The Tigers beat Tulane 36–7, then prepared to meet Iowa State in the Sun Bowl. In a game that catapulted Jones onto the national scene, he hit 12 of 18 passes to lead LSU to a 33–15 win. But the big story coming out of El Paso involved McClendon.

The Tiger coach confirmed a report that he had been offered $1 million to become the head man at Texas A & M. McClendon stayed, however, after Governor John McKeithen and the Board of Supervisors gave him a new contract that guaranteed added security. And McClendon would need that security in the upcoming years.

The game that set back relations, if not clocks, between Louisiana and Mississippi. Bert Jones throws his last-second touchdown to beat Ole Miss 17–16 (1972).

The 1972 season began with *Sports Illustrated* picking LSU as the number one team in the nation. The Tigers began to live up to the magazine's expectations with six wins, including easy victories over Auburn, Texas A & M, and Wisconsin. The next game was *The Game* against Ole Miss. The Rebels were not having a good year. However, they put it all together against the Tigers, and behind the all-round play of quarterback Norris Weese they led 16–10 late in the game. Now it was Bert Jones's turn to steal the show. Jones trotted out on the field with 3:02 left in the game and the ball 80 yards from the Rebels' goal line. The Tigers converted two fourth-down plays and found themselves with a first down on the Rebel 20 with ten seconds left in the game and no time-outs remaining. Ole Miss was called for pass interference at the 10-yard line, stopping the clock with just four seconds left. Jones threw quickly to Jimmy LeDoux at the goal line on what all assumed was the last play of the game, but when the ball was batted away one second still remained on the clock. The Tigers then lined up with both wide receivers split and tailback Brad Davis in the slot. Davis headed straight for the flag, and Jones hit him just before he reached the goal line. Davis bobbled the ball, then held on to it and backed across the goal line at the flag.

After the hysteria died down—and it took a while—Rusty Jackson's extra point gave the Tigers an incredible 17–16 come-from-behind win, one that was so unbelievable to many on both sides that a few months after the game the state of Mississippi put up a sign at the border between the two states that read: "You Are Now Entering Louisiana. Please Set Your Watches Back 4 Seconds."

In a nationally televised game the following week against Alabama, Jones was again outstanding, but the Crimson Tide prevailed, 35–21. Weather was a big factor the next two weeks. It rained all day prior to the Mississippi State game. But, adhering to the adage that it never rains in Tiger Stadium on Saturday night, the rain stopped just before kickoff, and LSU pulled out a 28–14 win.

The elements did not cooperate in Gainesville the next week, as the Tigers and Gators battled in a torrential downpour that ended in a 3–3 tie. Play was highlighted by All-American cornerback Mike Williams pulling down speedster Nat Moore from behind on the 1-yard line, then recovering a Gator fumble on the next play to preserve a tie.

A sluggish 9–3 win over Tulane was followed by a game against an old nemesis, Tennessee, in the Astro-Bluebonnet Bowl. The Vols dominated the first half, the Tigers the second. But Tennessee pulled out a 24–17 win, and the Tigers ended with an overall record for 1972 of 9–2–1.

The following year Bert Jones was gone, and "Miracle Mike" Miley, a man with a flair for the big play, took over LSU's quarterbacking. The Tigers breezed through their first nine opponents undefeated. The Alabama game was set back to Thanksgiving Day for the convenience of television, and a national TV audience saw the Tide use the big play, scoring on two long passes for a 21–7 win.

The LSU faithful could tolerate a loss to Alabama, but they could not tolerate a loss to the next week's opponent, Tulane. In front of the largest crowd ever to see a football game in Dixie, 86,598 fans in Tulane Stadium, the emotionally charged Greenies shut down Miley and the LSU offense while scoring two touchdowns, for a 14–0 victory.

But the Tigers had already received a bid to play in

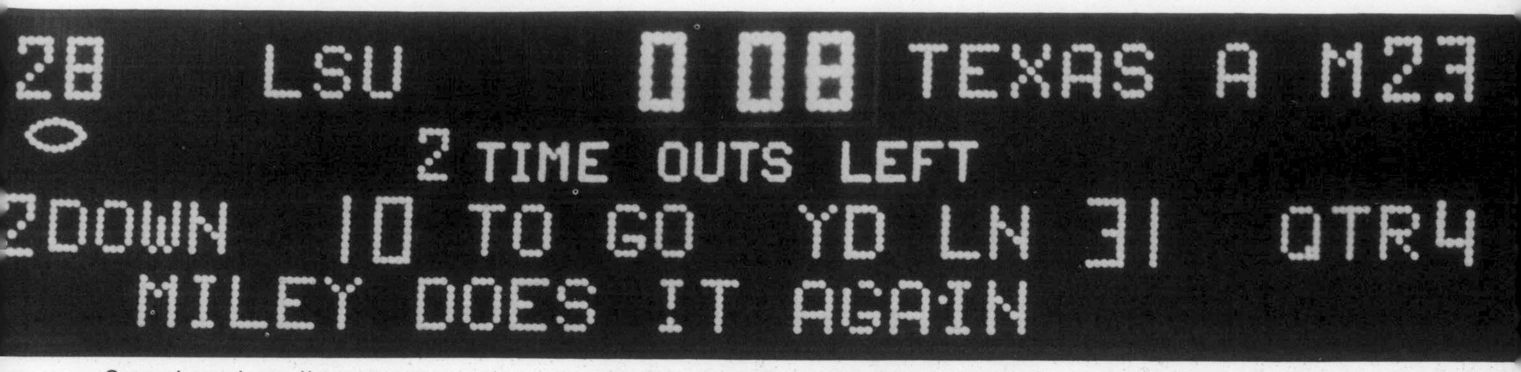

Scoreboard spells out yet another accomplishment of "Miracle Mike" Miley.

the Orange Bowl against Penn State and Heisman trophy winner John Cappelletti. LSU shut down the Heisman winner, but the Nittany Lions prevailed 16–9 in a topsy-turvy game, one in which LSU almost came back several times to win.

The 1974 season was a disappointing one for the Tigers, and it is difficult to pinpoint the reasons. Most of the team was returning, including so many running backs that McClendon switched the offense to the Veer. One possible explanation, albeit a simple one, is that the Tigers did not have an experienced quarterback to run the new offense. Miley, who had another year of eligibility, seemed a natural for the assignment, but he had signed a major league baseball contract during the summer.

The lack of an experienced quarterback did not seem to hurt the Tigers in their opening game against Colorado, as a flashy sophomore named Carl Otis Trimble ran wild in a 42–14 romp. But many noted that while Trimble ran the Buffs crazy, neither he nor the other quarterback, Billy Broussard, completed a pass.

The following week a powerful Texas A & M team stunned the Tigers 21–14. Then they had to hang on for a 10–10 tie with Rice in the season's third game. The only bright spots during the remainder of the season were a win over Tennessee, breaking the jinx, and a revenge victory over Tulane. The season also saw McClendon's first loss to his alma mater, Kentucky, and an embarrassing 30–0 defeat at the hands of Alabama on national television.

The season ended with a mediocre 5–5–1 record, McClendon's worst record since taking over the LSU reins. And it would get worse before it got better.

In 1975 the Tigers faced a murderous schedule with an inexperienced team meeting Nebraska, Texas A & M, and Florida in three of the first four games. The Tigers gave Nebraska all it could handle in Lincoln before falling 10–7, but the game seemed to take the starch out of the team, and they followed up the loss with two embarrassing defeats by scores of 39–8 and 34–6, sandwiched around a narrow win over Rice.

The Bengals dropped games against Ole Miss, Alabama and Mississippi State, then took out the season's frustrations on Tulane in the Louisiana Superdome, running up a 42–6 win, to finish up with a disappointing 4–7 record.

The Tigers' fortunes began to rise in 1976, as they fought Nebraska, the nation's number one–ranked team, to a 6–6 tie in the opening game. A strong defense and the superb running of Terry Robiskie were keys to the Tigers' relatively easy wins over Oregon State and Rice. Then they lost a heartbreaker to Florida, 28–23, when a pass from Pat Lyons to Bruce Hemphill just missed connecting for a last-minute touchdown.

The Tigers bounced back for a homecoming win over Vanderbilt, then played a frustrating game against Kentucky in Lexington, where they won virtually every battle, including the statistical one, but lost the all-important one on the scoreboard, 21–7. The team returned to early-season form the next week against Ole Miss. In a game where everything went right for the Tigers and wrong for the Rebels, Robiskie and sophomore sensation Charles Alexander both rushed for over 100 yards, as the Tigers won going away, 45–0.

Alabama continued its mastery over the Bengals in Birmingham the next week, and Mississippi State kept LSU's road jinx intact a week later, despite a wild comeback attempt in which freshman Steve Ensminger directed the offense back from a 21–0 deficit, only to see his team fall short and lose 21–13. Routine wins over Tulane and Utah followed, to round out a 6–4–1 season.

But despite their winning record, the Tigers had won only two Conference games and still had not won out of state since the 1973 Ole Miss game. McClendon was under fire from alumni, and in 1977 the pressure was really on to produce a successful season.

But McClendon was accustomed to such pressures, and he and the Tiger fans entered the 1977 season with cautious optimism, some of it based on the knowledge that they had one of the finest running backs in the nation in the person of junior Charles Alexander. In a wild season, featuring come-from-behind wins and Alexander's all-time SEC rushing total of 1686 yards, the team made a complete turn-around, finishing with an 8–3 regular season record and a bid to the Sun Bowl.

In the 1977 Sun Bowl, a pair of All-Americans, Alexander and Stanford quarterback Guy Benjamin, locked horns in a record-setting game that saw both the Sun Bowl's rushing and passing marks fall before Stanford pulled out a 24–14 win.

1978 was to be a watershed year in Tiger history, as many of those names which had contributed to LSU's greatness began to arrive or depart with a dizzying rapidity.

The first was former head coach Paul Dietzel. Just a decade and a half after he left LSU amidst recriminatory shouts of disloyalty, Dietzel was to return as director of athletics in the summer of 1978. Greeted as a prodigal son with open arms by Tiger followers with great memories and even greater hearts, this gregarious Ohio native made his homecoming an event to remember and proved Thomas Wolfe wrong: You can go home again—especially if home is LSU.

Terry Robiskie, the most prolific scorer in LSU history, scores another touchdown against Tulane in 42–6 win (1975).

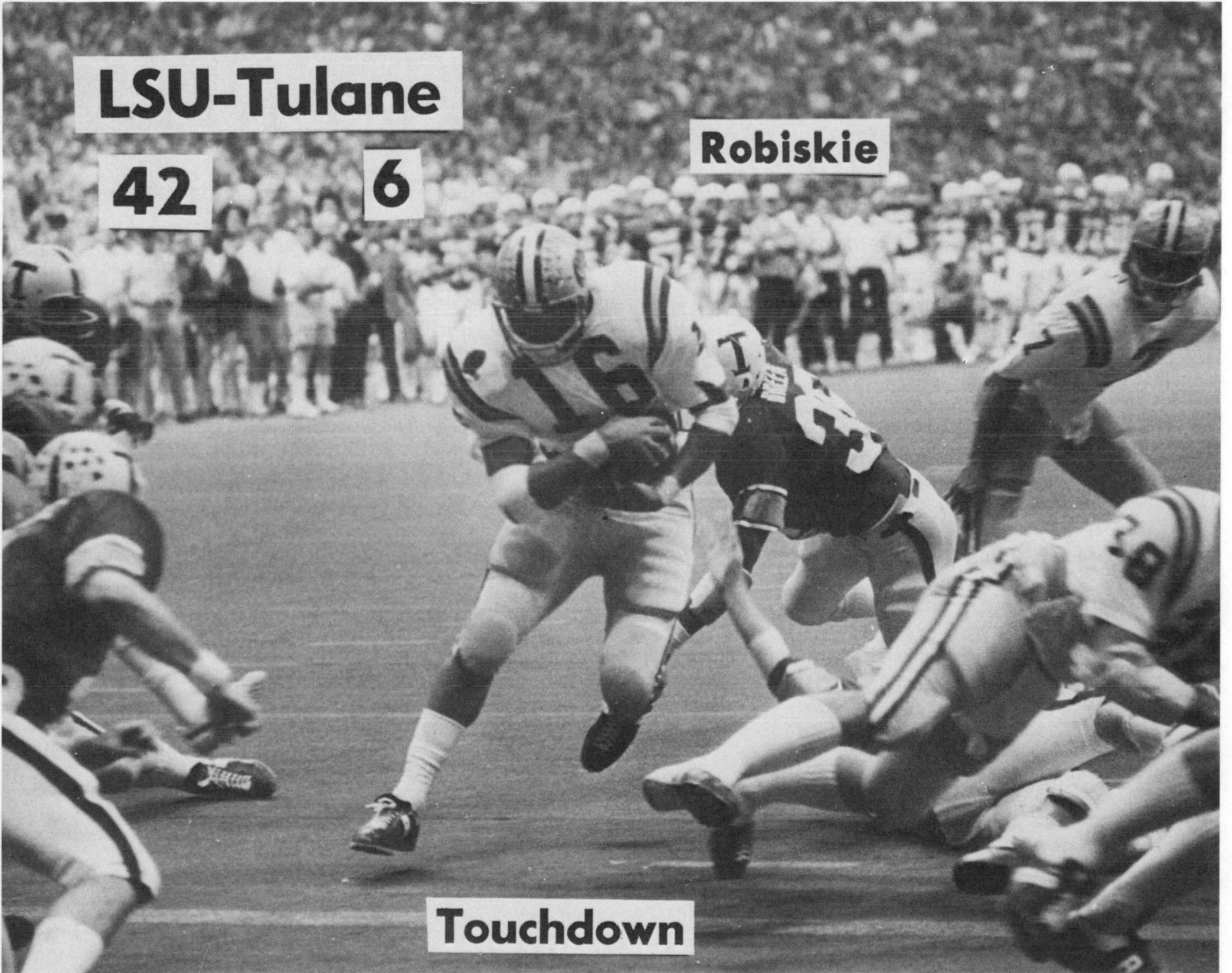

The second was Coach Charlie McClendon. After seventeen years at the helm of LSU's football fortunes, he had successfully conquered all the worlds he had set out to conquer as well as all those the alumni had set before him to conquer, and decided to retire at the end of the 1979 season. When he finally does step down, "Cholly Mac" will leave LSU with the task of filling more than just a position; they will have to fill a legacy as well.

And the third was All-American Charles Alexander. Not only would Alexander lead the Tigers to an 8–3 record and a Liberty Bowl berth by doing what he did best, running with the football, but this graduating senior would become the eighth man in NCAA history to rush for over 4000 yards in his career, breaking many of the LSU and SEC rushing records in the process. But while Alexander provided the firepower, there were other fireworks during 1978, including the longest scoring pass in Tiger history, an 82-yard bomb from quarterback Steve Ensminger to end Carlos Carson, Chris Williams's record-tying three interceptions against Rice, and the exciting second-half rally that fell just short of upsetting a great Missouri team in the Liberty Bowl.

And so another season had ended. Tiger fans would be looking forward to "next year." There would be pressure on the coach, rumors, a running back would be highly touted in the off-season, and the stadium would be expanding.

Charles Alexander takes off on another of his record-making jaunts.

Nothing much had really changed after all. The fans are still coming into Baton Rouge from all over—New Orleans, New Roads, Monroe, Mamou, Shreveport and Simmesport—meeting new friends and chatting with old. And waiting for the magic that is LSU football. . . .

The Golden Band from Tigerland.

University of Mississippi

by James "Bobo" Champion

From the rolling hills of the northern tip of the state to the swirling Gulf, they've come to the town of Oxford. Graduates of the flatlands, the Delta, natives of southeastern segments of the state, they've come. They've hailed from Boyle and Bude, Coldwater and Water Valley, Tie Plant and Shuqulak. And together they've toiled, played, hustled and sacrificed. Together they've changed from freckle-faced, sandy-haired boys into men who would be revered and respected across the nation. Together they form a living tradition known as Ole Miss football.

To trace the origin of the tradition requires looking back to 1893, when the first Mississippi team was organized. That fall, the University magazine reported: "The athletic fever has now taken full possession of the University . . . and the time is already here when, in order to rank high in college or in society, one must join the running crowd and play on the foot-ball team."

Dr. Alexander L. Bondurant, a Latin professor who in 1890 had written in the University magazine about the need for student participation in athletics, was the father of University football. In some reports Bondurant is cited as manager of the first team; in others, as coach. But while Bondurant is listed with the school's first-year record, he also should be credited with the recruitment of a mentor, J. W. S. Rhea, a prep school administrator who rode the train from Memphis to tutor the first Ole Miss team on weekends, as well as the foresight to see the wisdom of the manager's suggestion of colors for the team, cardinal red and navy blue. As Dr. Bondurant was later to recall, the team manager "suggested the union of the crimson of Harvard and the navy blue of Yale [which] would be very harmonious and that it would be very well to have the spirit of both of these good colleges."

The first game was staged on campus against Southwest Baptist University of Jackson, Tennessee (later Union), and the Rebels came out on top, 56–0. Their record for that inaugural year was 4–1, the first three triumphs all shutouts.

In Mississippi's embryonic stage, financial matters were handled by the manager, with support from the Athletic Association, which was composed of students and faculty members who all paid small fees. It was not uncommon for the Association to put on a minstrel show to alleviate the financial burden. And more than once games were canceled when opponents refused to pay their own traveling expenses.

The second year was more successful than the

Hemingway Stadium.

James "Bobo" Champion served as both assistant sports information director and sports information director at the University of Mississippi from 1972 through 1978.

first. After opening with two shutouts, the University concluded the 1894 season with a 6–1 record. The first game played in Jackson, the state's capital city—which over the years has become the Rebs' second home—was the 1894 tiff with Alabama.

Jackson's *Daily Clarion* took note of the 6–0 Ole Miss Fairgrounds win: "The game was witnessed by more than 1000 persons, but gate receipts totaled only $180. It is very evident that not one-half paid their entrance fee. It is not too late yet—they can hunt up the cashiers and pay their half-dollar without any trouble."

But if patrons had to hunt up cashiers, Mississippi did not have to hunt long for its first nickname. For the name Ole Miss first became part of University life during the year 1896, when it was selected in a contest to name the new student yearbook. The name—which stems from an old Southern colloquialism that dates back to the earliest days of plantation life, when family servants called the owner's wife "Ole Miss"—was suggested for the yearbook by Miss Elma Meek of Oxford. Originally used as the title of the yearbook, it ultimately became absorbed into the mainstream of the University, becoming synonymous with the school and, not incidentally, its teams.

In 1895 and 1896, a total of six games were played. After 2–1 and 1–2 seasons, the school went without football entirely in 1897 because of a yellow-fever epidemic that also delayed the opening of the fall term. The 1898 season was also cut to two games, which were split.

When a return to normalcy the next year showed student interest in football to be rampant, the faculty reacted harshly, imposing strict scholastic demands on athletes. (These pressures were, for the most part, lifted over the next few years.) The team played seven games, winning three.

The 1900 season witnessed just three games, all played on the road and all ending in defeats. The Red and Blue managed to score only five points in the three outings.

In 1901 Mississippi compiled a 2–4 record. Two head coaches saw service, and the series with current archrival Mississippi State (then Mississippi A & M) was inaugurated. The University went 4–3 in 1902, with all its victories shutouts, one of them a 21–0 dunking of A & M. Soon afterwards the Starkville school lured away the Ole Miss mentor, D. S. Martin. With enrollment reaching nearly three hundred in 1903, the team posted a 2–1–1 record. A year later they had a 4–3 season which included a staggering 114–0 shellacking of Southwest Baptist. Ole Miss should have saved some of its offense for the 1905 season, as the school dropped its only two encounters, failing to dent the scoreboard in either.

Mississippi returned to its winning ways in 1906, compiling a 4–2 record, but the roller coaster continued the next fall, with the team scoring just once in an 0–6 year.

Despite these dismal efforts, student support and spirit remained high. The 1908 squad faced keen opposition and finished 3–5. Halfback Ike Knox, the captain, supplied the offensive thrust in an era when depth was virtually unheard of.

The ensuing three years were significant in that Mississippi began playing a full schedule. At the helm was Dr. Nathan Stauffer, an ear, nose and throat specialist who left his medical practice and his job as assistant coach at the University of Pennsylvania to come to Oxford. Stauffer's first aggregation compiled a 4–3–2 record. Then the year everyone had been waiting for arrived: Dr. Stauffer's outfit was literally a "sight for sore eyes" as it shut out seven opponents in an eight-game schedule. The lone blemish was a 9–2 setback at the hands of Vanderbilt in Nashville, a loss that prevented the Red and Blue from winning the Southern Intercollegiate Athletic Association (SIAA) championship. Stauffer's team picked up in 1911 where it had left off the previous year, claiming three straight shutouts. But injuries saddled Ole Miss over the last five games, and it lost three of them, ending with a respectable 6–3 slate.

Over the next three years, the University had consecutive winning seasons. The 1913 and 1914 seasons were played under Bill Driver, a Missouri grad who picked up the pieces of a program severely hurt by the state legislature, which banned fraternities on college campuses and charged that paid players were infiltrating the college ranks. Morale among students, players and alumni alike was virtually nonexistent.

There was no place to go but up after the seven seasons 1915 through 1921, during which Ole Miss won eighteen and lost thirty-two and played under three head coaches. Despite a lackluster 3–5 mark in 1921, the team was invited to its first post-season clash: a game against the University of Havana in Havana, Cuba. However, Ole Miss lost 14–0 in the New Year's Eve skirmish.

The 1922 through 1924 seasons were particularly discouraging, as Ole Miss suffered consecutive defeats at the hands of A & M, a string that had reached twelve by 1924.

But alumni support was rejuvenated in 1925. The Athletic Committee was established, with members drawn from alumni and faculty. Since that time, the school has had eight head coaches, and three of the eight have also served as directors of athletics.

With a new outlook toward football, the University turned to Rutgers All-American Homer Hazel for field generalship in 1925. Hazel, who would coach for five years, lifted the Rebs to the .500 level for the first time since 1920, compiling a 5–5 record during his first season.

Although Hazel's second-season record of 5–4 was only a slight improvement, the fifth victory could have put him in the running for chancellor. After thirteen straight defeats, the Red and Blue finally halted A & M in a 7–6 struggle decided by Webb Burke's extra point. In the melee that followed, Ole Miss supporters scrambled for pieces of the goal posts. To save life, limb and goal posts, the joint student bodies purchased a Golden Egg cast in the size and shape of a football, and it became the symbol of the schools' seasonal supremacy.

The 1927 team, referred to as "the Mighty Mississippians," was as competitive a group as has ever taken the field. Its final record was 5–3–1, mediocre by some standards, but the three setbacks were by margins of twelve points, fourteen points and one point. In addition, the season produced the Red and Blue's second win in as many years over A & M, 20–12. Hazel's 1928 team, with seniors "Tad" Smith and "Pie" Vann providing leadership, had a topsy-turvy campaign, winning five and dropping four and continuing their mastery over A & M.

In 1929 Ole Miss fell to 1–6–2, the lone win being a 26–24 squeaker over Loyola of New Orleans in the school's first game played under the lights. Hazel's five-year record against A & M was 3–1–1, including a tie in 1929.

Hazel was succeeded in 1930 by Ed Walker, a Stanford grad who practiced what he had been taught by his mentor, the immortal Pop Warner. Armed with formations and plays foreign to Deep South football, Walker set about his task with a team known to its partisans as "the Flood." He launched his career with a 64–0 tattooing of Union, but a week later his team lost by the same score to Alabama. Four more losses and a tie preceded closing wins over Southwestern and A & M. It was the fifth straight year the Aggies had failed in their bid to beat Ole Miss.

In 1931, suffering from a lack of manpower, Mississippi finished 2–6–1. A record was established that year which still stands: Jack Burke's 109-yard kickoff return against Alabama. A & M was again beaten, 25–14, to end a down year on an upbeat note.

A year later, the team began seeing the light at the end of the tunnel. A 49–0 win over Mississippi Teachers (now Southern Mississippi) kicked off the season. The final 1932 scorecard read 5–6, and the unbeaten streak over A & M reached seven.

Walker's fourth campaign, and his first in the newly formed SEC, was his best thus far. The 1933 season started inauspiciously with a 6–6 stalemate against Southwestern of Memphis, and then Mississippi Teachers was bombed 45–0 for the second straight year. But more significant than the win over Mississippi Teachers was a 0–0 deadlock with pre-season SEC favorite Alabama. The game marked the first time Ole Miss had held the Tide scoreless since beating 'Bama 16–0 in 1910. After the Alabama tilt, Walker's team won four in a row, then dropped three straight before a rousing 31–0 romp over Mississippi State that closed out a respectable 6–3–2 year.

The 1934 campaign was one that Walker, his staff, and most University supporters would rather have forgotten. What many had felt would be a peak year was marred by numerous valleys. A 4–5–1 season opened as expected with wins over West Tennessee Teachers (now Memphis State) and Southwestern, both shutouts. Tennessee started the Ole Miss slide with a 27–0 blasting, and thereafter the season was

Frank M. "Bruiser" Kinard, the first player from Ole Miss to be named All-Southeastern and the first Mississippian to be selected as an All-American (1936 and 1937).

earmarked by solid defense and little offense. The game against State was played in Jackson for the first time since 1925, but the move did not help State, as Ole Miss kept its winning streak alive, this time by a 7–3 margin.

"What a difference a year makes!" could have been the team's battle cry in 1935. Ed Walker's sixth Mississippi team was not only his best; it was also the first Mississippi team ever to win nine games in a single season. And the season was garnished with a trip to a bowl.

Ole Miss started out like a house afire, winning its first five games, four of them shutouts, and rolling up 205 points in the process. But then Marquette threw a damper on the season by beating Ole Miss 33–7, and hopes of a first SEC title went up in smoke when Tennessee eked out a 14–13 win in Memphis, thanks to a blocked PAT attempt. But Mississippi bounced back to collar a State team that had entered the traditional season-ending game sporting an 8–2 record—including a stunning 13–7 upset win over mighty Army—beating them by the score of 14–6. The Red and Blue then capped the phenomenal 9–2 season by accepting an invitation to play in the fourth annual Orange Bowl game against Catholic University of Washington, D.C.—the first time the University of Miami had not played host in the second-oldest New Year's Day classic.

Playing without star fullback Clarence Hapes, who was out with a knee injury, Ole Miss finished ahead of Catholic University in every category except the final score. The team outgained the Cardinals 15–5 in first downs, and gained 300 yards in total offense to just 153 for the contingent from Washington. But they still lost to an opportunistic rival who capitalized on an intercepted pass to set up a first quarter touchdown, scored in the second quarter on a long pass, and then, even though they did not make a first down in the second half, converted a blocked punt into the decisive six points, to beat Ole Miss 20–19.

Graduation depleted the star-stocked 1935 platoon, and in 1936 the Rebels—the new nickname selected for the squad in a contest sponsored by the student newspaper, *The Mississippian*—carved out a .500 record, 5–5–2, with Mississippi State finally snapping the Reb domination. Junior Ray Hapes was a fleet halfback, and the line was anchored by Frank M. "Bruiser" Kinard, who gained All-American recognition in his junior year.

The year 1937 was Walker's final one as Mississippi head coach. Starting his valedictory season right, he preserved his perfect record of never having lost an opening game by downing Louisiana Tech 13–0. But while Kinard was enjoying national recognition as football's premier lineman—recognition that culminated in his repeating as the state's first All-American—he received precious little help from his teammates, and Ole Miss finished with a mediocre 4–5–1 record.

Still the 1937 Rebels made history of sorts when, on September 30, 1937, they became the first football team to fly en masse to a game, flying to Philadelphia for an October 1 encounter with Temple, coached by Walker's former mentor Pop Warner. The game itself was anticlimactic, ending in a scoreless tie. Five weeks later the Rebs repeated their history-making travel by flying to Washington, D.C., to face George Washington University, who had held them to a scoreless tie the year before. This time the flight turned into a pleasure trip, as they beat the Colonials 27–6.

Walker, who also doubled as athletic director, wound up his head-coaching chores with a perfectly symmetrical 38–38–8 record. Kinard, after putting in nine illustrious years as an NFL great and subsequently being elected to both the College Football and Pro Football Halls of Fame, returned to Mississippi in 1948 as line coach and served twenty-three years on the Ole Miss coaching staff and three as athletic director.

Walker was followed as head coach by Harry Mehre, a former pupil of Knute Rockne at Notre Dame. Mehre, coach and athletic director from 1938 to 1945, supplied Ole Miss with an era of football it had not known before: during his first four years, his record was 31–8–1.

In the 1938 opener, Mehre sent the Rebs out a twenty-point underdog against LSU, a team that had not surrendered a point to Ole Miss during the previous two seasons. This year was different, however.

Coach Harry Mehre, whose 1938–1941 teams lost just eight of forty games.

Parker Hall launched a successful bid for All-American honors that night in Baton Rouge, and the Rebs pulled off a stunning 20–7 upset, the first Rebel win over the Bengals since 1927 and only LSU's second SEC loss in four years. Over 1300 students—almost the entire student body—turned out to greet the team upon its return.

Mehre's first squad rolled to an impressive 9–2 season, garnering national ink with a 25–0 pounding of previously unbeaten, untied and unscored-upon George Washington.

The 1939 team pulled more surprises. It beat LSU 14–7 in Tigertown, posted three straight shutouts before falling to Tulane, and then dealt a 14–7 thumping to Vanderbilt for the first time in its history. A closing defeat to Mississippi State produced a final mark of 7–2. The team had lost only four times in two years, a rare record in the Rebel camp, and much of the prosperity was owed to the famed "H" boys, fullback Merle Hapes and halfback Junie Hovious. Mehre called Hapes "the best fullback I ever coached."

Mehre's 1940 congregation stayed in the headlines, with Hapes and Hovious continuing to excel. The Rebs gained their third straight win over LSU in Baton Rouge (19–6), and then whipped Duquesne 14–6 in the only defeat suffered by the Dukes in three seasons. After Arkansas eked out a 21–20 win in Memphis, the Rebs retaliated by downing Vanderbilt 13–7, their first win ever over the Commodores in Nashville. A 28–14 triumph over Georgia in Athens, where Mehre had coached before coming to Oxford, made a 9–2 ledger that much sweeter.

Tailback Parker Hall, All-American (1938).

Fullback Merle Hapes, All-SEC (1941).

Junie Hovious, three-time All-SEC (1939–1940–1941) and all-time All-Southeastern halfback.

The 1941 campaign produced some lightning bolts as well as an impressive 6–2–1 record. Georgetown was the first surprise, going down 16–6 in Washington. Tulane was beaten 20–13 in New Orleans; it was the Rebels' first win over the Greenies in twenty-five years. Then Mehre's youngsters, with Wobble Davidson and Larry Hazel as co-captains, once more turned the tables on LSU. The Bengals were beaten 13–12 in Tiger Stadium, giving Ole Miss the honor of becoming the first, and only, school to administer four consecutive spankings to LSU in Baton Rouge.

The war years were lean years. World War II cheated Ole Miss of its football potential a year before the general exodus hit most college squads. Three members of the 1941 freshman team who were summoned to duty, Barney Poole, Charley Conerly and Doug Kenna, all earned All-American honors several years later, either at Army or at Ole Miss.

Ray Poole, All-SEC end (1946) and later on OM assistant coach.

The 1942–45 record of 8–18 was uncharacteristic of Mehre's teams. But then again, the conditions were trying ones. The 1942 bunch was 2–7, even with Conerly operating out of the Notre Dame box. Louisiana State broke its losing streak, and Mississippi State continued its winning streak with four straight wins over Ole Miss. In 1943 football was abolished in all state-supported institutions by the Board of Trustees. Ole Miss wound up the 1944 season 2–6, drubbing Florida 26–6 in Jacksonville and finally taming a good Mississippi State team 13–8.

The 1945 season produced a 4–5 record, the third straight sub-par record for Mehre's teams. Kentucky was stopped 21–7 in Memphis to open the show, but the fireworks after that were few and far between. Just as in 1944, however, an aroused Reb brigade turned back Allyn McKeen's talented Mississippi State group, 7–6.

Mehre bowed out in January 1946, returning to Atlanta to enter private business. According to Hovious, who later coached on the Rebel staff for nearly thirty years, Harry Mehre gave Ole Miss "its first winning tradition." Mehre's overall record was a more-than-respectable 39–26–1.

In the post-war restoration program, C. M. "Tad" Smith, who had starred at halfback from 1926 through 1928 and then stayed on to coach, succeeded Mehre as director of athletics, and Harold "Red" Drew of Bates, long time Alabama end coach, became head football coach. The appointments

Coach Harold "Red" Drew.

John H. Vaught, Ole Miss coach for a quarter of a century.

marked the first time the two positions were separated, and Smith became the first alumnus to serve as athletic director. He held the position for twenty-five years, retiring on February 1, 1971.

Drew had developed several outstanding ends for Frank Thomas at Alabama, Don Hutson and Paul "Bear" Bryant among them. But his assignment now was difficult—to reconstruct a successful football program. He inherited just twelve lettermen, plus a host of eager war returnees. Experience and depth were practically nil. Drew's six-man staff included a future household word in Southern football, John Vaught.

The 1946 Rebs struggled as expected, winning just two games in nine starts, yet they were never embarrassed. They whipped Florida 13–7 and toppled Arkansas 9–7. A margin of twelve points in three losing outings prevented a winning season.

When Frank Thomas retired at Alabama in January 1947, the Tide sent out a call to Drew, who opted for Tuscaloosa over Oxford. Drew went on to serve as head coach of the Crimson Tide for eight seasons. His successor at Ole Miss was his line coach, John Vaught.

Some Mississippi-watchers say that football at the University of Mississippi began with the appointment of Vaught. A former line coach at North Carolina and a veteran of Naval programs in North Carolina and Texas, the ex–TCU All-American developed an outstanding rapport with the players in his first year at Ole Miss. He also developed something else—he redesigned the old Notre Dame shift pattern to take full advantage of Charley Conerly's aerial prowess.

Hall of Famer Charley Conerly, SEC Player of the Year (1947).

The first foe for Vaught and the Rebs in 1947 was Kentucky, a team that had beaten Ole Miss 20–6 the previous year. By the time the dust had settled in Oxford's Hemingway Stadium, the Rebels had a rare opening Homecoming win, 14–7; future All-Americans Conerly and Barney Poole had picked the 'Cats' defense clean, and Conerly had outdueled George Blanda. The 1947 team rolled to an 8–2 record, along the way waylaying favored LSU 20–18, destroying South Carolina 33–0, and scoring the school's first victory ever over Tennessee, 43–13.

Barney Poole, two-time All-American end (1947 and 1948) and member of the Hall of Fame.

Conerly throws another of his eighteen touchdown passes in 1947 to lead the Rebels to their first SEC title.

Smith and Vaught had signed for the Delta Bowl contest in midsummer. Playing before 28,000 fans in Memphis's Crump Stadium against TCU, Ole Miss spotted the Horned Frogs a 9–0 lead for three quarters, then won 13–9 on two Conerly touchdown passes.

The 1947 campaign produced a series of unprecedented firsts: the Rebels won their first SEC crown; Vaught was the first freshman coach to win the Conference championship and to be named the SEC Coach of the Year; and the bowl win was Mississippi's first post-season triumph.

With Conerly entering pro ball and other front-line personnel lost to graduation, Vaught introduced split-T football to Dixie in 1948. And the Rebs rambled to an 8–1 season, percentage-wise the best in the school's history to that point. Only a fourth-game loss to Tulane (20–7) on a steamy afternoon in New Orleans cost Ole Miss a chance to repeat as Conference champions.

Two-platoon football, which entered the picture in 1949, had a devastating effect on Ole Miss's football fortunes. Only nineteen lettermen were on hand, with inexperience the rule rather than the exception. Added to this debilitating disaster were the dual plagues of "fumbleitis" and leaky pass defense, and the Red and Blue became members of the walking wounded, skidding to a 4–5–1 record and an eighth-place tie in the Conference. Rebel flags, which had been waving high after opening 40–7 victories over Memphis State and Auburn, drooped perceptibly after Kentucky drubbed the Rebs 47–0 in the third game, setting the tone for the rest of the season. The only highlight of an otherwise long year was the rushing of Kayo Dottley, who rushed for 1312 yards, setting a Conference record that stood till 1977.

Injuries set the tone for much of the 1950 campaign. From September on, twenty-nine Rebs were injured, eighteen of them first-team personnel. Inexperience was once again a handicap, with only seventeen lettermen returning. Though the overall record leveled at 5–5, the league finish was a dismal eleventh. Dottley capped his career with an emotional 27–20 win over Mississippi State, gaining 127 yards on 23 carries.

If nothing else, the 1951 season hinted at what was around the corner. Vaught's fifth assemblage compiled a 6–3–1 record, and enthusiasm was building. It was, to say the least, an unpredictable campaign. Kentucky, a twenty-point favorite, was shaded 21–17; Tulane was thrashed 25–6; and leading 20–7 into the fourth stanza against Vanderbilt, the Rebs fell 34–20. Oft-injured "Showboat" Boykin, who played in Dottley's shadow throughout his career, ripped apart Mississippi State's touted defense for seven touchdowns in a 49–7 rout—his longest scamper covered 85 yards—for an NCAA record that has stood the test of time.

The 1952 season was less than encouraging coming out of the blocks. In the first four weeks, the Rebs gained two wins and two ties. But the walking days were over. It was now high-flying time, as four straight wins preceded a showdown with number three–ranked Maryland in Hemingway Stadium. With over 32,000 fans looking on, Ole Miss and quarterback Jimmy Lear disregarded their underdog role and plowed to a 21–14 shocker over the Terps in what the Associated Press pegged The Sports Upset of the Year. (For Rebel trivia buffs, the Maryland upset, the 1969 crunch of Tennessee, and the 1977 overthrow of Notre Dame, not necessarily in that order, rank as three of the biggest moments in Ole Miss grid history.) Immediately after the Maryland victory, Athletic Director Smith accepted an invitation to the Sugar Bowl, and two weeks later the Red and Blue pounced on Mississippi State 20–14, to complete their first unbeaten campaign. Kline Gilbert carted off All-American recognition at offensive tackle, and Mississippi was ranked number seven by all three major polling services.

Kline Gilbert, All-American tackle (1952).

Georgia Tech burst the Rebel bubble in the Sugar Bowl. But there was grumbling among Reb diehards that was heard not only throughout the State, but back in Peach country as well. Ole Miss tallied first and was marching for an apparent second tally when a disputed call halted the drive a foot shy of the goal line. The ruling seemed to take the wind out of the Magnolia sails. Other hairline calls prompted Mississippi Governor Hugh White to publicly protest the game. But the 24–7 loss remained, the Rebels' second disappointment in three bowl encounters.

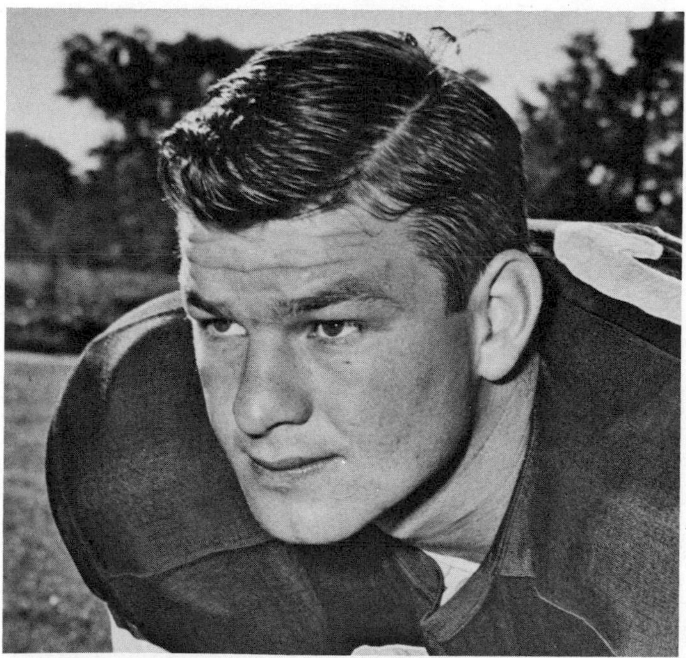

Crawford Mims, All-American guard (1953).

The success of the 1953 season was keyed to filling several positions, among them that of quarterback. The partially rebuilt team sailed out and won its first two games by convincing scores, then came a cropper against Auburn, as the Plainsmen broke OM's thirteen-game regular-season unbeaten streak. Bouncing back with five consecutive victories, the Rebels went to College Park, Maryland, to play the number one–ranked Terrapins, hoping to catch lightning in a bottle once again and repeat their 1952 stunner. However, this time they were not even in the proverbial ballpark, losing to Maryland 38–0. Still, as they came to the final weekend of the year and their annual game against State, a lot more than the Golden Egg was riding on the outcome of the game: a possible Conference championship and a likely bowl bid. But for the first time in seven years, the Rebs came away without a win. The 7–7 tie spoiled whatever chance they had for a Conference championship or a bowl bid.

In its 1954 pre-season ratings, *Collier's* magazine went out on a limb and tagged Ole Miss number one. And a well-balanced team came within an eyelash of fulfilling the prophecy. After reeling off five straight wins, the number five–ranked Rebs met the number seven–ranked Arkansas Razorbacks in Little Rock, in a game that was designated as an SEC game in order to give the Rebs a sufficient number of games to compete for the Conference championship. Although OM lost to Arkansas 6–0, other contenders also fell, and Ole Miss's closing four triumphs locked up its second SEC championship and a number six national ranking. Anchored by All-American tackle Rex Reed Boggan, the Johnny Rebs surrendered just forty-seven points in regular-season play and were first in the land in total defense.

Rex Reed Boggan, All-American tackle (1954).

Vaught and Co. made their second Sugar Bowl appearance in three years, this time against Navy. But an aroused Middie team—called "The Team Named Desire"—emerged victorious over an uninspired Rebel team, 21–0.

In 1955 it was a whole new ballgame, and the Rebels sought to make the most of it. The only flaw in an otherwise perfect record was an early-season upset loss to Kentucky. Following their defeat by the Wildcats, the Rebs reeled off eight straight victories, including a 29–26 victory over LSU, a 27–13 win over Tulane, and a 26–0 shutout over Mississippi State, as they marched to their third SEC championship and the first undisputed repeat title for a reigning Conference champion since 1943–44. Now ranked ninth or tenth nationally, depending on the poll, Ole Miss accepted its first invitation to play in the Cotton Bowl.

The Cotton Bowl itself was all it was cracked up to be and more—especially for Rebel fans. Ole Miss spotted TCU and All-American Jim Swink a 13–0 second-period advantage and then stormed from

Paige Cothren, two-time All-SEC fullback.

behind on the arm of Eagle Day, the legs of Paige Cothren, and the all-around play of guard Buddy Alliston. With the Rebels ahead 14–13 and with time running out, Eddie Crawford shrugged off an injury to intercept a pass and preserve a 14–13 win over the Horned Frogs. Day was voted the game's Outstanding Back and Alliston the Outstanding Lineman.

The team that went "cotton pickin'" was a talented cast: Fullback Cothren, who led the SEC in scoring with seventy-four points and set a national field-goal record with six three-pointers in a season, became the third Rebel to win the Jacobs trophy, presented to the best blocker in the SEC; Eagle Day, pegged the "Mississippi Gambler," ran the show from the quarterback spot; and halfback Billy Kinard excelled on offense and defense.

Eagle Day, the "Mississippi Gambler."

The Red and Blue began the 1956 season with four straight wins, the defense allowing only seven points. Then Tulane withstood a late rally to derail the Reb Express in Jackson, 10–3, and a week later Arkansas staged a 14–0 upset. Two wins soothed the Rebels' wounds, which Tennessee proceeded to reopen in Knoxville with a 27–7 win. Again it was catch-up against State, but the Maroons were edged 13–7. Key injuries began to take their toll: Cothren's left leg never fully mended following an operation performed over the summer; Billy Lott was plagued by leg and knee ailments; and Crawford could not shake his recurring shoulder problems. Despite the injuries, the Rebels compiled a respectable 7–3 record.

The Johnny Rebs steamrolled to an 8–1–1 year in 1957, as the defense grudgingly gave up a mere seven points to their first five opponents and just fifty-two in the ten-game schedule. With a powerful offensive line anchored by All-Americans Jackie Simpson and Gene Hickerson, the Rebs led the SEC in total offense for the sixth time since 1948. Arkansas administered the team's sole loss, 12–6. And a 7–7 stalemate with Mississippi State held the Rebels back from a share of the Conference championship.

Mississippi did not deviate from its ground-oriented offense against Texas in the 1958 Sugar Bowl, a 39–7 rout that gave OM its first New Orleans win in three tries. The Rebels sprinted to a 26–0 margin behind quarterbacks Raymond Brown and Bobby Franklin; then the 'Horns tallied and threatened again, only to have Brown come to the fore. First he picked off a pass at the Reb 7. Moments later, when he was about to punt, he avoided an onrushing end and set sail on a 92-yard sprint that put the icing on the cake and also locked up the game's Outstanding Player award—in a vote that was unanimous for the first and only time in Sugar Bowl history.

The 1958 campaign brought special focus on Deep South football when Ole Miss and LSU hooked up in Baton Rouge on November 1, with the Bengals the nation's number one power and the Rebs tagged number three. Vaught's charges had attained that rung with six consecutive wins, the sixth an exciting 14–12 squeaker over Arkansas. Tiger Stadium shook from side to side during the struggle, as 68,000 watched the two giants, who allowed each other less than 200 yards total offense. The Bengals scored once before halftime, then tacked on a fourth-quarter touchdown for a 14–0 showpiece. Two weeks later, in Knoxville, the Rebs were outpointed by an underdog Tennessee team 18–16, and hopes for another SEC championship were shattered. But a victory over Mississippi State brought the record to 8–2 and won OM their first visit to the Gator Bowl, to play Florida.

Bobby Franklin, chosen the game's Most Valuable Player, marched his team 70 yards after the opening kickoff and scored the contest's only touchdown. The Gators retaliated immediately with three points, but the 7–3 score stood up, for the Rebs' second straight bowl win.

Football fever at the University of Mississippi in 1959 was at an epidemic pitch even before the opening kickoff at Houston. Nothing like it had ever touched the Magnolia State before. But when the Rebs whitewashed both the Cougars and Kentucky by identical scores (16–0), temperatures soared to the breaking point. Four more teams fell: Memphis State (43–0), Vanderbilt (33–0), Tulane (53–7), and Arkansas (28–0). Now the entire state was a collective candidate for the intensive care ward.

Then came the game billed as the "Game of the Year." To some it was the "Game of the Decade," and to a few of the most feverish fans, given to hyperbole, the "Game of the Century." For the seventh game on Ole Miss's schedule was a classic confrontation pitting the third-ranked Rebels, unbeaten, untied and virtually unscored upon, having surrendered a mea-

Bobby Franklin, Most Valuable Player in Ole Miss's Gator Bowl win over Florida (1958).

ger seven points in six games, against LSU, the number one-ranked team, also undefeated, untied and even stingier, having given up just a pair of field goals in six games.

On a night meant only for the strong of heart, tickets were harder to find than good moonshine. Edgy scalpers bartered and ran for the hills. Tickettakers saw more cheerleaders and band members parade in than they had ever dreamed existed, as every scam known to man was tried by fans attempting to gain admittance to Tiger Stadium. Once inside the 68,000-seat madhouse—unaffectionately known as Death Valley and Heartbreak Hollow—viewers discarded costumes and scrambled madly for seats, as even standing room was at a premium.

The spectators were not disappointed. The game was everything it had promised to be. And more. A 22-yard field goal by Bob Khayat in the first period gave Mississippi the lead, one that held up until the final fifteen minutes. Then, with Jake Gibbs punting on third down, Heisman trophy winner Billy Cannon fielded the ball on his 11 and raced 89 yards, virtually untouched, for a touchdown. Once the uproar had subsided—and that took a while, as the whole of Louisiana exploded in celebration—Vaught called on sophomore quarterback Doug Elmore, his number three signal-caller, to make the stretch drive. Elmore responded by leading the Rebs straight down the field to the Tiger 2, where he stopped on fourth down with only seconds left, a fitting finale for the game between the two titans of collegiate football.

Jake Gibbs, SEC Player of the Year (1960).

Tackle Bob Khayat, whose three-pointer accounted for all of Ole Miss's points in the "Game of the Decade."

Mississippi ended the season with three straight wins, a 9–1 record, and a Sugar Bowl bid to once again lock horns with LSU in an encore of their earlier cliffhanger. Although the rematch was billed by some as "Son of Game of the Year," it had none of the pyrotechnics of the earlier game. In fact, it was no game at all, as Ole Miss determined early that it was not going to be ambushed again by Cannon or LSU. Led by defensive stalwart Larry Grantham, it held the vaunted LSU offense to just 74 yards in total offense—minus 15 yards rushing—with Cannon netting a meager 8. The Red and Blue offense, sparked by Franklin, Gibbs, Charlie Flowers and George Blair, twisted the Tigers' tail for a one-sided 21–0 Ole Miss win that not only avenged their previous close encounter, but took them past the Bengals in the national polls to the number two ranking.

But if the 1959 team was one of Mississippi's all-time great squads, the 1960 outfit saw it—and raised it one. Coming into their seventh game of the season, the all-winning Rebels were the second-rated team in the nation and heavy favorites to down oft-beaten LSU in their quest for an undefeated and untied season. In one of only two televised contests to emanate from Hemingway Stadium, the Tigers clung to a precarious 6–3 lead when placekicker Allen Green—thanks to All-American Gibbs's passing and the catching wizardry of Bobby Crespino and Co.—got his chance from 41 yards out and booted the three-pointer that provided not only a 6–6 tie but also an eventual fourth SEC championship. It was to be the only taint on an otherwise perfect season for Ole Miss; but the season was not without its close calls. Only a week before his heroics against LSU, Green had been the center of controversy when, following the aerial acrobatics of Gibbs and Crespino, he kicked a last-second 39-yard field goal to nudge OM past Arkansas 10–7. However, Green was forced to kick twice because of a signaled time-out just as the ball was snapped. To this day Razorback partisans vow that the second attempt was wide left.

Charlie Flowers, All-American fullback (1959).

Bobby Crespino, one of Ole Miss's top receivers (1958–1960).

Following their 14–6 Sugar Bowl win over Rice, their fifth straight bowl victory, the Rebs were acclaimed the 1960 national champions by the Football Writers Association of America—a fitting climax to a great year.

Vaught and his Mississippi team continued on their charted course in 1961. Some Rebel followers still say that that year's contingent was his best. Again it was old nemesis LSU who spoiled a perfect season, but with Elmore and Glynn Griffing at the throttle, the offense was the most prolific in the school's history, resetting or tying sixteen team marks and reeling off 419.2 yards per game, tops in the country. Defensively, big Jim Dunaway and his linemates, ranked third nationally, giving up a scant forty points in ten games. The 9–1 season opened with a nationally

Tackle Jim Dunaway, All-American (1962).

televised 16–0 carving of Arkansas that christened Mississippi Memorial Stadium in Jackson. Five more wins propelled the Rebs to a number two ranking. Then they headed into the Tigers' den, where the number six-ranked Bengals lay in wait. A chance to take over as the NCAA King of the Mountain vanished when LSU went ahead to stay, 10–7, late in the third quarter. In the fourth stanza, the Rebels paraded all over the field except into the promised land. A string of twenty-one games without a defeat came to an end. Three wins in the final three games sent Ole Miss to the Cotton Bowl, a jaunt made without All-American fullback Billy Ray Adams. Adams had suffered back, knee and internal injuries in an auto accident just two days after the finale with State, while returning from an awards banquet in Jackson. And in first-period action against Texas in the Cotton Bowl, his replacement, Buck Randall, departed with a knee injury. Griffing sparked the Rebel offense to over 300 yards, decidedly more than the Longhorns amassed, but the Texans stymied two OM scoring bids with interceptions and came away with a 12–7 upset, ending the all-winning OM bowl streak at five.

The 1962 brigade surpassed even the heroics of 1961, as for the first time the Rebels finished with a perfect season: a 9–0 mark in regular-season play that was extended to 10–0 after a post-season win. For the second straight year, the defense held opponents to just forty points in the regular season, with mammoth All-American Dunaway the giant on the combine that finished first nationally in defense. In the Dixieland Classic against LSU, Griffing, who also earned All-American honors, passed and ran over the Bengals in a 15–7 win in Baton Rouge that broke the Tiger jinx. Only a busted bootleg play by sophomore quarterback Jim Weatherly late in the contest against Mississippi State enabled the Johnny Rebs to cop a 13–6 decision. Weatherly's fourth-quarter heroics propelled Mississippi to its fifth SEC championship and sixth bowl game in as many years. The Rebels, ranked third in the polls, were back in New Orleans and the Sugar Bowl for a contest against Arkansas.

On paper, the Pokers were no match. On Tulane Stadium turf, it was another matter. Griffing was at his best, and he had to be. The Culkin senior accounted for 257 yards in total offense and 2 touchdowns, and won the Outstanding Player Award. The Griffing–Louis Guy combo went for 18 and 43 yards through the air to set up the go-ahead six-pointer in the third period. A successful defensive struggle ensued in the final quarter, but at game's end the Rebels had a hard-fought 17–13 victory.

Billy Ray Adams, All-SEC fullback (1961).

Glynn Griffing, All-American quarterback (1962).

The 1963 story can be summarized in one word: ties. Memphis State surprised everyone with a 0–0 stalemate in Crump Stadium, and Mississippi State, with only three first downs, forced a fourth-quarter field goal by Billy Carl Irwin for a 10–10 tie. However, Ole Miss packed away its sixth league title—its most recent—and went bowling for the seventh consecutive season. WIth their 7–0–2 record, the Rebs ran their string of unbeaten regular-season games to twenty-one and finished seventh in the polls, dropping from third after the tie with State. The defense was again the key, bettering the 1962 and 1961 standout platoons by permitting a mere thirty-three points in nine games and once again leading college football in that department. The annual struggle with LSU, set in Baton Rouge, was shifted to the afternoon for television, and the result was a surprisingly easy 37–3 romp for the Rebels. Even more embarrassing to LSU than the score was the way sophomore guard Stan Hindman caught fleet Joe Labruzzo from behind at the Rebel 1, only to see the Tigers give the ball up four plays later at the 5.

Perry Lee Dunn, quarterback of the 1963 SEC titlists.

As a rare snowfall descended upon New Orleans that New Year's Day 1964, an even rarer occurrence took place on Tulane University's field. Mississippi was facing Alabama in the thirtieth annual Sugar Bowl game, the first time the two schools had met since 1933. Plagued by eleven fumbles, six of which they coughed up to the Tide, and with the brilliant passing of Perry Lee Dunn neutralized, Ole Miss fell to 'Bama and substitute Tide quarterback Steve Sloan (filling in for the benched Joe Namath), four field goals to one touchdown, 12–7.

Ole Miss approached 1964 as the pre-season favorite to repeat as Conference champions. Off and running against a tough Memphis State team 30–0, the Rebels had their hopes for an undefeated season dashed by Kentucky in Jackson, 27–21. From that point on, it was an up-and-down season, with LSU winning 11–10 via a two-point conversion, and Mississippi State a 20–17 winner at Hemingway on national TV. It was the first MSU defeat of a Vaught-coached team and its first victory over OM since 1946. The 5–4–1 campaign, which missed being a 9–1 record by thirteen points, was climaxed with a reputation-rewarding berth in the Bluebonnet Bowl, where Tulsa went airborne with passes from Jerry Rhome to Howard Twilley, for a 14–7 upset.

Sideline shot of Coach John Vaught, at the right with hat, backed up by Junie Hovious, Ray Poole (wearing headset), and fullback Don Street.

Twelve months later, the Rebs beat Memphis State 34–14, and enthusiasm mounted for another successful campaign. However, Larry Seiple raced 70 yards from punt formation in Jackson to lead Kentucky to a 16–7 upset, and the early enthusiasm waned. A win over Alabama in Birmingham could have provided the stimulus for another outstanding season, but a hairline interference call on a fourth-down attempt by 'Bama, as well as fine play by the Tide's field general Sloan, led to a 17–16 'Bama win. Florida made it three losses in a row with a 17–0 scorcher over an emotionally drained team on Homecoming Day. But All-Americans Stan Hindman and Bill Clay, guard and safety, and a parcel of sophomores, including big Jim Urbanek, Dan Sartin and Jimmy Keyes, rallied the Rebels, who went on to capture five of the last six games and a berth in the 1965 Liberty Bowl. Included in the late-season revival was a 23–0 clouting of nationally ranked LSU.

In the Liberty Bowl, moved to Memphis after trials in Philadelphia and Atlantic City, Ole Miss and Auburn drew a then record crowd of 38,607. Two field goals by Keyes and a sack of Auburn quarterback Alex Bowden by Keyes, Urbanek and Co. at the Rebel 9 with only thirty-three seconds left closed the 1965 season with a 13–7 Red and Blue win. That left the Rebs with an overall record—including the bowl victory—of 7–4.

Defense was the hallmark of the 1966 squadron, which ranked third nationally against the pass and run combined. With Keyes, Urbanek and Jerry Richardson at the seams, the defensive unit yielded only forty-six points in an 8–2 regular season that gave hope of a return to the glory days. While the defense sparkled, the offense sputtered as Vaught weeded through quarterback nominees. Eventually the job went to heady Bruce Newell, a converted safety. Following shutout wins over Memphis State and Kentucky, narrow losses to Alabama and Georgia leveled off the high hopes of Reb followers. And Southern Mississippi was threatening to run the losing skein to three, as in 1965, when speedster Doug Cunningham snapped the spell with a 57-yard punt return for a touchdown and followed up with another score moments later for a 14–7 comeback win. From that point on, five opponents dropped in order. Gerald Warfield grabbed three passes against Houston, and Richardson and fellow end Bobo Uzzle tag-teamed Tennessee's Dewey Warren in a tackle-fumble-touchdown episode in Knoxville that led to a 14–7 victory and Regional Lineman honors for both.

Against Texas in the Bluebonnet Bowl, the Rebs were flat and flattened. The final score was 19–0 for

Defensive tackle Jim Urbanek, three-time All-SEC selection (1965–1966–1967).

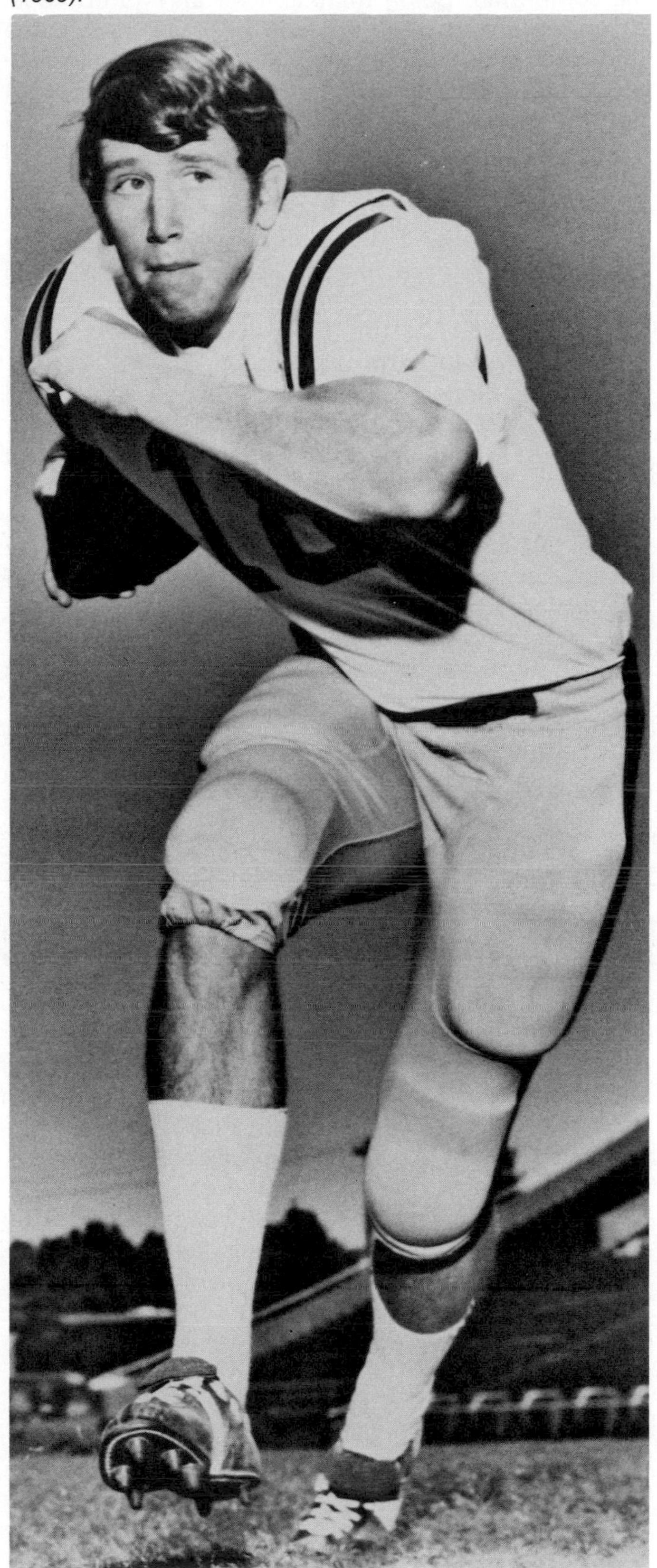
Archie Manning, Outstanding College Back in America (1969).

Bill Bradley and the 'Horns, who scored on drives of 89, 68 and 53 yards. Mississippi was hurt by four interceptions and mounted just two serious threats, the deepest thrust stalling at the Texas 8. It was a bad day even for the defense.

It was even gloomier in Memphis on September 23, 1967—on the Ole Miss side, that is. That evening Memphis State broke into the win column against the Rebs 27–17—the Tigers' first triumph in twenty-two tries. Another generation arrived on the scene, as sophomore running back Bo Bowen, son of 1947 Jacobs trophy winner Buddy Bowen, scored a touchdown the first time he touched the pigskin. Kentucky's Wildcats were tamed 26–13, but Alabama capitalized on five Reb fumbles for a 21–7 win on national television. The Rebs regrouped for a 29–20 win over unbeaten and nationally ranked Georgia, with Keyes and defensive backs Tommy James and Glenn Cannon stealing the show. But Tennessee halted OM's eight-game domination with a 20–7 win in the only other setback of the 6–3–1 regular season.

Then it was on to El Paso and the Rebels' first visit to the Sun Bowl. In their eleventh consecutive bowl game, before a packed house of some 35,000, the Rebs faced a Texas–El Paso team that was probably their toughest foe of 1967. Mac McClure's interception and run set up Newell's 1-yard sneak, making it 7–0, until UTEP hit through the air for one six-pointer and then moved in for the clincher after a Rebel bobble at their own 23, to beat the Red and Blue 14–7.

In 1968 a new kid, thin, weak-looking, and red-headed, arrived on the block. A lightly recruited prepster, Archie Manning was contacted by just three major colleges, but he would rapidly emerge as one of the school's finest players and continue the tradition of great quarterbacks as well as restore that certain something to Rebel football—pizzazz all Mississippi fans would come to know and love.

Manning's coming-out party met with an unusual delay, and Vaught was not the least bit unhappy about the postponement. The annual Red-Blue spring intrasquad game set for March 23, 1968, was canceled when sixteen inches of snow paralyzed Oxford and the campus. So in Ole Miss style, the 1968 football season kicked off in Memphis with a Peabody Hotel pep rally, ducks and all, and hours later, in Memorial Stadium in the Bluff City, Manning-mania was born.

Thirty-five sophomores and ten new offensive starters took the field against Memphis State. Manning directed the Rebs to three touchdowns in a five-minute span in the third quarter, and behind veteran linebacker Frank Trapp's fiery play, Ole Miss came out on top 21–7. Kentucky and Alabama were victims two and three, before injuries began hobbling key operators such as Manning, Trapp and Cannon. Georgia capitalized on the injuries, winning 21–7 on regional TV. Southern Mississippi was topped, but Houston proved to be too awesome and won 29–7 in Jackson. Then Archie sprang into the national limelight with Back of the Week laurels, as he accounted for a total of 362 yards in a 27–24 thriller over LSU. Many a Reb backer was headed for the exit gate at Tiger Stadium en route to New Orleans's Bourbon Street when Manning heaved a 65-yard bomb to Floyd Franks that ignited the winning rally. Two weeks later in Knoxville, Manning was intercepted six times in a 31–0 rout by Tennessee.

Ole Miss took a less-than-awesome 6–3–1 mark into the Liberty Bowl against Virginia Tech. It was Ole Miss's fifteenth bowl appearance in seventeen years. The Gobblers grabbed a 17–0 lead on an afternoon that was better designed for Eskimos than for football players. Manning hurled two scoring aerials, Steve Hindman raced 79 yards to paydirt, monsterman Robert Bailey scooted 70 yards on a pass interception, and Van Brown booted two field goals (one a 46-yarder), for a 34–17 comeback victory.

Rebel temperatures shot up in 1969. The team would not lose inside the state nor win under the lights. Just as the Magnolia State was the Rebs' playground of success, Jackson's Mississippi Memorial Stadium was their inviolate turf. Three powerhouses, all with national rankings, fell in the capital-city edifice.

The season opened on a encouraging note with a 28–3 trampling of Memphis State. But then the note began to sour, as the Rebels lost a couple of one-point games that eventually cost them a share of the Conference crown. In the first game, Kentucky capitalized on a pair of fourth-quarter fumbles, one at the Wildcats' 3, for a 10–9 upset in Lexington. The second one-point loss was harder to take—a 33–32 heartbreaker against Alabama. It was a "shoot-out" pure and simple, a combination of OK Corral, High Noon and Black Rock, as twenty-four national, SEC and team records were set. Manning and Scott Hunter thrilled the crowd with their aerial exploits, but in the end an errant extra point in the third quarter spelled the difference. Despite the loss, Manning was chosen national Back of the Week, an unheard-of honor for a losing quarterback. But then again, he had performed like a winner; it was the team that was the loser that night.

The next week Mississippi hosted Georgia at Jackson for the first time. With Manning in the dressing room undergoing treatment for an injured neck, the sixth-ranked Bulldogs held a 17–13 lead in the third quarter. But almost from the very second the Redhead returned, with seven minutes left in the third period, things began to happen. Ole Miss not only looked like a winner, but played like one as well. And when, with three minutes gone in the closing stanza, Manning engineered the Rebs' last score, OM had a come-from-behind 25–17 victory, with no small help coming from Cloyce Hinton's record-setting 59-yard field goal. After steamrolling over Southern Mississippi 69–7, the high-flying Rebels were brought down to earth by Houston, 25–11.

Then undefeated LSU, ranked number eight in the nation, traveled to Jackson. Ole Miss and Manning spotted the Bengals a 23–13 lead early in the second half, then notched two third-period touchdowns for a 26–23 lead. With 1:09 to play, LSU had fourth and 8 on the OM 23; eschewing a field goal and a tie, they put the ball in the air. But safety Glenn Cannon and linebackers Paul Dongieux and Freddie Brister foiled the "Hail Mary" go-for-all pass attempt. The 26–23 triumph became part of Ole Miss lore, as Jimmy Bryan of the *Birmingham News* reported, "On a gray, windy November day, Mississippi's one horseman rode again . . ."

Two weeks later, the opponent was third-ranked Tennessee, with its 7–0 record. The Vols were seemingly Orange Bowl–bound and possessed one of the nation's top defensive units. The Rebs were still boiling from their 31–0 defeat a year earlier in Knoxville and from a remark by UT linebacker Steve Kiner that Ole Miss had mules rather than the horses in 1969. The University was in an uproar. *The Daily Mississippian,* the student newspaper, headlined the "Big Orange Serial" all week long. Pep rallies raged nightly, and female students were given special late permission from their curfew of 10:30 P.M. to lead their own rallies. A rock group walked off the Coliseum stage after one student shouted, "Go to Hell, Tennessee!" causing one of the band members to reply, "All you people think about is football." He was right!

Finally, *The Game* arrived. The prize Big Orange defense succumbed early to the Reb rushing attack. Only two passes were thrown in the first scoring drive, which covered 83 yards. Ole Miss, amassing 392 yards in total offense, led 21–0 at the end of the first period, 24–0 at the half, 31–0 after three quarters, and won going away, with a final score of 38–0. A Sugar Bowl bid was extended and quickly accepted two days later. Against archrival Mississippi

Manning rolls out in 38–0 rout of Tennessee (1969).

State in the season finale, the Red and Blue broke a 14–14 halftime tie and went on to a resounding 48–22 victory. Manning passed for two touchdowns—one covering 58 yards to Vernon Studdard—Bowen rushed for 149 yards on nineteen trips, and Randy Reed rushed for 84 more.

In the Sugar Bowl for the eighth time, OM faced old rival Arkansas, ranked number three in the land. Mississippi forged a 24–12 halftime lead behind Manning's running and throwing, Bowen's rushing (a 69-yard touchdown gallop), and Hinton's kicking (two field goals, one a record 52-yarder). And while Manning copped the Outstanding Player award, it was Glenn Cannon who thwarted Arkansas's fourth-quarter rally. The All-American safety intercepted two passes and knocked down three passes in a row in the waning moments, preserving a 27–22 lead.

The man of the hour—or the day, the week, or even the entire year—was none other than the Drew Workhorse, Archie Manning, who not only had his "Army" of followers, but even had a record in his honor entitled "The Ballad of Archie Who." Named everybody's All-Everything in 1969, he was the beneficiary of advance publicity that had him one of the favorites for the 1970 Heisman trophy.

However, the year everyone had been anticipating never happened, even though it started like it would. With Manning clicking on seventeen of twenty-two passes and scoring two touchdowns, Ole Miss rolled over a hopelessly outclassed Memphis State team 47–13 to open the 1970 campaign. Kentucky was next, and it fell 20–17, although Manning came out of the game with a groin injury that hampered his performance for the remainder of the year. OM's third game, a nationally televised contest against Alabama, was a game the Rebs had been pointing toward for 365 days, and nights. Manning personally took charge of the Ole Miss attack, accounting for five touchdowns, and linebacker Crowell Armstrong spent the entire evening in the 'Bama backfield, as the Red and Blue turned back the Crimson Tide 48–23. The next week the streak kept building, with Georgia falling 31–21 to the combined heroics of Manning, Vernon Studdard, Jimbo Poole and Floyd Franks. It looked as though nothing could stop the Mississippi juggernaut.

But the Thursday before the Southern Mississippi game, Athletic Director Tad Smith was felled by a mild heart attack. It was a portent of things to come. Number four-ranked Mississippi was a 35-point favorite over Southern Miss, but USM spoiled the party as well as the newly installed Astroturf at Hemingway, overturning a Rebel halftime lead for a shocking 30–14 win, despite Manning's thirty completions. The plague continued. The following Tuesday night Vaught suffered an angina attack and was hos-

Manning executes one of his thirty-three completions against Alabama for an SEC record (1969).

pitalized. Then Vanderbilt was conquered in the rain in Nashville. With Houston up next, Vaught returned, but only for two days before he fell ill again. The Cougars were caged 24–13 in a tremendous victory for the Rebs, but it was a costly one. Five minutes into the third quarter, two Houston linemen hit Manning, breaking his left arm just above the wrist. Reliever Shug Chumbler fired four touchdown passes in an execution of Chattanooga, then two pass-interference calls for Mississippi State deep in Rebel territory led to a 19–14 Bulldog upset.

An Orange Bowl bid and an SEC championship all hung in the balance as the Red and Blue went out to do battle with LSU on December 5, 1970. Manning tried valiantly to play, but he just was not the same Superman(ning), with his left arm immobilized by a specially designed protective sleeve extending from shoulder to hand. Ole Miss led 7–0, then 10–7, before the Tigers ran wild, literally, running back three punt returns for touchdowns, in a 61–17 debacle.

Still, the Rebels' 1970 record of 7–3 merited a Gator Bowl invitation. The contest was an ideal matchup between Manning and Auburn's Pat Sullivan. Even with his left arm encased, Manning was still amazing, completing nineteen of twenty-eight passes before running out of gas. He and Chumbler accounted for 256 yards in a 35–28 action-packed loss, the highest-scoring donnybrook in Gator Bowl history.

In January 1971, after twenty-five years at the helm of OM's football fortunes, Vaught—holder of a 185–57–12 record, six Conference titles, and one national title—was advised by his doctors to retire from coaching. He had left the sidelines after the clobbering by Southern Mississippi midway through the 1970 campaign, with his longtime line coach, Frank M. "Bruiser" Kinard, the former All-American, taking over the coaching reins for the rest of the season.

Vaught retired with emeritus status, and Smith, who had planned to remain as director of athletics one more year, also decided to retire because of illness. The University Athletic Committee tabbed Kinard as athletic director.

The head-coaching job was offered to Billy Kinard, an assistant coach at Arkansas who had been a regular halfback for the Rebs in the mid-fifties. Billy Kinard was almost twenty years younger than his brother "Bruiser," but his desire to set Ole Miss football back on a championship course was just as strong. He now set out to accomplish his mission, relying more on discipline than on disciples.

The Rebels turned many things around, critics included, during the 1971 season. Picked in pre-season polls for the league cellar—primarily because of the loss of sixteen starters, including Manning—OM turned more than a few heads with a 9–2 finish. Injuries claimed key personnel, including Randy Reed, wingback Leon Felts, and ends Preston Carpenter and Allen LeBlanc, for extended periods. Yet with a host of youngsters, the Rebs beat Long Beach State, Memphis State and Kentucky before succumbing to Alabama and Georgia. Sophomore quarterback Kenny Lyons was leading the SEC in total offense when a shoulder injury sidelined him in the Southern Mississippi game. But his replacement, Norris Weese, was even better, guiding Ole Miss to seven straight decisions, including a 24–22 upset victory over previously unbeaten and nineteen-point favorite LSU. OM concluded its season with a forty-two-point second quarter in a 48–0 trouncing of rival Mississippi State, and immediately accepted a bid to play Georgia Tech in the Peach Bowl, for the Rebs' fifteenth consecutive bowl appearance. On a sloppy night in a steady downpour, the Red and Blue played as nearly perfect a game as was humanly possible, drubbing Tech 41–18 and ending the highest-scoring season in Mississippi history.

Ole Miss huddles before the 1971 LSU game, which they won 24–22 over the nineteen-point favorite Tigers.

The 1972 edition of the Red and Blue won its first three games. The team held South Carolina to just one first down, the same number the Gamecocks had managed the last time the two teams had played, twenty-five years before. A ten-game winning streak ended in Jackson, of all places, when Auburn

Tailback Greg Ainsworth puts a move on an LSU defender in 1971 LSU game.

Norris Weese, Ole Miss's signal-caller (1971–1973).

squeezed by the Rebs 19–13. The next week's game was also played in Jackson. The score was even closer, but the results were the same: OM lost to Georgia, 14–13. After bouncing back to beat Vandy, the Rebs took on unbeaten LSU in Tigertown. Throughout the evening Norris Weese matched All-American Bert Jones pass for pass, and the Rebs were in front 16–10, with 3:02 to go. But then Jones—and the element of time—worked against Mississippi. Jones began a drive from the Tiger 20 that took the ball to the OM 10, with but four seconds left to play. Jones took the ball and dropped back 10 yards. His pass fell incomplete across the middle. The game was over—or so it seemed to Rebel fans. But the officials ruled that one second still remained on the clock, and Jones had another opportunity. Given a new lease on life, Jones stepped back and fired the ball into the end zone for the tying touchdown, and the PAT gave LSU the game in a controversial 17–16 decision. The by now dispirited Rebels lost their next outing to Tennessee 17–0, and then salvaged what was left of the season with a 51–14 trouncing of Mississippi State for the Golden Egg and state "braggin' rights." But their 5–5 record gave OM its first nonwinning year since 1950, and a streak of fifteen consecutive bowl games was at an end.

But if 1972 was a "bummer," 1973 was worse, if that was possible. After an opening 24–6 win over Villanova—a costly victory, inasmuch as Weese was forced to leave the game in the very first quarter with torn ligaments—Missouri blanked Ole Miss 17–0. Then Memphis State scored one of its infrequent victories over OM, 17–13. That was enough for the Athletic Committee. Two days after the humiliating Memphis State loss, the University of Mississippi relieved Billy Kinard of his duties as coach after two-plus years and an overall record of 16–9, though just 6–7 in the Conference. At the same time, Bruiser Kinard was also released as athletic director.

Chancellor Porter L. Fortune, Jr., persuaded the man who personified Mississippi's great winning tradition, John Vaught, to come out of retirement and take over both positions. When the second-winningest coach in SEC history took his place on the sidelines prior to the Southern Mississippi game, the throng in Hemingway Stadium rose to its collective feet in an extemporaneous ovation some say could be heard on the square in Oxford more than a mile away. Not incidentally, his presence also inspired the Rebs to a 41–0 victory over Southern Mississippi. But the Herculean task facing Vaught was one that would have defeated a lesser man: Lyons could not shake a leg injury; Stan Bounds was hobbled by an ailing knee; Weese, hurt in the opener, did not return until the eighth game of the season; and Mississippi had yet to face seven SEC teams, four of them undefeated in overall play. In the face of all-but-insurmountable odds, Vaught led the Red and Blue to five wins in its last eight games, including 28–18 and 38–10 victories over Tennessee and Mississippi State in his final two games.

Coach Vaught returned in 1973 to add a successful postscript to the second-best coaching record in the history of the SEC.

After leading Ole Miss back to a respectable 6–5 record, on December 21, 1973 Vaught once again relinquished the coaching reins, retaining the title of athletic director. A month later, Ken Cooper, who had played for and coached at Georgia and was the Rebels' offensive line coach, was elevated to the position of head football coach.

Injuries to key players plagued the Rebs during Cooper's first year, a 3–8 season. Injuries struck veteran Lyons, talented tackles Gentle Ben Williams (OM's first black varsity member and three-time All-SEC selection) and Pete Robertson (who enjoyed an outstanding frosh season), speedy Paul Hofer, and rugged Gary Turner, the latter bowing out at a crucial point in the finale against Mississippi State. The squad also lacked depth, as evidenced by their being even through the first half in nine of the eleven games. With the scheduled opener at Tulane postponed because of Hurricane Carmen, the Red and Blue eased by eighteenth-ranked Missouri 10–0 to get things going. But Memphis State rallied in the second half for a rare win. Southern Mississippi was toppled 20–14 in the closing minutes, after a "must" 23-yard pass from Lyons to Bill Small on fourth and 22 from the Reb 36. Then the Red and Blue embarked on a seven-game losing skein that was finally broken with the 26–10 makeup-game victory over Tulane.

Quarterback Tim Ellis rolls out against Mississippi State.

Those five wins in its final six outings gave Ole Miss a 6–5 overall record and a record of 5–1 in the SEC, good for a second-place tie. Cooper was selected SEC Coach of the Year by three polls and Major College Coach of the South by another.

The 1975 season began with road losses to Baylor (20–10), Texas A & M (7–0), and Tulane (14–3). The team's "get up and go" appeared to have gotten up and gone. Southern Mississippi was whacked to slow the slide, but Alabama capitalized on countless mistakes for a 32–6 victory. The team caught its second wind the following Saturday when Cotton Bowl-bound Georgia was upset in Oxford. South Carolina momentarily quieted things with a 35–29 nailbiter in Jackson; then trimmings of Vanderbilt, Tennessee, LSU and Mississippi State put Ole Miss back on the right track to a winning season.

Hoppy Langley kicks the winning field goal in the 10–7 upset of Alabama (1976).

For a while during the 1976 season, the Rebs were fighting for the pole spot in the SEC; there was talk of a possible seventh Conference title. Ole Miss led Memphis State 13–0 before losing 21–16. Pandemonium broke loose a week later, when the Rebs clipped Alabama 10–7 and moved into the nation's top twenty. Their stock increased with two more victories. However, Auburn handled the offense with surprising ease and won 10–0 in Jackson. Underdogs against Georgia, Cooper's team came out a 21–17 winner over the eventual SEC champs, as defensive tackle Mike Pittman was chosen National Lineman of the Week. But then South Carolina applied the backbreaker, a 10–7 decision in Columbia that featured a disputed goal-line fumble in the closing seconds. The team regrouped to whip Vanderbilt, but LSU, Tennessee and Mississippi State all won going away. The 5–6 year resulted from lack of depth in critical positions and injuries to frontline personnel, including second-team All-SEC Lawrence Johnson, who was bounced from his defensive tackle slot in the first game with a bad knee; All-American nominee Gary Turner, who tore up a knee against USM; veteran Robertson who was hobbled in the game against Georgia; and Michael Sweet, the team's leading rusher, who underwent surgery after the South Carolina match.

Most pre-season polls picked the Rebels to finish no higher than eighth or ninth in the SEC in 1977. These less-than-optimistic prognoses were based on the fact that twenty-seven lettermen had been lost from the 1976 squad; Sweet had not recovered from surgery, leaving the tailback slot to inexperienced sophomores; and Danny Fischer, the pesky all-purpose punt returner and receiver, was out for the season with injuries. To make matters worse, the schedule was one of the toughest in OM's history. In short, the outlook did not exactly look bright for the Oxford eleven.

Mississippi opened with a 7–3 squeaker over Memphis State, as senior fullback James Storey rushed for over a hundred yards. But the sweet taste of victory was shortlived, as OM then faced the seemingly impossible task of getting up on successive Saturdays to meet the two leading football powerhouses in the nation—Alabama and Notre Dame. The first shoe fell when 'Bama recovered an early fumble in Rebel territory and converted it into a touchdown, going on to crush Ole Miss 34–13.

Now came the game Mississippians had been pointing to for almost six years—ever since the original announcement of a game between Ole Miss and the Fighting Irish. A crowd of 48,200, the largest ever to witness a sporting event in the state, flooded into Mississippi's Memorial Stadium, the site of the memorable scalpings of 1969 led by chief engineer Archie Manning. They hoped for more of the same, but it was a faint hope at best.

The coin toss at the start of the historic Ole Miss–Notre Dame game (1977).

Mississippi hardly played like a fourteen-point underdog against the future national champion. In fact, the Rebs played like a team possessed. Led by Bobby Garner, a gimpy-kneed junior southpaw, and veteran Tim Ellis, who had been relegated to back-up quarterbacking duties, Ole Miss took a 10–7 halftime lead into the locker room. But the Irish came storming out in the second half to capitalize on Rebel mistakes and finally go ahead on two field goals with just under five minutes left to play. Then Ellis came off the bench and piloted the Rebs 80 yards for the go-ahead touchdown, 48 of those yards coming on a pass to tight end L. Q. Smith, who tightrope-walked down the sidelines and outmaneuvered Irish defenders to take the ball deep into Notre Dame territory.

Storey, who caught Ole Miss's first touchdown pass from Garner, showed no favoritism to quarterbacks as he hauled in Ellis's decisive six-pointer with just 3:28 left. Hoppy Langley contributed his second field goal for the final three points, in the 20–13 win, and Ole Miss had an upset to rank with any in its long and glorious history. The effects of the win were staggering: Ellis and Garner were named Regional

Tight end L. Q. Smith's legendary run against top-ranked Notre Dame (1977).

Backs of the Week, defensive tackle Charlie Cage was selected as Regional Lineman, linebacker Brian Moreland was *Sports Illustrated*'s National Defensive Player, and Cooper was picked as National Coach of the Week. As the Ole Miss band harmonized in the stands long after the final whistle, former coach John Vaught, who had witnessed the classic from the Memorial Stadium press box, called the win "the greatest since the Maryland game of '52."

Either they were overconfident or just out-hustled, but in the game with Southern Mississippi the following week the Rebs lost a 19–7 halftime lead to a twenty-point third-quarter explosion, and the Notre Dame celebration was short-circuited by the 27–19 Southern Mississippi triumph. Narrow setbacks to Auburn and Georgia were suffered before a 17–10 Ellis-inspired win over South Carolina. Vanderbilt fell, and then, on regional TV, Ole Miss squandered a 21–0 lead over LSU, as the Tigers came charging back to reclaim a 28–21 win. Two weeks later, it was a different Ole Miss team that played Tennessee in Memphis, as the Rebs pounded, with 433 yards in total offense, Johnny Majors's first Vol contingent 43–14. Then, in a rainy finale, the Rebs jumped ahead of Mississippi State 14–0, only to have the Bulldogs fight back for an 18–14 victory. The final mark was another 5–6, both later changed to 6–5 when Mississippi State forfeited its victory because of an eligibility violation.

It was Cooper's most disappointing season. In the face of rising pressure, he resigned on November 30. Two days later, the school's twenty-ninth football coach was given a hero's welcome by a packed house at the athletic dormitory. The new coach was Steve Sloan, the same Steve Sloan who had so ably led Alabama to a victory over Mississippi in the 1964 Sugar Bowl game and come back to guide 'Bama to a 17–16 win over Ole Miss in the 1965 thriller.

Now Ole Miss and Steve Sloan were together on the same team. And once more Mississippi stood on the threshold of a new era, one which seemed to be coming when the 1978 team, despite a rash of injuries which saw Ole Miss lose three of its biggest offensive linemen early in the season, posted a 5–6 record, including an important 27–7 season-ending win over archrival Mississippi State.

With the steady progress that seems to be a Steve Sloan trademark, most Rebel fans feel that the day is not far away when howling, cheering students, like their fathers and grandfathers before them, will be able to celebrate an OM all-winning season in pregame pep rallies by shouting:

> "Hoddy toddy, gosh almighty,
> Who in the hell are we, hey!
> Flim flam, bim bam,
> Ole Miss, by damn!"

Coach Steve Sloan.

Mississippi State University

by Bob Hartley

Football as an intercollegiate sport made its appearance at Mississippi Agricultural and Mechanical College (now Mississippi State University) in October 1895, when W. M. Matthews, a student from Texas, organized and coached the team that on November 16 of that year represented the school in its first game of football. The game, played in Jackson, Tennessee, against Southwestern Baptist University (now Union University), resulted in a 21–0 defeat for A & M.

The student body had heard that every college had its colors; hence they requested that the football team select a suitable combination. The team considered such a task an honor, and they bestowed it upon Matthews, who holds the distinction of being the school's first football captain. On the eve of the first game, and without hesitation, Matthews chose maroon and white as the school colors.

The second—and last—game of the 1895 season was played in Memphis, Tennessee, on December 7, against the Memphis Athletic Club. Matthews's team lost again, only this time the score was closer, 16–0.

James Bell Hilderbrand, a Vanderbilt graduate, was hired the following season as the first paid coach. The student body, with some help from the townspeople, contributed money for Hilderbrand's employment.

But the addition failed to improve the team's record, as it went winless in its four-game schedule, failing to score a point for the second straight year.

Football had arrived, though, and during the 1896 season the student body viewed its first football game, when A & M played Union at the racetrack in Starkville, losing 8–0.

Because of an outbreak of yellow fever in the state in 1897, no attempt was made to field a football team; nor was any enthusiasm generated for a team in the subsequent three years. And so Mississippi A & M was without football from 1896 through 1900.

Interest was revived in the fall of 1901, when L. B. Harvey of Washington, D.C., a Georgetown grad, took charge of the football squad and coached the school's first successful team. The 1901 team won two games (the first in history, fittingly, against Ole Miss and the second over Meridian Athletic Club), lost a pair (against Tulane and Alabama), and played a scoreless tie with Christian Brothers College.

Since 1901, football has had an uninterrupted career at Mississippi State.

The 1903 team, coached by Dan Martin of Auburn, finished the season with a record of three wins and a pair of ties, and four years later Fred Furman of Cornell coached the Bulldogs to a 6–3 record, five of those victories—including a win over Ole Miss—shutouts.

W. D. Chadwick of Marietta, who later had a long and successful tenure as athletic director, followed Furman with a five-year stint, posting a winning record each year. In 1910 the record was 7–2; in 1911 it was 7–2–1; in 1913 it was 6–1–1.

E. C. "Billy" Hayes, who was to gain fame as the Indiana University track coach, served as head football coach during the 1914–16 seasons. He also met with considerable success—after 6–2 and 5–2–1

Bob Hartley has served as the sports information director of Mississippi State for the past thirty-three years and has been awarded the prestigious Arch Ward Award from the College Sports Information Directors of America and been selected for the Helms Hall of Fame for College Sports Information Directors.

seasons, his 1916 team had a break-even campaign, 4–4–1.

Stanley Robinson of Colgate, who later went on to a lengthy and productive career at Mississippi College, handled the coaching reins during the 1917–19 seasons, winning fifteen games and losing just five.

The next two seasons, 1920 and 1921, F. J. Holtkamp of Ohio State coached the Bulldogs to a 9–7–1 record.

(An historical aside: Mississippi A & M was originally a member of the Southern Intercollegiate Athletic Association [SIAA], until a number of the member schools, including A & M, withdrew from the mother organization to form the old Southern Conference.

(The formation of the Southern Conference was the result of a movement that had been brewing for several years before it came to a head in 1920. At the annual meeting of the old SIAA in Gainesville, Florida, on December 12 and 13, S. V. Sanford of the University of Georgia called together a few athletic directors and faculty athletic committee members from the larger institutions and laid plans for a second meeting, which was held in Atlanta, Georgia, on February 25 and 26. Representatives of fifteen of the state universities, colleges and technical schools in the South took part in the meeting, which gave birth to the Southern Intercollegiate Conference. [The name was later changed to the Southern Conference on December 7, 1923.])

Clark Randolph "Dudy" Noble, who served the school in every capacity in the athletic department over a span of almost half a century, coached the team during the 1922 season. Best known as baseball coach and athletic director, he was named to both the Helms Hall of Fame and the College Baseball Coaches Hall of Fame. Noble was also one of the few four-sport lettermen in the school's history (1911–15), and after graduation coached at both Ole Miss and Mississippi College. He returned to Mississippi State in 1919 and served the institution until January 15, 1959, when he retired at the age of sixty-five. During his long career, Noble had a great influence on hundreds of Mississippi State athletes and played a major role in the naming of many head coaches.

The late C. R. "Dudy" Noble, right, who served MSU for almost half a century in various capacities, with assistant athletic director Bob Hartley.

Following Noble as football coach at State was Earl C. Abell, who had been a teammate of Stanley Robinson at Colgate, where he was selected on Walter Camp's 1915 All-American team as a tackle. Abell put together winning seasons in 1923 and 1924, posting a 5–2–2 mark his first season and a 5–4 record his second, and final, year.

When Abell returned to Colgate, Minnesota grad Bernie Bierman, an assistant at Tulane, was hired to direct the football program. His 1925 team had a 3–4–1 record, and the Bulldogs enjoyed a 5–4 record in 1926, Bierman's final year in Starkville. He left to become head coach at Tulane, and took the Greenwave to the Rose Bowl in 1932 before returning to Minnesota, where he built several national championship teams during a long career with the Gophers.

John W. Hancock, an All-American at Iowa who was serving as an assistant at Colorado State, signed on to succeed Bierman. His 1927 team enjoyed a winning season, finishing 5–3. But the next two years saw the record drop to 2–4–2 and 1–5–2.

Hancock resigned in January 1930, to be succeeded as head coach by the legendary Christian (Chris) "Red" Cagle, who had just finished a brilliant collegiate career at West Point and been named All-American three times by Grantland Rice—and "Onward Christian" by the nation's sportswriters in tribute to his unerring ability to move the ball toward the enemy goal by whatever means he had at his disposal. Cagle assumed the head position at State with no previous coaching experience. Unfortunately, the magic he had demonstrated carrying the ball was not transferrable to coaching. When he resigned, with one game left to play in the 1930 season, the Bulldogs had a dismal 2–6 record on their way to a final 2–7.

Ray Dauber of Iowa, an assistant under Hancock for three seasons, coached for two seasons after Cagle departed and met with the same lack of success as his predecessor—the 1931 team ending up with a 2–6 record and the '32 team with 3–5.

Ross McKechnie came on to coach the 1933 team, State's first entry in the newly organized Southeastern Conference. State's first SEC team posted a 3–6–1 record, beating only Sewanee and tying Vanderbilt in Conference competition, and losing five intra-Conference games. The next year, McKechnie's last, State posted an imperceptibly better 4–6–0 record, but went winless in five Conference games.

Following McKechnie was the colorful Major Ralph Sasse, a former coach at Army who came to Mississippi State as Professor of Military Science and Tactics and head football coach. Sasse wasted little time in putting Mississippi State on the gridiron map.

Major Ralph Sasse, whose three Maroon teams (1935–1937) went 20–10–2 and also went to MSU's first bowl—the 1937 Orange Bowl.

His 1935 team surprised almost everyone with an 8–3 record, breaking even in four Conference games. During the season, Mississippi State gained one of its greatest football victories, a startling 13–7 upset over a previously undefeated Army team.

According to William W. Sorrels in his book *The Maroon Bulldogs:*

"State scored first, marching 77 yards behind the running of Fred Hight, Bobby Thames and Ike Pickle. With a first down on the four, Thames went outside right guard for the score. Pickle kicked it to 7–0.

"Coach Gar Davidson's Black Knights struck back in the second quarter, scoring on a 26-yard pass from Monk Meyer to Grove. Army then tied the game on Grove's kick.

"A serious Army threat in the third quarter ended when Pickle intercepted at the State 10.

"Only two minutes of the fourth quarter had elapsed before Sasse sent in his pitcher, Pee Wee Armstrong. State had the ball on its own 20. Armstrong, the passer, immediately sliced two yards off tackle. On the next play he passed 13 yards up the middle to Fred Walters, putting the ball on the State 35."

The late David Bloom of the Memphis *Commercial Appeal* wrote that the next play "provided the Maroons with the greatest victory in their athletic history." Bloom saw it this way:

"From his 35-yard line, Armstrong faded back and back. He found Walters cutting across the field to his right. Meyer, the Army safety man, was sucking in, and Walters got his hands on the ball just behind him. He juggled it for a second, gained control and started for the goal line. Meyer made a futile grab like a drowning man reaching for a straw.

"It was too late. Walters, pride of Laurel, shook himself loose and galloped across the goal line with the strides of Colossus and to the everlasting glory of the Maroons."

After the success of 1935, Mississippi State had high hopes for 1936. And with good reason, since most of the players who had whipped mighty Army were returning—Armstrong, Walters, Thames, Pickle and Hight, to name a few. Among the missing was guard Willie Stone, captain of the 1935 team. The 1936 team did not disappoint the Bulldog faithful, finishing with a 7–3–1 record, including a narrow 13–12 loss to Duquesne in the Orange Bowl, State's very first bowl appearance. The Bulldogs had a 3–2 Conference record, posting wins over Sewanee, Ole Miss and Florida, while losing to Alabama and LSU.

Despite its loss to Duquesne, State made an impressive appearance. The United Press said:

"A 55-yard pass by Boyd Brumbaugh to Ernest Hefferle in a desperate back-to-the-wall stand gave Duquesne a 13–12 win over Mississippi State today in the annual Orange Bowl football game.

"A shouting, shirt-sleeved crowd of 12,000 went wild when Brumbaugh's bull's-eye in the final period pulled the Dukes from almost certain defeat."

The back-to-back winning seasons in 1935 and 1936 were Mississippi State's best since J. W. Hancock's 1927 team went 5–3 for the campaign. And expectations for 1937, Sasse's third season, were higher than ever. At least one national publication picked Mississippi State as the top team in the nation.

After opening the season with two one-sided shutout victories, the Bulldogs lost to Texas A & M 14–0. The team never recovered, and visions of a national championship faded as the team struggled to a 5–4–1 record.

On November 9, 1937, following a 41–0 loss to LSU in Baton Rouge in the seventh game of the season, Sasse, suffering from the stress of a disappointing season, resigned. The team finished the season under assistant coaches Johnny Stokes, D. W. Aiken and Frank Carideo, beating Sewanee 12–0 and Ole Miss 9–7, before losing again to Duquesne, this time 9–0.

Sasse was gone, but his memory lived on. He had gained national recognition for Mississippi State in less than three years, and he had laid the foundation for many more good years to come.

The one-year tenure of Emerson "Spike" Nelson, however, was not such a year. Nelson had a splendid reputation as an LSU assistant coach, but his brief stay in Starkville was not successful (4–6).

The 1938 Bulldogs got off to a fine start, winning their first three games and four of the first five. Howard (now Samford University), Florida and Louisiana Tech, the trio of opening foes, did not score a point. State, meanwhile, scored a total of eighty-nine points. The final half of the season, however, was an unmitigated disaster, as the Bulldogs, plagued by player disenchantment, folded in a hurry. They lost their last five games: Tulane, LSU, Centenary, Southwestern and Ole Miss.

On February 1, 1939, following a 4–6 season that had started on such a high note, Nelson resigned. Six weeks later, after strong rumors that Dr. John "Jock" Sutherland, famed Pittsburgh coach, would be Nelson's successor, Athletic Director Noble announced the signing of Allyn McKeen to a three-year contract.

McKeen, highly recommended by Tennessee Coach Major Bob Neyland, had led West Tennessee State (now Memphis State) to a 10–0 record in 1938. His team was the highest-scoring undefeated and untied team in the nation. Some loyalists were disappointed that a "name" coach had not been selected, but the hiring of McKeen turned out to be one of the best decisions the school ever made, as the former Tennessee standout became the most successful coach in the history of Mississippi State University

Allyn McKeen, MSU coach during the Maroons' Glory Years—his ten teams lost just nineteen of eighty-seven games for a .764 record.

football. In nine seasons—1939 through 1948 (the Bulldogs did not field a team during the war year of 1943)—McKeen's teams posted an overall record of 65–19–4.

McKeen met with almost instant success. His 1939 team brought joy to thousands of Mississippi State alumni and fans with a sparkling 8–2 record. At the start of the campaign the Bulldogs were off to the races with impressive shutouts over Howard, Arkansas and Florida. Then, after losing a close 7–0 decision to Auburn, the State team bounced back with an easy win over Southwestern. Then came the only other defeat, a 7–0 setback to Alabama in Tuscaloosa. The 1939 team finished strong, closing out the campaign with victories over Birmingham, Southern, LSU, Millsaps and Ole Miss. The McKeen era was in high gear.

McKeen's 1940 team is the only undefeated team in the school's long history. The Bulldogs closed out the regular campaign with a 9–0–1 record, followed by a 14–7 Orange Bowl victory over Georgetown University. The lone blemish on the slate was a 7–7 standoff with Auburn at Legion Field in Birmingham.

The string of victories was impressive. An opening 27–7 win over Florida was followed by a 20–0 win over Southwestern Louisiana. Then came the tie with Auburn. The Bulldogs got back in the victory column with impressive wins over Howard (40–7), N.C. State (26–10), Southwestern (13–0), LSU (22–7), Millsaps (46–13), Ole Miss (19–0), and Alabama (13–0). Climaxing the nearly perfect season was the Bulldogs' second appearance in Miami's Orange Bowl.

Guard Hunter Corhern was captain of the 1940 squad, regarded by most alumni as the best team in the school's history. End Buddy Elrod became the first Mississippi State All-American and was tabbed the Southeastern Conference's Most Valuable Player in the Nashville *Banner* poll. McKeen was easily the choice as Coach of the Year.

End Buddy Elrod, Mississippi State's first All-American (1940).

The tie with Auburn cost Mississippi State a share of the Conference title, won by Tennessee with a 5–0 league record. The Vols of Bob Neyland finished the regular season with an unbeaten and untied 10–0 record. Tennessee went on to the Sugar Bowl, where they lost to Boston College.

Corhern earned second-team All-American honors and was joined by Elrod on the first-team All-SEC eleven. Tailback Harvey Johnson, another all-time great, and stalwart tackle John Tripson were named second-team All-SEC, while tailback Billy Jefferson was a third-team choice.

But many, many players on the 1940 team contributed greatly to its outstanding success. The team was closely knit and still gathers annually. Many team members were present in Jackson, Mississippi, on March 28, 1978, when Coach McKeen was inducted into the Mississippi Sports Hall of Fame.

The 1941 Mississippi State team, captained by tackle Bill Arnold, captured the school's first and only Southeastern Conference football championship. The team posted an 8–1–1 overall record, defeating Florida (6–0), Alabama (14–0) and Ole Miss (6–0) and fighting LSU to a scoreless deadlock. Non-Conference victories included wins over Union (56–7), Southeastern (20–6), Millsaps (49–6) and San Francisco (26–13). The lone blemish on the schedule was a 16–0 loss to Duquesne in the seventh game of the season.

The Bulldogs' 4–0–1 SEC record edged Tennessee's 3–1 Conference mark, the Vols' lone setback being a 9–2 loss to Alabama.

With the Conference title hinging on the outcome of the Bulldogs' game against its archrival Ole Miss, blocking back Jennings Moates scored the game's only touchdown on a 38-yard quarterback sneak, catching the Rebels by complete surprise.

Ole Miss owned wins over Tulane and LSU and had battled Georgia to a 14–14 tie. A win over Mississippi State would have given Coach Harry Mehre's Rebels the Conference crown. The loss, however, dropped Ole Miss to a fifth-place finish in the tightly bunched SEC.

A week after the Ole Miss game, the Bulldogs traveled west to defeat San Francisco 26–13. A day later, en route to Starkville, the Bulldogs were stranded in Los Angeles when Pearl Harbor was bombed by the Japanese.

J. T. "Blondy" Black, one of the best running backs in MSU history, cavorted in the 1941 backfield, along with Lamar Blount, Sonny Bruce, Walter "Bones" Craig, Wilbur Dees, Moates, Billy "Spook" Murphy, Hillard Thorpe, Collins Wohner, Charley

Yancey and Claiborne Bishop. Indeed, there was no lack of backfield talent.

The 1942 team, which McKeen always felt "was one of our best teams," completed the campaign with an 8–2 record, after losing two early-season games to Alabama and LSU without the services of the injured Black.

Bulldog victims included Union University, Vanderbilt, Florida, Auburn, Tulane, Duquesne, Ole Miss and San Francisco. It was against Duquesne that Black faked a punt deep in his own end zone and ran 107 yards for a touchdown.

1943 was a war year, and only five SEC teams fielded football squads. State was not one of the five. And so the team McKeen felt could have been one of the great ones was called on account of the war. By 1944, even though the war was still very much in progress, all twelve SEC schools had teams back on the field.

A freshman tailback from Meridian, Mississippi, by the name of Thomas E. "Shorty" McWilliams ran rampant for the Bulldogs in 1944, leading them to a successful, albeit abbreviated, 6–2 season. State finished fifth in the Conference with a 3–2 record, with Georgia Tech taking top laurels with a 4–0–0 mark. Tennessee had five SEC wins, but a scoreless deadlock with Alabama cost the Vols the title.

All-American tailback Tom "Shorty" McWilliams, SEC Most Valuable Player (1944).

McWilliams earned first-team All-SEC recognition and was named to the second-team All-American squad. Shortly after the close of the season, Shorty received an appointment to West Point, and in 1945 played in the Army backfield with Blanchard, Davis and Tucker.

The 1945 team, minus McWilliams, had a brand-new star in freshman tailback Harper Davis, a Clarksdale native who had gained attention while playing for a Navy service team on the West Coast. End Bill Hildebrand, who later became head coach at Wake Forest, was captain of the 1945 team, which wound up with a 6–3 record.

With many players returning from military service, the 1946 team, captained by Billy "Spook" Murphy—now athletic director at Memphis State after a long career as the Tigers' head coach—won eight games, losing only to LSU and Alabama. The 1946 team scored a 3–2 Conference record by defeating Auburn, Tulane and Ole Miss, good enough for a fifth-place finish in the Conference.

At the close of the 1946 season, Bowden Wyatt, a member of McKeen's staff since 1939 (with time out for Naval duty during the war), departed to take over the head-coaching post at Wyoming. Wyoming President Dr. George Duke Humphrey, who had been president at Mississippi State when McKeen was first hired, quickly decided that Wyatt, the former Tennessee All-American end, was the person needed to direct the Cowboy football program. Wyatt later accepted the coaching berth at Arkansas before returning to his alma mater, Tennessee.

W. D. "Dub" Garrett, an All-Conference tackle, captained the 1947 Mississippi State team to a 7–3 record. The Bulldogs finished fourth in the SEC, dividing four games: they won over Tulane and Auburn, but lost to LSU and Ole Miss.

When the 1948 Mississippi State team could do no better than a break-even season, finishing 4–4–1 overall and 3–3 in the SEC, the McKeen era came to an end. The three remaining years of McKeen's contract were bought up by the school. Yet McKeen never had a losing season and still remains the school's winningest football coach.

Dudy Noble began his search for a successor to McKeen. It was not long before Bernie Moore, who had only recently become SEC Commissioner after a lengthy period as LSU coach, recommended his former aide Arthur "Slick" Morton. Morton, an ex–LSU great born in Louisiana but raised as an

Arthur "Slick" Morton, MSU head coach from 1949 through 1951.

orphan at French Camp Academy in Mississippi, had just completed his second season as head coach at Virginia Military Institute. Before taking over the head position at VMI, he had installed the revolutionary T-formation for Moore at LSU, after studying its implementation at Cornell.

In three seasons Morton's teams compiled an 8–18–1 record. His first team, in 1949, failed to win a game, losing eight and salvaging what remained of the season by tying Clemson 7–7. The captain of Morton's winless first team was Jim Pittman, who later became head coach at Tulane after long service as Darrell Royal's assistant at Texas. Pittman was head coach at TCU when he died on the sidelines during a game against Baylor.

Morton's 1950 team had nowhere to go but up. And that's what, winning four games and losing five. One of those victories was a tremendous 7–0 upset of nationally ranked Tennessee at Scott Field; halfback Tom "Dutch" Rushing scored the game's lone touchdown. A loss to State was Tennessee's only blemish on an otherwise spotless slate, and the mighty Vols went on to beat Texas in the Cotton Bowl and finish the season as the number three–ranked team in the country. Another of the four wins was a 13–7 triumph over LSU, as Frank "Twig" Branch, a mighty mite of a quarterback—weighing in at all of

The late Jim Pittman, former Bulldog captain who served as an assistant coach at MSU and head coach at Tulane and TCU.

126 pounds, soaking wet—directed the Bulldogs to an upset win over Coach Morton's alma mater in Baton Rouge.

The 1951 team compiled the same record as the 1950 team: 4–5. The wins included important victories over Georgia and Tulane. Bill Stewart, a stocky fullback, later to become a casualty in the Korean War, was elected captain of the 1951 team at the end of the season.

Alumni and Bulldog fans were restless, and Morton decided to resign, declining an opportunity to remain as coach for at least one more season. While Morton's MSU coaching career was not successful by won-lost standards, he is remembered as the originator of the Mississippi High School all-star football game (1950). After Morton's resignation, sponsorship of the game was taken over by the Jackson Touchdown Club.

Noble did not waste any time in choosing a successor to Morton. He placed a quick call to West

Head coach Murray Warmath (1952 and 1953).

Point, and Murray Warmath, a top aide on Colonel Red Blaik's Army staff, quickly accepted the offer to coach the Bulldogs.

Warmath, formerly a standout lineman at Tennessee, was, along with Bowden Wyatt, one of the original members of McKeen's first MSU staff. Warmath and Noble had built a lasting friendship, and so for Warmath coming to MSU was like coming home.

A bruising two-way fullback by the name of Joe Fortunato, a Mingo Junction, Ohio, native who had transferred to State from VMI, teamed with a junior college quarterback, Jackie Parker, to make the Warmath years memorable for Mississippi State supporters. Parker, a native of Knoxville, Tennessee, had played for another Knoxvillian, Paul Davis, at Jones Junior College in Ellisville and was heavily recruited by Warmath aides Spooky Murphy and Jim Pittman.

As his quarterback coach, Warmath brought in young Darrell Royal, a former Oklahoma All-American. Royal's magic immediately began to rub off on Parker, who had played tailback at Jones.

The 1952 edition of the Bulldogs, however, did not exactly set the world on fire, compiling a 5–4 record. The Bulldogs whipped Arkansas State, North Texas State, Kentucky, Auburn and LSU, but lack of depth and a porous defense contributed heavily to losses to Tennessee, Alabama, Tulane and Ole Miss. The Bulldogs put 225 points on the scoreboard, but they gave up almost as many—186.

One of the more memorable games in Warmath's first season was the 49–34 win over Auburn at Auburn's Cliff Hare Stadium. It was Auburn's second season under the legendary Ralph "Shug" Jordan.

Parker, the blond bomber from Knoxville, ran for three touchdowns, passed for three more, set up the other Bulldog touchdown, and kicked six extra points (the other "conversion" came on a fumbled snap from center, which was picked up by Bobby Collins and passed for the extra point).

In the final game of the season, Parker scored all fourteen State points in a 20–14 loss to Ole Miss,

All-SEC fullback Joe Fortunato (1951).

Hall of Famer Jackie Parker, holder of the SEC record for most points scored in a single season and twice SEC Most Valuable Player (1952 and 1953).

boosting his season's point total to 120 points, a record that still stands in the Southeastern Conference. The 1952 team scored every time it had the football inside the opponents' 20-yard line, a record that is a credit to Parker and Fortunato, the backfield mainstays. Both players earned All-American laurels. Fortunato graduated after the 1952 season and began a long career as defensive captain for the Chicago Bears. And Darrell Royal departed for Canada to become coach of the Edmonton Eskimos.

In 1953, without Fortunato, the Bulldogs enjoyed a 5–2–3 record, losing only to Kentucky and Texas Tech, while defeating Memphis State, Tennessee, North Texas State, Tulane and LSU. The team played Auburn, Alabama and Ole Miss to standoffs. The 21–21 tie with Auburn is unforgettable, as the Bulldogs led 21–0 at the start of the second half, only to see Auburn earn a tie as the final whistle blew.

Parker, inducted into the National Football Hall of Fame in 1976, was the Nashville *Banner* choice for SEC Player of the Year in both 1952 and 1953. He was one of only four players to win the honor twice; the others were Tennessee's John Majors, LSU's Billy Cannon and Auburn's Pat Sullivan.

The popular Warmath shocked Bulldog fans when, following the 1953 season, he accepted the head-coaching post at Minnesota. While Dudy Noble hated to see Warmath depart, he was not worried about conducting a lengthy search for a successor. He had the right man in mind, and all it took was a telephone call to Darrell Royal in Edmonton, Canada. Royal had always wanted to coach a major college team, and he jumped at the chance to return to Starkville. The official announcement of his selection was made on February 1, 1954.

Darrell Royal, MSU head coach (1954 and 1955).

Jackie Parker was gone, but the Bulldogs still had some outstanding football talent. Bobby Collins, Parker's understudy at quarterback (now head coach at Southern Mississippi), was the captain of Royal's first college team. And there were other outstanding players, including Billy Dooley (now head coach at Virginia Tech), Hal Easterwood, Scott Suber, Ron Bennett, Art Davis, Charles "Dinky" Evans, Billy Fulton, Jim Barron, Bill Stanton, William Earl Morgan, Jim Harness, Levaine Hollingshead and George Suda, just to name a few.

Easterwood, Suber and Davis went on to earn All-American honors. Davis, a brother of Harper Davis, who had played under McKeen, was the Nashville *Banner's* Southeastern Conference Most Valuable

All-American halfback Art Davis receives the Nashville Banner *award as SEC Most Valuable Player from* Banner *publisher E. B. Stahlman (1955).*

Player of the Year in 1954. He was the fourth Mississippi State player to win the award since Buddy Elrod first won it in 1940.

The 1954 team won four of its first six games and went on to a 6–4 campaign record, highlighted by victories over Alabama and LSU. Davis ran wild against the Tigers in Baton Rouge, scoring all four Bulldog touchdowns in a 25–0 win.

Hal Easterwood, All-American center (1955).

The 1955 team, co-captained by Barron and Bennett, won six consecutive games after an opening 20–14 loss to Florida. The Bulldogs then dropped a heartbreaker to Auburn, 27–26, and lost the last two games to LSU and Ole Miss.

After compiling a 12–8 record in two years, Royal resigned to accept the top post at the University of Washington, where he remained for one season before moving on to Texas and lasting fame. The coaching reins were handed to Wade Walker, a member of Royal's staff and a former All-American tackle at Oklahoma.

Walker, now athletic director at Oklahoma, will never forget his first game as head coach. The Bulldogs opened the 1956 campaign at home against Florida, and Gator defensive back Joe Brodsky intercepted four passes, running one of them back 100 yards, for a 26–0 Florida victory. Quarterback Billy Stacy, who had his baptism in the SEC that afternoon, went on to earn All-SEC honors and All-American laurels during an outstanding career.

All-American quarterback Billy Stacy (1957).

Victories over Georgia and LSU highlighted Walker's 4–6 first season. The Bulldogs dropped a one-point verdict to Alabama, 13–12, and lost by a touchdown to both Tulane and Auburn.

Walker had one winning season and one break-even campaign during his six-year stint as head coach. His 1957 team, his second at State, went 6–2–1, losing to Tennessee by five points, to Auburn by eight, and tying Ole Miss in the final game, 7–7.

The Bulldogs had wins over Memphis State, Arkansas State, Florida, Alabama, Tulane and LSU. Walker was named SEC Coach of the Year, but the Bulldogs were disappointed when they did not receive a bowl invitation.

The outlook for 1958 was bullish, with several national publications predicting a lofty finish for the Bulldogs. *Look* magazine went so far as to predict a third-place national finish.

The team started on the right track, beating Florida 14–7. After losing a narrow decision to Tennessee, MSU beat Memphis State and Arkansas State handily. But the Bulldogs would not win another game for the rest of the season, losing the remaining five Conference games, to finish 3–6.

All-American center Tom Goode (1960).

Over the course of the next two seasons, the Bulldogs won just four games, while losing thirteen and tying one. In 1961 the Bulldogs broke even in ten games. But after six years and an overall record of 22–32–2, Walker's coaching career was over.

He continued as athletic director, a post he had assumed when Noble retired in 1959. Paul Davis, Walker's top assistant in 1961, assumed the head-coaching role, and he led the Bulldogs to a 3–6 record his first season, with wins over Tennessee, Tulane and Houston—all in the first four games.

Picked to finish ninth in the Conference, the Bulldogs were the Cinderella team of 1963, finishing fourth in the SEC with a 4–1–2 mark and an overall record of 6–2–2. Like Walker before him, Davis was the SEC Coach of the Year in his second season.

Paul Davis, head coach 1961 through 1966.

Some of the stars on that great State team included quarterback Sonny Fisher, halfback Ode Burrell, tackle Tommy Neville, guards Pat Watson and Justin Canale, and fullback Hoyle Granger.

In one of the most memorable games of that campaign, the Bulldogs whipped sixth-ranked Auburn 13–10 in Jackson. The game turned on an intercep-

Two of the unsung stars of the 1963 Cinderella Team —guard Pat Watson and tackle Tommy Neville.

tion of an errant Jimmy Sidle pass by Fisher, who played both ways, to set up a game-winning 36-yard field goal by Canale in the closing seconds.

State went on to cap one of its most successful seasons in years by accepting an invitation to play Atlantic Coast Conference co-champion North Carolina State in the Liberty Bowl—the last Liberty Bowl game to be played in Philadelphia.

The game itself was an extension of State's exciting year, as end Bill McGuire blocked a North Carolina State punt and Tommy Inman picked up the rolling ball at the 11 and dashed into the end zone for a Bulldog touchdown in the first quarter. Later in the opening stanza, Fisher faked a hand-off and took it across from the 3-yard line for State's second touchdown. Canale missed one of his two conversions, but made up for it with a 43-yard field goal into the wind, to give State a hard-fought 16–12 victory.

Burrell, one of the most exciting runners in MSU history, was selected as the game's Outstanding Player. Watson, now an assistant coach at Virginia Tech, was selected as the Outstanding Lineman.

Ode Burrell, second-team All-SEC and Outstanding Player in the Liberty Bowl (1963).

Hopes were high again as the team looked forward to the 1964 season. But success was denied the Bulldogs until the final game, the annual Golden Egg classic against Ole Miss. The game, played on a bitter cold day, was seen on national television, and the Bulldogs came up with a big 20–17 upset victory over Ole Miss.

It was State's first win over the Rebels since 1946, though the rivals had played three tie games in the intervening years: 7–7 in 1953 and 1957, and 10–10 in 1963. The final record for 1964 was just 4–6, with the Bulldogs finishing eighth in the SEC with a 2–5 mark.

The big win over Ole Miss in the final game left Bulldog spirits high; some State fans even envisioned a bowl bid in 1965. Indeed, the 1965 season started with a bang, with impressive wins over Houston, Florida, Tampa and Southern Mississippi. After four games, the national polls had State ranked in the top ten.

Students quickly coined a slogan: "Catch Us if You Can." The dam burst, however, when Memphis State, led by Billy Fletcher, caught and "whupped" the Bulldogs to the tune of 33–13.

The season was over except for the shouting. Beginning with the Memphis State contest, the Bulldogs lost the final six games of the season, compiling a 4–6 record and sharing the SEC cellar with Vanderbilt and Tulane, all three having identical 1–5 Conference records.

The end of the Paul Davis regime was at hand. Davis, regarded as an outstanding defensive coach, was relieved by President William L. Giles after the 1966 team posted a 2–8 record, again tying Vanderbilt for the SEC cellar. Wade Walker, the athletic director, was also relieved on December 10, 1966, which was also the signing date for SEC football scholarships.

After Bill Dooley turned down the head-coaching job, the combination assignment of head coach and athletic director was offered to Charley Shira, longtime Darrell Royal aide. Shira had played at Texas A & M and West Point and had been an assistant under both Royal and Walker during two previous coaching tenures at Mississippi State. He was with Royal in Canada in 1953, after first coming to State as a graduate assistant under Warmath in 1952. He returned to MSU when Royal took the head job in 1954, and stayed under Walker in 1956 when Royal went to the University of Washington. When Darrell accepted the Texas post in 1957, Shira accompanied him to Austin.

Shira, upon accepting the job at MSU, said: "I'm

Charley Shira, head coach 1967 through 1972.

approaching this thing with the idea that hard work will get the job done." Indeed, he was dedicated and a hard worker, but getting the job done was a monumental task, as he would soon discover.

His first team, the 1967 edition, won only one game—a 7–3 win over Texas Tech—and lost nine. In six years, Shira's teams won sixteen, lost forty-five and tied two.

For some reason, though, the tall, quiet Texan had Tech's number. During Shira's coaching tenure, the Bulldogs whipped Texas Tech three times and played to a 28–28 tie.

The Bulldogs failed to win a game in 1968, losing eight and tying two. In addition to tying Texas Tech, State gained a satisfying 17–17 standoff with archrival Ole Miss in the last game of the season.

The 1969 Mississippi State team won three games and lost seven. But two of the losses—to Houston and LSU—were by the embarrassing scores of 74–0 and 61–6.

State's only winning campaign under Shira came in 1970, when the Bulldogs finished with a 6–5 record. For his achievement in turning the team around, Shira was named by the Associated Press as SEC Coach of the Year. Two of State's wins were by one point: 14–13 over Oklahoma State and 7–6 over Georgia. And good ole Texas Tech fell by a score of 20–16. The other victims were Vanderbilt, Southern Missisippi and archrival Ole Miss. Against Ole Miss, MSU was led by Joe Reed, who had taken over the quarterbacking reins from Tommy Pharr, the Bulldogs' total offense leader the previous three seasons.

Quarterback Tommy Pharr, who holds most of the MSU passing records.

During the Shira era, the Bulldogs had two of the league's top pass receivers in Sammy Milner and David Smith. Milner led the SEC in 1968 with 64 receptions, while Smith set a school record and also led the SEC in 1970 with 74 receptions for 987 yards and 6 touchdowns.

The Bulldogs found the going tough in 1971, dropping to a 2–9 record. The Shira regime came to an end the following year, when the Bulldogs compiled a 4–7 mark.

All-American linebacker D. D. Lewis (1967).

One of the best players to perform at State under Shira was linebacker D. D. Lewis, currently a veteran member of the Dallas Cowboys. Despite State's 4–7 record, Lewis became an All-American. It was also during the Shira era that State recruited its first black football players, halfback Frank Dowsing of Tupelo and tackle Robert Bell of Meridian, both freshmen in 1969.

After retiring as head coach, Shira remained as athletic director until his untimely death in January 1976. He turned the coaching chores over to Bob Tyler, who had come from Bear Bryant's staff at Alabama and was Shira's offensive coordinator in 1972.

Tyler had gained a reputation as a miracle worker as a result of his phenomenal high school coaching record of ninety-one wins, nineteen losses and six ties, a winning percentage of .810 over an eleven-year span. He was what the doctor ordered for an ailing football program.

His record in his first season, 1973, was 4–5–2, with victories over Vanderbilt, Florida, Florida State and Louisville. The Bulldogs opened with a 21–21 tie against Northeast Louisiana and later fought Southern Mississippi to a 10–10 standoff. The Tyler era was under way; it was one that would soon pay big dividends.

A native of Water Valley, Mississippi, the soft-spoken Tyler was known for his motivation, organ-

Mississippi State head coach Bob Tyler.

izational ability and teaching expertise. He was the school's twenty-seventh head football coach and only the second native Mississippian to serve in this capacity.

In just five seasons at the helm of the Bulldogs, Tyler became the school's second-winningest coach. Only Allyn McKeen fashioned a better record, and McKeen was at the throttle of nine MSU teams.

Evidence of Tyler's coaching magic was seen in 1974, when he led the Bulldogs to an 8–3 regular-season record, followed by a 26–24 Sun Bowl victory over North Carolina. Mind you, this was with just two years to rebuild MSU gridiron fortunes.

The Bulldogs, with All-Southeastern Conference quarterback Rockey Felker at the controls, thrashed William and Mary 49–7 in the opening game, then soundly whipped Georgia. After losing to Florida, State bounced back with consecutive victories over Kansas State, Lamar, Memphis State and Louisville, then lost to Alabama and Auburn.

In a real offensive thriller against Auburn, MSU came ever so close, finally losing 24–20. But the Sun

Coach Bob Tyler with two of the standouts on MSU's 1974 Sun Bowl team: quarterback Rockey Felker (number 18) and tackle Jimmy Webb, both All-SEC members.

Bowl invitation was wrapped up, and the Bulldogs made the El Paso bowl officials look good with closing wins over LSU and Ole Miss.

But the one game that had the most bearing on the 1974 team's success was played in Memphis Memorial Stadium on Saturday night, October 19, 1974. Although the win over Army under Sasse in 1935 may have brought the school more national attention, the 29–28 win over Memphis State has to be remembered as the most exciting game ever played by a Mississippi State football team.

With 3:06 remaining, Mississippi State was backed up to its own 2-yard line as a result of a booming Tiger punt. The game seemed safely tucked away for Memphis, with State down 21–28 and 98 yards away from paydirt.

The Bulldogs had moved the ball well all night, piling up 418 yards total offense. But seven fumbles, five of them recovered by Memphis State, had given the lead to the fired-up home club.

To the surprise of 38,557 spectators, Felker directed his never-give-up Bulldogs 98 yards in thirteen plays, to move within a point of the Tigers, 28–27. Stan Black, a wide receiver in 1974 and later one of the best defensive backs ever to perform for Mississippi State; Walter Packer, the school's all-time ground gainer; Dennis Johnson; Terry Vitrano; and Melvin Barkum all contributed key plays in the final scoring drive. Johnson scored the important touchdown, but it was Felker's score on the two-point conversion that provided State with the most thrilling victory in its football history.

In his book *The Maroon Bulldogs,* Sorrels reports that Tyler later told him: "That game in Memphis meant as much to our program as anything else that has happened. It sealed down the possibilities in the minds of the players.

"They had seen at work some of the real mental plus. They realize that if you keep on, good things will happen."

After the comeback win over Memphis State, the Bulldogs encountered few problems in winning three of their final five games, losing only to Alabama and the squeaker to Auburn. The Sun Bowl win over North Carolina followed much the same pattern as the Memphis State game. The winning margin was two points this time, as State beat the Tarheels 26–24.

Freshman halfback Terry Vitrano was voted the Sun Bowl's Outstanding Player, edging teammate Walter Packer, who had 183 yards rushing, a Sun Bowl record. Vitrano rushed for 164 yards against

Walter Packer, MSU's all-time rushing leader.

North Carolina. Jimmy Webb, one of the best defensive tackles in MSU history and now a standout with the San Francisco 49ers, was the Sun Bowl's Outstanding Defensive Player.

In 1975, when the school began a two-year probation for recruiting irregularities, the Bulldogs finished with a 6–4–1 record. After an opening win over Memphis State, the team lost on successive weekends to Georgia and Florida before bouncing back with consecutive wins over Southern Mississippi, Rice, North Texas State, and Louisville. Following a 21–10 loss to Alabama, the Bulldogs fought Auburn to a 21–21 standoff and beat LSU 16–6 before losing the final game to Ole Miss. Packer, MSU's career rushing leader with 2820 yards, led the 1975 Bulldogs with 1012 yards. Wayne Jones, fullback on Tyler's first team in 1973, is the all-time single-season MSU rushing leader with 1193 yards.

Tyler became only the second Mississippi State coach to win nine games in a season when his 1976 Bulldog team went 9–2, the best record for an MSU team since Allyn McKeen's 1940 team went 9–0–1 in the regular season and then beat Georgetown in the Orange Bowl.

The only losses in 1976 were to Florida in a high-scoring affair, 34–30, and to Alabama, 34–17. Bulldog victims included North Texas State, Louisville, Cal Poly, Kentucky, Memphis State, Southern Mississippi, Auburn, LSU and Ole Miss.

Both the 1974 and the 1976 teams were ranked among the nation's top twenty, but the successful 1976 team was denied a bowl invitation because the school was finishing its probation period.

After the 1976 season, center Richard Keys earned All-SEC laurels for the second straight year, while three members of the defensive team, Stan Black, Harvey Hull and Ray Costict, were selected for the All-Conference team. Costict was chosen by UPI as the SEC Defensive Player of the Year.

The Bulldogs launched the 1977 campaign with a hard-earned triumph over rugged North Texas State, then scored one of their most impressive victories, a 27–18 win over future Rose Bowl champion Washington. The Bulldogs lost in the closing seconds to Florida, 24–22, in a game seen on regional television, and then came back in the final minute to defeat Kansas State, 24–21, in one of the most physical games ever played by an MSU team. Injuries to key players dealt a blow to the Bulldogs' chances for a winning season. Following the win over Kansas State, the Bulldogs dropped four consecutive games, losing to Kentucky, Memphis State, Southern Mississippi and Alabama.

The week of the Kentucky game Tyler decided to discard the Wishbone offense and install the pro-set. While the score of the Alabama game was not close, 37–7, the Bulldogs consistently moved the ball. The switch in offense paid off with a pair of important victories over Auburn and Ole Miss. And LSU had to kick a field goal in the closing minutes to escape with a 27–24 victory.

Bruce Threadgill, who took over at quarterback following the graduation of Rockey Felker, piloted the 1975, 1976 and 1977 teams, while Dennis Johnson, James Jones and Len Copeland served as key running backs. State unveiled a pair of excellent freshmen pass receivers: Mardye McDole, who led the team with 29 receptions for 510 yards and 2 touchdowns; and Breck Tyler, son of the coach, who caught 11 for 22 yards, despite being handicapped part of the season with an injured foot.

Quarterback Bruce Threadgill, who holds the Bulldog record for consecutive passes without an interception (fifty-one in 1975).

But just when it appeared that Bob Tyler's "Let's-Win-Something-Today" philosophy of winning had taken hold and that Mississippi State had come all the way back to where their athletic facilities were equal to those of any other school in the Conference, something happened.

To understand that "something," you have to go back to September 17, 1975, when Mississippi State was slapped by the NCAA with a two-year probation for violations in the conduct of its intercollegiate football program. The two-year probation not only included sanctions that prevented the football team from participating in post-season competition—such as preventing the 1976 Bulldog team, which finished with the most regular season wins for an MSU team since 1940, from going to a bowl—but also from appearing on any NCAA-televised event.

But that wasn't the end of it. Mississippi State was further penalized by the NCAA for allowing an athlete to play after its Committee on Infractions found that he had been provided with clothing at a discount, a discount now allowed regular students.

On the motion of Mississippi State, a Mississippi chancery court granted a restraining order permitting the athlete to play during the 1975, 1976, and 1977 seasons. However, the NCAA later won an appeal in the Mississippi Supreme Court overturning the chancery court decision, and applied section 10 of the NCAA enforcement code, which held that any schools which used athletes under court orders, which orders are eventually overturned, are liable to

Dave Marler, Mississippi State's 1978 All-SEC quarterback.

punishment. The "other shoe" came during its April 1978 meeting, when the NCAA council ruled that the NCAA enforcement program should be enforced against Mississippi State and that the Bulldogs should forfeit nineteen games—eighteen wins and one tie—during the three years in question.

Then, after a so-so year in 1978 despite the incredible efforts of quarterback Dave Marler and end Mardye McDole—both of whom led the SEC—Bob Tyler resigned as football coach, ending an era filled with enthusiasm, effort and controversy.

One week later Carl Maddox, who had just retired as LSU athletic director, was named MSU athletic director and promptly named Emory Bellard, former Texas A & M coach, as the Bulldogs' twenty-eighth head football coach.

Bellard, known as "The Father of the Wishbone Offense," compiled a six-year-plus record at Texas A & M of forty-eight victories and twenty-seven losses, including three bowl appearances and a share of the Southwest Conference title.

With forty-eight lettermen returning from the 1978 team which beat fourteenth-ranked LSU and sixteenth-ranked Florida State, Bulldog partisans have begun looking toward the future again, believing that the best years in MSU football are here now, and that the future looms even brighter!

MSU's new head coach, Emory Bellard, "Father of the Wishbone Offense."

The Bulldogs have arrived!

University of Tennessee

by Haywood Harris

When Johnny comes marching home again . . .

The movie projection room at Stokely Athletic Center, headquarters of the University of Tennessee Athletic Department, was jammed to capacity for the Saturday afternoon press conference. A guard was posted outside by the Sports Information Office to make sure only newsmen and a few invited guests entered. A total of one hundred twenty-one reporters, photographers and television technicians squeezed inside the room to record the historic moment when Johnny Majors assumed command of his alma mater's football program.

And so Saturday, December 4, 1976, was an "Orange"-letter day in Knoxville, Tennessee—and wherever Big Orange fans congregated. Novelty entrepreneurs quickly put their handiwork on display: "Johnny Comes Marching Home" T-shirts, together with "Back Johnny" bumper stickers, sold at a fast clip along the Strip, a five-block area of Cumberland Avenue adjacent to the campus.

One of the worst-kept secrets in the annals of sports history had become official the day before—Johnny Majors, an All-American two decades earlier, a dazzling triple-threat tailback who had led Tennessee to its last undefeated season, was returning now to lead again, this time in the capacity of head coach. The decline of the Volunteers over the previous four years dictated the move. The Big Orange—or, as it had been referred to derisively of late, the Little Orange—had indeed come upon hard times. From the dizzying heights of an 11–1 record in Bill Battle's first year as head coach in 1970, Tennessee had steadily drifted downhill: 10–2 in 1971, 10–2 in 1972, 8–4 in 1973, 7–3–2 in 1974, 7–5 in 1975, and 6–5 in 1976.

Tennessee fans, probably neither more nor less impatient than their counterparts at other schools that pride themselves on strong football programs, were discouraged by the downward spiral. A note in

Haywood Harris has been sports information director at the University of Tennessee since 1961 and twice has served as president of the Southeastern Conference Publicity Directors Association.

Coach Johnny Majors, Tennessee's nineteenth head football coach.

Sports Illustrated's Scorecard section in 1975 illustrated the decline in Tennessee's football fortunes by asking, in reference to a recently completed study by the NCAA: Guess which school is number one for the past fifty years. Notre Dame? Alabama? Southern California? Ohio State? Give up? Well, Tennessee, that's who.

At the end of the 1976 season an embattled Bill Battle had seen the handwriting on the wall, and Johnny Majors was summoned to take his place. It was a scenario that many people affiliated with Tennessee, Battle included, had believed was inevitable for a long time. John Terrill Majors, legendary Volunteer hero of 1956, became the nineteenth head football coach at the University of Tennessee, after turning around weak football programs at Iowa State and Pittsburgh. He turned Pittsburgh's around so completely that in 1976 the Panthers were proclaimed national champions and Majors Coach of the Year.

Battle resigned on Monday, November 22, two days after the Vols lost to Kentucky for the first time since 1964. Athletic Director Bob Woodruff met with Majors the following Sunday, and the announcement that Majors had accepted the Tennessee head-coaching job was made on Friday, December 3. Majors's mission was plain: restore Tennessee football to the heights that had earned it recognition as the nation's winningest team over the past half-century.

Such prominence, however, did not come early or easily. Before the advent of Bob Neyland, national fame was reserved for a select few, such as the Ivy League schools, Michigan, and, closer to home, Vanderbilt and Sewanee. Tennessee's start to the top was, at best, a tentative one, beginning with a 24–0 loss to Sewanee in its only game in 1891. However, the school did make one concrete contribution to future teams with its adoption in that inaugural year of the school colors orange and white, the colors of the common American daisy that grew in profusion on The Hill. But colors or no, the football program was doomed to early failure because of the absence of a full-time coach. As an example of how the Volunteers floundered early on, consider the 1893 season: the Vols suffered consecutive losses of 56–0 to Kentucky A & M, 64–0 to Wake Forest, 70–0 to Duke, and 60–0 to North Carolina. UT had a long way to go to achieve gridiron glory. And it could only go up!

But there were some bright moments along the tortuous path to the top. The 1907 team featured Hall-of-Fame guard Nathan "Nate" Dougherty, who later played a leading role in the formation of the Southeastern Conference and was a prominent figure in Tennessee athletics until his death in 1977. Dougherty and his 1907 teammates posted a 7–2–1 record, to become the first outstanding Vol club.

The 1914 team may have been one of the nation's best, even though there were no wire service polls in those days to substantiate the claim. Coached by Zora G. Clevenger, the Vols had their first banner year, fashioning a 9–0 record, including a 16–14

All-Southern guard Nathan W. Dougherty (1907–1908), later head of the UT Athletics Committee, president of the old Southern Conference and Founding Father of the SEC.

Undefeated 1914 team, SIAA champions and first UT team to beat Vanderbilt.

triumph over Dan McGugin's Vanderbilt Commodores. Tennessee captured the Southern Intercollegiate Athletic Association championship for the first title of any kind in the school's history. The win over Vanderbilt was celebrated by cancellation of classes for a day, leading the chancellor of Vandy to charge Tennessee with overemphasis of athletics and underemphasis of academics.

Another bright spot in those early years was the 1916 club, which had a shot at a tie with Georgia Tech for the SIAA crown but was denied a share of the title after a scoreless tie with Kentucky in a final game. That season the team finished with a sparkling 8–0–1 record. The season was also noteworthy in that Georgia Tech, which edged out Tennessee for the SIAA championship that year, set an all-time single-game scoring record with a 222–0 win over little Cumberland College.

The Vols had several good early years: they were 7–2 in 1920, 6–2–1 in 1921, and 8–2 in 1922. A significant development in the 1922 season was the introduction of orange jerseys on the backs of formerly black-clad Tennessee players. The change was the innovation of team captain Roy "Pap" Striegel, who, like Dougherty, played a prominent role in Tennessee athletics for half a century.

The state of Tennessee football in the pre-Neyland days can be demonstrated by the fact that Coach John R. Bender left Tennessee in 1920 to take a job at Knoxville High School, and Coach M. B. Banks resigned in 1925 to move on to Knoxville Central High School.

Tennessee's rise to prominence is tied directly to the coattails of Robert Reece Neyland, who, except for a coincidence of timing, might have worked his coaching magic at any one of dozens of other schools across the nation that had ROTC programs on campus. Fortunately, in 1925 the University of Tennessee had a vacancy in its military department at the same time an assistant football coach was needed. Dean N. W. Dougherty, chairman of the Athletics Board, wrote the head coach at West Point, John J. McEwan, asking that he recommend a man for the two jobs.

McEwan responded with the recommendation of Bob Neyland, an end at West Point, a standout pitcher for the Cadets' baseball team, and the

General Robert R. Neyland, legendary Tennessee coach. In a career that spanned twenty-one years, his teams won one hundred seventy-three games—once losing only two games in seven seasons—and went through eight seasons without a regular-season loss.

heavyweight boxing champion at the Academy. After a visit to the campus, Neyland agreed to come to Tennessee, thus beginning the process that would one day take the Volunteers to the top echelon of collegiate football.

The young West Point graduate became famous as a coach, but he never forgot his military training. Twice he left the University at the peak of his career to return to the Army for active duty. A brilliant engineer, Neyland rose in rank from captain (at the time he came to Tennessee) to general (when he returned to the campus after World War II).

His precise engineer's mind was reflected in his single-wing offense, a system that depended on timing and strength. The single-wing offense was durable and underwent very little change during the period Neyland served as head coach (1926–52). Neyland's achievements with offense were notable, but he seemed to delight even more in developing defensive strategies. His principles of defense have stood the test of time and are still in practice today at both college and high school levels.

At the time of Neyland's death in 1962, ten years after he hung up his coaching togs and adjusted to a semi-retired life as athletic director, Arthur Daley, the respected sports editor of the *New York Times,* penned an eloquent column about the man whose twenty-one-year record as head coach was an amazing 173 victories, 31 defeats and 12 ties. The column read, in part:

"Deep was the imprint that Neyland left on college football.

"For more than a quarter of a century the General was the nonpareil strategist in the collegiate ranks as he turned out one powerhouse after another at Tennessee. So sound were his methods and so beautifully drilled were his teams that Neyland pupils were in constant demand as coaches upon graduation. At one time he had 88 in head coaching jobs. They regarded their old boss with a respect that bordered on awe and they never quite got over being scared of him.

"The General was a steely-eyed, square-jawed disciplinarian who was never satisfied with less than perfection. He remained dignified and aloof. He was much like Jock Sutherland, another great coach. Beneath the façade of each, though, was a warm and vibrant human being, something that few were privileged to discover.

"The General was an arch-conservative who scorned the razzle-dazzle football of the present day. Being a West Point graduate, he reduced everything to military principles. 'The team that makes the fewer mistakes will win,' he insisted.

"Tennessee made few mistakes and it kept such relentless pressure on the opposition that it forced mistakes by the enemy. One reason for this was the emphasis the hard-bitten General gave to defense.

"The General wore his players to the nub in practice. No play is any good until it's been rehearsed 500 times, he used to say."

At the time Neyland was named head coach in 1926, probably the greatest source of irritation to Tennessee fans was the failure of their football team to hold its own against Vanderbilt, its intrastate rival. Neyland was expected to do something to correct the imbalance in the series between the two schools. To say that Neyland straightened the situation out is an understatement: his overall record against Vanderbilt was a highly satisfying 16–3–2.

When did Tennessee football attain big-time status under Neyland? Tennessee lore says 1928, and it pinpoints one particular game, the 15–13 victory over Alabama at Tuscaloosa. Alabama, already established as a Southern power, had pulverized Mississippi and Mississippi State and was rated about four touchdowns better than Tennessee. Supremely confident Alabama fans reportedly were offering 5–1 odds that 'Bama would win, even money that the margin would be more than twenty-eight points, and even money that the Vols would be shut out.

Neyland, who was never accused of publicly underestimating an opponent, approached Alabama Coach Wallace Wade before the game and suggested that to avoid an embarrassing rout of Tennessee the third and fourth quarters should be shortened. Wade told his young coaching rival that he would agree to cut the time, provided Alabama was enjoying a substantial lead.

The opening kickoff hinted at the monumental upset in the making. Gene McEver, regarded as one of the best backs ever to play under Neyland, took the kick at his 2-yard line and headed straight upfield. Nine Alabama defenders fell, as the Vols' crisscross blocking worked to perfection. The remaining two Alabama tacklers zeroed in on McEver at midfield. Gene blasted between them, sending the pair reeling, and scampered the remaining distance for a 98-yard touchdown return.

Halfback Gene "Mac" McEver, Tennessee's first All-American (1929) and half of the fabled "Hack 'n Mack" backfield.

It did not take Alabama long, however, to narrow the margin. The Tide needed only four plays and two minutes to score, but a missed extra point left Tennessee on top, 7–6. UT's Hobo Thayer pounced on a fumble outside the end zone for a safety, to up the Vols' margin to 9–6. Bobby Dodd tossed a short touchdown pass for a 15–6 lead, but the Tide came back for a touchdown before halftime, making the score 15–13. The score stayed that way, as Tennessee's tough defense wrapped up the victory that landed it squarely in the big time of college football.

McEver later told Russ Bebb, author of *The Big Orange,* about the play that set the tone of the game:

"After our guys put nine of theirs on the ground, I saw those two Alabama players up there in the alley about midfield. I went right between them, split them. I just bowed my neck and let 'em have it. That's all I could do. I don't know to this day whether anybody chased me to the goal. I don't think there is any question that that game put Tennessee on the football map."

McEver was one-half of the Vols' famed "Hack 'n Mack" halfback combination and the first of a long line of great UT players. Neyland later described the man known as "Mack"—and nicknamed by his teammates "the Wild Bull"—and Buddy Hackman, the other half of the great backfield duo, as follows:

"Hack and Mack were as totally different as any two athletes on earth. Mack is dark and his face is set. His legs are short and his chin determined, whereas Hackman is a smiling blond, built like an

J. S. "Buddy" Hackman, All-Southern Conference (1930) and "Hack" of the "Hack 'n Mack" duo.

antelope and easygoing. Both of them have the highest spirit imaginable. Neither has the slightest bit of prima donna about him. That counts a lot. Mack doesn't do anything Hack can't do. They're just 'Hack 'n Mack' and they win ball games for us."

And win they did, powering Tennessee to unbeaten seasons in 1928 and 1929. Then when knee surgery forced McEver to the sidelines in 1930, Hackman led the club to a 9–1 record, its only loss coming against Alabama. But McEver returned to action in 1931, and without Hackman, he sparked the Vols to another unbeaten season, their third in four seasons—the only blotch on their unbeaten record in each of those seasons known as "the McEver Years" was a tie with Kentucky. "I'm still trying to figure out those Wildcat games," McEver was to say years later.

But as great as McEver and Hackman were, other contributions by members of Neyland's "Flaming Sophomores" of 1928 were also needed to transform Tennessee into one of the nation's football powerhouses. One of those contributing was All-Southern tackle Ray Saunders. Another was quarterback Bobby Dodd. And still another was the most famous lineman in the history of Southern football, Herman Hickman.

Hickman was a sturdily built 225-pound guard whose name always graces all-time teams alongside

Bobby Dodd, All-Southern Conference back (1929) and one of Neyland's "Flaming Sophomores."

Herman Hickman, called the most famous lineman in the history of Southern football.

Yale's great "Pudge" Heffelfinger. He could outrun anybody on the team with the exception of McEver, and, on a good day, Hackman. His speed, agility and brute power from a squat position turned him into a human cannonball when he fired off the line of scrimmage, piling up everything in his wake—blockers and ballcarrier alike—into one gigantic mass of humanity. On offense, his speed and power made him a powerful, if not awesome, blocker. When the Vols played NYU in a 1931 post-season charity game in New York's Yankee Stadium, Hickman put on a one-man show, singlehandedly wrecking one of the finest lines in college football.

The man who had the misfortune to play opposite Hickman that day was Galahad Grant, a tackle of imposing presence. When NYU Coach Chick Meehan removed Grant from the game to save him from being committed to the Home for Bewildered Football Players, he asked Grant paternally, "Tell me, son, is this Hickman really as good as the papers say he is?"

The thoroughly exhausted Grant could only answer, "Coach, that big Southerner just called me a Yankee sonofabitch, and I didn't even answer him back. That's how good he is!"

The loss of such stars as Hickman and McEver, however, did not leave Neyland with a bare cupboard. Beattie "Big Chief" Feathers, who had played behind McEver in 1931 as a sophomore—scoring on 60- and 80-yard runs against Mississippi, 70 yards against Kentucky, 65 yards against NYU and 65 yards against Duke—finally came into his own in 1932. Named by George Trevor, the respected football editor of the old New York *Sun,* as halfback on his all-time Southern team, Feathers combined speed and a great final burst of energy to show his heels to many of the Vols' opponents, leading UT to its second straight 9–0–1 record. Feathers went on to set the NFL record for most yards gained per carry during a season (9.94 yards)—a record that still stands—and later joined McEver in college football's hallowed Hall of Fame. But it was his punting duel with Alabama's great Johnny Cain in 1932 that was to serve as the anchor of his fame.

The game was played before 20,000 frigid fans at Birmingham's Legion Field in a steady rain. Both teams played conservatively, relying on their dependable kickers for field position. Cain averaged 43 yards on 19 punts, Feathers 46 yards on 23 boots. When Feathers backed Alabama to its 1-yard line in the fourth quarter, the stage was set for a Tennessee victory.

Hall of Famer Beattie "Big Chief" Feathers, named to many all-time Southern teams.

Cain hurried the return kick because of a bad snap from center, and the ball carried only to the 12-yard line. Three plays later, Feathers knifed across for the score. Herman "Breezy" Wynn's extra point made it 7–3 Tennessee, a score that held up the rest of the way.

Guard Bob Suffridge, selected by AP and the Football Writers to their all-time All-American team.

Returning from military duty in Panama in 1936, Neyland immediately began forming the nucleus of a team that would create an era called "the Glory Years." By 1937 he had gathered a group of players he referred to as his second group of "Flaming Sophomores." Included in this fine group of prospects were such future stalwarts as Bob Suffridge, Ed Cifers, Bob Foxx, Ed Molinski, George Cafego, Jimmy Coleman, Abe Shires and Buist Warren. Together they were to lead the Volunteers to thirty-three consecutive regular-season victories, three undefeated, untied seasons, and three SEC championships.

The leader of the all-winning Vol teams of 1938–40 was a player described by Coach Neyland as "the only practice bum I ever coached who was a genuine All-American football player. In practice, he couldn't do anything right, but for two hours on a Saturday afternoon, he did everything an All-American is supposed to do"—George "Bad News" Cafego. The SEC Player of the Year in 1938, Cafego sparked Tennessee to a 13–0 win over defending champion Alabama in its pivotal game—its first win over 'Bama in six years—and a 10–0 record, piling up 276 points to but 16 for its opponents. But Cafego was not the whole story. He was joined on the All-SEC team by captain and end Bowden Wyatt and by Bob Suffridge, the best of the pulling single-wing guards on offense and such a terror on defense that UT's arch-enemy Kentucky once awarded him an honorary "K" for having spent more time in the Wildcats' backfield than any of their own players. Thanks largely to the talents of these men and of second-team All-SEC back Len Coffman and third-team members Ed Molinski and Babe Wood, the unbeaten Orangemen not only finished second in the Associated Press's national poll, but merited an invitation to Tennessee's first post-season bowl game, the Orange Bowl, to play fourth-ranked Oklahoma.

The game is memorable not only because Tennessee's 17–0 victory gave the team national exposure, but because the game is regarded as one of the roughest, no-holds-barred bowl games ever played. In fact, the mayhem was so extreme that one journalist insisted it should have been called the "Orange Brawl."

George Cafego, All-American tailback (1939).

Bowden Wyatt, captain and end on the unscored-on 1939 team.

The great UT tailback George Cafego was involved in an opening salvo that set the tone for the rough play that followed. On the first play, Cafego blocked All-American Waddy Young, sending the Sooner star sprawling and out of the game. Neyland grew alarmed at the disruptive tone the game was taking, so he sent one of the team's cooler heads, reserve center Joe Little, to settle his teammates down and get their minds back on football.

Little had good intentions, but on his first play, as he snapped the ball back for a punt, he was greeted by an uppercut to the chin. Little, the designated peacemaker, chased his attacker downfield and delivered an equally vicious blow. He then stood over the fallen Sooner and dared him to get up. The referee threw Little out of the game less than a minute after he had been sent into battle to cool things down. As Little approached the sidelines, he screamed an apology to his coach.

Bobby Foxx and Babe Wood scored touchdowns and Wyatt kicked a field goal, to provide a 17–0 margin. Neyland would win only one other bowl game in his career, the 1951 Cotton Bowl against Texas.

If the 1928 win over Alabama established Tennessee as a football powerhouse and a contender for national honors, the 1939 match with the Tide in

Johnny Butler's great run against Alabama in 1939.

Knoxville produced the most memorable play ever recorded at Neyland Stadium—or Shields-Watkins Field, as it was then called. The play involved reserve sophomore tailback Johnny "Blood" Butler, who was sent into the game after Tennessee had built an early lead. Grantland Rice was in the press box that October afternoon, and the noted writer described Butler's twisting, turning run without benefit of blocking as the greatest he had ever witnessed. Although most of the 'Bama players had a shot at Butler on that 56-yard scamper, none managed to lay a hand on him. One account read: "From the Vol 44, Butler slashed off tackle, cut back, and then started zigging and zagging, dodging and weaving, darting and dancing."

Bob Suffridge, who was on the bench at the time, described the run as follows: "That was the greatest run I ever saw. Butler went 56 yards from scrimmage, but I guess Johnny must have scampered around 200 yards dodging people."

While Butler's 56-yard run provided the offensive highlight of the 21–0 shutout the Vols dealt the Crimson Tide that afternoon, it paled beside the accomplishments of the defensive unit, which registered its ninth straight shutout. The defense, led by "Suff," would go through the entire regular schedule without surrendering a single point—only the fourteenth, and the last, school in modern collegiate football history to do so.

Only a 14–0 loss to Southern Cal in a Rose Bowl game that saw 1939 All-American tailback George Cafego hobbled by a bad knee spoiled the Vols' otherwise letter-perfect season.

The 1940 team, led by Bob Foxx, John Butler, Marshall Shires, Bob Suffridge, Ed Molinski and Ed Cifers, added yet another 10–0 record and a third straight SEC title to Tennessee's proud escutcheon. The Vols were invited to the Sugar Bowl for the first time, where they faced fifth-ranked Boston College, the class of the East. Before the kickoff, Boston's great blocking back, Tarzan Toczylowski, sought out one of the members of the Tennessee team and said:

"We're just a bunch of Polish boys whose fathers weren't even in America when your ancestors fought the Union. What I want to know is, do you want to fight the Civil War all over again today, or just have a good, hard football game?"

Despite the mile-high emotional buildup for the classic confrontation, the Vol player could not resist a smile. "Let's just settle for a football game," he replied. And they did, although it turned into a war of sorts, with the damnyankees finally prevailing 19–13 on one of Charlie O'Rourke's famed running passes.

When Neyland went to India on active military duty in 1942, John Barnhill took over the coaching reins and went on to enjoy spectacular success, compiling a 32–5–2 record, with two bowl appearances. When Neyland returned for the 1946 season, Barnhill went to Arkansas as head coach.

In Neyland's absence the T-formation had grown in popularity, but the General stayed with the offense he knew best, the single wing, and by the time of his retirement he had turned the Tennessee attack into an awesome machine.

Before he put together one of his greatest teams for a national championship in 1951, Neyland had many memorable games, perhaps the greatest being the opening game of 1946 against tough Georgia Tech. Billed as master against pupil, the game matched the brilliant Neyland against one of his brightest former players, Bobby Dodd, who was only in his second year as head coach of the Yellow Jackets.

The game between the two master strategists produced one of Neyland's shrewdest gambits, a spectacular play that is credited with preserving a vital Vol victory and a piece of the SEC championship. With time running out after three and a half periods of fairly equal give and take, Tennessee had a scant 13–7 lead. But Tech had pushed the Vols back toward their own goal line and appeared to have one more chance to get the ball—in good scoring position.

Tennessee's legion of grandstand quarterbacks was a mite unhappy when Neyland ordered three straight line plunges before the expected fourth-down punt. They wanted something more daring than merely falling on the ball. And they got it!

On fourth down, tailback Walter Slater lined up in punt formation deep in his own end zone. He took the snap from center, but, instead of kicking the ball, tucked it under his arm and began zig-zagging through his end zone, eating up precious seconds as Georgia Tech linemen desperately lunged at him. Slater eluded the grasp of the swarming Yellow Jackets as long as he could, and finally stepped out of the end zone, giving Tech a safety and two points—but, more importantly, giving Tennessee a free kick from its own 20. The kick put the ball back on Tech's 49-yard line, 51 yards away from paydirt, rather than deep in UT territory. After two incomplete passes and a completion to the Vol 35, the clock ran out, and Tennessee had a hard-fought—and masterfully stage-managed—13–9 win.

Tennessee experienced relatively hard times in 1947 and 1948. Some fans began calling for the scalp of the man experts rank as one of the great coaches of all time, perhaps the greatest. Critics said that his single-wing offense was outdated, that he could no longer recruit, and that he had lost his feel for coaching.

The ever-confident General set out to prove his critics wrong by mounting a campaign to recruit the best talent available for UT. His 1948 class of recruits was perhaps the greatest ever to grace the Tennessee campus; it included guard Ted Daffer, tackle Bill Pearman, linebackers Gordon Polofsky and Bill Jasper, wingback Bert Rechichar, fullback Andy Kozar, blocking back Jimmy Hahn, center Bob Davis, tailback Herky Payne, and Neyland's prize prospect, Hank Lauricella, a picture-perfect tailback from New Orleans. It was a carefully selected group that Neyland would mold into the 1951 national champions.

There are many, however, who insist that the 1950 Volunteer team was superior, at least defensively. They rest their case on two games that took place during that memorable season. The first was played November 25 at Knoxville against undefeated and top-ranked Kentucky, coached by Paul "Bear" Bryant and led by the Most Valuable Player in the SEC, Vito "Babe" Parilli. And although Tennessee had come on strong after an early-season loss to Mississippi State, winning seven in a row and eight of nine to rank ninth in the country, the writers were forced to ask: How could Tennessee cope with a team that had racked up eighty-three points the previous week and had already locked up the SEC championship and a Sugar Bowl bid?

The answer was supplied by Tennessee's proud defensive unit, comprised of Bill Pearman, Ted Daffer, Bud Sherrod and Doug Atkins, who kept Parilli at bay all day with their fierce pass rush. Meanwhile, the polished Lauricella completed a touchdown pass of 27 yards to Bert Rechichar for all the points Tennessee needed for a 7–0 victory. Bryant never won a game against Neyland, and the 1950 defeat was

Doug Atkins, All-American tackle (1952).

Tailback Hank Lauricella, who led the Vols to the 1951 national title.

probably the most galling of all, spoiling Kentucky's chance for its first undefeated season in fifty-one years.

With a victory over Kentucky, and, in the last game of the season, a win over rival Vanderbilt, the third-ranked Vols were invited to the Cotton Bowl to play second-ranked Texas. The size of the Longhorns, exemplified by giant guard "Bud" McFadin, contrasted sharply with that of the Volunteers. Pre-game speculators felt that Tennessee would have to build an early lead in order to withstand Texas's overwhelming physical strength up front, which they felt was sure to take its toll in the second half.

But it did not work out that way at all. A superbly executed 75-yard run by Lauricella set up a Tennessee touchdown. But the Longhorns countered with two touchdowns before intermission, sending the teams into the locker room with Texas on top, 14–7. Employing the buck lateral series that gave the single wing as much deception as the T, Tennessee took charge late in the third period and dominated the rest of the game. Lauricella and Kozar took turns lugging the ball, with captain Jack Stroud and other blockers clearing a path through the bulkier Texans. After Kozar scored Tennessee's second touchdown early in the fourth period, Pat Shires, a kicking specialist before such functionaries became commonplace, was sent in to tie the score. Shires, however, suffered one of his rare misses and was fighting back tears as he returned to the bench.

"Don't worry about it, Pat," General Neyland told his dejected placekicker. "We didn't come out here to tie them." Shortly thereafter the Vols drove 43

All-SEC fullback Andy Kozar, hero of the 1951 Cotton Bowl victory over Texas and now executive assistant to UT President Ed Boling.

Lauricella's 75-yard run in the 1951 Cotton Bowl.

yards for the winning touchdown, with Kozar knifing across. This time Shires kicked the point, and Neyland's sleek greyhounds had beaten Texas's bulky behemoths 20–14, using the supposedly outdated single wing.

To many of Tennessee's most fervent followers, the 20–14 victory established the Vols as the nation's best football team—even if the AP and UP did not agree. It was as simple as ABC: After Bowl Contests. Tennessee had won its post-season bowl, and the two teams ahead of it—Oklahoma and Texas—had both lost theirs. But the polls had closed before the bowl games, and Tennessee's claim to the mythical championship would have to wait for a year. Ironically, when UT's day as King of the College Football Mountain came, it was because of the closing of the polls before the bowl games. Tennessee reigned as 1951's college king after a 10–0 season, despite being upset in the Sugar Bowl by Maryland, 28–13.

A third straight bowl appearance climaxed Neyland's twenty-six-year head-coaching career, but the General was a spectator when the Volunteers met Texas in a rematch on January 1, 1953. Doctors conducting tests on Neyland were alarmed by his white-corpuscle count and ordered him to relinquish the coaching reins at the end of the 1952 regular season. Fittingly, the last game he actively coached produced a victory over archrival Vanderbilt, 46–0.

General Robert Neyland retired from the active coaching ranks after the 1952 season, assuming the duties of athletic director, which he retained until his death in 1962. But the legacy he left will be remembered for a long time. It will be remembered in the 80,250-seat Neyland Stadium, the fourth-largest football plant in the nation. It will be remembered for his winning tradition: in a career spanning twenty-one years, his teams won 173 of 216 games—during one seven-year span his teams had a 61–2–5 record—making his won-lost percentage .829, the highest of any coach in the history of the SEC. And it will be remembered for his leadership: no less than one hundred of his disciples were coaching at one time throughout the country. But most of all General Neyland will be remembered for being, in the words of Knute Rockne, "football's greatest coach."

The thankless task of succeeding the legendary General fell to his long-time aide Harvey Robinson, a man who had never aspired to be a head coach but whose brilliance and gentlemanly demeanor made him the logical heir to Neyland. Under Robinson, Tennessee had lackluster records in 1953 and 1954, and the stage was set—as it would be twenty-two years later—for the return to the campus of a former Vol football hero who had made his mark nationally

Bowden Wyatt, SEC Coach of the Year (1956).

as head coach. This time the man was Bowden Wyatt.

Wyatt appeared to be born to the orange. After serving as captain of the first great Vol team, the all-winning 1938 squad, Wyatt had gone on to employ the Neyland tactics at Wyoming and Arkansas, winning championships at both schools. Now the return of one of Tennessee's all-time legendary players ignited visions of UT's return to football preeminence.

At his first public appearance in Knoxville after his selection as head coach, the ruggedly handsome Wyatt gave voice to the hopes of Volunteer fans everywhere: "I'll win with boys who have orange in their blood," he told an assembled crowd of five hundred fifty at a team banquet. " 'Boy, you're now a Volunteer,' I'll tell those football players who come to play at Tennessee. It's a rare privilege to be a Volunteer, and the greatest pleasure in my career—including tonight—was at this same banquet seventeen years ago when I was elected captain for 1938. You don't know how happy I am to be back home."

The inspirational new head coach tried in vain to temper the enthusiasm of Tennessee's die-hard fans, who fully expected an era of Volunteer football comparable to the glorious days enjoyed under Neyland. "We hope to give our friends and fans good football during the 1955 season, but we hope they are not too optimistic, because we are a long way from being a championship team," Wyatt warned.

But despite his own timetable for success, in just two seasons Wyatt had guided Tennessee to its first SEC title since 1951, when Neyland's team was the toast of Dixie. And the player most responsible for the reestablishment of UT's credentials as a Southeastern power was the man who himself would come to Tennessee two decades later on the same mission that brought Wyatt to Knoxville in 1955—Johnny Majors.

Johnny Majors, two-time SEC Player of the Year (1955 and 1956).

Although Wyatt's first year record of 6–3–1 was hardly anything to write home about, there were several moments that gave promise of great things to come—most notably the closing game against Vanderbilt. The Vols' intrastate rival came into the traditional closer against UT under a full head of steam, having won its last six games by the cumulative score of 167–20 and clinched a bid to the Gator Bowl, its first-ever bowl bid. But Wyatt had the Vols up for the game, and after the Commodores' sophomore fullback Phil King battered the Vols' line for huge chunks of yardage in the first half, UT stiffened and then uncorked its own offensive fireworks. Operating out of the time-honored balanced single wing that Neyland had developed into a thing of beauty and Wyatt had perfected, Majors fired a pass to Buddy Cruze. Cruze somehow managed to catch the pass in a one-handed circus fashion that still defies retelling, and Al Carter fired a touchdown strike to wingback Bill Anderson. When the dust had settled, Tennessee had scored more points than Vandy had allowed any team all year, and had pulled off a come-from-behind 20–14 upset win. It was a portent of what 1956 held in store for Vol fans.

Wyatt's 1956 team ran through, around and over six straight opponents, and with four games left found itself atop the SEC—along with Georgia Tech. The two unbeaten schools would face each other in a showdown in early November to determine SEC and national honors. It was a classic—a game that was to be called by many the second most exciting game in college football history.

In a battle that was as close as football would ever get to Armageddon, both Wyatt and Tech Coach Dodd drew from their vast coaching experience as well as from the strategies of their mutual mentor, General Robert Neyland, throwing everything they had into the fray—and more. The battle finally turned on two passes from Majors to Cruze in the third period which set up a 1-yard touchdown plunge by Tommy Bronson. The extra point was missed, and the score stood 6–0 Tennessee. As the tense struggle wound down, the Vols clung to their slim lead, helped in no small measure by the brilliant punting of tailback Bobby Gordon. Finally it was over, and an exhausted Tennessee team left the field with a 6–0 victory over an equally exhausted Tech team. And even though the game was played in Atlanta, two hundred miles away from Knoxville, cars with horns blaring paraded bumper to bumper down Knoxville's Gay Street throughout the night in celebration of the Vols' epic victory.

But the euphoria was shortlived; Tennessee's perfect 10–0 record was marred by a 13–7 loss to Baylor in the Sugar Bowl, UT's seventh bowl loss in ten appearances.

After the heady heights of the 1956 season, Tennessee's football fortunes took a turn for the worse, and Wyatt, faced with the all-but-impossible task of repeating his success of 1956, saw his team's record slide to 8–3 in 1957, 4–6 in 1958, and 5–4–1 in 1959. But there was one moment that would be remembered by all in those years of frustration: a landmark victory over LSU at Shields-Watkins Field in 1959.

LSU, coached by Paul Dietzel, was the defending national champion, winners of nineteen straight games and victors the previous week over an equally tough Ole Miss team. Led by Heisman trophy candidate Billy Cannon and his speedy running mate Johnny Robinson, the number one-ranked Tigers were prohibitive favorites over the floundering Vols, and they proved it by running the Orange ragged in the first half. But despite its obvious superiority, LSU could only manage to put seven points up on the scoreboard by halftime.

Tennessee, whose players had vowed before the season that they would leave fans something to remember them by, staved off one Tiger scoring drive after another. Then lightning struck early in the third period, when the Vols' Jim Cartwright picked off a Warren Rabb pass and raced 59 yards for the touchdown that tied the game 7–7. The crowd, which had watched the proceedings in deepening gloom, began to brighten noticeably at the quick turn of events and then went into pandemonium when a Tiger fumble after the ensuing kickoff gave UT possession at the LSU 26.

Tennessee capitalized on the turnover just four plays later, when alternate captain Neyle Sollee darted through a hole over left tackle and raced 14 yards for a touchdown, to give the Vols a 14–7 lead. Then it was LSU's turn. The Tigers recovered a bobbled punt at the UT 2-yard line and promptly scored, setting up a two-point conversion attempt that will be remembered even longer than Butler's legendary touchdown run in the 1939 'Bama game. Everyone in the stadium knew that LSU would go for the two points and victory. They also knew that the ball would be entrusted to none other than Billy Cannon. And they were right! LSU's Mr. All-Everything got the ball on an off-tackle play and started to his right. Then he cut inside. But there Vol tackle Joe Schaffer met him head on and slowed down his progress. Then Wayne Grubb and Charley Severance, aided by Bill Majors, all converged on the driving Cannon and finally hauled him down just inches short of the goal line, to preserve a 14–13 victory for the Vols—one of the few UT bright spots in an otherwise dismal period between 1958 and 1964.

The Bowden Wyatt era, which began with such high hopes in 1955, ended in sorrow and despair, as poor health and other factors forced him to resign as head coach in 1963, after compiling three more mediocre years in 1960, 1961 and 1962. It was a sad exit for the man who had seemed destined to carry on the great winning tradition of General Neyland. During his eight years at the helm, Wyatt's teams had compiled an overall record of 49–29–4, won the SEC and national championships, and earned him the National Coach of the Year award in 1956.

Wyatt's departure came at an awkward time—between the end of spring practice and the start of fall workouts. UT officials, shut out of the normal December-January coaches' market, reached into the ranks of the Vol staff, selecting Jim McDonald to serve as interim coach for the 1963 season. While the Vols struggled to a 5–5 record under McDonald, as much interest centered on the eventual resolution of the unsettled coaching situation as on the achievements of the team.

Athletic Director Bob Woodruff.

A critical stage in UT football history had arrived: for the first time since 1926, Tennessee was involved in the delicate business of selecting a head football coach with neither Robert Neyland nor a logical successor waiting offstage to fill the vacuum. Fortunately, one of the wisest men in college athletics had moved into the vacant athletic director's position at the same time McDonald had assumed the head coaching duties. University officials quickly turned over the problem of choosing McDonald's successor to Bob Woodruff, a former head coach at Baylor and Florida, who had also been a member of the Tennessee staff when Wyatt was deposed. The deep-thinking and methodical Woodruff wasted little time inquiring about the availability of a bright young quarterback he had coached at Florida in the early 1950s, now reportedly a man on the rise as a coaching assistant for Frank Broyles at Arkansas. Woodruff placed a call to Fayetteville, Arkansas, to talk to Douglas Adair Dickey.

"I knew Doug as a man of unusual intelligence, and you can't overestimate the value of brains," said Woodruff as he introduced the new head coach before the start of the 1964 season. Reflecting back to his coaching days at Florida, Woodruff added: "Doug could see things as a game rolled along that showed me he had the makings of a smart coach."

When Dickey emerged from the meeting with the Athletic Board, there was a feeling among the membership that Tennessee was on the way back under the quick-thinking, six-foot-three Dickey, who bore the all-business look of the man in the gray flannel suit.

Doug Dickey, twice SEC Coach of the Year (1965 and 1967).

Dickey's first year was a rebuilding year. The Vols suffered through a 4–5–1 record; their offense generated a meager eighty points and was shut out three times in ten games. But 1965 was to be different. And when the unbeaten Vols tied the defending national champs, Alabama, in their first away game, Tennessee fans rejoiced at the first concrete sign of UT's gridiron resurgence.

However, it was to be shortlived jubilation, for two days later tragedy struck. The car carrying three young UT coaches to their Neyland Stadium office was hit by a train, killing Bill Majors and Bobby Jones instantly and fatally injuring Charlie Rash. Still, the Vols managed to pull themselves together to post a 7–1–2 record, and capped their comeback year with a 27–6 victory over Tulsa in the 1965 Bluebonnet Bowl, their first bowl in eight years and the first of ten straight post-season appearances.

But it was not the victory over Tulsa that will be remembered by Vol fans as Tennessee's greatest game of the 1965 season; that distinction was reserved for the season's finale against UCLA, one of the most extraordinary contests in UT football history.

The early December meeting in Memphis was viewed by both schools as somewhat of a nuisance, and by the press as the "Rosebonnet Bowl"—a snide reference to the fact that Tennessee had already wrapped up a bid to the Bluebonnet Bowl and UCLA was Rose Bowl–bound. The game between the two top-ten-rated teams was a seesaw battle that produced a total of seventy-one points and went right down to the final minute of play. There it was decided by UT's Dewey Warren, the most unlikely candidate to break up a ballgame with his running. For although Warren was known as a superb passer, he was described as "one who ran as though his feet were enmeshed in molasses." But regardless of his credits, with the ball on the UCLA 1-yard line, fourth down and only a minute left, it was Warren who tucked the ball under his arm and began circling left end . . . and circling . . . and circling . . . and circling. Finally, after what seemed like an eternity, Warren managed to hurl himself toward the goal line. It was ruled a touchdown, and the Volunteers had a hard-fought 37–34 win over a UCLA team that would go on to beat the number one team in the country, Michigan State, in the Rose Bowl in just three weeks.

Dewey Warren, possessor of many UT passing records and at least one memorable running feat.

UCLA Coach Tommy Prothro was livid after the game. His fiery remarks probably did almost as much to make the game a memorable one as events on the field. Prothro was infuriated not so much by the close call on Warren's disputed touchdown as by a couple of calls that had stopped the clock during Tennessee's drive preceding the touchdown. The UCLA coach gained a measure of revenge when his Bruins, led by Gary Beban, whipped Tennessee, 20–16, in the 1967 season opener in Los Angeles.

That inaugural loss to UCLA was hardly an indicator of the season to come. Given an extra week off because of an open date, the Vols used the time to make a series of adjustments that turned the team into a solid unit. Dickey installed future All-Americans Steve Kiner and Jack Reynolds at the linebacker spots, and the Vols began to roll. They roared through the remainder of their 1967 schedule, overcoming a couple of pesky nemeses along the way.

Particularly gratifying to Tennessee fans was the 24–13 victory over defending national champion Alabama. It not only marked the first time since 1960 that the Vols had beaten a Bear Bryant–coached team; it also avenged the galling loss of 1966, when Gary Wright's field-goal attempt had gone wide in the closing moments and UT had lost to 'Bama 11–10. Now, with substitute quarterback Bubba Wyche ably filling in for the injured Dewey Warren, and his back-up Charlie Fulton and defensive halfback Albert Dorsey intercepting three errant 'Bama passes in the fourth quarter, the Vols had their revenge—and broke a twenty-five-game Tide winning streak as well.

A second triumph during 1967 that especially delighted Big Orange followers took place on November 18, in Memphis, when Tennessee completed its giant quinella and defeated Ole Miss, thereby snapping a winless famine that dated back to 1958. Fulton, tailback Walter Chadwick, and wingback Richmond Flowers halted UT's dry spell at eight as they ran behind the talented offensive blocking of Bob Johnson, John Boynton and Charles Rosenfelder, to carry the Vols to a 20–7 win over Mississippi.

The Dickey regime at Tennessee was in full bloom when the Vols notched the 1967 Southeastern Conference championship and then followed two years later with a second title. Vol fans were exultant. Not only had their orange-clad heroes won two league titles in three years, but the horizon held unlimited promise for the seasons ahead. Tennessee's ecstatic fans, however, had not figured on the backstage intrigue that would take Doug Dickey overnight from Knoxville to Gainesville.

The holiday atmosphere that prevailed in Jacksonville before the 1969 Gator Bowl game against Florida was dampened by a rumor that would not go away: after the Gator Bowl, Dickey would resign and take over as head coach at his alma mater, Florida. The rumor had Ray Graves, the current Florida coach, tendering his resignation, effective immediately following the bowl game. At first Tennessee partisans were inclined to ignore the rumor. But when no denials were forthcoming, they began to take it seriously.

The rumors grew so strong that by game time there was more concern over the potential coaching changeover than over finding a way to beat Florida. A lackluster performance against Florida followed, resulting in a 14–13 loss. And that, in turn, was followed by confirmation of the rumor. Dickey was indeed headed for his alma mater. The storybook switch met with more than slight criticism: many Tennessee fans believed that Dickey had violated ethics by discussing a coaching position with officials of a school he was preparing to play, while many Florida followers felt that the Gator head-coaching job should have gone to Graves's assistant, Gene Ellenson.

Once again Woodruff and other UT officials were faced with the task of selecting a new head coach. Based on Tennessee's two SEC titles over the past three years, Woodruff saw advantages in maintaining continuity by staying within Dickey's staff for a new head man. Woodruff let it be known that three top prospects from within the staff were Jimmy Dunn, the offensive coordinator and, like Dickey, a former Florida quarterback under Woodruff; Doug Knotts, the defensive coordinator, with a background as player and coach at Duke; and a surprise candidate, twenty-eight-year-old Bill Battle.

The changing of the guard: Doug Dickey in the foreground and his successor, young Bill Battle, behind him.

To the surprise of everyone, Woodruff settled on Battle, whom most observers expected to be passed over because of his age. But Woodruff saw in the youthful Alabama graduate signs of maturity beyond his years. And he observed other characteristics that would be beneficial in guiding the Volunteer football machine to continued success. In the years immediately ahead, events followed the blueprint to the letter.

The 1970 season, Battle's first as head coach, was interpreted as a harbinger of continued Vol prosperity. Quarterback Bobby Scott and fullback Curt Watson for the offense and linebacker Jackie Walker and safety Bobby Majors for the defense played key roles as Tennessee bounced back from an early-season loss to Auburn to post an 11–1 record. Included among accomplishments that earned the Vols number four national ranking were Tennessee's first shutout victory over Alabama since 1959, a particularly sweet 38–7 triumph over a Florida team coached by Doug Dickey, and a 34–13 rout of Air Force in the Sugar Bowl—a satisfying season to be sure.

When slick quarterback Condredge Holloway enrolled in 1971 and a crowd of more than 31,000 showed up to watch Holloway weave his magic against Notre Dame in a freshman game, Vol fans were convinced Tennessee would be a top-ten team for many years to come.

In 1971 and 1972 the record dropped a notch, to 10–2, and in 1973 it fell even further, to 8–4. Tennessee fans grew a bit less confident of the future. And in 1974, when a series of miracle catches by gifted Larry Seivers were required to pull out a 7–3–2 record, the first serious rumblings of discontent were heard among the masses. Overall Battle's record was a more-than-creditable 59–22–2 over seven years, but the downward drift, uninterrupted by any upward surges, sealed Battle's fate. Battle was so well liked and respected that people desiring his termination went out of their way to precede their comments with "He's a nice guy, but. . . ." In fact, instead of being ridden out of town on the proverbial rail, Battle became perhaps the first deposed coach in history to depart the premises in a new car provided by the local quarterback club.

Coach Bill Battle, whose seven Volunteer teams had a winning percentage of .723, including four wins in five bowl appearances.

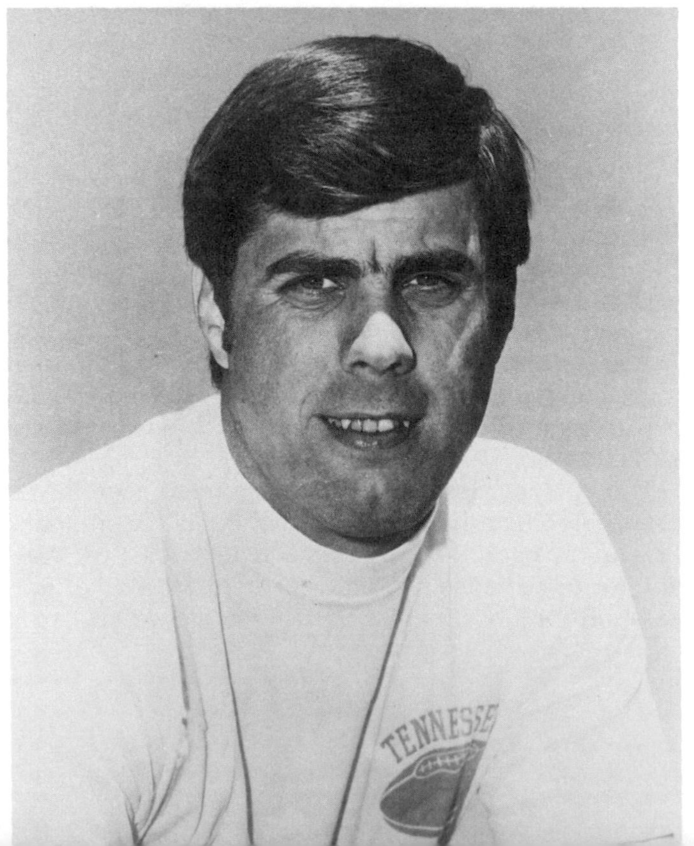

The call went out for home-state hero Majors to right the good ship Volunteer. Emphasizing that he considered himself "a hard worker, not a miracle worker," Majors turned his vast energies to the problem he considered foremost among Tennessee's weaknesses: recruiting. Seldom has a football staff worked harder or spent more time on the road than Volunteer coaches in the weeks leading up to the scholarship signing date in 1977.

According to impartial, objective sources, the campaign was a huge success. Ratings of recruiting success ranked Tennessee's cache of prospects anywhere from first to third in the nation. But one group of prospects does not a winner make, and the hoped-for "miracle" was not yet forthcoming, as 1977 proved, when Majors's first team turned in a 4–7 season.

1978 looked like a repeat of 1977. Tennessee went down in its 1978 opener to UCLA, barely managed to tie Oregon State with a miracle finish, and then took a brutal beating from Auburn to get off to a less-than-rousing 0–2–1 start. A win over outmanned Army didn't do much to brighten the picture. When mighty Alabama came to town for the annual midseason classic, Vol fans expected the worst. And they got it: 30–13. Then came another beating, this time by Mississippi State, and UT's record was now 1–4–1.

But there was some ray of hope in the black clouds, as Tennessee watchers saw the Vols come on strong in both the 'Bama and MSU losses, outscoring the Tide 13–0 in the final period and slicing eighteen points off the Bulldogs' margin in the last quarter. Good things were beginning to happen, although you had to look hard to see them.

When the Vols beat Duke 34–0 and went into the locker room at halftime owning a 7–6 lead over nationally ranked Notre Dame, Majors and his staff started talking about "turning the corner." And although Notre Dame finally overcame Tennessee's lead and tenacity to win, it looked like Majors might be right.

Needing to win the remaining three games against old SEC rivals to avoid a second consecutive losing season, Majors rallied the Vols and they met the challenge, blasting Ole Miss 41–17, Kentucky 29–14, and Vanderbilt 41–15.

Vol fans were beaming for the first time since 1974, when they last visited a bowl. The lobby of the team's motel headquarters in Nashville for the Vandy game was packed on Saturday morning, reminding long-

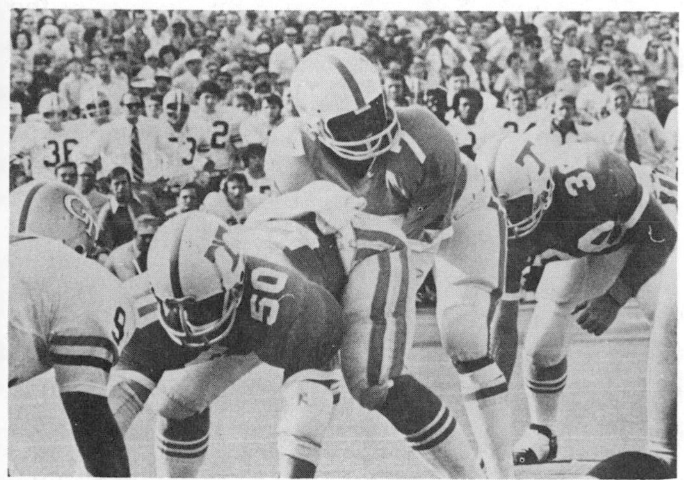

All-SEC quarterback Condredge Holloway (1973).

time followers of a bygone era of crowded lobbies in the Tutwiler in Birmingham, the Peabody in Memphis, the Phoenix in Lexington, and other old familiar stops during the team's Glory Years.

Tennessee fans are confident that the Big Orange is on its way back to its rightful place as one of the winningest teams in college football.

For the symbolic "Torch" that is the spirit of the state and the university has passed from the hands of General Robert Neyland into the hands of Johnny Majors. And hopefully, now that Majors has taken it in his firm grasp, it will guide the way to greatness for future Tennessee teams—lighting the way to what the legions of Volunteer followers hope and believe will become known as "Majors's Dynasty."

Majors leads his team into packed Neyland Stadium.

Johnny Majors, an All-America hero of two decades ago returned to his alma mater in January 1977 as the University of Tennessee's nineteenth head football coach.

The all-time greatest Volunteer game, UT fans voted, was the classic 1956 victory over Georgia Tech, high point of Majors' senior season.

Majors, tailback in the single wing offense, led the Volunteers through an undefeated season in 1956 and was acclaimed national back of the year.

The new Tennessee staff put the Orange forces through an intense spring practice.

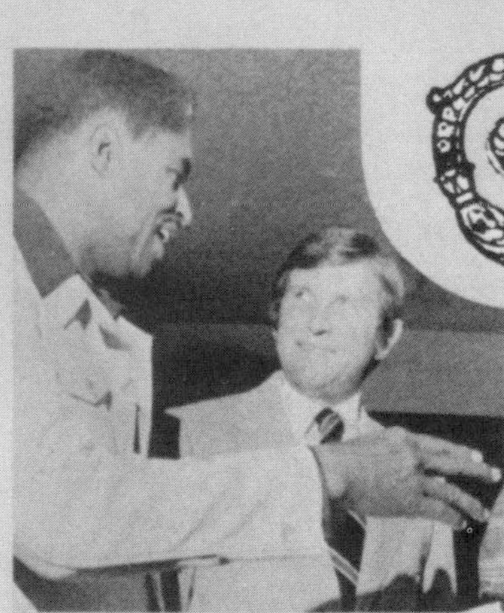

Majors, coach of the year in 1976, received congratulations from American Football Coaches Assn. officer Eddy Robinson of Grambling College.

As coach of 1976 national champion Pittsburgh, Majors guided the Panthers to an undefeated season and a Sugar Bowl victory over Georgia.

The front cover of the 1977 University of Tennessee Football Guide heralding Majors's return.

Vanderbilt University

by John Tishler

The 1924 Vanderbilt squad of some thirty players gathered around Coach Dan McGugin. The Commodores were in Minneapolis to play the powerful University of Minnesota Gophers, who the week before had beaten Illinois and "Red" Grange for Grange's first collegiate loss.

Dan McGugin's teams were the scourge of the South during his thirty years at Vanderbilt. From 1904 to 1934 his teams won one hundred ninety-seven games and had four undefeated seasons.

John Tishler, a Vanderbilt Sports Information Office student assistant, is a recipient of one of three scholarships awarded annually by the Alabama chapter of Sigma Delta Chi Society of professional journalists.

McGugin, always soft-spoken, quietly began preparing his team psychologically. He said:

"Men, those people in the stands out there haven't heard of Southern football. When they think about the South, they think about the Civil War—they think about pain, suffering and death. Many people have no idea of what Southern manhood is all about. Today we can show them. When your mothers looked on you sleeping in your cradles twenty years ago, they wondered when the time would come when you could bring honor to the South. That time has arrived!"

Indeed, the time had arrived for Vanderbilt and Southern football. The Commodores went out and whipped the favored Gophers 16–0. Jess Neely, captain of the undefeated 1922 squad, calls McGugin "the greatest coach for preparing a team psychologically that I've ever known."

Dan McGugin symbolizes "the Golden Era" (1890–1934) of Vanderbilt football, the Commodores' most successful years on the gridiron.

On November 13, 1890, Peabody Normal College, also known as Nashville University, challenged Vanderbilt to a football game. Elliott H. Jones was put in charge of organizing the Vanderbilt squad to play Nashville on November 27, Thanksgiving Day, on the Sulphur Dell Grounds.

Led by Horace E. Bemis, a quarter-miler on the track team, Vanderbilt downed the Nashville squad 40–0. It seems, however, that Vanderbilt had an unusual advantage over its opponents: Vandy players Pat Estes and Jones had hidden in a tree overlooking Nashville's practice field and gathered what the 1891 Vanderbilt yearbook, *The Comet,* termed "useful information" about their opponents.

In 1894 Vanderbilt hired its first football coach, former University of Pennsylvania guard Henry Thornton. His salary was $400, a rather paltry sum compared to the princely coaching salaries of today.

Vanderbilt was partially responsible for a rule change in 1895. An Auburn halfback pushed the ball down the back of teammate Reynolds Tichenor's jersey during the Tiger-Commodore tussle in Nashville. While the entire Vanderbilt team converged on an apparent dive play, Tichenor trotted around end for Auburn's only touchdown. Perhaps proving that justice triumphs, Vanderbilt still managed to prevail, 9–6. Football rules after 1895, however, outlawed such "hidden ball" tricks.

In 1904 Dan McGugin of Michigan was hired as football coach, and he became the most successful coach in Vanderbilt history, compiling a 197–55–19 record in thirty years at the Commodore helm. Perhaps even more remarkable is the fact that football was only McGugin's avocation. His occupation was, in reality, the practice of law.

Dan McGugin, Jr., a prominent Nashville attorney, recalls:

"My father played for Fielding 'Hurry-Up' Yost's first two 'point-a-minute' teams at Michigan in 1901 and 1902. After receiving his law degree in 1902, he set up a practice in Detroit. By this time Yost was a famous coach and many colleges wrote him asking for recommendations from among his former players for head coaching jobs around the country. Yost recommended my father to Western Reserve University in Cleveland, Ohio, and Vanderbilt.

"Some of my father's fondest memories were of his father, a Civil War veteran, gathering the children around a big fire in their Iowa farmhouse, telling about the warmth and hospitality of the South he had encountered while with General Sherman in Georgia. This had stirred my father's interest in the South, so he decided to take the Vanderbilt job."

Amazingly, McGugin continued his law practice in Detroit for approximately his first five years as a coach, taking off three months a year to coach Vanderbilt and then returning to Michigan for the other nine to practice law. In 1910, however, McGugin moved his law practice to Nashville permanently, discontinuing his commuting between jobs.

When McGugin arrived in Nashville in 1904, he brought with him Yost's formula of "a punt, a pass and a prayer." McGugin believed in making the punt an offensive weapon. His teams could not overwhelm the opposition with their size, so they wore down stronger but slower teams with their speed instead.

McGugin, who had played guard for Michigan's 1902 Rose Bowl champions under Yost, had developed a close and lasting relationship with his former coach. When McGugin got married in Nashville in 1905, Yost was his best man. McGugin introduced Yost to his wife's sister, and a year and a half later Yost and McGugin were brothers-in-law.

Vanderbilt so dominated Southern football during McGugin's first five years at Vandy that the Commodores were undefeated (34–0–1) against Southern opposition until the last game of 1909.

"My father would plan games way ahead of time," said the younger McGugin. "He often would get weather reports and gauge his offense accordingly."

McGugin was also a scholar of Civil War and military history. He perceived each game as a military battle and planned his strategy the way a general would that of an army.

Life as a Vanderbilt football player was not easy in those days. According to Jess Neely:

"We would have a job in the morning, classes from one to four in the afternoon, practice from four until dark, and sometimes work at a job at night.

"Coach McGugin would always close up his law office at four every afternoon and come over to Vanderbilt and change from his suit to an old baseball uniform in Furman Hall. Our practices and games were held on what is now called Curry Field. We called it Dudley Field then."

McGugin's first Commodore squad went undefeated, with only one field goal scored against it. Vanderbilt's 9–0 record prompted Southern football historian Fuzzy Woodruff to say, "McGugin stood out in the South like Gulliver among the native sons of Lilliput. The best teams of the section scheduled Vanderbilt simply as a method of gaining football instruction."

The Commodores' first intersectional game was played in 1905 against McGugin's alma mater, Michigan. Though the Commodores came out on the short end of an 18–0 score, Vanderbilt finished the season 7–1–0.

The first time Vanderbilt defeated an intersectional rival was in 1906, when Vandy upset the Carlisle Indians, 4–0. In addition, the Commodores came close to beating Michigan, tying the score 4–4 in the last quarter before losing 10–4.

Navy had a powerhouse team in 1907, but Vanderbilt traveled to Annapolis and tied the Midshipmen, 6–6. The game ended with Vandy on the Naval Academy's 18-yard line.

From 1904 to 1907 Vanderbilt claimed three Southern Intercollegiate Athletic Association (SIAA) championships. Dr. William Dudley, dean of the Vanderbilt Medical School from 1895 to his death in 1914, was responsible for founding the SIAA.

For the first time in three years, Vandy did not win the SIAA title in 1908. Sewanee tied Vanderbilt 6–6 in the schools' annual Thanksgiving Day battle, and the title went to undefeated Auburn.

In 1909 Sewanee again played the spoiler's role, beating Vanderbilt 16–5 to claim the SIAA title. The Purple Tigers became the first Southern team to beat a McGugin-coached team.

The 1910 Commodore team gained national recognition by playing powerful Yale to a 0–0 tie in New Haven, Connecticut.

Recalls 1910 reserve J. Holmes Anderson:

"Most of us hadn't been out of Tennessee, and we were in awe of New York and the East. When we came out of our hotel for breakfast the morning before the game, newspapermen taunted us about the South, cotton, and slaves.

"We got to the gymnasium and began to change our clothes. Yale was right next to our dressing room. They started stomping their feet on the concrete and making a lot of racket to intimidate us, but it only served to fire us up more.

"Ray Morrison, who in 1911 made All-American at quarterback, kept us in that game. They had a great punter named Deming who would kick the ball real high, and real far, making it hard to catch. Morrison always fielded the ball for Vanderbilt and never dropped one. He had the surest hands on the team."

Led by All-American quarterback Ray Morrison, undefeated Vanderbilt brought widespread acclaim to Southern football by tying national powerhouse Yale 0–0 in 1910.

Vanderbilt gained three times as much yardage as the Elis, but could not put any points on the scoreboard against a tenacious Bulldog defense. It was during this game, though, that Yale Coach Ted Coy chose Morrison for the 1911 All-American team. Upon Morrison's graduation, McGugin called him "the best quarterback I have ever seen."

The 1915 team was known for its scoring ability, tight defense, and ironclad stomachs. Led by All-American Josh Cody and Irby "Rabbit" Curry, Vanderbilt was a genuine "point-a-minute" team, av-

Josh Cody, tackle on Vandy's 1915, 1916 and 1919 teams, was named to the Football Writers all-time All-American team in 1969.

Picture of the legendary Irby "Rabbit" Curry (captain of the 1916 Commodore squad) that hung in Coach McGugin's office.

eraging 51 points per fifty-minute game. The 1915 squad scored a total of 514 points. Only 38 points were scored by opponents, 35 of them by Virginia in Vanderbilt's only loss of the season.

On the way to Memphis to play Mississippi that year, Vanderbilt's caravan was stopped by a freight train. The delay was so long that the players finally convinced student manager Jimmy Stahlman to go look for something to eat.

Stahlman found an orchard nearby and returned carrying armfuls of green apples. Stahlman, who demonstrated his resourcefulness that day, later became owner and publisher of the Nashville *Banner* and was a dynamic figure in the Nashville community until his death in 1976. Showing no ill effects from their delay, the Commodores clobbered the Rebels the next day, 91–0.

Curry played his finest game in the 1915 season finale against Sewanee. Going into the fourth quarter, Vandy trailed 3–0, and Curry, only five foot eight and 130 pounds, came off the field with three broken ribs. With "Rabbit" watching painfully from the sidelines, the Commodores were unable to get an offensive drive started. Finally Curry went to McGugin and asked to be put in.

"I know I can score a touchdown, Coach," he said. McGugin put him in, and the diminutive quarterback scored two touchdowns, as Vanderbilt came from behind to win the game 28–3.

Curry served as a fighter pilot in World War I, perishing when his plane was shot down in 1918.

Recalled 1921 center Alfred Sharp:

"McGugin always kept three pictures in his office. On the left he had Abraham Lincoln, in the middle, Rabbit Curry, and to the right, Robert E. Lee. He loved Rabbit; but then, McGugin loved all his players.

"In 1921 we went out to Dallas twenty-point underdogs to Texas. They were big. McGugin got us all in a room while we were dressing. He could have been a Shakespearean actor—his pre-game speeches were that eloquent, but everyone knew he wasn't putting on an act. He felt what he said.

"McGugin began by saying how we would meet a test that day, and he told us how Rabbit had met many tests—even his death. Rabbit's father had come to the game [Curry was from Marlin, Texas] and Coach McGugin finally asked him to say a few words.

"He got up, tried to talk, but finally burst out crying. We all cried that day. McGugin reminded us that Rabbit's spirit would be with us that day. I guess it was. We beat 'em, 20–0."

Following the successful 1921 season (7–0–1), Vanderbilt built the first stadium in the South to be

Jess Neely (right), captain of the great 1922 team that tied Michigan in the dedication game of Dudley Field, returns as athletic director after forty years of coaching to receive plaque commemorating his many contributions to football. The plaque was presented by the mayor of Nashville and Alfred Sharp (center of the undefeated 1922 team, left).

used exclusively for football. McGugin invited Michigan down for the inaugural game in 22,000-seat Dudley Stadium, named after the founder of the SIAA.

Neely, the team captain, said:

"We were ready for that game with Michigan. Just before the game began, an airplane was flying overhead to drop the game ball. Coach McGugin had us all around him and he was squatting with his hands out in front of him, palms up. The plane dropped the ball at the center of the field; it took a high bounce, then landed right in Coach McGugin's outstretched hands. He didn't even have to reach for it. It was a good omen."

Indeed, it was an omen of good things to come: the Commodores threw up an inspired goal-line defense to end the first half and played the Wolverines to a 0–0 tie, the eighth time McGugin was to play his alma mater—and his brother-in-law—and the closest he was to come to victory.

Captain Neely remembered:

"They [Michigan] got down to our 2-yard line and

Hall of Famer Bill Spears, one of the South's all-time great quarterbacks, led the 1925–1926–1927 teams, which lost just five of twenty-nine games.

had a first down. Before their first snap, I looked up into the west stands and saw about a thousand handkerchiefs waving. I shouted to the team to look at the handkerchiefs, and it inspired the whole team. They didn't gain an inch in four tries. They couldn't have moved us out with a bulldozer—we were that fired up."

Neely went on from Vanderbilt to become one of college football's most successful coaches, winning 207 games at Southwestern, Clemson and Rice. He is a member of the National Football Hall of Fame, as are McGugin; 1902–03 back John Tigert; 1914–16, 1919 All-American tackle Josh Cody; 1923 All-American end Lynn Bomar; 1927 All-American quarterback Bill Spears; 1935–39 head football coach Ray Morrison; and 1937 All-American center Carl Hinkle.

The 1927 Vanderbilt squad went 8–1–2, losing only to Texas. The Commodores were headed by All-

American quarterback Bill Spears, who ended his career in a 14–7 victory over Alabama by outgaining the entire Crimson Tide team and fullback Jimmy Armistead, who was the nation's high scorer that year, with 138 points on 23 touchdowns.

Sharp said:

"I remember one incident that happened in 1927," Vandy center Alfred Sharp laughingly recalled. "My brother Vernon was captain that year. Ralph 'Peck' Owen was in Vanderbilt's backfield, and he was a very fast runner. Against Maryland, he broke out into the open on one play.

"Maryland had this player named Schneider who ran after Peck and finally caught him around the Maryland 15-yard line. Peck was wearing silk pants that were very slick, and it made it hard to tackle him. However, this Schneider grabbed Peck's belt. But Peck kept running.

"Unfortunately, Peck's pants didn't go with him. While Schneider was around the 15-yard line holding Peck's belt, Peck was still running to about the 10. All this time, those pants kept stretching and tearing, until they came down around his knees."

McGugin had an interesting friendship with Huey Long, longtime governor and senator of Louisiana.

One year, after Vanderbilt had completed its season, McGugin was watching LSU play archrival Tulane. The Tigers' head coach was a former Vandy player and captain.

The Green Wave was having an outstanding year and led LSU 7–0 late in the fourth quarter. The Tigers, however, were playing an inspired game, and with a couple of minutes remaining they took over the football deep in their own territory. Long, who had reportedly fired an LSU coach at halftime of one game only to rehire him after the game, began criticizing the Tigers and their head coach for being too cautious with the football.

After Long loudly voiced his opinion that LSU should begin filling the air with passes in a desperate effort to tie Tulane, McGugin, in a stern tone, explained that LSU had very little chance of scoring. Instead, he pointed out, the Green Wave might intercept an LSU pass and put the Tigers completely out of the game.

Long was silent for a moment and then admitted, "By God, I believe you are right!" The two were fast friends from that point on.

In 1934 LSU had an outstanding team. Both Vanderbilt and the Tigers went into their championship-deciding clash in Nashville undefeated. Long decided that part of the LSU student body and the band should go to the game, so he made a veiled threat to raise taxes on railroads and bridges if the railroad did not let students ride the train from Baton Rouge to Nashville and back for $6. The railroad agreed, and 5000 students followed their team to Nashville. Long led the LSU band as it paraded down West End Avenue to Dudley Stadium, where the Tigers shut out the Commodores, 29–0.

The Golden Era of Vanderbilt football came to a close in 1934, when Dan McGugin stepped down as the Commodore coach. McGugin died in January of 1936.

From 1890 to 1934, Vanderbilt compiled a highly impressive 268–83–26 record. Few schools, if any, could boast of such a mark during that—or any—period.

Former All-American quarterback and National Football Hall-of-Famer Ray Morrison returned to Vanderbilt in 1935. Morrison was named head coach after McGugin stepped down, and he made quite a coaching debut, guiding the Commodores to seven victories, including a 13–7 win over Tennessee and General Bob Neyland. Not only was Morrison selected SEC Coach of the Year, but in end Willie Geny he produced the first of five Commodores to be named SEC Player of the Year. Other Vandy players to win the honor were center Carl Hinkle in 1937, fullback Jack Jenkins in 1941, All-American quarterback Bill Wade in 1951, and split end Bob Goodridge in 1967.

Hall of Famer Carl Hinkle, the Most Valuable Player in the SEC (1937), receives congratulations from Commodore supporter Tennessee governor Gordon Browning after leading Vandy to a 13–7 win over rival Tennessee—the last game the Vols were to lose for four years.

Although the 1936 team did not roll up huge margins of victory over its opponents, only an upset loss to Georgia Tech kept the Commodores from entering a Thanksgiving Day showdown with Alabama for the Southeastern Conference crown undefeated.

One of the season's highlights was a successful "hidden ball" trick against LSU. This, needless to say, was *not* the one outlawed in 1895 after Auburn used it against Vanderbilt.

Three minutes into the game, Vanderbilt got the ball on the Tigers' 38-yard line. Vandy halfback Clarence Reinschmidt received the ball from center, spun, concealed the ball on the ground behind a Vanderbilt lineman, then faked cleverly around his left end. The LSU team and the game officials went with Reinschmidt, while tackle Greer Ricketson scooped up the ball and ran for the winning touchdown in a 7–6 win.

Alabama entered the 1937 Thanksgiving Day game against Vanderbilt undefeated. Neither team knew at the time that a Rose Bowl bid was riding on the outcome of the contest. With six minutes left in the game, Vanderbilt led 7–6. However, Crimson Tide substitute end Sandy Sanford kicked a perfect 23-yard field goal for a 9–7 Alabama win. Ironically, before the end of the first half, the Commodores had tried the "hidden ball" trick that had been so successful against LSU. Unfortunately, this time Alabama recovered the football and drove to the Tide's lone touchdown of the day.

Morrison followed the 1937 season with consecutive 6–3–0 and 2–7–1 records. In 1940 Morrison announced he would not sign the one-year contract Vanderbilt offered him and instead would become head coach and athletic director at Temple University.

After several days of deliberation, the Vanderbilt Athletic Committee chose two finalists for the head coaching position: Georgia Tech Coach Bobby Dodd and Henry "Red" Sanders, 1927 back-up quarterback to Spears. Chiefly because of his youth (he was only thirty-five) and the fact that he had been a backfield coach, the committee decided on Sanders as Vanderbilt's eleventh head football coach.

Vanderbilt Vice-Chancellor C. Madison Sarratt once recalled his thoughts on hiring Sanders, a close friend. "It was considered a tremendous risk, hiring an untested man to coach a team when he was only thirty-five," Sarratt admitted. "His career at Vanderbilt was highlighted by his ability to pick students who could play football and do their schoolwork too."

Sanders acquired his nickname "Red" not for the color of his hair, but because as a boy playing sandlot football in Nashville he always wore a red sweater. One day, after watching him play, the elder Sanders started calling his son "my red-jerseyed bull." The nickname was shortened to Red, and even though he did not have a red hair on his head, Sanders's nickname stuck with him throughout his life.

Henry "Red" Sanders's teams won thirty-six games in six years, including his last eight games at Vanderbilt before he left to take over the head-coaching position at UCLA.

Red had been a member of the 1927 Vandy football squad and had played second fiddle to future Hall-of-Famer Spears. After lettering for the Commodores in football, basketball and baseball, Sanders became a backfield assistant at Clemson. He was a Tiger six months a year and played professional baseball the other six months. As it turned out, Sanders was as versatile as a coach as he had been as an athlete.

He left Clemson in 1931 to become head coach at Columbia Military Academy. In 1934 he moved to Riverside Prep, where he compiled a 55–4–2 record in four years. In 1938 he became the freshman coach at Florida, and in 1939 backfield coach at LSU.

Sanders's 1940 Vandy team quickly established a trademark that was to be Sanders's strong point throughout his seventeen-year coaching stint at Vanderbilt and UCLA: a tough-as-nails defense. Though the 1940 squad won only three games, the Commodores outscored their ten opponents 101–98.

It was during the 1940 season that a Vanderbilt line coach by the name of Paul "Bear" Bryant got his first chance at head coaching. Bryant had followed Sanders to Vanderbilt in 1940, after serving as an assistant at Alabama for six years.

The Commodores had ripped Washington and Lee 19–0 in the season opener before falling to two-touchdown favorite Princeton by a 7–6 margin. The Thursday before the third game of the season, against Kentucky, Sanders had to be rushed to the hospital for an emergency appendectomy. The head-coaching responsibility fell to Bryant.

Vandy scored on a Mickey Flanigan pass to Binks Bushmiaer in the first quarter. Leading 7–0 at halftime, the Commodores received an inspirational talk from Sanders via a telephone hookup from his hospital bed.

With three minutes left in the game, the score still stood 7–0 in favor of Vanderbilt. Kentucky, however, scored from the 7-yard line, and the game ended in a tie. Sanders considered the game a moral victory, and it helped launch Bryant's fantastic coaching career.

The 1941 Vanderbilt squad posted an 8–2–0 record and was one of the nation's strongest teams. The Commodores beat Purdue, Georgia Tech and Alabama and finished second only to Tulane in the SEC. Sanders was selected SEC Coach of the Year by his peers for his masterful job.

In 1942 Sanders enlisted for naval duty in World War II. When he returned in 1946, Commodore fortunes were at a low ebb. There was a push for Vandy to deemphasize football or totally disband the program. Sanders, however, guided a small, physically outmanned Commodore team to a 5–4 record, including wins over Mississippi, Florida and Auburn.

The 1947 team pulled upsets over Harry Gilmer-led Alabama, the SEC champs, and Charlie Conerly and the Rebels of Mississippi, finishing with a strong 6–4–0 mark.

Sanders's 1948 team ranks with the finest in Vanderbilt history. After sputtering to a 0–2–1 start, Vandy roared to eight straight wins, including a 28–6 shellacking of Tennessee, the first victory over the Vols since 1937.

Former Vanderbilt and professional football standout Herb Rich remembers the Sanders style:

"We never went on the field that year with any idea except winning. We had no halftime pep talks, either. Coach Sanders usually had a word or two about strategic changes, but the gist of his conversations was usually humorous.

"I recall once when we were playing horribly the first two quarters. At halftime, Coach Sanders came to the dressing room and said: 'You guys cut short your summer vacations to come here and practice football. You've worked your heads off every morning and afternoon. If you're silly enough to goof off out there for an hour and waste it all, if you can't dig inside you and get it up, then you're just not very smart!' "

Sanders had pulled Rich after he made two mistakes in the Kentucky game in 1947. Sanders challenged Rich to do better, saying that otherwise he would play very little that year.

"I told him I'd do my best," Rich said. "He said my best wasn't good enough." Rich responded to the challenge by earning All-SEC honors as a defensive back in 1948 and 1949. He later played pro football and was a member of the New York Giants' 1956 NFL championship team.

Sanders always retained a sense of humor along with his knowledge of the perils of the coaching profession. In 1950, when Florida asked him to leave UCLA to coach the Gators, a horde of students descended on his apartment chanting over and over, "Don't go, Red!"

"No coach in the world is worth all this excitement," Sanders told them. However, knowing full well the hazards of coaching, he turned to his wife and joked, "Which one of them has the rope?"

Though the 1948 Vanderbilt team had been one of his finest, Sanders was unhappy with the rumblings of the alumni during the squad's slow September start. In December UCLA offered him the head coaching job. Although the Bruins had traditionally been a Pacific Coast Conference also-ran, Sanders saw the job as a challenge. He accepted it and headed for the Coast, leaving Vanderbilt—and a six-year winning percentage of .617—behind.

Sanders continued his success in Los Angeles. In 1954 his Bruin team won the national championship and went to the Rose Bowl undefeated. There UCLA lost to Michigan State, 28–20, but Sanders was named national Coach of the Year by his fellow coaches.

He took UCLA to the Rose Bowl again in 1956. The Bruins fell to Michigan State again, this time on a field goal in the last seven seconds.

Sanders died of a heart attack in Los Angeles in 1958. Perhaps the best tribute to the man who guided Vanderbilt football fortunes during the 1940s was given by longtime Commodore business manager and assistant athletic director Pete Naylor: "To me, Red Sanders wrote the textbook on success. Red Sanders was the Robert E. Lee of Southern football. He accomplished so much with less than adequate troops."

Coach Art Guepe takes one of his many victorious journeys across the gridiron on the shoulders of his players. Here, guard Larry Hayes (left) and center Barry Heywood (right) carry Guepe off after Vanderbilt's 26–0 win over Tennessee in 1954.

Vanderbilt football went through four mediocre seasons to begin the 1950s. Starting in 1953, under Coach Art Guepe, however, the Commodores began to rise to national prominence again.

"The 1955 football team had a lot of character," Guepe, who lives in Nashville, remembered. "We didn't have a lot of depth, but we had good talent. It was a real dedicated group."

At the end of the 1955 season, Vandy sported a 7–3–0 record. However, a season-ending loss to Tennessee and an elbow injury to starting quarterback Don Orr seemed to preclude a bowl offer.

Yet the Sunday after the Tennessee game Guepe received a phone call in Nashville from Gator Bowl President George Olsen, offering Vandy a match with SEC rival Auburn.

"I was very excited," Guepe recalled. "I called a special meeting of the team for nine o'clock that night. I wanted the players to decide whether or not to go. Chancellor Harvie Branscomb showed up at the meeting. He had been under pressure from some of the University's academicians, who were afraid a bowl trip would hurt Vanderbilt's prestige as an outstanding academic institution.

"Just as Chancellor Branscomb was about to voice this opinion, guard Larry Hayes got up and said, 'Chancellor Branscomb, you can talk all day, but we want to go and we're going.' That settled the issue right then and there."

Guepe flew to Jacksonville, signed the contract, and was handed a box with Vandy's allotment of 5000 tickets for the bowl game. He remembered his feelings at the time:

"Each ticket was worth eight dollars, so I was carrying around $40,000 with me! I flew to Atlanta, but

Coach Guepe confers with quarterback Don Orr before the 1955 Gator Bowl, the first bowl game Vanderbilt ever participated in. Orr, Most Valuable Player, led the Commodores to a 25–13 win over Auburn despite an injured arm.

the next flight to Nashville didn't leave until the next morning.

"I had a dilemma: did I check into a hotel room with the tickets, or did I take the train? I chose the train. However, I could only get an upper berth on the train so, to keep the tickets safe that night, I had to put them to bed with me!"

In the game itself, Hayes and Larry Frank harassed the Auburn quarterback all day long, as the Commodores triumphed in their first bowl appearance, 25–13. Guepe calls the game "perfect."

Though the Commodores' performance in the Gator Bowl may have been a little surprising, Don Orr's return to form was simply incredible.

Guepe remembered:

"We had to tape Orr's arm to his side during practice. It was his passing arm, so we couldn't pass any when he practiced with us. I didn't know if he'd start until right before the game started. We took the tape off his elbow and he said he could go. He said he could go with tears in his eyes—that's how ready he was—and he really went."

Indeed he went. He passed, ran and punted his way to the Gator Bowl's Most Valuable Player award. Orr completed 4 of 6 passes for 67 yards and 1 touchdown, rushed 10 times for 43 yards and 2 more touchdowns, and even punted for a 32-yard average.

A late bloomer on the Gator Bowl squad was Tommy Woodroof, the Vandy placekicker. He performed his duties to perfection in Jacksonville. Two years previously, however, as a sophomore, he had experienced great anguish. As he had approached the ball on an extra-point attempt, his foot had hit the turf in front of the ball, making the ball skim harmlessly along the grass in front of the uprights.

"He came a long way," Guepe said.

Guepe had a unique attitude toward the two-point conversion rule passed by the NCAA during his term as head coach at Vanderbilt. "I'll get the ruling from the stands," Guepe joked. "That way I won't be put on the spot. I think the head coach is put on the spot enough times as it is, now. If I get the ruling from the stands, that will put the fans on the spot."

Guepe resigned from coaching in 1962 and was replaced by Jack Green, a former All-American guard who had paved the way for Doc Blanchard and Glenn Davis at West Point. In 1964 Green's Commodores upset Tennessee 7–0 on the only touchdown of senior halfback Bob Sullins's Vanderbilt career.

Sullins recounted:

"I had lettered as a punter in 1961," recounted Sullins, "was the starting halfback in 1962 when I was injured early in the season, and broke a leg in the fall of 1963. I started in 1964 and was the seventh leading rusher in the Conference, but I still hadn't scored a touchdown until the Tennessee game.

All-SEC fullback Phil King (1956).

"The week before the game, Coach Green put in the 'Sally Rand,' the Vanderbilt version of the Statue of Liberty play, where the quarterback goes back into the pocket, cocks his arm as if he is going to throw it, and then an end or wingback comes behind him to take it around on a naked reverse.

Vanderbilt halfback Bob Sullins scored the only touchdown of his career in the 7–0 Vanderbilt victory over Tennessee in 1964.

"Against Tennessee the next Saturday, we were on our 40-yard line when Coach Green called the 'Sally Rand.' Our wingback, Toby Wilt, took the ball to the UT 2-yard line on that play. From there I rammed it over in two tries. That was all the scoring of the game, but it sure was a sweet one."

Vanderbilt's 7–0 win over the Vols was the last Commodore win over its intrastate rival until 1975. Green went 2–7–1 and 1–9–0 in 1965 and 1966, and he was replaced by Bill Pace, a bright young Arkansas assistant, in 1967.

Pace guided the Black and Gold to a 5–4–1 record in 1968 and in 1969 pulled an amazing 14–10 upset over Paul "Bear" Bryant and his Alabama team at Dudley Stadium.

"We thought we could win," recalled Watson Brown, the Vanderbilt quarterback that night. "Alabama was number two in the country and undefeated through three games. But after watching them on film, it was obvious we could beat them. We knew we were better."

Vanderbilt fell behind, 3–0, on an Alabama field goal in the first quarter. But the Commodores came back to take a 7–3 lead at halftime on halfback Doug Matthews's 6-yard pass to Dave Strong.

Alabama went back on top in the third quarter and led 10–7 late in the fourth period.

Pat Toomay, who anchored the Vanderbilt line during the 1967–1969 seasons, went on to stardom in the NFL as part of Dallas's "Doomsday Defense."

"It was third down, and we were 10 yards from the Alabama goal," Brown said. "I called a play-action pass where Jimmy Cunningham crossed over the middle. It was a very simple play. Alabama knew we were going to have to pass, but Jimmy just outran their defender and I hit him right on the numbers for the winning touchdown."

Unfortunately for the Commodores, not many more upsets came their way that season, and the 1969 team finished 4–6. Pace suffered through three more losing seasons before being replaced by Steve Sloan in 1973.

The twenty-nine-year-old Sloan, a former All-American quarterback for Bear Bryant at Alabama, led the Commodores to a Peach Bowl tie in 1974.

Following a 5–6 record in 1973, which included a stunning upset of Georgia at Dudley Field, Vanderbilt posted a 7–3–1 regular-season record and tied Texas Tech in the 1974 Peach Bowl, 6–6. It was Vandy's first bowl appearance in nineteen years.

Before 34,000 partisan fans in Dudley Field, quarterback Watson Brown led the Commodores to a stunning 14–10 upset over previously undefeated Alabama in 1969.

Young Alabama assistant coach Steve Sloan came to Vanderbilt in 1973 to revive Commodore football fortunes and in two years had taken Vandy to the Peach Bowl.

Sloan said:

"That 1974 squad was a collection of individuals who typified pure determination and will. I don't think I've ever been a part of a team that had that much will, determination and sheer disregard for anything but success. That team had excellent practice habits. They were the hardest practicing group I've had.

"An example of their determination was the Georgia game in 1974: they got behind 31–14 and fought back to tie it 31–31 with only a minute to go. Then, even though they lost that game in the last seconds, they bounced back the next week to beat Ole Miss."

One of the keys to the Commodores' success that year was back-up quarterback David Lee, who successfully stepped in for injured starter Fred Fisher. Lee went on to lead the SEC in passing in 1974, completing 85 of 159 passes for 1173 yards and 7 touchdowns and rushing for 225 yards and 5 more touchdowns.

"David's ability to put the team before personal goals," Sloan said, "and his winning attitude were important to our successes that season."

Lee, who came from Pensacola, Florida, made his home state's university sorry they had not recruited him, especially after the Gators and Commodores tangled in 1974. When fifth-ranked Florida came to

Vanderbilt's all-time rushing leader Jamie O'Rourke follows the block of center Bill Holby (50) for a few tough yards in the 6–6 Peach Bowl tie with Texas Tech.

Quarterback David Lee, who led the SEC in passing in 1974.

Vanderbilt on October 12, Vandy, led by Lee—who rushed for 30 yards and 1 touchdown and completed 8 of 11 passes for 128 yards and another touchdown—beat the Gators, 24–10.

Two-time All-American Barry Burton was also instrumental in Vandy's success in 1974 and 1975. In the 1973 Georgia upset, Burton got off the longest punt in Commodore history—79 yards. "Barry's punting created good field position for us that year," Sloan said.

A genuine throwback to the triple-threat days of yore, Burton was also a key pass receiver from his tight-end spot and was virtually unstoppable on the end-around play.

Amazingly, Burton faced the same situation against the same team, Tennessee, three straight years. And he proved that three times on a gridiron—as opposed to three on a match—can be lucky.

Sloan recalled:

"Against Tennessee in 1974, he dropped a punt, they recovered the ball, scored a touchdown, and tied the game 21–21. In 1973, with his back to the goal line late in the game—the same situation as in 1974—he had to run with the punt and was stopped short of the first down when we were tied with the Vols. Tennessee went from there, kicked a field goal, and won 20–17. It was just a coincidence that he had had that same thing happen two years in a row."

Make that three years in a row—almost. The coach this time was Fred Pancoast, who had coached Memphis State to a 20–12–1 mark the previous three years. He was hired after Sloan accepted the head-coaching job at Texas Tech. It was late in the fourth quarter of the 1975 edition of the traditional season finale against Tennessee, the Commodores were leading their archrivals, and Burton was punting from deep in his own end zone at Neyland Stadium in Knoxville. A deafening din arose, as 65,000 Vol partisans, remembering the last two years, began chanting, "Punt, Barry, punt!"

All-SEC and All-American Barry Burton was a triple threat—punter, runner and receiver—and led the Commodores to several wins, including their 1975 victory over Tennessee.

"The score was 17–14. Even the public address announcer got in on the act, saying: 'Now punting for Vanderbilt, *out of the end zone,* Barry Burton!'" Pancoast recalled, half jokingly.

"Not only did he get a beauty of a punt off, but when Vol back Stanley Morgan broke the return down the sideline, Barry made the tackle on our 35. He was the last man between Morgan and our goal."

Vandy went on to hold Tennessee on the 35-yard line and successfully defend against a field-goal attempt, to defeat the Vols in Knoxville for the first time in sixteen years. That particular game had a special theme, according to Pancoast:

"Fourteen thousand Vanderbilt fans followed us to Knoxville. They had come faithfully for the past eight times we had been in Knoxville, only to face a long ride back to Nashville after a loss.

"Kenny Starr had just written and recorded a popular song 'Blind Man in the Bleachers.' According to the song, a blind man came faithfully to every game, and even though he knew he'd never see his son play, his son knew he would be there for moral support. Then one night he failed to appear at the game. His son, a benchwarmer, was notified of his father's death at halftime, as the song goes, and went on to star and win the game. I told the squad the story of the song in the dressing room that day. Our team played with great enthusiasm." And finished the season with a 7–4 record.

From the McGugin era to the "Blind Man in the

Coach Fred Pancoast assumed the coaching reins in 1975 and promptly gave Vandy fans what they had been waiting for since 1964: a 17–14 win over arch-rival Tennessee. Here, Pancoast is carried off the field after Vanderbilt's first win over the Vols in eleven years.

6'8" 272-pound Dennis Harrison lettered all four of his years at Vanderbilt and was named the Outstanding Defensive Player of the Peach Bowl Game after he blocked a Texas Tech field goal attempt.

twenty-five years ago and have gone on to make outstanding contributions to their communities through academics or business. Dr. Bill Mac Jones, President of Memphis State University and a member Bleachers," Vanderbilt football has come a long way. And just this year it came even further, with the hiring of its twentieth head coach, George MacIntyre, former defensive coordinator at Ole Miss and Steve Sloan's secondary coach at Vandy in 1973–1974.

But despite its appreciation of football and its place in a successful overall program, Vanderbilt has remained unique in combining sports and academics. Its rich heritage is best exemplified by the fact that three former Vanderbilt football players have won the NCAA's Silver Anniversary award, an honor conferred on athletes who finished their eligibility

of the 1948 and 1949 football teams, received the honor in 1975, and Ernest J. "Bucky" Curtis of Chicago and Bill Wade, a prominent Nashville businessman, won the honor in 1976 and 1977, respectively. Through these men and others like them Vanderbilt has proven, both in the past and in the present, that it's possible for a man to be both a scholar and an athlete.

All-SEC quarterback (1951) and holder of most of Vandy's passing records, Bill Wade is the recipient of the NCAA's Silver Anniversary award, representative of Vanderbilt's successful combination of sports and academics.

SEC Records

The SEC

SEC Annual Football Standings—1933 to 1978

1933

School	Conference W-L-T	Pct.	Pts.	Opp.	Overall W-L-T	Pts.	Opp.
Alabama......	5-0-1	.917	69	15	7-1-1	130	17
L.S.U...........	3-0-2	.800	73	20	7-0-3	176	27
Georgia.......	3-1-0	.750	53	33	8-2-0	148	86
Tennessee..	5-2-0	.714	134	37	7-3-0	176	47
Tulane.........	4-2-1	.643	127	55	6-3-1	160	68
Auburn.........	2-2-0	.500	40	43	5-5-0	133	104
Mississippi...	2-2-1	.500	78	66	6-3-2	167	79
Vanderbilt....	2-2-2	.500	56	74	4-3-3	126	107
Florida.........	2-3-0	.400	50	53	5-3-1	114	53
Kentucky.....	2-3-0	.400	14	87	5-5-0	91	116
Ga. Tech.....	2-5-0	.286	62	55	5-5-0	117	83
Miss. State..	1-5-1	.214	39	143	2-7-1	69	149
Sewanee.....	0-6-0	.000	36	158	3-6-0	75	165

1934

School	Conference W-L-T	Pct.	Pts.	Opp.	Overall W-L-T	Pts.	Opp.
Tulane.........	8-0-0	1.000	148	49	9-1-0	195	69
Alabama......	7-0-0	1.000	223	32	9-0-0	287	32
Tennessee..	5-1-0	.833	98	32	8-2-0	175	58
L.S.U...........	4-2-0	.667	113	41	7-2-2	172	77
Georgia.......	3-2-0	.600	51	33	7-3-0	141	56
Vanderbilt....	4-3-0	.571	66	94	6-3-0	105	100
Florida.........	2-2-1	.500	52	74	6-3-1	113	110
Mississippi...	2-3-1	.417	39	78	4-5-1	114	98
Kentucky.....	1-3-0	.250	30	73	5-5-0	123	86
Auburn.........	1-6-0	.143	37	87	2-8-0	58	107
Sewanee.....	0-4-0	.000	12	105	2-7-0	40	147
Miss. State..	0-5-0	.000	6	94	4-6-0	79	126
Ga. Tech.....	0-6-0	.000	42	125	1-9-0	56	187

1935

School	Conference W-L-T	Pct.	Pts.	Opp.	Overall W-L-T	Pts.	Opp.
L.S.U...........	5-0-0	1.000	95	15	9-1-0	221	38
Vanderbilt....	5-1-0	.833	103	42	7-3-0	179	68
Mississippi...	3-1-0	.750	87	26	9-2-0	292	66
Auburn.........	5-2-0	.714	118	39	8-2-0	201	46
Alabama......	4-2-0	.667	106	48	6-2-1	185	55
Tulane.........	3-3-0	.500	86	87	6-4-0	156	123
Kentucky.....	3-3-0	.500	80	68	5-4-0	167	94
Ga. Tech.....	3-4-0	.429	123	123	5-5-0	162	142
Miss. State..	2-3-0	.400	73	63	8-3-0	190	76
Tennessee..	2-3-0	.400	34	84	4-5-0	98	155
Georgia.......	2-4-0	.333	54	81	6-4-0	169	88
Florida.........	1-6-0	.143	51	134	3-7-0	113	154
Sewanee.....	0-6-0	.000	0	189	2-7-0	15	228

1936

School	Conference W-L-T	Pct.	Pts.	Opp.	Overall W-L-T	Pts.	Opp.
L.S.U...........	6-0-0	1.000	143	13	9-0-1	281	33
Alabama......	5-0-1	.917	89	29	8-0-1	168	35
Auburn.........	4-1-1	.750	58	44	7-2-2	160	63
Tennessee..	3-1-2	.667	79	25	6-2-2	147	52
Miss. State..	3-2-0	.600	101	25	7-2-1	220	25
Georgia.......	3-3-0	.500	74	133	5-4-1	115	159
Ga. Tech.....	3-3-1	.500	164	63	5-5-1	251	103
Tulane.........	2-3-1	.417	73	91	6-3-1	163	117
Vanderbilt....	1-3-1	.300	33	59	3-5-1	115	87
Kentucky.....	1-3-0	.250	13	55	6-4-0	179	84
Florida.........	1-5-0	.167	40	98	4-6-0	99	125
Mississippi...	0-3-1	.125	12	46	5-5-2	150	98
Sewanee.....	0-5-0	.000	13	211	0-6-1	20	230

1937

School	Conference W-L-T	Pct.	Pts.	Opp.	Overall W-L-T	Pts.	Opp.
Alabama......	6-0-0	1.000	145	20	9-0-0	225	20
L.S.U...........	5-1-0	.833	108	21	9-1-0	234	27
Auburn.........	4-1-2	.714	95	23	5-2-3	121	36
Vanderbilt....	4-2-0	.667	80	36	7-2-0	121	42
Miss. State..	3-2-0	.600	42	94	5-4-1	119	117
Ga. Tech.....	3-2-1	.583	64	34	6-3-1	177	54
Tennessee..	4-3-0	.571	130	47	6-3-1	189	47
Florida.........	3-4-0	.429	46	59	4-7-0	86	89
Tulane.........	2-3-1	.417	66	50	5-4-1	164	69
Georgia.......	1-2-2	.400	13	50	6-3-2	151	64
Mississippi...	0-4-0	.000	14	68	4-5-1	127	106
Kentucky.....	0-5-0	.000	0	104	4-6-0	93	130
Sewanee.....	0-6-0	.000	7	204	2-7-0	78	213

1938

School	Conference W-L-T	Pct.	Pts.	Opp.	Overall W-L-T	Pts.	Opp.
Tennessee..	7-0-0	1.000	167	9	10-0-0	276	16
Alabama......	4-1-1	.750	82	33	7-1-1	149	40
Tulane.........	4-1-1	.750	107	9	7-2-1	211	53
Mississippi...	3-2-0	.600	85	73	9-2-0	232	120
Ga. Tech.....	2-1-3	.583	47	51	3-4-3	72	84
Vanderbilt....	4-3-0	.571	54	49	6-3-0	84	49
Florida.........	2-2-1	.500	25	54	4-5-1	112	149
Auburn.........	3-3-1	.500	84	49	4-5-1	110	88
Georgia.......	1-2-1	.375	39	57	5-4-1	145	143
L.S.U...........	2-4-0	.333	58	83	6-4-0	160	89
Miss. State..	1-4-0	.200	41	98	4-6-0	123	131
Kentucky.....	0-4-0	.000	31	105	2-7-0	150	160
Sewanee.....	0-6-0	.000	9	159	1-8-0	59	213

1939

School	Conference W-L-T	Pct.	Pts.	Opp.	Overall W-L-T	Pts.	Opp.
Tennessee..	6-0-0	1.000	120	0	10-0-0	212	0
Ga. Tech...	6-0-0	1.000	74	25	7-2-0	129	49
Tulane.........	5-0-0	1.000	128	26	8-0-1	181	46
Miss. State..	3-2-0	.600	47	32	8-2-0	216	32
Mississippi...	2-2-0	.500	40	50	7-2-0	230	64
Kentucky.....	2-2-1	.500	47	58	6-2-1	161	64
Auburn.........	3-3-1	.500	48	40	5-5-1	71	69
Alabama......	2-3-1	.417	53	47	5-3-1	101	53
Georgia.......	1-3-0	.250	12	35	5-6-0	113	98
L.S.U...........	1-5-0	.167	58	109	4-5-0	111	116
Vanderbilt....	1-6-0	.143	57	120	2-7-1	96	165
Florida.........	0-3-1	.125	16	48	5-5-1	78	66
Sewanee.....	0-3-0	.000	7	117	3-5-0	43	150

1940

	Conference				Overall		
School	W-L-T	Pct.	Pts.	Opp.	W-L-T	Pts.	Opp.
Tennessee..	5-0-0	1.000	122	12	10-0-0	319	26
Miss. State..	4-0-1	.900	88	21	9-0-1	233	51
Mississippi...	3-1-0	.750	60	46	9-2-0	251	100
Alabama......	4-2-0	.667	89	80	7-2-0	166	80
Auburn.........	3-2-1	.583	89	70	6-4-1	170	153
L.S.U...........	3-3-0	.500	55	82	6-4-0	139	112
Georgia.......	2-3-1	.417	82	106	5-4-1	209	134
Florida.........	2-3-0	.400	48	81	5-5-0	136	141
Kentucky.....	1-2-2	.400	40	79	5-3-2	190	107
Tulane.........	1-3-0	.250	41	60	5-5-0	144	126
Vanderbilt....	1-5-1	.214	55	91	3-6-1	101	98
Ga. Tech.....	1-5-0	.167	72	93	3-7-0	139	160
Sewanee.....	0-1-0	.000	0	20	3-5-0	132	125

1941

	Conference				Overall		
School	W-L-T	Pct.	Pts.	Opp.	W-L-T	Pts.	Opp.
Miss. State..	4-0-1	.900	40	7	8-1-1	191	55
Tennessee..	3-1-0	.750	61	29	8-2-0	182	73
Alabama......	5-2-0	.714	105	51	8-2-0	234	64
Georgia.......	3-1-1	.700	75	44	8-1-1	279	59
Mississippi...	2-1-1	.625	47	45	6-2-1	131	67
Vanderbilt....	3-2-0	.600	81	82	8-2-0	260	89
L.S.U...........	2-2-2	.500	47	33	4-4-2	119	93
Tulane.........	2-3-0	.400	93	72	5-4-0	220	95
Ga. Tech.....	2-4-0	.333	62	96	3-6-0	82	130
Florida.........	1-3-0	.250	24	42	4-6-0	149	97
Auburn.........	0-4-1	.100	28	88	4-5-1	123	115
Kentucky.....	0-4-0	.000	35	109	5-4-0	151	154

1942

	Conference				Overall		
School	W-L-T	Pct.	Pts.	Opp.	W-L-T	Pts.	Opp.
Georgia.......	6-1-0	.857	238	56	10-1-0	367	76
Ga. Tech.....	4-1-0	.800	89	48	9-1-0	212	73
Tennessee..	4-1-0	.800	85	15	8-1-1	245	54
Miss. State..	5-2-0	.714	118	62	8-2-0	200	77
Alabama......	4-2-0	.667	80	41	7-3-0	209	76
L.S.U...........	3-2-0	.600	62	70	7-3-0	192	117
Auburn.........	3-3-0	.500	79	60	6-4-1	174	133
Vanderbilt....	2-4-0	.333	61	113	6-4-0	232	113
Florida.........	1-3-0	.250	25	121	3-7-0	106	185
Tulane.........	1-4-0	.200	47	113	4-5-0	121	154
Kentucky.....	0-5-0	.000	19	101	3-6-1	155	154
Mississippi...	0-5-0	.000	33	136	2-7-0	132	163

1943

	Conference				Overall		
School	W-L-T	Pct.	Pts.	Opp.	W-L-T	Pts.	Opp.
Ga. Tech.....	3-0-0	1.000	123	7	7-3-0	280	124
Tulane.........	1-1-0	.500	27	33	3-3-0	92	94
L.S.U...........	2-2-0	.500	68	102	5-3-0	143	144
Georgia.......	0-3-0	.000	33	109	6-4-0	264	153
Vanderbilt....	0-0-0	.000	0	0	5-0-0	145	33

1944

	Conference				Overall		
School	W-L-T	Pct.	Pts.	Opp.	W-L-T	Pts.	Opp.
Ga. Tech.....	4-0-0	1.000	119	13	8-2-0	241	75
Tennessee..	5-0-1	.917	120	27	8-0-1	173	48
Georgia.......	4-2-0	.667	121	103	7-3-0	269	130
Alabama......	3-1-2	.667	128	47	5-1-2	246	54
Miss. State..	3-2-0	.600	73	59	6-2-0	219	79
L.S.U...........	2-3-1	.417	79	80	2-5-1	92	101
Mississippi...	2-3-0	.400	59	95	2-6-0	77	178
Tulane.........	1-2-0	.333	29	72	4-3-0	113	125
Kentucky.....	1-5-0	.167	59	134	3-6-0	125	147
Florida.........	0-3-0	.000	18	104	4-3-0	108	136
Auburn.........	0-4-0	.000	47	118	4-4-0	181	137
Vanderbilt....	0-0-0	.000	0	0	3-0-1	67	23

1945

	Conference				Overall		
School	W-L-T	Pct.	Pts.	Opp.	W-L-T	Pts.	Opp.
Alabama......	6-0-0	1.000	265	60	9-0-0	396	66
Tennessee..	3-1-0	.750	100	25	8-1-0	238	52
L.S.U...........	5-2-0	.714	172	80	7-2-0	245	92
Georgia.......	4-2-0	.667	164	66	8-2-0	294	94
Mississippi...	3-3-0	.500	68	112	4-5-0	100	183
Ga. Tech.....	2-2-0	.500	68	56	4-6-0	157	165
Miss. State..	2-3-0	.400	79	96	6-3-0	221	108
Auburn.........	2-3-0	.400	46	89	5-5-0	172	129
Vanderbilt....	2-4-0	.333	40	175	3-6-0	71	215
Florida.........	1-3-1	.300	32	79	4-5-1	155	100
Tulane.........	1-3-1	.300	41	113	2-6-1	93	212
Kentucky.....	0-5-0	.000	38	162	2-8-0	96	217

1946

	Conference				Overall		
School	W-L-T	Pct.	Pts.	Opp.	W-L-T	Pts.	Opp.
Georgia.......	5-0-0	1.000	151	34	10-0-0	372	100
Tennessee..	5-0-0	1.000	57	29	9-1-0	175	89
L.S.U...........	5-1-0	.833	140	101	9-1-0	240	123
Ga. Tech.....	4-2-0	.667	128	75	8-2-0	243	108
Miss. State..	3-2-0	.600	80	44	8-2-0	271	71
Alabama......	4-3-0	.571	85	84	7-4-0	186	110
Vanderbilt....	3-4-0	.429	66	43	5-4-0	108	43
Kentucky.....	2-3-0	.400	50	69	7-3-0	233	97
Tulane.........	2-4-0	.333	106	110	3-7-0	179	209
Auburn.........	1-5-0	.167	53	164	4-6-0	132	210
Mississippi...	1-6-0	.143	61	130	2-7-0	77	144
Florida.........	0-5-0	.000	46	140	0-9-0	104	264

1947

	Conference				Overall		
School	W-L-T	Pct.	Pts.	Opp.	W-L-T	Pts.	Opp.
Mississippi...	6-1-0	.857	157	82	8-2-0	256	101
Ga. Tech.....	4-1-0	.800	88	21	9-1-0	220	35
Alabama......	5-2-0	.714	122	61	8-2-0	203	74
Miss. State..	2-2-0	.500	54	54	7-3-0	169	89
Georgia.......	3-3-0	.500	104	81	7-4-0	192	115
Vanderbilt....	3-3-0	.500	72	58	6-4-0	182	85
Tulane.........	2-3-2	.429	88	100	2-5-2	94	192
L.S.U...........	2-3-1	.417	95	121	5-3-1	149	161
Kentucky.....	2-3-0	.400	53	40	7-3-0	151	59
Tennessee..	2-3-0	.400	38	93	5-5-0	164	152
Auburn.........	1-5-0	.167	33	151	2-7-0	78	204
Florida.........	0-3-1	.125	33	75	4-5-1	125	156

1948

	Conference				Overall		
School	W-L-T	Pct.	Pts.	Opp.	W-L-T	Pts.	Opp.
Georgia.......	6-0-0	1.000	175	51	9-1-0	278	100
Mississippi...	6-1-0	.857	160	73	8-1-0	226	93
Tulane.........	5-1-0	.833	124	40	9-1-0	207	60
Vanderbilt....	4-2-1	.643	170	67	8-2-1	328	73
Ga. Tech.....	4-3-0	.571	126	62	7-3-0	226	69
Alabama......	4-4-1	.500	153	164	6-4-1	228	170
Miss. State..	3-3-0	.500	62	59	4-4-1	103	87
Tennessee..	2-3-1	.417	59	77	4-4-2	140	98
Kentucky.....	1-3-1	.300	60	96	5-3-2	199	128
Florida.........	1-5-0	.167	78	153	5-5-0	213	206
L.S.U...........	1-5-0	.167	52	178	3-7-0	99	271
Auburn.........	0-7-0	.000	29	228	1-8-1	68	262

1949

	Conference				Overall		
School	W-L-T	Pct.	Pts.	Opp.	W-L-T	Pts.	Opp.
Tulane.........	5-1-0	.833	155	61	7-2-1	251	142
Kentucky.....	4-1-0	.800	126	6	9-2-0	304	53
Tennessee..	4-1-1	.750	97	64	7-2-1	214	104
Ga.Tech......	5-2-0	.714	134	99	7-3-0	197	129
L.S.U...........	4-2-0	.667	122	53	8-2-0	231	74
Alabama......	4-3-1	.563	145	96	6-3-1	227	130
Vanderbilt....	4-4-0	.500	144	170	5-5-0	177	183
Auburn.........	2-4-2	.375	114	168	2-4-3	134	188
Mississippi...	2-4-0	.333	107	151	4-5-1	246	243
Florida.........	1-4-1	.250	86	156	4-5-1	180	218
Georgia.......	1-4-1	.250	47	94	4-6-1	177	134
Miss.State...	0-6-0	.000	25	184	0-8-1	38	224

1950

	Conference				Overall		
School	W-L-T	Pct.	Pts.	Opp.	W-L-T	Pts.	Opp.
Kentucky.....	5-1-0	.833	157	48	10-1-0	380	62
Tennessee..	4-1-0	.800	99	16	10-1-0	315	57
Alabama......	6-2-0	.750	214	101	9-2-0	328	107
Tulane.........	3-1-1	.700	118	66	6-2-1	260	97
Ga.Tech......	4-2-0	.667	89	95	5-6-0	182	193
Georgia.......	3-2-1	.583	65	44	6-2-3	158	65
Miss.State...	3-4-0	.429	95	123	4-5-0	169	137
L.S.U...........	2-3-2	.429	107	88	4-5-2	165	151
Vanderbilt....	3-4-0	.429	128	178	7-4-0	252	216
Florida.........	2-4-0	.333	90	137	5-5-0	157	181
Mississippi...	1-5-0	.167	75	169	5-5-0	207	183
Auburn.........	0-7-0	.000	17	189	0-10-0	31	255

1951

	Conference				Overall		
School	W-L-T	Pct.	Pts.	Opp.	W-L-T	Pts.	Opp.
Ga.Tech......	7-0-0	1.000	175	41	10-0-1	278	76
Tennesee....	5-0-0	1.000	150	61	10-0-0	373	88
L.S.U...........	4-2-1	.643	63	71	7-3-1	128	111
Mississippi...	4-2-1	.643	181	130	6-3-1	254	157
Kentucky.....	3-3-0	.500	102	68	7-4-0	294	114
Auburn.........	3-4-0	.429	101	164	5-5-0	180	212
Vanderbilt....	3-5-0	.375	147	167	6-5-0	201	195
Alabama......	3-5-0	.375	116	140	5-6-0	263	188
Georgia.......	2-4-0	.333	73	97	5-5-0	176	184
Florida.........	2-4-0	.333	88	96	5-5-0	174	131
Miss.State...	2-5-0	.286	23	107	4-5-0	82	127
Tulane.........	1-5-0	.167	40	117	4-6-0	143	172

1952

	Conference				Overall		
School	W-L-T	Pct.	Pts.	Opp.	W-L-T	Pts.	Opp.
Ga. Tech.....	6-0-0	1.000	124	26	11-0-0	301	52
Tennessee...	5-0-1	.917	142	36	8-1-1	259	63
Mississippi...	4-0-2	.833	122	69	8-0-2	237	96
Alabama......	4-2-0	.667	121	85	9-2-0	264	133
Georgia........	4-3-0	.571	108	131	7-4-0	226	208
Florida.........	3-3-0	.500	127	84	7-3-0	290	109
Miss State...	3-4-0	.429	170	172	5-4-0	225	186
Tulane.........	3-5-0	.375	107	132	5-5-0	188	146
Kentucky......	1-3-2	.333	75	121	5-4-2	161	173
L.S.U...........	2-5-0	.286	101	138	3-7-0	148	214
Vanderbilt....	1-4-1	.250	55	145	3-5-2	151	199
Auburn.........	0-7-0	.000	75	188	2-8-0	139	208

1953

	Conference				Overall		
School	W-L-T	Pct.	Pts.	Opp.	W-L-T	Pts.	Opp.
Alabama......	4-0-3	.786	91	51	6-2-3	172	124
Ga. Tech.....	4-1-1	.750	140	44	8-2-1	246	92
Mississippi...	4-1-1	.750	129	62	7-2-1	236	113

School	W-L-T	Pct.	Pts.	Opp.	W-L-T	Pts.	Opp.
Kentucky......	4-1-1	.750	137	89	7-2-1	201	116
Auburn.........	4-2-1	.643	136	99	7-2-1	257	138
Miss State...	3-1-3	.643	121	80	5-2-3	196	219
Tennessee...	3-2-1	.583	95	80	6-4-1	240	153
L.S.U...........	2-3-3	.438	123	138	5-3-3	194	159
Florida.........	1-3-2	.333	69	79	3-5-2	200	113
Vanderbilt....	1-5-0	.167	59	172	3-7-0	131	258
Georgia........	1-5-0	.167	71	149	3-8-1	155	250
Tulane.........	0-7-0	.000	68	196	1-8-1	129	228

1954

	Conference				Overall		
School	W-L-T	Pct.	Pts.	Opp.	W-L-T	Pts.	Opp.
Mississippi*..	5-1-0	.833	119	29	9-1-0	283	47
Ga. Tech.....	6-2-0	.750	145	63	7-3-0	175	91
Florida.........	5-2-0	.714	94	66	5-5-0	115	128
Kentucky......	5-2-0	.714	90	95	7-3-0	151	125
Georgia........	3-2-1	.583	40	69	6-3-1	89	89
Auburn.........	3-3-0	.500	124	54	7-3-0	243	73
Miss. State..	3-3-0	.500	58	47	6-4-0	192	120
Alabama......	3-3-2	.500	74	74	4-5-2	123	104
L.S.U..........	2-5-0	.286	66	115	5-6-0	125	173
Tulane..........	1-6-1	.188	26	124	1-6-3	46	144
Vanderbilt.....	1-5-0	.167	68	91	2-7-0	134	169
Tennessee...	1-5-0	.167	39	116	4-6-0	105	164

1955

	Conference				Overall		
School	W-L-T	Pct.	Pts.	Opp.	W-L-T	Pts.	Opp.
Mississippi...	5-1-0	.833	135	73	9-1-0	251	97
Auburn.........	5-1-1	.786	123	92	8-1-1	211	98
Ga. Tech.....	4-1-1	.750	87	33	8-1-1	182	46
Tennessee...	3-2-1	.583	74	57	6-3-1	188	92
Vanderbilt....	4-3-0	.571	123	66	7-3-0	215	73
Miss. State..	4-4-0	.500	120	135	6-4-0	173	142
Kentucky......	3-3-1	.500	89	108	6-3-1	178	131
Tulane.........	3-3-1	.500	101	94	5-4-1	163	136
L.S.U..........	2-3-1	.417	106	81	3-5-2	139	149
Florida.........	3-5-0	.375	77	119	4-6-0	111	126
Georgia........	2-5-0	.286	91	123	4-6-0	173	170
Alabama......	0-7-0	.000	36	181	0-10-0	48	256

1956

	Conference				Overall		
School	W-L-T	Pct.	Pts.	Opp.	W-L-T	Pts.	Opp.
Tennessee...	6-0-0	1,000	139	28	10-0-0	268	75
Ga. Tech.....	7-1-0	.875	211	26	9-1-0	227	33
Florida.........	5-2-0	.714	124	58	6-3-1	158	98
Mississippi...	4-2-0	.667	122	68	7-3-0	207	82
Auburn.........	4-3-0	.571	108	110	7-3-0	174	117
Kentucky......	4-4-0	.500	72	105	6-4-0	119	105
Tulane..........	3-3-0	.500	56	83	6-4-0	124	123
Vanderbilt.....	2-5-0	.286	72	91	5-5-0	147	113
Alabama......	2-5-0	.286	53	152	2-7-1	85	208
Miss. State..	2-5-0	.286	104	119	4-6-0	148	152
L.S.U..........	1-5-0	.167	50	158	3-7-0	104	197
Georgia........	1-6-0	.143	30	143	3-6-1	66	162

1957

	Conference				Overall		
School	W-L-T	Pct.	Pts.	Opp.	W-L-T	Pts.	Opp.
Auburn.........	7-0-0	1.000	90	7	10-0-0	207	28
Mississippi...	5-0-1	.917	128	26	8-1-1	232	52
Miss. State..	4-2-1	.643	118	81	6-2-1	175	100
Florida.........	4-2-1	.643	92	70	6-2-1	133	70
Tennessee...	4-3-0	.571	82	62	7-3-0	161	75
Vanderbilt....	3-3-1	.500	47	81	5-3-2	113	108
L.S.U...........	4-4-0	.500	126	76	5-5-0	159	110
Ga. Tech.....	3-4-1	.438	62	71	4-4-2	75	71
Georgia........	3-4-0	.429	72	71	3-7-0	93	150
Tulane.........	1-5-0	.167	41	135	2-8-0	94	195
Alabama......	1-6-1	.188	40	143	2-7-1	69	173
Kentucky......	1-7-0	.125	48	120	3-7-0	128	127

*See page 229, "Appointed Conference Games."

1958

	Conference				Overall		
School	W-L-T	Pct.	Pts.	Opp.	W-L-T	Pts.	Opp.
L.S.U...........	6-0-0	1.000	138	23	10-0-0	275	53
Auburn.........	6-0-1	.929	102	40	9-0-1	173	62
Mississippi*..	4-2-0	.667	83	46	8-2-0	215	65
Vanderbilt....	2-1-3	.583	45	30	5-2-3	131	71
Tennessee...	4-3-0	.571	64	77	4-6-0	77	122
Alabama......	3-4-1	.438	63	69	5-4-1	106	75
Kentucky......	3-4-1	.438	65	109	5-4-1	136	115
Florida.........	2-3-1	.417	66	56	6-3-1	171	93
Ga. Tech.....	2-3-1	.417	53	60	5-4-1	98	91
Georgia........	2-4-0	.333	70	64	4-6-0	196	114
Tulane.........	1-5-0	.167	35	148	3-7-0	105	189
Miss. State..	1-6-0	.143	61	123	3-6-0	127	129

1959

	Conference				Overall		
School	W-L-T	Pct.	Pts.	Opp.	W-L-T	Pts.	Opp.
Georgia........	7-0-0	1.000	123	53	9-1-0	214	89
L.S.U...........	5-1-0	833	79	23	9-1-0	164	29
Mississippi....	5-1-0	.833	184	21	9-1-0	329	21
Alabama......	4-1-2	.714	65	45	7-1-2	95	52
Auburn.........	4-3-0	.571	90	33	7-3-0	174	58
Vanderbilt....	3-2-2	.571	57	79	5-3-2	138	106
Ga. Tech.....	3-3-0	.500	76	69	6-4-0	129	107
Tennessee...	3-4-1	.438	60	111	5-4-1	112	118
Florida.........	2-4-0	.333	60	62	5-4-1	169	107
Kentucky......	1-6-0	.143	45	97	4-6-0	140	107
Tulane.........	0-5-1	.083	39	143	3-6-1	94	176
Miss. State..	0-7-0	.000	19	161	2-7-0	96	198

1960

	Conference				Overall		
School	W-L-T	Pct.	Pts.	Opp.	W-L-T	Pts.	Opp.
Mississippi...	5-0-1	.917	138	37	9-0-1	266	64
Florida.........	5-1-0	.833	93	57	8-2-0	144	74
Alabama......	5-1-1	.786	81	47	8-1-1	180	53
Auburn.........	5-2-0	.714	68	52	8-2-0	155	80
Tennessee...	3-2-2	.571	85	58	6-2-2	209	79
Georgia........	4-3-0	.571	88	95	6-4-0	174	118
Ga. Tech.....	4-4-0	.500	102	78	5-5-0	118	97
L.S.U...........	2-3-1	.417	42	37	5-4-1	105	50
Kentucky......	2-4-1	.357	79	81	5-4-1	206	81
Tulane.........	1-4-1	.250	57	84	3-6-1	132	139
Miss. State..	0-5-1	.084	41	96	2-6-1	101	119
Vanderbilt....	0-7-0	.000	7	159	3-7-0	74	193

1961

	Conference				Overall		
School	W-L-T	Pct.	Pts.	Opp.	W-L-T	Pts.	Opp.
Alabama......	7-0-0	1.000	178	15	10-0-0	287	22
L.S.U...........	6-0-0	1.000	143	27	9-1-0	234	50
Mississippi...	5-1-0	.833	176	33	9-1-0	326	40
Tennessee...	4-3-0	.571	128	114	6-4-0	221	149
Ga. Tech.....	4-3-0	.571	90	42	7-3-0	162	50
Florida.........	3-3-0	.500	57	92	4-5-1	97	146
Auburn.........	3-4-0	.429	94	109	6-4-0	174	137
Kentucky......	2-4-0	.333	81	101	5-5-0	138	123
Georgia........	2-5-0	.286	60	128	3-7-0	84	177
Miss. State..	1-5-0	.167	34	112	5-5-0	111	135
Tulane.........	1-5-0	.167	20	175	2-8-0	60	225
Vanderbilt....	1-6-0	.143	51	163	2-8-0	95	220

1962

	Conference				Overall		
School	W-L-T	Pct.	Pts.	Opp.	W-L-T	Pts.	Opp.
Mississippi...	6-0-0	1.000	117	19	9-0-0	230	40
Alabama......	6-1-0	.857	187	27	9-1-0	272	39
L.S.U...........	5-1-0	.833	113	25	8-1-1	162	34
Ga. Tech.....	5-2-0	.714	141	511	7-2-1	201	83
Florida.........	4-2-0	.667	106	74	6-4-0	204	132
Auburn.........	4-3-0	.571	88	134	6-3-1	173	168
Georgia........	2-3-1	.417	68	123	3-4-3	109	174
Kentucky......	2-3-1	.417	32	54	3-5-2	85	101
Miss. State..	2-5-0	.286	60	101	3-6-0	76	132
Tennessee...	2-6-0	.250	108	120	4-6-0	179	134
Vanderbilt....	1-6-0	.143	34	141	1-9-0	62	215
Tulane.........	0-7-0	.000	43	228	0-10-0	76	293

1963

	Conference				Overall		
School	W-L-T	Pct.	Pts.	Opp.	W-L-T	Pts.	Opp.
Mississippi...	5-0-1	.917	146	27	7-0-2	207	33
Auburn.........	6-1-0	.857	119	74	9-1-0	189	103
Alabama......	6-2-0	.750	177	63	8-2-0	215	88
Miss. State..	4-1-2	.714	96	65	6-2-2	169	82
L.S.U...........	4-2-0	.667	78	57	7-3-0	135	98
Ga. Tech.....	4-3-0	.571	101	76	7-3-0	173	89
Florida.........	3-3-1	.500	61	71	6-3-1	130	120
Tennessee...	3-5-0	.375	85	108	5-5-0	168	121
Georgia........	2-4-0	.333	61	95	4-5-1	133	151
Vanderbilt....	0-5-2	.143	23	113	1-7-2	73	146
Kentucky......	0-5-1	.083	41	109	3-6-1	142	168
Tulane.........	0-6-1	.071	23	153	1-8-1	43	191

1964

	Conference				Overall		
School	W-L-T	Pct.	Pts.	Opp.	W-L-T	Pts.	Opp.
Alabama......	8-0-0	1.000	188	60	10-00	233	67
Georgia........	4-2-0	.667	59	59	6-3-1	123	98
Florida.........	4-2-0	.667	101	64	7-3-0	181	98
Kentucky......	4-2-0	.667	95	97	5-5-0	150	194
L.S.U...........	4-2-1	.643	83	70	7-2-1	115	79
Auburn.........	3-3-0	.500	43	65	6-4-0	123	91
Mississippi...	2-4-1	.357	113	104	5-4-1	210	113
Miss. State..	2-5-0	.286	82	102	4-6-0	155	143
Vanderbilt....	1-4-1	.250	37	67	3-6-1	79	122
Tennessee...	1-5-1	.214	32	87	4-5-1	80	121
Tulane.........	1-5-0	.167	31	82	3-7-0	79	147

1965

	Conference				Overall		
School	W-L-T	Pct.	Pts.	Opp.	W-L-T	Pts.	Opp.
Alabama......	6-1-1	.813	161	65	8-1-1	217	79
Auburn.........	4-1-1	.750	113	115	5-4-1	165	162
Florida.........	4-2-0	.667	126	76	7-3-0	221	129
Tennessee*.	3-1-2	.667	73	40	7-1-2	193	92
Mississippi...	5-3-0	.625	129	77	6-4-0	166	108
L.S.U...........	3-3-0	.500	144	109	7-3-0	251	157
Kentucky......	3-3-0	.500	120	90	6-4-0	202	160
Georgia*......	3-3-0	.500	81	90	6-4-0	186	158
Vanderbilt....	1-5-0	.167	40	125	2-7-1	85	180
Tulane.........	1-5-0	.167	37	192	2-8-0	71	268
Miss. State..	1-5-0	.167	78	123	4-6-0	202	172

1966

	Conference				Overall		
School	W-L-T	Pct.	Pts.	Opp.	W-L-T	Pts.	Opp.
Alabama......	6-0-0	1.000	149	37	10-0-0	267	37
Georgia*......	6-0-0	1.000	132	61	9-1-0	211	89
Florida*........	5-1-0	.800	140	78	8-2-0	238	135
Mississippi...	5-2-0	.714	116	33	8-2-0	170	46
Tennessee*.	4-2-0	.667	130	61	7-3-0	222	87
L.S.U.*.........	3-3-0	.500	75	80	5-4-1	135	124
Kentucky......	2-4-0	.333	65	119	3-6-1	107	196
Auburn.........	1-5-0	.167	60	127	4-6-0	104	162
Miss. State..	0-6-0	.000	45	129	2-8-0	75	176
Vanderbilt*...	0-6-0	.000	28	144	1-9-0	72	237

1967

	Conference				Overall		
School	W-L-T	Pct.	Pts.	Opp.	W-L-T	Pts.	Opp.
Tennessee...	6-0-0	1.000	146	68	9-1-0	259	115
Alabama......	5-1-0	.833	96	61	8-1-1	188	111
Florida.........	4-2-0	.667	123	120	6-4-0	201	161
Georgia*......	4-2-0	.667	138	70	7-3-0	250	105
Mississippi...	4-2-1	.643	120	97	6-3-1	174	151
L.S.U...........	3-2-1	.583	155	50	6-3-1	248	114
Auburn.........	3-3-0	.500	126	79	6-4-0	237	123
Kentucky......	1-6-0	.143	65	187	2-8-0	111	230
Vanderbilt*...	0-6-0	.000	71	143	2-7-1	165	241
Miss. State..	0-6-0	.000	10	168	1-9-0	49	259

1968

	Conference				Overall		
School	W-L-T	Pct.	Pts.	Opp.	W-L-T	Pts.	Opp.
Georgia........	5-0-1	.917	173	47	8-0-2	282	98
Tennessee...	4-1-1	.750	106	68	8-1-1	248	110
Alabama......	4-2-0	.667	108	63	8-2-0	174	104
L.S.U.*.........	4-2-0	.667	108	79	7-3-0	190	144
Auburn.........	4-2-0	.667	123	75	6-4-0	223	149
Florida*........	3-2-1	.583	98	120	6-3-1	151	175
Mississippi...	3-2-1	.583	91	115	6-3-1	178	180
Vanderbilt*...	2-3-1	.417	61	94	5-4-1	163	147
Miss. State*.	0-4-2	.167	88	142	0-8-2	146	260
Kentucky......	0-7-0	.000	59	150	3-7-0	141	206

1969

	Conference				Overall		
School	W-L-T	Pct.	Pts.	Opp.	W-L-T	Pts.	Opp.
Tennessee...	5-1-0	.833	174	127	9-1-0	315	165
L.S.U...........	4-1-0	.800	162	77	9-1-0	349	91
Auburn.........	5-2-0	.714	238	123	8-2-0	363	137
Florida.........	3-1-1	.700	144	112	8-1-1	329	187
Mississippi...	4-2-0	.667	178	105	7-3-0	307	140
Georgia........	2-3-1	.417	106	79	5-4-1	212	101
Vanderbilt....	2-3-0	.400	111	137	4-6-0	242	264
Alabama......	2-4-0	.333	121	175	6-4-0	281	221
Kentucky......	1-6-0	.143	61	224	2-8-0	104	295
Miss. State..	0-5-0	.000	95	231	3-7-0	193	385

1970

	Conference				Overall		
School	W-L-T	Pct.	Pts.	Opp.	W-L-T	Pts.	Opp.
L.S.U...........	5-0-0	1.000	144	49	9-2-0	277	96
Tennessee...	4-1-0	.800	154	49	10-1-0	336	103
Auburn.........	5-2-0	.800	247	128	8-2-0	355	149
Mississippi...	4-2-0	.667	156	157	7-3-0	285	220
Florida.........	3-3-0	.500	118	190	7-4-0	224	256
Georgia........	3-3-0	.500	131	85	5-5-0	242	153
Alabama......	3-4-0	.429	176	151	6-5-0	310	240
Miss. State..	3-4-0	.429	72	189	6-5-0	171	264
Vanderbilt....	1-5-0	.167	60	159	4-7-0	201	213
Kentucky......	0-7-0	.000	72	173	2-9-0	131	233

*See page 229, "Appointed Conference Games."

1971

	Conference				Overall		
School	W-L-T	Pct.	Pts.	Opp.	W-L-T	Pts.	Opp.
Alabama......	7-0-0	1.000	238	45	11-0-0	362	84
Auburn.........	5-1-0	.833	160	94	9-1-0	313	132
Georgia........	5-1-0	.833	200	56	10-1-0	353	112
Mississippi...	4-2-0	.667	147	127	9-2-0	322	204
Tennessee...	4-2-0	.667	94	82	9-2-0	256	108
L.S.U...........	3-2-0	.600	122	61	8-3-0	320	138
Vanderbilt....	1-5-0	.167	70	146	4-6-0	136	208
Florida.........	1-6-0	.143	79	232	4-7-0	174	298
Kentucky......	1-6-0	.143	84	186	3-8-0	144	284
Miss. State..	1-7-0	.125	80	251	2-9-0	120	311

1972

	Conference				Overall		
School	W-L-T	Pct.	Pts.	Opp.	W-L-T	Pts.	Opp.
Alabama......	7-1-0	.875	258	97	10-1-0	393	133
Auburn.........	6-1-0	.857	120	103	9-1-0	185	138
L.S.U...........	4-1-1	.750	114	75	9-1-1	235	121
Tennessee...	4-2-0	.667	94	44	9-2-0	273	83
Georgia........	4-3-0	.571	82	96	7-4-0	174	163
Florida.........	3-3-1	.500	121	76	5-5-1	218	144
Mississippi...	2-5-0	.286	124	104	5-5-0	192	142
Kentucky......	2-5-0	.286	45	141	3-8-0	131	232
Miss. State..	1-6-0	.143	81	202	4-7-0	197	254
Vanderbilt....	0-6-0	.000	60	161	3-8-0	129	243

1973

	Conference				Overall		
School	W-L-T	Pct.	Pts.	Opp.	W-L-T	Pts.	Opp.
Alabama......	8-0-0	1.000	268	19	11-0-0	454	89
L.S.U...........	5-1-0	.833	156	72	9-2-0	258	153
Mississippi...	4-3-0	.571	124	137	6-5-0	202	177
Tennessee...	3-3-0	.500	127	136	8-3-0	272	219
Florida.........	3-4-0	.429	89	141	7-4-0	180	171
Kentucky......	3-4-0	.429	148	130	5-6-0	226	196
Georgia........	3-4-0	.429	128	114	6-4-1	207	150
Auburn.........	2-5-0	.286	73	140	6-5-0	153	159
Miss. State..	2-5-0	.286	133	205	4-5-2	219	255
Vanderbilt....	1-5-0	.167	87	181	5-6-0	181	262

1974

	Conference				Overall		
School	W-L-T	Pct.	Pts.	Opp.	W-L-T	Pts.	Opp.
Alabama......	6-0-0	1.000	168	50	11-0-0	318	83
Auburn.........	4-2-0	.667	120	88	9-2-0	260	126
Georgia........	4-2-0	.667	155	122	6-5-0	317	264
Kentucky......	3-3-0	.500	139	128	6-5-0	248	194
Florida.........	3-3-0	.500	128	123	8-3-0	251	184
Miss. State..	3-3-0	.500	109	121	8-3-0	301	200
Vanderbilt....	2-3-1	.417	122	144	7-3-1	307	193
Tennessee...	2-3-1	.417	90	114	6-3-2	204	178
L.S.U...........	2-4-0	.333	77	91	5-5-1	202	168
Mississippi...	0-6-0	.000	65	192	3-8-0	135	241

1975

	Conference				Overall		
School	W-L-T	Pct.	Pts.	Opp.	W-L-T	Pts.	Opp.
Alabama......	6-0-0	1.000	174	40	10-1-0	361	66
Mississippi...	5-1-0	.833	104	78	6-5-0	170	162
Georgia........	5-1-0	.833	147	70	9-2-0	289	166
Florida.........	5-1-0	.833	182	47	9-2-0	302	104
Tennessee...	3-3-0	.500	89	110	7-5-0	253	193
Vanderbilt....	2-4-0	.333	47	156	7-4-0	119	200
L.S.U. f.........	2-4-0	.333	62	128	5-6-0	159	202
Auburn f......	2-4-0	.333	80	138	4-6-1	174	243
Kentucky......	0-6-0	.000	59	131	2-8-1	132	188
Miss. State f	0-6-0	.000	70	116	2-9-0	165	166

f-Includes forfeit imposed by NCAA and SEC.

1976

	Conference				Overall		
School	W-L-T	Pct.	Pts.	Opp.	W-L-T	Pts.	Opp.
Georgia........	5-1-0	.833	183	55	10-1-0	324	118
Kentucky f...	5-1-0	.833	84	61	8-3-0	188	151
Alabama......	5-2-0	.714	169	99	8-3-0	291	134
Florida.........	4-2-0	.667	142	159	8-3-0	314	255
Mississippi f.	4-3-0	.571	68	142	6-5-0	153	180
L.S.U. f.......	3-3-0	.500	138	118	7-3-1	255	149
Auburn f......	3-3-0	.500	93	146	4-7-0	194	267
Tennessee...	2-4-0	.333	104	101	6-5-0	237	162
Vanderbilt....	0-6-0	.000	47	161	2-9-0	131	282
Miss. State f	0-6-0	.000	138	118	0-11-0	269	178

f-Includes forfeit imposed by NCAA and SEC.

1977

	Conference				Overall		
School	W-L-T	Pct.	Pts.	Opp.	W-L-T	Pts.	Opp.
Alabama......	7-0-0	1.000	209	76	10-1-0	345	133
Kentucky......	6-0-0	1.000	152	50	10-1-0	252	111
Auburn f......	5-1-0	.833	131	130	6-5-0	204	243
L.S.U...........	4-2-0	.667	135	131	8-3-0	375	196
Florida.........	3-3-0	.500	108	135	6-4-1	251	235
Mississippi f.	3-4-0	.429	145	143	6-5-0	208	196
Georgia........	2-4-0	.333	79	132	5-6-1	157	191
Tennessee...	1-5-0	.167	112	136	4-7-0	229	229
Vanderbilt...	0-6-0	.000	67	172	2-9-0	141	276
Miss. State f	0-6-0	.000	105	138	0-11-0	193	227

f-Included forfeit by NCAA and SEC.

1978

	Conference				Overall		
	W-L-T	Pct.	Pts.	Opp.	W-L-T	Pts	Opp.
Alabama	6-0-0	1.000	204	97	10-1-0	331	161
Georgia	5-0-1	.917	160	90	9-1-1	268	162
Auburn	3-2-1	.583	129	104	6-4-1	238	291
LSU	3-3-0	.500	126	100	8-3-0	264	166
Tennessee	3-3-0	.500	159	139	5-5-1	251	209
Florida	3-3-0	.500	138	104	4-7-0	249	223
Kentucky	2-4-0	.333	123	104	4-6-1	193	189
Mississippi	2-4-0	.333	107	154	5-6-0	181	240
Miss. State	2-4-0	.333	71	137	6-5-0	232	205
Vanderbilt	0-6-0	.000	72	260	2-9-0	164	418

(Ties count a half-game won and a half-game lost.)

*Appointed Conference Games

While the SEC rule requiring six football games with member schools was in effect some 16 games with outside schools were appointed to serve as conference games to avoid a violation for the members. The rule was negated in 1969.

The entire list of "appointed" conference games follows:

1954 Ole Miss vs. Arkansas, 0-6
1958 Ole Miss vs. Houston, 56-7
1965 Georgia vs. Clemson, 23-9
Tennessee vs. S. Carolina, 24-3
1966 Florida vs. Tulane, 31-10
Georgia vs. N. Carolina, 28-3
L.S.U. vs. Tulane, 21-7
Tennessee vs. S. Carolina, 29-17
Vanderbilt vs. Tulane, 12-13
1967 Georgia vs. Clemson, 24-17
Vanderbilt vs. Tulane, 12-13
1968 Florida vs. Tulane, 24-3
L.S.U. vs. T.C.U., 10-7
L.S.U. vs. Tulane, 34-10
Miss. State vs. Tex. Tech, 28-28
Vanderbilt vs. Tulane, 21-7

Bowl Games of SEC Members

(Listed by Schools)

ALABAMA
(Won 14, lost 13, tied 2)

1-1-35	Rose Bowl	29 Stanford	13
1-1-38	Rose Bowl	0 California	13
1-1-42	Cotton Bowl	29 Texas A&M	21
1-1-43	Orange Bowl	37 Boston Coll.	21
1-1-45	Sugar Bowl	26 Duke	29
1-1-46	Rose Bowl	34 Sou. Calif.	14
1-1-48	Sugar Bowl	7 Texas	27
1-1-53	Orange Bowl	61 Syracuse	6
1-1-54	Cotton Bowl	6 Rice	28
12- 9-59	Liberty Bowl	0 Penn State	7
12-17-60	Bluebonnet	3 Texas	3
1-1-62	Sugar Bowl	10 Arkansas	3
1-1-63	Orange Bowl	17 Oklahoma	0
1-1-64	Sugar Bowl	12 Mississippi	7
1-1-65	Orange Bowl	17 Texas	21
1-1-66	Orange Bowl	39 Nebraska	28
1-2-67	Sugar Bowl	34 Nebraska	7
1-1-68	Cotton Bowl	16 Texas A&M	20
12-28-68	Gator Bowl	10 Missouri	35
12-13-69	Liberty Bowl	33 Colorado	47
12-31-70	Bluebonnet	24 Oklahoma	24
1-1-72	Orange Bowl	6 Nebraska	38
1-1-73	Cotton Bowl	13 Texas	17
1-1-74	Sugar Bowl	23 Notre Dame	24
1-1-75	Orange Bowl	11 Notre Dame	13
12-31-75	Sugar Bowl	13 Penn State	6
12-20-76	Liberty Bowl	36 UCLA	6
1-2-78	Sugar Bowl	35 Ohio State	6
1-1-79	Sugar Bowl	14 Penn State	7

AUBURN
(Won 6, lost 7, tied 1)

1-1-37	Rhumba Bowl	7 Villanova	7
1-1-38	Orange Bowl	6 Mich. State	0
1-1-54	Gator Bowl	13 Texas Tech	35
12-31-54	Gator Bowl	33 Baylor	13
12-31-55	Gator Bowl	13 Vanderbilt	25
1-1-64	Orange Bowl	7 Nebraska	13
12-18-65	Liberty Bowl	7 Mississippi	13
12-28-68	Sun Bowl	34 Arizona	10
12-31-69	Bluebonnet	7 Houston	36
1-2-71	Gator Bowl	35 Mississippi	28
1-1-72	Sugar Bowl	22 Oklahoma	40
12-30-72	Gator Bowl	24 Colorado	3
12-29-73	Sun Bowl	17 Missouri	34
12-30-74	Gator Bowl	27 Texas	3

FLORIDA
(Won 5, lost 6)

1-1-53	Gator Bowl	14 Tulsa	13
12-27-58	Gator Bowl	3 Mississippi	7
12-31-60	Gator Bowl	13 Baylor	12
12-28-62	Gator Bowl	17 Penn State	7
1-1-66	Sugar Bowl	18 Missouri	20
1-2-67	Orange Bowl	27 Ga. Tech	12
12-27-69	Gator Bowl	14 Tennessee	13
12-22-73	Tangerine	7 Miami, O.	16
12-31-74	Sugar Bowl	10 Nebraska	13
12-29-75	Gator Bowl	0 Maryland	13
1-2-77	Sun Bowl	14 Texas A&M	37

GEORGIA
(Won 9, lost 9, tied 1)

1-1-42	Orange Bowl	40 T.C.U.	26
1-1-43	Rose Bowl	9 U.C.L.A.	0
1-1-46	Oil Bowl	20 Tulsa	6
1-1-47	Sugar Bowl	20 N. Carolina	10
1-1-48	Gator Bowl	20 Maryland	20
1-1-49	Orange Bowl	28 Texas	41
12-9-50	Presidential	20 Texas A&M	40
1-1-60	Orange Bowl	14 Missouri	0
12-26-64	Sun Bowl	7 Texas Tech	0
12-31-66	Cotton Bowl	24 S.M.U.	9
12-16-67	Liberty Bowl	7 N.C. State	14
1-1-69	Sugar Bowl	2 Arkansas	16
12-20-69	Sun Bowl	6 Nebraska	45
12-31-71	Gator Bowl	7 N. Carolina	3
12-28-73	Peach Bowl	17 Maryland	16
12-20-74	Tangerine	10 Miami, O.	21
1-1-76	Cotton Bowl	10 Arkansas	31
1-1-77	Sugar Bowl	3 Pittsburgh	27
12-31-78	Bluebonnet	22 Stanford	25

KENTUCKY
(Won 4, lost 1)

12-6-47	Great Lakes	24 Villanova	14
1-2-50	Orange Bowl	13 Santa Clara	21
1-1-51	Sugar Bowl	13 Oklahoma	7
1-1-52	Cotton Bowl	20 T.C.U.	7
12-31-76	Peach Bowl	21 N. Carolina	0

LOUISIANA STATE
(Won 9, lost 11, tied 1)

1-1-36	Sugar Bowl	2 T.C.U.	3
1-1-37	Sugar Bowl	14 Santa Clara	21
1-1-38	Sugar Bowl	0 Santa Clara	6
1-1-44	Orange Bowl	19 Texas A&M	14
1-1-47	Cotton Bowl	0 Arkansas	0
1-2-50	Sugar Bowl	0 Oklahoma	35
1-1-59	Sugar Bowl	7 Clemson	0
1-1-60	Sugar Bowl	0 Mississippi	21
1-1-62	Orange Bowl	25 Colorado	7
1-1-63	Cotton Bowl	13 Texas	0
12-21-63	Bluebonnet	7 Baylor	14
1-1-65	Sugar Bowl	13 Syracuse	10
1-1-66	Cotton Bowl	14 Arkansas	7
1-1-68	Sugar Bowl	20 Wyoming	13
12-30-68	Peach Bowl	31 Fla. State	27
1-1-71	Orange Bowl	12 Nebraska	17
12-18-71	Sun Bowl	33 Iowa State	15
12-30-72	Bluebonnet	17 Tennessee	24
1-1-74	Orange Bowl	9 Penn State	16
12-31-77	Sun Bowl	14 Stanford	24
12-23-78	Liberty Bowl	15 Missouri	20

MISSISSIPPI
(Won 11, lost 9)

1-1-36	Orange Bowl	19 Catholic U.	20
1-1-49	Delta Bowl	13 T.C.U.	9
1-1-53	Sugar Bowl	7 Ga. Tech	24
1-1-55	Sugar Bowl	0 Navy	21
1-2-56	Cotton Bowl	14 T.C.U.	13
1-1-58	Sugar Bowl	39 Texas	7
12-27-58	Gator Bowl	7 Florida	3
1-1-60	Sugar Bowl	21 L.S.U.	0
1-2-61	Sugar Bowl	14 Rice	6
1-1-62	Cotton Bowl	7 Texas	12
1-1-63	Sugar Bowl	17 Arkansas	13
1-1-64	Sugar Bowl	7 Alabama	12
12-19-64	Bluebonnet	7 Tulsa	14
12-18-65	Liberty Bowl	13 Auburn	7
12-17-66	Bluebonnet	0 Texas	19
12-30-67	Sun Bowl	7 UT El Paso	14
12-14-68	Liberty Bowl	34 Va. Tech	17
1-1-70	Sugar Bowl	27 Arkansas	22
1-2-71	Gator Bowl	28 Auburn	35
12-30-71	Peach Bowl	41 Ga.Tech 18	

MISSISSIPPI STATE
(Won 3, Lost 1)

1-1-37	Orange Bowl	12 Duquesne	13
1-1-41	Orange Bowl	14 Georgetown	7
12-21-63	Liberty Bowl	16 N.C. State	12
12-28-74	Sun Bowl	26 N. Carolina	24

TENNESSEE
(Won 10, lost 11)

Date	Bowl	Score	Opponent	Score
1-1-39	Orange Bowl	17	Oklahoma	0
1-1-40	Rose Bowl	0	Sou. Calif.	14
1-1-41	Sugar Bowl	13	Boston Coll.	19
1-1-43	Sugar Bowl	14	Tulsa	7
1-1-45	Rose Bowl	0	Sou. Calif.	25
1-1-47	Orange Bowl	0	Rice	8
1-1-51	Cotton Bowl	20	Texas	14
1-1-52	Sugar Bowl	13	Maryland	28
1-1-53	Cotton Bowl	0	Texas	16
1-1-57	Sugar Bowl	7	Baylor	13
12-28-57	Gator Bowl	3	Texas A&M	0
12-18-65	Bluebonnet	27	Tulsa	6
12-31-66	Gator Bowl	18	Syracuse	12
1-1-68	Orange Bowl	24	Oklahoma	26
1-1-69	Cotton Bowl	13	Texas	36
12-27-69	Gator Bowl	13	Florida	14
1-1-71	Sugar Bowl	34	Air Force	13
12-20-71	Liberty Bowl	14	Arkansas	13
12-30-72	Bluebonnet	24	L.S.U.	17
12-29-73	Gator Bowl	19	Texas Tech	28
12-16-74	Liberty Bowl	7	Maryland	3

VANDERBILT
(Won 1, lost 0, tied 1)

Date	Bowl	Score	Opponent	Score
12-31-55	Gator Bowl	25	Auburn	13
12-28-74	Peach Bowl	6	Texas Tech	6

SEC All-Time Scoring Leaders

Year	Player	Team	TD	PAT	FG	Pts.
1976	Jackie Parker	Miss. State	16	24	0	120
1969	Tommy Durrance	Florida	18	2	0	110
1977	Charles Alexander	L. S. U.	17	2	0	104*
1971	Johnny Musso	Alabama	16	4	0	100
1978	Joe Cribbs	Auburn	16	0	0	98
1943	Steve Van Buren	L. S. U.	14	14	0	98
1942	Frank Sinkwich	Georgia	16	0	0	96
1978	Charles Alexander	L.S.U.	16	0	0	96
1961	Wendell Harris	L. S. U.	8	28	6	94
1962	Cotton Clark	Alabama	15	2	0	92
1977	Tony Nathan	Alabama	15	2	0	92
1941	Jack Jenkins	Vanderbilt	12	15	1	90
1948	Joe Geri	Georgia	9	36	0	90

SEC Season Scoring Leaders—1933 to 1978

Year	Name, School	TD	PAT	FG	Pts.
1933	Beattie Feathers, Tenn	13	0	0	78
1934	Claude Simons, Tul	10	9	0	69
1935	Ray Hapes, Miss	12	2	0	74
1936	Bob Davis, Ky	11	0	0	66
1937	Pinky Rohm, LSU	9	0	0	54
	Bob Davis, Ky	9	0	0	54
1938	Parker Hall, Miss	11	6	0	72
1939	Harvey Johnson, Miss St	10	2	0	62
1940	Merle Hapes, Miss	12	0	0	72
1941	Jack Jenkins, Vandy	12	15	1	90
1942	Frank Sinkwich, Ga	16	0	0	96
1943	Steve Van Buren, LSU	14	14	0	98
1944	Tom McWilliams, Miss St	14	0	0	84
1945	Fred Grant, Ala	11	0	0	66
1946	Charlie Trippi, Ga	14	0	0	84
1947	Charlie Conerly, Miss	9	0	0	54
1948	Joe Geri, Ga	9	36	0	90
1949	John Dottley, Miss	14	0	0	84
1950	Al Bruno, Ky	10	0	0	60
	Wilbur Jamerson, Ky	10	0	0	60
	Al Lary, Ala	10	0	0	60
1951	Hal Payne, Tenn	14	0	0	84
1952	Jackie Parker, Miss St	16	24	0	120
1953	Jimmy Wade, Tenn	12	0	0	72
1954	Joe Childress, Aub	7	20	1	65
1955	Paige Cothren, Miss	6	20	6	74
1956	Jim Taylor, LSU	8	8	1	59
1957	Jim Taylor, LSU	12	14	0	86
1958	Billy Cannon, LSU	11	4	0	74*
1959	Charley Flowers, Miss	11	0	0	66
1960	Tom Mason, Tul	13	0	0	78
1961	Wendell Harris, LSU	8	26	6	94*
1962	Cotton Clark, Ala	15	0	0	92*
1963	Billy Lothridge, Ga Tech	3	15	12	69
1964	Doug Moreau, LSU	4	6	13	73*
1965	Rodger Bird, Ky	13	0	0	78
1966	Bobby Etter, Ga	0	21	12	57
1967	Dicky Lyons, Ky	11	4	1	73
1968	Dicky Lyons, Ky	11	0	0	66
1969	Tommy Durrance, Fla	18	2	0	110
1970	Terry Beasley, Aub	12	0	0	72
1971	Johnny Musso, Ala	16	4	0	100
1972	Haskel Stanback, Tenn	13	0	0	78
1973	Sonny Collins, Ky	13	0	0	80*
1974	Stanley Morgan, Tenn	14	0	0	84
1975	David Posey, Fla	0	37	9	64
1976	Terry Robiskie, LSU	12	0	0	72
1977	Charles Alexander, LSU	17	0	0	104*
1978	Joe Cribbs, Aub	16	0	0	98*

SEC Annual Top Ten Scorers—1933 to 1978

1933

Position, Player School	TD	PAT	FG	Pts
TB Beattie Feathers, Tenn	13	0	0	78
FB Cy Grant, Ga	8	10	0	58
HB Dixie Howell, Ala	9	0	0	54
TB Alex Weliford, Sewanee	7	1	0	43
FB George Gunter, Miss	6	3	0	39
FB Floyd Roberts, Tul	5	8	0	38
TB Abe Mickal, LSU	3	14	2	38
HB George Chapman, Ga	6	0	0	36
HB Farrell Thomas, Tul	5	2	0	32
HB Bobby Oliver, Vandy	5	1	0	31
FB Earl Hutson, Miss	5	1	0	31

1934

Position, Player, School	TD	PAT	FG	Pts
HB Claude Simons, Tul	10	9	0	69
TB Dixie Howell, Ala	10	0	0	60
HB Bert Johnson, Ky	9	1	0	55
HB Julius Brown, Fla	8	0	0	48
FB Joe Demyanovich, Ala	7	0	0	42
HB Rab Rodgers, Miss	7	0	0	42
QB Riley Smith, Ala	3	23	0	41
HB Young Boozer, Ala	6	0	0	36
TB Phil Dickens, Tenn	6	0	0	36
End Don Hutson, Ala	5	2	0	32

1935

Position, Player, School	TD	PAT	FG	Pts
HB Ray Hapes, Miss	12	2	0	74
HB Bob Davis, Ky	11	0	0	66
HB Rab Dodgers, Miss	10	0	0	60
QB Riley Smith, Ala	7	9	1	54

*Includes 2-pt PATs.

Position, Player, School	TD	PAT	FG	Pts
HB Bill Grass, LSU	6	9	0	45
HB Wilton Kilgore, Aub	6	0	0	36
TB Pinky Rohm, LSU	6	0	0	36
HB Barney Mintz Tul	5	5	0	35
FB Dave Bernard, Miss	5	1	0	31

(Nine players scored 30 points)

1936

Position, Player School	TD	PAT	FG	Pts
HB Bob Davis, Ky	11	0	0	66
HB Dutch Konemann, Ga T	10	1	0	61
TB Joe Kiligrow, Ala	5	22	0	52
End Gaynell Tinsley, LSU	8	0	0	48
HB Rock Reed, LSU	7	0	0	42
TB Pinky Rohm, LSU	7	0	0	42
RB George Edwards, Ga T	7	0	0	42
HB Harry Appleby, Ga Tech	7	0	0	42
HB Guy Milner, LSU	6	5	0	41
FB Bill Crass, LSU	5	10	0	40
HB Ike Pickle, Miss St	5	10	0	40

1937

Position, Player, School	TD	PAT	FG	Pts
TB Pinky Rohm, LSU	9	0	0	54
HB Bob Davis, Ky	9	0	0	54
HB Jabbo Howell, LSU	8	0	0	48
HB Vassa Cate, Ga	8	0	0	48
HB Dutch Konemann, Ga Tech	7	1	0	43
TB Joe Kilgrow, Alabama	5	12	0	42
TB Fleycher Sims, Ga Tech	5	11	0	41
HB Bill Steadman, Miss St	6	3	0	39
HB Burton Banker, Tul	6	0	0	36
HB George Cafego, Tenn	6	0	0	36

1938

Position, Player, School	TD	PAT	FG	Pts
TB Parker Hall, Miss	11	6	0	72
HB Jim Fordham, Ga	8	0	0	48
End Bowden Wyatt, Tenn	5	11	1	44
HB Warren Brunner, Tul	7	0	0	42
HB Jack Nix, Miss St	6	0	0	36
FB Leonard Coffman, Tenn	6	0	0	36
HB Burton Banker, Tul	5	5	0	35
End Ken Kavanaugh, LSU	5	1	0	31
Back Vic Bradford, Ala	3	10	1	31
Back Bobby Johnson, Fla	5	1	0	31

1939

Position, Player, School	TD	PAT	FG	Pts
HB Harvey Johnson, M St	10	2	0	62
HB Bob Kellogg, Tul	8	7	0	55
E Ken Kavanaugh, LSU	9	0	0	54
WB Bob Foxx, Tenn	6	5	0	41
FB Leslie Dodson, Miss	5	10	0	40
HB Paul Spencer, Ala	6	0	0	36
HB Jim Fordham, Ga	6	0	0	36
E Bob Ison, Ga Tech	5	0	0	30
FB David Zoeller, Ky	4	5	0	29
HB Jack Nix, Miss St	4	4	0	28
HB Junior Jones, Ky	4	4	0	28

1940

Position, Player, School	TD	PAT	FG	Pts
FB Merle Hapes, Miss	12	0	0	72
HB John Hovious, Miss	9	11	0	65
FB Fred Newman, Tenn	6	15	0	51
E Ralph Plaster, Ga Tech	7	8	0	50
HB Paul Spencer, Ala	8	0	0	48
HB Dave Brown, Ala	7	1	0	43
HB Noah Mullins, Ky	7	0	0	42
HB Adrian Dodson, LSU	7	0	0	42
WB Bob Foxx, Tenn	5	11	0	41
HB Dick McGowen, Aub	4	13	1	40

1941

Position, Player, School	TD	PAT	FG	Pts
FB Jack Jenkins, Vandy	12	15	1	90
WB Lamar Davis, Ga	12	1	0	73
HB Bob Glass, Tul	8	3	0	51
HB Lou Thomas, Tul	7	8	0	50
TB Jimmy Nelson, Ala	8	0	0	48
TB Frank Sinkwich, Ga	7	0	1	45
HB Ty Irby, Auburn	7	3	0	45
HB Sonny Bruce, Miss St	4	19	0	43
HB Noah Mullins, Ky	7	0	0	42
HB Blondy Black, Miss St	7	0	0	42

1942

Position, Player, School	TD	PAT	FG	Pts
TB Frank Sinkwich, Ga	16	0	0	96
FB Jack Jenkins, Vandy	7	15	0	57
TB Jim Reynolds, Aub	9	0	0	54
HB Charlie Kuhn, Ky	6	17	0	53
WB Lamar Davis, Ga	8	0	0	48
TB Charlie Trippi, Ga	8	0	0	48
C Leo Costa, Ga	0	43	0	43
HB Russ Craft, Ala	7	0	0	42
HB Lou Thomas, Tul	4	8	2	38
TB Walt Slater, Tenn	5	7	0	37

1943

Position, Player, School	TD	PAT	FG	Pts
TB Steve Van Buren, LSU	14	14	0	98
TB Eddie Prokop, Ga Tech	8	24	0	72
TB Johnny Cook, Ga	12	0	0	72
HB Billy Rutland, Ga	7	0	0	42
FB Harry Robinson, Vandy	7	0	0	42
HB Charlie Smith, Ga	6	0	0	36
QB Frank Broyles, Ga Tech	5	1	0	31
HB Ed Scharfschwerdt, Ga T	5	0	0	30
HB W. A. Jones, Tul	4	1	0	25
HB Jim Shriver, Tul	4	1	0	25
HB Carlos Izzaguirre, Vandy	4	1	0	25
FB Mickey Logan, Ga T	4	1	0	25

1944

Position, Player, School	TD	PAT	FG	Pts
TB Tom McWilliams, M St	14	0	0	84
TB Buster Stephens, Tenn	10	0	0	60
HB Curtis Kuykendall, Aub	9	0	0	54
HB Bobby Forbes, Fla	9	0	0	54
HB Allen Bowen, Ga Tech	4	21	1	48
HB George Mathews, Ga T	8	0	0	48
HB Billy Bryan, Georgia	3	29	0	47
HB W. A Jones, Tul	5	12	1	45

(Six players scored 36 points)

1945

Position, Player, School	TD	PAT	FG	Pts
FB Fred Grant, Ala	11	0	0	66
HB Hugh Morrow, Ala	3	46	0	64
WB Lowell Tew, Ala	10	0	0	60
TB Charlie Trippi, Ga	9	0	0	54
TB Harper Davis. M St	9	0	0	54
FB Gene Knight, LSU	7	6	1	51
FB Norwood Hodges, Ala	8	0	0	48
HB Charlie Smith, Ga	8	0	0	48
WB Bob Lund, Tenn	8	0	0	48
TB Harry Gilmer, Ala	7	0	0	42
E Reid Moseley, Ga	7	0	0	42
HB Don Robinson, M St	7	0	0	42

1946

Position, Player, School	TD	PAT	FG	Pts
TB Charlie Trippi, Ga	14	0	0	84
HB John Donaldson, Ga	10	0	0	60
TB Travis Tidwell, Aub	8	0	0	48
G George Jernigan, Ga	0	47	0	47
HB Allen Bowen, Ga Tech	4	19	0	43
TB John Rauch, Ga	7	0	0	42
WB Pat McHugh, Ga T	7	0	0	42
WB Don Phelps, Ky	7	0	0	42
HB Larry Matulich, M St	7	0	0	42
E Ed Heider, Tul	4	13	0	37

1947

Position, Player and School	TD	PAT	FG	Pts
TB Charlie Conerly, Miss	9	0	0	54
HB Bobby Forbes, Fla	9	0	0	54
FB Bobby Berry, Vandy	8	0	0	48
E Barney Poole, Miss	8	0	0	48
TB Harper Davis, M St	7	0	0	42
TB Harry Gilmer, Ala	7	0	0	42
FB Dean Davidson, Vandy	6	0	0	36
TB Tom McWilliams, M St	6	0	0	36
HB Floyd Reid, Ga	6	0	0	36
HB Joe Geri, Georgia	2	24	0	36

1948

Position, Player, School	TD	PAT	FG	Pts
HB Joe Geri, Georgia	9	36	0	90
HB Charles Hunsinger, Fla	11	0	0	66
FB Eddie Price, Tul	10	0	0	60
TB Ed Salem, Alabama	5	27	1	60
FB Dean Davidson, Vandy	9	0	0	54
B John Cox, Florida	7	0	0	42
HB Allen Bowen, Ga Tech	4	16	0	40
WB Zack Clinard, Vandy	0	40	0	40
E Dick Sheffield, Tul	3	19	0	37

1949

Position, Player, School	TD	PAT	FG	Pts
FB John Dottley, Miss	14	0	0	84
HB Charles Hunsinger, Fla	12	0	0	72
FB Eddie Price, Tul	11	0	0	66
TB Ed Salem, Alabama	4	27	0	51
QB Billy Mustin, Miss	8	0	0	48
FB Gordon Polofsky, Tenn	8	0	0	48
FB Bobby North, Ga Tech	5	14	1	47
WB Bert Rechichar, Tenn	4	16	2	46
WB Don Phelps, Kentucky	7	1	0	43
HB Carroll Griffith, LSU	2	27	0	39

1950

Position, Player, School	TD	PAT	FG	Pts
E Al Bruno, Kentucky	10	0	0	60
HB Wilbur Jamerson, Ky	10	0	0	60
E Al Lary, Alabama	10	0	0	60
TB Ed Salem, Alabama	8	9	0	57
FB Andy Kozar, Tenn	9	0	0	54
HB George Kinek, Tulane	9	0	0	54
HB Bobby Marlow, Ala	9	0	0	54
E Bucky Curtis, Vandy	9	0	0	54
TB Pat Shires, Tenn	2	35	1	50
HB Hal Waggoner, Tul	8	0	0	48

*Includes 2-pt PATs.

1951

Position, Player, School	TD	PAT	FG	Pts
TB Hal Payne, Tenn	14	0	0	84
HB Bobby Marlow, Ala	12	0	0	72
FB Andy Kozar, Tenn	11	0	0	66
HB Harry Jones, Ky	5	27	1	60
FB Showboat Boykin, Miss	10	0	0	60
QB Jimmy Lear, Miss	6	23	0	59
HB Dick Foster, Vandy	5	19	2	55
TB Hank Lauricella, Tenn	8	0	0	48
E Steve Meilinger, Ky	8	0	0	48
E Buck Martin, Ga Tech	8	0	0	48

1952

Position, Player, School	TD	PAT	FG	Pts
QB Jackie Parker, M St	16	24	0	120
HB Buford Long, Fla	14	0	0	84
HB Bobby Luna, Ala	6	33	1	72
FB Rick Casares, Fla	6	19	3	64
QB Pepper Rogers, Ga Tech	1	36	4	54
HB Bobby Marlow, Ala	9	0	0	54
HB Corky Tharp, Ala	9	0	0	54
HB Leon Hardeman, Ga Tech	8	0	0	48
E Steve Meilinger, Ky	8	0	0	48
HB Wilson Dillard, Miss	8	0	0	48
WB Harol Lofton, Miss	8	0	0	48

1953

Position, Player, School	TD	PAT	FG	Pts
TB Jimmy Wade, Tenn	12	0	0	72
QB Jackie Parker, M St	8	17	0	65
QB Bobby Freeman, Aub	9	0	0	54
HB Jerry Marchand, LSU	8	0	0	48
HB Tommy Haddock, Fla	8	0	0	48
FB Bobby McCool, Miss	7	0	0	42
HB Earl Blair, Miss	7	0	0	42
HB Jimmy Patton, Miss	5	9	0	39
HB Danny Byers, Vandy	6	0	0	36
HB Fob James, Auburn	6	0	0	36
FB Bobby Duke, Auburn	6	0	0	36

1954

Position, Player, School	TD	PAT	FG	Pts
FB Joe Childress, Aub	7	20	1	65
HB Arthur Davis, M St	10	0	0	60
HB Allen Muirhead, Miss	10	0	0	60
QB Bobby Freeman, Aub	8	0	0	48
HB Charlie Horton, Vandy	7	0	0	42
HB Jimmy Patton, Miss	6	1	0	37
HB Corky Tharp, Ala	6	0	0	36
HB Fob James, Aub	6	0	0	36
FB Paige Cothren, Miss	4	7	0	31
FB Tom Tracy, Tenn	4	7	0	31
E Jim Pyburn, Aub	5	1	0	31

1955

Position, Player and School	TD	PAT	FG	Pts
FB Paige Cothren, Miss	6	20	6	74
HB Charley Horton, Vandy	12	1	0	73
QB Bob Hardy, Kentucky	9	8	0	62
HB Ron Quillian, Tul	10	0	0	60
FB Joe Childress, Aub	6	11	0	47
HB Fob James, Auburn	7	1	0	43
HB Wm Earl Morgan M St	5	13	0	43
QB Howell Tubbs, Aub	5	6	1	39
QB Toppy Vann, Ga Tech	6	1	0	37
E. H. Schnellenberger, Ky	6	0	0	36
TB Johnny Majors, Tenn	6	0	0	36

*Includes 2-pt PATs.

1956

Position, Player, School	TD	PAT	FG	Pts
FB Jim Taylor, LSU	8	8	1	59
QB Raymond Brown, Miss	8	4	0	52
FB Tommy, Bronson, Tenn	8	0	0	48
HB Phil King, Vandy	7	5	0	47
FB Paige Cothren, Miss	2	16	6	46
WB Al Carter, Tenn	7	0	0	42
TB Johnny Majors, Tenn	7	0	0	42
QB Howell Tubbs, Auburn	4	15	0	39
QB Toppy Vann, Ga Tech	5	9	0	39
FB Carl Smith, Tenn	6	1	0	37

1957

Position, Player, School	TD	PAT	FG	Pts
FB Jim Taylor, LSU	12	14	0	86
FB Billy Atkins, Aub	11	13	1	82
TB Bobby Gordon, Tenn	9	0	0	54
HB Bernie Parrish, Fla	5	14	0	44
HB Molly Halbert, M St	7	0	0	42
QB Raymond Brown, Miss	7	0	0	42
HB Billy Cannon, LSU	6	0	0	36
HB Cowboy Woodruff Miss	5	0	0	30
HB Jim Rountree, Fla.	5	0	0	30
HB Robert Collins, M St	5	0	0	30
E Jimmy Phillips, Aub	5	0	0	30
FB Theron Sapp, Ga	5	0	0	30

1958

Position, Player, School	TD	PAT	FG	Pts
HB Billy Cannon, LSU	11	4	0	74*
HB Calvin Bird, Ky	10	5	0	65
HB Bobby Jackson, Ala	7	0	0	44*
HB Johnny Robinson, LSU	7	0	0	42
QB Bobby Franklin, Miss	6	3	0	39
T Robert Khayat, Miss	0	22	4	34*
FB Tommy Davis, LSU	3	11	1	34
QB Richie Petitbon, Tul	5	0	0	30
E Larry Grantham, Miss	5	0	0	30
FB Eddie Dyas, Auburn	4	4	0	28

1959

Position, Player and School	TD	PAT	FG	Pts
FB Charley Flowers, Miss	11	0	0	66
HB Tommy Moore, Vandy	10	0	0	60
HB Jerry Bird, Ky	8	7	0	55
QB Bobby Hunt, Aub.	7	0	0	44*
FB Ed Dyas, Auburn	3	14	4	44
HB Billy Cannon, LSU	7	0	0	44*
QB Jake Gibbs, Miss	7	0	0	42
T Robert Khayat, Miss	0	25	5	40
HB Jack Westbrook, Fla	6	0	0	36
HB Durward Pennington, Ga	0	26	2	32

1960

Position, Player, School	TD	PAT	FG	Pts
HB Tom Mason, Tul	13	0	0	78
FB Ed Dyas, Auburn	2	12	13	63
TB Glenn Glass, Tenn	8	0	0	48
FB James Anderson, Miss	7	0	0	42
HB Durward Pennington, Ga	0	16	8	40
HB Fred Brown, Georgia	6	0	0	38*
HB Wendell Harris, LSU	2	10	4	34
HB Tommy Wells, Ga Tech	0	10	8	34
E Cotton Letner, Tenn	1	18	3	33
C Allen Green, Miss	0	19	4	31

1961

Position, Player, School	TD	PAT	FG	Pts
HB Wendell Harris, LSU	8	26	6	94*
FB Billy R. Adams, Miss	10	0	0	60
QB Pat Trammell, Ala	9	0	0	56*
E Wes Sullivan, Miss	4	18	3	51
PK Tim Davis, Ala	0	22	9	49
QB Billy Lothridge, Ga Tech	3	16	4	46
HB Lindy Infante, Fla	7	0	0	42
QB Bobby Hunt, Aub	6	0	0	36
PK Woody Woodall, Aub	0	19	5	36*
TB Mallon Faircloth, Tenn	6	0	0	36

1962

Position, Player, School	TD	PAT	FG	Pts
HB Cotton Clark, Ala	15	0	0	92*
QB Billy Lothridge, Ga	9	20	5	89
HB Jerry Stovall, LSU	11	0	0	66
HB Louis Guy, Miss	8	0	0	48
FB Larry Dupree, Fla	7	0	0	42
PK Woody Woodall, Aub	0	17	8	41
PK Tim Davis, Ala	0	22	4	34
QB Lynn Amedee, LSU	0	18	5	33
HB Don Porterfield, Ga	5	0	0	30
HB Odie Burrell, M St	5	0	0	30

1963

Position, Player, School	TD	PAT	FG	Pts
QB Billy Lothridge, Ga Tech	3	15	12	69
HB Benny Nelson, Ala	10	0	0	62*
QB Jimmy Sidle, Aub	10	0	0	60
HB Ode Burrell, M St	7	0	0	42
PK Woody Woodall, Aub	0	23	6	41
End Billy C. Irwin, Miss	1	23	3	38
Gd Justin Canaie, M St	0	16	7	37
PK Tim Davis, Ala	0	24	4	36
FB Don Schwab, LSU	6	0	0	36
HB Mike Dennis, Miss	6	0	0	36

1964

Position, Player, School	TD	PAT	FG	Pts
End Doug Moreau, LSU	4	6	13	73*
HB David Ray, Alabama	2	23	12	71
HB Roger Bird, Ky	10	0	0	60
FB Steve Bowman, Ala	9	0	0	54
End Billy C. Irwin, Miss	0	21	7	42
HB Marcus Rhoden, Miss St	7	0	0	42
HB Jack Harper, Florida	7	0	0	42
QB Joe Namath, Alabama	6	0	0	36
End Rick Kestener, Ky	6	0	0	36
QB Pres Ridlehuber, Ga	6	0	0	36
HB Mike Dennis, Miss	6	0	0	36

1965

Position, Player, School	TD	PAT	FG	Pts
HB Rodger Bird, Ky	13	0	0	78
End Doug Moreau, LSU	3	30	3	59*
HB Larry Seiple, Ky	9	0	0	56*
HB David Ray, Alabama	1	21	7	50*
HB Mike Dennis, Miss	8	0	0	48
End Charles Case, Fla	8	0	0	48
PK Bobby Etter, Georgia	0	16	10	46
FB Wayne Barfield, Fla	0	26	6	44
Gd Jimmy Keyes, Miss	1	19	6	43
HB Marcus Rhoden, M St	7	0	0	42

1966

Position, Player, School	TD	PAT	FG	Pts
PK Bobby Etter, Ga	0	21	12	57

PK Steve Davis, Ala	0	25	10	55
FB Larry Smith, Fla	9	0	0	54
Guard Jimmy Keyes, Miss	0	20	10	50
Flk Richard Trapp, Fla	7	0	0	44*
End Austin Denney, Tenn	7	0	0	42
HB D. Cummingham, Miss	7	0	0	42
End Ray Perkins, Ala	7	0	0	42
PK Gary Wright, Tenn	0	28	4	40
FB Wayne Barfield, Fla	0	27	4	39

1967

Position, Player, School	TD	PAT	FG	Pts
FB Dicky Lyons, Ky	11	4	1	73
TB Walt Chadwick, Tenn	11	0	0	66
PK Karl Kremser, Tenn	0	30	10	60
FB Larry Smith, Florida	10	0	0	60
Flk Dennis Homan, Ala	9	0	0	54*
PK Jim McCullough, Ga	0	31	7	52
PK John Riley, Auburn	0	16	9	43
FB Ron Jenkins, Georgia	7	0	0	42
QB Kirby Moore, Georgia	7	0	0	42
PK Steve Davis, Alabama	0	18	8	42

1968

Position, Player, School	TD	PAT	FG	Pts
TB Dicky Lyons, Ky	11	0	0	66
PK John Riley, Auburn	0	25	12	61
PK Jim McCullough, Ga	0	31	7	52
PK Karl Kremser, Tenn	0	28	6	46
FB Larry Smith, Florida	7	0	0	42
HB Mike Currier, Auburn	7	0	0	42
End Tim Christian, Aub	7	0	0	42
WB Dave Strong, Vandy	7	0	0	42
HB Steve Hindman, Miss	7	0	0	42
WB Richmond Flowers, Tenn	7	0	0	42

1969

Position, Player, School	TD	PAT	FG	Pts
TB Tommy Durrance, Fla	18	2	0	110
QB Archie Manning, Miss	14	2	0	86
TB Johnny Musso, Ala	13	0	0	78
FL Carlos Alvarez, Fla	12	4	0	76
PK John Riley, Aub	0	39	10	69
PK George Hunt, Tenn	0	35	10	65
PK Mark Lumpkin, LSU	0	38	8	62
QB Watson Brown, Vandy	9	4	0	58
PK Rich Franco, Fla	0	33	6	51
FL Dave Strong, Vandy	8	2	0	50

1970

Position, Player, School	TD	PAT	FG	Pts
SE Terry Beasley, Aub	12	0	0	72
PK George Hunt, Tenn	0	42	10	72
PK Gardner Jett, Aub	0	41	10	71
PK Kim Braswell, Ga	0	22	13	61
QB Steve Burger, Vandy	10	0	0	60
QB Pat Sullivan, Aub	9	0	0	54
PK Richard Ciemny, Ala	0	26	10	56
TB Johnny Musso, Ala	9	0	0	54
PK Mark Lumpkin, LSU	0	32	7	53
TB Bobby Knight, Miss	8	0	0	48

1971

Position, Player, School	TD	PAT	FG	Pts
TB Johnny Musso, Ala	16	4	0	100
QB Andy Johnson, Ga	13	0	0	78
PK Bill Davis, Ala	0	36	13	75
WR Terry Beasley, Aub	12	0	0	72
TE Jay Michaelson, ISU	2	39	7	72
PK George Hunt, Tenn	0	30	12	66
TB Greg Ainsworth, Miss	11	0	0	66
PK Kim Braswell, Ga	0	38	7	9
TB Jimmy Poulos, Ga	9	4	0	58
FB Curt Watson, Tenn	9	0	0	54

1972

Position, Player, School	TD	PAT	FG	Pts
TB Haskel Stanback, Tenn	13	0	0	78
TB Terry Henley, Aub	11	0	0	66
TB Nat Moore, Fla	13	0	0	78
PK Ricky Townsend, Tenn	0	31	12	67
TB Steve Bisceglia, Ala	10	0	0	60
PK Bill Davis, Ala	0	46	5	61
QB Terry Davis, Ala	9	0	0	54
TB Butch Veazey, Miss	8	0	0	48
PK Gardner Jett, Aub	0	21	8	45
HB Wilbur Jackson, Ala	8	0	0	48

1973

Position, Player, School	TD	PAT	FG	Pts
TB Sonny Collins, Ky	13	2-pt	0	80
PK Bill Davis, Ala	0	51	8	75
PK Ricky Townsend, Tenn	0	27	11	60
PK Hawkins Golden, Vandy	0	11	12	47
PK Steve Lavinghouze, Miss	0	25	9	52
HB Wilbur Jackson, Ala	8	2-pt	0	50
PK Allan Leavitt, Ga	0	25	8	49
PK Vic Nickels, M St	0	23	8	47
PK Rusty Jackson, LSU	0	28	6	46

1974

Position, Player, School	TD	PAT	FG	Pts
TB Stanley Morgan, Tenn	14	0	0	84
TB Jamie O'Rourke, Vandy	13	0	0	78
TB Horace King, Ga	12	0	0	72
PK Mark Adams, Vandy	0	34	11	67
QB Mike Fanuzzi, Ky	11	0	0	66
PK Davis Posey, Fla	0	27	12	63
PK Alan Leavitt, Ga	0	40	7	61
PK John Pierce, Ky	0	25	11	58
TB Brad Davis, LSU	9	0	0	54
FB Calvin Culliver, Ala	8	0	0	48

1975

Position, Player, School	TD	PAT	FG	Pts
PK David Posey, Fla	0	32	9	64
TB Terry Robiskie, LSU	10	2-pt	0	62
RB Kevin McLee, Ga	10	0	0	60
TB Stanley Morgan, Tenn	10	0	0	60
QB Richard Todd, Ala	9	0	0	54
PK Kinney Jordan, M St	0	14	13	53
PK Neil O'Donoghue, Aub	0	13	12	49
PK Steve Lavinghouze, Miss	0	18	10	48
PK Danny Ridgeway, Ala	0	35	4	47
PK Mark Adams, Vandy	0	11	12	47

1976

Position, Player, School	TD	PAT	FG	Pts
TB Terry Robiskie, LSU	12	0	0	72
PK Allan Leavitt, Ga	0	37	11	70
WB Stanley Morgan, Tenn	11	2-pt	0	68
PK David Posey, Fla	0	34	10	64
PK Kinney Jordan, M St	0	31	10	61
SE Wes Chandler, Fla	10	0	0	60
HB Willie Wilder, Fla	10	0	0	60
QB Ray Goff, Ga	10	0	0	60
QB Derrick Ramsey, Ky	10	0	0	60
PK Mike Conway, LSU	0	30	9	57

1977

Position, Player, School	TD	PAT	FG	Pts
TB Charles Alexander, LSU	17	2-pt	0	104
RB Tony Nathan, Ala	15	2-pt	0	92
QB Derrick Ramsey, Ky	13	2-pt	0	80
WR Wes Chandler, Fla	12	0	0	72
FB James Storey, Miss	10	0	0	60
RB Beri Yepremian, Fla	0	29	12	65
PK Jorge Portela, Aub	0	19	15	64
PK Roger Chapman, Ala	0	30	11	63
WR Carlos Carson, LSU	10	0	0	60
PK Dave Marler, M St	0	18	13	57

*Total includes 2-pt PATs

1978

Position, Player, School	TD	PAT	FG	Pts
B Joe Cribbs, Aub	16	2-pt	0	98
B Charles Alexander, LSU	16	0	0	96
B James Jones, Miss St	13 3	2pt	0	84
B Willie McClendon, Ga	13	0	0	78
K Rex Robinson, Ga	0	29	15	74
K Berj Yepremian, Fla	0	25	16	73
K Mike Conway, LSU	0	26	14	68
K Alan Duncan, Tenn	0	26	13	65
B Cris Collinsworth, Fla	10	2-pt	0	62
B Jimmy Streeter, Tenn	10	0	0	60

*Includes 2-pt PATs.

SEC All-Time Passing Leaders (Yardage)

	Completions	Yards	Yds per Compl
John Reaves, Fla, 1969	222	2896	13.04
Pat Sullivan, Aub, 1970	167	2586	15.48
John Reaves, Fla, 1970	188	2549	13.56
Dave Marler, Miss St, 1978	163	2422	14.86
Scott Hunter, Ala, 1969	157	2188	13.94
John Reaves, Fla, 1971	193	2104	10.90
Steve Spurrier, Fla, 1966	179	2012	10.42
Pat Sullivan, Aub, 1971	162	2012	12.42
Steve Spurrier, Fla, 1965	148	1893	12.79
Tommy Pharr, Miss St, 1968	173	1838	10.62
Zeke Bratkowski, Ga, 1952	131	1824	13.92
Rick Norton, Ky, 1965	113	1823	16.13

SEC All-Time Passing Leaders (Completions)

	Attempts	Completions	Yards
John Reaves, Fla, 1969	396	222	2896
John Reaves, Fla, 1971	356	193	2104
John Reaves, Fla, 1970	376	188	2549
Steve Spurrier, Fla, 1966	291	179	2012
Tommy Pharr, Miss St, 1968	319	173	1838
Pat Sullivan, Aub, 1970	281	167	2586
Dave Marler, Miss St, 1978	287	163	2422
Pat Sullivan, Aub, 1971	281	162	2012
Scott Hunter, Ala, 1969	266	157	2188
Archie Manning, Miss, 1969	265	154	1762

SEC All-Time Passing Leaders (Percentage)*

	Attempts	Completions	Percent
Ken Stabler, Ala, 1966	114	74	.649
Joe Namath, Ala, 1964	100	64	.640
Watson Brown, Vandy, 1969	111	69	.622
Steve Spurrier, Fla, 1966	291	179	.615
Francis Tarkenton, Ga, 1959	102	62	.608
Condredge Holloway, Tenn, 1972	120	73	.608
Jake Gibbs, Miss, 1960	109	66	.606
Steve Sloan, Ala, 1965	160	97	.606
Dewey Warren, Tenn, 1966	229	136	.602
Jeff Rutledge, Ala, 1977	107	64	.598

(*100 or more attempts)

SEC Seasonal Passing Leaders

		Attempts	Completions	Interceptions	Gain	Touchdowns	Percent
1948	John Rauch, Ga	141	71	13	1307	5	.504
1949	Babe Parilli, Ky	150	81	13	1081	8	.540
1950	Babe Parilli, Ky	203	114	12	1627	23	.561
1951	Babe Parilli, Ky	239	136	12	1643	19	.569
1952	Zeke Bratkowski, Ga	262	131	16	1824	12	.500
1953	Zeke Bratkowski, Ga	224	113	23	1461	6	.504
1954	Bob Hardy, Ky	108	57	11	887	5	.528
1955	Dick Young, Ga	97	48	8	875	8	.495
1956	Raymond Brown, Miss	84	40	3	653	8	.476
1957	Boyce Smith, Vandy	98	49	10	664	8	.500
1958	Richie Petitbon, Tul	125	66	10	728	3	.528
1959	Jake Gibbs, Miss	94	46	2	755	6	.489
1960	Francis Tarkkenton, Ga	185	108	12	1189	7	.584
1961	Pat Trammell, Ala	133	75	2	1035	8	.564
1962	Joe Namath, Ala	146	76	8	1192	13	.520
1063	Larry Rakestraw, Ga	209	103	14	1297	7	.493
1964	Rick Norton, Ky	202	106	10	1514	9	.525
1965	Steve Spurrier, Fla	287	148	13	1893	14	.516
1966	Steve Spurrier, Fla	291	179	8	2012	16	.615
1967	Loran Carter, Aub	178	85	17	1307	9	.478

1968	Tommy Pharr, Miss St	319	173	18	1838	9	.542
1969	John Reaves, Fla	396	222	19	2896	24	.561
1970	Pat Sullivan, Aub	281	167	12	2586	17	.594
1971	John Reaves, Fla	356	193	21	2104	17	.542
1972	David Bowden, Fla	229	108	12	1481	12	.472
1973	Fred Fisher, Vandy	234	128	5	1450	11	.547
1974	Matt Robinsaon, Ga	121	60	10	1317	8	.496
1975	Randy Wallace, Tenn	145	72	11	1318	8	.497
1976	Jimmy Fisher, Fla	146	83	8	1511	10	.568
1977	Mike Wright, Vandy	211	106	7	1383	5	.502
1978	Dave Marler, Miss St	287	163	17	2422	11	.568

SEC All-Time Pass Receiving Leaders (Receptions)

		Receptions	Yards
1969	Carlos Alvarez, Fla	88	1329
1967	Bob Goodridge, Vandy	79	1114
1970	David Smith, Miss St	74	987
1968	Sammy Milner, Miss St	64	909
1969	Sammy Milner, Miss St	64	745
1966	Richard Trapp, Fla	63	872
1965	Charley Casey, Fla	58	809
1967	Richard Trapp, Fla	58	708
1969	Dave Bailey, Ala	56	781
1971	Terry Beasley, Aub	55	846
1970	Dave Bailey, Ala	55	790

SEC All-Time Pass Receiving Leaders (Yardage)

		Receptions	Yards	Yards per Reception
1969	Carlos Alvarez, Fla	88	1329	15.1
1967	Bob Goodridge, Vandy	79	1114	14.1
1970	Terry Beasley, Aub	52	1051	20.2
1978	Mardye McDole, Miss St	48	1035	21.6
1970	David Smith, Miss St	74	987	13.3
1968	Sammy Milner, Miss St	64	909	14.2
1966	Richard Trapp, Fla	63	872	13.8
1970	Andy Hamilton, LSU	39	870	22.3
1971	Andy Hamilton, LSU	45	854	19.0
1975	Larry Seivers, Tenn	41	840	20.4

SEC Seasonal Pass Receiving Leaders

		Receptions	Yards
1948	Jim Powell, Tenn	36	452
1949	Gene Lorendo, Ga	28	391
1950	Al Lary, Ala	35	756
	Al Bruno, Ky	35	532
1951	Harry Babcock, Ga	41	666
1952	John Carson, Ga	32	467
1953	John Carson, Ga	45	663
1954	Jim Pyburn, Aub	28	460
1955	Jimmy Orr, Ga	24	443
1956	Jimmy Phillips, Aub	23	383
1957	Jimmy Orr, Ga	16	237
1958	Calvin Bird, Ky	21	373
	Pete Abanie, Tul	21	266
1959	Bobby Towns, Ga	18	263
1960	Fred Brown, Ga	31	275
1961	Tom Hutchinson, Ky	32	543
1962	Clem Dellenger, Tul	39	375
1963	Pat Hodgson, Ga	24	375
1964	Charley Casey, Fla	47	673
1965	Charley Casey, Fla	58	809
1966	Richard Trapp, Fla	63	872
1967	Bob Goodridge, Vandy	79	1114
1968	Sammy Milner, Miss St	64	909
1969	Carlos Alvarez, Fla	88	1329
1970	David Smith, Miss St	74	987
1971	Terry Beasley, Aub	55	846
1972	Bill Buckley, Miss St	47	776
1973	Bill Buckley, Miss St	41	661
1974	Lee McGriff, Fla	36	698
1975	Larry Seivers, Tenn	41	840
1976	Larry Seivers, Tenn	51	737
1977	Martin Cox, Vandy	48	783
1978	Mardye McDole, Miss St	48	1035

SEC All-Time Rushing Leaders

Year	Player	Attempts	Yards	Average
1977	Charles Alexander, LSU	311	1686	5.4
1978	Willie McClendon, Ga	287	1312	4.6
1949	John Dottley, Miss	208	1312	6.3
1975	Jimmy DuBose, Fla	191	1307	6.8
1973	Sonny Collins, Ky	224	1213	5.4
1973	Wayne Jones, Miss St	212	1193	5.6
1948	Eddie Price, Tul	186	1178	6.3
1975	Sonny Collins, Ky	248	1150	4.6
1970	Johnny Musso, Ala	226	1137	5.0
1949	Eddie Price, Tul	171	1137	6.6

SEC Seasonal Rushing Leaders

Year	Player	Attempts	Yards	Average
1948	Eddie Price, Tul	186	1178	6.3
1949	John Dottley, Miss	208	1312	6.3
1950	John Dottley, Miss	191	1007	5.3
1951	Hank Lauricella, Tenn	111	818	7.9
1952	Bobby Marlow, Ala	176	950	5.3
1953	Jerry Merchand, LSU	137	696	5.1
1954	Joe Childress, Aub	148	836	5.6
1955	Fob James, Aub	123	879	7.1
1956	Tommy Lorino, Aub	82	692	8.4
1957	Jimmy Taylor, LSU	162	762	4.7
1958	Billy Cannon, LSU	115	686	6.0
1959	Charley Flowers, Miss	141	733	5.2
1960	Tom Mason, Tul	120	663	5.5
1961	Mike Fracchia, Ala	130	652	5.0
1962	Larry Dupree, Fla	113	604	5.3
1963	Jimmy Sidle, Aub	185	1006	5.4
1964	Don Schwab, LSU	160	683	4.3
1965	Steve Bowman, Ala	153	770	5.0
1966	Larry Smith, Fla	162	742	4.6
1967	Steve Hindman, Miss	215	829	3.9
1968	Rich Pickens, Tenn	133	736	5.5
1969	Doug Mathews, Vandy	167	849	5.1
1970	Johnny Musso, Ala	226	1137	5.0
1971	Johnny Musso, Ala	191	1088	5.7
1972	Haskel Stanback, Tenn	183	890	4.9
1973	Sonny Collins, Ky	224	1213	5.4
1974	Walter Packer, Miss St	157	994	6.3
1975	Jimmy DuBose, Fla	191	1307	6.8
1976	Terry Robiskie, LSU	224	1117	5.0
1977	Charles Alexander, LSU	311	1686	5.4
1978	Willie McClendon, Ga	287	1312	4.6

Associated Press All-SEC Teams

1933

First Team	Second Team	Third Team
E—Graham Batchelor, Ga	Jimmy Slocum, Ga Tech	Don Hutson, Ala
T—Jack Torrance, LSU	Bill Lee, Ala	Clyde Williams, Ga Tech
G—LeRoy Moorehead, Ga	J. B. Ellis, Tenn	Sam Brown, Vandy
C—Sheriff Maples, Tenn	Homer Robinson, Tul	Welcome Shearer, Fla
G—Tom Hupke, Ala	Boots Chambless, Aub.	Dave Wilcox, Ga Tech
T—Bob Tharpe, Ga Tech	Hal Starbuck, Fla.	Jesse Flowers, Miss
E—Gump Ariail, Aub	Joe Rupert, Ky.	Bart Herrington, Miss
B—Ripper Williams, Aub	Rand Dixon, Vandy	Casey Kimbrell, Aub
B—Beattie Feathers, Tenn	Floyd Roberts, Tul	Homer Key, Ga
B—Dixie Howell, Ala	Cy Grant, Ga	R. H. Herrington, Miss St
B—Ralph Kercheval, Ky	Jack Phillips, Ga Tech	George Chapman, Ga

1934

First Team	Second Team	Third Team
E—Don Hutson, Ala	Paul Bryant, Ala	Joe Rupert, Ky
T—Justin Rukas, LSU	C. W. Williams, Ga Tech	William Stark, Fla
G—Murray Warmath, Tenn	John Brown, Ga	Buck Brown, LSU
C—Homer Robinson, Tul	John McKnight, Ga	Walter Gilbert, Aub
G—Charlie Marr, Ala	George Tessier, Tul	Mike Welch, Aub
T—Bill Lee, Ala	Howard Bailey, Tenn	Rannie Throgmorton, Vandy
E—Bennie Fenton, Aub	Gene Rose, Tenn	Willie Geny, Vandy
B—Dixie Howell, Ala	Rand Dixon, Vandy	Riley Smith, Ala
B—Bert Johnson, Kentucky	Charlie Vaughan, Tenn	Jess Fatherree, LSU
B—Abe Mickal, LSU	Julius Brown, Fla	Shorty Roberts, Ga Tech
B—Claude Simons, Tul	Joe Demyanovich, Ala	George Chapman, Ga.

1935

First Team	Second Team	Third Team
E—Gaynell Tinsley, LSU	Gene Rose, Tenn	Paul Bryant, Ala
T—Haygood Paterson, Aub	Sterling Richardson, Miss	Stanley Nevers, Ky
G—Frank Johnson, Ga	Samuel Brown, Vandy	Willie Stone, Miss St
C—Walter Gilbert, Aub	Kavanaugh Francis, Ala	Marvin Stewart, LSU
G—J. M. FitzSimons, Ga Tech	Frank Gantt, Aub	Arthur White, Ala
T—James Whatley, Ala	Justin Rukas, LSU	Rannie Throgmorton, Vandy
E—Willie Geny, Vandy	Charles Gelatka, Miss St	Warren Barrett, LSU
B—Riley Smith, Ala	Rand Dixon, Vandy	Barney, Mintz, Tul
B—Ike Pickle, Miss St	Bob Davis, Ky	Ray Hapes, Miss
B—Jess Fatherree, LSU	Rab Rodgers, Miss	Billy Chase, Fla
B—Bill Crass, LSU	Abe Mickal, LSU	Dutch Konemann, Ga Tech

1936

First Team	Second Team	Third Team
E—Gaynell Tinsley, LSU	Perron Shoemaker, Ala	Chuck Gelatka, Miss St
T—Frank Kinard, Miss	William Moss, Tul	Paul Carroll, LSU
G—Arthur White, Ala	Dewitt Weaver, Tenn	Frank Gantt, Aub
C—Walter Gilbert, Aub	Marvin Stewart, LSU	Carl Hinkle, Vandy
G—Wardell Leisk, LSU	J. M. FitzSimons, Ga Tech	Pete Tinsley, Ga
T—Rupert Colmore, Sew	Stanley Nevers, Ky	Alex Lott, Miss St
E—Joel Eaves, Aub	Otis Maffett, Ga	Dick Plasman, Vandy
B—Joe Riley, Ala	Walter Mayberry, Fla	Billy May, LSU
B—Phil Dickens, Tenn	Joe Kilgrow Ala	Bill Crass, LSU
B—Howard Bryan, Tul	Clarence Hapes, Miss	Bob Davis, Ky
B—Dutch Konemann, Ga Tech	Pat Coffee, LSU	Wilton Kilgore, Aub

1937

First Team	Second Team	Third Team
E—Bill Jordon, Ga Tech	Ralph Wenzel, Tul	Bowden Wyatt, Tenn
T—Frank Kinard, Miss	"Bo" Russell, Aub	Ben Friend, LSU
G—Leroy Monsky, Ala	Ed Merlin, Vandy	Norman Hall, Tul
C—Carl Hinkle, Vandy	Quinton Lumpkin, Ga	Jack Chivington, Ga Tech
G—Ralph Sivell, Aub	Ed Sydnor, Ky	Pete Tinsley, Ga
T—Eddie Gatto, LSU	Buford Ray, Vandy	Jim Ryba, Ala
E—Erwin Warren, Ala	Perron Shoemaker, Ala	Ken Kavanaugh, LSU
B—Fletcher Simms, Ga Tech	George Cafego, Tenn	Lunsford Hollins, Vandy
B—Joe Kilgrow, Ala	Pinky Rohm LSU	Jim Fenton, Aub
B—Walter Mayberry, Fla	Bob Davis, Ky	Dutch Konemann, Ga Tech
B—Bill Hartman, Ga	Charles Holm, Ala	Guy Milner, LSU

1938

First Team	Second Team	Third Team
E—Bowden Wyatt, Tenn	Ralph Wenzel, Tul.	Perron Shoemaker, Ala
T—Eddie Gatto, LSU	Maurice Holdgraf, Vandy	Malcolm Gray, Miss St
G—Jimmy Brooks, Ga Tech	John Goree, LSU	Ed Molinski, Tenn
C—Quinton Lumpkin, Ga	Jack Chivington, Ga Tech	Sherman Hinkebein, Ky
G—Bob Suffridge, Tenn	Milton Howell, Aub	Frank Kocsis, Fla
T—"Bo" Russell, Aub	Ray Miller, Tul	Walter Merrill, Ala
E—Ken Kavanaugh, LSU	Marvin Franklin, Vandy	Billy McCubbin, Ky
B—George Cafego, Tenn	Vic Bradford, Ala	Kimble Bradley, Miss
B—Parker Hall, Miss	Spec Kelly, Aub	Babe Wood, Tenn
B—Warren Brunner, Tul	Dave Zoeller, Ky	Jim Fordham, Ga
B—Charles Holm, Ala	Len Coffman, Tenn	Bert Marshall, Vandy

1939

First Team	Second Team	Third Team
E—Bob Ison, Ga Tech	Ralph Wenzel, Tul	Harold Newman, Ala
T—Harley McCollum, Tul	John Eibner, Ky	Clark Goff, Fla
G—Ed Molinski, Tenn	Bob Suffridge, Tenn	Tom O'Boyle, Tul
C—James Rike, Tenn	John Goolsby, Miss St	Winkey Autrey, Miss
G—John Goree, LSU	Milton Howell, Aub	Neil Cavette, Ga Tech
T—Marshall Shires, Tenn	Fred Davis, Ala	Walter Merrill, Ala
E—Ken Kavanaugh, LSU	Erwin Elrod, Miss St	Bill McCubbin, Ky
B—George Cafego, Tenn	Sam Bartholomew, Tenn	Buck Murphy, Ga Tech
B—Bob Foxx, Tenn	John Hovious, Miss	Junius Plunkett, Vandy
B—Bob Kellog Tul	Dick McGowen, Aub	Jack Nix, Miss St
B—Bill Schneller, Miss	Howard Ector, Ga Tech	Fred Gloden, Tul

1940

First Team	Second Team	Third Team
E—Erwin Elrod, Miss St	Edward Cifers, Tenn	Forrest Ferguson, Fla
T—Marshall Shires, Tenn	Charles Dufour, Tul	John Eibner, Ky
G—Bob Suffridge, Tenn	Ed Molinski, Tenn	Julius Battista, Fla
C—Bob Gude, Vandy	Bert Ackermann, Tenn	Warren Averitte, Ala
G—Hunter Corhern Miss St	Ed Hickerson, Ala	John Goree, LSU
T—Fred Davis, Ala	John Tripson, Miss St	John Barrett, LSU
F—Holt Rast, Ala	Bob Ison, Ga Tech	Harold Newman, Ala
B—Bob Foxx, Tenn	Harvey Johnson, Miss St	Charles Ishmael, Ky
B—John Hovious, Miss	John Butler, Tenn	Johnny Bosch, Ga Tech
B—Jimmy Nelson, Ala	Jim Thibaut, Tul	Rufus Deal, Aub
B—Dick McGowen, Aub	Merle Hapes, Miss	Billy Jefferson, Miss St

1941

First Team	Second Team	Third Team
E—Holt Rast, Ala	Forrest Ferguson, Fla	Bill Hornick, Tul
T—Ernest Blandin, Tul	Bill Arnold, Miss St	Milton Hull, Fla
G—John Wyhonic, Ala	Jack Tittle, Tul	Walter Ruark, Ga
C—Bob Gude, Vandy	Bernie Lipkis, LSU	Ray Graves, Tenn
G—Homer Hazel, Miss	Oscar Britt, Miss	George Hecht, Ala
T—Don Edmiston, Tenn	Charles Sanders, Ga Tech	Chet Kozel, Miss
E—Bill Eubanks, Miss	George Webb, Ga Tech	George Poschner, Ga
B—Jack Jenkins, Vandy	Lloyd Cheatham, Aub	Cliff Kimsey, Ga
B—Frank Sinkwich, Ga	John Hovious, Miss	Tom Harrison, Fla
B—Jimmy Nelson, Ala	Blondy Black, Miss St	Bob Glass, Tul
B—Merle Hapes, Miss	Walt McDonald, Tul	Noah Mullins, Ky

1942

First Team	Second Team	Third Team
E—George Poschner, Ga	Martin Comer, Tul	Sam Sharpe, Ala
T—Clyde Johnson, Ky	Mitchell Olenski, Ala	Gene Ellenson, Ga
G—Harvey Hardy, Ga Tech	Raymond Ray, Miss St	Oscar Britt, Miss
C—Joe Domnanovich, Ala	George Manning, Ga Tech	Jim Talley, LSU
G—Walter Ruark, Ga	George Hecht, Ala	Curtis Patterson, Miss St
T—Don Whitmire, Ala	Denver Crawford, Tenn	Dick Huffman, Tenn
F—Albert Hust, Tenn	Bob Patterson, Miss St	Jack Marshall, Ga Tech
B—Jack Jenkins, Vandy	Walt McDonald, Tul	Lou Thomas, Tul
B—Monk Gafford, Aub	Blondy Black, Miss St	Alvin Dark, LSU
B—Clint Castleberry, Ga Tech	Russ Craft, Ala	Lamar Davis, Ga
B—Frank Sinkwich, Ga	Bob Cifers, Tenn	Bernie Rohling, Vandy

1943

First Team	Second Team	Third Team
E—Phil Tinsley, Ga Tech	Charles Webb, LSU	Jim Wilson, Ga Tech
T—Joe Hartley, LSU	Fred Roseman, Tul	W. N. Smith, Ga Tech
G—John Steber, Ga Tech	Carl Janneck, LSU	Mike Castronis, Ga
C—Buddy Gatewood, Tul	George Manning, Ga Tech	Ed Claunch, LSU
G—Gaston Bourgeois, Tul	Frank Beall, Ga Tech	Charley Hoover, Ga Tech
T—Bill Chambers, Ga Tech	G. E. Jones, Tul	Ralph Hunt, LSU
E—Ray Olsen, Tul	Walt Kilzer, Ga Tech	Ken Tarzetti, Tul
B—Joe Renfroe, Tul	Leonard Finley, Tul	Bobby Hague, Ga
B—Eddie Prokop, Ga Tech	Harry Robinson, Vandy	W. A. Jones, Tul
B—Johnny Cook, Ga	Charlie Smith, Ga	Joe Nagata, LSU
B—Steve Van Buren, LSU	Mickey Logan, Ga Tech	Frank Broyles, Ga Tech

(Only Four Teams Played Due to the War)

1944

First Team	Second Team	Third Team
E—Phil Tinsley, Ga Tech	Ralph Jones, Ala	Bill Hildebrand, Miss St
T—Hillery Horne, Miss St	Andy Perhach, Ga	Tom Whitley, Ala
G—Herb St. John, Ga	Maurice Furchgott, Ga Tech	Roland Phillips, Ga Tech
C—Tex Warrington, Aub	Vaughn Mancha, Ala.	Russ Morrow, Tenn
G—Bob Dobelstein, Tenn	Gaston Bourgeois, Tul	Gerald Bertucci, LSU
T—Wash Serini, Ky	Dub Garrett, Miss St	Mike Castronis, Ga
E—Ray Olsen, Tul	Reid Moseley, Ga	Bob McCain, Miss
B—Buster Stephens, Tenn	Harry Gilmer, Ala	Norman Klein, Ky
B—Tom McWilliams, Miss St	Alan Bowen, Ga Tech	Bobby Forbes, Fla
B—W. A. Jones, Tul	Bill Bevis, Tenn	George Mathews, Ga Tech
Frank Broyles, Ga Tech	Curtis Kuykendall, Aub.	Gene Knight, LSU

1945

First Team	Second Team	Third Team
E—Rebel Steiner, Ala	Reid Moseley, Ga	Buddy Pike, Tenn
T—Tom Whitley, Ala	Wash Serini, Ky	Jack White, Fla
G—Bob Dobelstein, Tenn	Jack Green, Ala	George Hills, Ga Tech
C—Vaughn Mancha, Ala	Paul Duke, Ga Tech	Hugh Bowers, Tul
G—Felix Trapani, LSU	Gaston Bourgeois, Tul	Herb St. John, Ga
T—Bobby Davis, Ga Tech	Mike Castronis, Ga	Dub Garrett, Miss St
E—Bill Hildebrand, Miss St	Clyde Lindsey, LSU	Walter Kilzer, Ga Tech
B—Harry Gilmer, Ala	Curtis Kuykendall, Aub	Bill Bevis, Tennessee
B—Harper Davis, Miss St	Buster Stephens, Tenn	Jim Cason, LSU
B—Charlie Trippi, Ga	George Mathews, Ga Tech	Bill Fuqua, Vandy
B—Gene Knight, LSU	Lowell Tew, Ala	Graham Bramlett, Miss St

1946

First Team	Second Team	Third Team
E—Wallace Jones, Ky	Frank Hubbell, Tenn	Broughton Williams, Fla
T—Bobby Davis, Ga Tech	Dub Garrett, Miss St	Alf Satterfield, Vandy
G—Herb St. John, Ga	Bill Healy, Ga Tech	Gaston Bourgeois, Tul
C—Paul Duke, Ga Tech	Vaughn Mancha, Ala	Jay Rhodemyre, Ky
G—Wren Worley, LSU	Tex Robertson, Vandy	Mike Harris, Miss St
T—Dick Huffman, Tenn	Ed Champagne, LSU	Jack Bush, Ga
E—Ray Poole, Miss	Joe Tereshinski, Ga	Ted Cook, Ala
B—Charlie Trippi, Ga	Charles Conerly, Miss	Dan Sandifer, LSU
B—Harry Gilmer, Ala	Travis Tidwell, Aub	Pat McHugh, Ga Tech
B—Frank Broyles, Ga Tech	John Rauch, Ga	Harper Davis, Miss St
B—Tom McWilliams, Miss St	Y. A. Tittle, LSU	Walter Slater, Tenn

1947

First Team	Second Team	Third Team
E—Barney Poole, Miss	John North, Vandy	Rebel Steiner, Ala
T—Bobby Davis, Ga Tech	Bill Erickson, Miss	Charles Compton, Ala
G—John Wozniak, Ala	Herb St. John, Ga	Wren Worley, LSU
C—Jay Rhodemyre, Ky	Vaughn Mancha, Ala	Louis Hook, Ga Tech
G—Bill Healy, Ga Tech	Tex Robertson, Vandy	Leo Yarutis, Ky
T—Dub Garrett, Miss St	Wash Serini, Ky	Denver Crawford, Tenn
E—Dan Edwards, Ga	Abner Wimberly, LSU	George Brodnax, Ga Tech
B—Charles Conerly, Miss	John Rauch, Ga	Bobby Berry, Vandy
B—Harry Gilmer, Ala	Bobby Forbes, Fla	Harper Davis, Miss St
B—Rip Collins, LSU	Lowell Tew, Ala	Allen Bowen, Ga Tech
B—Tom McWilliams, Miss St	Y. A. Tittle, LSU	Eddie Price, Tul

1948

First Team	Second Team	Third Team
E—Barney Poole, Miss	Abner Wimberly, LSU	Wallace Jones, Ky
T—Paul Lea, Tul	Porter Payne, Ga	Dutch Cantrell, Vandy
G—Bill Healy, Ga Tech	Ken Cooper, Vandy	Homer Hobbs, Ga
C—John Clark, Vandy	Hal Herring, Aub	Ed Claunch, LSU
G—Jimmy Crawford, Miss	Dennis Doyle, Tul	Jim Vugrin, Ga Tech
T—Norman Meseroll, Tenn	Robert Gain, Ky	Clay Matthews, Ga Tech
E—George Brodnax, Ga Tech	Jim Powell, Tenn	Dick Sheffield, Tul
B—John Rauch, Ga	Farley Salmon, Miss	Harper Davis, Miss St
B—Charles Hunsinger, Fla	Hal Littleford, Tenn	Bob McCoy, Ga Tech
B—Tom McWilliams, Miss St	Herb Rich, Vandy	Bill Cadenhead, Ala
B—Eddie Price, Tul	Frank Ziegler, Ga Tech	Joe Geri, Ga

1949

First Team	Second Team	Third Team
E—Bud Sherrod, Tenn	Bob Walston, Ga	Bucky Curtis, Vandy
T—Bob Gain, Ky	Tom Coleman, Ga Tech	Marion Campbell, Ga
G—Allen Hover, LSU	Dennis Doyle, Tul	Mike Mizerany, Ala
C—Harry Ulinski, Ky	Jerry Taylor, Miss St	Jimmy Kynes, Fla
G—Ed Holdnak, Ala	Jimmy Crawford, Miss	Ted Daffer, Tenn
T—Paul Lea, Tul	Ray Collins, LSU	Carl Copp, Vandy
E—Sam Lyle, LSU	Jack Stribling, Miss	Dick Harvin, Ga Tech
B—Eddie Price, Tul	Babe Parilli, Ky	Don Phelps, Ky
B—Travis Tidwell, Aub	Jimmy Jordan, Ga Tech	Floyd Reid, Ga
B—John Dottley, Miss	Herb Rich, Vandy	Butch Avinger, Ala
B—Charles Hunsinger, Fla	Zollie Toth, LSU	Lee Nalley, Vandy

1950

First Team	Second Team	Third Team
E—Bucky Curtis, Vandy	Al Lary, Ala	John Weigle, Ga Tech
T—Bob Gain, Ky	Bill Pearman, Tenn	Marion Campbell, Ga
G—Mike Mizerany, Ala	Rocco Principe, Ga	Tom Banks, Aub
C—Pat O'Sullivan, Ala	Doug Moseley, Ky	Bob Bossons, Ga Tech
G—Ted Daffer, Tenn	Bill Wannamaker, Ky	Pat James, Ky
T—Paul Lea, Tul	Russ Faulkinberry, Vandy	Charles LaPradd, Fla
E—Bud Sherrod, Tenn	Al Bruno, Ky	Bill Stribling, Miss
B—Babe Parilli, Ky	Haywood Sullivan, Fla	Billy Mixon, Ga
B—John Dottley, Miss	Bill Wade, Vandy	Butch Avinger, Ala
B—Ed Salem, Ala	Bill Leskovar, Ky	Wilbur Jamerson, Ky
B—Ken Konz, LSU	Hank Lauricella, Tenn	Bobby North, Ga Tech

1951

OFFENSE

First Team	Second Team	Third Team
E—Harry Babcock, Ga	Buck Martin, Ga Tech	Lee Hayley, Aub
T—Lum Snyder, Ga Tech	Jerome Helluin, Tul	Hal Miller, Ga Tech
G—John Michels, Tenn	Ed Bauer, Aub	Ed Duncan, Aub
C—Doug Moseley, Ky	Carroll McDonald, Fla	Bob Davis, Tenn
G—Gene Donaldson, Ky	Sid Fournet, LSU	Jerry Watford, Ala
T—Bob Werckle, Vandy	Jim MacKenzie, Ky	Ray Potter, LSU
E—Steve Meilinger, Ky	Ben Roderick, Vandy	Warren Virgets, LSU
B—Hank Lauricella, Tenn	Bobby Marlow, Ala	Leon Hardeman, Ga Tech
B—Babe Parilli, Ky	Bert Rechichar, Tenn	Hal Payne, Tenn
B—Bill Wade, Vandy	Andy Kozar, Tenn	Haywood Sullivan, Fla
H—Darrell Crawford, Ga Tech	Zeke Bratkowski, Ga	Jimmy Lear, Miss

DEFENSE

First Team	Second Team	Third Team
E—Doug Atkins, Tenn	Bobby Flowers, Fla	Jesse Yates, LSU
T—Lamar Wheat, Ga Tech	Charlie LaPradd, Fla	Marion Campbell, Ga
G—Ted Daffer, Tenn	Joe D'Agostino, Fla	Art Kleinschmidt, Tul
C—George Tarasovic, LSU	Ralph Carrigan, Ala	Larry Morris, Ga Tech
G—Ray Beck, Ga Tech	Jess Richardson, Ala	John Cheadle, Vandy
T—Bill Pearman, Tenn	Billy Pyron, Miss St	Bill Turnbeaugh, Aub
E—Harold Maxwell, Miss	Red Lutz, Ala	Bob Fry, Ky
B—Bobby Marlow, Ala	George Morris, Ga Tech	Emery Clark, Ky
B—Bert Rechichar, Tenn	Vince Dooley, Aub	Mickey Lakos, Vandy
B—Claude Hipps, Ga	Jim Roshto, LSU	Jim Barton, LSU
B—Joe Fortunato, Miss St	Gordon Polofsky, Tenn	Bobby Wilson, Ala

1952

OFFENSE

First Team	Second Team	Third Team
E—Harry Babcock, Ga	Buck Martin, Ga Tech	Lee Hayley, Aub
T—Kline Gilbert, Miss	Jim Haslam, Tenn	Bob Fry, Ky
G—John Michels, Tenn	Jake Shoemaker, Ga Tech	Jerry May, Miss
C—Pete Brown, Ga Tech	Bo Reid, Miss St	Larry Stone, Vandy
G—Jerry Watford, Ala	Al Robelot, Tul	Ed Gossage, Ga Tech
T—Hal Miller, Ga Tech	Travis Hunt, Ala	Dewayne Douglas, Fla
E—Steve Meilinger, Ky	Ben Roderick, Vandy	Jeff Knox, Ga Tech
B—Jack Parker, Miss St	Zeke Bratkowski, Ga	Jimmy Lear, Miss
B—Leon Hardeman, Ga Tech	Rick Casares, Fla	Buford Long, Fla
B—Bobby Marlow, Ala	Corky Tharp, Ala	Billy Teas, Ga Tech
B—Andy Kozar, Tenn	Joe Fortunato, Miss St	Max McGee, Tul

DEFENSE

First Team	Second Team	Third Team
E—Sam Hensley, Ga Tech	Joe O'Malley, Ga	Jim Mask, Miss
T—Charlie La Pradd, Fla	Bill Turnbeaugh, Aub	Paul Miller, LSU
G—Joe D'Agostino, Fla	Crawford Mims, Miss	Chris Filipkowski, Ga
LB—George Morris, Ga Tech	Ralph Carrigan, Ala	Arlen Jumper, Fla
LB—Larry Morris, Ga Tech	Tommy Adkins, Ky	Bill Barbish, Tenn
G—Francis Holohan, Tenn	Orville Vereen, Ga Tech	Tony Sardisco, Tul
T—Doug Atkins, Tenn	Ed Culpepper, Ala	Bob Sherman, Ga Tech
E—Mack Franklin, Tenn	Bob Hines, Vandy	Roger Rotroff, Tenn
HB—Bobby Moorhead, Ga Tech	Charles Ware, Fla	Charlie Brannon, Ga Tech
HB—Cecil Ingram, Ala	Bobby Jordan, Aub	Charley Oakley, LSU
S—Art Decarlo, Ga	George Brancato, LSU	Don Gleisner, Vandy

1953

First Team	Second Team	Third Team
E—John Carson, Ga	Roger Rotroff, Tenn	Mack Franklin, Tenn
T—Sid Fournet, LSU	Bob Fisher, Tenn	Tom Morris, Miss St
G—Crawford Mims, Miss	Joe D'Agostino, Fla	Al Robelot, Tul
C—Larry Morris, Ga Tech	Ralph Carrigan, Ala	Hal Easterwood, Miss St
G—Ray Correll, Ky	George Atkins, Aub	Pete Williams, Vandy
T—Frank D'Agostino, Aub	Bob Sherman, Ga Tech	Dan Hunter, Fla
E—Jim Pyburn, Aub	Joe Tuminello, LSu	Sam Hensley, Ga Tech
B—Jackie Parker, Miss St	Zeke Bratkowski, Ga	Bobby Freeman, Aub
B—Corky Tharp, Ala	Leon Hardeman, Ga Tech	Bill Teas, Ga Tech
B—Steve Mellinger, Ky	Jimmy Wade, Tenn	Hal Lofton, Miss
B—Glenn Turner, Ga Tech	Ralph Paolone, Ky	Jerry Marchand, LSU

1954

First Team	Second Team	Third Team
E—Jim Pyburn, Aub	Joe Tuminello, LSU	Howard Schnellenberger, Ky
T—Sid Fournet, LSU	Darris McCord, Tenn	George Mason, Ala
G—Bobby Goodall, Vandy	Don Shea, Ga	George Atkins, Aub
C—Hal Easterwood, Miss St	Larry Morris, Ga Tech	Steve DeLaTorre, Fla
G—Franklin Brooks, Ga Tech	Bryan Bunthorne, Tul	Bill Dooley, Miss St
T—Rex Reed Boggan, Miss	Frank D'Agostino, Aub	Pud Mostellor, Ga
E—Henry Hair, Ga Tech	Joe O'Malley, Ga	Ray Brown, Fla
B—Bob Hardy, Ky	Eagle Day, Miss	Bobby Freeman, Aub
B—Arthur Davis, Miss St	Allen Muirhead, Miss	Charley Horton, Vandy
B—Tom Tracy, Tenn	Corky Tharp, Ala	Jimmy Thompson, Ga Tech
B—Joe Childress, Aub	Mal Hammack, Fla	Bobby Garrard, Ga

1955

First Team	Second Team	Third Team
E—Joe Tuminello, LSU	Joe Stephenson, Vandy	Nick Germanos, Ala
T—Frank D'Agostino, Aub	M. L. Brackett, Aub	Jim Barron, Miss St
G—Scott Suber, Miss St	Tony Sardisco, Tul	Larry Frank, Vandy
C—Steve DeLaTorre, Fla	Gene Dubisson, Miss	Bob Scarbrough, Aub
G—Franklin Brooks, Ga Tech	Buddy Alliston, Miss	Bryan Bunthorne, Tul
T—Earl Leggett, LSU	Charles Rader, Tenn	Lou Michaels, Ky
E—H. Schnellenberger, Ky	Jimmy Phillips, Aub	Roy Wilkins, Ga
B—John Majors, Tenn	Bob Hardy, Ky	Eagle Day, Miss
B—Fob James, Aub	George Volkert, Ga Tech	Jackie Simpson, Fla
B—Charley Horton, Vandy	Art Davis, Miss St	Billy Kinard, Miss
B—Paige Cothren, Miss	Joe Childress, Aub	Ronnie Quillian, Tul

1956

First Team	Second Team	Third Team
E—Buddy Cruze, Tenn	Jimmy Phillips, Aub	Roger Urbano, Tenn
T—Lou Michaels, Ky	J. T. Frankenberger, Ky	Carl Vereen, Ga Tech
G—John Barrow, Fla	Allen Ecker, Ga Tech	Ernest Danjean, Aub
C—Don Stephenson, Ga Tech	Dave Kuhn, Ky	Jerry Stone, Miss
G—John Gordy, Tenn	Paul Ziegler, LSU	Charles Duck, Miss
T—Billy Yelverton, Miss	Dalton Truax, Tul	Art Demmas, Vandy
E—Ron Bennett, Miss St	Jerry Nabors, Ga Tech	John Wood, LSU
B—Billy Stacy, Miss St	Gene Newton, Tul	Toppy Vann, Ga Tech
B—Johnny Majors, Tenn	Tommy Lorino, Aub	Phil King, Vandy
B—Paige Cothren, Miss	Paul Rotenbery, Ga Tech	Jimmy Rountree, Fla
B—Ken Owen, Ga Tech	Ronny Quillian, Tul	Bob Dougherty, Ky

1957

First Team	Second Team	Third Team
E—Jimmy Phillips, Aub	Bob Laws, Vandy	Don Fleming, Fla
T—Lou Michaels, Ky	Charlie Mitchell, Fla	Nat Dye, Ga
G—Bill Johnson, Tenn	Billy Rains, Ala	Zeke Smith, Aub
C—Don Stephenson, Ga Tech	Jackie Burkett, Aub	Jack Benson, Miss St
G—Jackie Simpson, Miss	George Deiderich, Vandy	Cicero Lucas, Ga
T—Gene Hickerson, Miss	Ben Preston, Aub	Sam Latham, Miss St
E—Jerry Wilson, Aub	Jerry Nabors, Ga Tech	John Benge, Miss St
B—Billy Stacy, Miss St	Ray Brown, Miss	Boyce Smith, Vandy
B—Bobby Gordon, Tenn	Phil King, Vandy	Tommy Lorino, Aub
B—Jim Rountree, Fla	Bobby Cravens, Ky	Billy Lott, Miss
B—Jimmy Taylor, LSU	Billy Atkins, Aub	Theron Sapp, Ga

1958

First Team	Second Team	Third Team
E—Jerry Wilson, Aub	Larry Grantham, Miss	Dave Hudson, Florida
E—Don Fleming, Fla	Billy Hendrix, LSU	Gerald Burch, Ga Tech
T—Vel Heckman, Fla	Nat Dye, Ga	Dave Sington, Ala
T—Cleve Wester, Aub	Charles Strange, LSU	Bob Lindon, Ky
G—Zeke Smith, Aub	Don Cochran, Ala	Bobby Urbano, Tenn
G—George Deiderich, Vandy	Jack Benson, Miss St	Larry Kahlden, LSU
C—Jackie Burkett, Aub	Max Fugler, LSU	Max Baughan, Ga Tech
B—Waren Rabb, LSU	Richie Petitbon, Tul	Billy Stacy, Miss St
B—Billy Cannon, LSU	Tom Moore, Vandy	Tommy Lorino, Aub
B—John Robinson, LSU	Bobby Cravens, Ky	Floyd Faucette, Ga Tech
B—Charlie Flowers, Miss	Theron Sapp, Ga	J. W. Brodnax, LSU

1959

First Team	Second Team	Third Team
E—Larry Grantham, Miss	John Brewer, Miss	Dave Hudson, Fla
E—Jimmy Vickers, Ga	Mickey Mangham, LSU	LaVelle White, Miss St
T—Ken Rice, Aub	Larry Wagner, Vandy	Lynn LeBlanc, LSU
T—Joe Rice, Aub	Toby Deese, Ga Tech	Danny Royal, Fla
T—Joe Schaffer, Tenn	Don Cochran, Ala	Billy Roland, Ga
G—Marvin Terrell, Miss	Pat Dye, Ga	Bob Talamini, Ky
G—Zeke Smith, Aub	Tom Goode, Miss St	Jackie Burkett, Aub
C—Maxie Baughan, Ga Tech	Jake Gibbs, Miss	Bobby Hunt, Aub
B—Francis Tarkenton, Ga	Calvin Bird, Ky	Johnny Robinson, LSU
B—Billy Cannon, LSU	Bobby Walden, Ga	Lamar Rawson, Aub
B—Tom Moore, Vandy	Ed Dyas, Aub	Taz Anderson, Ga Tech
B—Charles Flowers, Miss		

1960

First Team	Second Teacm	Third Team
E—Johnny Brewer, Miss	Pat Patchen, Fla	Ralph Smith, Miss
E—Tom Hutchinson, Ky	Gerald Burch, Ga Tech	Mike Lasorsa, Tenn
T—Ken Rice, Aub	Billy Wilson, Aub	Pete Case, Ga
T—Billy Shaw, Ga Tech	Bob Benton, Miss	Jim Beaver, Fla
G—Vic Miranda, Fla	Pat Dye, Ga	Billy Neighbors, Ala
G—Richard Price, Miss	Roy Winston, LSU	Lloyd Hodge, Ky
C—Tom Goode, Miss St	Charles Strange, LSU	Mike Lucci, Tenn
B—Jake Gibbs, Miss	Larry Libertore, Fla	Phil Nugent, Tul
B—Tom Mason, Tul	Fred Brown, Ga	Jim Cartwright, Tenn
B—Francis Tarkenton, Ga	Billy Williamson, Ga Tech	Leon Fuller, Ala
B—Ed Dyas, Aub	James Anderson, Miss	Don Goodman, Fla.

1961

First Team	Second Team	Third Team
E—Tom Hutchinson, Ky	Ralph Smith, Miss	Gene Sykes, LSU
E—Dave Edwards, Aub	Johnny Baker, Miss St	Tommy Brooker, Ala
T—Billy Neighbors, Ala	Billy Booth, LSU	Jim Beaver, Fla
T—Jim Dunaway, Miss	Pete Case, Ga	Ernie Colquett, Tul
G—Roy Winston, LSU	Harold Ericksen, Ga Tech	Billy Ray Jones, Miss
G—Dave Watson, Ga Tech	Monk Guillot, LSU	Howard Benton, Miss St
C—Mike Lucci, Tenn	Lee Roy Jordan, Ala	Wayne Frazier, Aub
B—Pat Trammell, Ala	Doug Elmore, Miss	Hank Lesene, Vandy
B—Billy Ray Adams, Miss	Jerry Stovall, LSU	Billy Williamson, Ga T
B—Wendell Harris, LSU	Mallon Faircloth, Tenn	Don Goodman, Fla
B—Mike Fracchia, Ala	Bill McKenny, Ga	Earl Gros, LSU

1962

First Team	Second Team	Third team
E—Tom Hutchinson, Ky	Billy Martin, Ga Tech	Richard Williamson, Ala
E—Johnny Baker, Miss St	Clem Dellenger, Tul	Sam Holland, Fla
T—Fred Miller LSU	Jim Dunaway, Miss	Larry Stallings, Ga Tech
T—Junior Hawthorne, Ky	Frank Lasky, Fla	Ernie Colquette, Tul
G—Rufus Guthrie, Ga Tech	Robbie Hucklebridge, LSU	Larry Travis, Fla
G—Don Dickson, Miss	Steve DeLong, Tenn	Dave Watson, Ga Tech
C—Lee Roy Jordan, Ala	Dennis Gaubatz, LSU	Jim Price, Aub
B—Jerry Stovall, LSU	Larry Rakestraw, Ga	Lindy Infante, Fla
B—Glynn Griffing, Miss	Joe Namath, Ala	Mike McNames, Ga Tech
B—Billy Lothridge, Ga Tech	Cotton Clark, Ala	Chuck Morris, Miss
B—Larry Dupree, Fla	Darrell Cox, Ky	Louis Guy, Miss

1963

First Team	Second Team	Third Team
E—Billy Martin, Ga Tech	Billy Truax, LSU	Pat Hodgson, Ga
E—Allen Brown, Miss	Howard Simpson, Aub	Clem Dellenger, Tul
T—Whaley Hall, Miss	Ray Rissmiller, Ga	Mike Calamari, Tul
T—Tommy Neville, Miss St	Dennis Murphy, Fla	Ralph Pere, LSU
G—Steve DeLong, Tenn	Stan Hindman, Miss	Al Lewis, Ala
G—Rob Hucklebridge, LSU	Pat Watson, Miss St	Bill Van Dyke, Aub
C—Kenny Dill, Miss	Dave Simmons, Ga Tech	Bill Cody, Aub
B—Billy Lothridge, Ga Tech	Larry Rakestraw, Ga	Joe Namath, Ala
B—Jimmy Sidle Aub	Ode Burrell, Miss St	Larry Rawson, Aub
B—Benny Nelson, Ala	Tucker Frederickson, Aub	Don Schwab, LSU
B—Larry Dupree, Fla.	Perry Lee Dunn, Miss	Hoyle Granger, Miss St

1964

OFFENSE First Team	OFFENSE Second Team	DEFENSE First Team	DEFENSE Second Team
E—Doug Moreau, LSU	Tommy Inman, Miss St	E—Rick Kestner, Ky	Lynn Matthews, Fla
E—Charley Casey, Fla	Tommy Tolleson, Ala	E—Allen Brown, Miss	Barry Wilson, Ga
T—Jim Wilson, Ga	Ray Rissmiller, Ga	T—Jack Thornton, Aub	George Patton, Ga
T—George Rice, LSU	Gary Hart, Vandy	T—Dan Kearley, Ala	Tommy Neville, Miss St
G—Wayne Freeman, Ala	Stan Hindman, Miss	G—Steve DeLong, Tenn	Leon Verriere, Tul
G—Larry Gagner, Fla	Justin Canale, Miss St	G—Bill Richbourg, Fla	Pat Watson, Miss St
C—Richard Granier, LSU	Gay McCollough, Ala	LB—Mike Vincent, LSU	Frank Emanuel, Tenn
Q—Joe Namath, Ala	Jim Weatherly, Miss	LB—Bill Cody, Aub	Paul Crane, Ala
H—Roger Bird, Ky	Larry Dupree, Fla	DB—T. Frederickson, Aub	Allen Trammell, Fla
H—Mike Dennis, Miss	Marcus Rhoden, Miss St	DB—Bruce Bennett, Fla	Dave Malone, Vandy
F—Steve Bowman, Ala	Hoyle Granger, Miss St	DB—Wayne Swinford, Ga	Steve Sloan, Ala

1965

OFFENSE First Team	OFFENSE Second Team	DEFENSE First Team	DEFENSE Second Team
E—Tommy Tolleson, Ala	Barry Brown, Fla	E—Creed Gilmer, Ala	Lynn Mathews, Fla
E—Charles Casey, Fla	Pat Hodgson, Ga	E—Bobby Frazier, Tenn	Lane Wolbe, Vandy
T—Sam Ball, Ky	Jim Harvey, Miss	T—Jack Thornton, Aub	George Rice, LSU
T—Dave McCormick, LSU	Andy Gross, Aub	T—Jim Urbanek, Miss	Dick Lemay, Vandy
G—Stan Hindman, Miss	Doug Davis, Ky	G—George Patton, Ga	Grady Bolton, Miss St
G—Larry Beckman, Fla	Bobby Gratz, Tenn	LB—Frank Emanuel, Tenn	Tom Fisher, Tenn
C—Paul Crane, Ala	Forrest Blue, Aub	LB—Bill Goss, Tul	Mike McGraw, Ky
B—Steve Spurrier, Fla	Steve Sloan, Ala	LB—Bill Cody, Aub	Tim Bates, Ala
B—Steve Bowman, Ala	Hoyle Granger, Miss St	B—Bobby Johns, Ala	Marv Cornelius, Miss St
B—Roger Bird, Ky	Larry Seiple, Ky	B—Bruce Bennett, Fla	Terry Beadles, Ky
B—Mike Dennis, Miss	Joe Labruzzo, LSU	B—Lynn Hughes, Ga	Bobby Beaird, Aub

1966

OFFENSE First Team	OFFENSE Second Team	DEFENSE First Team	DEFENSE Second Team
E—Johnny Mills, Tenn	Austin Denny, Tenn	E—John Garlington, LSU	Jeff Van Note, Ky
E—Ray Perkins, Ala	Wayne Cook, Ala	E—Larry Kohn, Ga	Jerry Richardson, Miss
T—Cecil Dowdy, Ala	Jerry Duncan, Ala	T—George Patton, Ga	Bill Stanfill, Ga
T—Edgar Chandler, Ga	Bubba Hampton, Miss St	T—Jim Urbanek, Miss	Richard Cole, Ala
G—Bob Johnson, Tenn	Jim Benson, Fla	G—Jimmy Keyes, Miss	Bobby Morel, Tenn
G—Don Hayes, Ga	Scott Hall, Vandy	LB—Paul Naumoff, Tenn	Gusty Yearout, Aub
C—Bill Carr, Fla	Chuck Hinton, Miss	LB—George Bevan, LSU	Doug Archibald, Tenn
QB—Steve Spurrier, Fla	Dewey Warren, Tenn	LB—D. D. Lewis, Miss St	Chip Healy, Vandy
RB—Larry Smith, Fla	Ronnie Jenkins, Ga	B—Lynn Hughes, Ga	Dicky Lyons, Ky
RB—D. Cunningham, Miss	Charlie Fulton, Tenn	B—Bobby Johns, Ala	Jerry Davis, Ky
FL—Richard Trapp, Fla	Freddie Hyatt, Aub	B—Gerry Warfield, Miss	Sammy Grezaffi, LSU

1967

OFFENSE First Team	OFFENSE Second Team	DEFENSE First Team	DEFENSE Second Team
E—Dennis Homan, Ala	Freddie Hyatt, Aub	E—John Garlington, LSU	Jerry Richardson, Miss
E—Bob Goodridge, Vandy	Mac Haik, Miss	E—Mike Ford, Ala	Nick Showalter, Tenn
T—Edgar Chandler, Ga	Alan Bush, Miss	T—Bill Stanfill, Ga	Charlie Collins, Aub
T—John Boynton, Tenn	Elliot Gammage, Tn	T—Jim Urbanek, Miss	Glenn Higgins, Miss St
G—Guy Dennis, Fla	Bruce Stevens, Ala	G—Gusty Yearout, Aub	Don Giordano, Fla
G—C. Rosenfelder, Tenn	Don Hayes, Ga	G—Mike Hall, Ala	Dan Sartin, Miss
C—Bob Johnson, Tenn	Barry Wilson, LSU	LB—D. D. Lewis, Miss St	Steve Kiner, Tenn
QB—Ken Stabler, Ala	Nelson Stokley, LSU	LB—Jimmy Keyes, Miss	Robert Margeson, Tub
RB—Larry Smith, Fla	Steve Hindman, Miss	DB—Albert Dorsey, Tenn	Buddy McClinton, Aub
FL—Richard Trapp, Fla	Richmond Flowers, Tn	DB—Sammy Grezaffi, LSU	Tommy James, Miss
FB—Ronnie Jenkins, Ga	Walter Chadwick, Tn	DB—Jake Scott, Ga	Mike Jones, Tenn
PK—Wayne Barfield, Fla	Karl Kremser, Tenn	P—Eddie Ray, LSU	Julian Fagan, Miss

1968

OFFENSE

First Team	Second Team
E—Dennis Hughes, Ga	Ken Delong, Tenn
E—Tim Christian, Aub	Donnie Sutton, Ala
T—David Rholetter, Ga	Bob Asher, Vandy
T—Bill Fortier, LSU	Jerry Gordon, Aub
G—C. Rosenfelder, Tenn	Guy Dennis, Fla
G—Alvin Samples, Ala	Johnny McDonald, Aub
C—Chip Kell, Tenn	G. Zaundrecher, LSU
QB—Tommy Pharr, Miss St	Mike Cavan, Ga
HB—Dicky Lyons, Ky	Richmond Flowers, Tn
FL—Sammy Milner, Miss St	Kent Lawrence, Ga
FB—Richard Pickens, Tenn	Larry Smith, Fla
PK—John Riley, Aub	Jim McCoullough, Ga

DEFENSE

First Team	Second Team
E—Billy Payne, Ga	Neal McMeans, Tenn
E—Mike Ford, Ala	Dick Palmer, Ky
T—Bill Stanfill, Ga	Dick Williams, Tenn
T—David Campbell, Aub	Randy Barron, Ala
G—Sam Gellerstedt, Ala	David Roller, Ky
LB—Steve Kiner, Tenn	Mike Anderson, LSU
LB—Mike Hall, Ala	Frank Trapp, Miss
LB—Mike Kolen, Aub	Happy Dicks, Ga
DB—Jake Scott, Ga	Steve Tannen, Fla
DB—Buddy McClinton, Aub	Gerry Kent, LSU
DB—Glenn Cannon, Miss	Jim Weatherford, Tn
P—Spike Jones, Ga	Julian Fagan, Miss

1969

OFFENSE

First Team	Second Team
E—Carlos Alverez, Fla	Floyd Franks, Miss
E—Sammy Milner, Miss St	Terry Beasley, Aub
T—Bob Asher, Vandy	Mac Steen, Fla
T—Danny Ford, Ala	Richard Cheek, Aub
G—Chip Kell, Tenn	Don Williams, Fla
G—Alvin Samples, Ala	Skip Jernigan, Miss
C—Tom Banks, Aub	Mike Bevans, Tenn
B—Archie Manning, Miss	Pat Sullivan, Aub
B—John Reaves, Fla	Johnny Musso, Ala
B—Curt Watson, Tenn	Tom Durrance, Fla
B—Eddie Ray, LSU	Con Frederick, Aub

DEFENSE

First Team	Second Team
E—Hap Farber, Miss	Dick Palmer, Ky
E—D. Ghesquiere, Fla	Neal Dettmering, Aub
T—David Roller, Ky	Buz Morrow, Miss
T—Steve Greer, Ga	Frank Yanossy, Tenn
LB—Steve Kiner, Tenn	Larry Thomas, Miss
LB—George Bevan, LSU	Chip Wisdom, Ga
LB—Mike Kolen, Aub	Joe Federspiel, Ky
LB—Jack Reynolds, Tenn	Bob Strickland, Aub
DB—Buddy McClinton, Aub	Tim Priest, Tenn
DB—Glenn Cannon, Miss	Steve Tannen, Fla
DB—Tommy Casanova, LSU	L. Willingham, Aub

1970

OFFENSE

First Team	Second Team
SE—Terry Beasley, Aub	David Bailey, Ala
TE—Jim Yancey, Fla	Jim Poole, Miss
T—Worthy McClure, Miss	Johnny Hannah, Ala
T—Royce Smith, Ga	Danny Speigner, Aub
G—Chip Kell, Tenn	Mike Demarie, LSU
G—Skip Jernigan, Miss	Jimmy Speigner, Aub
C—Mike Bevans, Tenn	Tommy Lyons, Ga
QB—Pat Sullivan, Aub	Archie Manning, Miss
RB—Johnny Musso, Ala	Art Cantrelle, LSU
RB—Curt Watson, Tenn	Randy Reed. Miss
FL—David Smith, Miss St	Floyd Franks, Miss
PK—Gardner Jett, Aub	Kim Braswell, Ga

DEFENSE

First Team	Second Team
E—Jack Youngblood, Fla	Dave Hardt, Ky
E—Dennis Coleman, Miss	Chuck Heard, Ga
T—John Sage, LSU	Ronnie Estay, LSU
T—Dave Roller, Ky	Larry Brasher, Ga
LB—Mike Anderson, LSU	Chip Wisdom, Ga
LB—Jackie Walker, Tenn	Fred Brister, Miss
LB—Bobby Strickland, Aub	Chuck Dees, Miss St
B—Tommy Casanova, LSU	Tim Priest, Tenn
B—Bobby Majors, Tenn	Craig Burns, LSU
B—Larry Willingham, Aub	Ray Heidel, Miss
B—Buzy Rosenberg, Ga	Ken Phares, Miss St
P—Steve Smith, Vandy	Frank Mann, Ala

1971

OFFENSE

First Team	Second Team
SE—Terry Beasley, Aub	Dick Schmalz, Aub
Te—David Bailey, Ala	Carlos Alvarez, Fla
LT—Jim Krapf, Ala	Eric Hoggat, Miss St
RT—Tom Nash, Ga	Danny Speigner, Aub
LG—Royce Smith, Ga	Fred Abbott, Fla
RG—John Hannah, Ala	Mike Demarie, LSU
C—Kendall Keith, Ga	Bill Emendorfer, Tenn
QB—Pat Sullivan, Aub	Jimmy Grammer, Ala
RB—Johnny Musso, Ala	John Reaves, Fla
RB—Art Cantrelle, LSU	Curt Watson, Tenn
Fl—Andy Hamilton, LSU	Andy Johnson, Ga
PK—George Hunt, Tenn	Jay Michaelson, LSU

DEFENSE

First Team	Second Team
LE—Robin Parkhouse, Ala	Mixon Robinson, Ga
RE—Bob Brown, Aub	George Abernethy, Vandy
LT—Ronnie Estay, LSU	Chuck Heard, Ga
RT—Elmer Allen, Miss	Tommy Yearout, Aub
LB—Joe Federspiel, Ky	Chip Wisdom, Ga
LB—Bob Nettles, Tenn	Jeff Rouzie, Ala
LB—Tom Surlas, Ala	Jackie Walker, Tenn
BK—Bobby Majors, Tenn	Paul Dongieux, Miss
BK—Steve Higginbotham, Ala	Johnny Simmons, Aub
BK—Frank Dowsing, Miss St	Conrad Graham, Tenn
BK—Buzy Rosenberg, Ga	Ken Stone, Vandy
Punter—David Beverly, Aub	Greg Gantt, Ala

1972

OFFENSE

First Team	Second Team
WR—Bill Buckley, Miss St	Gerald Keigley, LSU
WR—Wayne Wheeler, Ala	Walter Overton, Vandy
TE—Butch Veazey, Miss	Brad Boyd, LSU
T—Mac Lorendo, Aub	Paul Parker, Fla
T—Don Leathers, Miss	L. T. Southall, Vandy
G—John Hannah, Ala	Tyler Lafauci, LSU
G—Bill Emendorfer, Tenn	Art Bressler, Miss
C—Jim Krapf, Ala	Chris Hammond, Ga
QB—Terry Davis, Ala	Bert Jones, LSU
RB—Nat Moore, Fla	Haskel Stanback, Tenn
RB—Terry Henley, Aub	Steve Bisceglia, Ala
PK—Ricky Townsend, Tenn	Gardner Jett, Aub

DEFENSE

First Team	Second Team
E—Danny Sanspree, Aub	Ricky Browne, Fla
E—John Mitchell, Ala	John Croyle, Ala
T—John Wood, LSU	Skip Kubelius, Ala
T—John Wagster, Tenn	Benny Sivley, Aub
LB—Jamie Rotella, Tenn	Ken Bernich, Aub
LB—Warren Capone, LSU	John David Calhoun, Miss St
LB—Fred Abott, Fla	Art Reynolds, Tenn
B—Bobby McKinney, Ala	Darryl Bishop, Ky
B—Conrad Graham, Tenn	Jim Revels, Fla
B—Ken Stone, Vandy	Ken Phares, Miss St
B—Dave Beck, Aub	Mike Williams, LSU
Punter—Greg Gantt, Ala	Rusty Jackson, LSU

1973

OFFENSE

First Team	Second Team
WR—Wayne Wheeler, Ala	WR—Lee McGriff, Fla
TE—Brad Boyd, LSU	TE—Butch Veazey, Miss
T—Buddy Brown, Ala	T—Harvey Sword, Ky
T—Tyler Latauci, LSU	T—Richard Brooks, LSU
G—Mac McWhorter, Ga	G—Lee Gross, Aub
G—Art Bressler, Miss	G—Burton Lawless, Fla
C—Steve Taylor, Aub	C—Jimmy Ray Stephens, Fla
QB—Condredge Holloway, Tenn	QB—Gary Rutledge, Ala
RB—Sonny Collins, Ky	RB—Brad Davis, LSU
RB—Wayne Jones, Miss St	RB—Haskel Stanback, Tenn
RB—Wilbur Jackson, Ala	RB—Paul Hofer, Miss
PK—Hawkins Golden, Vandy	

DEFENSE

First Team	Second Team
E—Ricky Browne, Fla	E—Mike Dubose, Ala
E—Binks Miciotto, LSU	E—Jimmy Webb, Miss St
T—Mike Raines, Ala	T—David Hitchcock, Fla
T—Benny Sivley, Aub	T—Ben Williams, Miss
LB—Warren Capone, LSU	G—Danny Jones, Ga
LB—Woodrow Lowe, Ala	LB—Jim Stuart, Miss
LB—Ralph Ortega, Fla	LB—Ken Bernich, Aub
B—Eddie Brown, Tenn	LB—Bo Harris, LSU
B—Mike Washington, Ala	B—Darryl Bishop, Ky
B—Jim Revels, Fla	B—Harry Harrison, Miss
Kick returner—Mike Fuller, Aub	B—Mike Williams, LSU
Punter—Greg Gantt, Ala	

1974

OFFENSE

First Team	Second Team
WR—Lee McGriff, Fla	WR—Gene Washington, Ga
TE—Barry Burton, Vandy	TE—Richard Appleby, Ga
T—Craig Hertwig, Ga	T—Chuck Fletcher, Aub
T—Warren Bryant, Ky	T—Paul Parker, Fla
G—Gene Moshier, Vandy	G—Burton Lawless, Fla
G—John Rogers, Ala	G—Sam Nichols, Miss St
C—Lee Gross, Aub	C—Rick Nuzum, Ky
QB—Rockey Felker, Miss St	QB—Mike Fanuzzi, Ky
RB—Sonny Collins, Ky	RB—Willie Shelby, Ala
RB—Glynn Harrison, Ga	RB—Stanley Morgan, Tenn
RB—Walter Packer, Miss St	RB—Jamie O'Rourke, Vandy
PK—Mark Adams, Vandy	Rb—Horace King, Ga

DEFENSE

First Team	Second Team
E—Leroy Cook, Ala	E—Mike Dubose, Ala
E—Rusty Deen, Aub	E—David McKnight, Ga
T—Jimmy Webb, Miss St	T—Ben Williams, Miss
T—Steve Cassidy, LSU	T—Robert Pulliam, Tenn
LB—Ken Bernich, Aub	LB—Ralph Ortega, Fla
LB—Glenn Cameron, Fla	LB—Sylvester Boler, Ga
LB—Woodrow Lowe, Ala	LB—Harvey Hull, Miss St
B—Mike Washington, Ala	LB—Tom Galbierz, Vandy
B—Ricky Davis, Ala	B—Jim McKinney, Aub
B—Mike Fuller, Aub	B—Mike Williams, LSU
B—Jay Fuller, Aub	B—Steve Curnutte, Vandy
B—Jay Chesley, Vandy	B—Wayne Fields, Fla
Punter—Neil Clabo, Tenn	Punter—John Tatterson, Ky

1975

OFFENSE

First Team	Second Team
SE—Larry Seivers, Tenn	SE—Rick Kimbrough, Miss
TE—Barry Burton, Vandy	SE—Jeff Gilligan, Aub
T—Warren Bryant, Ky	TE—Tommy West, Tenn
T—Mike Williams, Fla	T—Mike Wilson, Ga
G—Randy Johnson, Ga	T—Chuck Fletcher, Aub
G—David Gerasimchuck, Ala	G—Gerald Loper, Fla
C—Richard Keys, Miss St	G—Sam Nichols, Miss St
QB—Richard Todd, Ala	C—Robbie Moore, Fla
RB—Jimmy DuBose, Fla	QB—Don Gaffney, Fla
RB—Glynn Harrison, Ga	RB—Walter Packer, Miss St
RB—Sonny Collins, Ky	RB—Johnny Davis, Ala
PK—David Posey, Fla	RB—Stanley Morgan, Tenn
	RB—Kevin McLee, Ga
	PK—Mark Adams, Vandy

DEFENSE

First Team	Second Team
E—Leroy Cook, Ala	E—Gary Turner, Miss
E—Kenny Bordelon, LSU	E—Ron McCartney, Tenn
T—Bob Baumhower, Ala	T—Darrell Carpenter, Fla
T—Steve Cassidy, LSU	T—Lawrence Johnson, Miss
T—Rick Telhiard, Aub	MG—Harvey Hull, Miss St
MG—Ben Williams, Miss	LB—Ben Zambiasi, Ga
LB—Sammy Green, Fla	LB—Jim Kovach, Ky
LB—Conley Duncan, Ala	LB-Ray Costict, Miss St
LB—Andy Spiva, Tenn	B—Henry Davis, Fla
B—Mike Mauck, Tenn	B—Bill Krug, Ga
B—Wayne Rhodes, Ala	B—Stan Black, Miss St
B—Jay Chesley, Vandy	P—Bill Farris, Miss
P—Clyde Baumgartner, Aub	

1976

OFFENSE

First Team	Second Team
WR—Larry Seivers, Tenn	WR—Gene Washington, Ga
WR—Wes Chandler, Fla	WR—Stanley Morgan, Tenn
TE—Ozzie Newsome, Ala	TE—Jimmy Stephens, Fla
T—Mike Wilson, Ga	T—K. J. Lazenby, Ala
T—Warren Bryant, Ky	T—Bobby Dugas, LSU
G—Joel Parrish, Ga	T—David Forrester, Fla
G—Dave Gerasimchuk, Ala	G—Sam Nichols, Miss St
C—Richard Keys, Miss St	G—Dave Ostrowski, Aub
QB—Ray Goff, Ga	C—Robbie Moore, Fla
RB—Terry Robiskie, LSU	QB—Phil Gargis, Aub
RB—Kevin McLee, Ga	RB—Johnny Davis, Ala
PK—Allan Leavitt, Ga	RB—Dennis Johnson, Miss St
	PK—Neil O'Donoghue, Aub

DEFENSE

First Team	Second Team
E—Lew Sibley, LSU	E—Paul Harris, Ala
E—Art Still, Ky	E—Jeff McCollum, Aub
T—Charles Hannah, Ala	T—Bob Baumhower, Ala
T—A. J. Duhe, LSU	T—Darrell Carpenter, Fla
MG—Harvey Hull, Miss St	LB—Kem Coleman, Miss
LB—Ben Zambiasi, Ga	LB—Freddie Smith, Aub
LB—Ray Costict, Miss St	LB—Jon Streete, LSU
LB—Andy Spiva, Tenn	LB—Jim Kovach, Ky
DB—Stan Black, Miss St	B—Brenard Wilson, Vandy
DB—Bill Krug, Ga	B—Alvin Cowans, Fla
DB—Clinton Burrell, LSU	B—Mike Siganos, Ky
P—Craig Colquitt, Tenn	B—Charlie Moss, Miss
	P—Clyde Baumgartner, Aub

1977

OFFENSE	DEFENSE
WR—Wes Chandler, Fla	E—Art Still, Ky
WR—Martin Cox, Vandy	E—George Plasketes, Miss
TE—Ozzie Newsome, Ala	T—Larry Gillard, Miss St
T—Robert Dugas, LSU	T—Ronnie Swoopes, Ga
T—Jim Bunch, Ala	MG—Scott Hutchinson, Fla
G—Tom Dornbrook, Ky	LB—Ben Zambiasi, Ga
G—Lynn Johnson, Aub	LB—Freddie Smith, Aub
C—Dwight Stephenson, Ala	LB—Ed Smith, Vandy
QB—Derrick Ramsey, Ky	LB—Scott Brantley, Fla
RB—Charles Alexander, LSU	DB—Mike Siganos, Ky
RB—Johnny Davis, Ala	DB—Dallas Owens, Ky
PK—Jorge Portella, Aub.	DB—James McKinney, Aub
	P—Craig Colquitt, Tenn.

1978

OFFENSE	DEFENSE
WR—Mardye McDole, Miss St	E—John Adams, LSU
WR—Chris Collinsworth, Fla	E—E. J. Junior, Ala
T—Robert Dugas, LSU	T—Marty Lyons, Ala
T—Mike Burrow, Aub	T—Frank Warren, Aub
G—Mike Brock, Ala	LB—Scot Brantley, Fla
G—Mack Guest, Ga	LB—Barry Kraus, Ala
C—Robert Shaw, Tenn	LB—Ricky McBride, Ga
C—Dwight Stephenson, Ala	LB—Jim Kovach, Ky
QB—Dave Marler, Miss St	DB—Roland James, Tenn
RB—Charles Alexander, LSU	DB—Murray Legg, Ala
RB—Willie McClendon, Ga	DB—Chris Williams, LSU
RB—Joe Cribbs, Aub	P—Jim Miller, Miss
PK—Berj Yepremian, Fla.	

School Records

University of Alabama

Location: Tuscaloosa, Alabama
Enrollment: 17,000
Nickname: Crimson Tide
Colors: Crimson and White
Stadium: Bryant-Denny (59,000)

University of Alabama Head Coaching Records

COACH	YEARS	WON	LOST	TIED
E. N. Beaumont	1892	2	2	0
Eli Abbott	1893-'95; 1902	5	11	0
Otto Wagonhurst	1896	2	1	0
Allen McCants	1897	1	0	0
W. A. Hartin	1899	3	1	0
M. Griffin	1900	2	3	0
M. H. Harvey	1901	2	1	2
J. O. Heyworth	1902	2	2	0
W. B. Blount	1903-'04	10	7	0
Jack Leavenworth	1905	6	4	0
J. W. H. Pollard	1906-'09	21	4	5
Guy S. Lowman	1910	4	4	0
D. V. Graves	1911-'14	21	12	3
Thomas Kelly	1915-'17	17	7	1
Xen C. Scott	1919-'22	29	9	3
Wallace Wade	1923-'30	61	13	3
Frank W. Thomas	1931-'42; 1944-'46	115	24	7
Harold (Red) Drew	1947-'54	54	29	7
J. B. Whitworth	1955-'57	4	24	2
Paul (Bear) Bryant	1958-'78	192	38	7

University of Alabama All-Time Scores

1892

56 B'ham HS 0
4 B'ham AC 5
14 B'ham AC 0
22 Auburn 32

96 (2-2-0) 37

1893

0 B'ham AC 4
8 B'ham AC 10
0 Sewanee 20
16 Auburn 40

24 (0-4-0) 74

1894

0 Ole Miss 6
18 Tulane 6
24 Sewanee 4
18 Auburn 0

60 (3-1-0) 16

1895

6 Georgia 30
0 Tulane 22
6 LSU 12
0 Auburn 48

12 (0-4-0) 112

1896

30 B'ham AC 0
6 Sewanee 10
20 Miss State 0

56 (2-1-0) 10

1897

6 Tuscaloosa AC 0

1898—No Team

1899

16 Tuscaloosa AC 5
16 M'gomery AC 0
7 Ole Miss 5
0 N Orleans AC 21

39 (3-1-0) 31

1900

35 Taylor Sch 0
12 Ole Miss 6
0 Tulane 6
5 Auburn 53
0 Clemson 35

52 (2-3-0) 100

1901

41 Ole Miss 0
0 Georgia 0
0 Auburn 17
45 Miss State 0
6 Tennessee 6

92 (2-1-2) 23

1902

57 B'ham HS 0
81 Marion 0
0 Auburn 23
0 Georgia 5
27 Miss State 0
0 Texas 10
26 Ga Tech 0
0 LSU 11

191 (4-4-0) 49

1903

0 Vanderbilt 30
0 Miss State 11
18 Auburn 6
0 Sewanee 23
18 LSU 0
0 Cumberland 44
24 Tennessee 0

60 (3-4-0) 114

1904

29 Florida 0
0 Clemson 18
6 Miss State 0
17 Nash Univ 0
16 Georgia 5
5 Auburn 29
0 Tennessee 5
11 LSU 0
6 Tulane 0
10 Pensacola AC 5

100 (7-3-0) 62

1905

17 Maryville 0
0 Vanderbilt 34
34 Miss State 0
5 Ga. Tech 12
0 Clemson 25
36 Georgia 0
21 Centre 0
30 Auburn 0
6 Sewanee 42
29 Tennessee 0

178 (6-4-0) 113

1906

6 Maryville 0
14 Howard 0
0 Vanderbilt 78
16 Miss State 4
10 Auburn 0
51 Tennessee 0

97 (5-1-0) 82

1907

17 Maryville 0
20 Ole Miss 0
4 Sewanee 54
0 Georgia 0
12 Centre 0
6 Auburn 6

6 LSU 4
5 Tennessee 0
70 (5-1-2) 64

1908

27 Wetumpka 0
17 Howard 0
16 Cincinnati 0
6 Ga Tech 11
23 Chattanooga 6
6 Georgia 6
9 Haskell Inst 8
4 Tennessee 0
108 (6-1-1) 31

1909

16 Union 0
14 Howard 0
3 Clemson 0
0 Ole Miss 0
14 Georgia 0
10 Tennessee 0
5 Tulane 5
6 LSU 12
68 (5-1-2) 17

1910

25 B'ham Sou 0
26 Marion 0
0 Georgia 22
0 Ga. Tech 36
0 Ole Miss 16
0 Sewanee 30
5 Tulane 3
9 Wash & Lee 0
65 (4-4-0) 107

1911

24 Howard 0
47 B'ham Sou 5
3 Georgia 11
6 Miss State 6
0 Ga Tech 0
35 Marion 0
0 Sewanee 3
22 Tulane 0
16 Davidson 6
153 (5-2-2) 31

1912

52 Marion 0
62 B'ham Sou 0
3 Ga Tech 21
0 Miss State 7
9 Georgia 13
7 Tulane 0
10 Ole Miss 9
6 Sewanee 6
7 Tennessee 0
156 (5-3-1) 56

1913

27 Howard 0
81 B'ham Sou 0
20 Clemson 0
0 Georgia 20
26 Tulane 0
21 Miss College 3
7 Sewanee 10
6 Tennessee 0
0 Miss State 7
188 (6-3-0) 40

1914

13 Howard 0
54 B'ham Sou 0
13 Ga Tech 0
7 Tennessee 17
58 Tulane 0
0 Sewanee 18
63 Chattanooga 0
0 Miss State 9
3 Carlisle 20
211 (5-4-0) 64

1915

44 Howard 0
67 B'ham Sou 0
40 Miss College 0
16 Tulane 0
23 Sewanee 10
7 Ga Tech 21
0 Texas 20
53 Ole Miss 0
250 (6-2-0) 51

1916

13 B'ham Sou 0
80 Sou Univ 0
13 Miss College 7
16 Florida 0
27 Ole Miss 0
7 Sewanee 6
0 Ga Tech 13
0 Tulane 33
0 Georgia 3
156 (6-3-0) 62

1917

7 Ohio Am Corp 0
13 Maron 0
46 Miss College 0
64 Ole Miss 0
3 Sewanee 3
2 Vanderbilt 7
27 Kentucky 0
6 Camp Gordon 19
168 (5-2-1) 29

1918—No Team

1919

27 B'ham Sou 0
49 Ole Miss 0
48 Howard 0
61 Marion 0
40 Sewanee 0
12 Vanderbilt 16
23 LSU 0
6 Georgia 0
14 Miss State 6
280 (8-1-0) 22

1920

59 Sou Mil Inst. 0
49 Marion 0
45 B'ham Sou 0
57 Miss College 0
33 Howard College 0
21 Sewanee 0
14 Vanderbilt 7
21 LSU 0
14 Georgia 21
24 Miss State 7
40 Case Inst. 0
377 (10-1-0) 35

1921

34 Howard 14
27 Spring Hill 7
55 Marion 0
95 Bryson (N.C.) 0
0 Sewanee 17
7 L.S.U. 7
0 Vanderbilt 14
2 Florida 9
0 Georgia 22
7 Miss. State 7
14 Tulane 7
241 (5-4-2) 104

1922

110 Marion 0
41 Oglethorpe 0
7 Ga. Tech 33
7 Sewanee 7
10 Texas 19
9 Pennsylvania 7
47 L.S.U. 3
0 Kentucky 6
10 Georgia 6
59 Miss. State 0
300 (6-3-1) 81

1923

12 Union 0
56 Ole Miss 0
0 Syracuse 23
7 Sewanee 0
59 Spring Hill 0
0 Ga. Tech 0
16 Kentucky 8
30 L.S.U. 3
36 Georgia 0
6 Florida 16
222 (7-2-1) 50

1924

55 Union 0
20 Furman 0
51 Miss. College 0
14 Sewanee 0
14 Ga. Tech 0
61 Ole Miss 0
42 Kentucky 7
0 Centre 17
33 Georgia 0
290 (8-1-0) 24

1925

53 Union 0
50 B'ham-Sou. 7
42 L.S.U. 0
27 Sewanee 0
7 Ga. Tech 0
6 Miss. State 0
31 Kentucky 0
34 Florida 0
27 Georgia 0
277 (9-0-0) 7

Rose Bowl

20 Washington 19

1926

54 Millsaps 0
19 Vanderbilt 7
26 Miss. State 7
21 Ga. Tech 0
2 Sewanee 0
24 L.S.U. 0
14 Kentucky 0
49 Florida 0
33 Georgia 6
242 (9-0-0) 20

Rose Bowl

7 Stanford 7

1927

46 Millsaps 0
31 Presbyterian 0
0 L.S.U. 0
0 Ga. Tech 13
24 Sewanee 0
13 Miss. State 7
21 Kentucky 6
6 Florida 13
6 Georgia 20
7 Vanderbilt 14
154 (5-4-1) 73

1928

27 Ole Miss 0
46 Miss. State 0
13 Tennessee 15
42 Sewanee 12
0 Wisconsin 15
14 Kentucky 0
13 Ga. Tech 33
19 Georgia 0
13 L.S.U. 0
187 (6-3-0) 75

1929

55 Miss. College 0
22 Ole Miss 7
46 Chattanooga 0
0 Tennessee 6
35 Sewanee 7
0 Vanderbilt 13
24 Kentucky 13
14 Ga. Tech 0
0 Georgia 12
196 (6-3-0) 58

1930

43 Howard 0
64 Ole Miss 0
25 Sewanee 0
18 Tennessee 6
12 Vanderbilt 7
19 Kentucky 0
20 Florida 0
33 L.S.U. 0
13 Georgia 0
247 (9-0-0) 13

Rose Bowl

24 Wash. State 0

1931

42 Howard 6
55 Ole Miss 6
53 Miss. State 0
0 Tennessee 25
33 Sewanee 0
9 Kentucky 7
41 Florida 0
74 Clemson 7
14 Vanderbilt 6
46 Chattanooga 0
170 (9-1-0) 57

1932

45 Southwestern 6
53 Miss. State 0
28 Geo. Wash. 6
3 Tennessee 7
24 Ole Miss 13
12 Kentucky 7
9 Va. Tech 6
0 Ga. Tech 6
20 Vanderbilt 0
6 St. Mary's 0
200 (8-2-0) 51

1933

34 Oglethorpe 0
0 Ole Miss. 0
18 Miss. State 0
12 Tennessee 6
0 Fordham 2
20 Kentucky 0
27 Va. Tech 0
12 Ga. Tech 9
7 Vanderbilt 0
130 (7-1-1) 15

1934

24 Howard 0
35 Sewanee 6
41 Miss. State 0
13 Tennessee 6
26 Georgia 6
34 Kentucky 14
40 Clemson 0
40 Ga. Tech 0
34 Vanderbilt 0
287 (9-0-0) 32

Rose Bowl

29 Stanford 13

1935

7 Howard 7
39 Geo. Wash. 0
7 Miss. State 20
25 Tennessee 0
17 Georgia 7
13 Kentucky 0
33 Clemson 0
38 Ga. Tech 7
6 Vanderbilt 14
185 (6-2-1) 55

1936

34 Howard 0
32 Clemson 0
7 Miss. State 0
0 Tennessee 0
13 Loyola (N.O.) 6
14 Kentucky 0
34 Tulane 7
20 Ga. Tech 16
14 Vanderbilt 6
168 (8-0-1) 35

1937

41 Howard 0
65 Sewanee 0
20 S. Carolina 0
14 Tennessee 17
19 Geo. Wash. 0
41 Kentucky 0
9 Tulane 6
7 Ga. Tech 0
9 Vanderbilt 7
225 (9-0-0) 20

Rose Bowl

0 California 13

1938

19 Sou. Calif. 7
34 Howard 0
14 N. C. State 0
0 Tennessee 13
32 Sewanee 0
26 Kentucky 6
3 Tulane 0
14 Ga. Tech 14
7 Vanderbilt 0
149 (7-1-1) 40

1939

21 Howard 0
7 Fordham 6
20 Mercer 0
0 Tennessee 21
7 Miss. State 0
7 Kentucky 7
0 Tulane 13
0 Ga. Tech 6
39 Vanderbilt 0
101 (5-3-1) 53

1940

26 Spring Hill 0
20 Mercer 0
31 Howard 0
12 Tennessee 27
25 Kentucky 0
13 Tulane 6
14 Ga. Tech 13
25 Vanderbilt 21
0 Miss. State 13
166 (7-2-0) 80

1941

47 SW Louisiana 6

0 Miss. State 14
61 Howard 0
9 Tennessee 2
27 Georgia 14
30 Kentucky 0
19 Tulane 14
20 Ga. Tech 0
0 Vanderbilt 7
21 Miami 7

234 (8-2-0) 64

Cotton Bowl
29 Texas A&M 21

1942
54 SW Louisiana 0
21 Miss. State 6
27 Pscla. NAS 0
8 Tennessee 0
14 Kentucky 0
10 Georgia 21
29 S. Carolina 0
0 Ga. Tech 7
27 Vanderbilt 7
19 Ga. Navy P-F 35

209 (7-3-0) 76

Orange Bowl
37 Boston College 21

1943—No Team

1944
27 L.S.U. 27
63 Howard 7
55 Millsaps 0
0 Tennessee 0
41 Kentucky 0
7 Georgia 14
34 Ole Miss 6
19 Miss. State 6

224 (5-1-2) 60

Sugar Bowl
26 Duke 29

1945
21 Keesler AFB 0
26 L.S.U. 7
55 S. Carolina 0
25 Tennessee 7
28 Georgia 14
60 Kentucky 19
71 Vanderbilt 0
55 Pscla. NAS 6
55 Miss. State 13

396 (9-0-0) 66

Rose Bowl
34 Sou. Calif. 14

1946
26 Furman 7
7 Tulane 6
14 S. Carolina 6
54 SW Louisiana 0
0 Tennessee 12
21 Kentucky 7
0 Georgia 14
21 L.S.U. 31
12 Vanderbilt 7
7 Boston College 13
24 Miss. State 7

186 (7-4-0) 110

1947
34 Sou. Miss. 7
20 Tulane 21
7 Vanderbilt 14
26 Duguesne 0
10 Tennessee 0
17 Georgia 7
13 Kentucky 0
14 Ga. Tech. 7
41 L.S.U. 12
21 Miami 6

203 (8-2-0) 74

7 Texas 27

1948
14 Tulane 21
14 Vanderbilt 14
48 Duquesne 6
6 Tennessee 21
10 Miss. State 7
0 Georgia 35
27 Sou. Miss. 0
14 Ga. Tech 12
6 L.S.U. 26
34 Florida 28
55 Auburn 0

228 (6-4-1) 170

1949
14 Tulane 28
7 Vanderbilt 14
48 Duquesne 8
7 Tennessee 7
35 Miss. State 6
14 Georgia 7
20 Ga. Tech 7
34 Sou. Miss. 26
35 Florida 13
13 Auburn 14

227 (6-3-1) 130

1950
27 Chattanooga 0
26 Tulane 14
22 Vanderbilt 27
34 Furman 6
9 Tennessee 14
14 Miss. State 7
14 Georgia 7
53 Sou. Miss 0
54 Ga. Tech 19
41 Florida 13
34 Auburn 0

328 (9-2-0) 107

1951
89 Delta State 0
7 L.S.U. 20
20 Vanderbilt 22
18 Villanova 41
13 Tennessee 27
7 Miss. State 0
16 Georgia 14
40 Sou. Miss. 7
7 Ga. Tech 27
21 Florida 30
25 Auburn 7

263 (5-6-0) 188

1952
20 Sou. Miss. 6
21 L.S.U. 20
21 Miami 7
33 Va. Tech 0
0 Tennessee 20
42 Miss. State 19
34 Georgia 19
42 Chatt. 28
13 Ga. Tech 7
27 Maryland 7
21 Auburn 0

264 (9-2-0) 133

Orange Bowl
61 Syracuse 6

1953
19 Sou. Miss. 25
7 LSU 7
21 Vanderbilt 12
41 Tulsa 13
0 Tennessee 0
7 Miss. State 7
33 Georgia 12
21 Chatt. 14
13 Ga. Tech 6
0 Maryland 21
10 Auburn 7

172 (6-2-3) 124

Cotton Bowl
6 Rice 28

1954
2 Sou. Miss. 7
12 L.S.U. 0
28 Vanderbilt 14
40 Tulsa 0
27 Tennessee 7
7 Miss. State 12
0 Georgia 0
0 Tulane 0
0 Ga. Tech 20
7 Miami 23
0 Auburn 28

123 (4-5-2) 104

1955
0 Rice 20
6 Vanderbilt 21
0 T.C.U. 21
0 Tennessee 20
7 Miss. State 26
14 Georgia 35
7 Tulane 27
2 Ga. Tech 26
12 Miami 34
0 Auburn 26

48 (0-10-0) 256

1956
13 Rice 20
7 Vanderbilt 32
6 T.C.U. 23
0 Tennessee 24
13 Miss. State 12
13 Georgia 16
13 Tulane 7
0 Ga. Tech 27
13 Sou Miss. 13
7 Auburn 34

85 (2-7-1) 208

1957
0 L.S.U. 28
6 Vanderbilt 6
0 T.C.U. 28
0 Tennessee 14
13 Miss. State 25
14 Georgia 13
0 Tulane 7
7 Ga. Tech 10
29 Sou Miss. 2
0 Auburn 40

69 (2-7-1) 173

1958
3 L.S.U. 13
0 Vanderbilt 0
29 Furman 6
7 Tennessee 14
9 Miss. State 7
12 Georgia 0
7 Tulane 13
17 Ga. Tech 8
14 Memphis St. 0
8 Auburn 14

106 (5-4-1) 75

1959
3 Georgia 17
3 Houston 0
7 Vanderbilt 7
13 Chattanooga 0
7 Tennessee 7
10 Miss. State 0
19 Tulane 7
9 Ga. Tech 7
14 Memphis St. 7
10 Auburn 0

95 (7-1-2) 52

Liberty Bowl
0 Penn St. 7

1960
21 Georgia 6
6 Tulane 6
21 Vanderbilt 0
7 Tennessee 20
14 Houston 0
7 Miss. State 0
51 Furman 0
16 Ga. Tech 15
34 Tampa 6
3 Auburn 0

180 (8-1-1) 53

Bluebonnet Bowl
3 Texas 3

1961
32 Georgia 6
35 Vanderbilt 6
9 Tulane 0
26 N. C. State 7
34 Tennessee 3
17 Houston 0
24 Miss. State 0
66 Richmond 0
10 Ga. Tech 0
34 Auburn 0

287 (10-0-0) 22

Sugar Bowl
10 Arkansas 3

1962
35 Georgia 0
44 Tulane 6
17 Vanderbilt 7
14 Houston 3
27 Tennessee 7
35 Tulsa 6
20 Miss. State 0
36 Miami 3
6 Ga. Tech 7
38 Auburn 0

272 (9-1-0) 39

Orange Bowl
17 Oklahoma 0

1963
32 Georgia 7
28 Tulane 0
21 Vanderbilt 6
6 Florida 10
35 Tennessee 0
21 Houston 13
20 Miss. State 19
27 Ga. Tech 11
8 Auburn 10
17 Miami 12

215 (8-2-0) 88

Sugar Bowl
12 Ole Miss 7

1964
31 Georgia 3
36 Tulane 6
24 Vanderbilt 0
21 N. C. State 0
19 Tennessee 8
17 Florida 14
23 Miss. State 6
17 L.S.U. 9
24 Ga. Tech 7
21 Auburn 14

233 (10-0-0) 67

Orange Bowl
17 Texas 21

1965
17 Georgia 18
27 Tulane 0
17 Ole Miss 16
22 Vanderbilt 7
7 Tennessee 7
21 Fla. State 0
10 Miss. State 7
31 L.S.U. 7
35 S. Carolina 14
30 Auburn 3

217 (8-1-1) 79

Orange Bowl
39 Nebraska 28

1966
34 La. Tech 0
17 Mississippi 7
26 Clemson 0
11 Tennessee 10
42 Vanderbilt 6
27 Miss. State 14
21 L.S.U. 0
24 S. Carolina 0
34 Sou. Miss. 0
31 Auburn 0

267 (10-0-0) 37

Sugar Bowl
34 Nebraska 7

1967
37 Fla. State 37
25 Sou. Miss. 3
21 Ole Miss 7
35 Vanderbilt 21
13 Tennessee 24
13 Clemson 10
13 Miss. State 0
7 L.S.U. 6
17 S. Carolina 0
7 Auburn 3

188 (8-1-1) 111

Cotton Bowl
16 Texas A&M 20

1968
14 Va. Tech 7
17 Sou. Miss. 14
8 Ole Miss 10
31 Vanderbilt 7
9 Tennessee 10
21 Clemson 14
20 Miss. State 13
16 L.S.U. 7
14 Miami 6
24 Auburn 16

174 (8-2-0) 104

Gator Bowl
10 Missouri 35

1969
17 Va. Tech 13
63 Sou. Miss. 14
33 Ole Miss 32
10 Vanderbilt 14
14 Tennessee 41
38 Clemson 13

23	Miss. State	19
15	L.S.U.	20
42	Miami	6
26	Auburn	49
281	(6-4-0)	221
	Liberty Bowl	
33	Colorado	47
	1970	
21	Sou. Calif.	42
51	Va. Tech	18
46	Florida	15
23	Ole Miss	48
35	Vanderbilt	11
0	Tennessee	24
30	Houston	21
35	Miss. State	6
9	L.S.U.	14
32	Miami	8
28	Auburn	33
310	(6-5-0)	240
	Bluebonnet Bowl	
24	Oklahoma	24
	1971	
17	Sou. Calif.	10
42	Sou. Miss.	6
38	Florida	0
40	Ole Miss	6
42	Vanderbilt	0
32	Tennessee	15
34	Houston	20
41	Miss. State	10
14	L.S.U.	7
31	Miami	3
31	Auburn	7
362	(11-0-0)	84
	Orange Bowl	
6	Nebraska	38
	1972	
35	Duke	12
35	Kentucky	0
48	Vanderbilt	21
25	Georgia	7
24	Florida	7
17	Tennessee	10
48	Sou. Miss.	11
58	Miss. State	14
35	L.S.U.	21
52	Va. Tech	13
16	Auburn	17
393	(10-1-0)	133
	Cotton Bowl	
13	Texas	17
	1973	
66	California	0
28	Kentucky	14
44	Vanderbilt	0
28	Georgia	14
35	Florida	14
42	Tennessee	21
77	Va. Tech	6
35	Miss. State	0
43	Miami	13
21	L.S.U.	7
35	Auburn	0
454	(11-0-0)	89
	Sugar Bowl	
23	Notre Dame	24
	1974	
21	Maryland	16
52	Sou. Miss.	0
23	Vanderbilt	10
35	Ole Miss	21
8	Fla. State	7
28	Tennessee	6
41	T.C.U.	3
35	Miss. State	0
30	L.S.U.	0
28	Miami	7
17	Auburn	13
318	(11-0-0)	83
	Orange Bowl	
11	Notre Dame	13
	1975	
7	Missouri	20
56	Clemson	0
40	Vanderbilt	7
32	Ole Miss	6
52	Washington	0
30	Tennessee	7
45	T. C. U.	0
21	Miss. State	10
23	LSU	10
27	Sou. Miss.	6
28	Auburn	0
361	(10-1-0)	66
	Sugar Bowl	
13	Penn State	6
	1976	
7	Ole Miss	10
56	SMU	3
42	Vanderbilt	14
0	Georgia	21
24	Sou. Miss.	8
20	Tennessee	13
24	Louisville	3
34	Miss. State	17
28	LSU	17
18	Notre Dame	21
38	Auburn	7
291	(8-3-0)	134
	Liberty Bowl	
36	UCLA	6
	1977	
34	Mississippi	13
24	Nebraska	31
24	Vanderbilt	12
18	Georgia	10
21	So. Cal.	20
24	Tennessee	10
55	Louisville	6
37	Miss. State	7
24	LSU	3
36	Miami	0
48	Auburn	21
345	(10-1-0)	133
	Sugar Bowl	
35	Ohio State	6
	1978	
20	Nebraska	3
38	Missouri	20
14	So. Cal.	24
51	Vanderbilt	28
20	Washington	17
23	Florida	12
30	Tennessee	17
35	Virginia Tech	0
35	Miss. State	14
31	LSU	10
34	Auburn	16
331	(10-1-0)	161
	Sugar Bowl	
14	Penn State	7

University of Alabama Football Lettermen—1892 to 1978

A

ABBOTT, Eli, 1892-93
ABBRUZZESE, Raymond, 1960-61
ABSTON, Bill, 1948-49
ADAMS, George, 1935
ADKINSON, Wayne, 1970-71-72
ALAND, Jack, 1942
ALBRIGHT, George, 1944
ALLEN, Charles G., 1957-58-59
ALLEN, John, 1907
ALLEN, Steve, 1961-62-63
ALLISON, Scott, 1978
ALLMAN, Phil, 1976-77-78
ANDREWS, Mickey, 1963-64
ANGELICH, James Dykes, 1933-34-35
ARANT, Hershel W., 1908
ARTHUR, Paul, 1949
AUGUST, Johnny, 1942-46-47
AUSTILL, Huriescsco, 1904
AUSTILL, Jere, 1908
AVERITTE, Warren, 1938-39-40
AVINGER, Clarence "Butch", 1948-49-50
AYDELETTE, William Leslie "Buddy", 1977-78

B

BAILEY, David, 1969-70-71
BAKER, George, 1921
BALLARD, Clarence Bingham, 1901-02
BANKHEAD, M. H., 1895
BANKHEAD, Wm. Brockman, 1892-93
BANKS, R. R., 1901
BARKER, Troy, 1931-32-33
BARNES, Emile "Red", 1925-26
BARNES, Ronnie Joe, 1973-74
BARNES, W. A., 1912
BARNES, Wiley, 1978
BARNETT, Henry Herndon, 1911
BARRON, Marvin, 1970-71-73
BARRON, Randy, 1966-67-68
BARRY, Dick, 1951
BARTLETT, Charles, 1920-21
BASWELL, Ben, 1935
BATES, C. F., 1914
BATES, Tim, 1964-65
BATEY, Joseph Dwight "Bo", 1976
BATTLE, Wm "Bill", 1960-61-62
BATY, William C., Jr., 1921-22
BAUGHMAN, Bill, 1946
BAUMHOWER, Robert Glenn, 1974-75-76
BEALLE, Sherman "Bucky", 1929
BEAN, Dickie, 1966
BEARD, Jeff, 1969-70-71
BEARD, Ken, 1963
BEARD, Silas "Buddy", 1937-38
BECK, Ellis, 1971-72-73
BECK, Willie, 1956-57
BEDDINGFIELD, David, 1969
BEDWELL, David, 1965-66-67
BELL, Stanley, 1959
BENTLEY, Edward K., Jr., 1970
BERREY, Fred Benjamin "Bucky", 1974-75-76
BILLINGSLEY, Randy, 1972-73-74
BIRD, Ron, 1963
BIRES, Andy, 1942
BISCEGLIA, Steve, 1971-72
BLACKMON, Sumpter, 1941
BLACKWELL, Gene, 1937-38-39
BLACKWOOD, J. E., 1921
BLAIR, Bill, 1968-69-70
BLAIR, Elmer, 1917
BLAIR, J. W., 1897
BLALOCK, Ralph, 1956-57
BLEVINS, James Allen, 1957-58-59
BLITZ, Jeff, 1972
BOLDEN, Ray, 1974-75
BOLER, Clark, 1962-63
BOLES, John "Duffy", 1973-75
BOLTON, Bruce, 1976-77-78
BOMAN, T. D., 1914-15
BONE, George, 1968
BOOKMEIER, Robert L., 1956
BOONE, Alfred Morgan "Dan", 1917-18-19
BOONE, Isaac M "Ike", 1919
BOOTH, Baxter, 1956-57-58
BOOTHE, Vince, 1977-78
BOOZER, Young, 1934-35-36
BORDERS, Tom, 1939
BOSCHUNG, Paul, 1967-68-69
BOSTICK, Lewis, 1936-37-38
BOSWELL, Charley, 1938-39
BOWDOIN, James L. "Goofy", 1927-28
BOWDOIN, Jimmy, 1954-55-56
BOWMAN, Steve, 1963-64-65
BOX, Jimmy, 1960
BOYD, Thomas, 1978
BOYKIN, Dave, 1928-29
BOYKIN, Gideon Frierson, 1894
BOYLE, R. E., 1893
BOYLES, J. V., 1904
BOYLSTON, Robert W. "Bobby", 1959-60
BRADFORD, James J. "Jim", 1977
BRADFORD, Vic, 1937-38
BRAGAN, Dale, 1976
BRAGGS, Byron, 1977-78
BRANNAN, Troy Crampton, 1914
BRANNEN, Jerre Lamar, 1957-58
BRASFIELD, Davis, 1927
BREWER, Richard, 1965-66-67
BRITT, Gary, 1977
BROCK, Mike, 1977-78
BROOKER, Wm. T. "Tommy", 1959-60-61
BROOKS, Wm. S. "Billy", 1954-55-56
BROWN, Billy, 1928
BROWN, Carl Abercrombie, 1898-99
BROWN, Dave, 1940-41-42
BROWN, Halver "Buddy", 1971-72-73
BROWN, Jack, 1948-49-50-51
BROWN, Jerry, 1974-75
BROWN, Johnny Mack, 1923-24-25
BROWN, Marshall, 1955-56-57
BROWN, Randall R., 1908-09
BROWN, Randy, 1968
BROWN, Robert C., 1916-17
BROWN, T. L., 1919-20
BROWN, Tolbert "Red", 1926-27
BRUNGARD, David A., 1970
BRYAN, Richard, 1972-74
BRYANT, Paul W. "Bear", 1933-34-35

BUCHANAN, Richard Woodruff "Woody", 1976
BUCK, Oran, 1969
BUCKLER, Wm. E. "Bill", 1923-24-25
BUMGARDNER, Robert H., 1909-10
BUNCH, Jim, 1976-77-78
BURKART, C. T., 1920
BURKETT, Jim, 1949-50
BURKS, Auxford, 1903-04-05
BURKS, Basil Manly, 1913-14
BURKS, Henry Thomas, 1906-07-08
BURNETT, Hunter Tennille, 1914-15
BURR, Borden, 1893-94
BUSBEE, Kent, 1967
BUSBY, Max, 1977
BUSH, Jeff, 1933-34
BUSH, Jim, 1945-46
BUTLER, Clyde, 1970

C

CADENHEAD, Billy, 1946-47-48-49
CAIN, Jim, 1945-46-47-48
CAIN, Johnny, 1930-31-32
CALDWELL, Blackie, 1936
CALDWELL, Herschel, 1925-26
CALLAWAY, Neil, 1975-77
CALLIES, Kelly, 1977
CALVERT, John, 1965-66
CALVIN, Tom, 1948-49-50
CAMP, Joseph "Pete", 1923-24-25
CAMPBELL, John, 1928-29-30
CAMPBELL, Tilden "Happy", 1934-35
CANTERBURY, Frank, 1964-65-66
CARGILE, C. J., 1914
CARRIGAN, Ralph, 1951-52-53
CARROLL, Jimmy, 1965-66
CARY, Robert H. Jr. "Robin", 1972-73
CASH, Jerauld Wayne "Jerry", 1970-71
CASHIO, Gri, 1947
CASSIDY, Francis, 1944-45-46-47
CAUSEY, Joe, 1931
CAVAN, Peter Alexander, 1975-76-77
CHAFFIN, Phil, 1968-69-70
CHAMBERS, Jimmy, 1967
CHAPMAN, Herb, 1947
CHAPMAN, Roger, 1977-78
CHAPPELL, Howard, 1931-32-33
CHATWOOD, David, 1965-66-67
CHILDERS, Morris, 1960
CHILDS, Bob, 1966-67-68
CHIODETTI, Larry, 1950-51
CHRISTIAN, Knute Rockne, 1954-55
CIEMNY, Richard, 1969-70
CLARK, Cotton, 1961-62
CLARK, Frank Barnard, 1903-04
CLARK, Phil, 1956
CLARK, Tim, 1978
CLAY, Hugh Stephen, 1969
CLEMENS, Al, 1921-22
CLEMENT, C. B. "Foots", 1928-29-30
CLEMENTS, Mike, 1978
CLORFELINE, Julius, 1911
COCHRAN, Bob, 1947-48-49
COCHRAN, Donald G., 1957-58-59
COCHRAN, Ralph, 1949
COCHRANE, David, 1931
COCHRANE, Henry, 1937
COHEN, Andy, 1923-24
COKELY, Donald, 1970-71
COLE, Richard, 1964-65
COLEMAN, Michael, 1978
COLLINS, Danny, 1976-77
COMPTON, Ben E., 1923-24-25
COMPTON, Charley, 1942-46-47
COMPTON, Joe, 1949-50-51
COMSTOCK, Charles Dexter, 1895-96
COMSTOCK, Donald, 1956
CONNOR, Don, 1955
CONWAY, Bob, 1950-51-52
COOK, Elbert, 1960-61-62
COOK, Leroy, 1972-73-74-75
COOK, Ted, 1942-46
COOK, Wayne, 1964-65-66
COOPER, Ernest "Shorty", 1921-22-23
COPE, Robert, 1892-93
CORBITT, James "Corky", 1945-46
COUCH, L. B., 1949-50
COUNTESS, C. C., 1907-08
COWELL, Vince, 1978
COX, Allen, 1972
COX, Carey, 1937-38-39
COYLE, Don Joseph, Jr., 1955-56
CRAFT, Russ, 1940-41-42
CRANE, Paul, 1963-64-65
CREEN, Cecil L., 1916
CRENSHAW, Curtis, 1961
CROOM, Sylvester, 1972-73
CROSS, Andy, 1972
CROW, John David, Jr., 1975-76-77
CROWSON, Roger, 1968
CROYLE, John, 1971-72-73
CRUMBLEY, Allen, 1976-78
CRYDER, Robert J., 1975-76-77
CULLIVER, Calvin, 1973-74-75-76
CULPEPPER, Ed, 1951-52-53-54
CULWELL, Ingram, 1961-62
CUMMINGS, Joe, 1952-53
CUNNINGHAM, E. A. "Jim", 1955-56
CURTIS, Joe, 1950-51-52
CURTIS, Nathan Stephenson, 1906

D

DAVIDSON, James Lafayette, 1900
DAVIS, Alvin "Pig", 1937-38
DAVIS, Bill, 1971-72-73
DAVIS, Charley, 1948-49
DAVIS, Fred, 1938-39-40
DAVIS, Fred, Jr., 1964
DAVIS, Jim, 1951-52-53
DAVIS, Johnny Lee, 1975-76-77
DAVIS, Mike, 1975
DAVIS, Ricky, 1973-74
DAVIS, Steve, 1965-66-67
DAVIS, Terry Ashley, 1970-71-72
DAVIS, Terry Lane, 1970
DAVIS, Tim, 1961-62-63
DAVIS, William, 1978
DAVIS, William "Junior", 1967-68
DAWSON, Jimmy Dale, 1973
DEAN, Mike, 1967-68-69
DEAN, Steve, 1972-73
DeLAURENTIS, Vincent, 1952-53
DEMPSEY, Benny, 1956-57
DEMYANOVICH, Joe, 1932-33-34
DeNIRO, Gary, 1978
DeSHANE, Charley, 1940
DiCHIARA, Ron, 1974
DILDY, Jim, 1931-32-33
DILL, Jimmy, 1962-63
DIXON, Dennis, 1967-68
DOBBS, Edgar, 1928-30
DOMNONOVICH, Joe, 1940-41-42
DONALD, Joseph Glenn, 1905-06
DONALDSON, Paul, 1954
DORAN, Stephen Curtis, 1969-70
DOTHEROW, Autrey, 1930-31
DOWDY, Cecil, 1964-65-66
DRENNEN, Earle, 1900-01
DRINKARD, Reid, 1968-69-70
DUBOSE, Mike, 1972-73-74
DUKE, Jim, 1967-68-69
DUNCAN, Conley, 1973-74-75
DUNCAN, Jerry, 1965-66
DURBY, Ron, 1963-64
DYAR, Warren E., 1972-73
DYE, George, 1927
DYESS, Marlin, 1957-58-59

E

EBERDT, Jess, 1929-30
ECKENROD, Michael Lee, 1973
ECKERLY, Charles, 1952-53-54
EDWARDS, Bryant B., 1906
EDWARDS, Marion "Buddy", 1944
ELLETT, Alvin, 1955
ELLIS, Billy, 1928
ELLIS, Raiford, 1934
ELMORE, Albert, Jr., 1953-54-55
ELMORE, Albert, Sr., 1929-30
ELMORE, Grady, 1962-63-64
EMERSON, Ken, 1969-70
EMMETT, J. H. 1919-20-21-22
EMMONS, James Thomas, 1954
ENIS, Ben, 1926

F

FAUST, Donald W., 1975-76-77
FAUST, Douglas, 1972
FEDAK, Frank, 1945
FERGUSON, Burr, 1892-93
FERGUSON, Charles M. 1968-69
FERGUSON, Hill, 1895-96
FERGUSON, Mitch, 1977
FERGUSON, Richard, 1969
FICHMAN, Leon, 1941-42
FIELDS, William H., 1944
FILIPPINI, Bruno, 1944-45-46-47
FINLAY, Louis Malone, 1909-10
FINNELL, Edward Judson, 1911
FIORETTE, Anthony Raymond, 1920
FLANAGAN, Thad, 1974-75-76
FLETCHER, Maurice, 1937
FLOWERS, Dick, 1946-47-48
FLOWERS, Lee, 1945
FORBUS, Roy, 1956
FORD, Danny, 1967-68-69
FORD, Mike, 1966-67-68
FORD, Steven, 1973-74
FORMAN, James R., 1901-02
FORTUNATO, Steve, 1946-47-48
FOSHEE, Jess, 1937-38
FOWLER, Conrad, 1966-67-68
FOWLER, Les, 1976
FRACCHIA, Mike, 1960-61-63
FRALEY, Robert, 1974-75
FRANCIS, Kavanaugh "Kay", 1934-35
FRANK, Milton, 1958-59
FRANK, Morris, 1962
FRANKLIN, Arthur, 1906
FRANKO, Jim, 1947-48-49
FRAZER, Thomas Sydney, 1893
FREEMAN, Wayne, 1962-63-64
FRENCH, Buddy, 1963-64
FREY, Calvin, 1931-32-33
FULLER, Jimmy, 1964-65-66
FULLER, Leon, 1959-60

G

GAGE, Fred Harrison, 1916
GAMBRELL, D. Joe, 1945-46
GAMMON, George, 1941-42
GANDY, Joseph Maury, 1912-13
GANDY, Ralph, 1932-33-34-35
GANTT, Greg, 1971-72-73
GARRETT, Broox Cleveland, 1909
GARRETT, Coma, Jr., 1905-06
GELLERSTEDT, Sam, 1968
GERASIMCHUK, David, 1975-76
GERBER, Elwood, 1940
GERMANOS, Nicholas "Nick", 1954-55
GIBBONS, James Booth, 1914
GIBSON, Richard, 1945
GILBERT, Danny, 1968-69-70
GILLILAND, Rickey, 1976-77-78
GILLIS, Grant, 1924-25
GILMER, Creed, 1964-65
GILMER, Harry, 1944-45-46-47
GODFREE, Newton, 1930-31-32
GORNTO, Jack "Red", 1938
GOSSETT, Don Lee, 1969
GOTHARD, Andrew "Andy", 1975-76
GRAHAM, Glen W., 1955-56
GRAMMER, James W., 1969-71
GRAMMER, Richard, 1967-68-69
GRANADE, James Napoleon, 1898-99
GRANT, Fred, 1944-45-46
GRANTHAM, Jim, 1945-46
GRAVES, Bibb, 1892-93
GRAY, Charlie, 1956-57-58
GRAYSON, David Allison, 1892-93
GREEN, Jack, 1945
GREEN, Louis E., 1974-76-77
GREENE, Edgar D., 1907-08
GREER, Charles West, 1910-11
GRESHAM, Owen Garside, 1908-09
GRYSKA, Clem, 1947-48
GWIN, James C. B., 1903

H

HAGLER, Ellis, 1927-28
HALL, Mike, 1966-67-68
HALL, Randy Lee, 1972-73-74
HALL, Wayne, 1971-72-73
HAMER, Norris, 1967-68
HAMILTON, Wayne, 1977-78
HAMNER, Robert Lee, 1925-26-27
HAND, Mike, 1968-69-70
HANNAH, Charles, 1974-75-76
HANNAH, David, 1975-77-78
HANNAH, Herb, 1948-49-50
HANNAH, John, 1970-71-72
HANNAH, William C., 1957-58-59
HANNON, Emile "Chick", 1907
HANRAHAN, Gary, 1973
HANSEN, Cliff, 1940-41
HANSON, John, 1939-40
HARKINS, Grover, 1937-38
HARPOLE, Allen "Bunk", 1965-66-67
HARRELL, Billy, 1940
HARRIS, Charles, 1965-66-67
HARRIS, Don, 1968-69-70
HARRIS, Hudson, 1962-63-64

HARRIS, Jim Bob, 1978
HARRIS, Joe Dale, 1975
HARRIS, Paul, 1974-75-76
HARRISON, Bill, 1976
HARSH, Griffin R., 1914
HARSH, William L., 1914-15
HAYDEN, Neb, 1969-70
HEARD, Victor John, 1910
HEARD, Virgil Willis, 1911
HEATH, Donnie, 1960
HECHT, George, 1940-41-42
HELMS, Sandy, 1949-50
HENDERSON, S.W., 1892
HENDERSON, Wm. T. "Bill", 1975-77
HENRY, Butch, 1961-62-63
HEWES, Willis, 1931-32
HICKERSON, Ed, 1938-40
HICKS, Billy, 1928-29
HICKS, J.W., 1912-13
HIGGINBOTHAM, Robert, 1967-68
HIGGINBOTHAM, Steve, 1969-70-71
HILL, Marvin "Buster", 1952-54
HILMAN, R. G., 1895
HINES, Edward T., 1970-72
HINTON, Robert Poole, 1922-23
HITE, John H., 1944
HOBBS, Sam, 1907
HOBSON, Clell, 1950-51-52
HODGES, Bruce, 1977
HODGES, Norwood, 1944-45-46-47
HOLDER, Harry, 1927
HOLDNAK, Ed, 1948-49
HOLLEY, Hillman D., 1930-31-32
HOLLIS, William C., 1954-55
HOLM, Bernard "Tony", 1927-28-29
HOLM, Charlie, 1937-38
HOLMES, Gordon "Sherlock", 1926
HOLSOMBACK, Roy, 1959-60
HOLT, Darwin, 1960-61
HOLT, James Jay "Buddy", 1977
HOMAN, Dennis, 1965-66-67
HOOD, Bob, 1946-47-48
HOOD, E. P., 1919-20
HOPPER, Mike, 1961-62-64
HORTON, Jimmy, 1971
HOUSTON, Ellis "Red", 1930-31-32
HOVATER, Dexter Louis, 1914-15
HOVATER, Jack, 1919-20-21
HOVATER, Walter E., 1917-18-19
HOWARD, Frank, 1928-29-30
HOWELL, Millard "Dixie", 1932-33-34
HOWLE, G. D., 1907
HUBBARD, Colenzo, 1974-75-76
HUBERT, A. T. S. "Pooley", 1922-23-24-25
HUDSON, Ben A., 1923-24-25
HUDSON, H. Clayton, 1921-22
HUFSTETLER, Thomas R. Jr., 1977-78
HUGHES, Hal, 1937-38
HUGHES, Howard, 1941
HUGHES, Larry, 1931-32-33
HUNDERTMARK, John, 1933
HUNT, Ben, 1921-22
HUNT, Morris Parker, 1972-73
HUNT, Travis, 1950-51-52
HUNTER, Scott, 1968-69-70
HUPKE, Tom, 1931-32
HURD, Clarence S., 1908-09
HURLBUT, Jack, 1962-63
HURST, Tim, 1975-76-77
HURT, Cecil A., 1927-28-29
HUSBAND, Hunter, 1967-68-69
HUSBAND, Woodward A. "Woodie", 1969-70
HUTSON, Don, 1932-33-34

I

IKNER, Lou, 1977-78
INGRAM, Cecil, "Hootie", 1952-53-54
ISRAEL, Jimmy Kent, 1966
ISRAEL, Thomas Murray, 1969
IVY, Hyrle, Jr., 1951-52

J

JACKSON, Billy, 1978
JACKSON, Bobby, 1957-58
JACKSON, Max, 1930-31
JACKSON, Wilbur, 1971-72-73
JAMES, Kenneth Morris, 1969-70
JENKINS, John Felix, 1894-95
JENKINS, Jug, 1949-50-51
JENKINS, Tom "Bobby", 1942
JILLEBA, Pete, 1967-68-69
JOHNS, Bobby, 1965-66-67
JOHNSON, Billy, 1965-66-67
JOHNSON, Cornell, 1959-60
JOHNSON, D. B., 1892
JOHNSON, Forney, 1899
JOHNSON, Harold, 1951
JOHNSON, James, 1924-25
JOHNSTON, Donny, 1966-69
JOHNSTON, J. Goree, 1915-16
JOHNSTON, Sidney, 1919-20
JOHNSTON, Wm. McDow, 1914
JONES, Brice Sidney, 1906-07
JONES, Bruce, 1923-24-25
JONES, H. H., 1901
JONES, Howard Criner, 1914
JONES, Joe, 1978
JONES, Kevin, 1977-78
JONES, Paul B., 1907
JONES, Ralph, 1944
JONES, Ralph Lee, 1917-18-19
JONES, Raymond Wm., 1912
JONES, Terry Wayne, 1975-76-77
JOPLIN, Charles West, 1911-12
JORDAN, Lee Roy, 1960-61-62
JORDAN, Lint, 1950-51
JUNIOR, E. J. III, 1977-78

K

KEARLEY, Dan, 1962-63-64
KELLER, Phillips Brooks, 1911
KELLEY, Joe, 1966-67-68
KELLEY, Leslie, 1964-65-66
KELLEY, Max, 1954-55-56
KELLY, William Milner, 1920-21
KERR, Dudley, 1966-67
KILGROW, Joe, 1935-36-37
KILLGORE, Terry, 1965-66-67
KILROY, William, 1952
KIMBALL, Morton, 1941
KINDERKNECHT, Donald H., 1955-56
KING, Tyrone, 1972-73-74-75
KIRBY, Lelias E., 1920-21
KIRKLAND, B'Ho, 1931-32-33
KNAPP, David, 1970-71-72
KNIGHT, William, 1957
KRAMER, Michael T., 1975-76-77
KRAPF, James Paul, 1970-71-72
KRAUSS, Barry, 1976-77-78
KROUT, Bart, 1978
KUBELIUS, Skip, 1972-73
KULBACK, Steve Joseph, 1973-74
KYZER, G. H., 1893

L

LaBUE, John, 1976
LaBUE, Joseph II, 1970-71-72
LAMBERT, Buford, 1976
LAMBERT, Randolph, 1973-74
LANGDALE, Noah, 1940-41
LANGHORNE, Jack, 1922-23-24
LANGSTON, Griff, 1968-69-70
LANIER, M. B., 1905
LARY, Al, 1948-49-50
LARY, Ed, 1949-50-51
LASLIE, Carney, 1930-31-32
LAUER, Larry, 1948-49-50
LAW, Phil, 1971
LAWLEY, Lane, 1970
LAYTON, Dale, 1962
LAZENBY, K. J., 1974-75-76
LEACH, Foy, 1931-32-33
LEE, Bill, 1932-33-34
LEE, Harry C., 1951-52-53-54
LEE, Mickey, 1968-69
LEETH, Wheeler, 1941-42
LEGG, Murray, 1976-77-78
LENOIR, E. B. "Mully", 1917-18-19
LEON, Tony, 1941-42
LETCHER, Marion, 1893-94
LETT, Frank Montague, 1901-02
LEWIS, Al, 1961-62-63
LEWIS, Tommy, 1951-52-53
LITTLE, Poc, 1920
LITTLE, W. G., 1892-93
LOCKRIDGE, Doug, 1948-49
LOFTIN, James, 1956-57
LONG, Charles Allen, 1913-14
LONG, Leon, 1929-30-31
LOVE, Henry Benton, 1912
LOWE, Woodrow, 1972-73-74-75
LOWMAN, Joseph Allen, 1916-17
LUMLEY, Wade H., 1907
LUMPKIN, Billy Neal, 1955
LUNA, Robert K. "Bobby", 1951-52-53-54
LUSK, Thomas Joseph III, 1970-72
LUTZ, HAROLD "Red", 1949-50-51
LYLES, Warren, 1978
LYNCH, Curtis, R., 1953-54-55
LYON, Samuel Hamilton, 1934-35
LYONS, Martin A. "Marty", 1977-78

M

MACHTOLFF, Jack, 1937
MADDOX, Sam H. 1976-77
MALCOLM, Charles, 1952
MANCHA, Vaughn, 1944-45-46-47
MANLEY, Harold, 1950-51
MANN, Frank, 1968-69-70
MANNING, Thomas, 1910-11
MARCELLO, Jerry, 1973
MARCUS, Van J., 1950-51-52
MARLOW, Bobby, 1950-51-52
MARR, Charles, 1933-34
MARSH, Griffith, 1913-14-15
MARSH, William "Bill", 1915-16
MARSHALL, Fred H., 1970-71
MARTIN, Gary, 1961-62-63
MARTIN, Kenny, 1966-67
MASON, George L., 1952-53-54
MAURO, John, 1978
MAXWELL, Raymond Edward, 1973-74-75
MAY, Walter, 1949
MAYFIELD, Dave, 1949-50
MAYNOR, E. W., 1915-16
MELTON, James "Bimbo", 1949-50-51
MERRILL, Walter, 1937-38-39
MERRILL, William Hoadley, 1910
MIKEL, Bobby, 1976
MILLER, Andrew McMurray, 1914
MILLER, Floyd, 1948-49
MILLER, Hugh, 1929-30
MILLER, John, 1928-29-30
MILLER, Noah Dean, 1973
MIMS, Carl, 1941
MIMS, Fred, 1951-52
MITCHELL, David Dewey, 1975-76-77
MITCHELL, John, 1971-72
MITCHELL, Ken "TANK", 1964
MIZERANY, Mike, 1948-49-50
MONSKY, Leroy, 1936-37
MONTGOMERY, Greg, 1972-73-74-75
MONTGOMERY, Robert M., 1970
MONTGOMERY, Wm. Gabriel, 1920-21
MOODY, Farley, 1912
MOODY, Wash, 1906
MOONEYHAM, Marlin, 1962
MOORE, Harold, 1965-66
MOORE, Jimmy, 1928-29-30
MOORE, John, 1962
MOORE, Mal, 1962
MOORE, Pete, 1968-69
MOORE, Randy, 1970-73
MOORER, Jefferson, 1953-54
MORGAN, Ed, 1966-67-68
MORRISON, Duff, 1958-59-60
MORRISON, William, 1926
MORROW, Bob Ed, 1934
MORROW, Hugh, 1944-45-46-47
MORROW, Hugh, 1893
MORTON, Farris, 1962
MORTON, L. D., 1916
MOSELEY, Elliott, 1960
MOSELEY, Frank "Chesty", 1931-32-33
MOSLEY, Herschel "Herky", 1937-38-39
MOSLEY, John, 1964-65-66
MOSLEY, Norman "Monk", 1942-46-47
MOSLEY, Russ, 1942
MOSS, Stan, 1965-66-67
MOYE, Lamar, 1934-35-36
MUDD, Joseph Paul, 1908-09
MURPHY, Phillip, 1973
MUSSO, Johnny, 1969-70-71

Mc

MacAFEE, Ken, 1951
MacCARTEE, Allen Graham, 1922-23
McBEE, Jerry, 1955
McCAIN, George, 1950-51
McCANTS, A. G., 1892-94
McCLENDON, Frankie, 1962-63-64
McCLINTOCK, Graham, 1925-27
McCOLLOUGH, Gaylon, 1962-63-64
McCOMBS, Eddie, 1978
McCONVILLE, John, 1944
McCORQUODALE, John C., 1902

McCORVEY, Gessner T., 1900-01
McDONALD, James T., 1927
McDOWELL, Holt Andrews, 1911-12
McELROY, Alan, 1978
McGAHEY, T. A. "Son", 1934-35
McGEE, Barry, 1975
McGILL, Larry, 1962-63
McGRIFF, Curtis, 1977-78
McINTYRE, David, 1975-76
McKEWEN, Jack, 1941-42
McKEWEN, Jack II, 1968
McKINNEY, Robert B., Jr., 1970-71-72
McKOSKY, Ted, 1942
McLAIN, Rick, 1974-75
McLEOD, Ben, 1965
McLEOD, Ben W., 1934-35-36
McMAKIN, David, 1971-72-73
McMILLIAN, Thomas E., 1933
McNEAL, Don, 1977-78
McRIGHT, Ralph, 1928-29-30
McWHORTER, Jim, 1942

N

NAMATH, Joe Willie, 1962-63-64
NATHAN, R. L., 1912-13
NATHAN, Tony, 1975-76-77-78
NEAL, Rick, 1976-77-78
NEIGHBORS, Billy, 1959-60-61
NEIGHBORS, Sidney, 1956-57
NELSON, Benny, 1961-62-63
NELSON, Charles, 1956
NELSON, Jimmy, 1939-40-41
NELSON, Rod, 1974-75-76
NESMITH, C. C., 1892-93-94
NEWMAN, Hal, 1938-40
NEWSOME, Ozzie, 1974-75-76-77
NEWTON, Tom, 1920-21-22
NISBET, James "Bubba", 1934-35-36
NOLAND, John Phillip, 1917-18
NOOJIN, Augustus Young, 1908
NOONAN, L. W. "Red", 1946-47-48-49
NORMAN, Haywood Eugene "Butch", 1973
NORRIS, Lanny S., 1970-71-72
NORTHINGTON, M. P., 1893

O

OATES, W. C., 1906
O'CONNOR, J. T., 1919-20
O'DELL, Richard, 1959-60-62
ODOM, Ernest Lavont, 1973
OGDEN, Ray, 1962-63-64
OGILVIE, Morgan Oslin "Major", 1977-78
OLENSKI, Mitchell, 1942
O'LINGER, John, 1959-60-61
OLIVER, W. S. "Country", 1925
OLIVER, William, 1952-53
OLIVER, William "Brother", 1960-61
O'REAR, Jack, 1974-76-77
OSER, Gary
O'STEEN, Robert "Gary", 1957-58-59
O'SULLIVAN, Pat, 1947-48-49-50
OWEN, Wayne, 1966-67-68
OWENS, Donald, 1956-57

P

PAGET, Manchester, 1920
PALMER, Dale, 1978
PALMER, Thomas W., 1908-09
PAPIAS, Julius, 1941
PAPPAS, Peter George, 1973
PARKER, Calvin, 1976-78
PARKHOUSE, Robin, 1969-70-71
PARSONS, Don, 1958
PATTERSON, Jim, 1971
PATTERSON, Steve, 1972-73-74
PATTON, David Dare, 1898-99-1900
PATTON, James "Jap", 1959-61
PAYNE, Leslie, 1925-26-27
PEARCE, Clarke "Babe", 1926-27-28
PEARL, James H., 1944
PEAVY, John Roberts, 1902-03-04
PEEBLES, Emory Bush, 1908-10
PELL, Charles R., 1960-61-62
PEPPER, Raymond W., 1926-27
PERKINS, Ray, 1964-65-66
PERRY, Anthony "Lefty", 1973
PERRY, Claude, 1925
PETER, G. F., 1892
PETERS, William E., 1936-37
PETTEE, Robert A. "Bob", 1959-61-62
PETTUS, Gordon, 1945-46-48
PHARO, Edward, 1952-56
PHILLIPS, Gary, 1958-59-60
PICKHARD, Frederick, 1926-27
PIPER, Billy, 1960-62-63
PITTMAN, Alec Noel, 1970
PIZZITOLA, Alan, 1973-74-75
POOLE, John Paul, 1955-58
POPE, Herman "Buddy", 1973-74-75
POTTS, Douglas, 1954-55-56
POWE, Frank Houston, 1899-1900-01
POWELL, Harold Mustin, 1910-11
PRATT, Derrill B., 1908-09
PRATT, G. W., 1907-09
PRATT, Henry Merrill, 1892-93-94
PRESTWOOD, Thomas A., 1975
PRITCHETT, James P., 1955
PROM, John, 1951
PROPST, Clyde "Shorty", 1922-23-24
PROPST, Eddie, 1966-67
PRUDHOMME, John Mark, 1973-74-75
PUGH, George, 1972-73-74-75
PUGH, Keith Harrison, 1977-78

Q

QUICK, Cecil Van, 1970

R

RABURN, Gene, 1965-66
RADFORD, James Solomon, 1935-36
RAINES, Billy, 1956-57
RAINES, James Patrick, 1970-71-72
RAINES, Vaughn Michael, 1972-73
RANAGER, George, 1968-69-70
RANKIN, Carlton, 1962
RAST, Holt, 1939-40-41
RAY, David, 1964-65
REAVES, Pete, 1958
REDDEN, Guy, 1904-05
REDDEN, Jake, 1937-38
REESE, Kenny, 1942
REIDY, Thomas, 1907-08
REILLY, Mike, 1966-67-68
REITZ, John David, 1965-66-67
RHOADS, Wayne R., 1969-70
RHODES, D. Wayne, Jr., 1973-74-75
RICE, William, Jr. "Bill", 1959-60-61
RICH, Jerry, 1959
RICHARDSON, Jesse, 1950-51-52
RICHARDSON, Ron, 1971
RICHARDSON, W. E., 1959-60-61
RICHESON, Ray, 1946-47-48
RIDDLE, Charles D., 1912-13
RIDGEWAY, Danny Howard, 1973-74-75
RILEY, Joe, 1934-35-36
RILEY, Mike, 1974
RIPPETOE, Benny, 1971
ROBBINS, Joe, 1978
ROBERTS, James "Babs", 1940-42
ROBERTS, Johnny, 1937
ROBERTS, Kenneth, 1956-57-58
ROBERTSON, James, 1944-45-46
ROBERTSON, Ronald Dale, 1973-74
RODDAM, J. D., 1949
RODDAM, Ronnie, 1968-69
ROGERS, Eddie Bo, 1966-67
ROGERS, John David, 1972-73-74
ROGERS, Isaac "Ike", 1916-17-18-19
ROGERS, O'Neal, 1927
ROGERS, Richard, 1973
ROHRDANZ, Clarence, 1935
RONSONET, Norbie, 1958-59-60
ROOT, Steve, 1971
ROSENFELD, Max, 1920-21
ROSENFIELD, David, 1925-26
ROSSER, Jimmy Lynn, 1969-70-71
ROUZIE, Jefferson Carr, 1970-71-73
ROWAN, Robert "Robby", 1972
ROWE, Harry, 1919
ROWELL, Terry, 1969-70-71
RUFFIN, Larry Joe, 1973-74-75
RUSTIN, Nathan, 1966-67
RUTLEDGE, Gary, 1972-73-74
RUTLEDGE, Jack, 1959-60-61
RUTLEDGE, Jeffrey R., 1975-76-77-78
RYBA, Jim, 1937

S

SABO, Al, 1940-41-42
SADLER, David A., 1975-76-77
SALEM, Ed, 1948-49-50
SALEM, George, 1956
SALLS, Don, 1940-41-42
SAMFORD, Conner, 1916
SAMPLES, Alvin, 1967-68-69
SANFORD, Donald, 1930-31-32
SANFORD, Hayward "Sandy", 1936-37
SANSING, Walter, 1958
SARTAIN, Harvey, 1904
SASSER, Mike, 1966-69
SAUL, Calhoun "Sunbeam", 1916
SAVAGE, Frank, 1892-93
SAWYER, Bubba, 1969-71
SCALES, Lou, 1942-45
SCHAMUN, Russ, 1974-76
SCHUMANN, Eric, 1977
SCOTT, Arthur, 1957
SCOTT, James Alfred, 1910
SCOTT, Randy, 1978
SCROGGINS, Billy, 1967-68
SEARCEY, Bill, 1978
SEAY, Buddy, 1969-70
SEBASTIAN, Mike, 1978
SELF, Hal, 1944-45-46
SELMAN, Tom, 1950
SESSIONS, Tram, 1917-19-20
SEWELL, J. Luke, 1919-20
SEWELL, Joe, 1917-18-19
SEWELL, Ray, 1976
SEWELL, Toxey, 1913-14
SHANKLES, Don, 1967
SHARPE, Jimmy, 1960-61-62
SHARPE, Joe F., 1929-30-31
SHARPE, Sam, 1940-41-42
SHARPLESS, John Waylon, Jr., 1972-73
SHEALY, Steadman, 1977-78
SHELBY, Willie, 1973-74-75
SHEPHERD, Joe Ruffus, 1935-36
SHERRILL, Jackie, 1963-64-65
SHERRILL, Wm. Swift, 1901-02-03
SHIPP, Billy, 1949-52-53
SHIRLEY, Patrick Kyle, 1910
SHOEMAKER, Perron "Tex", 1937-38-39
SIDES, John "Brownie", 1966-67
SIMMONS, Jim, 1962-63-64
SIMMONS, Jim, 1969-70-71
SIMS, T. S., 1905-06
SIMS, Wayne, 1958-59
SIMS, William Comer, 1931-32
SINGTON, Dave, 1956-57-58
SINGTON, Fred, 1928-29-30
SINGTON, Fred, Jr., 1958-59
SISIA, Joseph, 1960
SKELTON, Robert "Bobby", 1957-59-60
SKIDMORE, Jim, 1928
SLEMONS, Billy, 1937-38
SLOAN, Steve, 1963-64-65
SLONE, Samuel Byron, 1893-94-95-96
SMALLEY, Jack, 1951-52-53
SMALLEY, Jack, Jr., 1976-77
SMALLEY, Roy, 1950
SMITH, Barry S., 1977-78
SMITH, Ben, 1929-30-31
SMITH, Bobby, 1956-57-58
SMITH, Bobby, 1978
SMITH, D. H., 1892-93
SMITH, Earl, 1926-27-28
SMITH, Jack, 1949
SMITH, James Sidney, 1974-75-76
SMITH, Molton, 1928-29
SMITH, Riley H., 1934-35
SMITH, Sammy Wayne, 1957
SMITH, Truman A., 1903-04
SNODERLY, John M., 1952-56
SOMERVILLE, Tom, 1965-66-67
SPEED, Elliott, 1948-49-50
SPENCER, Paul, 1939-40
SPIVEY, Paul Randall, 1972-73
SPRAYBERRY, Steve, 1972-73
SPRUIELL, Jerry, 1960
STABLER, Ken "Snake", 1965-66-67
STANFORD, Robert "Bobby", 1969-72
STAPLES, John, 1942-46
STAPP, Charlie, 1935
STAPP, Laurien "Goodie", 1958-59-60
STARLING, Hugh, 1928-29
STARR, Bryan Bartlett, 1952-53-54-55
STEAKLEY, Rod, 1971
STEINER, Rebel, 1945-47-48-49
STEPHENS, Bruce, 1965-66-67
STEPHENS, Charles, 1962-63-64
STEPHENS, Gerald, 1962
STEPHENSON, Dwight, 1977-78
STEPHENSON, Lovick Leonidas, 1915-16
STEPHENSON, Riggs, 1917-18-19

STEVENS, Wayne, 1966
STEWART, Arthur Walter, 1901
STEWART, Vaughn, 1941
STICKNEY, Enoch Morgan, 1912
STICKNEY, Frederick Grist, 1901-02
STICKNEY, Ravis "Red", 1957-59
STOCK, Mike, 1973-74-75
STOKES, Ralph Anthony 1972-74
STONE, G. E., 1894
STONE, Rocky, 1969
STONE, William J., 1953-54-55
STOWERS, Max Frederick, 1916-17
STRICKLAND, Charles "Chuck", 1971-72-73
STRICKLAND, Lynwood, 1965
STRICKLAND, William Ross, 1970
STRUM, Richard, 1957
STURDIVANT, Raymond, 1906-07
SUGG, Joseph Cullen, 1938-39
SULLIVAN, Johnny, 1964-65-66
SURLAS, Tom, 1970-71
SUTHER, John Henry, 1928-29-30
SUTTON, Donnie, 1966-67-68
SUTTON, Mike, 1978
SWAFFORD, Bobby "Hawk", 1967-68
SWAIM, R.M., 1931-32

T

TAYLOR, Archie, 1926-27
TAYLOR, J. K., 1914-15
TAYLOR, James E., 1973-74-75
TAYLOR, Paul, 1948
TERLIZZI, Nicholas, 1945
TEW, Lowell, 1944-45-46-47
THARP, Thomas "Corky", 1951-52-53-54
THERIS, Bill, 1948
THOMAS, Daniel Martin, 1970
THOMAS, Lester, 1921
THOMASON, Frank Boyd, 1919
THOMPSON, Louis, 1965-66
THOMPSON, Richard "Dickey", 1965-66-67
THOMPSON, Wesley, 1951-55-56
TIDWELL, Robert Earl, 1903-04
TILLMAN, Homer Newton "Chip", 1976-77
TILLMAN, Tommy, 1952-53-54
TIPTON, Jim, 1936-37
TODD, Richard, 1973-74-75
TOLLESON, Tommy, 1963-64-65
TRAMMELL, Pat, 1959-60-61
TRAVIS, Timothy Lee "Tim", 1976-77-78
TRIMBLE, Wayne, 1964-65-66
TUCK, Floyd, 1927
TUCKER, John, 1930-31
TUCKER, Michael V., 1975-76-77
TUCKER, Richard Glenn "Ricky", 1977-78
TURPIN, John R., 1977-78
TURPIN, Richard "Dick", 1973-74-75
TUTWILER, Edward McGruder, 1898

U

UMPHREY, Woody, 1978

V

VAGOTIS, Chris, 1966
VALLETTO, Carl, 1957-58
VANDEGRAAFF, Adrian V., 1912
VANDEGRAAFF, Hargrove, 1913
VANDEGRAAFF, W. T. "Bully", 1912-13-14-15
VARNADO, Carey Reid, 1970
VEAZY, Louis, 1955
VERSPRILLE, Eddie, 1961-62-63
VICKERY, Roy Leon, 1956
VINES, Jay, 1978
VINES, Melvin, 1926-28-29

W

WADE, Steve, 1971-72
WADE, Tommy, 1967-68-70
WAITES, W. L., 1938
WALKER, Bland, Jr., 1957
WALKER, Erskine "Bud", 1931-32-33
WALKER, Hilmon, 1936
WALKER, James E., 1935
WALKER, M. P., 1892
WALKER, Noojin, 1955
WALKER, Wayne D., 1944
WALKER, William Mudd, 1892-94
WALL, Larry "Dink", 1961-62-64
WALLS, Clay, 1955-56-57
WARD, Wm. LaFayette, 1904-05
WARREN, Erin "Tut", 1937-38-39
WASHCO, Gerard George, 1973-74-75
WASHINGTON, Mike, 1972-73-74
WATFORD, Jerry, 1950-51-52
WATKINS, David, 1971-72-73
WATSON, Rick, 1974-75-76
WATSON, William C., 1908
WEAVER, Sam, 1928-29
WEEKS, George, 1940-41-42
WEIGAND, Tommy, 1968
WELSH, Clem, 1948
WERT, Thomas William, 1899
WESLEY, L. O., 1922-23
WESLEY, Wm. Earl "Buddy", 1958-59-60
WHALEY, Frank, 1965-66
WHATLEY, James W., 1933-34-35
WHATLEY, Seaborn Thornton, 1906
WHEELER, Wayne, 1971-72-73
WHITAKER, Hulet, 1925
WHITE, Arthur P. "Tarzan", 1934-35-36
WHITE, Ed, 1947-48-49
WHITE, Frank S., Jr., 1897-98-99
WHITE, Gus, 1974-75-76
WHITE, Jack, 1971
WHITE, Tommy, 1958-59-60
WHITLEY, Tom, 1944-45-46-47
WHITMAN, Steven K., 1977-78
WHITMIRE, Don, 1941-42
WHITTLELSEY, C. S., 1916-17
WHITWORTH, J. B. "Ears", 1930-31
WICKE, Dallas, 1938-39
WIESEMAN, Bill, 1962-63
WILBANKS, Danny, 1957
WILCOX, George Spigener, 1903-04
WILDER, Ken, 1968-69
WILGA, Bob, 1951-52-53
WILHITE, Al, 1949-50-51
WILKINS, Red, 1961
WILKINSON, Everett, 1909-10-12-13
WILLIAMS, Billy, 1951-52
WILLIAMS, John Byrd, 1965-66
WILLIAMS, Steven Edward, 1969-70
WILLIAMSON, Richard, 1961-62
WILLIAMSON, Temple, 1935
WILLIS, Perry, 1967
WILLIS, Virgil "Bud", 1951-52
WILSON, Bobby, 1950-51-52
WILSON, George "Butch", 1960-61-62
WILSON, Jimmy, 1961-62
WINDHAM, Edward Price, 1897
WINGO, Richard Allen "Rich", 1976-77-78
WINSLETT, Hoyt "Wu", 1924-25-26
WISE, Mack, 1958
WOOD, Bobby, 1937-38
WOOD, William B., 1957
WOOD, William Dexter, 1970-72
WOODRUFF, Glen, 1971
WOZNIAK, John, 1944-45-46-47
WRIGHT, Steve, 1962-63
WYATT, W. S., 1903-04
WYHONIC, John, 1939-40-41

Y

YATES, Ollie Porter, 1954
YELVINGTON, Gary, 1973-74
YOUNG, Cecil Hugh, 1902-03
YOUNG, William A., 1936
YOUNGLEMAN, Sid, 1952-53-54

Z

ZIVICH, George, 1938-39

Auburn University

Location: Auburn, Alabama
Enrollment: 17,523
Nickname: Tigers
Colors: Burnt Orange and Navy Blue
Stadium: Jordan-Hare (61,261)

Auburn University Head Coaching Records

COACH	YEAR	WON	LOST	TIED
Dr. George Petrie	1892	2	2	0
G. R. Harvey	1893	3	0	1
D. M. Balleit	1893	0	0	1
F. M. Hall	1894	1	3	0
John W. Heisman	1895-'99	12	4	2
Billy Watkins	1900-'01	6	2	1
R. S. Kent	1902	2	1	1
Mike Harvey	1902	0	3	0
Billy Bates	1903	4	3	0
Mike Donahue	1904-'06; 1908-'22	97	35	4
W. S Keinholz	1907	6	2	1
Boozer Pitts	1923-'24; 1927	7	11	2
Dave Morey	1925-'27	10	10	1
George Bohler	1928-'29	3	11	0
John Floyd	1929	0	4	0
Chet Wynne	1930-'33	22	15	2
Jack Meagher	1934-'42	48	37	10
Carl Voyles	1944-'47	15	22	0
Earl Brown	1948-'50	3	22	4
Ralph (Shug) Jordan	1951-'75	175	83	7
Doug Barfield	1976-'78	14	18	1

Auburn University All-Time Scores

Auburn	Opponent	Opp.
	1892	
10	Georgia	0
6	Trinity	34
0	N. Carolina	64
26	Ga. Tech	0
42	(2-2-0)	98
	1893	
32	Alabama	22
30	Vanderbilt	10
14	Sewanee	14
40	Alabama	16
0	Ga. Tech	0
126	(3-0-2)	62
	1894	
4	Vanderbilt	20
94	Ga. Tech	0
8	Georgia	10
0	Alabama	18
106	(1-3-0)	48
	1895	
6	Vanderbilt	9
48	Alabama	0
16	Georgia	6
70	(2-1-0)	15
	1896	
46	Mercer	0
45	Ga. Tech	0
38	Sewanee	6
6	Georgia	12
135	(3-1-0)	18
	1897	
26	Mercer	0
14	Nash. Univ.	4
0	Sewanee	0
40	(2-0-1)	4
	1898	
29	Ga. Tech	6
0	N. Carolina	24
18	Georgia	17
47	(2-1-0)	47
	1899	
63	Ga. Tech	0
41	M'tgomery AC	0
34	Clemson	0
0	Georgia	0
10	Sewanee	11
148	(3-1-1)	11
	1900	
28	Nash. Univ.	0
23	Tennessee	0
53	Alabama	5
44	Georgia	0
148	(4-0-0)	5
	1901	
5	Nash. Univ.	23
0	Vanderbilt	44
17	Alabama	0
28	L.S.U.	0
0	Georgia	0
50	(2-2-1)	67
	1902	
18	Ga. Tech	6
23	Alabama	0
0	Tulane	0
0	L.S.U.	5
0	Sewanee	6
0	Clemson	16
5	Georgia	12
46	(2-4-1)	45
	1903	
26	M'tgomery AC	0
58	Howard	0
6	Alabama	18
0	Sewanee	47
12	L.S.U.	0
10	Ga. Tech	5
13	Georgia	22
125	(4-3-0)	92
	1904	
5	Clemson	0
10	Nash. Univ.	0
12	Ga. Tech	0
29	Alabama	5
17	Georgia	6
73	(5-0-0)	11
	1905	
0	Davidson	6
18	Miss. State	0
0	Vanderbilt	54
0	Clemson	6
0	Alabama	30
20	Georgia	0
38	(2-4-0)	96
	1906	
5	Sewanee	10
0	Ga. Tech	11

4	Clemson	6
0	Alabama	10
15	Gordon MA	0
0	Georgia	4
24	(1-5-0)	41

	1907	
23	Howard	0
29	Maryville	0
63	Mercer	0
12	Clemson	0
34	Gordon	0
8	Sewanee	12
6	Alabama	6
12	Ga. Tech	6
0	Georgia	6
158	(6-2-1)	30

	1908	
18	Howard	0
42	Gordon MA	0
2	L.S.U.	10
23	Mercer	0
6	Sewanee	0
44	Ga. Tech	0
23	Georgia	0
158	(6-1-0)	10

	1909	
11	Howard	0
46	Gordon MA	0
23	Mercer	5
0	Vanderbilt	17
11	Sewanee	12
17	Georgia	5
9	Ga. Tech.	0
117	(5-2-0)	39

	1910	
78	Howard	0
6	Miss. State	0
17	Clemson	0
0	Texas	9
16	Ga. Tech	0
26	Georgia	0
33	Tulane	0
176	(6-1-0)	9

	1911	
29	Mercer	0
20	Clemson	0
0	Texas A&M	16
11	Miss. State	5
5	Texas	18
0	Georgia	0
11	Ga. Tech	5
85	(4-2-1)	45

	1912	
56	Mercer	0
27	Florida	13
27	Clemson	6
7	Miss. State	0
27	Ga. Tech	7
7	L.S.U.	0
7	Vanderbilt	7
6	Georgia	12
164	(6-1-1)	45

	1913	
53	Mercer	0
55	Florida	0
34	Miss. State	0
20	Clemson	0
7	L.S.U.	0
20	Ga. Tech	0
13	Vanderbilt	6
21	Georgia	7
223	(8-0-0)	13

	1914	
39	Marion	0
20	Florida	0
28	Clemson	0
60	N. Ala. AC	0
19	Miss. State	0
14	Ga. Tech	0
6	Vanderbilt	0
0	Georgia	0
7	Carlisle	0
193	(8-0-1)	0

	1915	
78	Marion	0
7	Florida	0
14	Clemson	0
20	Miss. State	0
12	Georgia	0
45	Mercer	0
0	Vanderbilt	17
0	Ga. Tech	7
184	(6-2-0)	24

	1916	
35	Howard	0
92	Mercer	0
28	Clemson	0
7	Miss. State	3
3	Georgia	0
20	Florida	0
9	Vanderbilt	20
7	Ga. Tech	33
201	(6-2-0)	56

	1917	
53	Howard	0
13	Cp. Sherman	0
7	Clemson	0
13	Miss. State	6
68	Florida	0
6	Davidson	31
31	Vanderbilt	7
0	Ohio State	0
7	Ga. Tech	68
198	(6-2-1)	112

	1918	
58	Oglethorpe	0
0	Cp. Greenleaf	26
20	Marion	7
6	Cp. Gordon	14
0	Vanderbilt	21
0	Ga. Tech	41
0	Cp. Sheridan	7
84	(2-5-0)	116

	1919	
37	Marion	0
19	Howard	6
7	Clemson	0
6	Vanderbilt	7
7	Georgia	0
10	Spring Hill	0
7	Miss. State	0
14	Ga. Tech	7
107	(7-1-0)	20

	1920	
27	Marion	0
88	Howard	0
21	Clemson	0
56	Vanderbilt	6
0	Georgia	7
49	B'ham-Sou.	0
77	Wash. & Lee	0
0	Ga. Tech	34
318	(6-2-0)	47

	1921	
35	Howard	3
44	Spring Hill	3
56	Clemson	0
14	Ft. Benning	7
0	Georgia	7
14	Tulane	0
0	Centre	21
0	Ga. Tech	14
163	(5-3-0)	52

	1922	
61	Marion	0
72	Howard	0
19	Spring Hill	6
6	Army	19
50	Mercer	6
30	Ft. Benning	0
7	Georgia	3
19	Tulane	0
6	Centre	0
6	Ga. Tech	14
276	(8-2-0)	48

	1923	
0	Clemson	0
20	B'ham-Sou.	0
30	Howard	0
6	Army	28
34	Ft. Benning	0
0	Georgia	7
6	Tulane	6
0	Centre	17
0	Ga. Tech.	0
96	(3-3-3)	58

	1924	
7	B'ham-Sou.	0
13	Clemson	0
0	Va. Tech	0
3	L.S.U.	0
17	Howard	0
0	Vanderbilt	13
6	Tulane	14
0	Georgia	6
0	Ga. Tech	7
46	(4–4-1)	40

	1925	
25	B'ham-Sou.	6
13	Clemson	6
19	Va. Tech	0
0	Texas	33
7	Howard	6
0	Tulane	13
0	Georgia	34
10	Vanderbilt	9
7	Ga. Tech	7
81	(5-3-1)	114

	1926	
15	Chattanooga	6
47	Clemson	0
33	Howard	14
0	L.S.U.	10
2	Tulane	0
9	Sewanee	0
6	Georgia	16
3	Marquette	19
7	Ga. Tech	20
122	(5-4-0)	85

	1927	
0	Stetson	6
0	Clemson	3
6	Florida	33
0	L.S.U.	9
3	Georgia	33
9	Howard	9
6	Tulane	6
6	Miss. State	7
0	Ga. Tech	18
30	(0-7-2)	124

	1928	
0	B'ham-Sou.	6
0	Clemson	6
0	Florida	27
0	Ole Miss	19
25	Howard	6
0	Georgia	13
12	Tulane	13
0	Miss. State	13
0	Ga. Tech	51
37	(1-8-0)	154

	1929	
7	B'ham-Sou.	0
7	Clemson	26
0	Florida	19
2	Vanderbilt	41
6	Howard	0
0	Tennessee	27
0	Tulane	52
0	Georgia	24
6	Ga. Tech	19
28	(2-7-0)	208

	1930	
0	B'ham-Sou.	7
13	Spring Hill	0
0	Florida	7
12	Ga. Tech	14
7	Georgia	39
38	Wofford	6
0	Tulane	21
6	Miss. State	7
0	Vanderbilt	27
25	S. Carolina	7
101	(3-7-0)	135

	1931	
24	B'ham-Sou.	6
7	Wisconsin	7
13	Ga. Tech	0
12	Florida	13
27	Spring Hill	7
0	Tulane	27
12	Sewanee	0
6	Georgia	12
13	S. Carolina	6
114	(5-3-1)	98

	1932	
61	B'ham-Sou.	0
77	Erskine	0
18	Duke	7
6	Ga. Tech	0
19	Tulane	7
14	Ole Miss	7
25	Howard	0
21	Florida	6
14	Georgia	7
20	S. Carolina	20
275	(9-0-1)	54

	1933	
20	B'ham-Sou.	7
19	Howard	0
6	Ga. Tech	16
6	Geo. Wash.	19
13	Tulane	7
7	Duke	13
27	Oglethorpe	6
14	Georgia	6
7	Florida	14
14	S. Carolina	16
133	(5-5-0)	104

	1934	
0	B'ham-Sou.	7
15	Oglethorpe	0
0	Tulane	13
6	La. State	20
6	Vanderbilt	7
0	Kentucky	9
6	Duke	13
18	Ga. Tech	6
7	Florida	14
0	Georgia	18
58	(2-8-0)	107

	1935	
25	B'ham-Sou.	7
10	Tulane	0
6	Tennessee	13
23	Kentucky	0
7	Duke	0
0	L.S.U.	6
33	Ga. Tech	7
51	Oglethorpe	0
19	Georgia	7
27	Florida	6
201	(8-2-0)	46

	1936	
45	B'ham-Sou.	0
0	Tulane	0
6	Tennessee	0
6	Detroit	0
20	Georgia	13
0	Santa Clara	12
13	Ga. Tech	12
6	L.S.U.	19
44	Loyola	0
13	Florida	0
153	(7-2-1)	56

	Rhumba Bowl	
7	Villanova	7

	1937	
19	B'ham-Sou.	0
0	Tulane	0
0	Villanova	0
33	Miss. State	7
21	Ga. Tech	0
7	Rice	13
20	Tennessee	7
7	L.S.U.	9
0	Georgia	0
14	Florida	0
127	(5-2-3)	36

	Orange Bowl	
6	Mich. State	0

	1938	
14	B'ham-Sou.	0
0	Tulane	0
0	Tennessee	7
20	Miss. State	6
6	Ga. Tech	7
0	Rice	14
12	Villanova	25
28	L.S.U.	6
23	Georgia	14
7	Florida	9
110	(4-5-1)	88

	1939	
6	B'ham-Sou.	0
0	Tulane	12
7	Miss. State	0
0	Manhattan	7
6	Ga. Tech	7
7	Boston Col.	13
10	Villanova	9
21	L.S.U.	7
7	Georgia	0
7	Florida	7
0	Tennessee	7
71	(5-5-1)	69

	1940	
27	Howard	13
20	Tulane	14
7	Miss. State	7
13	S.M.U.	20
16	Ga. Tech	7
13	Georgia	14
21	Clemson	7
13	L.S.U.	21

7 Boston College 33
20 Florida 7
13 Villanova 10

170 (6-4-1) 153

1941

13 Howard 0
0 Tulane 32
34 La. Tech 0
7 S.M.U. 20
14 Ga. Tech 28
0 Georgia 7
7 Miss. State 14
7 L.S.U. 7
13 Villanova 0
28 Clemson 7

123 (4-5-1) 115

1942

20 Chattanooga 7
0 Ga. Tech 15
27 Tulane 13
0 Florida 6
6 Georgetown 6
14 Villanova 6
0 Miss. State 6
14 Ga. Navy P-F 41
25 L.S.U. 7
27 Georgia 13
41 Clemson 13

174 (6-4-1) 133

1943
(No Team)

1944

32 Howard 0
7 Ft. Benning 0
0 Ga. Tech 27
13 Tulane 16
57 Presbyterian 0
21 Miss. State 26
13 Georgia 49
38 Miami 19

180 (4-4-0) 137

1945

38 Howard 0
0 Maxwell Fld. 7
0 Miss. State 20
20 Tulane 14
7 Ga. Tech 20
19 Florida 0
52 SW La 0
0 Georgia 35
29 La. Tech 0
7 Miami 33

172 (5-5-0) 129

1946

13 Sou. Miss. 12
26 Furman 6
27 St. Louis 7
0 Tulane 32
6 Ga. Tech 27
0 Vanderbilt 19
0 Miss. State 33
0 Georgia 41
13 Clemson 21
47 Florida 12

132 (4-6-0) 210

1947

13 Sou. Miss. 19
14 La. Tech 0
20 Florida 14
7 Ga. Tech 27
0 Tulane 40
0 Vanderbilt 28
0 Miss. State 14
6 Georgia 28
18 Clemson 34

78 (2-7-0) 204

1948

20 Sou. Miss. 14
13 La. Tech 13
9 Florida 16
0 Ga. Tech 27
6 Tulane 21
0 Vanderbilt 47
0 Miss. State 20
14 Georgia 42
6 Clemson 7
0 Alabama 55

68 (1-8-1) 262

1949

7 Ole Miss 40
14 Florida 14
21 Ga. Tech 35
6 Tulane 14
7 Vanderbilt 26
25 Miss. State 6
20 Georgia 20
20 Clemson 20
14 Alabama 13

134 (2-4-3) 188

1950

14 Wofford 19
0 Vanderbilt 41
0 SE Louisiana 6
7 Florida 27
0 Ga. Tech 20
0 Tulane 28
0 Miss. State 27
10 Georgia 12
0 Clemson 41
0 Alabama 34

31 (0-10-0) 255

1951

24 Vanderbilt 14
30 Wofford 14
14 Florida 13
7 Ga. Tech 27
21 Tulane 0
49 La College 0
14 Mississippi 39
14 Georgia 46
0 Clemson 34
7 Alabama 25

180 (5-5-0) 212

1952

7 Maryland 13
7 Ole Miss 20
54 Wofford 7
0 Ga. Tech 33
6 Tulane 21
21 Florida 31
34 Miss. State 49
7 Georgia 13
3 Clemson 0
0 Alabama 21

139 (2-8-0) 208

1953

47 Stetson 0
13 Ole Miss 0
21 Miss. State 21
6 Ga. Tech 36
34 Tulane 7
16 Florida 7
29 Miami 20
39 Georgia 18
45 Clemson 19
7 Alabama 10

157 (7-2-1) 138

Gator Bowl

13 Texas Tech 35

1954

45 Chattanooga 0
13 Florida 19
14 Kentucky 21
7 Ga. Tech 14
33 Fla. State 0
27 Tulane 0
14 Miami 13
35 Georgia 0
27 Clemson 6
28 Alabama 0

243 (7-3-0) 73

Gator Bowl

33 Baylor 13

1955

15 Chattanooga 6
13 Florida 0
14 Kentucky 14
14 Ga. Tech 12
52 Furman 0
13 Tulane 27
27 Miss. State 26
16 Georgia 13
21 Clemson 0
26 Alabama 0

211 (8-1-1) 98

Gator Bowl

13 Vanderbilt **25**

1956

7 Tennessee 35
41 Furman 0
13 Kentucky 0
7 Ga. Tech 28
12 Houston 0
0 Florida 20
27 Miss. State 20
20 Georgia 0
13 Fla. State 7
34 Alabama 7

117 (7-3-0) 117

1957

7 Tennessee 0
40 Chattanooga 7
6 Kentucky 0
3 Ga. Tech 0
48 Houston 7
13 Florida 0
15 Miss. State 7
6 Georgia 0
29 Fla. State 7
40 Alabama 0

207 (10-0-0) 28

1958

13 Tennessee 0
30 Chattanooga 8
8 Kentucky 0
7 Ga. Tech 7
20 Maryland 7
6 Florida 5
33 Miss. State 14
21 Georgia 6
21 Wake Forest 7
14 Alabama 8

173 (9-0-1) 62

1959

0 Tennessee 3
35 Mardin-Sim. 12
33 Kentucky 0
7 Ga. Tech 6
21 Miami 6
6 Florida 0
31 Miss. State 0
13 Georgia 14
28 Sou. Miss. 7
0 Alabama 10

174 (7-3-0) 58

1960

3 Tennessee 10
10 Kentucky 7
10 Chattanooga 0
9 Ga. Tech 7
20 Miami 7
10 Florida 7
27 Miss. State 12
9 Georgia 6
57 Fla. State 21
0 Alabama 3

155 (8-2-0) 80

1961

24 Tennessee 21
12 Kentucky 14
35 Chattanooga 7
6 Ga. Tech 7
24 Clemson 14
21 Wake Forest 7
10 Miss. State 11
10 Georgia 7
32 Florida 15
0 Alabama 34

174 (6-4-0) 137

1962

22 Tennessee 21
16 Kentucky 6
54 Chattanooga 6
17 Ga. Tech 14
17 Clemson 14
3 Florida 22
9 Miss. State 3
21 Georgia 30
14 Fla. State 14
0 Alabama 38

173 (6-3-1) 168

1963

21 Houston 14
23 Tennessee 19
14 Kentucky 13
28 Chattanooga 0
29 Ga. Tech 21
19 Florida 0
10 Miss. State 13
14 Georgia 0
2 Fla. State 15
10 Alabama 8

189 (9-1-0) 103

Orange Bowl

7 Nebraska 13

1964

30 Houston 0
3 Tennessee 0
0 Kentucky 20
33 Chattanooga 12
3 Ga. Tech 7
14 Sou. Miss. 7
0 Florida 14
12 Miss. State 3
14 Georgia 7
14 Alabama 21

123 (6-4-0) 91

1965

8 Baylor 14
13 Tennessee 13
23 Kentucky 18
30 Chattanooga 7
14 Ga. Tech 23
0 Sou. Miss. 3
28 Florida 17
25 Miss. State 18
21 Georgia 19
3 Alabama 30

165 (5-4-1) 162

Liberty Bowl

7 Ole Miss 13

1966

20 Chattanooga 6
0 Tennessee 28
7 Kentucky 17
14 Wake Forest 6
3 Ga. Tech 17
7 T.C.U. 6
27 Florida 30
13 Miss. State 0
13 Georgia 21
0 Alabama 31

104 (4-6-0) 162

1967

40 Chattanooga 6
13 Chattanooga 27
48 Kentucky 7
43 Clemson 21
28 Ga. Tech 10
0 Miami 7
26 Florida 21
36 Miss. State 0
0 Georgia 17
3 Alabama 7

237 (6-4-0) 123

1968

28 S.M.U. 37
26 Miss. State 0
26 Kentucky 7
21 Clemson 10
20 Ga. Tech 21
31 Miami 6
24 Florida 13
28 Tennessee 14
3 Georgia 17
16 Alabama 24

223 (6-4-0) 149

Sun Bowl

34 Arizona 10

1969

57 Wake Forest 0
19 Tennessee 45
44 Kentucky 3
51 Clemson 0
17 Ga. Tech 14
20 L.S.U. 21
38 Florida 12
52 Miss. State 13
16 Georgia 3
49 Alabama 26

363 (8-2-0) 137

Bluebonnet Bowl

7 Houston 36

1970

33 Sou. Miss 14
36 Tennessee 23
33 Kentucky 15
44 Clemson 0
31 Ga. Tech 7
9 L.S.U. 17
63 Florida 14
56 Miss. State 0
17 Georgia 31
33 Alabama 28

355 (8-2-0) 149

Gator Bowl

35 Ole Miss 28

1971

60 UT Chattanooga 7
10 Tennessee 9
38 Kentucky 6
27 Sou. Miss. 14
31 Ga. Tech 14
35 Clemson 13
40 Florida 7

30	Miss. State	21
35	Georgia	20
7	Alabama	31
313	(9-1-0)	142

Sugar Bowl

22	Oklahoma	40

1972

14	Miss. State	3
14	UT Chattanooga	7
10	Tennessee	6
19	Ole Miss	13
7	L.S.U.	35
24	Ga. Tech	14
27	Fla. State	14
26	Florida	20
27	Georgia	10
17	Alabama	16
185	(9-1-0)	138

Gator Bowl

24	Colorado	3

1973

18	Oregon St.	9
31	UT Chattanooga	0
0	Tennessee	21
14	Ole Miss	7
6	L.S.U.	20
24	Ga. Tech	10
7	Houston	0
8	Florida	12
31	Miss. State	17
14	Georgia	28
0	Alabama	35
153	(6-5-0)	159

Sun Bowl

17	Missouri	34

1974

16	Louisville	3
52	UT-Chatt.	7
21	Tennessee	0
3	Miami	0
31	Kentucky	13
31	Ga. Tech	22
38	Fla. State	6
14	Florida	25
24	Miss. State	20
17	Georgia	13
13	Alabama	17
260	(9-2-0)	126

Gater Bowl

27	Texas	3

1975

20	Memphis St.	31
10	Baylor	10
17	Tennessee	21
16	Va. Tech	23
15	Kentucky	9
31	Ga. Tech	27
17	Fla. State	14
14	Florida	31
*21	Miss. State	21
13	Georgia	28
0	Alabama	28
174	(3-6-2)	243

*Won by forfeit

1976

19	Arizona	31
14	Baylor	15
38	Tennessee	28
10	Ole Miss	0
27	Memphis St.	28
10	Ga. Tech	28
31	Fla. State	19
19	Florida	24
*19	Miss. State	28
0	Georgia	28
7	Alabama	38
194	(3-8-0)	267

*Won by forfeit

1977

21	Arizona	10
13	Sou. Miss.	24
14	Tennessee	12
21	Mississippi	15
15	N. C. State	17
21	Ga. Tech	38
3	Fla. State	24
29	Florida	14
*13	Miss. State	27
33	Georgia	14
21	Alabama	48
204	(6-5-0)	243

*Won by forfeit

1978

45	Kansas State	32
18	Virginia Tech	7
29	Tennessee	10
15	Miami	17
49	Vanderbilt	7
10	Ga. Tech	24
21	Wake Forest	7
7	Florida	31
6	Miss. State	0
22	Georgia	22
16	Alabama	34
238	(6-4-1)	191

Auburn University Football Lettermen—1891-1978

A

ABRAHAM, William, 1945
ABREU, Arnaldo, 1974-75-76
ADAMS, Johnny, 1953-54-55
ADAMS, Thurston, 1925-26-27-28
ADCOCK, John, 1947-48-49
ALDRIDGE, L. L., 1925
ALFORD, Mike, 1962-63-64
ALFORD, William Percy, Jr., 1950-52
ALLEN, E. H., 1922-26
ALLEN, Ricky, 1977-78
ALLEY, John T., Jr., 1946
ALLISON, H. A., 1902-03-04
ANDERSON, Willis, 1947
ANDRESS, H. C., 1926-27
ANDREWS, Joe, 1929
ANDREWS, William, 1976-77-78
ANTLEY, Lester, 1935-36-37
ARDILLO, Nick, 1940
ARIAIL, David, 1931-32-33
ARNOLD, Danny, 1974-76-77
ARNOLD, Ted, 1911-12-13-14
ARTHUR, Robert C., 1930
ATKINS, George, 1952-53-54
ATKINS, William, 1956-57
AUSTIN, Billy, 1956-57
AUTREY, Max, 1944-47-48-49
AYERS, Bucky, 1965-66-67

B

BAGBY, Milton, 1937
BAGGETT, Bill, 1960
BAKER, Ed, 1951-52-53
BAKER, Tim, 1955-56-57
BALL, William S., 1944-46-47
BANKS, Thomas Sidney, 1948-49
BANKS, Tom, 1967-68-69
BARKER, Harold, 1944
BARLEY, Breece Houston, 1950
BARNWELL, Charles H., 1891-92
BARTON, Billy D., 1941-42
BARTON, Coker Hugh, 1947-48-49
BASKIN, W. O., 1926
BATSON, S. R., 1905-06-07-08
BAUGHN, Joe William, 1960-61-62
BAUMGARTNER, Clyde, 1974-75-76
BAYNES, Ronald L., 1962-64-65
BEAIRD, Robert L., 1964-65-66
BEARDEN, Paul, 1945
BEASLEY, Jerry, 1977-78
BEASLEY, Terry, 1969-70-71
BEAVER, J. J., 1910
BECK, Dave, 1970-71-72
BECK, Gary, 1975
BELLAMY, Rodney, 1975-76-77-78
BENNETT, Edwin, 1918
BENTLEY, Danny, 1969
BENTON, Duncan, 1948-49
BENTON, Philip M., 1934
BERNICH, Ken, 1972-73-74
BEVERLY, David, 1970-71-72
BICKERSTAFF, Hugh, 1894
BIDEZ, Paul R., 1912-13-14-15
BLACKERBY, Don, 1950
BLACKMON, Scott, 1969-70
BLACKSHEAR, Gil W., 1917
BLAKE, Robert, F., 1934-36
BLAKENEY, Larry Clinton, 1966-67-68
BLUE, Forest, 1965-66-67
BODNAR, Michael, 1965
BOGUE, F., 1925
BOHLERT, Allen J., 1963-64
BONNER, James, Jr., 1961
BONNER, M. L., 1917
BONNER, T. H., 1918-19-20
BOUCHILLON, James, 1965-66-67
BOWDEN, Alex, 1965
BOWLES, Billy, 1944
BOWLIN, Vincent, 1968-69
BRACKETT, M. L., 1953-54-55
BRADLEY, Bob, 1976-77
BRAME, Albert W., 1952-53-54
BRANCH, Butch, 1968
BRASWELL, Bill, 1964-65-66
BRASWELL, Don, 1957-58
BRAUSE, Donald, 1946
BRENNEN, Terry, 1966-67-68
BRESLER, Alvin, 1969-70
BRICE, Ralph, 1923-24
BRIGGS, Robert, 1949
BRISENDINE, Dwight, 1968
BRISTOW, Don, 1969-70-71
BROOKS, James, 1977-78
BROOKS, Jim, 1949
BROWN, Bob, 1969-70-71
BROWN, David, 1973
BROWN, J. V., 1892-93-94
BROWN, Red, 1920
BROWN, Thomas, 1930-31-32
BROWNE, Lott, 1969-70
BRUCE, Billy, 1974
BRUCE, Guy H., 1950-51-52
BRYAN, Tom, 1964-65-66
BRYANT, Phillip, 1973
BULGER, C. N., 1938-39-40
BULLARD, E. W., 1897-98
BULLOCK, J. K., 1918-19-20
BURBANK, Bill, 1955
BURFORD, Oscar, 1936-37-38
BURGESS, Bill, 1962
BURKETT, Jackie, 1957-58-59
BURKS, Ken, 1973-74-75
BURNS, G. O., 1916
BURNS, George Robert, 1951-52
BURNS, Herman W., 1964-65-66
BURNS, James T., 1945-48
BURNS, T. Howard, 1939
BURNS, Vernon, 1938
BURNS, W. M., 1926-27
BURNS, Wayne, 1963-64-65
BURROW, Mike, 1976-77-78
BURSON, Jimmy, 1960-61-62
BURT, Joe B., 1928-29-30
BUSH, J. D., 1929-30-31
BUSH, T. G., 1898
BUTLER, Bob, 1977
BUTLER, Ed, 1972-73-74-75
BUTLER, Rufus White, 1898-99-1904
BYLSMA, Bruce, 1969-70-71
BYRD, Rusty, 1976-77-78
BYRUM, L. E., 1896

C

CAHOON, Jack, Jr., 1944-45
CALDWELL, Hamlin, 1972-73-74
CALHOUN, Dennis, 1951-52
CALLAHAN, Mark, 1977
CALLAHAN, Porter, 1927-28-29
CAMP, K. H., 1903
CAMP, N. G., 1921
CAMPBELL, B. G., 1924
CAMPBELL, Bill, 1965-66
CAMPBELL, David, 1967-68
CAMPBELL, Joseph, 1964-65-66
CAMPBELL, Robert, 1914-15
CANNON, Robert, 1945-46-47-48
CANNON, Sandy, 1971-72
CANTRELL, G. W., 1937-39
CARPENTER, Lee, 1972-73
CARTER, H. J., 1926-27-28
CARTER, J. E., 1927
CARTER, Jimmy, 1965-66-67
CARTER, John F., 1921
CARTER, Loran, 1966-67-68
CASEY, Jay, 1970-71-72
CASSEDY, Coley Boyd, 1960
CASTELLOW, Eugene, 1944
CATON, E. L., 1909-10-11
CAZONERI, Fagan, 1942-43
CHADWICK, Ray, 1966-67
CHALKLEY, Johnnie, 1940-41
CHAMBLESS, Boots, 1931-32-33
CHAMPION, Mac, 1957
CHANDLER, Walter, 1938-39
CHAPPELLE, Earl Howard, 1929
CHASTAIN, Rick, 1970-71
CHATEAU, L. A., 1942
CHEANAULT, Rick, 1976-77
CHEATAM, H. Lloyd, 1940-41
CHEEK, Richard, 1967-68-69
CHESSHER, Chet, 1977-78
CHILDRESS, Joe, 1953-54-55

CHRIETZBERG, Abb, 1938-39-40
CHRIETZBERG, W. D., 1931-32-33
CHRISTIAN, Tim, 1966-67-68
CHRISTIAN, Wallace, 1972-73
CHRISTY, Foster, 1976-77-78
CLAPP, G. W., 1958-59-61
CLARK, Wallace, 1968-69-70
CLAY, Berney S., 1911
CLAYTON, Aubrey, 1941-42
CLEMENT, Mark, 1977-78
CLINE, Chester, 1948-49
CLINE, James, 1951
COCHRAN, John, 1963-64-65
COCHRAN, Leon Thomas, 1945-46-47
CODY, Bill, 1963-64-65
COGDELL, Homer, 1908-09-10-11
COLEMAN, T. W., 1921
COLLEY, Jere, 1970
COLLINS, Charles, 1965-66-67
COMER, Hubert, 1966
COOK, James, 1955-56
COOK, William C., 1946
COPTSIAS, Reges, 1952
CORNELIUS, William D., 1941-42
CORR, Mark, Jr., 1936
COSPER, James, 1927
COSTELLOS, Vic, 1941-42
CRANE, John, 1977
CRANE, T. R., 1923-25
CRAWFORD, J. B., 1927-28-29
CRAWFORD, Mac, 1968-69
CREEL, Homer J., 1923
CREEL, Jackie, 1951
CREEL, John Paul, 1917-18-19-20
CREMER, Theodore, 1940
CRIBBS, Joe, 1976-77-78
CRIMMINS, Francis, 1940-41
CROLLA, John, 1949-50-51
CRUSE, S. R., 1910-11
CUNNINGHAM, Bill, 1975-76
CUMMINGHAM, R. E., 1926
CURRIER, Mike, 1967-68-69

D

D'AGASTINO, Frank, 1953-55
DANJEAN, Ernest, 1954-55-56
DAVIDSON, M. V., 1929-30-31
DAVIDSON, W. M., Jr., 1959-60-61
DAVIS, Bobby, 1973-74
DAVIS, George, 1949-50
DAVIS, Howard, 1901
DAVIS, Joe Brown, 1951-52-53
DAVIS, John Eayres, 1937-38
DAVIS, John Eayres, Sr., 1908-09-10-11
DAVIS, John Elliott, 1923
DAVIS, Michael E., 1964-65-66
DAVIS, Rett, 1972-73
DAVIS, Robert, 1959-60-61
DAVISON, George H., 1967
DEAL, Rufus, 1940
DEAN, C. Ross, 1935
DEEN, Rusty, 1972-73-74
DENNIS, Jep, 1951
DENSON, John W., 1905
DETTMERING, Neal, 1968-69-70
DICKEY, George Oliver, 1897
DILLION, Jim Leo, 1952
DIXON, Duncan P., 1896-97
DOLAN, Joe, 1959-60
DONAHUE, William F., 1917-18
DOOLEY, Vince, 1951-52-53
DOUGLASS, Andrew, 1947
DOVER, Rick, 1976-77-78
DOWNEY, Mitch, 1974
DOWNS, Don, 1960-61-62
DUART, Fredrick, 1947-49-50
DUKE, Robert C., 1952-53
DUNCAN, Lloyd, 1951-52-53
DuPREE, Sterling, 1931-32-33
DUPUY, Harold Burke, 1944-45
DYAS, Ed, 1958-59-60

E

EARNEST, J. M., 1926
EAVES, Joel, 1934-35-36
EDDINS, Jo Jo, 1940-41-42
EDDINS, Liston, 1973-74-75
EDGE, Billy, 1962-63-64
EDGE, Harvey Arnold, 1922
EDWARDS, Dave, 1959-60-61
EDWARDS, Tommy, 1950
EGGE, George, 1929-30-31
EICHELBERGER, P. M., 1894-1902
ELAM, Scotty, 1969-70-71
ELLIOTT, Gerald, 1951-54-55-56
ELLIS, George, 1925-26-27
ELLIS, Larry, 1966-67-68
ESSLINGER, Harry W., 1907-08-09
ESSLINGER, Monroe S., 1912-13
EVANS, Bill, 1973-74-75-76
EVANS, Bruce, 1972-73-74
EVERETT, Brad, 1977-78

F

FAGEN, Arnold, 1947-48-49
FAIRCHILD, Gerry, 1938-39
FARQUHAR, Andy, 1972-73
FARRIOR, Bob, 1972-73
FAULK, Teedie, 1946
FEAGIN, Arthur Henry, 1898-99-1900
FEAGIN, C. E., 1901
FEAGIN, Joel D., 1920
FEAGIN, William F., 1892-93
FENTON, Jimmy, 1935-36-37
FENTON, William Vincent, 1932-33-34
FERGUSON, Sonny, 1967-68-69
FERRELL, J. F., 1941-42
FINNEY, Charlie, 1941-42
FISHER, Marvin, 1926
FITZHUGH, Mike, 1969-70
FLETCHER, Carl, 1946
FLETCHER, Chuck, 1973-74-75
FLOURNEY, Dickie, 1948-49-50
FLOURNOY, Josiah, 1903-04
FLYNN, Mike, 1971-73-74
FORD, Flivver, 1921-22-23
FORET, Bobby, 1960-61
FORET, Teddy, 1957-58-59
FOWLER, Julian, 1939
FOY, Humphrey, 1904-05-06
FOY, Robert, 1891-92-93
FRANCIS, T. M., 1909-10-11
FRANKLIN, Byron, 1977-78
FRAZIER, Wayne, 1959-60-61
FREDERICK, Connie, 1967-68-69
FREDERICKSON, Tucker, 1962-63-64
FREEMAN, Bobby, 1951-52-53-54
FREEMAN, Rick, 1975-76-77
FRICKS, R. M., 1915-16
FRIDDLE, Joe, 1968-69
FULFORD, Danny, 1964-65-66
FULGHUM, Robert, 1965-66-67
FULLER, Franklin Dee, 1963-65
FULLER, Mike, 1972-73-74
FULLER, Rusty, 1972-73
FULLER, Terry, 1975-76-77
FULLINGTON, James, 1952
FULMER, Floyd, 1946-47

G

GAFFORD, Frederick, 1948
GAFFORD, Monk, 1940-41-42
GAITHER, Eric, 1961-62
GALLOWAY, Sam, 1961
GANTT, Frank, 1934-35-36
GARGIS, Phil, 1974-75-76
GARLAND, Peter, 1921-22
GARNER, L. C., 1944
GARRAMONE, Pasco, 1945
GATES, Mike, 1972-73-74
GATSKI, Frank, 1945
GAUM, Carl Gilbert, 1908
GAUNTT, James G., 1906-08
GENDUSA, A. J., 1942
GIBSON, Charles, 1921-22
GIBSON, U. F., 1917
GIDDENS, Winkey, 1960-61-62
GIFFIN, Roger Allen, 1966-67-68
GILBERT, Walter Beasley, 1934-35-36
GILCHRIST, Philip, 1935
GILCHRIST, Philip P., 1969-70-71
GILLIAM, Fred, 1935-37
GILLIAM, John R., 1948
GILLIGAN, Jeff, 1975
GILREATH, Ted, 1957
GIVENS, Donnie, 1977-78
GLENN, Charlie, 1966-67
GOETZ, Ludwig, 1959
GOLDEN, Bobby, 1949-50-51
GOODWIN, John, 1915-16
GORDON, Glenn, 1971
GORDON, Jerry, 1967-68
GOSSOM, Thomas, 1972-73-74
GRANGER, John, 1925
GRANGER, W. G., 1927-28-29
GRANT, Bob, 1969-70-71
GRANT, Russell, 1930-31-32
GRAY, Jeff, 1976-77-78
GREEN, H. L., 1928
GREEN, Keith, 1968-69-70
GREENE, Carson, 1923-24-25
GRIFFIN, Bobby, 1951
GRIFFITH, Doc, 1962-63-64
GRIFFITH, Lee, 1960-61
GRIMMETT, Clarence, 1941-42
GRISHAM, William, 1920-24
GROAT, Tommy, 1966-67
GROOVER, Mike, 1960
GROSS, Andy, 1964-65-66
GROSS, George, 1960-61-62
GROSS, Lee, 1972-73-74
GRUBB, Charles, 1944-45-46-47
GULLEDGE, Jerry, 1959-60-61
GUTHRIE, Richard, 1961
GWIN, Terry, 1899
GWIN, W. H., 1900-01-02

H

HAAS, Howard, 1960-61
HAGAN, Larry K., 1967
HAGOOD, M. H., 1924
HALL, Hank, 1965-66-67
HALL, James S., 1955-56-57
HALL, Jim, 1952-53
HAM, Harold, 1967-68
HAMRICK, Hal, 1968-69-70
HANKS, Samuel, 1950-51-52
HAPPER, Carl, 1938-39-40
HARALSON, Jonathan, 1898
HARBUCK, Rick, 1975
HARDIN, Alan, 1976-77-78
HARDY, Carl, 1965-66
HARDY, Henry, 1973
HARDY, Ken, 1977-78
HARDY, Zac, 1977-78
HARE, F. W., 1898
HARKINS, C. D., 1928-29-30
HARKINS, E. M., 1920-21-22-23
HARKINS, Hawk, 1940-41-42
HARMAN, William, 1908-09-10
HARPER, Charles, 1946
HARREY, F. D., 1891-96
HARRIS, A. J., 1893
HARRIS, Harold, 1950
HARRIS, Rabbitt, 1906-07-08-09
HARRIS, Ralph, 1944
HARRIS, Red, 1912-13-14
HARRIS, W. F., 1945
HARRISON, Joe, 1973
HARRISON, Joseph L., 1923-24
HARRISON, Max Lamar, 1937
HARTSELLE, J. L., 1927
HARVARD, Bryant, 1957-59-60
HATAWAY, Charles C., 1951-52-53
HATAWAY, Daniel D., 1944-45
HATCHER, Reginald Marvin, 1929
HATFIELD, Lindley Lucius, 1929-30-31
HAWKINS, Herbert, 1944
HAYES, Frank Jeep, 1949
HAYES, Richard A., 1947
HAYLEY, Dick, 1976-77-78
HAYLEY, Lee, 1951-52
HAYNIE, E. C., 1903
HAYNIE, Larry, 1964-65-66
HAYNIE, Lawrence S., 1964-65
HAYWORTH, John, 1969-70-71
HEAD, T. R., 1933
HEATH, Walter, 1936-37
HELLER, Donald Lee, 1962-63-64
HELMS, Mike, 1962-63-64
HENLEY, Terry, 1970-71-72
HEPLER, Wayne, 1946
HERREN, Daniel, 1909-10
HERRING, Hal M., 1946-47-48
HEWLETT, Marvin McClay, 1946
HICKS, Tommy, 1976-77
HILL, David Harris, 1961-62
HILL, G. B., 1902-03
HILL, H. H., 1920-21
HILL, Larry, 1969-70-71
HILL, Lucien Aubrey, 1934
HILL, W. W., 1930
HITCHCOCK, Billy, 1935-36-37
HITCHCOCK, James Franklin, 1930-31-32
HITT, Dwight, 1949-50-51
HOBBIE, J. M., 1903
HOBDY, J. B., 1897
HODGES, W. A., 1925-26-27
HOFFMAN, Murray, 1925
HOFFMAN, Ralph, 1944
HOGARTH, Bill, 1949-50
HOLCOMBE, Walter Pearce, 1896-97

HOLDCROFT, George Thomas, 1929
HOLLEY, W. R., 1907-08
HOLMAN, Freddie W., 1935-36-37
HOLMES, J. Crawford, 1937-38-39
HOLMES, M. C., 1933
HOLTZCLAW, Mike, 1967-68-69
HONEYCUTT, Eugene, 1925
HOPPE, Robert, 1955-56-57
HOUSE, Edwin, 1945
HOUSTIN, N. G., 1933-34
HOWARD, Bucky, 1966-67-68
HOWARD, C. S., 1919-20-21
HOWARD, R. B., 1926
HOWARD, Thomas Herman, 1951-52
HOWE, Fox, 1921-22-23
HOWELL, Milton L., 1937-38-39
HOWLE, Thomas Blake, 1915
HUBBARD, Carl, 1973-74-75
HUBBARD, Mike, 1977
HUFF, John, 1939-40
HUGHES, David, 1971-72-73
HUGHES, Edward, 1911-12-13
HUGULEY, Ed, 1898-99-1900
HUNT, Bobby, 1959-60-61
HUNT, Phillip, 1962-63
HURSTON, Chuck, 1962-63-64
HURSTON, Dwight, 1966-67-68
HUTCHINSON, Jerry, 1958
HYATT, Freddie, 1965-66-67

I

INGLE, Jim, 1963
INGRAM, Rupert, 1927-28
INGWERSEN, Dick, 1969
INMAN, Russell L., 1949
IRBY, L. E., 1940-41-42
IRVIN, Donald Charles, 1960-61

J

JACKSON, Clay, 1920-21
JACKSON, Edward B., 1956-57
JACKSON, Hubert, 1924
JACKSON, Mike, 1973
JACKSON, Mitzi, 1973-74-75
JACKSON, Oliver, 1933
JAMES, Bill, 1967-68-69
JAMES, D. T., 1930
JAMES, Fob, 1952-53-54-55
JAMES, Louie, 1928-29
JEFFERS, James, 1949
JEFFREY, James E. 1957-58
JENKINS, B. S., 1942
JENKINS, Frank, 1964-65-66
JENKINS, George C., 1932-33
JENKINS, Z. T., 1942-47
JERKINS, Marrell, 1969-70
JETT, Gardner, 1970-71-72
JOHNS, Kenneth R., 1956
JOHNSON, C. J., 1900-01
JOHNSON, George Lee, 1930-32
JOHNSON, Lynn, 1973-74-75-77
JOHNSTON, George E., 1918-19-20-21
JOHNSTON, Richard M., 1919
JOHNSTON, Skip, 1977-78
JONES, Anthony, 1975-76-77
JONES, Charles A., 1915-16
JONES, Donald T., 1930-32
JONES, Doug, 1964
JONES, Frank, 1904-05
JONES, Frank E., 1949
JONES, Herman J., 1929-30
JONES, James Allen, 1961-62
JONES, Jimmy, 1966-67
JONES, John Allen, 1892
JONES, Ken, 1965-66-67
JONES, Miles, 1971-72
JONES, Pat, 1974-75
JONES, Ronnie, 1974-75-76
JORDAN, Herbert, 1952
JORDAN, James, 1959
JORDAN, James Ralph, 1929-30-31
JORDAN, Robert C., 1951-52
JUSTO, Charles L., 1950

K

KARAM, James, 1934
KEARLEY, Richard, 1910-11-12-13
KELLY, Barry, 1975-76
KELLY, Spec, 1936-37-38
KEMP, William T., 1932-33
KENMORE, George V., 1937-38-39
KENT, Mailon, 1961-62-63
KERN, John A., 1957-58-59
KIDD, Weyman L., 1966-67
KIEFER, Chuck, 1967-68
KILGORE, Jon, 1962-63-64
KILGORE, Wilton, 1934-35-36
KILPATRICK, William W., 1951-52
KIMBRELL, Casey, 1932-33
KING, Kelly O., 1963
KIRKWOOD, John Kenneth, 1919-20-21
KIRKWOOD, W. R., 1928
KIRSCH, C. F., 1942
KITCHENS, Billy Wilson, 1956-57-58
KLOETI, R. P., 1942
KNAPP, A. D., 1922-23
KNIGHT, Walter Douglas, 1923
KOLEN, Mike, 1967-68-69
KRAL, Louis, 1973
KUYKENDALL, Curtis, 1942-43-44

L

LACEY, Edward Philip, 1902-03-04-05
LACEY, Tim, 1972-73
LAFFOON, William, 1945
LALLAR, L. W., Jr., 1919
LAMB, B. J., 1910-11-12
LAMBERT, Jack Eddie, 1948-49
LANG, Nolan, 1944-45
LANGFORD, Jack, 1952
LANGNER, Charlie A., 1948-49-50
LANGNER, David, 1971-72-73
LANIER, Gaines, 1972-73-74
LANNOM, Harold, 1946-47
LARIMORE, William H., 1952
LaROCK, Pat, 1975
LaRUSSA, Frank Joseph, 1956-57-58
LASTER, James Walker, 1957-58
LASTER, Larry T., 1961-62
LAUDER, Robert N., 1957-58-60
LAWRENCE, J. D., 1921-22-23-24
LEACH, Sydney, 1893
LEDBETTER, Lowell, 1956-57
LEE, Jimmy Smith, 1957-58-59
LEE, Robert W., 1961
LEICHTNAM, Joseph, 1958-59-60
LeNOIR, Jim, 1938-39-40
LEVI, Irving, Jr., 1934-35
LEWIS, Aubrey, 1931
LEWIS, Don, 1963-64-65
LIGHTFOOT, Ben, 1952
LIND, E. W., 1909
LINDERMAN, Chris, 1972-73
LINDSEY, E. M., 1913
LIPTAK, John Paul, 1945-46-47
LITTLE, Charles A., 1951-52-53
LOCKE, T. C., 1907-08-09
LOCKLEAR, Jack, 1951-52-53-54
LOCKLEAR, Mike, 1977-78
LOCKWOOD, F. W., 1912-13-14
LOFLIN, Wesley B., 1935-36
LOFTON, James Curtis, 1951
LONG, G. J., 1928-29
LONG, Howell G., 1927-28-29
LONG, Hunter Allen, 1890
LONG, James Wallace, 1951-52-53
LONG, S. R., 1924-25-26
LONG, Scotty, 1964-65-66
LONG, Tony, 1975-76
LORENDO, Mac, 1970-71-72
LORINO, Tommy, 1956-57-58
LOVELACE, Jonathon B., 1913
LOWRY, Tommy, 1969-70-71
LUKA, Bill, 1971-72-73
LUKE, James M., 1911
LUNCEFORD, Tommy, Jr., 1965-66-67
L'UPTON, Frank Allen, 1891
LUTZ, Earle G., 1923
LYLE, Tim, 1967-68
LYON, David M., 1942
LYON, Dave, 1971

M

MACHEN, Don, 1959-60-61
MAJOR, J. P., 1910-11-12
MALONE, Robert L., 1911
MANTHRONE, Dan, 1948-49
MARGESON, Robert, 1965-66-67
MARKET, Joe, 1924-25-26
MARTIN, C. B., 1913-14
MARTIN, Dan S., 1898-99-1900-01
MARTIN, Philip, 1967-68
MASON, Sam, 1930
MAXIME, Chuck, 1954-55-56
MAY, Don, 1956
MacEACHERN, Gordon, 1938-39-40
McADORY, Issac Sadler, 1901-02-03
McAFEE, John, 1963-64-65
McCALL, Mac, 1970-71-72
McCALL, Reese, 1975-76-77
McCAY, Don, 1965-66-67
McCLENDON, Tommy, 1975-76
McCLINTON, Buddy, 1967-68-69
McCLOUD, Mike, 1975-76
McCLURKIN, J. H., 1940-41-42
McCLURKIN, Sam P., 1945-46
McCOLLUM, F. G., 1931-32-33
McCOLLUM, Jeff, 1974-75-76
McCOY, C. L., 1907-08-09-10
McCRACKEN, Spence, 1969-70-71
McCRARY, I. H., 1920-21
McCRAW, Harrison, 1966
McCROSKEY, Sam E., 1934-35-36
McDANIEL, James E., 1944-45-46-47
McDAVID, Ben, 1964-65-66
McDONALD, Johnny, 1968-69-70
McDUFFIE, Francis D., 1961
McELDERRY, J. W., 1925
McENIRY, William Hugh, 1903
McFADEN, Earl, 1924-25-26
McGEEVER, John, 1959-60-61
McGEHEE, C. H., 1939-40
McGOWEN, Dick, 1938
McGOWEN, Jim, 1947-48
McGRAW, Joseph, 1965-66
McGUIRE, Bill, 1948-49
McINTYRE, Secdrick, 1973-74-75-76
McKAY, Don, 1965-66-67
McKAY, W. C., 1918
McKINNEY, James, 1976-77-78
McKINNEY, Jim, 1972-73-74
McKINNEY, Tom, 1946
McKISSICK, A. H., 1892-93-94
McKISSICK, Rex, 1935-36-37-38
McLENNAN, J. Alan, 1923
McLURE, J. T., 1906-07-08
McMAHEN, Royce L., 1947
McMAHON, C. E., 1939-40
McMANUS, Bill, 1969-70-71
McMILLAN, L. E., 1921
McMURRY, William E., 1950-51-52
McNEILL, Fats, 1925
McQUAIG, Mike, 1976-77
McREE, J. L., 1929
McSWEEN, Clyde J., 1951
MEADOWS, M. E., 1911-12-13
MEADOWS, W. T., 1965-66
MEAGHER, Patrick C., 1956-57
MEDLIN, Phillip, 1962
MERCER, Ray, 1952
MERKEL, A. W., 1903-04
MIDDLETON, David Hinton, 1952-53-54
MILLER, Bogue, 1964-65
MILLER, H. R., 1931-32-33
MILLER, Robert L., 1964-65-66
MILLS, Ernest, 1938-39-40
MIMS, David, 1925
MIMS, W. D., 1937-38-39
MINOR, William Ray, 1954
MIRACLE, Joe, 1962-63-64
MITCHAM, George Nathan, 1896-97-98
MITCHELL, Henry G., 1905
MITCHELL, Holley, 1946
MITCHELL, Jack, 1903
MITCHELL, Joe Bob, 1934-35
MITCHELL, Roger, 1971-72-73
MITCHELL, Sam, 1961
MOLPUS, C. E., 1930-31
MONSEES, Henry, 1940
MOON, Joe, 1970
MOON, W. P., 1901-02-03-04
MOORE, Adolphus, 1911
MOORE, Allen, 1970
MOORE, George, 1946-47-48-49
MOORE, J. Allen, 1920
MOORE, Ray, 1946-47-48-49
MORGAN, Malvern, 1937-38-39
MORRIS, M. K., 1933-34-35
MORRIS, Max, 1941
MOSS, Ben, 1944
MOTLEY, J. W., 1907-08
MOULTON, John L., 1945-47
MOULTON, William Patrick, 1926
MULHALL, Eugene F., 1950-51
MUMMERT, Gordon, 1952-53-54-55
MUSGROVE, W. T., 1932-33-34
MYERS, Leon H., 1958-59-60

N

NADER, Sam, 1967

NAFTEL, James, Jr., 1956-57
NALL, James, 1915-16
NALOR, George, 1945
NEEL, Mike, 1970-71-72
NEEL, Rick, 1973-74-75
NELSON, L. L., 1926
NETTLEMAN, Tom, 1975-76-77
NEURA, Ted, 1952-53-54
NEWELL, James Kirk, 1910-11-12
NEWSON, Douglas, 1925
NEWTON, Bill, 1971-72-73
NEWTON, Bob, 1971-72-73
NEWTON, J. B., 1930
NICHOLS, Bill, 1937-38-39
NIX, Lloyd, 1956-57-58
NIX, Paul, 1967-68–69
NIXON, Charles, 1900
NIXON, Glenn, 1948-49
NOBLE, A. S., 1908-09-10
NOLL, W. L., 1900
NORMAN, Eugene, 1945
NORTON, Clarence A. 1948-49
NUGENT, Dan, 1972-73-74

O

O'CAIN, Richard, 1946
O'DONOGHUE, Neil, 1975-76
OGLESBY, Julian, 1892-93
O'GWYNN, Ralph, 1936-37-38
OLLINGER, G. B., 1923-25
OLLINGER, Rodney M., 1918-19-20-21
O'ROURKE, D. D., 1935
OSBURNE, Steve, 1963
OSTROWSKI, Dave, 1973-74-75-76
OVERTON, Joe, 1961-62
OWEN, Hunter, 1944
OWENS, James, 1970-71-72

P

PADUCH, Kenneth, 1957-58
PAGE, J. M., 1904-05-06
PAGE, Terry, 1971
PAGE, W. G., 1911
PARK, Henry Bigham, 1898
PARKER, W. D., 1930-31-32
PARKS, Allan L., 1950-51
PARTIN, James, 1963-64
PATE, R. H., 1930
PATERSON, J. Haygood, 1903-04-05
PATERSON, J. P., 1932-34-35
PATERSON, W. W., 1925-26-27
PATERSON, Wallace B., 1907
PATERSON, William B., 1900
PATTON, Jim, 1976-77
PEAKE, Edward, 1927-28
PEARCE, James G., 1920-21-22
PEARCE, Marvin, 1896-97
PEARCE, T. H., 1926-27
PEARSON, Gus, 1938-39
PELFREY, Raymond H., 1947
PELHAM, Morris, 1898-99-1900
PENTON, George, 1905-06-08-09
PENTON, John, 1897
PERILLARD, Michael, 1965-66-67
PERKINS, N. Snow, 1893
PETERSON, S. D., 1922
PETRIE, George, 1892
PETTUS, James, 1958-59-60
PHARR, Jim, 1946-47
PHILLIPS, Red, 1955-56-57
PHIPPS, W. E., 1931-32-33
PICKETT, F. E., 1912
PIERCE, L. W., 1902-03
PITMAN, Eddie, 1958
PITTMAN, Richard, 1966-67-68
PITTS, Jim, 1973-74-75
PITTS, John E., 1908-09-10
PLAGGE, Richard, 1965-66-67
POPWELL, Jerry, 1963-64-65
PORTELA, Jorge, 1977-78
POSS, Summie, 1945
POUNDSTONE, Phillip, 1946-47
POWELL, Francis, 1945
POWELL, James, 1955
POWELL, Ray, 1976-77-78
PREIS, Louis, 1956
PRENDERGAST, F. H., 1913-14-15-16
PRESLEY, Dan Jasper, 1956-57
PRESTON, Ben, 1955-56-57
PRICE, Gary, 1961-62-63
PRICE, James, 1960-61-62
PRIM, Red, 1930-31-32
PRUETT, E. A., 1925-26
PRUETT, Roger, 1971-72-73
PRUITT, C. A., 1919-22-23-24
PUMMER, Pete, 1969-70
PURIFAY, Jon, 1895
PUTMAN, Jimmy 1960-61
PYBURN, Jim, 1953-54
PYBURN, Ralph, 1946-48-49

R

RANDOLPH, Don, 1966
RANIER, J. M., 1918
RAINER, Mark, 1942
RAWSON, David, 1962-63
RAWSON Lamar, 1957-58-59
RAWSON, Larry, 1961-62-63
RAY, W. M., 1921-22
REAGAN, Frank A., 1920-23
REDDING, S. Arthur, 1893-94
REESE, John Lewis, 1923
REEVES, Frank, 1954-55-56
REVINGTON, George, 1916-17
REYNOLDS, James, 1957-58-59
REYNOLDS, James A., 1940-41-42
REYNOLDS, Walker, 1907-08-09
RHED, Bobby, 1950
RHODES, Bob, 1976-77-78
RICE, Ken, 1958-59-60
RICE, Virgil Preston, 1941
RICKETTS, Jimmy, 1956-57-58
RIDDLE, Obie, 1907-08
RIDGEWAY, Dave, 1950-51
RIGSBY, Robert, 1966-67
RILEY, Frank, 1956
RILEY, John Sellers, 1967–68-69
RILEY, Marshall, 1977-78
RIVINGS, Franklin Carlisle, 1899
ROBBS, Ronnie, 1957-58
ROBERT, Greg, 1968-69
ROBERTSON, J. P., 1918
ROBBINS, Mark, 1977-78
ROBINETT, Robby, 1969-70-71
ROBINSON, Abe, 1925
ROBINSON, Carey, 1914-15-16-17
ROBINSON, Henry W., 1911-12-13-14
ROBINSON, Moye Ardath, 1949
RODGERS, Hugh, 1934-35-36
ROGERS, Don Luther, 1952
ROGERS, Foreman,
ROGERS, R. C., 1918-19-20
ROGERS, Robert William, 1962
ROGERS, Tres, 1971
ROGERS, W. A., 1931-32-33
ROGERS, William George, 1953-54
ROLLINS, Ray, 1976-77-78
ROSE, George, 1961-62-63
ROSE, Jimmy, 1942-46
ROSS, John, 1956-57
ROSS, Ronnie, 1968-69-70
ROTON, Herbert Carl, 1935-36
RUSSELL, Bo, 1936-37-38
RUSSELL, Erskine, 1946-47-48-49
RUSSELL, William Francis, 1924

S

SALTER, H. V., 1924-25-26
SAMFORD, James D., 1917
SAMFORD, James H., 1939-40-41
SAMFORD, Jim, 1967-68
SAMFORD, Yetta G., 1915
SAMPLE, A. D., 1914-15-16
SANDA, Francis, 1961-62
SANDERS, Ricky, 1974-75
SANSOM, Gerald, 1954-55-56
SANSPREE, Danny, 1970-71-72
SARGENT, H. O., 1896
SAUERBREY, Erich L., 1950-51
SAULS, Durward, 1968-69
SAVAGE, Morris, 1957-58
SCARBROUGH, Robert L., 1952-53-54-55
SCARBROUGH, Sidney, 1934-35-36
SCHLICH, Carl L., 1928-29
SCHMALZ, Dick, 1969-70-71
SCHULER, William, 1941
SCOTT, Charles, 1920-21-22-23
SEIBERT, Robert, 1946
SELF, Geddis, 1923-24-25
SELLERS, Clyde, 1927
SELLERS, Kim, 1974-75-76-77
SENN, Cary Lamar, 1930-31-32
SEXTON, Leo, 1967-68-69
SHACKELFORD, J. G., 1930
SHANKS, R. G., 1894
SHANNON, E., 1928
SHAW, Joe, 1975-76-77
SHELBY, David, 1971
SHELL, Alton, 1954-55
SHERIDAN, F. L., 1924
SHERLING, E. C., 1918-19-20-21
SHERLING, W. G., 1910-11-12
SHIREY, John, 1919-20-21-22
SHIRLEY, Merrill, 1967-68-69
SHORT, David, 1970
SHOTTS, Tom, 1925-26-27
SHOWS, Mike, 1967-68
SIDLE, Jimmy, 1962-63-64
SILVERBERG, Arnold, 1944
SIMMONS, Johnny, 1970-71-72
SIMMONS, Michael Stephens, 1956-57-58
SIMPSON, Howard, 1961-62-63
SIRMANS, Jim, 1972-73
SISTRUNK, John, 1976
SITZ, Pilham, 1937-38
SITZ, W. C., 1922-23-24
SIVELL, James, 1935-36-37
SIVLEY, Benny, 1971-72-73
SIZEMORE, Emmett, 1917-18-20
SKEGGS, Henry H., 1898-99
SKELTON, Mike, 1976-77
SLONEY, John, 1919
SMALLEY, Harley, 1945
SMITH, A. Chapman, 1926
SMITH, C. E., 1938
SMITH, E. R., 1929
SMITH, Freddie, 1976-77-78
SMITH, George W., 1930
SMITH, Harry Howell, 1894-95
SMITH, Henry, 1913
SMITH, John, 1975-76-77
SMITH, Osmo, 1936-37-38
SMITH, Roger, 1957-58-59
SMITH, Sammy, 1968-69
SMITH, Zac T., 1902-03
SNAPP, W. T., 1923
SNELL, Denvard, 1944-45-46-48
SNIDER, Ralph M., 1918-19
SNIDER, Snitz, 1926-27
SPEIGNER, Danny, 1969-70-71
SPEIGNER, Jimmy, 1968-69-70
SPENCE, Dudley L., 1951-52
SPENCER, James, 1959
SPENCER, John C., 1942
SPINKS, Leslie, 1923-24-25
SPINKS, Pete, 1926-27-28
SPIVEY, Rob, 1973-74-75
SPRAGUE, Edmond Scott, 1937
SPRAGUE, Joseph Miles, 1941
STANALAND, Steve, 1973-74-75
STANLEY, Royden, Keith, 1906
STEADHAM, John B., 1910
STEED, George, 1913
STEELE, Andy, 1972-73-74
STEWART, Daniel, 1947-48-49
STEWART, Jack, 1930-31-32
STEWART, Joseph, 1934-36
STICKNEY, W. A., 1916
STILES, Burt, 1917
STOREY, David, 1971-72-73
STOREY, Ron, 1967--68-69
STRAIN, Jimmy, 1954-55-56
STREIT, C. W., 1904-05
STREIT, J. Bradley, 1909-10
STRICKLAND, Ben, 1973-74-75
STRICKLAND, Bobby, 1968-69-70
STRINGER, Raymond, 1945
STOWERS, Tim, 1977-78
STUBBS, Francis, 1918-19-20
SUELL, Doug, 1967
SULLIVAN, Pat, 1969-70-71
SUMNER, Johnny, 1973-74
SUTTON, Mickey, 1962-63-64
SWEET, Henry W., 1924

T

TALLEY, M. P., 1931-32-33
TATUM, Roy, 1965-66-67
TAYLOR, Erquiet, 1929-30
TAYLOR, Larry, 1971-72
TAYLOR, Steve, 1972-73
TELHIARD, Tick, 1973-74-75
TERRY, Paul Edwin, 1954-55-56
THAGGARD, F. J., 1907
THAXTON, Steve, 1964-65-66
THIGPEN, J. H., 1912-13-14-15
THOMASON, W. D., 1923
THOMPSON, Foy C., 1950-51-52
THOMPSON, Larry, 1971
THORNTON, Jack, 1963-64-65
THORPEK, William, 1937-38-39

TIBURZI, Joseph M., 1950-51
TICHENOR, Walker Reynolds, 1894-95-96
TIDWELL, Donnie, 1970
TIDWELL, Travis, 1946-47-48-49
TILLERY, Don Edward, 1945
TIPPER, John Paul, 1934-35-36
TONEY, Clifford, 1977-78
TOOMER, Sheldon Lyne, 1892
TRAMMELL, A. Taymond, 1924
TRAPANI, R. R., 1944
TRAPANI, U. L., 1942
TRAPP, John Herman, 1917-18-19
TRAYLOR, Tommy, 1968-69-70
TROTMAN, Charlie, 1977-78
TROTMAN, John M., 1944-45
TROTT, Marvin, 1975-76-77
TUBBS, M. Howell, 1954-55-56
TUCKER, Marvin, 1965-66-67
TUCKER, William Francis, 1949-50
TURK, C. H., 1924
TURNBAOUGH, Bill, 1951-52
TURNER, Raymond, 1927
TUXWORTH, F. E., 1925-26-28

U

UNGER, Harry, 1970-71

V

VACARELLA, Chris, 1973-74-75-76
VALENTINE, Johnny, 1968-69-70
VAN DYKE, Bill, 1962-63
VAN YPEREN, Jack, 1970
VARANO, Theodore, 1949-50
VAUGHN, B. W., 1926
VAUGHN, Terry, 1958
VENABLE, Willie, 1904-05

W

WADDAIL, Bill, 1946-47-48
WAGNON, Troy, 1977
WAID, Richard, 1962-63-64
WALKER, Gene, 1969-70-71
WALKER, Marion, 1937-38
WALKER, Sullivan, 1973
WALL, Hindman Putman, 1957
WALLIS, Johnny, 1948-49-50
WALLS, Randy, 1972-73
WALSH, James, 1954-55-56
WALTON, Robert L., 1963-64-65
WARD, Glen, 1974-75
WARD, Harry, 1973-74
WARD, James Luther, 1927
WARE, Robert Young, 1905-06-07
WARREN, C. C., 1918-19-20
WARREN, Frank, 1977-78
WARREN, James Earnest, 1962-63-64
WARREN, Ordell, 1953
WARRICK, Haywood, 1957-58-59
WARRINGTON, Caleb Van, 1944
WASDEN, Bobby, 1957-58-59
WATKINS, James Harold, 1944
WATWOOD, Johnnie, 1926
WEAVER, Bobby, 1947-48
WEBB, Donald Edward, 1967-68-69
WEBB, James S., 1902-03
WEBB, Judson, 1901
WEEKLEY, John Francis, 1955-56-57
WELCH, Eddie, 1970-71-72
WELCH, Michael C., 1957
WELCH, Michael C., 1932-33-34
WENDLING, Bud, 1939-40
WERT, Thomas, 1898
WESLEY, Homer, 1950
WEST, Hershel C., 1933
WEST, Willis, 1944
WESTER, Cleve, 1956-57-58
WHATLEY, Hancie, 1937
WHATLEY, John Calvin, 1957
WHATLEY, Wade, 1972-73
WHEELER, George, 1897-98
WHITE, H. T., 1907
WILKES, Don, 1945
WILKES, Herman, 1962
WILKINSON, Mark, 1971-72-73
WILLETT, Dennis V., 1948-49-50
WILLIAMS, David, 1972-73-74
WILLIAMS, E. E., 1923-24-25
WILLIAMS, George W., 1931-32-33
WILLIAMS, H. D., 1935-36
WILLIAMS, Homer E., 1949-50-51
WILLIAMS, Jack, 1940-41
WILLIAMS, James Ray, 1946-47
WILLIAMS, Marvin, 1977-78
WILLIAMS, William, 1894-95-96
WILLINGHAM, Larry, 1968-69-70
WILLS, Will, 1897
WILSON, Bill, 1946
WILSON, Bobby, 1966-67-68
WILSON, Chris, 1972-73-74
WILSON, David, 1892
WILSON, Gerald Roscoe, 1956-57-58
WILSON, John Wesley, 1929
WILSON, Steve, 1970-72
WILSON, William W., 1959-60-61
WINGO, Thomas, 1911
WISE, Warren Wallace, 1939-40
WOLFF, George, 1937-38-39
WOOD, Billy, 1975
WOOD, Charles, 1976-77-78
WOOD, Richard, 1965-66-67
WOOD, Richard M., 1958-59
WOOD, William C., 1930-31-32
WOOD, William T., 1923-24
WOODALL, Woody, 1961-62-63
WOODRUFF, Bobby, 1969
WOODRUFF, Charles W., 1906-07-08
WOODWARD. Dave, 1959-60-61
WOZNIAK, Joe, 1944
WREN, Edward, 1915-16
WRIGHT, A. Z., 1893-94
WYNN, E. L., 1921-22

Y

YARBROUGH, F. R., 1898-99-1900
YARBROUGH, F. R., Jr., 1929
YARBROUGH, Ron, 1967-68-69
YATES, Bruce, 1963-64-65
YEAROUT, Gusty, 1965-66-67
YEAROUT, Tommy, 1969-70-71
YEAROUT, W. T., 1940
YORK, James A., 1907
YOUNG, F. Leo, 1929

Z

ZOFKO, Mickey, 1968-69-70

University of Florida

Location: Gainesville, Florida
Enrollment: 28,500
Nickname: Gators
Colors: Orange and Blue
Stadium: Florida Field (62,800)

University of Florida Head Coaching Records

COACH	YEAR	WON	LOST	TIED
Jack Forsythe	1906-'08	14	6	2
G. E. Pyle	1909-'13	26	7	3
Charles McCoy	1914-'16	9	10	0
A. L. Busser	1917-'19	7	8	0
William Kline	1920-'22	19	8	2
J. A. VanFleet	1923-'24	12	3	4
H. L. Sebring	1925-'27	17	11	2
Charles Bachman	1928-'32	27	18	3
D. K. (Dutch) Stanley	1933-'35	14	13	2
Josh Cody	1936-'39	17	24	2
Tom Lieb	1940-'45	20	26	1
Ray (Bear) Wolf	1946-'49	13	24	2
Bob Woodruff	1950-'59	54	41	6
Ray Graves	1960-'69	70	31	4
Doug Dickey	1970-'78	58	42	2

University of Florida All-Time Scores

1906		
16	Gnsvl. AC	6
3	Mercer	27
6	Rollins	0
19	Jksnvl. AC	0
2	Savannah AC	27
10	Athens AC	0
0	Rollins	6
39	Jksnvl. AC	0
95	(5-3-0)	66

1907		
6	Columbia AC	0
0	Mercer	6
21	Jksnvl. AC	0
9	Rollins	4
17	Jksnvl. AC	0
0	Rollins	0
53	(4-1-1)	10

1908		
0	Mercer	24
4	Jax AC	0
37	Gnsvl. AC	5
0	Rollins	6
6	Columbia AC	0
6	Stetson	5
37	Jksnvl. AC	0
0	Stetson	0
90	(5-2-1)	40

1909		
5	Gnsvl. AC	0
14	Rollins	0
O	Stetson	26
28	Rollins	3
11	Olympics	0
5	Stetson	5
28	Olympics	0
26	Tallahassee	0
117	(6-1-1)	34

1910		
23	Gnsvl. Grds.	0
0	Mercer	13
52	Georgia A&M	0
6	Citadel	2
38	Rollins	0
34	Charleston	0
33	Columbia Col.	0
186	(6-1-0)	15

1911		
15	Citadel	3
6	S. Carolina	6
6	Clemson	5
9	Columbia Col.	0
27	Stetson	0
21	Charleston	0
84	(5-0-1)	14

1912		
13	Auburn	27
10	S. Carolina	6
7	Ga. Tech	14
78	Charleston	0
23	Stetson	7
0	Mercer	0
44	Tampa AC	0
28	Vedado Club	0
203	(5-2-1)	54

1913		
144	Southern	0
0	Auburn	55
39	Maryville	0
3	Ga. Tech	13
0	S. Carolina	13
18	Citadel	13
24	Mercer	0
228	(4-3-0)	94

1914		
0	Auburn	20
36	Kings Col.	0
0	Sewanee	26
59	Southern	0
36	Wofford	0
7	Citadel	0
14	Mercer	0
152	(5-2-0)	46

1915		
0	Auburn	7
0	Sewanee	7
45	Southern	0
0	Georgia	39
6	Citadel	0
14	Tulane	7
34	Mercer	7
99	(4-3-0)	67

1916		
0	Georgia	21
0	Alabama	16
0	Tennessee	24
0	Auburn	20
3	Indiana	14
3	(0-5-0)	95

1917		
21	S. Carolina	13
0	Tulane	52
19	Southern	7
0	Auburn	68
7	Clemson	55
0	Kentucky	52
47	(2-4-0)	247

1918		
2	Cp. Johnson	14

1919		
33	Georgia A&M	2
48	Mercer	0
0	Georgia	16
0	Southern	7
2	Tulane	14

64 Stetson 0
13 S. Carolina 0
14 Oglethorpe 7

174 (5-3-0) 46

1920

21 Newberry 0
13 Southern 0
30 Mercer 0
0 Tulane 14
26 Stetson 0
0 Georgia 56
21 Stetson 0
0 Oglethorpe 21
1 Rollins 0

112 (5-3-0) 91

*Forfeit

1921

6 U.S. Infantry 0
33 Rollins 0
0 Carlstrom Fly 19
7 Mercer 0
0 Tennessee 9
34 Howard 0
7 S. Carolina 7
9 Alabama 2
7 Miss. College 7
21 Oglethorpe 3
10 N. Carolina 14

134 (6-3-2) 61

1922

6 Furman 7
19 Rollins 0
14 Amer. Legion 0
57 Howard 0
12 Oglethorpe 0
47 Clemson 14
0 Harvard 24
27 Tulane 6
58 Miss. College 0

240 (7-2-0) 51

1923

0 Army 20
7 Ga. Tech 7
28 Rollins 0
16 Wake Forest 7
19 Mercer 7
27 Stetson 0
53 Southern 0
13 Miss. State 13
18 Alabama 6

179 (6-1-2) 60

1924

77 Rollins 0
7 Ga. Tech 7
34 Wake Forest 0
7 Texas 7
27 Southern 0
7 Army 14
0 Mercer 10
27 Miss. State 0
10 Drake 0
16 Wash. & Lee 6

212 (6-2-2) 44

1925

24 Mercer 0
9 Southern 0
22 Hmptn.-Sidney 6
7 Ga. Tech 23
24 Wake Forest 3
65 Rollins 0
42 Clemson 0
0 Alabama 34
12 Miss. State 0
17 Wash. & Lee 14

222 (8-2-0) 80

1926

16 Southern 0
6 Chicago 12
7 Ole Miss 12
3 Mercer 7
13 Kentucky 18
9 Georgia 32
33 Clemson 0
0 Alabama 49
0 Hmptn.-Sydney 0
7 Wash. & Lee 7

94 (2-6-2) 137

1927

26 Southern 7
0 Davidson 12
33 Auburn 6
27 Kentucky 6
6 N. C. State 12
32 Mercer 6
0 Georgia 28
13 Alabama 6
20 Wash. & Lee 7
7 Maryland 6

164 (7-3-0) 96

1928

26 Southern 0
27 Auburn 0
73 Mercer 0
14 N. C. State 7
71 Sewanee 6
26 Georgia 6
27 Clemson 6
60 Wash. & Lee 6
12 Tennessee 13

336 (8-1-0) 44

1929

54 Southern 0
18 V.M.I. 7
19 Auburn 0
6 Ga. Tech 19
0 Harvard 14
18 Georgia 6
13 Clemson 7
20 S. Carolina 7
25 Wash. & Lee 7
20 Oregon 6

119 (8-2-0) 73

1930

45 Southern 7
27 N. C. State 0
7 Auburn 0
19 Chicago 0
13 Furman 14
0 Georgia 0
0 Alabama 20
27 Clemson 0
55 Ga. Tech 7
6 Tennessee 13

199 (6-3-1) 61

1931

35 N. C. State 0
0 N. Carolina 0
12 Syracuse 33
13 Auburn 12
6 Georgia 33
0 Alabama 41
6 S. Carolina 6
0 Ga. Tech 23
0 U.C.L.A 13
2 Kentucky 7

74 (2-6-2) 168

1932

19 Sewanee 0
27 Citadel 7
6 N. C. State 17
12 Georgia 33
13 N. Carolina 18
6 Auburn 21
0 Ga. Tech 6
13 Tennessee 32
12 U.C.L.A 2

108 (3-6-0) 136

1933

28 Stetson 0
31 Sewanee 0
0 N. C. State 0
9 N. Carolina 0
6 Tennessee 13
0 Georgia 14
7 Ga. Tech 19
14 Auburn 7
19 Maryland 0

114 (5-3-1) 53

1934

13 Rollins 2
20 Va. Tech 13
12 Tulane 28
14 N. C. State 0
0 Maryland 21
0 Georgia 14
13 Ole Miss 13
14 Auburn 7
13 Ga. Tech 12
14 Stetson 0

113 (6-3-1) 110

1935

34 Stetson 0
7 Tulane 19
6 Ole Miss 27
6 Maryland 20
0 Georgia 7
6 Kentucky 15
20 Sewanee 0
6 Ga. Tech 39
6 Auburn 27
22 S. Carolina 0

113 (3-7-0) 154

1936

20 Citadel 14
0 S. Carolina 7
32 Stetson 0
0 Kentucky 7
7 Maryland 6
8 Georgia 26
18 Sewanee 7
14 Ga. Tech 38
0 Auburn 13
0 Miss. State 7

99 (4-6-0) 125

1937

0 L.S.U. 19
18 Stetson 0
6 Temple 7
21 Sewanee 0
13 Miss. State 14
7 Maryland 13
6 Georgia 0
9 Clemson 10
0 Ga. Tech 12
0 Auburn 14
6 Kentucky 0

86 (4-7-0) 89

1938

14 Stetson 16
0 Miss. State 22
10 Sewanee 6
7 Miami 19
33 Tampa 0
0 Boston Col. 33
6 Georgia 19
21 Maryland 7
0 Ga. Tech 0
9 Auburn 7
12 Temple 20

112 (4-6-1) 149

1939

21 Stetson 0
0 Texas 12
0 Miss. State 14
7 Boston Col. 0
7 Tampa 0
14 Maryland 0
0 S. Carolina 6
2 Georgia 6
13 Miami 6
7 Ga. Tech 21
7 Auburn 7

78 (5-5-1) 66

1940

7 Miss. State 27
23 Tampa 0
0 Villanova 28
19 Maryland 0
0 Tennessee 14
18 Georgia 13
46 Miami 6
16 Ga. Tech 7
7 Auburn 20
0 Texas 26

136 (5-5-0) 141

1941

26 Rndlph.-Macon 0
0 Miss. State 6
46 Tampa 6
0 Villanova 6
12 Maryland 13
7 L.S.U. 10
3 Georgia 19
14 Miami 0
14 Ga. Tech 7
27 U.C.L.A. 30

149 (4-6-0) 97

1942

7 Jax NAS 20
45 Rndlph.-Macon 0
26 Tampa 6
6 Auburn 0
3 Villanova 13
12 Miss. State 26
0 Maryland 13
0 Georgia 75
0 Miami 12
7 Ga. Tech 20

106 (3-7-0) 185

1943-No Team

1944

36 Mayport NAS 6
6 Ole Miss 26
16 Jax NAS 20
0 Tennessee 40
13 Maryland 6
13 Miami 0
12 Georgia 38

96 (4-3-0) 136

1945

31 Cp. Blanding 2
26 Ole Miss 13
6 Tulane 6
0 Vanderbilt 7
6 Miami 7
45 SW Louisiana 0
0 Auburn 19
0 Georgia 34
41 Presbyterian 0
0 US Amphibs 12

155 (4-5-1) 100

1946

7 Ole Miss 13
13 Tulane 27
0 Vanderbilt 20
13 Miami 20
19 N. Carolina 40
14 Georgia 33
20 Villanova 27
6 N. C. State 37
12 Auburn 47

104 (0-9-0) 264

1947

6 Ole Miss 14
12 N. Texas St. 20
14 Auburn 20
7 N. C. State 6
7 N. Carolina 35
34 Furman 7
6 Georgia 34
7 Tulane 7
7 Miami 6
25 Kansas State 7

125 (4-5-1) 156

1948

0 Ole Miss 14
28 Tulsa 14
16 Auburn 9
41 Rollins 12
7 Ga. Tech 42
39 Furman 14
12 Georgia 20
15 Kentucky 34
27 Miami 13
28 Alabama 34

213 (5-5-0) 206

1949

13 Citadel 0
40 Tulsa 7
14 Auburn 14
17 Vanderbilt 22
14 Ga. Tech 43
28 Furman 27
28 Georgia 7
0 Kentucky 35
13 Miami 28
13 Alabama 35

180 (4-5-1) 218

1950

7 Citadel 3
27 Duquesne 14
13 Ga. Tech 16
27 Auburn 7
31 Vanderbilt 27
19 Furman 7
6 Kentucky 40
0 Georgia 6
14 Miami 20
13 Alabama 41

157 (5-5-0) 181

1951

13 Wyoming 0
27 Citadel 7
0 Ga. Tech 27
40 Loyola (Calif.) 7
13 Auburn 14
33 Vanderbilt 13
6 Kentucky 14
6 Georgia 7
6 Miami 21
30 Alabama 21

174 (5-5-0) 131

1952

33 Stetson 6
14 Ga. Tech 17
33 Citadel 0
54 Clemson 13
13 Vanderbilt 20
30 Georgia 0
31 Auburn 21
12 Tennessee 26
43 Miami 6

27 Kentucky 0
290 (7-3-0) 109

Gator Bowl
14 Tulsa 13

1953
16 Rice 20
0 Ga. Tech 0
13 Kentucky 26
45 Stetson 0
60 Citadel 0
21 L.S.U. 21
7 Auburn 16
21 Georgia 7
7 Tennessee 9
10 Miami 14
200 (3-5-2) 113

1954
14 Rice 34
13 Ga. Tech 12
19 Auburn 13
7 Clemson 14
21 Kentucky 7
7 L.S.U. 20
7 Miss. State 0
13 Georgia 14
14 Tennessee 0
0 Miami 14
115 (5-5-0) 128

1955
20 Miss. State 14
7 Ga. Tech 14
0 Auburn 13
28 Geo. Wash. 0
18 L.S.U. 14
7 Kentucky 10
19 Georgia 13
0 Tennessee 20
6 Vanderbilt 21
6 Miami 7
111 (4-6-0) 126

1956
26 Miss. State 0
20 Clemson 20
8 Kentucky 17
7 Rice 0
21 Vanderbilt 7
21 L.S.U. 6
20 Auburn 0
28 Georgia 0
0 Ga. Tech 28
7 Miami 20
158 (6-3-1) 98

1957
27 Wake Forest 0
14 Kentucky 7
20 Miss. State 29
22 L.S.U. 14
0 Auburn 13
22 Georgia 0
14 Vanderbilt 7
0 Ga. Tech 0
14 Miami 0
133 (6-2-1) 70

1958
34 Tulane 14
7 Miss. State 14
21 U.C.L.A. 14
6 Vanderbilt 6
7 L.S.U. 10
5 Auburn 6
7 Georgia 6
51 Ark. State 7
21 Fla. State 7
12 Miami 9
171 (6-3-1) 93

Gator Bowl
3 Ole Miss 7

1959
30 Tulane 0
14 Miss. State 13
55 Virginia 10
13 Rice 13
6 Vanderbilt 13
0 L.S.U. 9
0 Auburn 6
10 Georgia 21
18 Fla. State 8
23 Miami 14
169 (5-4-1) 107

1960
30 Geo. Wash. 7
3 Fla. State 0
18 Ga. Tech 17
0 Rice 10
12 Vanderbilt 0
13 L.S.U. 10
7 Auburn 10
22 Georgia 14
21 Tulane 6
18 Miami 0
144 (8-2-0) 74

Gator Bowl
13 Baylor 12

1961
21 Clemson 17
3 Fla. State 3
14 Tulane 3
10 Rice 19
7 Vanderbilt 0
0 L.S.U. 23
0 Ga. Tech 20
21 Georgia 14
15 Auburn 32
6 Miami 15
97 (4-5-1) 146

1962
19 Miss. State 9
0 Ga. Tech 17
21 Duke 28
42 Texas A&M 6
42 Vanderbilt 7
0 L.S.U. 23
22 Auburn 3
23 Georgia 15
20 Fla. State 7
15 Miami 17
204 (6-4-0) 132

Gator Bowl
17 Penn State 7

1963
0 Ga. Tech 9
9 Miss. State 9
35 Richmond 28
10 Alabama 6
21 Vanderbilt 0
0 L.S.U. 14
0 Auburn 19
21 Georgia 14
27 Miami 21
7 Fla. State 0
130 (6-3-1) 119

1964
24 S.M.U. 8
16 Miss. State 13
30 Ole Miss 14
37 S. Carolina 0
14 Alabama 17
14 Auburn 0
7 Georgia 14
7 Fla. State 16
12 Miami 10
20 L.S.U. 6
181 (7-3-0) 98

1965
24 Northwestern 14
13 Miss. State 18
14 L.S.U. 7
17 Ole Miss 0
28 N. C. State 6
17 Auburn 28
14 Georgia 10
51 Tulane 13
13 Miami 16
30 Fla. State 17
221 (7-3-0) 129

Sugar Bowl
18 Missouri 20

1966
43 Northwestern 7
28 Miss. State 7
13 Vanderbilt 0
22 Fla. State 19
17 N. C. State 10
28 L.S.U. 7
30 Auburn 27
10 Georgia 27
31 Tulane 10
16 Miami 21
238 (8-2-0) 135

Orange Bowl
27 Ga. Tech 12

1967
14 Illinois 0
24 Miss. State 7
6 L.S.U. 37
35 Tulane 0
27 Vanderbilt 22
21 Auburn 26
17 Georgia 16
28 Kentucky 12
16 Fla. State 21
13 Miami 20
201 (6-4-0) 161

1968
23 Air Force 20
9 Fla. State 3
31 Miss. State 14
24 Tulane 3
7 N. Carolina 22
14 Vanderbilt 14
13 Auburn 24
0 Georgia 51
16 Kentucky 14
14 Miami 10
151 (6-3-1) 175

1969
59 Houston 34
47 Miss. State 35
21 Fla. State 6
18 Tulane 17
52 N. Carolina 2
41 Vanderbilt 20
12 Auburn 38
13 Georgia 13
31 Kentucky 6
35 Miami 16
329 (8-1-1) 187

Gator Bowl
14 Tennessee 13

1970
21 Duke 19
34 Miss. State 13
15 Alabama 46
14 N.C. State 6
38 Fla. State 27
30 Richmond 0
7 Tennessee 38
14 Auburn 63
24 Georgia 17
24 Kentucky 13
13 Miami 14
224 (7-4-0) 256

1971
6 Duke 12
10 Miss. State 13
0 Alabama 38
13 Tennessee 20
7 L.S.U. 48
17 Fla. State 15
27 Maryland 23
7 Auburn 40
7 Georgia 49
35 Kentucky 24
45 Miami 16
174 (4-7-0) 298

1972
14 S.M.U. 21
28 Miss. State 13
42 Fla. State 13
7 Alabama 24
16 Ole Miss 0
20 Auburn 26
7 Georgia 10
40 Kentucky 0
3 L.S.U. 3
17 Miami 6
24 N. Carolina 28
218 (5-5-1) 144

1973
21 Kansas St. 10
14 Sou. Miss. 13
12 Miss. State 33
3 L.S.U. 24
14 Alabama 35
10 Ole Miss 13
12 Auburn 8
11 Georgia 10
20 Kentucky 18
14 Miami 7
49 Fla. State 0
180 (7-4-0) 171

Tangerine Bowl
7 Miami (0) 16

1974
21 California 17
17 Maryland 10
29 Miss. State 13
24 L.S.U. 14
10 Vanderbilt 24
21 Fla. State 14
30 Duke 13
25 Auburn 14
16 Georgia 17
24 Kentucky 41
31 Miami 7
251 (8-3-0) 184

Sugar Bowl
10 Nebraska 13

1975
40 S.M.U. 14
7 N. C. State 8
27 Miss. State 10
34 LSU 6
35 Vanderbilt 0
34 Fla. State 8
24 Duke 16
31 Auburn 14
7 Georgia 10
48 Kentucky 7
15 Miami 11
302 (9-2-0) 104

Gator Bowl
0 Maryland 13

1976
21 N. Carolina 24
49 Houston 14
34 Miss. State 30
28 LSU 23
33 Fla. State 26
20 Tennessee 18
24 Auburn 19
27 Georgia 41
9 Kentucky 28
50 Rice 22
19 Miami 10
314 (8-3-0) 255

Sun Bowl
14 Texas A&M 37

1977
48 Rice 3
24 Miss. State 22
14 LSU 36
17 Pittsburgh 17
27 Tennessee 17
14 Auburn 29
22 Georgia 17
7 Kentucky 14
38 Utah 29
31 Miami 14
9 Florida State 37
251 (6-4-1) 235

1978
25 SMU 35
34 Miss. State 0
21 LSU 34
12 Alabama 23
31 Army 7
13 Ga. Tech 17
31 Auburn 7
22 Georgia 24
18 Kentucky 16
21 Florida State 38
21 Miami 22
249 (4-7-0) 223

University of Florida Football Lettermen—1906 to 1978

A

ABBOTT, Frederic Marshall, 1970-71-72
ABDELHOUR, Thomas Allen, 1967-68-69
ADAMS, Lawrence Herbert, 1971-74
ADAMS, Roger, 1944
ADKINS, Mitty, 1948-49
ADKINS, Robert Maurice, 1974-77
AGEE, Joseph Ryan, III, 1969
ALBERTSON, Arthur, 1906
ALBURY, Charles D., 1968-69
ALDERMAN, Tom, 1906
ALLEN, Major General Chester, 1928
ALLEN, Joseph Louis, 1973-74-75
ALLEN, Richard Archer, 1959
ALLEN, Richard B., 1955
ALVAREZ, Carlos, 1969-70-71
AMELUNG, Frank Albert, Jr., 1967-68-69
ANDERSON, Anthony Leon, 1973-74
ANDERSON, B. G., 1920
ANDERSON, C. A., 1919-20
ANDERSON, Jerry David, 1964-65-66
ANDERSON, Kris Hoffman, 1971-72-73
ANDERSON, R. T., 1931
ANDERSON, Tom, 1931
ANDERSON, W. F., 1925
ARFARAS, Nicholas John, 1960-61
ASH, Terry Dean, 1970
AUST, Clifton Elwood, 1971-72-73
AYDT, Timothy E., 1975-76-77
AYERS, William, 1957-58

B

BAESZLER, Marquis C., 1964-65-66
BAGWELL, Archie, 1940
BAKER, Henry, 1908-09
BAKER, P. O., 1916-19-20
BALAS, Leonard Charles, 1950-51-52
BALL, Clinton Robert, 1973-74-75
BARBER, John, 1942
BARBER, Vernon Stanley, 1973-74-75-76
BARCHAN, Joseph, 1922
BARFIELD, John Wayne, 1965-66-67
BARKER, Allie, 1931
BARNES, Donald L., 1952
BARNHART, David L., 1968
BARR, Jimmy Darrell, 1969-71
BARRINGTON, Glenn, 1942
BARROW, John B., 1956
BARRS, Albert, 1906
BARTLESON, Charles, 1908
BASS, Billy, 1952-53-54
BATTEN, Thomas E., Jr., 1961
BATTISTA, Julius B., 1938-39-40
BEACH, James Eldridge, 1948
BEAVER, James Edward, 1959-60-61
BECK, Cecil, 1925-26-27
BECK, George, 1933
BECKMAN, Lars Eric, 1964-65
BECKWITH, Jack, 1933-34-35
BEELER, P. R., 1912
BELDEN, Douglas R., 1947
BELL, Reed, 1944
BELL, William Richard, 1977-78
BENNEK, William Joseph, 1977-78
BENNETT, Bruce, 1964-65
BENNETT, Franklin, 1936
BENO, Andy, 1939
BENSON, James Edward, Jr., 1964-65-66
BENTFROU, W., 1921
BERNHARD, Drayton, 1931-32-33
BERNHARDT, James Thomas, III, 1964
BERRY, John J., 1938
BETHEA, L. R., 1930
BEUSSE, Carl, 1965-66
BEVIS, first name unknown, 1909
BIE, O. A., 1922
BILINSKI, Leo, 1933
BILYK, Gerald L., 1952-53-54
BISHOP, Homer, 1925
BISHOP, Howard, 1925-26-27
BISHOP, Thomas W., 1946-47
BLAIR, Richard Howard, 1957
BLAIR, Steven Starnes, 1975-76-77
BLALOCK, Jack, 1937-38
BLANK, Ralph, 1941
BLAVI, Richard H., 1957
BLUDWORTH, David Howard, 1961
BOARDMAN, Hollis Cassell, 1971-72-73
BOEDY, Robert Frederick, 1972-73
BOLTON, William Oakley, Jr., 1954-55-56
BOND, John S., Jr., 1924
BOND, William B., 1928
BONEY, Clark Howell, Jr., 1955-56-57
BONO, Louis, 1927-28
BOOKER, William Edward, 1956-57-58
BOOTH, James Kenneth, 1971
BOWDEN, David Raymond, 1972-73
BOWEN, Hunter Stephen, 1969-70
BOWYER, Ernest J., 1926-27-28
BRACKEN, Andrew J., 1941-42
BRANCH, Harold T., 1946
BRANNON, C. S., 1917
BRANNON, Hill, 1950-51-52
BRANTLEY, John Walter, 1977-78
BRANTLEY, Richard Allen, 1957-58-59
BRANTLEY, Scot Eugene, 1976-77-78
BRAY, H. Thompson, 1947-48
BRETSCH, Kenneth P., 1957
BRINSON, Larry Sylvesta, 1973-74-75-76
BROADUS, Loren A., 1947-48-49-50
BROCK, Paul, 1936-37
BRODSKY, Joe, 1953-54-55-56
BRODSKY, Joseph, Jr., 1978
BROOKS, Hubert E., 1950-51-52
BROOKS, Rodney Andrew, 1978
BROWN, Aaron, 1948-49
BROWN, Donald E., 1949-50-51
BROWN, J. Alton, 1933-34-35
BROWN, Joseph Barry, 1964-65
BROWN, Merrell Russell, 1961-62-63
BROWN, Paul, 1932
BROWN, Ray Thomas, 1952-53-54-55
BROWN, Richard, 1923-24-25
BROWN, Trell, 1977
BROWN, Wallace, 1933-34
BROWNE, Richard Scott, 1971-72-73
BRUMBAUGH, Carl, 1927-28
BRUMBY, Robert, 1924
BRYAN, Joe, 1927-28
BRYAN, William Emory, 1932-33
BRYANT, G. K., 1925
BUCHA, Mike, 1938-39-40
BUCHANAN, Richard Alvin, 1969-70-71
BUCK, Shaw, 1931
BUIE, A. P., 1910-11-12-13
BULLOCK, Carlos E., 1933
BULLOCK, J. R., 1911-12-13
BURCH, Shannon Leonard, 1978
BURDGESS, Derrick E., 1977-78
BURFORD, Robert Ray, 1954-55-56
BURGESS, John E., 1952-53-54-55
BURKE, William C., 1954
BURNETT, John, 1925
BURNETT, R. H., 1921
BURNS, Jack C., 1968-69-70
BURROUGHS, John, 1935
BUSHNELL, Byron, 1915
BUTLER, Alvin Bernard, 1972-73-74
BUTLER, Gene, 1932
BUTZ, Clyde Owen, 1959
BYERS, Bernarr M., 1968
BYRD, C. Y., 1922
BYRGE, Earl, 1965

C

CAHILL, Leo, 1939-40-41
CAIN, Herbert Allen, 1976
CAIN, John Jeffrey, 1976
CALLAHAN, Melton Victor, 1965
CAMERON, Glenn Scott, 1972-73-74
CANOVA, W. F., 1917
CANSLER, Dale Bruce, 1958-59
CAPPLEMAN, H. L., 1909-14
CARD, Jack Dennis, 1964-65-66
CARLTON, James M., 1952
CARLTON, R. A., 1922
CARLTON, T. Hoyt, 1920-21
CARPENTER, Darrell Franklin, 1973-74-75-76
CARR, Earl, 1975-76-77
CARR, William Curtis, 1964-65-66
CARTE, B. S., 1944-45-46
CARVER, Corlis, R., 1947-48-49
CARY, Stanley, 1942
CASARES, Richard J., 1951-52-53
CASE, Lawrence, 1923
CASEY, Charles Arthur, 1964-65
CASH, William K., 1960-61-62
CASSIDY, Arch W., 1953-54
CAWEN, William, 1941
CAWTHON, Rainey, 1927-28-29
CHAMPLON, Ralph, 1925
CHANDLER, Don Gene, 1954-55
CHANDLER, Wesley Sandy, 1974-75-76-77
CHAPLIN, Charlie, 1930
CHAPLIN, James, 1924-25-26
CHAPMAN, Howard Garland, 1952-53
CHARLES, William, 1932
CHASE, L. C., 1922
CHASE, W. W., 1933-34-35
CHENEY, Andrew Bruce, 1969-70
CHERRY, H. Spurgeon, 1930-31
CHESSER, Joe E., 1945-46-47
CHORNIEWY, Thomas Francis, 1973
CHRISTIAN, Floyd, 1934-35-36
CHRISTIAN, Floyd T., Jr., 1966-67-68
CHRISTIE, W. M., 1912
CIANCI, Tony, 1939-40-41
CLARK, Carroll Harvin, Jr., 1969-70-71
CLARK, Michael Hugh, 1978
CLARKE, Hagood, III, 1961-62-63
CLEMONS, Gordon, 1917-18-19
CLEMONS, Justin, 1926-27-28
CLEMONS, W. N., 1928-29-30
CLIETT, Gary, 1964-65
CLIFFORD, John Jerome, 1970-71-72
CLIFFORD, Thomas Alan, 1973-74-75
CLIFTON, William, 1962
CLINE, James Lawrence, 1974-75-76-77
COARSEY, J. M., 1911-12-13
COBBE, Charles T., 1932
COBURN, Henry Kyle, 1977-78
COCHRAN, James, 1949
CODY, Ernest, 1938
COE, Harry, 1906
COLE, John, 1964-65-66
COLE, Marshall, 1969-70
COLE, Samuel, 1948
COLEMAN, Robert Wesley, 1968-69
COLEMAN, Ronald L., 1976-78
COLLINS, Chester T., Jr., 1959-60-61
COLLINS, Juan Lorenzo, 1977-78
COLLINS, P. F., 1915-16
COLLINSWORTH, Anthony Cris 1977-78
COLSON, Gordon Wallace, 1964-65
CONDON, Thomas Franklin, 1971
CONNELL, H. R., 1917-18-19
CONOVER, William L., 1978
CONRAD, Gene Gray, 1970-71
COONS, John D., 1966-67
CORBETT, Roy, 1906-07-08
CORNWALL, Sam, 1923-24
CORRY, William W., 1940-41-42
COWANS, Alvin Jeffrey, 1973-74-75-76
COWEN, J. William, 1939-40-41
COWSERT, J. T., 1914
COX, Abner, 1935
COX, Asa Joseph, 1957-58-59
COX, John O'Neal, 1921
COX, John O'Neal, Jr., 1948-49
CRABTREE, Clyde, 1927-28-29
CRABTREE, John M., 1937-38
CRAWFORD, Jeff, 1961
CROSS, William Timothy, 1976
CULLER, John, 1931
CULPEPPER, J. Blair, 1957-58
CULPEPPER, Philip Bruce, 1960-61-62
CUMMINGS, Robert C., 1951
CUMMINS, John R., 1951
CUMMINS, Richard, 1951
CURTIS, Reid A., 1932
CUTFLIFFE, C. Paige, 1966

D

D'AGOSTINO, Joe A., 1951-52-53
D'AGUILE, Frank, 1942

DANIEL, Marvin Raymond, 1957
DARBY, Alvis Russell, 1973-74-75
DATY, Arthur, 1922
DAVID, Claude Lee, 1952
DAVIDSON, Peter Bertel, 1956-57-58
DAVIS, Calvin Jerome, 1978
DAVIS, Clyde, 1924-25-26
DAVIS, F. G., 1909-10-11
DAVIS, Henry Arthur, 1974-75
DAVIS, Joseph P., 1951
DAVIS, Nelson P., 1937
DAVIS, Robert Gene, 1952-53-54
DAVIS, Robert Stanley, 1973
DAVIS, Sam F., 1931-32-33
DEAL, Don Lee, 1958-59-60
DEAN, George R., 1966-67-68
DEAN, Thomas Floyd, 1960-61
DEARING, William Howard, 1953
DEDGE, Al, 1929
DeHOFF, Donald, 1927
DeHOFF, Willie, 1926-27-28
DeLANEY, Paul, 1937
DeLaTORRE, Stephen J., 1952-55
DEMPSEY, James Frank, 1946-47-48-49
DENNIS, Guy Durrell, 1966-67-68
DENT, John C., 1961-62-63
DeVANE, O. C., 1915-16-19
DEWELL, John, 1937
DICKEY, Donald Bruce, 1975-76
DICKEY, Douglas Adair, 1952-53
DIDIO, Nick, 1964-65-66
DILTS, Russell Joseph, 1958-59
DINGMAN, Virgil, 1945
DIXON, Ray C., 1922
DODD, Frank, 1918
DODD, Robert Lee, Jr., 1960-61
DODDRIDGE, Rock Edward, 1970
DODDS, Frank, 1918
DOEL, Duane Paul, 1970
DOLFI, Thomas Nello, 1975
DOLL, Ronald David, 1972
DONNELLY, Jay, 1965
DORMINY, Albert Clayton, 1972
DORSETT, Luke M. 1929-30-31-32
DORSEY, William J., 1966-67-68
DOTY, Arthur E., 1921-22
DOUGLAS, E. Dewayne, 1951-52
DOWDY, William Ernest, 1969-70-71
DOWLING, Ham, 1915
DOWNS, Bobby C., 1966-67
DREW, Horace, 1945
DRIGGERS, R., 1920
DuBOSE, Jimmy Dewayne, 1973-74-75
DuHART, Paul, 1942
DUNCAN, Fred H., 1921-22
DUNN, Edgar McAuley, Jr., 1961
DUNN, James Howard, 1956-57-58
DUNN, Henry Hampton, Jr., 1969
DUPREE, L. B., Jr., 1945
DUPREE, Lawrence Wallace, 1962-63-64
DUPREE, Michael Daniel, 1976–77-78
DURRANCE, Thomas Louis, 1969-70-71
DUVEN, Gary G., 1966-67-68
DYAL, Lawrence E., 1952
DYE, Dewey, 1918
DYER, James A., 1944-45

E

EARMAN, J. B., 1906
EASTMAN, Ward Taylor, 1973
EATON, James Millard, 1955-56
ECKDAHL, Jack Lee, 1967-68-69
EDGINGTON, Dan Thomas, 1957-58-59
EDMONDS, Maurice, 1950-51-52
EGGART, Dan, 1964
EGGERTON, D. C., 1909-10
ELLENBURG, James S., 1958-59
ELLER, Paul, 1938-39-40-41
ELY, Mark M., 1967-68-69
ELY, Stephen, 1968
EMBRY, W. E., 1914-15
EMMELHAINZ, Allen E., 1931
ENCLADE, Ronald, 1974-75-76-78
ENTZMINGER, Percy, 1941
ENTZMINGER, Wade Denton, 1961
EPPERT, Kenneth, 1934-35
EVANS, Frank, 1923
EVANS, James H., 1941
EVANS, John, 1937
EWALDSEN, Paul H., 1965-66
EWELL, Cecil Davis, Jr., 1960-61

F

FAIX, John W., 1968-70-71
FANNIN, David Earle, 1958-59
FARMER, Henry B., Jr., 1961-62
FARRIOR, J. Rex, Jr., 1913-14-15-16
FAVATA, Dr. John J., 1945
FEIBER, John Kincaid, 1964-65
FERNALD, G. F., 1917
FERRAZZI, S. W. 1931-32-33
FERRIGNO, Carmen, 1939-40-41
FIELD, Michael Scott, 1970
FIELDS, Charles, 1942-46-47
FIELDS, Wayne Gazelle, 1972-73-74-75
FIORILLO, William Stephen, 1978
FISHER, James Douglas, 1974-75-76
FISHER, Robin Lynn, 1978
FLEMING, Charles, 1933
FLEMING, Dan, 1958
FLEMING, Dennis Wayne, 1976
FLOURNOY, Melvin A., 1976-77
FLOWERS, Robert J., 1950-51
FLOYD, John Patrick, 1974
FOLDBERG, Henry Christian, 1971-72-73
FORBES, Robert G., 1944-46-47
FORCE, Wilbur H., 1947
FORD, Herbert G., 1920
FORRESTER, David Dee, 1975-76-77
FORRESTER, Dennis Dee, 1975-76-77
FOSTER, R. Edmund, III, 1968
FOUNTAIN, Johnny, 1931
FRANCO, Richard Joseph, 1969-70-71
FREEMAN, H. E., 1914
FREEMAN, Judson, 1934
FREEMAN, Wilson, 1938
FRENCH, James, 1949-50-51
FROMANG, Vernon Brian, 1976
FULLER, A. H., 1914-15-16-17
FULLER, General Tom, 1927
FULLER, William Leonard, 1970-71

G

GAFFNEY, Derrick Tyrone, 1975-76-77
GAFFNEY, Donald George, 1973-74-75
GAFFNEY, Johnny Anthony, 1978
GAFFNEY, Warren B., 1975-76-78
GAGNER, Larry, 1964-65
GAILEY, Thomas Chandler, 1971-72-73
GAISFORD, William J., 1967-68
GALLOWAY, David Lawrence, 1977-78
GALLOWAY, Harold, 1978
GARDNER, Alex, 1947-48-49
GARDNER, Earl, 1936
GARDNER, Gordon, 1937-38
GARRETT, Curtis Lamar, 1978
GEIGER, Carey Harris, 1971-72-73
GEORGE, Leonard, 1970-71-72
GERBER, Myron, 1949
GETZEN, James Glenn, 1970
GHESQUIERE, George David, Jr., 1967-68-69
GHOLSEN, Davis, 1942
GIANNAMORE, Lawrin Ferd, 1957-58-59
GIBBS, W. W., 1906-07-08
GILBERT, John W., 1946-47-48
GILBERT, Lewis Howe, Jr., 1975-76-77
GILBERT, Robert W., 1946
GILES, Donald Ralph, 1958
GILL, Charles Wilson, Jr., 1960
GILMARTIN, W. H., Jr., 1944-45
GIORDANO, Donald M., 1965-66-67
GLENN, Thomas E., 1967
GODWIN, Russell, 1948-49
GOFF, Clark, 1937-38-39
GOLDEN, Ben, 1936
GOLDEN, Timothy George, 1978
GOLDSTEIN, Goldy, 1923-24-25
GOLDSTEIN, Mark, 1926-27
GOLSBY, Jack K., 1914-15-16-19
GOODBREAD, Royce, 1927-28-29
GOODMAN, Donald Eugene, 1959-60-61
GOODYEAR, E D., 1931-32-33
GOWLAND, Jan Eric, 1970-71-72
GRAHAM, Joe G., 1944
GRAMLING, Donnie Lamar, 1968
GRANDOFF, Bert, 1928
GRANDY, Stuart George, 1964-65-66
GRAVES, Homer Eugene, 1958-59
GREBE, Daniel Eugene, 1976
GREEN, Kaye Carl, 1954-55
GREEN, Napoleon Jr., 1976-77
GREEN, Samuel Lee, 1972-73-74-75
GREEN, Tom, 1925-26
GREEN, Tony Edward, 1974-75-76-77
GREENE, Bobby Joe, 1958-59
GREENE, Harry, 1928-29
GREGORY, Leo, 1933
GREGORY, Thomas Ray, 1960-61
GRIFFETH, James Kenneth, Jr., 1975
GRIFFIN, H. H., 1946-47-48-49
GRIFFIN, James A., 1962
GRIFFIN, Skil, 1964
GRIFFITH, Clinton Douglas, Jr., 1972-73-74
GRIFFITH, Todd Wayne, Jr., 1967-68-69
GROVES, Cecil Timothy, 1977-78
GROVES, Fletcher, 1944-46-47-48
GRUETZMACHER, Robert, 1947-48-49
GUIDO, Michael Francis, 1977
GUNN, Errett F., 1921-22
GUNN W. W., 1919-20
GUNTER, William Bruce, 1971
GURKIN, Van Michael, 1970

H

HACKNEY, Robert Ross, 1972
HADDOCK, Thomas Eugene, 1952-53
HADLEY, James Frederick, 1967-68
HAGER, Teddy C., 1968-69-70
HAINES, Webber, 1929
HALL, Brady, 1945
HALL, H. E., 1917
HALL, James Elwood, Jr., 1962-63-64
HALL, Joe, 1930
HALL, John Lewis, Jr., 1950-51-52
HALL, Kenneth, 1944
HAMILTON, Elton Cecil, 1955
HAMILTON, Kenneth, 1944-45
HAMMACK, Malcolm, 1953-54
HAMMOCK, John Ellis, 1951-52
HANCOCK, A. Roy, 1910-13-14
HANCOCK, Frank, 1934
HANDCOCK, Tom, 1906
HANNA, E. B., 1939
HANSBERRY, William, 1969
HANSENBAUER, Edward P., 1941-42
HARDEN, M. C., 1945
HARDWICK, Joe, 1936
HARLOW, Joseph Greg, 1970-72
HARPER, Jack Riley, 1964-65
HARRELL, James Clarence, 1977-78
HARRELL, Robert Steven, 1969-70-71
HARRISON, John B., 1941
HARRISON, Thomas, 1939-40-41
HARRY, Cadillac, 1925
HASSETT, Buswell, 1937
HATCH, Charles Edwin, 1976-77-78
HATCH, Donald James, 1952-53-54
HATCHER, F., 1916
HAUGHTON, Mal, 1906-07-08
HAUSENBAUER, E. P. 1942
HAWKINS, Joe, 1948
HAWKINS, Robert Alexander, 1958-59
HAYGOOD, Attice Curt, 1952-53-54
HAYMAN, W. P., 1917
HAZELWOOD, Harold, 1948-49
HEALEY, Michael Joseph, 1967-68
HECKMAN, Velles Alvin, 1956-57-58
HEIDT, William Steven, 1964-65-66
HEINER, Webber, 1929
HELTON, Charles Kimberlin, 1967-68-69
HENDERSON, Jack, 1933
HENDERSON, W. B., 1913-14-15-16
HENDRICKS, Ray, 1944
HENDRICKS, T. M., 1936
HENRY, Robert, 1942
HERGERT, Joseph Martin, 1956-57-58
HESTER, Grant, 1944
HESTER, H. S., 1911-12-13
HEWKO, Eric, 1976
HEWLETT, Robert F., 1951
HICKENLOOPER, Walter Andrew, 1960-61-62
HICKLAND, A. J., 1933-34-35
HICKS, Dashwood, 1928-29
HICKS, Donald Henry, 1955-56-57
HICKS, Louis Edwin, 1961

HILL, Buster Eugene, 1954
HILL, O'Neal, 1942
HINTON, Dozyier, 1976-78
HIPP, Brian, 1968
HITCHCOCK, David Philip, 1971-72-73
HOBBS, Harry M., 1945-46
HOBBS, Russell D., 1944
HODGES, G. H., 1920-22
HOGAN, Fred, 1945
HOKENSTAD, Lloyd, 1922
HOLLAND, Walter Samuel, 1960-61-62
HONTAS, Mark James, 1972
HOOD, Charles Henry, 1970
HOOD, William Kenneth, 1958-59-60
HOOVER, Robert Raymond, 1960-61-62
HORNER, Ray, 1939-40
HORSEY, James F., Jr., 1942
HORTON, Robert Elmore, 1950-51-52
HORVATH, Robert D., 1949
HOSACK, Robert Lee, 1961-62
HOUGH, Wallace Oliver, Jr., 1978
HOUGHTALING, Doc, 1913
HOUSER, M. S., 1928-29
HOUSTON, Hubert, 1939-40
HOWARD, first name unknown, 1909
HOWELL, E. G., 1938
HOWELL, W. E., 1937-38
HOYE, Francis O., 1965
HUDSON, William David, 1957-58
HUERTA, Marcelino, 1947-48-49
HUGGINS, Floyd, 1950-51
HUGHES, Carlisle, 1934-35
HUGHES, Jimmie E., 1931-32-33
HULL, Milton, 1939-40-41
HUNGERBUHLER, Tom J., 1966-67
HUNSINGER, Charles Ray, 1946-47-48-49
HUNTER Daniel M., 1950-51-52-53
HUNTER, Jim, 1908
HURSE, William D., 1952
HUTCHERSON, Dale Lee, 1969-70-71
HUTCHINSON, Scott Rawls, 1974-75-76-77

I

IANNARELLI, Ronald John, 1972
IHRIG, Elmer, 1925
INFANTE, Gelindo, 1961-62
IVES, Thomas Wilbur, 1953
IVEY, R. H., 1935-36

J

JACKSON, James, 1949-50
JACKSON, R. B., 1964-65
JACKSON, Willie B., 1970-71-72
JACOBSEN, Edward Par, 1977
JACOBSON, first name unknown, 1909
JAMES, J. Wilbur, 1928-29
JAMES, James A., 1949
JAMES, John Wilbur, Jr., 1970-71
JAMES, Vernon Levone, 1976-77-78
JAMISON, W. K., 1942-46
JENKINS, Joe P., 1935
JETTER, Brian L., 1965-66-67
JOHNS, Edwin C., 1957
JOHNSON, David James, 1977-78
JOHNSON, E. Julian, Jr., 1965
JOHNSON, Fal L., 1947-48-49
JOHNSON, James Waring, 1978
JOHNSON, John W., 1956-57
JOHNSON, Leslie, 1910
JOHNSON R.G., 1910
JOHNSON, Robert F., 1938
JOHNSTON, Kent, 1906
JOHNSTON, Pat, 1906
JONES, A. J., 1941-42
JONES, C. Jerome, 1961-62-63
JONES, Edgar C., 1923-24-25
JONES, Jackie Dwight, 1959
JONES, Jesse D., 1934
JONES, Richard E., III, 1961-62
JONES, Roger Darrell, 1977-78
JORDAN, Jimmy Andrew, 1964
JUMPER, Arlen N., 1951-52

K

KANTER, Jeffrey Dean, 1975-76-77
KAPLAN, Phillip, 1942
KARAPHILLIS, Mike John, 1953
KATZ, Jack, 1962-63-64
KELLEY, James Michael, 1968-69-70
KELLEY, Tommy Rogers, 1961-62
KELLY, Mikey, 1950-52-53
KELLY, T. Paine, Jr., 1931-32
KELLY, William James, 1970
KELMAN, Ralph, 1938-39
KENDRICK, Preston, 1972-73-74
KENDRICK, Vincent, 1971-72-73
KENNELL, Thomas Henry, 1969
KENSLER, Richard Byard, 1970-71
KICLITER, Harry J., 1935-36
KIEFER, Steven Robert, 1976
KILEY, James Michael, 1968-69
KILLER, Clyde, 1964
KING, Mark, 1971
KING, Roswell, 1911
KING, Sylvester, 1975-76-77
KING, William Curtis, 1950-51-52
KIRCHNER, Clarence, 1927
KIRK, Dick, 1964-65
KIRK, James, 1906
KIRKPATRICK, Wesley, 1961
KLICKOVICK, Walter, 1941
KLUTKA, Nick, 1940-41-42
KNAPP, Donald Otis, 1964-65-66
KNIGHT, Robert V., 1950-51-54
KNOWLES, Hanford, 1949
KOCSIS, Frank, 1936-37-38
KONESTY, Floyd, 1940-41-42
KREIS, James Daryl, 1977-78
KREIJCIER, Charles, 1936-37
KRUSE, Jim Pane, 1973
KUSS, Ferdinand, 1945
KYNES, James Hiatt, 1972-73-74
KYNES, James W., Jr., 1946-47-48-49
KYNES, William Leland, 1975-76

L

LACER, John Barbour, 1971-72-73
LAGER, Willie, 1962-63
LAMB, Doug, 1966
LANCE, Robert F., 1954-55
LANE, Benny, 1939-40-41
LANE, Julian, 1934-35-36
LANE, Thomas, 1932-33
LaPETE, Frank Leroy, 1974-75
LaPRADD, Charles W., 1950-51-52
LASKY, Francis J., 1962-63
LASMIS, H. E., 1917
LATSKO, William, 1940-41-42
LAURENT, Eugene, 1936
LAVIN, Charles G., 1933
LAWLER, S. W., Jr., 1911-12
LAWLESS, Richard Burton, 1972-73-74
LeCOUNT, Terry, 1975-76-77
LEE, Eugene, O., 1942
LEE, Herbert C., 1957
LEE, William L., Jr., 1969
LEMON, Samuel, 1976
LENARD, Gary Wayne, 1976-77
LENFESTY, Sidney G., 1933
LEWIS, Lazarous, 1947-48-49
LIBERTORE, Lawrence Paul, Jr., 1960-61-62
LIGHTBOWN, Lynn E., 1937-38
LIGHTSEY, Spec, 1923-24
LITHERLAND, C. J., 1931
LITTLE, David Lamar, 1977-78
LIVINGSTON, Archibald, 1925
LOCKHART, Welton Perry, 1953-54
LOGAN, Kevin Richard, 1974-75
LONG, Buford Eugene, 1950-51-52
LOOMIS. H. E., 1917
LOPER, Gerald Calvin, 1973-74-75
LORENZO, Frank M., 1946-47-48-49
LOTSPIECH, A. A., 1913-14-15
LUCAS, Leonard LaVann, 1971
LUCEY, Don Truesdale, 1958-59
LUCKIE, Dock, 1977-78
LUCZKO, George, 1975
LYLE, Robert Telford, Jr., 1962-63-64

M

MacBETH, Jon Lowell, 1958-59-60
MACK, Joe, 1939-40-41
MACK, Sam Harry, 1961
MacLEAN, Sydney Wade, 1962-63-64
MADIGAN, James, 1932
MADISON, W., 1918
MAGGIO, Phillip James, 1965-66
MAHOOD, Jack, 1965-66
MALISKA, Paul Wm., 1967-68-69
MALLORY, LeRoy Thornton, 1971
MANN, Thomas David, 1967-68
MANNING, C. W., 1910
MANNING, Charles H., 1952-53-54
MANNING, Ed., Jr., 1936-37
MANRY, Daniel S., Jr., 1965
MARSHALL, A. P., 1917
MARTIN, Bruce, 1945
MARTIN, Hubert Bodie, Jr., 1952-53-54-55
MARTIN, Richard Charles, 1953-54
MATHENY, Charles, 1935
MATTHEWS, Jack, 1923
MATTHEWS, Lynn, 1964-65
MATTHEWS, Preston, 1966
MAY, Aurist, 1951-52-53
MAY, Jon Mardi, 1956
MAYBERRY, Walter, 1935-36-37
MAYNARD, Jack, 1937
MAYNARD, Zollie, 1934-35
MAYNOR, James Mark, 1974-75-76
McANLY, Herbert, 1933-35
McBRIDE, William A., 1968
McCALL, Wayne C., 1964-66-67
McCAMPBELL, George, 1932-33-34
McCANN, George H., 1966-67
McCARRON, Pat, 1965-66
McCARTY, John, 1936
McCLELLAN, Broward, 1930-31
McCLURE, James, 1957
McCORD, Guyte, 1906
McCOUN, Joseph Chrisman, 1971-72-73
McCRAVY, Daniel Wesley, 1971
McDANIEL, Ray, 1939
McDONALD, Carroll Wilks, 1949-50-51
McEWEN, J. Milton, 1928-29-30
McGHEE, Warren, 1937
McGONIGAL, Elroy Edward, 1956
MCGOWAN, William Albert, 1950-51
McGRIFF, Lee Colson, 1972-73-74
McGRIFF, Perry Colson, Jr., 1958-59
McIVER, Larry Leroy, 1954
McKEEL, Frederick Graham, 1964-66-67
McLEAN, Cecil, 1932
McLEAN, Kenneth, 1944
McMILLAN, Ralph Wendell, 1970
McMILLAN, Red, 1908
McNEAL, Raymond, 1941
McRAE, W. A., 1928-29-30
McRAE, Walter A., Jr., 1941-42
McTHENY, Guy Corbett, 1967-68-69
MEDVED, George P., 1953
MEISCH, Edmond, 1920
MERRIN, George, 1925-26
MERRIN, J. F., 1919-20-21
MERRIN, Joe, 1923-24
MERRITT, G., 1912
MIDDEN, Mark Brian, 1977-78
MIDDEN, Ray E., 1955-56-57
MIDDLEKAUF, Walter, 1933-34
MIDDLEKAUF, William, 1923-24-27
MILBY, Robert Vance, 1958-59
MILLER, H. M., 1945
MILLER, Hugo, 1942-45
MILLER, Waring T., 1935
MIMS, William O., 1942
MIRANDA, Victor Russell, 1957-58-60
MITCHELL, Carl, 1939-40-41
MITCHELL, Charles Foster, 1955-56-57
MITCHELL, Fondren, 1940-41-42
MITCHELL, Dr. W. H., 1908
MITCHUM, William Jewell, 1950-51
MONTSDEOCA, Fred, 1948-49-50
MOODY, John, 1908
MOONEY, Ottis A., 1944-45
MOORE, Eddy Lynn, 1970-71-73
MOORE, Michael Lindsey, 1971-72-73
MOORE, Nathaniel, 1972-73
MOORE, Robert Lewis, 1974-75-76
MORGAN, Jimmy S., 1962-63
MORGAN, L. Z., 1918-19
MORGAN, Ralph, 1946
MORGAN, Robert Edward II, 1974-75-76
MORRIS, Billy Frank, 1950-51-52
MORRIS, John, 1964
MORRIS, Ralph Larry, 1970-72
MORRIS, Terry E., 1966-67-68
MORRISON, Sherwood C., 1972-73-74
MORTELLARO, Paul, 1944-45-46-47
MOSELEY, G. R., 1913-14
MOUNTS, Mervin, 1921-22
MOYE, George, 1932-33-34
MUETH, Robert Henry, 1952
MULCAHY, James, 1937

MULLINIKS, Bruce Allan, 1974-75-76
MULLINS, L. D., 1936-37-38
MUNIZ, Frank L., 1946
MURPHREE, John A. H., 1923-24
MURPHY, Alvin Dennis, 1962-63-64

N

NALLS, Ronnie, 1961-62
NATYSHAK, John, 1948-49
NEILSON, ALfred, 1906
NEWBERN, William Alfred, 1956-57-58
NEWCOMER, Gerald Carl, 1962-63-64
NEWMAN, Mark Lester, 1976
NEWTON, R. D., 1921-22-23-24
NICHOLS, Jack Clyde, 1950-51-52
NOLAN, Jimmy, 1928-29-30
NORFLEET, Joe, 1930-31
NORRIS, Kenneth Leroy, 1959-60
NORTH, Merle, 1930-31
NORTON, Clyde, 1923-24-25
NORTON, Oscar H., 1918-19-20
NUGENT, William Scott, 1972-73

O

O'BRIAN, Jack E., 1951-52-53
OCCHIUZZI, Anthony, 1945
ODHAM, Glenn, 1945
ODOM, Gerald Spessard, 1960-62-63
O'DONNELL, James Dennis, 1961-62-63
OLIVA, John Ernest, 1961
OOSTERHOUDT, Frank, 1924-26
OOSTERHOUDT, Sam, 1950-51-52
ORTEGA, Ralph, 1972-73-74
OSGOOD, Simon, 1931
OSWALD, Douglas H., 1948-49
OVERMAN, C. H., 1909
OWENS, George, 1936
OWENS, Tom, 1926-27-28
OXFORD, James, 1936-37

P

PADGETT, Aubrey Gary, Jr., 1972-73
PAGE, Edward Eugene, 1959-60
PALAHACH, Michael, 1969
PALMER, first name unknown, 1909
PAPPAS, Jackie Louis, 1950-51
PARHAM, Harry, 1940-41
PARKER, Joseph Lee, 1971-72-73
PARKER, Paul, 1908
PARKER, Paul Plenge, 1972-74
PARKER, Wendell C., 1946-47-48
PARKER, W. E., 1948
PARNELL, Ed, 1952
PARNELL, Edward, 1929-30-31
PARNELL, Sidney, 1938-40
PARRISH, Alvin Leonard, 1975-76
PARRISH, Bernie Paul, 1956-57
PARTIN, Walter Douglas, 1958-59-60
PASTERIS, Joseph D., 1966-67
PATCHEN, Patrick N., 1958-59-60
PATSY, John, 1950-51
PAULSON, Gunnar Fortune, 1969
PAYNE, W. D., 1916
PEACOCK, Harold E., 1968
PEARSON, James Fred, 1961-62-63
PEDRICK, Jack, 1951
PEDRICK, Jack, 1927
PEEK, David Hudgins, 1970-71
PEEK, Eugene G., 1967-68
PEEK, Scott I., 1951
PEEK, Scott Irving, Jr., 1977
PELHAM, Louis Daniel, 1956-57
PENNINGTON, Fonia, 1936-37
PERRY, Carl E., 1916-19-20-21
PERRY, Henry, 1921
PETERS, Anton Berdette, Jr., 1961-62
PETERSEN, Gary Lee, 1970-71
PETTEE, Roger, 1962-63-64
PETTY, Richard Allen, 1950-51
PHARR, George M., 1945
PHARR, Phillip, 1978
PHEIL, Clarence E., 1929-30-31
PHILLIPS, James C., 1978
PICKELS, Richard Clayton, 1957
PILCHER, Ray C., Jr., 1970-71
PIOMBO, John, 1938-39-40
PIPPIN, Charles, 1966
PITTMAN, O. W., 1924
PLATT, Eugene A., 1942
PLATT, Harry T., Jr., 1941-42
PLESS, Glenn, 1927
POE, Alan, 1964-65
POFF, William David, 1970-71-72
POMEROY, Stewart, 1921-22-23
PORCH, Ben, 1935
PORTALE, Joseph James, 1976-77-78
POSEY, David Ellsworth, 1973-74-75-76
POUCHER, Gordon Leroy, 1950
POUNDS, Hoyle, 1911-12
POWELL, Brad, 1968-69-70
PRACEK, Robert Louis, 1959
PRATT, E. A., 1942
PRATT, Ralph Cleon, Jr., 1976-78
PRESTON, John Harvey, 1964-65-66
PRICE, Carl A., 1924
PRICE, J. C., 1912
PRICE, T. E., 1909-11-13
PRIEST, Ernest, 1934
PROCTOR, Carlos, 1929-30
PROCTOR, Ralph, 1925
PULESTON, Charles, 1906
PUPELLO, Joseph Charles, 1974-75-76
PURCELL, 1909
PURCELL, Robert Eugene, 1955
PURSELL, Ron, 1964-65

Q

QUINN, Reed G., 1951-52

R

RAASCH, Ezra, 1924
RABORN, W. W., 1946
RADAR, Ralph, 1906-08
RAMSDELL, A. W., 1913-14-15
RAMSEY, James, 1930
RAMSEY, Watson, 1938
RAWLS, Dr. James A., Jr., 1951
RAWLS, Vernon C., 1926
RAYBORN, William, 1941-42-46
REAVES, Thomas Johnson, 1969-70-71
REBOL, Richard, 1968-69
REDDELL, Billy, 1951
REEN, Patrick, 1938-40
REEVES, A. J., 1950-51
REEVES, Alex, 1927-28-29
REID, A. L., 1914
RENFROE, W., 1921
RENTZ, Ralph Larry, 1966-67-68
REVELS, James C., III, 1971-72-73
REYNOLDS, Joseph Robert, 1975
RHYNE, James Robert, 1958-59
RICH, Michael Lee, 1969-70-71
RICHARDS, Henry, 1931
RICHARDS, James Thomas, 1973-74-75
RICHBOURG, William Britton, 1962-63-64
RINGGOLD, Donald Wayne, 1960-61
RIPLEY, Wayne, 1926
RITTGERS, Rex Von, 1966
ROBERTS, Charles Avery, 1956-57-58
ROBINSON, Harold, 1933
ROBINSON, James, 1946
ROBINSON, Leffie Fred, 1952-54
ROBINSON, Rocky, 1970
ROBINSON, Tony Lewis, 1977-78
ROBINSON, W. M., 1921-22-23
ROBINSON, William B., 1941
ROBLES, O. S., 1915-16
ROGERO, A. L., 1930-31
ROGERS, Charles B., 1932-33-34
ROOD, R. S., 1916
ROOT, Charles, 1934-35-36
ROSE, J. R., 1924
ROSENHOUSE, M., 1921
ROSENTHAL, J. D., 1916
ROSS, Hugh A., 1944
ROSS, Ira Joseph, 1954
ROUBLES, O. S., 1916
ROUNTREE, James Woodrow, 1955-56-57
ROWE, Harold, 1934-35-36
ROWE, Richard Lew, 1950
ROYAL, Robert Daniel, Jr., 1958-59-60
ROZELLE, Frederick Edward, 1950
RUSHING, Dewell, 1944-47
RUSSELL, Kenneth Wayne, 1962-63-64
RUTH, Richard Eugene, 1976-77

S

SANTILLE, D. Michael, 1966
SAPP, E. B., Jr., 1944-45
SARRA, Lamar, 1924-25-26
SARRIS, George Tony, 1952
SAUERS, Robert, 1939-40
SAULS, Charles F., 1928-29-30
SAUNDERS, J. L., 1930-31
SAWYER, Ross C., 1905
SCARBOROUGH, Earl, 1945
SCARBOROUGH, Truman C., 1935
SCHANBACHER, Stephen F., 1977
SCHIRMER, Ernest, 1932
SCHMIDT, Carl Frederic, 1970
SCHMIDT, Robert, 1944
SCHNEBLY, John Martin, 1969-70-71
SCHROEDER, Douglas Wayne, 1976-77-78
SCHUCHT, Hubert, 1934-35
SCHULER, Scott Allan, 1975-76
SCHULTZ, Fred William, 1956-58
SCHUMAN, Carl, 1932-33
SCHWARTZBURG, Jim H., 1952-53-54
SCOTT, Ivan W., 1921-22
SCOTT, James, 1925
SCOTT, Laurence Clyde, 1952-53-54
SCOTT, Tom, 1938-39
SCOTT, William R., 1940
SEAL, Howard Kensel, 1974
SEALS, Roger Kyle, 1959-60
SEARS, Edwin R., 1955-56-57
SEAY, Homer, 1929-30-31
SENTERFITT, Donald Richmond, 1959-60
SEVER, Tyson Lee, 1972-73-74
SEVER, William Glenn, 1973-74
SEWELL, first name unknown, 1918
SEYMOUR, Harold Daily, 1964-65
SEYMOUR, Kenneth Earle, 1957
SHACKLEFORD, T. W., 1910
SHANDS, A. G., 1913
SHANDS, William A., 1908
SHANNON, Thomas Joseph, Jr., 1962-63-64
SHEARER, Welcome, 1932-33-34
SHEER, Thomas Lee, 1956-58
SHEPPARD, Joseph Earl, 1971-72
SHORTER, N. W., 1910
SHOUSE, A. G., 1933-34
SIKES, Michael Daniel, 1956
SILMAN, John Spencer, 1970
SILSBY, Link W., 1929-30-31
SIMPSON, Clay, 1931-32
SIMPSON, Jackie M., 1953-54-55-56
SINARDI, Nick Joseph, 1969
SKALASKI, Charles Wm., III, 1976-77
SKELLY, Richard James, 1960
SKOLDOWSKI, Ziggy, 1945
SKRIVANEK, Britt Edward, 1967-68-69
SLACK, Arthur Ronald, 1958-59-60
SMITH, first name unknown, 1909
SMITH, Charles Edward, 1950
SMITH, Glenn, 1944
SMITH, Horace, 1923-24
SMITH, James, 1949
SMITH, John G., 1938-39
SMITH, Johnny Wayne, 1978
SMITH, Michael Bernard, 1973-74-75
SMITH, Mills, 1927
SMITH, Robert Dean, 1954
SMITH, Thomas Ruel, Jr., 1959-60-61
SMITH, W. Lawrence, 1966-67-68
SMOAK, D. Frank, 1938-39-40
SNEED, Neal, 1964-65
SORENSON, Douglas, 1969-70-71
SPARKMAN, James K., 1914-15-16-19
SPEARS, Harry Gordon, 1953-56
SPIERS, W. H., 1931
SPLANE, T. Douglas, 1965-66-67
SPURRIER, Stephen Orr, 1964-65-66
STADLER, John, 1929
STANFIELD, Michael David, 1972-73-74
STANLEY, Dennis K., 1926-27-28
STANLEY, Will A., 1925
STANLY, George, 1921
STANLY, Richard Lee, 1921
STAPLES, Russell F., 1961-62
STARBUCK, Hal, 1932-33-34
STARK, William D., 1932-33-34
STARKEY, David Bruce, 1972-73
STARLING, Bruce Cordell, 1960-61
STEELE, Jimmy, 1928-29-30
STEEN, Malcolm Everett, 1967-68-69
STEPHENS, G. H., 1960
STEPHENS, Jimmy Ray, 1973-75-76
STEPHENS, Robert Louis, 1971
STEPHENS, Tony Roderick, 1976-77-78

STEPHENS, William B., 1935
STEPHENSON, George Kay, 1966
STEVENS, Kent S., 1950-52
STEWART, Jack, 1924-25-26
STOCKTON, C. A., 1915-16
STOLZ, Charles, 1932-33-34
STONE, W. E., 1917
STONER, Ronald Eugene, 1961
STORTER, Neil S., 1909-10-11
SUBERS, James Innes, 1978
SULLIVAN, George Theodore, 1975
SULLIVAN, Haywood C., 1950-51
SUMMERS, Jacob Anderson, 1972-73-74
SUMNER, Kenneth Milton, 1951-52
SUTHERLAND, George, 1942-46
SUTTON, Clifford, 1946-47-48-49
SUTTON, John, 1912-13
SUTTON, Yancey M., 1977-78
SWAFFORD, Donald L., 1976-77-78
SWANSON, E., 1919
SWANSON, R. M., 1920-21
SWANSON, T. J., 1910-11-13-14
SWANZ, Robert James, 1975-76-77
SWINK, P. C., 1917
SYMANK, John Richard, 1955-56

T

TAGGERT, George Eric, 1970
TALBOT, Randy William, 1972-73-74
TANNEN, Steven Olson, 1967-68-69
TATE, Charlie, 1939-40-41
TATUM, Earl, 1956
TATUM, Jim, 1956
TAYLOR, Earl A., 1908-10-11-12
TAYLOR, J., 1908
TAYLOR, James, J., 1952
TAYLOR, Ted, 1938
TENNELL, Gregory Lee V., 1975-77
TENNEY, Louis Earl, 1910-11-12-13
THOMAS, Clarence S., 1917-19
THOMAS, Gary, 1964-65
THOMAS Owen Jerome, 1951
THOMAS, Philip E., 1921
THOMPSON, Charlie, 1906-08
THOMPSON, Harry W., 1914-15
THOMPSON, Jack Bernard, III, 1961-62-63
THOMPSON, John Clark, 1960
THOMPSON, Tim Ewell, 1974
THRASHER, first name unknown, 1909
TODD, Edgar R., 1924-25
TOLBERT, H. L., 1921
TOTTEN, Mark Alan, 1975-76-77
TRAMMELL, Allen Raymond, Jr., 1964-65
TRAPP, Richard E., 1965-66-67
TRAVIS, Larry Lee, 1960-61
TREADGOLD, R. J., 1931-32
TRIBBLE, Keith Reginald, 1974-75-76
TRUEHEART, Harold S., Jr., 1961-62
TUCKER, Charles, 1926-27
TUCKER, D. A., 1916
TUCKER, John, 1964
TURMAN, Lloyd A., 1967-68
TURNER, James Morris, 1944
TURNER, Jess L., 1931
TURNER, William E., 1946-47-48-49
TURNER, William F., 1933-34-35

U

USPENSKY, Michael Nicholas, 1969

V

VACCARO, Gasper V., 1946-47-48-49
VAN CAMP, R. K., 1914
VANDERGRIFF, J. H., 1920
VAN FLEET, Richard, 1908
VANGELAS, Thomas, 1945
VANSICKEL, Dale, 1927-28-29
VARGECKO, Paul John, 1959-60-61
VAUGHN, Lane Waring, 1974
VAUGHN, Sidney, 1945
VETTER, Emerson, 1939
VICKERY, Charles, 1929
VIDAL, James H., 1908
VINESETT, Jerry D., 1968-69-70
VISSER, Robert Henry, 1955
VOOR, Joseph Bernard, 1978
VOSLOH, Robert Paul, 1954-55-56

W

WAGES, Harmon, L., 1966-67
WAGGENER, J. A., 1910
WAHLBERG, Joel David, 1956-57
WALDRON, Jesse C., 1931
WALKER, Barry Steven, 1977-78
WALKER, Garry L., 1968-69-70
WALKER, Ion, 1926-27
WALKER, L. B., 1938
WALKER, Tom B., 1936-37-38
WALKER, W. S., 1909
WALTON, W. L., 1938-39-40
WARBRITTON, William Randolph, 1970
WARE, Charles Edward, 1950-51-52
WARE, Melton, 1934
WARNER, Edwin R., 1966
WARNER, Henry, 1919
WARREN, W. T., 1934-35-36
WATERS, Anthony Nealy, 1977-78
WATERS, Dale, 1928-29-30
WATSON, Richard O., 1952
WAXMAN, Mike, 1964-65
WEBSTER, H. Allison, 1947
WEBSTER, W. J., 1951
WEHKING, Robert Jean, 1959-60-61
WELCH, James John, 1969
WELLES, Frank, 1936
WESLEY, Larry Eustace, 1954-55-56
WESTBROOK, Jack Eugene, 1958-59
WESTER, William J., 1951
WHATLEY, John, 1964-65
WHIDDON, Clifford, 1937
WHITE, Jack, 1944-45-46
WHITE, Paul Edward, 1959-60-61
WHITEHEAD, James Orlin, 1954
WHITTAKER, Glenn, 1925
WHITTAKER, John Lee, 1978
WHITTINGTON, Arling, 1944
WICKLINE, Gregory Joe, 1978
WIGGINS, Lloyd Gregory, 1970
WILDER, Willie B., 1975-76-77
WILDMAN, Charles Frederick, 1973-75
WILKINSON, S. A., 1915-16-17
WILLIAM, Buton C., 1923-24-25
WILLIAMS, Alan Kenton, 1976-77
WILLIAMS, Angus, 1945-48-49-50
WILLIAMS, Bill, 1936-37
WILLIAMS, Bud, 1964-65
WILLIAMS, Burton C., 1965
WILLIAMS, Charles, 1974-75-76-77
WILLIAMS, Charles Broughton, 1942-46
WILLIAMS, Daniel Marvin, 1969-70
WILLIAMS, Donald E., 1968-69-70
WILLIAMS, John Daniels, 1972-73-75
WILLIAMS, Roderic Michael, 1973-74-75
WILLIAMS, Terry Claitte, 1978
WILLIAMSON, H. E., 1932
WILLIAMSON, J. D., 1930-31
WILLIAMSON, Kendrick Wayne, 1957-58-59
WILLIAMSON, Larry Cline, 1969
WILLIS, Frank, 1936
WILLIS, Kenneth, 1935-36-37
WILSKY, C., 1921
WILSON, C., 1921
WILSON, R. Borden, 1912
WINDHAM, Joseph Nathan, 1956-57-58
WING, Harry Fannin, 1952
WINNE, Ross Wesley, Jr., 1952-53-54
WINTERS. Alex Prior, 1975
WOLFE, Stanley, 1926
WOOD, G. P., 1916
WOOD, Sidney, 1942
WRIGHT, Arthur J., 1951-52-53
WRIGHT, David Alexander, 1975-76-77
WRIGHT, Joe Lawrence, 1950
WRIGHT, Weldon, 1945
WUNDERLY, Joseph Alan, 1973-74
WUTHRICH, E. B., 1917-18-19-21
WYNN, Milton, 1944

Y

YANCEY, Harvey, 1930
YANCEY, James, 1947-48-49
YANCEY, James Mitchell, 1969-70-71
YANCEY, Malcolm, 1919
YARBROUGH, James, 1966-67-68
YEATS, James Melvin, 1955-56-57
YEPREMIAN, Berj Sarkis, 1977-78
YINSHANIS, Frank, 1938
YON, E. M., 1914-15
YORK, M. E., 1952
YOUNG, James Winston, 1959-60-61
YOUNGBLOOD, Herbert Jackson, 1968-69-70

Z

ZUKLEY, Jack Ed, 1975-76

University of Georgia

Location: Athens, Georgia
Enrollment: 22,000
Nickname: Bulldogs
Colors: Red and Black
Stadium: Sanford (59,200)

University of Georgia Head Coaching Records

COACH	YEARS	WON	LOST	TIED
Dr. Charles Herty	1892	1	1	0
Ernest Brown	1893	2	2	1
Robert Winston	1894	5	1	0
Glenn S. "Pop" Warner	1895-'96	7	4	0
Charles McCarthy	1897-'98	6	3	0
Gordon Saussy	1899	2	3	1
E. E. Jones	1900	2	4	0
Billy Reynolds	1901-'02	5	7	3
M. M. Dickinson	1903; 1905	4	9	0
Charles A. Barnard	1904	1	5	0
W. S. Whitney	1906-'07	6	7	2
Branch Bocock	1908	5	2	1
J. Coulter & Frank Dobson	1909	1	4	2
W. A. Cunningham	1910-1916; 1919	43	18	9
H. J. Stegeman	1920-'22	20	6	3
George Woodruff	1923-'27	30	16	1
Harry Mehre	1928-'37	59	34	6
Joel Hunt	1938	5	4	1
Wallace Butts	1939-'60	140	86	9
Johnny Griffith	1961-'63	10	16	4
Vince Dooley	1964-'78	112	50	6

University of Georgia All-Time Scores

1892

50	Mercer	0
0	Auburn	10
50	(1-1-0)	10

1893

6	Ga. Tech	28
0	Vanderbilt	35
0	Savannah AC	0
24	Augusta AC	0
22	Furman	8
52	(2-2-1)	71

1894

8	Sewanee	12
40	S.C. State	0
10	Wofford	0
66	Augusta AC	0
10	Auburn	8
22	Savannah AC	0
156	(5-1-0)	20

1895

34	Wofford	0
0	N. Carolina	6
6	N. Carolina	10
30	Alabama	6
22	Sewanee	0
0	Vanderbilt	6
6	Auburn	16
98	(3-4-0)	44

1896

34	Wofford	0
24	N. Carolina	16
26	Sewanee	0
12	Auburn	6
96	(4-0-0)	22

1897

24	Clemson	0
28	Ga. Tech	0
4	Virginia	17
56	(2-1-0)	17

1898

20	Clemson	8
14	Atlanta AC	0
15	Ga. Tech	0
4	Vanderbilt	0
0	N. Carolina	44
17	Auburn	18
70	(4-2-0)	70

1899

11	Clemson	0
0	Sewanee	12
20	Ga. Tech	0
0	Tennessee	5
0	Auburn	0
0	N. Carolina	5
31	(2-3-1)	22

1900

12	Ga. Tech	0
5	S. Carolina	0
6	Sewanee	21
5	Clemson	39
0	N. Carolina	55
0	Auburn	44
28	(2-4-0)	159

1901

10	S. Carolina	5
0	Vanderbilt	47
0	Sewanee	47
5	Clemson	29
0	N. Carolina	27
0	Alabama	0
6	Davidson	16
0	Auburn	0
21	(1-5-2)	171

1902

11	Furman	0
0	Ga. Tech	0
5	Alabama	0
0	Clemson	36
27	Davidson	0
0	Sewanee	11
12	Auburn	5
55	(4-2-1)	52

1903

0	Clemson	29
0	S. Carolina	17
38	Ga. Tech	0
0	Vanderbilt	33
5	Tennessee	0
0	Savannah AC	6
22	Auburn	13
65	(3-3-0)	98

1904

52	Florida	0
0	Clemson	10
0	S. Carolina	2
5	Alabama	16

6 Ga. Tech 23
6 Auburn 17
69 (1-5-0) 66

1905
0 Clemson 35
0 Cumberland 39
0 Alabama 36
16 Dahlonega 12
0 Ga. Tech 46
0 Auburn 20
16 (1-5-0) 188

1906
0 Davidson 15
0 Clemson 6
55 Mercer 0
0 Ga. Tech 17
0 Tennessee 0
4 Auburn 0
0 Svnh. AC 12
59 (2-4-1) 50

1907
57 Dahlonega 0
0 Tennessee 15
26 Mercer 6
0 Alabama 0
6 Ga. Tech 10
8 Clemson 0
0 Sewanee 16
6 Auburn 0
103 (4-3-1) 47

1908
16 Dahlonega 0
29 S. Carolina 6
0 Tennessee 10
10 Mercer 0
6 Clemson 0
6 Alabama 6
2 Davidson 0
0 Auburn 23
69 (5-2-1) 45

1909
0 Citadel 0
0 Davidson 0
3 Tennessee 0
0 Alabama 14
0 Clemson 5
6 Ga. Tech 12
5 Auburn 17
14 (1-4-2) 48

1910
101 Locust Grove 0
79 Gordon MA 0
22 Alabama 0
35 Tennessee 5
21 Mercer 0
12 Sewanee 15
0 Clemson 0
11 Ga. Tech 6
0 Auburn 26
281 (6-2-1) 52

1911
51 Ala. Presby 0
38 S. Carolina 0
11 Alabama 3
12 Sewanee 3
8 Mercer 5
0 Vanderbilt 17
23 Clemson 0
5 Ga. Tech 0
0 Auburn 0
148 (7-1-1) 28

1912
33 Chattanooga 0
33 Citadel 0
0 Vanderbilt 46
13 Alabama 9
13 Sewanee 13
27 Clemson 6
20 Ga. Tech 0
12 Auburn 6
151 (6-1-1) 80

1913
108 Ala. Presby 0
51 Dahlonega 0
20 Alabama 0
6 Virginia 13
19 N. Carolina 6
18 Clemson 15
14 Ga. Tech 0
7 Auburn 21
243 (6-2-0) 55

1914
81 Dahlonega 0
13 Citadel 0
7 Sewanee 6
6 N. Carolina 41
0 Virginia 28
0 Miss. State 9
13 Clemson 35
0 Ga. Tech 7
0 Auburn 0
120 (3-5-1) 126

1915
79 Newberry 0
64 Dahlonega 0
6 Chattanooga 6
35 Citadel 0
7 Virginia 9
0 Auburn 12
39 Florida 0
0 Ga. Tech 0
13 Clemson 0
243 (5-2-2) 27

1916
6 Citadel 0
26 Clemson 0
21 Florida 0
13 Virginia 7
3 Navy 20
0 Auburn 3
49 Furman 0
0 Ga. Tech 21
3 Alabama 0
121 (6-3-0) 51

1917
(NO TEAM)

1918
(NO TEAM)

1919
28 Citadel 0
14 S. Carolina 0
13 Sewanee 0
16 Florida 0
0 Auburn 7
7 Virginia 7
7 Tulane 7
0 Alabama 6
0 Clemson 0
85 (4-2-3) 27

1920
40 Citadel 0
37 S. Carolina 0
7 Furman 0
27 Oglethorpe 3
7 Auburn 0
0 Virginia 0
56 Florida 0
21 Alabama 14
55 Clemson 0
250 (8-0-1) 17

1921
28 Mercer 0
27 Furman 7
7 Harvard 10
14 Oglethorpe 0
7 Auburn 0
21 Virginia 0
7 Vanderbilt 7
22 Alabama 0
28 Clemson 0
0 Dartmouth 7
161 (7-2-1) 31

1922
82 Newberry 13
41 Mercer 0
0 Chicago 20
7 Furman 0
7 Tennessee 3
26 Oglethorpe 6
3 Auburn 7
6 Virginia 6
0 Vanderbilt 12
6 Alabama 10
178 (5-4-1) 77

1923
7 Mercer 0
20 Oglethorpe 6
0 Yale 40
17 Tennessee 0
7 Auburn 0
13 Virginia 0
7 Vanderbilt 35
0 Alabama 36
3 Centre 3
74 (5-3-1) 120

1924
26 Mercer 7
18 S. Carolina 0
6 Yale 7
23 Furman 0
3 Vanderbilt 0
33 Tennessee 0
7 Virginia 0
6 Auburn 0
0 Alabama 33
7 Centre 14
129 (7-3-0) 61

1925
32 Mercer 0
6 Virginia 7
7 Yale 35
21 Furman 0
26 Vanderbilt 7
7 Tennessee 12
34 Auburn 0
0 Ga. Tech 3
0 Alabama 27
133 (4-5-0) 62

1926
20 Mercer 0
27 Virginia 7
0 Yale 19
7 Furman 14
13 Vanderbilt 14
32 Florida 9
16 Auburn 6
14 Ga. Tech 13
6 Alabama 33
135 (5-4-0) 115

1927
32 Virginia 0
14 Yale 10
32 Furman 0
33 Auburn 3
31 Tulane 0
28 Florida 0
32 Clemson 0
26 Mercer 7
20 Alabama 6
0 Ga. Tech 12
248 (9-1-0) 38

1928
52 Mercer 0
6 Yale 21
7 Furman 0
20 Tulane 14
13 Auburn 0
6 Florida 26
12 L.S.U. 13
0 Alabama 19
6 Ga. Tech 20
122 (4-5-0) 113

1929
6 Oglethorpe 13
27 Furman 0
15 Yale 0
19 N. Carolina 12
6 Florida 18
15 Tulane 21
19 N.Y.U. 27
24 Auburn 0
12 Alabama 0
12 Ga. Tech 6
155 (6-4-0) 97

1930
31 Oglethorpe 6
51 Mercer 0
18 Yale 14
26 N. Carolina 0
39 Auburn 7
0 Florida 0
7 N.Y.U. 6
0 Tulane 25
0 Alabama 13
13 Ga. Tech 0
185 (7-2-1) 71

1931
40 Va. Tech 0
26 Yale 7
32 N. Carolina 6
9 Vanderbilt 0
33 Florida 6
7 N.Y.U. 6
7 Tulane 20
12 Auburn 6
35 Ga. Tech 6
0 Sou. Calif. 60
201 (8-2-0) 146

1932
6 Va. Tech 7
25 Tulane 34
6 N. Carolina 6
33 Florida 12
7 N.Y.U. 13
32 Clemson 18
7 Auburn 14
0 Ga. Tech 0
6 Vanderbilt 12
122 (2-5-2) 116

1933
20 N. C. State 10
26 Tulane 13
30 N. Carolina 0
13 Mercer 12
25 N.Y.U. 0
14 Florida 0
7 Yale 0
6 Auburn 14
7 Ga. Tech 6
0 Sou. Calif. 31
148 (8-2-0) 86

1934
42 Stetson 0
7 Furman 2
0 N. Carolina 14
6 Tulane 7
6 Alabama 26
14 Florida 0
14 Yale 7
27 N. C. State 0
18 Auburn 0
7 Ga. Tech 0
141 (7-3-0) 56

1935
31 Mercer 0
31 Furman 7
40 Chattanooga 0
13 N. C. State 0
7 Alabama 17
7 Florida 0
26 Tulane 13
0 L.S.U. 13
7 Auburn 19
7 Ga. Tech 19
169 (6-4-0) 88

1936
15 Mercer 6
13 Furman 0
7 L.S.U. 47
6 Rice 13
13 Auburn 20
0 Tennessee 46
26 Florida 8
12 Tulane 6
7 Fordham 7
16 Ga. Tech 6
115 (5-4-1) 159

1937
60 Oglethorpe 0
13 S. Carolina 7
14 Clemson 0
6 Holy Cross 7
19 Mercer 0
0 Tennessee 32
0 Florida 6
7 Tulane 6
0 Auburn 0
6 Ga. Tech 6
26 Miami 8
151 (6-3-2) 72

1938
20 Citadel 12
7 S. Carolina 6
38 Furman 7
28 Mercer 19
6 Holy Cross 29
19 Florida 6
6 Tulane 28
14 Auburn 23
0 Ga. Tech 0
7 Miami 13
145 (5-4-1) 143

1939
26 Citadel 0
0 Furman 20
0 Holy Cross 13
6 Kentucky 13
13 N.Y.U. 14
16 Mercer 9
6 Florida 2
33 S. Carolina 7
0 Auburn 7
0 Ga. Tech 13
13 Miami 0
113 (5-6-0) 98

1940
53 Oglethorpe 0

33 S. Carolina 2
14 Ole Miss 28
13 Columbia 19
7 Kentucky 7
14 Auburn 13
13 Florida 18
13 Tulane 21
21 Ga. Tech 19
28 Miami 7
209 (5-4-1) 134

1941

81 Mercer 0
34 S. Carolina 6
14 Ole Miss 14
7 Columbia 3
14 Alabama 27
7 Auburn 0
19 Florida 3
47 Centre 6
35 Dartmouth 0
21 Ga. Tech 0
269 (8-1-1) 59

Orange Bowl

40 T.C.U. 26

1942

7 Kentucky 6
14 Jax NAS 0
40 Furman 7
48 Ole Miss 13
40 Tulane 0
35 Cincinnati 13
21 Alabama 10
75 Florida 0
40 Chattanooga 0
13 Auburn 27
34 Ga. Tech 0
367 (10-1-0) 76

Rose Bowl

9 U.C.L.A. 0

1943

25 Presbyterian 7
27 L.S.U. 34
67 Tenn. Tech 0
7 Wake Forest 0
7 Daniel Field 18
6 L.S.U. 27
39 Howard 0
40 Presbyterian 12
46 Va. Tech 7
0 Ga. Tech 48
264 (6-4-0) 153

1944

7 Wake Forest 14
67 Presbyterian 0
13 Kentucky 12
53 Daniel Field 6
7 L.S.U. 15
14 Alabama 7
38 Florida 12
49 Auburn 13
21 Clemson 7
0 Ga. Tech 44
269 (7-3-0) 130

1945

49 Murray St. 0
20 Clemson 0
27 Miami 21
48 Kentucky 6
0 L.S.U. 32
14 Alabama 28
34 Chattanooga 7
34 Florida 0
35 Auburn 0
33 Ga. Tech 0
294 (8-2-0) 94

Oil Bowl

20 Tulsa 6

1946

35 Clemson 12
35 Temple 7
28 Kentucky 13
33 Okla. State 13
70 Furman 7
14 Alabama 0
33 Florida 14
41 Auburn 0
48 Chattanooga 27
35 Ga. Tech 7
372 (10-0-0) 100

Sugar Bowl

20 N. Carolina 10

1947

13 Furman 7
7 N. Carolina 14
35 L.S.U. 19
0 Kentucky 26
20 Okla. State 7
7 Alabama 17
21 Clemson 6
34 Florida 6
28 Auburn 6
27 Chattanooga 0
0 Ga. Tech 7
192 (7-4-0) 105

Gator Bowl

20 Maryland 20

1948

14 Chattanooga 7
14 N. Carolina 21
35 Kentucky 12
22 L.S.U. 0
42 Miami 21
35 Alabama 0
20 Florida 12
42 Auburn 14
33 Furman 0
21 Ga. Tech 13
276 (9-1-0) 100

Orange Bowl

28 Texas 41

1949

25 Furman 0
42 Chattanooga 6
14 N. Carolina 21
0 Kentucky 25
7 L.S.U. 0
9 Miami 13
7 Alabama 14
7 Florida 28
20 Auburn 20
40 Duquesne 0
6 Ga. Tech 7
177 (4-6-1) 134

Presidential Cup

20 Texas A&M 40

1950

27 Maryland 7
7 St. Mary's 7
0 N. Carolina 0
27 Miss. State 0
13 L.S.U. 13
19 Boston Col. 7
7 Alabama 14
6 Florida 0
12 Auburn 10
40 Furman 0
0 Ga. Tech 7
158 (6-2-3) 65

1951

33 Geo. Wash. 0
28 N. Carolina 16
0 Miss. State 6
7 Maryland 43
0 L.S.U. 7
35 Boston Col. 28
14 Alabama 16
7 Florida 6
48 Auburn 14
6 Ga. Tech 48
176 (5-5-0) 184

1952

19 Vanderbilt 7
21 Tulane 16
49 N.C. State 0
0 Maryland 37
27 L.S.U. 14
0 Florida 30
19 Alabama 34
34 Pennsylvania 27
13 Auburn 7
9 Ga. Tech 23
35 Miami 13
226 (7-4-0) 208

1953

32 Villanova 19
16 Tulane 14
12 Texas A&M 14
13 Maryland 40
6 L.S.U. 14
27 N. Carolina 14
12 Alabama 33
7 Florida 21
18 Auburn 39
0 Miss. Sou. 14
12 Ga. Tech 28
155 (3-8-0) 230

1954

14 Fla. State 0
14 Clemson 7
0 Texas A&M 6
21 N. Carolina 7
16 Vanderbilt 14
7 Tulane 0
0 Alabama 0
14 Florida 13
0 Auburn 35
3 Ga. Tech 7
89 (6-3-1) 89

1955

13 Ole Miss 26
14 Vanderbilt 13
7 Clemson 26
28 N. Carolina 7
47 Fla. State 14
0 Tulane 14
35 Alabama 14
13 Florida 19
13 Auburn 16
3 Ga. Tech 21
173 (4-6-0) 170

1956

0 Vanderbilt 14
3 Fla. State 0
7 Miss. State 19
26 N. Carolina 12
7 Miami 7
7 Kentucky 14
16 Alabama 13
0 Florida 28
0 Auburn 20
0 Ga. Tech 35
66 (3-6-1) 161

1957

7 Texas 26
6 Vanderbilt 9
0 Michigan 26
13 Tulane 6
14 Navy 27
33 Kentucky 14
13 Alabama 14
0 Florida 22
0 Auburn 6
7 Ga. Tech 0
93 (3-7-0) 160

1958

8 Texas 13
14 Vanderbilt 21
14 S. Carolina 24
28 Fla. State 13
28 Kentucky 0
0 Alabama 12
6 Florida 7
6 Auburn 21
76 Citadel 0
16 Ga. Tech 3
196 (4-6-0) 114

1959

17 Alabama 3
21 Vanderbilt 6
14 S. Carolina 30
35 Hardin-Simmons 0
15 Miss. State 0
14 Kentucky 7
42 Fla. State 0
21 Florida 10
14 Auburn 13
21 Ga. Tech 14
204 (9-1-0) 83

Orange Bowl

14 Missouri 0

1960

6 Alabama 21
18 Vanderbilt 7
39 S. Carolina 6
3 Sou. Calif. 10
20 Miss. State 17
17 Kentucky 13
45 Tulsa 7
14 Florida 22
6 Auburn 9
7 Ga. Tech 6
174 (6-4-0) 118

1961

6 Alabama 32
0 Vanderbilt 21
17 S. Carolina 14
0 Fla. State 3
10 Miss. State 7
16 Kentucky 15
7 Miami 32
14 Florida 21
7 Auburn 10
7 Ga. Tech 22
84 (3-7-0) 197

1962

0 Alabama 35
10 Vanderbilt 0
7 S. Carolina 7
24 Clemson 16
0 Fla. State 18
7 Kentucky 7
10 N.C. State 10
15 Florida 23
30 Auburn 21
6 Ga. Tech 37
109 (3-4-3) 174

1963

7 Alabama 32
20 Vanderbilt 0
27 S. Carolina 7
7 Clemson 7
31 Miami 14
17 Kentucky 14
7 N. Carolina 28
14 Florida 21
0 Auburn 14
3 Ga. Tech 14
133 (4-5-1) 157

1964

3 Alabama 31
7 Vanderbilt 0
7 S. Carolina 7
19 Clemson 7
14 Fla. State 17
21 Kentucky 7
24 N. Carolina 8
14 Florida 7
7 Auburn 14
7 Ga. Tech 0
123 (6-3-1) 98

Sun Bowl

7 Texas Tech 0

1965

18 Alabama 17
24 Vanderbilt 10
15 Michigan 7
23 Clemson 9
3 Fla. State 10
10 Kentucky 28
47 N. Carolina 35
10 Florida 14
19 Auburn 21
17 Ga. Tech 7
186 (6-4-0) 158

1966

20 Miss. State 17
43 V.M.I. 7
7 S. Carolina 0
9 Ole Miss 3
6 Miami 7
27 Kentucky 15
28 N. Carolina 3
27 Florida 10
21 Auburn 13
23 Ga. Tech 14
211 (9-1-0) 89

Cotton Bowl

24 S.M.U. 9

1967

30 Miss. State 0
24 Clemson 17
21 S. Carolina 0
20 Ole Miss 29
56 V. M. I. 6
31 Kentucky 7
14 Houston 15
16 Florida 17
17 Auburn 0
21 Ga. Tech 14
250 (7-3-0) 105

Liberty Bowl

7 N.C. State 14

1968

17 Tennessee 17
31 Clemson 13
21 S. Carolina 20
21 Ole Miss 7
32 Vanderbilt 6
35 Kentucky 14
10 Houston 10
51 Florida 0
17 Auburn 3
47 Ga. Tech 8
282 (8-0-2) 98

Sugar Bowl

2 Arkansas 16

1969

35 Tulane 0
30 Clemson 0
41 S. Carolina 16
17 Ole Miss 25
40 Vanderbilt 8
30 Kentucky 0
3 Tennessee 17
13 Florida 13
3 Auburn 16
0 Ga. Tech 6

212 (5-4-1) 101

Sun Bowl

6 Nebraska 45

1970

14 Tulane 17
38 Clemson 0
6 Miss. State 7
21 Ole Miss 31
37 Vanderbilt 3
19 Kentucky 3
52 S. Carolina 34
17 Florida 24
31 Auburn 17
7 Ga. Tech 17

242 (5-5-0) 153

1971

56 Oregon State 25
17 Tulane 7
28 Clemson 0
35 Miss. State 7
38 Ole Miss 7
24 Vanderbilt 0
34 Kentucky 0
24 S. Carolina 0
49 Florida 7
20 Auburn 35
28 Ga. Tech 24

353 (10-1-0) 112

Gator Bowl

7 N. Carolina 3

1972

24 Baylor 14
13 Tulane 24
28 N.C. State 22
7 Alabama 25
14 Ole Miss 13
28 Vanderbilt 3
13 Kentucky 7
0 Tennessee 14
10 Florida 7
10 Auburn 27
27 Ga. Tech 7

174 (7-4-0) 163

1973

7 Pittsburgh 7
31 Clemson 14
31 N. Carolina 12
14 Alabama 28
20 Ole Miss 0
14 Vanderbilt 18
7 Kentucky 12
35 Tennessee 31
10 Florida 11
28 Auburn 14
10 Ga. Tech 3

207 (6-4-1) 150

Peach Bowl

17 Maryland 16

1974

48 Oregon St. 35
14 Miss. State 38
52 S. Carolina 14
24 Clemson 28
49 Ole Miss 0
38 Vanderbilt 31
24 Kentucky 20
24 Houston 31
17 Florida 16
13 Auburn 17
14 Ga. Tech 34

317 (6-5-0) 264

Tangerine Bowl

10 Miami, O. 21

1975

9 Pittsburgh 19
28 Miss. State 6
28 S. Carolina 20
35 Clemson 7
13 Ole Miss 28
47 Vanderbilt 3
21 Kentucky 13
28 Richmond 24
10 Florida 7
28 Auburn 13
42 Ga. Tech 26

289 (9-2-0) 166

Cotton Bowl

10 Arkansas 31

1976

36 California 24
41 Clemson 0
20 S. Carolina 12
21 Alabama 0
17 Ole Miss 21
45 Vanderbilt 0
31 Kentucky 7
31 Cincinnati 17
41 Florida 27
28 Auburn 0
13 Ga. Tech 10

324 (10-1-0) 118

Sugar Bowl

3 Pittsburgh 27

1977

27 Oregon 16
6 Clemson 7
15 So. Carolina 13
10 Alabama 18
14 Mississippi 13
24 Vanderbilt 13
0 Kentucky 33
23 Richmond 7
17 Florida 22
14 Auburn 33
7 Georgia Tech 16

157 (5-6-0) 191

1978

16 Baylor 14
12 Clemson 0
10 So. Carolina 27
42 Mississippi 3
24 LSU 17
31 Vanderbilt 10
17 Kentucky 16
41 VMI 3
24 Florida 22
22 Auburn 22
29 Georgia Tech 28

268 (9-1-1) 162

Bluebonnet Bowl

23 Stanford 25

University of Georgia Lettermen—1892 to 1978

A

AARON, Phillip, 1978
ADAMS, Gary, 1965-66-67
ALEXANDER, Eugene P., 1944-45-46
ALLEN, Donnie, 1970-71-72
ALLEN, Ed, 1968-69
ALLEN, Heyward, 1939-40-41
ALLEN, Robert, 1960-61-62
ALLEN, V., 1902
AMBRESTER, Leon, 1962-63-64
AMTOWER, Frederick, 1960-61
ANDERSON, Alfred, 1934-35-36
ANDERSON, Charles, 1953
ANDERSON, Michael, 1956-57-58
ANDERSON, Paul K., 1920-22
ANGLIN, Bobby, 1950-51-52
ANSLEY, Abb, 1972-73-74
ANTHONY, Thurston L., 1919-20-21-23
APPLEBY, Richard, 1973-74-75
ARCHER, David, 1977
ARKWRIGHT, Charles, 1965-66
ARMSTRONG, W. B., 1892
ARNETTE, William T., 1911-12
ARNOLD, Anthony "Amp", 1977-78
ARNOLD, James W., 1904
ARRENDALE, James L., 1906-07
ARRINGTON, Rick, 1966
ARTHUR, Matthew, 1953-54-55
ASHE, Phillip, 1958-59-60
ASHE, Thomas, 1960
ASHFORD, Alex, 1933-34-35
ATKINSON, G., 1896
AUSTIN, Stafford L., 1919

B

BABB, Michael, 1961-62-63
BABCOCK, Harry, 1950-51-52
BADGETT, Willis, 1936-37-38
BAILEY, Robert, Jr., 1960
BAILEY, Sam M., 1944-45
BAKER, Jim, 1968-73-74-75
BAKER, Sam "Buck", 1972-73
BARBAS, Constino J., 1944
BARBER, Fred, Jr., 1962-63-64
BARBRE, Ned C., 1937-38
BARCHAN, Joe, 1919
BARRETT, Pearce, Jr., 1943
BARROW, Craig, 1893-95
BARROW, Thomas A., 1902
BATCHELOR, Graham, 1931-32-33
BATTEY, George M., 1906
BAXTER, Julian F., 1900-01-02
BEASLEY, Tom R., 1915-16
BEAVER, Sandy, 1901-02
BECKWITH, Charles, 1950-51
BEDINGFIELD, Walter, 1959-60
BELK, Robert, 1943
BELL, Greg, 1977-78
BELL, John, 1953-54-55
BELUE, Benjamin III, "Buck", 1978
BENNETT, Daniel P., 1921
BENNETT, Jasper C., Jr., 1930-31
BENNETT, Joe J., Jr., 1922-23
BENNETT, Joe L., Jr., 1920-21
BENNETT, Joseph, 1929
BENNETT, Paige, 1920
BENNETT, Roger, 1977-78
BENTON, Gene, 1943
BETSILL, Roy, 1959-60
BILYUE, Fred, 1950-51-52
BIRD, Wayne, 1967
BISHOP, Alan, 1956
BISSELL, Hal, 1971-72
BLACK, Charles H., 1898
BLACK, Dameron, 1904
BLACK, J. C., 1892-93
BLACKBURN, Donald, 1960-61-62
BLACKMAN, Joe W., 1919-20
BLANCH, Wright B., 1896
BLANCHARD, Elmer, 1961
BLANTON, Brooker, Jr., 1940
BOBO, Tim, 1978
BODINE, Alvin, 1947-48-49
BOERSIG, Dave, 1976-77-78
BOLAND, Frank K., Jr., 1924-26
BOLAND, Joseph H., 1927-28-29
BOLAND, Kels, Jr., 1925
BOLER, Sylvester, 1973-74
BOND, Ed V., 1897
BOND, John, 1933-34-35
BONEY, Sam M., 1921-22
BORN, Wade H., 1895
BOSTWICK, Henry G., 1908-09
BOSTWICK, Hugh, 1908-09
BOULEY, Laurent, 1944-45
BOWDEN, B. Limon, 1910-11
BOWDEN, Timon D., 1912
BOWEN, Marcus, 1966
BOWER, John D., 1902-03
BOWLES, Jesse, 1944
BOX, Aaron, 1957-58-59
BOX, Gary "Butch", 1973-74-75-76
BOYD, Benny, 1962-63
BOYD, Willard, 1942
BOYKIN, Richard, 1961-62-63
BOYNTON, Rooks, 1961
BRACCO, Nicholas, 1957-58
BRADBERRY, George, 1944-46-47-48
BRADLEY, Richard, 1959
BRADSHAW, William, 1947-48-49-50
BRAMLETT, Randy, 1975
BRANNEN, James, 1977
BRANNEN, Millard, 1968
BRANTLEY, Wayne, 1963-64-65
BRASHER, Larry, 1968-69-70
BRASWELL, Kim, 1970-71-72
BRASWELL, Matt, 1976-77-78
BRATKOWSKI, Edmund "Zeke", 1951-52-53
BRATTON, Edgar, 1943
BRAY, Mell, 1941-46
BRAY, Ralph, 1965
BRICE, Billy, 1968-70-71
BRICE, Frank, 1972-73
BRITT, Charles, 1957-58-59
BROADNAX, John E., 1926-27
BROOKS, Steve, 1977
BROWN, David, 1960
BROWN, Frederick, 1958-59-60
BROWN, Henry C., 1892-93
BROWN, James, 1954-55-56
BROWN, John, 1944
BROWN, John A., 1903-04-06
BROWN, John C., 1932-33-34
BROWN, Sam, 1932-33
BROWN, Stanley, 1978
BROWN, Steve, 1968-69
BROWN, William W., 1906
BROWN, Woodrow, 1939-40
BROYLES, Edwin N., 1912-13
BROYLES, N. A., 1919
BRUCE, Milton, 1971-72-73
BRUNSON, Lewis, 1947-48-49-50
BRYAN, William, Jr., 1944
BRYANT, Vernon H., 1928
BULLOCH, Cyprian, 1965
BURGAMY, Jeff, Jr., 1950-51

BURKE, Fred, 1943
BURKHALTER, Edward, 1956
BURNETT, Doug, 1971-72
BURNS, Bob, 1971-72-73
BURNS, Sam, 1970
BURSON, Joseph, 1962-64-65
BURT, Will, 1940-41
BURT, William, 1953
BUSH, Jackson, 1946-47-48
BUSH, Marion, 1956
BUTLER, George P., 1892-93-94
BUTLER, Jacob J., 1922-23-24-25
BYARS, Charles, 1956
BYRD, Gregg, 1970
BYRD, Henry, 1943
BYRD, Wayne, 1968-69

C

CAGLE, Jim, 1971-72-73
CALHOUN, Andrew, 1901
CALLAWAY, Tim, 1967-68-69
CAMPAGNA, James, 1952-53-54
CAMPBELL, John, 1952
CAMPBELL, Johnny, 1969-70
CAMPBELL, Marion, 1949-50-51
CAMPBELL, William H., Jr., 1919-20
CANDLER, Asa, 1934-35-36
CANNON, Keith, 1978
CAPRARA, Anthony, 1951-52
CARROLLTON, William, 1954-55
CARSON, Johnny, 1950-52-53
CARTER, Rusty, 1971-72
CASE, Clifford, Jr., 1960
CASE, Ronald L., 1959-60-61
CASEY, Patrick, 1957
CASTRONIS, Mike, J., 1943-44-45
CATE, Vassa, 1937-38-39
CAUSEY, Paul L., 1936
CAVAN, James, Jr., 1936-37
CAVAN, Mike, 1968-69-70
CAWTHON, Mike, 1971
CESCUTTI, Brad, 1974-75-76
CHAMBERLIN, Steve, 1969-71
CHANDLER, Bob, 1969
CHANDLER, Charles, 1952
CHANDLER, Edgar, 1965-66-67
CHANDLER, Eugene, Jr., 1946-47-48-49
CHANDLER, Spurgeon, 1929-30-31
CHAPMAN, George, 1932-33-34
CHAVIOUS, Charles, 1972
CHEEK, George, 1961
CHESNA, Joe L., 1945
CHEVES, James P., 1919-20
CHILDERS, Clyde, 1960-61
CHILDS, R. R., 1911
CHONKO, Bill, 1943-44-45
CHRISTIANSON, David, 1972-74
CLAMON, Joe, 1967-68
CLARK, Cleve, 1953-54-55
CLARK, Dicky, 1974-75-76
CLARK, Ralph, 1973
CLARK, Raymond, 1960-61-62
CLARKE, Arthur, 1897
CLARKE, T. Burton, 1897
CLARKE, W. W., 1894-95
CLAY, Frank, 1905
CLAY, Herbert, 1901
CLECKLEY, Hervey N., 1922-23
CLEMENS, Robert, 1952-53-54
CLEVELAND, Robert, 1957
CLOER, Billy, 1965
COATES, Jesse, 1892
COBB, Johnny, 1971
COLBY, Glenn, 1907
COLE, Bill, 1978
COLE, Mike, 1963
COLEMAN, John S., 1914-15-16
COLLIER, Barry, 1972-73-74
COLLIER, Steve, 1975-76-77
COLLINGS, David A., Jr., 1919-20-21-22
COLLINS, Bobby, 1978
COLLINS, George, 1975-76-77
COLLINS, Pat, 1977-78
COMFORT, Joseph, 1955-56-57
CONE, James, 1960-61
CONGER, Melvin, 1941
CONKLIN, Hughbert W., 1910-11-12-13
CONN, Dick, 1971-72-73
CONNALLY, Joe, 1948
CONNALLY, Joe B., 1895
CONYERS, James B., 1911-12-13-14-15
COOK, Buster, 1928
COOK, Harold D., 1953-56
COOK, Johnny, 1943-46
COOK, Malcolm, 1949-50-51
COOK, Randy, 1977-78
COOLEY, Jimmy, 1964-65-66
COOLEY, Michael, 1944-45-46-47
COOPER, Clenton, 1955-56-57
COOPER, David, 1966
COOPER, William, 1931-32-33
CORDELL, Lew, 1934
COSTA, Leonard, Jr., 1940-41-42
COTHRAN, Walter S., 1895-96
COUCH, Tommy, 1969-70-71
COVINGTON, Leon H., 1910-12
COX, Bryant, 1943
COX, Charles, 1903-04-06
COX, Harmon, 1898
COX, John B., 1909-10
CRAFT, Lawrence, 1974-75-76
CRANE, George S., 1893
CRAWFORD, Ray, Jr., 1962-63-64
CRAWFORD, Stanley, 1964-65-66
CREECH, Glenn, 1964-65
CRENSHAW, McCarthy, 1930-31
CRISP, Dan, 1976
CROOK, Melvin, 1962-63
CROUCH, Joe, 1932
CRUMP, Stephen A., 1911-12-13
CULPEPPER, Knox, 1954-55-56
CUMMING, D. R., 1909
CUMMINGS, David, 1959
CUNARD, Vernon, 1958
CURINGTON, Jim, 1971-72-73
CURRAN, Jack, 1924-25-26
CUSHENBERRY, Anthony, 1954-55-56

D

DANIEL, Lee, 1967-68-69
DANTZLER, Danny, 1971-72-73
DARBY, Billy, 1968-69-70
DARDEN, Joel, 1962-63-64
DAUGHERTY, Jim S., 1895
DAVID, William, 1932-33
DAVIDSON, John, 1929-30
DAVIS, B., 1908-09
DAVIS, Dan, 1960
DAVIS, Edward H., 1930
DAVIS, Glenn, 1968-69
DAVIS, Hinton, 1959-60
DAVIS, J. B., 1955-56-57
DAVIS, John, 1935-36-37
DAVIS, Ken, 1963-64-65
DAVIS, Lamar, 1940-41-42
DAVIS, Louis S., 1915
DAVIS, Paul Jack, 1965-66
DAVIS, R. Cooper, 1909
DAVIS, Steve, 1974-75-76
DAVIS, Van, 1940-41-42
DAY, A. M., 1919-20-21
DAY, T. Roosevelt, 1923-24
DEAN, Sidney, 1901
DEAVERS, Clayton, 1944-46-47
DeCARLO, Arthur, Jr., 1950-51-52
DeCHARLEROY, Albert, 1938
DeLaPIERRIERE, Arthur L., 1911-12-13
DeLaPIERRIERE, Herman, 1905-06-07-08
DELESKI, Gerald, 1945-46
DELLINGER, Robert, 1952
DeMERSSEMAN, Paul, 1975
DEMOS, George, 1970
DENNARD, Anthony, 1964-65-66
DENNEY, Jimmy, 1964-65
DENNIS, Steve, 1976-77-78
DENYER, Richard, 1977
DERRICK, Claude, 1908
DEZENDORF, E. H., 1915-16
DICHARRY, Ray, 1970
DICKENS, Marion, 1929-30-31
DICKENS, Pete, 1963-64-65
DICKINSON, Marvin D., 1900-01-02
DICKS, Robert "Happy", 1966-67-68
DILTS, Douglas "Bucky", 1974-75-76
DiPIETRO, Francis, 1951
DOBBS, George, 1950-51
DONALDSON, John C., 1945-46-47-48
DONALDSON, Ray, 1977-78
DONNELLY, William P., 1916
DORSEY, Cam D., 1900-01-02
DORSEY, Ed H., 1913
DORSEY, W., 1904
DOWNER, Austin J., Jr., 1929-30-31
DuBIGNON, Charles, 1898
DUDISH, Andrew, 1940-41-42
DUDLEY, Frank C., 1927-28
DUKE, John, 1948-49-50
DUKES, Henry, Jr., 1955-56-57
DUKES, LeRoy, 1962-63-64
DUMBLETON, Ken, 1970
DuPRIEST, Bob, 1967-68
DURAND, Robert, 1949-50
DYE, Nat, 1956-57-58
DYE, Patrick, 1958-59-60
DYE, Wayne, Jr., 1954-55-56

E

EARNEST, Charles, 1951-52-53
EAVES, Charles, 1943-44-45
ECHOLS, W. R., 1920
EDWARDS, Dan, 1944-45-46-47
EHRDARDT, Clyde, 1941-42
ELDREDGE, Knox, 1937-38-39
ELLENSON, Eugene, 1940-41-42
ELLSPERMANN, Lenny, 1971-72
ELROD, Craig, 1966-68-69
EPPERSON, Rusty, 1967-68
ESKEW, Sammy, 1970-71
ESTES, A. B., 1910
ESTES, Roy E., 1925-26-27
ETTER, Bobby, 1964-65-66
EUBANK, Nathan B., 1925-26
EVANS, Robert, 1966
EVANS, Vance, 1963-64-65
EZELLE, Percy P., 1893

F

FAIRCLOTH, MacArthur "Mack", 1961-63-64
FALES, Charlie, 1976-77-78
FARAH, Freddy, 1960
FARISH, James, 1951-52
FARNSWORTH, Rick, 1972-73
FARNSWORTH, Steve, 1967-68-69
FARRIBA, Mark, 1977
FARRIS, E., 1906
FAULKNER, Darrell, 1975
FEHER, Nick, 1947-48-49-50
FENDER, W. B., 1893
FERGUSON, J. P., 1916
FERRELL, Fortune C., 1895
FERSEN, Paul, 1970-71-72
FERST, Frank W., 1916
FIELD, Patrick, 1948-49-50
FILIPKOWSKI, Chris, 1951-52
FILIPOVITS, Edward, 1949-50-51
FINNEGAN, B. E., 1899
FISHER, Mike, 1978
FITTS, Sheldon, 1920
FITZGERALD, Hugh, 1904
FLEMING, Claude A., 1893
FLEMING, Thomas F., 1907
FLETCHER, John, 1973
FLETCHER, John H., 1921-22-23-24
FLOURNOY, Walker R., 1913
FORBES, Walter T., Jr., 1925-26
FORD, George, 1949-50
FORDHAM, James, 1937-38-39
FOREHAND, Bill, 1972
FOWLER, William, 1954-55
FOX, L. J., 1916
FRANCIS, Albert, 1957
FRANKLIN, Neal, 1978
FRANKLIN, Omer W., 1909-10
FREEDMAN, Louis, 1976-77-78
FRICKS, L. D., 1892
FRIER, W. R., Jr., 1923
FRISBIE,Theodore, 1927-28-29
FRUEHAUF, Ben, 1953-54
FURCHGOTT, Charles M., 1944-45

G

GAINES, Turner P., 1966
GALBREATH, Robert, 1958
GALLOWAY, Homer H., 1910
GARASIC, George, 1943
GARMANY, W. H., 1914-15
GARRARD, Robert, 1952-53-54-55
GARRARD, William T., 1914-15
GARRETT, Mike, 1977-78
GASTON, Marion, Jr., 1932-33
GATEWOOD, James, 1947
GEARRELD, William P., 1894
GEORGE, Carl, 1947-48
GERI, Joseph, 1946-47-48
GIBBS, Bobby, 1973-74

GILBERT, Paul, 1967-69-70
GILBERT, William, 1958
GILLESPIE, Marvin, 1936-37-38
GILLIAM, F. Roosevelt, 1977
GILMORE, Lloyd, 1930-31
GLASS, John, 1964-65
GLOVER, Gary, 1960
GODFREY, Aaron "Ben", 1959
GODFREY, David, 1960-61
GODWIN, William, 1941-42
GOFF, Ray, 1974-75-76
GOLDEN, Don, 1971-72-73
GOLF, S. B., 1899
GOODING, T. H., 1899
GOODMAN, Winfred, 1939-40-41
GOODWIN, Robert, 1977-78
GORDON, Hugh, 1969-70
GORDON, Hugh H., 1900
GORDON, James, 1945
GRAFF, Joseph, 1953-54
GRAHAM, Don, 1968-69
GRANT, Joseph A., 1954
GRANT, William, 1950-51
GRATE, Carl, 1940
GRAVES, Richard A., 1906
GRAY, Phillip, 1978
GRAY, Warren, 1959
GRAYSON, Spencer M., 1923
GREEN, Bobby, 1959-60-61
GREEN, Floyd, 1944
GREEN, Maurice, 1934-35-36
GREEN, Phillip, 1962
GREENE, Mike, 1969-70-71
GREENE, Thomas, 1939-40-41
GREENWAY, Edward, 1949-50-51
GREER, Robert, 1948-49-50
GREER, Steve, 1967-68-69
GRIFFIN, Gerald D., Jr., 1952-53-54-55
GRIFFIN, John, 1967-69
GRIFFIN, Tuck, 1903
GRIFFITH, Byron, Jr., 1932-33-34
GRIFFITH, Jim, 1975-76-77
GRIFFITH, Roy, 1908-10
GRIFFITH, Vernon, 1951-52
GRUBBS, Clayton, 1955
GUEST, C. B., Jr., 1939-40
GUEST, Mack, 1976-77-78
GUISLER, George, 1957-58-59
GUNBY, Cooper, 1974
GUNN, Earl, 1951-52
GUNNELS, Riley, 1956-57-58
GUNNELS, Sandy C., 1933-34
GURLEY, John, 1973-74
GUTHRIE, Carlton, 1961-62-63

H

HAGUE, Bobby, 1943
HALEY, Bill, 1944
HALEY, Eugene S., 1927-28
HALL, Burl F., 1915
HALL, James, 1934-35-36
HALL, Orville D., 1915
HALSEY, A. O., 1892
HALSEY, Lindsley, 1893-94
HAMILTON, W., 1899
HAMMOND, Chris, 1971-72-73
HAMPTON, Donnie, 1967-68-69
HAMRICK, Jim, 1930-31
HANDMACHER, Paul, 1966-67
HANSEN, George, 1957-58
HARBER, William, 1966
HARDY, Wilson M., 1901
HARGROVE, Lauren, 1950-51-52
HARMAN, Harry E., Jr., 1906-07
HARMAN, Harry, III, 1934-35-36
HARMON, W., 1902
HARPER, James K., 1919-20
HARPER, James, Jr., 1952-53-54-55
HARPER, Jeff, 1978
HARPER, Jimmy, 1971-72-73
HARRIS, Charles, 1954-55
HARRIS, Henderson, 1943
HARRIS, Keith, 1972-73-74
HARRIS, Robert "Chuck", 1975-76
HARRISON, Clyde, 1951
HARRISON, Glynn, 1973-74-75
HARTLEY, Hugh V., 1920
HARTLEY, Richard, 1921
HARTMAN, Kevin, 1973-75
HARTMAN, William, Jr., 1935-36-37
HARTRIDGE, Julian, 1905
HATCHER, Herbert C., 1907-08-09-10
HATCHER, Samuel B., 1906
HATCHER, William J., 1925-26
HAUSS, Leonard, 1961-62-63
HAY, Hafford, 1910
HAYES, Donald, 1965-66-67
HAYGOOD, Thomas, 1935-36-37
HAZELHURST, William, 1932
HEARD, Chuck, 1969-70-71
HEARIN, Gerald, 1960
HEARN, William, Jr., 1956-57
HEIDT, Jule, 1898
HELMS, Ken, 1974-75-76
HENDERSON, John G., 1912-13-14-15
HENDERSON, Johnny, 1975-76-77
HENDERSON, Terry, 1968
HENDERSON, William, 1946-47-48-49
HENDRIX, Hugh, 1974-75-76
HERLONG, Grig, 1967
HERRON, William, 1958-59
HERTWIG, Craig, 1972-73-74
HESTER, Dennis, 1971-72-73
HEWLETT, Samuel D., 1899-1900
HIDE, Glenn, 1952
HIERS, William L., Jr., 1944-45
HIGHSMITH, E. Way, 1919-20
HILL, B. Harvey, 1928
HILL, Jack, 1950-51-52
HIPP, Jeff, 1978
HIPPS, Claude, 1944-49-50-51
HIRSCH, D., 1893
HIRSCH, Harold, 1900
HIRSCH, Harold, 1934
HISE, Earl, 1938
HITCHCOCK, William E., 1912-13-14
HLEBOVY, Gus, 1949-50
HOBBS, Homer, 1946-47-48
HODGE, Marc, 1976-77-78
HODGES, Billy, 1944-46-47
HODGSON, Hutch, 1933
HODGSON, Morton S., 1906
HODGSON, Pat, 1963-64-65
HODGSON, Winston, 1938
HOGAN, Hank, 1973
HOKE, Eugene, 1903-04
HOLLAND, Randy, 1977
HOLLAND, Ward, 1973
HOLLINGSWORTH, Joe, 1943
HOLLIS, Howell T., 1924-25-26
HOLMES, Mark, 1966-67
HOLMES, Paul, Jr., 1960-61
HOLT, Tom, 1972-73
HONEYCUTT, Robert, 1970-71-72
HOOKS, Robert G., 1926-28
HOPE, Robert, 1976-77-78
HOPP, Clifford, 1948
HORNE, Everett, 1940-41
HORTON, Dwight, Jr., 1957
HUDSON, Harry, 1966
HUDSON, Nat, 1978
HUFF, Olin E., 1925-26-28
HUFF, James B., 1898
HUGGINS, Ronnie, 1967-68-69
HUGHES, Dennis, 1967-68-69
HUGHES, Lynn, 1964-65
HUGHES, Steve, 1939-40-41
HUGHES, Turner L., 1966
HULL, Augustus L., 1900
HUNNICUTT, Lynn, 1970-71-72
HUNNICUTT, Oliver, 1937-38-39
HUNNICUTT, Pat, 1964
HUNNICUTT, William, Jr., 1962
HURST, Marvin, 1963-64-65
HYDE, Glenn, 1950

I

INGLE, Wayne, 1965-66-67
INGRAM, Johnny, 1967
IVEY, William, 1960-61-62

J

JACKSON, Jerone, 1971-72-73
JACKSON, William, 1960
JACKURA, Joseph, 1944-47-48-49
JACOBSON, Roy H., 1927-28
JAMISON, Joe, 1940
JANKO, Morris, 1943
JEFFREY, Al, 1945
JENKINS, Donald, 1946
JENKINS, Ronald, 1965-66-67
JENNINGS, John, 1968-70-71
JERNIGAN, George, 1943-44-45-46
JOHNSON, Andy, 1971-72-73
JOHNSON, Brad, 1966-67-68
JOHNSON, Frank W., 1933-34-35
JOHNSON, Glenn, 1934-35-36
JOHNSON, H. F., Jr., 1926-27-28
JOHNSON, Howard, 1936-38-39
JOHNSON, Howard F., 1946-47-48
JOHNSON, Michael, 1978
JOHNSON, Randy, 1973-74
JOHNSON, Rodney, 1974-75-76
JOHNSON, Roy, 1926
JOHNSON, Sandy, 1966-67
JOHNSON, W. Franklin, 1965
JONES, A. C., 1897
JONES, Alvin, 1962
JONES, Danny, 1971-72-73
JONES, Hurley, Jr., 1951-52
JONES, John, 1934-35-36
JONES, Raymond, 1971
JONES, Robert P., 1898
JONES, Spike, 1967-68-69
JOSELOVE, Ike, 1922-23-24

K

KAIN, Thomas G., 1924-25-26
KASAY, John, 1965-66
KAVOUKLIS, Mike, 1975-76
KEITH, Kendall, 1969-70-71
KELLEY, Gorden, 1957-58-59
KELLEY, Richard, 1960-62
KELLY, Bob, 1978
KELLY, Howard, 1953-54
KELLY, Steve, 1978
KELLY, Weddington, 1929-30-31
KELTNER, Greene, Jr., 1939-41
KEMP, Bruce, 1967-68-69
KENNEDY, William, 1977
KENT, William B., 1894-95-96-97
KERSEY, Ben, Jr., 1938
KETRON, Grover C., 1906
KETRON, Harold, 1901-02-03-06
KEUPER, Kenneth, 1940-41-42
KEY, Homer, 1931-32-33
KIGHT, Tony, 1976
KILLORIN, Joseph I., 1894-95-1903-04
KILPATRICK, Martin E., 1923-24-25
KIMSEY, Cliff, 1939-40-41
KINSEY, Bucky, 1969
KING, Hardy, 1966-67
KING, Horace, 1972-73-74
KING, LaFayette, 1942
KING, Norman, 1958
KINNEBREW, Chuck, 1972-73-74
KITCHENS, Steve, 1969-70-71
KLUK, Paul, 1940
KNOWLES, William, Jr., 1961-62-63
KOHN, Larry, 1965-66-67
KOTES, Harry, 1954
KRUG, Bill, 1975-76-77
KUNIANSKY, Harry, 1941-42

L

LAKE, Rickey, 1970-71-72
LAMAR, Henry J. 1899-1901
LANCASTER, Larry, 1958-59
LANDRY, John, Jr., 1960-61
LANFORD, Leroy C., 1928
LANGLEY, Derwent, Jr., 1950-52-53
LANKEWICZ, Frank, 1962-63-64
LAURENT, Andy, 1964
LAUTZENHISER, Glenn, 1926-27-28
LAW, Robert, 1934-35-36
LAWHORNE, Tommy, 1965-66-67
LAWRENCE, Fred, 1958-59-60
LAWRENCE, Kent, 1966-67-68
LAYFIELD, Jimmy, 1967-68
LEATH, Dennis, 1970
LEATHERS, Milton, 1929-30-31
LEAVITT, Allan, 1973-74-75-76
LEE, James, 1941-42
LEE, Ryals, 1942-45
LEEBERN, Donald, 1936
LEEBERN, Donald, Jr., 1957-58-59
LEGG, Will, 1973-74-76
LENDERMAN, Lee, 1970
LEVIE, Marshall C., 1923-24-25
LEWIS, Jeff, 1975-76-77
LEWIS, Jim, 1941
LEWIS, Thomas, Jr., 1957-59
LINDSEY, Kiefer, 1898-99
LITTLETON, Eugene, 1956-57-58
LLOYD, David, 1957-58
LLOYD, Mayfield, 1942
LOCKE, James, 1952
LOEFFLER, Leroy, 1925-26
LOFTON, Wilbur, Jr., 1955-56-57
LOGAN, Harold, 1913
LONG, Cary B., 1977
LOPATKA, Mike, 1969-70

LORENDO, Eugene, 1947-48-49
LOVE, Henry, 1948-49
LOVEJOY, R. Hatton, 1896
LOWNDES, J. Dozier, 1905-06
LUCAS, Cicero, 1956-57-58
LUCAS, James E., 1907-08-09
LUCAS, W. M., 1909-10-11-12
LUCK, John, Jr., 1954-55-56
LUCKEY, J. Curtis, 1924-25-26
LUDWIG, Paul, 1932-33
LUMPKIN, Quinton, 1936-37-38
LYNDON, Ed, 1898
LYONS, Tommy, 1968-69-70

M

MacDONALD, Alexander, 1955-56
MADDOX, Arthur K., 1908-09-10-11
MADDOX, Ralph, 1929-30-31
MADDOX, Raymond, 1961-62-63
MADISON, Charles, 1952-53-54
MADRAY, Ashley, 1977-78
MADRAY, Clint, Jr., 1950-51
MAFFETT, Herbert S., 1928-29-30
MAFFETT, Otis, 1935-36-37
MAGONI, Charles, 1950-51
MAGUIRE, Walter, 1942
MAKOWSKI, Henry, 1951-52
MALINOWSKI, Francis, 1951-52-53
MALLOY, Harold, 1978
MALONE, Kirby S., 1911-12-13
MALONE, Tom, 1939-40
MANISERA, Conrad, 1951-55
MANNING, Carl E., 1956-57-58
MAPP, Armand, 1924
MARICICH, Eli, Jr., 1946-47-48-49
MARSHALL, Earl, 1941
MARTIN, Frank, 1904
MARTIN, Joe B., 1928
MARTIN, Tim, 1978
MATHEWS, Dooley, 1937-38-39
MATHIS, Buddy, 1952
MATTHEWS, Jack, 1940
MAXWELL, Richard, Jr., 1932
McARTHUR, Jim, 1971-72
McBRIDE, Ricky, 1975-76-77-78
McCALL, Kenneth, 1944-47-48-49
McCALLA, James, 1900
McCARLEY, Hugh, Jr., 1948-49
McCASKILL, Alex, 1938-39
McCLELLAND, W. F., 1910
McCLENDON, Willie, 1976-77-78
McCLUNG, Jerry, 1950-51
McCLURE, Ardie, 1942
McCONNELL, Bright, 1915-16
McCOY, E. T., 1905
McCOY, Mike, 1971
McCRARY, Herdis W., 1926-27-28
McCULLOUGH, David, 1932-33-34
McCULLOUGH, Jim, 1967-68-69
McCULLOUGH, William, 1962-63
McCUTCHEON, C. D., 1893
McCUTCHEON, Frank Kelly, 1899-1900
McDONALD, David, 1976-77
McDONALD, John N., 1905
McDONALD, Lilard, 1954
McEACHERN, John, 1960-62
McFALLS, Douglas, 1963-64-65
McGILL, Curtis, 1967-68-69
McHUGH, Jack, 1949
McINTIRE, Frank P., 1902
McINTOSH, John H., 1898-99
McKENNY, William, 1959-60-61
McKINNEY, Lee, 1939-40
McKINNON, D. T., 1913
McKNIGHT, David R., 1966-68-69
McKNIGHT, David W., 1972-73-74
McKNIGHT, John, 1933-34-35
McKNIGHT, Larry, 1970-71
McLAIN, C. M., 1910
McLAWS, W. H., 1916
McLEE, Kevin, 1975-76-77
McMANUS, Fred, 1949-50
McMICHAEL, Edward H., 1916
McMICKENS, Donnie, 1978
McPHEE, Richard, 1941-42-46
McPIPKIN, Jim, 1971-72-73
McPIPKIN, Joe, 1972-73
McPIPKIN, Paul, 1969-71
McSHEA, Pat, 1978
McTIGUE, Robert E., 1926-27
McWHORTER, Fonville, 1907
McWHORTER, J. Vason, 1903
McWHORTER, Mac, 1971-72-73
McWHORTER, R. B., 1899
McWHORTER, Robert L., 1910-11-12-13
McWHORTER, Thurmond, 1919-20
McWHORTER, Vason, Jr., 1930-31-32
McWHORTER, William H., 1965-66
MEATHERINGHAM, Mike, 1955-56-57
MEEKS, Calvin, 1943
MEROLA, Michael, 1949-50
METHVIN, Eugene, 1954
MIDDLEBROOKS, G. Percy, 1895-96
MIDDLETON, Keith, 1978
MILAM, Ed, 1973
MILLER, Fred, 1930-31-32
MILLER, James, 1941-42-45
MILLER, Mark, 1978
MILLER, Marvin, "Chip", 1974-75
MILLER, Thomas, 1957
MILLER, Wallace, Jr., 1937
MILNER, Thomas, 1935-37
MILO, Jim, 1977-78
MIMS, William, 1937-38-39
MINOT, Al, 1933-34-35
MITCHELL, George, 1954
MITCHELL, Mark, 1974-75-76
MIXON, Billy, 1948-49-50
MONAHAN, Johnny, 1901-02
MONK, Marion S., 1900-01
MONTGOMERY, Jack, 1969-70
MONTGOMERY, Lee, 1963
MONTI, Angelo, Jr., 1955-56
MOORE, Andrew C., Jr., 1923-24-25
MOORE, G. A., 1903-04
MOORE, Jonathan T., 1895-97
MOORE, Kirby, 1965-66-67
MOORE, Virlyn B., 1903-04
MOORE, W. W., 1916
MOOREHEAD, Leroy, 1932-33-35
MORAN, Tommy, 1929-31
MORENO, H. C., 1893
MOROCCO, Anthony, 1949-50-51
MORRIS, Fred, 1894-95
MORRIS, J. Robert, 1925-26-27
MORRIS, Robert, 1950-51
MORRISON, Tim, 1977-78
MORTON, George, 1924-25-26
MOSELEY, Reid, Jr., 1943-44-45-46
MOSHER, Stu, 1965-66-67
MOSTELLER, James, 1954-55-56
MOTT, Kennon, 1919
MOTT, Norman, 1930-31-32
MRVOS, Samuel, 1951-52-53
MULHERIN, William, 1953-55
MULVEHILL, Richard, 1922
MUNN, Edmund K., 1919
MURPHEY, Eugene F., 1893
MURRAY, Jessie, 1976-77
MURRAY, Mercer W., 1921

N

NALL, Hugh, 1977-78
NALLY, Rufus B., 1892-93-94-95-96
NAPIER, James, 1907-09
NASH, Thomas C., 1909
NASH, Tom, 1969-70-71
NASH, Tom A., 1925-26-27
NEATHERY, Milton, 1976
NELSON, Curtis, 1939
NELSON, Tom, 1923-24-25
NESTORAK, Stan, 1947
NEUHAUS, Steve, 1965-66
NEVILLE, Walter E., 1915-16
NEWKIRK, Duncan, 1964
NEWSOME, Erle T., 1907-08
NIX, Sidney J., 1901-02
NORRIS, Ulysses "Pay", 1976-77-78
NORTHCUTT, John R., 1909
NORWICKI, George, 1962-63-64
NOWELL, Robin, Jr., 1940
NUNLEY, Glen, 1956-58
NUNN, George A., 1905
NUNNALLY, Jerry, 1941-42
NUTT, Fred, Jr., 1953-54

O

OAKES, Mike, 1970
OBERDORFER, Donald, 1919-20
OGLETREE, Carl, 1946
O'MALLEY, Joseph, 1952-53-54
OPPER, Charles, 1932-33-34
ORGEL, Frank, 1959-60
ORR, James, Jr., 1955-56-57
ORRIS, Norman, 1952
OSBOLT, Terry, 1966-68
OUTLAR, Barry, 1970

P

PADDOCK, David F., 1912-13-14-15
PAGE, Ralph, 1973
PAINE, Thad A., 1916
PAINE, Trav, 1968-69
PALMER, Henry G., 1927-28
PARIS, Thomas, 1929
PARIS, Thomas H., Jr., 1958-59-60
PARKS, Tim, 1978
PARRISH, Joel, 1974-75-76
PARRISH, Joseph S., 1909-11
PASCALE, Donald, 1977
PASSAVANT, Oscar W., 1905
PASSMORE, Homer, 1940
PATTERSON, James, 1929-30-31
PATTON, George, 1964-65-66
PAUL, Jerry, 1973-74
PAULK, Jeff, 1978
PAYNE, Bully, 1966-67-68
PAYNE, Jimmy, 1978
PAYNE, Porter, 1946-47-48-49
PEACOCK, Albert, 1914
PEACOCK, David R., 1910-11-12
PEACOCK, Howell B., 1908-09
PEARCE, C. C., Jr., 1921
PEEPLES, Terry, 1970
PENNINGTON, Durward, Jr., 1959-60-61
PENNINGTON, Huey, 1966-67-68
PERHACH, Andrew, 1944-45-46-47
PERKINS, John, 1953
PERKINSON, Tom, 1933
PERL, Al, 1944
PERRY, Bill, 1943
PETRIE, Russell R., Jr., 1915-16
PETRISKO, Paul, 1976-77-78
PEW, Andrew, Jr., 1916-19-21
PHELPS, Morris, 1941
PHILLIPS, Benjamin C., 1944
PHILLIPS, Carlso, 1943-44-45
PHILLIPS, Dickie, 1964-65-66
PHILPOT, William K., 1923
PIERCE, Brooke, 1942
PILCHER, George, 1971-72
PILGRIM, Harold, 1954-56
PILLSBURY, Ken, 1964-65-66
PITTMAN, Marvin, Jr., 1940
PLANT, Frank, 1945
POLAK, Joe, 1942
POLLARD, Al, 1974-75-76
POMPEROY, Edgar E., 1895
PONDER, Ernest, 1978
POPE, Clarence, 1973
POPE, Thomas, 1945-47-48-49
PORTER, John H., 1908
PORTERFIELD, Donald, 1962-63-64
POSCHNER, George, 1940-41-42
POSEY, Wyatt, 1939-40-41
POSS, Bob, Jr., 1969-70-71
POSS, Dexter, 1950-51-52
POSS, Robert, 1942
POST, Dan M., 1922
POULOS, Jimmy, 1971-72-73
POWELL, John W., 1914-15
POWELL, Tom N., 1911-12
POWERS, Henry, 1939-41
PRICE, Fred O., 1894-95-96
PRICE, Kirk, 1973-76
PRINCE, Carmon, 1976-77-78
PRICE, George W., 1897
PRINCIPE, Rocco, 1949-50-51
PROSPERI, Raymond, 1948-49-50
PUTNAL, Rex, 1970-71-72
PUTNAM, I. M., 1900
PYBURN, Jeff, 1976-77-78

R

RABER, Mike, 1975-76
RABER, Richard, 1949-50-51
RAGSDALE, Randolph, 1951-52
RAJECKI, Peter, 1968-69-70
RAKESTRAW, Larry, 1961-62-63
RAMSEY, Carter, Jr., 1958-59
RANDALL, L. C., 1921-22-23-24
RANSOM, Eugene M., 1905-06
RAOUL, Loring, 1904
RAUCH, John, 1945-46-47-48
RAY, John, 1970-71-72
REED, Robert, 1953
REID, Andy, 1973-74-75
REID, Bernie, 1944-47-48
REID, Floyd, 1945-47-48-49
REIDER, Ric, 1973-74
REYNOLDS, James T., 1919-20-21

REYNOLDS, Owen G., 1916-19-21
RHOLETTER, David, 1966-67-68
RICHARDS, Leander, 1937
RICHARDSON, Dick, 1942
RICHARDSON, Sam L., 1921-22-23
RICHARDSON, William H., 1952-53
RICHTER, Frank, 1964-65-66
RIDLEHUBER, Preston, 1963-64-65
RIDLEY, Frank M., Jr., 1900-01-02
RIGDON, John, 1916-19
RINGWALL, Richard, 1952
RIOFSKI, Frank, 1942
RISSMILLER, Raymond, 1962-63-64
RITCHIE, Andrew J., 1899
RITCHIE, Horace B., 1902-03-04
RITCHIE, William R., 1898
ROBBINS, Gordon, 1973-74
ROBERTS, Jack, 1929-30-31
ROBERTS, James "Jack", 1950-51-52
ROBERTS, James, Jr., 1958
ROBERTS, Joe W., 1952
ROBERTS, Laneair, 1954-55-56
ROBERTS, William, 1963
ROBESON, E. J., 1909
ROBESON, L. S., 1905
ROBINSON, Matt, 1974-75-76
ROBINSON, Mike, 1973-74
ROBINSON, Mixon, 1969-70-71
ROBINSON, Noble "Rex", 1977-78
ROBISON, Dennard, 1968
ROCCO, Patsy, 1949-50
RODDENBERY, Andrew, 1935-36-37
RODRIQUE, Patrick, 1966-67-68
ROGERS, Danny, 1976-77-78
ROGERS, Ernest P., 1924-25-26
ROGERS, Ronnie, 1967-69-70
ROGERS, Steve, 1977
ROLAND, Billy, 1957-58-59
ROS, Frank, 1978
ROSE, Frank D., 1919
ROSE, Robert, 1929-30-31
ROSENBERG, Buzy, 1970-71-72
ROSSITER, Joseph A., 1904
ROTHE, E. S., 1919
ROTHSTEIN, Bennie, 1927-28-29
RUARK, Walter, 1940-41-42
RUCKER, Lamar, 1900
RUNYON, Thomas, 1962
RUSSELL, Jay, 1978
RUSSELL, John "Rusty", 1973-74-75
RUSSELL, Phillip, 1967-68-69
RUTLAND, James W., 1944
RUTLAND, William, 1943

S

SAGE, Dan Y., 1904-05-06
SALERNO, Frank, 1950-51-52
SALISBURY, Robert, 1937-38-39
SAMPSON, Bill, 1967
SANCKEN, George A., 1910-11-12
SANDERS, Jeff, 1974-75-76
SANDERS, Robert, 1945
SANDERSON, Fred, 1971
SAPP, Theron, 1956-57-58
SAUNDERS, Tom, 1974-75
SAYE, David, 1968-69-70
SAYE, Jake, 1960-61-62
SAYE, William, 1953-54-55
SCHOPEN, Joseph, 1955
SCHULTEZ, Kenneth, 1956-57
SCHWAK, David, 1973-74-75
SCICHILONE, Joseph, 1950-51-52
SCOTT, Jake, 1967-68
SCOTT, Lindsay, 1978
SCOTT, Robert B., 1907
SCOTT, Terry, 1961-62-63
SEALY, James, 1958
SEDLOCK, Robert, 1957
SELLERS, Terry, 1965-66-67
SELLERS, Weyman, 1945-46-47-48
SHACKELFORD, George O., 1893
SHAMBLIN, Jackson, 1959-60
SHANNON, Emory, 1898-1900
SHAW, Ken, 1968-69-70
SHEA, Donald, 1953-54-55
SHERLOCK, Cecil W., 1924-25-26
SHERRER, Bobby, 1952
SHI, Allen, 1933-34-35
SHIMKUS, Dennis, 1960
SHIRER, Jimmy, 1969-70-71
SHIVER, Ivy M., Jr., 1926-27
SHIVER, Ivy, III, 1949-50
SIMCOX, Horace, 1899
SIMON, Matthew, 1978
SIMONS, Walter, 1943
SIMONTON, Abner, 1939
SINGLETARY, Wilson E., 1944
SINKWICH, Frank, 1940-41-42
SKIPWORTH, George, 1944
SKIPWORTH, James, 1939-40
SLATER, J. F., 1909-10
SLAUGHTER, William, 1959
SLEEK, Steve, 1970-71-72
SMAHA, Jiggy, 1967
SMILEY, Dan, 1972
SMILEY, Julian, 1969-70
SMILEY, Ronnie, 1972
SMITH, Allen N., 1925-26
SMITH, Charles, 1943-44-45-46
SMITH, Don, 1957
SMITH, Henry E., 1925-26-27
SMITH, J. H., 1928
SMITH, Jim, 1963-65
SMITH, John, 1972
SMITH, Marion, 1901-02
SMITH, Patrick, 1959-60-61
SMITH, Paul, 1943
SMITH, Quinton, 1957
SMITH, R. Kyle, 1905-06-07
SMITH, Royce, 1969-70-71
SMITH, Talbot F., 1893
SMITH, Vern, 1972-73-74
SMITH, Vernon, Jr., 1929-30-31
SMOOK, Tommy, 1971-72
SNELL, Jerry, 1964
SNIDER, Billy, 1952
SNIDER, Leonard, 1894-95
SOBERDASH, Donald, 1957-58-59
SPADAFINO, Leonard, 1954-55
SPAIN, Frank, 1894
SPAIN, J. W., 1894-96
SPICER, James P., 1921
SPIVEY, Dan, 1973-74
SPOONER, Johnny, 1956
STANFILL, Bill, 1966-67-68
STAPLETON, Charles, 1974
STARGELL, Guy, 1978
STEBER, Joel, 1978
STEELE, Richard, 1949-50-51
STEELY, Harold, 1964-65
STEGEMAN, John, 1939
STEINER, Godfrey, 1945
STELLING, H. Cree, 1927-28-29
STEVENS, Harry, 1936-38
STEWART, Mark, 1966-67-68
STEWART, Ronnie, 1977-78
STILES, George, 1892
STINSON, Les, 1973-74
ST. JOHN, Herbert, 1944-45-46-47
STOINOFF, James M., 1930
STRIPLIN, Mike, 1974-75
STROTHER, Clinton, 1942
STRUMKE, William, 1956
STUBBS, Herbert W., 1893-94-95
SULLIVAN, Arthur R., 1903-04-05
SULLIVAN, Phil, 1969-70-71
SULLIVAN, Wendall, 1930-31
SWANSON, Ben, 1900
SWINDLE, Buck, 1968-69-70
SWINFORD, Gene, 1970-71-72
SWINFORD, Wayne, 1962-63-64
SWOOPES, Ronnie, 1974-75-76-77

T

TANNER, Fred A., 1919-20-21-22
TANNER, Hampton, 1948-49-50
TARKENTON, Francis, 1958-59-60
TARLETON, Wendell, 1954-55-56
TARRER, Harold, 1966-67-68
TASSAPOULAS, Spero, 1929-30
TATE, E. B., 1915-16
TAYLOR, Bob, 1963-64-65
TAYLOR, N. James, 1920-22-23-24
TAYLOR, Spafford, 1947-48
TAYLOR, Steve, 1972-73-74
TAYLOR, Wayne, 1959-60-61
TEDDER, Stan, 1975
TEEL, Kerry, 1968
TERESHINSKI, Joe, 1942-45-46
TERESHINSKI, Joe, Jr., 1974-75-76
TERESHINSKI, Wally, 1976-77
TERRY, John, 1946
TERRY, John Gordon, 1976-77-78
THOMAS, Carroll, 1937-38
THOMAS, John, 1974
THOMASON, James D., 1922-23-24
THOMPSON, Albert, 1949-50
THOMPSON, Billy Joe, 1957-58-59
THOMPSON, Brad, 1974-75
THOMPSON, Charlie E., 1912-14-15
THOMPSON, Clyde "Mac", 1978
THOMPSON, Homer, 1910
THOMPSON, Ralph, 1921-22-24-25
THOMPSON, Robert, 1975-76-77
THORNHILL, Thomas, 1959
THRASH, Tom A., 1914-15-16
THRASHER, Babe, 1898
THURMAN, Allen, 1906
TICHENOR, W. R., 1897
TIDMORE, Ronnie, 1966-67
TILLITSKI, John, 1948-49-50
TINSLEY, Elijah P., Jr., 1935-36-37
TODD, James, Jr., 1940-41-42
TOMBERLIN, Donald, 1960
TOOTLE, Marvin, 1965-66
TOWNS, Forrest, 1936-37
TOWNS, Robert, 1957-58-59
TOWNSEND, E. C., 1931
TOWNSEND, Glenn, 1977
TREADAWAY, Charlie, 1934-35
TRIPPI, Charles, 1942-45-46
TROUTMAN, Walter, 1936-37
TUCK, Reuben M., 1909
TUCKER, Doug, 1967
TUCKER, Mayo, 1969-70-71
TURBYVILLE, Charlie, 1933-34
TURNER, C. Lewis, 1906
TURNER, William R., 1901-02
TWITTY, W. C., 1903

U

ULLRICH, Andy, 1975

V

VAN BUREN, Robert, 1954
VANDIVER, J. H., 1919-20-21-22
VANDIVER, Sanford, Jr., 1936-37
VAN GIESEN, George, 1925-26
VANN, Kenneth, 1960-61-62
VARNADO, Jerry, 1964-65-66
VEAL, Gene, 1978
VELLA, Leonard, 1960-61
VICKERS, Jimmy, 1957-58-59
VICKERY, Farrar, 1942
VINESETT, Travis, 1956-57
VON GAMMON, Vonabalde, 1896-97

W

WADLEY, Bubba, 1974
WADLEY, L. R., 1904
WAGNON, Henry, 1933-34-35
WALDEN, Bobby, 1958-59-60
WALDEN, H. S., 1897-98
WALSH, William, Jr., 1950-51
WALSTON, Robert, 1947-48-49-50
WASHINGTON, Gene, 1973-74-75-76
WATKINS, Herbert, 1976-77
WATKINS, Newton, 1892-94
WATKINS, William, 1956
WATSON, Dennis, 1969-70-71
WATSON, Steve, 1971
WATSON, Young L., 1896-97
WATT, Josh, 1975
WAUGH, Armin, 1929-30
WEAVER, Eddie, Jr., 1978
WEIR, John B., Jr., 1908
WELCH, Clarence, 1941
WELLS, Don Ray, 1944
WELTON, Chris, 1978
WEST, John, 1932-33-34
WEST, Larry, 1972-73-74
WEST, Robert, 1950-51-52
WESTBURY, Gary, 1978
WESTMORELAND, Ralph, 1961
WHEATLEY, J. D., 1905
WHEELER, Charles Randy, 1965-66
WHELCHEL, Hugh C., 1919-20-21-22
WHIDDON, Ken C., 1965-66
WHIRE, Joseph, 1931
WHITE, Gene, 1951-52-53
WHITE, George, 1966-67-68
WHITE, Steve, 1970-71-72
WHITE, Walter, 1954-55
WHITEHEAD, James, 1962
WHITTEMORE, Charles, 1968-69-70
WHITTON, George, 1956-58
WHITWORTH, Keith, 1973
WIEHRS, Charles F., 1923-24
WILFONG, Walter, 1938-39
WILHITE, Clayton, 1938
WILKINS, Roy, 1953-54-55-56
WILLIAMS, Charles, 1938-39
WILLIAMS, Charles H., 1921
WILLIAMS, Garland, 1942-46

WILLIAMS, Greg, 1976-77-78
WILLIAMS, James, 1952-53-54
WILLIAMS, James, Jr., 1955
WILLIAMS, Langdale, 1959-60-61
WILLIAMS, Rayfield, 1974-75-76
WILLIAMS, Ronald, 1952
WILLIAMSON, Wallace, 1960-61-62
WILLINGHAM, Broadus E., 1908
WILLINGHAM, N., 1902
WILSON, Barry, 1962-63-64
WILSON, Duane "Bubba", 1973
WILSON, Jim, 1963-64
WILSON, Mark, 1974-75-76
WILSON, Mike, 1974-75-76
WILSON, Robert, 1974-75
WILSON, Steve, 1973-74-75
WIMBERLY, Bruce, 1952-53
WINGATE, Harry L., 1915-16
WINSETT, Gerald, 1963
WINSHIP, Blanton, 1892
WISDOM, Chip, 1969-70-71
WITT, Tom, 1939-40
WOERNER, Scott, 1977-78
WOLFSON, Louis, 1931
WOMACK, Jimmy, Jr., 1977-78
WOOD, Jimmy, 1968-69-70
WOOD, William "Butch", 1973
WOODALL, Luke, 1926
WOODALL, Woody, 1967-68
WOODRUFF, George C., 1907-08-10-11-12
WOODRUFF, Harry E., 1903-04
WOODS, Billy, 1974-75-76-77
WOODWARD, Brigham, 1961-62-63
WOODWARD, Steve, 1966-67-68
WORRELL, Billy, 1960
WRAY, C. B., 1905
WRIGHT, Louis M., 1901
WRIGLEY, G. Arthur, 1893

Y

YAWN, Bruce, 1966-67-68
YELVINGTON, Richard, Jr., 1948-49-50-51
YORK, Gus, 1910-11-12
YOUNG, Bruce, 1966
YOUNG, Dick, 1967
YOUNG, Hilton, 1976-77
YOUNG, Leroy, 1932-33
YOUNG, Lewis, 1936-37
YOUNG, Richard, 1954-55
YOUNG, William, 1952-53

Z

ZAMBIASI, Ben, 1974-75-76-77
ZIMMERLINK, Tom, 1974

University of Kentucky

Location: Lexington, Kentucky
Enrollment: 37,500
Nickname: Wildcats
Colors: Blue and White
Stadium: Commonwealth (58,000)

University of Kentucky Head Coaching Records

COACH	YEAR	WON	LOST	TIED
No coach	1881	1	2	0
No coach	1891	1	1	0
Prof. A. M. Miller, John A. Thompson	1892	2	4	1
John A. Thompson	1893	5	2	1
W. P. Finney	1894	5	2	0
Charles Mason	1895	4	5	0
Dudley Short	1896	3	6	0
Lyman B. Eaton	1897	2	4	0
W. R. Bass	1898-'99	12	2	2
W. H. Kiler	1900-'01	6	12	1
E. N. McLeod	1902	3	5	1
C. A. Wright	1903	7	1	0
F. E. Schacht	1904-'05	15	4	1
J. White Guyn	1906-'08	17	7	1
E. R. Sweetland	1909-'10; 1912	23	5	0
P. P. Douglass	1911	7	3	0
Alpha Brumage	1913-'14	11	5	0
J. J. Tigert	1915-'16	10	2	3
S. A. Boles	1917	3	5	1
Andy Gill	1918-'19	5	5	1
W. J. Juneau	1920-'22	13	10	2
J. J. Winn	1923	4	3	2
Fred J. Murphy	1924-'26	12	14	1
Harry Gamage	1927-'33	32	25	5
Chet Wynne	1934-'37	20	19	0
A. D. Kirwan	1938-'44	24	28	4
Bernie Shively	1945	2	8	0
Paul (Bear) Bryant	1946-'53	60	23	5
Blanton Collier	1954-'61	41	36	3
Charlie Bradshaw	1962-'68	25	41	4
John Ray	1969-'72	10	33	0
Fran Curci	1973-'78	35	30	2

University of Kentucky All-Time Scores

1881

7¼	Transylvania	1
3¼	Transylvania	3¾
10½	(1-2-0)	6¾

1891

8	Georgetown	2
0	Centre	10
8	(1-1-0)	12

1892

0	Transylvania	0
6	Central	8
4	Central	8
14	Louisville AC	10
0	V. M. I.	34
6	Central	10
10	Transylvania	4
36	(2-4-1)	66

1893

80	Georgetown	0
56	Tennessee	0
4	Centre	6
28	Transylvania	0
36	Central	48
14	Cincy YMCA	4
38	Transylvania	28
24	Indiana	24
280	(5-2-1)	110

1894

4	Cincinnati	32
40	Georgetown	6
66	Jeff'ville AC	0
28	Miami (O.)	6
44	Transylvania	0
0	Centre	67
38	Central	10
220	(5-2-0)	121

1895

10	Frankfort AC	0
0	Purdue	32
0	DePauw	18
6	Centre	0
0	Georgetown	10
26	Transylvania	0
6	Ohio State	8
16	Lexington AC	10
0	Centre	16
64	(4-5-0)	94

1896

0	Lexington AC	10
0	Vanderbilt	6
4	Cat'burg AC	6
36	Transylvania	6
0	Centre	32
62	Central	0
0	Centre	44
16	Georgetown	0
4	Lexington AC	30
122	(3-6-0)	134

1897

8	Transylvania	6
0	Ky. Wesleyan	4
32	Georgetown	0
20	Georgetown	4
0	Vanderbilt	50
0	Central	18
4	Georgetown	12

0	Centre	36
64	(3-5-0)	120

1898

18	Transylvania	0
28	Georgetown	0
59	8th. Mass. Com.	0
17	Louisville AC	0
6	Centre	0
17	160th Ind.	0
36	Newcastle AC	0
181	(7-0-0)	0

1899

23	Transylvania	6
18	Miami (O.)	5
11	Centre	11
0	Tennessee	12
0	Central	5
34	Georgetown	0
0	Wash. & Lee	0
6	Wash. & Lee	0
6	Alumni	5
98	(5-2-2)	44

1900

6	Cincinnati	20
12	L'ville YMCA	6
0	Centre	5
0	All-Kentucky	5
0	Central	6
12	L'ville YMCA	0
5	Avondale AC	11
12	Georgetown	0
0	Central	11
12	Transylvania	0
59	(4-6-0)	64

1901

0	Vanderbilt	22
0	Cincinnati	0
17	Georgetown	0
0	Transylvania	27
6	Avondale AC	17
0	L'ville YMCA	11
0	Central	5
0	Tennessee	5
16	Cincinnati	0
39	(2-6-1)	87

1902

22	Q. &. C. Rwy.	0
11	Miami (O.)	5
28	Georgetown	0
0	Nashville	11
0	Mooney School	23
0	Central	15
0	L'ville YMCA	17
6	Cincinnati	6
5	Vanderbilt	16
5	Transylvania	6
77	(3-6-1)	99

1903

39	Cynthiana	0
21	Xavier	0
17	Berea College	0
18	K. M. I.	0
47	Miami (O.)	0
51	Georgetown	0
11	Marietta	5
0	Transylvania	17
204	(7-1-0)	22

1904

28	Paris	0
12	Indiana	0
40	Centre	0
42	Berea	0
6	Bethany	0
0	Cincinnati	11
11	K. M. I.	0
35	Georgetown	0
81	Central	0
21	Transylvania	4
276	(9-1-0)	15

1905

52	Cynthiana	0
23	Catlettsburg	0
0	Indiana	29
12	K. M. I.	4
46	Berea	0
53	Marshall	0
0	W. Virginia	45
12	Cumberland	0
0	St. Louis	82
11	Central	11
209	(6-3-1)	171

1906

0	Vanderbilt	28
48	Eminence AC	0
16	K. M. I.	11
0	Marietta	16
21	Tennessee	0
19	Georgetown	0
6	Centre	12
110	(4-3-0)	67

1907

17	Ky. Wesleyan	0
6	Winchester AC	0
30	Manual HS	0
0	Vanderbilt	40
29	Morris-Harvey	0
40	Hanover	0
0	Tennessee	0
5	Maryville	2
38	Georgetown	0
11	Central	0
5	Transylvania	0
187	(9-1-1)	46

1908

17	Berea	0
0	Tennessee	7
18	Maryville	0
5	Miss. State	12
0	Sewanee	12
0	Michigan	62
12	Rose Poly	0
40	Centre	0
92	(4-4-0)	91

1909

18	Ky. Wesleyan	0
28	Berea	0
6	Illinois	2
17	Tennessee	0
6	N.C. State	15
43	Rose Poly	0
22	Georgetown	6
29	St. Mary's	0
77	Transylvania	0
15	Central	6
259	(9-1-0)	29

1910

112	Ohio Univ.	0
12	Maryville	5
11	N. Carolina	0
42	Ky. Wesleyan	0
37	Georgetown	0
10	Tulane	3
10	Tennessee	0
0	St. Louis	9
6	Central	12
140	(7-2-0)	29

1911

13	Maryville	0
12	Morris-Harvey	0
12	Miami (O.)	0
17	Lexington HS	0
0	Cincinnati	6
18	Georgetown	0
0	Vanderbilt	18
5	Transylvania	12
8	Central	5
12	Tennessee	0
97	(7-3-0)	41

1912

34	Maryville	0
13	Marshall	6
8	Miami (O.)	13
19	Cincinnati	13
41	Louisville	0
2	V.M.I.	3
64	Hanover	0
13	Tennessee	6
56	Cinn. YMI	0
250	(7-2-0)	41

1913

21	Butler	7
0	Illinois	21
0	Miss. State	31
21	Ohio Northern	0
27	Cincinnati	7
28	Earlham	10
33	Wilmington	0
20	Louisville	0
7	Tennessee	13
157	(6-3-0)	89

1914

87	Wilmington	0
80	Maryville	0
19	Miss. State	13
81	Earlham	3
7	Cincinnati	14
6	Purdue	40
42	Louisville	0
6	Tennessee	23
328	(5-3-0)	93

1915

33	Butler	0
54	Earlham	13
0	Miss. State	12
7	Sewanee	7
27	Cincinnati	6
15	Louisville	0
7	Purdue	0
6	Tennessee	0
149	(6-1-1)	38

1916

39	Butler	3
68	Centre	0
0	Vanderbilt	45
0	Sewanee	0
32	Cincinnati	0
13	Miss. State	3
0	Tennessee	0
152	(4-1-2)	51

1917

33	Butler	0
19	Maryville	0
0	Miami (O.)	0
0	Vanderbilt	5
0	Sewanee	7
0	Centre	3
0	Miss. State	14
0	Alabama	28
52	Florida	0
104	(3-5-1)	57

1918

24	Indiana	7
0	Vanderbilt	33
21	Georgetown	3
45	(2-1-4)	43

1919

12	Georgetown	0
0	Indiana	24
0	Ohio State	49
6	Sewanee	0
0	Vanderbilt	0
0	Cincinnati	7
0	Centre	56
13	Tennessee	0
31	(3-4-1)	136

1920

62	Sou. Presby.	0
31	Maryville	0
0	Miami (O.)	14
6	Sewanee	6
0	Vanderbilt	20
7	Cincinnati	6
0	Centre	49
7	Tennessee	14
113	(3-4-1)	109

1921

68	Ky. Wesleyan	0
28	Marshall	0
14	Vanderbilt	21
33	Georgetown	0
0	Sewanee	6
0	Centre	55
14	V. M. I.	7
0	Tennessee	0
157	(4-3-1)	89

1922

16	Marshall	0
15	Cincinnati	0
73	Louisville	0
40	Georgetown	6
7	Sewanee	0
8	Centre	27
0	Vanderbilt	9
6	Alabama	0
7	Tennessee	14
167	(6-3-0)	56

1923

41	Marshall	0
14	Cincinnati	0
6	Wash & Lee	6
28	Maryville	0
35	Georgetown	0
0	Centre	10
8	Alabama	16
3	Ga. Tech	3
0	Tennessee	18
135	(4-3-2)	53

1924

29	Louisville	0
42	Georgetown	0
7	Wash & Lee	10
7	Sewanee	0
0	Centre	7
7	Alabama	42
3	V. M. I.	10
27	Tennessee	6
7	W. Va. Wes.	24
129	(4-5-0)	99

1925

13	Maryville	0
0	Chicago	9
19	Clemson	6
0	Wash & Lee	25
14	Sewanee	0
16	Centre	0
0	Alabama	31
7	V. M. I.	0
23	Tennessee	20
92	(6-3-0)	97

1926

25	Maryville	0
6	Indiana	14
13	Wash. & Lee	14
18	Florida	13
13	Va. Tech	13
0	Alabama	14
9	V. M. I.	10
0	Centre	7
0	Tennessee	6
84	(2-6-1)	91

1927

6	Maryville	6
0	Indiana	21
13	Ky. Wesleyan	7
6	Florida	27
0	Wash. & Lee	25
6	Vanderbilt	34
6	Alabama	21
25	V. M. I.	0
53	Centre	0
0	Tennessee	20
115	(3-6-1)	161

1928

61	Carson-Nwmn.	0
6	Wash. & Lee	0
0	Northwestern	7
8	Centre	0
7	Vanderbilt	14
0	Alabama	14
18	V. M. I.	6
0	Tennessee	0
101	(4-3-1)	41

1929

40	Maryville	0
20	Wash. & Lee	6
58	Carson-Nwmn.	0
33	Centre	0
44	Clemson	6
13	Alabama	24
23	V. M. I.	12
6	Tennessee	6
237	(6-1-1)	54

1930

37	Sewanee	0
57	Maryville	0
33	Wash. & Lee	14
47	Virginia	0
0	Alabama	19
7	Duke	14
26	V. M. I.	0
0	Tennessee	8
207	(5-3-0)	55

1931

19	Maryville	0
45	Wash. & Lee	0
6	Maryland	6
20	Va. Tech	6
7	Alabama	9
0	Duke	7
20	V. M. I.	12
6	Tennessee	6
7	Florida	2
130	(5-2-2)	48

1932

23	V. M. I.	0
18	Sewanee	0
12	Ga. Tech	6
53	Wash. & Lee	7
0	Va. Tech	7
7	Alabama	12
0	Duke	13
3	Tulane	6
0	Tennessee	26
116	(4-5-0)	77

1933
46 Maryville 2
7 Sewanee 0
7 Ga. Tech 6
3 Cincinnati 0
0 Wash. & Lee 7
7 Duke 14
0 Alabama 20
21 V. M. I. 6
0 Tulane 34
0 Tennessee 27
91 (5-5-0) 116

1934
26 Maryville 0
0 Wash. & Lee 7
27 Cincinnati 0
7 Clemson 0
0 N. Carolina 6
9 Auburn 0
14 Alabama 34
33 Southwestern 0
7 Tulane 20
0 Tennessee 19
123 (5-5-0) 86

1935
60 Maryville 0
21 Xavier 7
6 Ohio State 19
25 Ga. Tech 6
0 Auburn 23
0 Alabama 13
15 Florida 6
13 Tulane 20
27 Tennessee 0
167 (5-4-0) 94

1936
54 Maryville 3
21 Xavier 0
38 V. M. I. 0
0 Ga. Tech 34
39 Wash. & Lee 7
7 Florida 0
0 Alabama 14
7 Manhattan 13
7 Clemson 6
6 Tennessee 7
179 (6-4-0) 84

1937
0 Vanderbilt 12
6 Xavier 0
0 Ga. Tech 32
41 Wash. & Lee 6
19 Manhattan 0
0 Alabama 41
27 S. Carolina 7
0 Boston Col. 13
0 Tennessee 13
0 Florida 6
93 (4-6-0) 130

1938
46 Maryville 0
66 Oglethorpe 0
7 Vanderbilt 14
0 Wash. & Lee 8
7 Xavier 26
6 Alabama 26
18 Ga. Tech 19
0 Clemson 14
0 Tennessee 46
150 (2-7-0) 160

1939
21 V. M. I. 0
21 Vanderbilt 13
59 Oglethorpe 0
13 Georgia 6
21 Xavier 0
7 Alabama 7
6 Ga. Tech 13
13 W. Virginia 6
0 Tennessee 19
161 (6-2-1) 64

1940
59 Bald. Wallace 7
13 Xavier 0
47 Wash. & Lee 12
7 Vanderbilt 7
24 Geo. Wash. 0
7 Georgia 7
0 Alabama 25
26 Ga. Tech 7
7 W. Virginia 9
0 Tennessee 33
190 (5-3-2) 107

1941
37 Va. Tech 14
7 Wash. & Lee 0
15 Vanderbilt 39
21 Xavier 6
18 W. Virginia 6
0 Alabama 30
13 Ga. Tech 20
33 Southwestern 19
7 Tennessee 20
151 (5-4-0) 154

1942
6 Georgia 7
35 Xavier 19
53 Wash. & Lee 0
6 Vanderbilt 7
21 Va. Tech 21
0 Alabama 14
27 George Wash. 6
7 Ga. Tech 47
0 W. Virginia 7
0 Tennessee 26
155 (3-6-1) 154

1943—No Team

1944
27 Ole Miss. 7
13 Tennessee 26
0 Mich. State 2
12 Georgia 13
26 V. M. I. 2
0 Alabama 41
0 Miss. State 26
40 W. Virginia 9
7 Tennessee 21
125 (3-6-0) 147

1945
7 Ole Miss 21
13 Cincinnati 7
6 Mich. State 7
6 Georgia 48
6 Vanderbilt 19
7 Cincinnati 16
19 Alabama 60
19 W. Virginia 6
13 Marquette 19
0 Tennessee 14
96 (2-8-0) 217

1946
20 Ole Miss 6
26 Cincinnati 6
70 Xavier 0
13 Georgia 28
10 Vanderbilt 7
7 Alabama 21
39 Mich. State 14
35 Marquette 7
13 W. Virginia 0
0 Tennessee 7
233 (7-3-0) 96

1947
7 Ole Miss 14
20 Cincinnati 0
20 Xavier 0
26 Georgia 0
14 Vanderbilt 0
7 Mich. State 6
0 Alabama 13
15 W. Virginia 6
36 Evansville 0
6 Tennessee 13
151 (7-3-0) 52

Great Lakes Bowl
24 Villanova 14

1948
48 Xavier 7
7 Ole Miss 20
12 Georgia 35
7 Vanderbilt 26
25 Marquette 0
28 Cincinnati 7
13 Villanova 13
34 Florida 15
0 Tennessee 0
25 Miami 5
199 (5-3-2) 128

1949
71 Sou. Miss. 7
19 L.S.U. 0
47 Ole Miss 0
25 Georgia 0
44 Citadel 0
7 S. M. U. 20
14 Cincinnati 7
21 Xavier 7
35 Florida 0
0 Tennessee 6
21 Miami 6
304 (9-2-0) 53

Orange Bowl
13 Santa Clara 21

1950
25 N. Texas St 0
14 L.S.U. 0
27 Ole Miss 0
40 Dayton 0
41 Cincinnati 7
34 Villanova 7
28 Ga. Tech 14
40 Florida 6
48 Miss. State 21
83 N. Dakota 0
0 Tennessee 7
380 (10-1-0) 62

Sugar Bowl
13 Oklahoma 7

1951
72 Tenn. Tech 13
6 Texas 7
17 Ole Miss 21
7 Ga. Tech 13
27 Miss. State 0
35 Villanova 13
14 Florida 6
32 Miami 0
37 Tulane 0
47 Geo. Wash 13
0 Tennessee 28
294 (7-4-0) 114

Cotton Bowl
20 T.C.U. 7

1952
6 Villanova 25
13 Ole Miss 13
10 Texas A&M 7
7 L.S.U. 34
14 Miss. State 27
14 Cincinnati 6
29 Miami 0
27 Tulane 6
27 Clemson 14
14 Tennessee 14
0 Florida 27
161 (5-4-2) 173

1953
6 Texas A&M 7
6 Ole Miss 22
26 Florida 13
6 L.S.U. 6
32 Miss. State 13
19 Villanova 0
19 Rice 13
40 Vanderbilt 14
20 Memphis St. 7
27 Tennessee 21
201 (7-2-1) 116

1954
0 Maryland 20
9 Ole Miss 28
7 L.S.U. 6
21 Auburn 14
7 Florida 21
13 Ga. Tech 6
28 Villanova 3
19 Vanderbilt 7
33 Memphis St. 7
14 Tennessee 13
151 (7-3-0) 125

1955
7 L.S.U. 19
21 Ole Miss 14
28 Villanova 0
14 Auburn 14
14 Miss. State 20
10 Florida 7
20 Rice 16
0 Vanderbilt 34
41 Memphis St. 7
23 Tennessee 0
178 (6-3-1) 131

1956
6 Ga. Tech 14
7 Ole Miss 37
17 Florida 8
0 Auburn 13
14 L.S.U. 0
14 Georgia 7
14 Maryland 0
7 Vanderbilt 6
35 Xavier 0
7 Tennessee 20
119 (6-4-0) 105

1957
0 Ga. Tech 13
0 Ole Miss 15
7 Florida 14
0 Auburn 6
0 L.S.U. 21
14 Georgia 33
53 Memphis St. 7
7 Vanderbilt 12
27 Xavier 0
20 Tennessee 6
128 (3-7-0) 127

1958
51 Hawaii 0
13 Ga. Tech 0
6 Ole Miss 27
0 Auburn 8
7 L.S.U. 32
0 Georgia 28
33 Miss. State 12
0 Vanderbilt 0
20 Xavier 6
6 Tennessee 2
136 (5-4-1) 115

1959
12 Ga. Tech 14
0 Ole Miss 16
32 Detroit 7
0 Auburn 33
0 L.S.U. 9
7 Georgia 14
22 Miami 3
6 Vanderbilt 11
41 Xavier 0
20 Tennessee 0
140 (4-6-0) 107

1960
13 Ga. Tech 23
6 Ole Miss 21
7 Auburn 10
55 Marshall 0
3 L.S.U. 0
13 Georgia 17
23 Fla. State 0
27 Vanderbilt 0
49 Xavier 0
10 Tennessee 10
206 (5-4-1) 81

1961
7 Miami 14
6 Ole Miss 20
14 Auburn 12
21 Kansas St. 8
14 L.S.U. 24
15 Georgia 16
20 Fla. State 0
16 Vanderbilt 3
9 Xavier 0
16 Tennessee 26
138 (5-5-0) 123

1962
0 Fla. State 0
0 Ole Miss 14
6 Auburn 16
27 Detroit 8
0 L.S.U. 7
7 Georgia 7
17 Miami 25
7 Vanderbilt 0
9 Xavier 14
12 Tennessee 10
85 (3-5-2) 101

1963
33 Va. Tech 14
7 Ole Miss 31
13 Auburn 14
35 Detroit 18
7 L.S.U. 28
14 Georgia 17
14 Miami 20
0 Vanderbilt 0
19 Baylor 7
0 Tennessee 19
142 (3-6-1) 168

1964
13 Detroit 6
27 Ole Miss 21
20 Auburn 0
6 Fla. State 48
7 L.S.U. 27
7 Georgia 21
21 W. Virginia 26
22 Vanderbilt 21
15 Baylor 17
12 Tennessee 7
150 (5-5-0) 194

1965

7 Missouri 0
16 Ole Miss 7
18 Auburn 23
26 Fla. State 24
21 L.S.U. 31
28 Georgia 10
28 W. Virginia 8
34 Vanderbilt 0
21 Houston 38
3 Tennessee 19

202 (6-4-0) 160

1966

10 N. Carolina 0
0 Ole Miss 17
17 Auburn 7
0 Va. Tech 7
0 L.S.U. 30
15 Georgia 27
14 W. Virginia 14
14 Vanderbilt 10
18 Houston 56
19 Tennessee 28

107 (3-6-1) 196

1967

10 Indiana 12
13 Ole Miss 26
7 Auburn 48
14 Va. Tech 24
7 L.S.U. 30
7 Georgia 31
22 W. Virginia 7
12 Vanderbilt 7
12 Florida 28
7 Tennessee 17

111 (2-8-0) 230

1968

12 Missouri 6
14 Ole Miss 30
7 Auburn 26
35 Oregon St. 34
3 L.S.U. 13
14 Georgia 35
35 W. Virginia 16
0 Vanderbilt 6
14 Florida 16
7 Tennessee 24

141 (3-7-0) 206

1969

30 Indiana 58
10 Ole Miss 9
3 Auburn 44
7 Va. Tech 6
10 L.S.U. 37
0 Georgia 30
6 W. Virginia 7
6 Vanderbilt 42
6 Florida 31
26 Tennessee 31

104 (2-8-0) 295

1970

10 N. Carolina 20
16 Kansas State 3
17 Ole Miss 20
15 Auburn 33
6 Utah St. 35
7 L.S.U. 14
3 Georgia 19
27 N.C. State 2
17 Vanderbilt 18
13 Florida 24
0 Tennessee 45

131 (2-9-0) 233

1971

13 Clemson 10
8 Indiana 26
20 Ole Miss 34
6 Auburn 38
6 Ohio Univ. 35
13 L.S.U. 17
0 Georgia 34
33 Va. Tech 27
14 Vanderbilt 7
24 Florida 35
7 Tennessee 21

144 (3-8-0) 284

1972

25 Villanova 7
0 Alabama 35
34 Indiana 35
17 Miss. State 13
20 N. Carolina 31
0 L.S.U. 10
7 Georgia 13
7 Tulane 18
14 Vanderbilt 13
0 Florida 40
7 Tennessee 17

131 (3-8-0) 232

1973

31 Va. Tech 26
14 Alabama 28
3 Indiana 17
42 Miss. State 14
10 N. Carolina 16
21 L.S.U. 28
12 Georgia 7
34 Tulane 7
27 Vanderbilt 17
18 Florida 20
14 Tennessee 16

226 (5-6-0) 196

1974

38 Va. Tech 7
3 W. Virginia 16
28 Indiana 22
10 Miami, O. 14
13 Auburn 31
20 L.S.U. 13
20 Georgia 24
30 Tulane 7
38 Vanderbilt 12
41 Florida 24
7 Tennessee 24

248 (6-5-0) 194

1975

27 Va. Tech 8
10 Kansas 14
10 Maryland 10
3 Penn State 10
9 Auburn 15
14 LSU 17
13 Georgia 21
23 Tulane 10
3 Vanderbilt 13
7 Florida 48
13 Tennessee 17

132 (2-8-1) 183

1976

38 Oregon St. 13
16 Kansas 37
14 W. Virginia 10
22 Penn State 6
*7 Miss. State 14
21 LSU 7
7 Georgia 31
14 Maryland 24
14 Vanderbilt 0
28 Florida 9
7 Tennessee 0

188 (7-4-0) 151

*Won by forfeit

Peach Bowl

21 N. Carolina 0

1977

10 N. Carolina 7
6 Baylor 21
28 West Virginia 13
24 Penn State 20
23 Miss. State 7
33 LSU 13
33 Georgia 0
32 Va. Tech 0
28 Vanderbilt 6
14 Florida 7
21 Tennessee 17

252 (10-1-0) 111

1978

14 So. Carolina 14
25 Baylor 21
3 Maryland 20
0 Penn State 30
24 Mississippi 17
0 LSU 21
16 Georgia 17
28 Va. Tech 0
53 Vanderbilt 2
16 Florida 18
14 Tennessee 29

193 (4-6-1) 189

University of Kentucky Lettermen—1892 to 1978

A

ABBOTT, Bob, 1967
ACHESON, Kevin, 1974
ADAIR, George, 1905-06-07
ADKINS, Tommy, 1951-52-53
ALAMAN, Paul, 1973, Mgr.
ALDRIDGE, Burton, 1930-32-33
ALEXANDER, James, 1975, Mgr.
ALFORD, Smith, 1893-94-95-96
ALLEN, Ermal, 1939-40-41
ALLEN, Rich, 1971-72-73
ALTHAUS, Carl, 1941-42
ALVAREZ, Jack, 1971-72-73
ANDERSON, H. C., 1893
ANDERSON, Tom, 1967
ANDREWS, Ken, 1929-30-31
ANDRIGHETTI, John, 1963-64-65
ANTONINI, Frank, 1964-65
ARENSTEIN, Leo, 1944
ARNOLD, Chuck, 1966
ARNSPARGER, Bill, 1944
ASHER, A. J., 1897
ASHER, G. M., 1895
ASHER, Letcher, 1932
ATKINS, Bob, 1909
ATKINS, Presley, 1902-04-05
AYERS, Clarence, 1933-34-35

B

BABB, Harvey, 1909-10-11
BABB, Jim, 1946-47
BABLITZ, August A., 1910-11
BACH, Stanley, 1932,33
BAER, Stanley, 1905-06
BAILEY, J. Yost "Bill", 1913-14
BAILEY, Joe, 1938-39-40
BAILEY, John, 1952
BAIR, Dave, 1967-68
BAIRD, Charles N., 1892
BAIRD, M., 1905
BALDWIN, John, 1950-51-52
BALL, Sam, 1963-64-65
BARBEE, Dick, 1907-08-09
BARGA, Ray, 1971-72-73
BARNETT, Jim, 1945
BARRINGTON, John, 1976, Mgr.
BARTLETT, Tom, 1918
BARTOS, Bill, 1973-74-75
BASSITT, Bob, 1952
BASTIN, A. L., 1918
BAUGH, Frank, 1921
BAUGH, Walter, 1917-18
BAUGHMAN, Bob, 1929-30
BAYLESS, T. Gardner, 1924
BEADLES, Terry, 1965-66-67
BEAL, Dick, 1944
BEARD, Dick, 1968-69
BEARD, T. W., 1904
BEATTY, Jerry, 1954
BECHERER, Tom, 1963-64-65
BECK, Norman, 1942
BEELER, Bob, 1940-41
BEIRNE, Mike, 1967
BELT, Sylvan, 1926-27
BENNETT, Bob, 1954-55-56
BENNETT, Leeman, 1958-59-60
BENSON, Pascal, 1957-58-59
BENTLEY, Charles, 1946-47-48-49
BENTLEY, Jerry, 1969-70-71
BEZUK, Bob, 1949
BICKEL, Arthur, 1927
BICKEL, George, 1930
BIRD, Billy, 1961
BIRD, Calvin, 1958-59-60
BIRD, Rodger, 1963-64-65
BISHOP, Darryl, 1971-72-73
BISHOP, Fred, 1973-74
BIVIN, Arvon, 1953
BLACK, Billy, 1940
BLACK, Harold, 1936-37-38
BLACK, Marvin, 1905
BLACKBURN, Charles, 1967-68
BLAND, Leroy, 1918
BLANDA, George, 1945-46-47-48
BLANTON, Jerry, 1974-75-76-77
BLEVINS, Ralph, 1932
BLOCKER, Dick, 1957-58
BOCARD, Ken, 1961-62-63
BOLLER, Bill, 1946-47-48-49
BOONE, George, 1957-58-59
BOSSE, Joe, 1935-36-37
BOSTON, Bill, 1937-39
BOSWELL, M. T., 1893
BOULWARE, Mike, 1967-68-69
BOW, John, 1976-77-78
BOWENS, Cecil, 1970-71
BOWIE, Jim, 1958
BOWLING, Willet L., 1901
BOYD, Berl, 1921
BOYD, Jim, 1910, Mgr.
BOYD, Lester, 1975-76-78
BOYD, Ritchie, 1977-78
BRADSHAW, Charlie, 1946-47-48-49
BRANDEL, Joe, 1961
BRANDSTETNER, "Brandy", 1911
BRANSOM, Ben, Jr., 1973-74
BRANSON, Don, 1905
BREWER, Bruce, 1904-05-06
BREWER, Ted, 1922
BRITTAIN, John, 1915-16-17
BRITTON, Donnie, 1966-67
BROCK, Lafayette, 1896, Mgr.
BROCKMAN, George, 1907
BRONAUGH, William, 1898, Mgr.
BRONSTON, Jake, 1929-30
BROOKS, Bobby, 1948-49
BROOKS, Randy, 1976-77-78
BROWN, Bob, 1962-63-64
BROWN, Dave, 1939-40-41
BROWN, Harry, 1937-38

BROWN, Herbert W., Jr., 1928
BROWN, Jack, 1971
BROWN, Locky, 1955
BROWN, Paul, 1913
BROWNING, Charles, 1946-47
BRUECK, Joe, 1959
BRUNO, Al, 1948-49-50
BRUSH, Tommy, 1961
BRYAN, John, 1892-93-94
BRYANT, Charles "Perky", 1961-62-63
BRYANT, Joe, 1976-77
BRYANT, Gene, 1934
BRYANT, Thomson, 1907, Mgr.
BRYANT, Warren, 1973-74-75-76
BUCHANAN, Don, 1957
BURKE, Randy, 1974-75-76
BURNAM, Buzz, 1970-71-72
BUSHONG, Bill, 1970-71
BUTLER, Bob, 1959-60-61
BUTLER, Jack, 1954-55-56

C

CAIN, Ronnie, 1957-58-59
CALLAHAN, Ray, 1953-54-55
CAMBRON, Jim, 1957-58
CAMMACK, A. B. "Red", 1922, Mgr.
CAMMACK, Jim "J. W.", 1921-22-23-25
CAMPASSI, Steve, 1972-73-74-75
CAMPBELL, J. 1909-10
CAMPBELL, James, 1897
CAMPBELL, Jim, 1978
CAMBPELL, Kenton, 1944-45
CAMPBELL, Mark, 1971
CAMPBELL, Tom, 1895-96
CAMPBELL, Walter, 1900-02
CARBONI, Steve, 1973
CARDWELL, Denny, 1963
CARDWELL, J. W., 1908
CAREY, George B., 1892-93-94
CARLIG, Clyde, 1952-55
CARNAHAN, James W., 1892-94-95
CARNES, Wilce, 1938-39
CARPENTER, Bruce, 1976
CARPENTER, W. T., 1897, Mgr.
CARR, Ray, 1973-74-75-76
CARRITHERS, William S., 1912
CARROLL, Arvel, Jr., 1970-71-72
CARROLL, Mike, 1966-67, Mgr.
CARSON, Don, 1961
CARTER, Larry, 1976-77-78
CARTWRIGHT, Bill, 1966-67-68
CASNER, Jack, 1942
CASON, Ron, 1974-75-76-77
CASSADY, Tom, 1932-33
CASSITY, Michael E., 1966
CASSITY, Michael L., 1973-74
CAVANA, James (Bud), 1929-30-31
CHAMBERS, Bill, 1944-45-46
CHAMBERS, J. S., 1909-10-11-12
CHANDLER, Mel, 1956-60-61
CHANEY, Robb, 1977-78
CHAPALA, Tom, 1965
CHAPMAN, Dave, 1961
CHARLES, Dick, 1957
CHISHOLM, O. B., 1906
CLAIBORNE, George, 1951
CLAIBORNE, Jerry, 1946-48-49
CLARK, Emery, 1949-50-51
CLARK, Terry, 1964-65
CLARK, W. F., 1907-08
CLARK, Tom, 1970-71-72
CLARKE, C. C., 1897-98-99-1900
CLAY, Jim, 1908
CLAYTON, R. S., 1915
CLEMENTS, Earle, 1916
CLYMER, Lee, 1971
COCHRAN, Gary, 1959-60-61
COLEMAN, Sam, 1905-06
COLEMAN, Tommy, 1936
COLKER, Max, 1928-29-30
COLLIER, Bob, 1955-56-57
COLLINS, Bill, 1911
COLLINS, Sonny, 1972-73-74-75
COLPITTS, William "Coley", 1919-20-21-22
COLVIN, Dick, 1941-42
COMBS, Carl "Hoot", 1938-39-40
COMBS, John, 1919
COMBS, W., 1902
CONDE, Bill, 1949-50-51
CONGER, Fred, 1967, 69
CONN, C. R., 1926, Mgr.
COOK, H., 1906
COONS, Joe, 1903-04
CORN, Franklin, 1914-15
CORNELIUS, John, 1955-56-57
CORRELL, Ray, 1951-52-53
COVINGTON, Will Ed, 1927-28-29
COYLE, Mike, 1961, Mgr.
COX, Darrell, 1961-62-63
CRAIG, Bill, 1899-1900
CRAIN, A. B., 1906-07
CRAVENS, Bobby, 1956-57-58
CRAVENS, J. T., 1901-02-03
CREECH, Ted, 1924-26
CROAN, Walter, B., 1914, Mgr.
CROWE, Tom, 1969-70-71
CRUTCHER, Maury, 1913-14-15-16
CULP, William, 1919
CURD, Cary, 1975
CURLING, Kerry, 1965-66-67
CURNUTTE, Duke, 1952-53-54-56
CURNUTTE, Ivan, 1956-57
CURRY, Larry, 1927
CUTCHIN, Phil, 1941-42-46
CUTLER, Tom, 1902

D

DABNEY, Al, 1900
DANKO, Don, 1964-65
DARBY, Darrell, 1930-31-32
DARNABY, Jim, 1932-34
DARNALL, F. H., 1904
DAVIDSON, O. L. "Bud", 1931-32-33
DAVIS, Bob, 1935-36-37
DAVIS, Dameron, 1936-37-38
DAVIS, Doug, 1963-64-65
DAVIS, Jerry, 1965-66
DAWSON, Bill, 1946-48-50
DEATON, Mike, 1977-78
DeBOW, Sam, 1894-95-96
DEES, Claire, 1926-27-28
DeHAVEN, Denver, 1924-25-26
DEMPSEY, C. F., 1915-16-17
DENHAM, Harry, 1940
DERRICK, Frank, 1924
DeSPAIN, James, 1972, Mgr.
DICKERSON, Charlie, 1976
DICKERSON, Jerry, 1959-60-61
DIEHL, Bud, 1976-77
DIPRE, Joe, 1973-74-76-77
DISHMAN, Tony, 1918-19
DIXON, Wayne, 1960-61
DOGGENDORF, Mike, 1970-71-72
DOMHOFF, Tom, 1971
DONALDSON, Gene, 1950-51
DONAN, A. L., 1906, Mgr.
DONIGAN, Shawn, 1978
DONLEY, Pat, 1973-74
DORNBROOK, Tom, 1974-75-76-77
DOUGHERTY, Bob, 1955-56
DOWNING, Clay, 1917
DOWNING, George, 1917
DOWNING, Gibson, 1911-12-13-14
DRINNEN, Dennis, 1967-68
DRURY, Bill "Pete", 1927-28-29
DRURY, John, 1932
DUFF, Noah, 1931-32
DUFFY, Tom, 1969
DUKE, Billy, 1967-68-69
DUNCAN, Dick, 1918, Mgr.
DUNCAN, Walter, 1895-96
DUNLAP, G. G., 1906-07-09-10
DUNNEBACKE, Howard, 1961-62
DURBIN, Raul, 1938, Mgr.
DURBIN, Ron, 1971, Asst. Trn.
DYER, Don, 1952
DYER, O. K., 1901-02-03
DYSARD, Bill, 1930

E

EARLE, Tom, 1908-09-10-11
EBLEN, Charles, 1942
ECKENROD, Pat, 1968-69-70
EDWARDS, Adolph, 1925-26
EDWARDS, George, 1942
EHLERS, Tom, 1972-73-74
EIBNER, John, 1938-39-40
EISAMAN, Jerry, 1958-59-60
ELGIN, Jeff, 1906-07
ELLINGTON, Russell "Duke", 1935-36-37
ELLIOTT, Cronley, 1900
ELLIOTT, Milward, 1896-97-98
ELLIS, Byrne, 1909
ELLIS, Ray, 1925-26-27
ELLISON, Robert, 1937, Mgr.
EMANUEL, Mike, 1973-74-75
ENGLISIS, Nick, 1944-45
EWELL, George, 1900-01
EWING, Tom, 1942

F

FADROWSKI, 1976-77-78
FALCONER, B. O., 1919
FANUZZI, Mike, 1971-73-74
FARLEY, Bill, 1950-51
FARMER, Tom, 1972-73-74
FARRELL, Bob, 1961
FARRIS, Jack, 1946-47
FARRIS, John, 1934
FAULCONER, B. O., 1919
FAULKNER, J. V., 1892-93
FEATHERSON, Lloyd, 1933, Mgr.
FEATHERSTON, Dan, 1970
FEDERSPIEL, Joe, 1969-70-71
FEE, Tom, 1964-66-67
FELCH, Allen, 1951-52
FERGUSON, Tom, 1967
FERGUSON, Walter, 1921-22
FERRELL, Doc, 1944-46-47-48
FERRIS, Fred, 1944
FEST, Fred, 1920-21-22
FILLION, Tom, 1951-52-53
FISH, Al, 1969-70
FISH, Bill, 1933
FISHER, Jim, 1959-60
FLEAHMAN, W. "Slugs", 1921
FOLEY, Jim, 1962-63-64
FORD, Roy, 1948
FORD, Warner, 1927-28-29
FORQUER, L. G. "Floppy", 1928-29-30
FORSTON, Stan, 1968-69-70
FOSTER, John, 1910
FOSTER, Mike, 1974
FOUSHEE, Gil, 1976
FOWLER, Dan, 1974-75-77-78
FRAMPTON, Don, 1948-49
FRANKENBERGER, J. T., 1954-55-56
FRANKLIN, Jim, 1973-75
FRANKLIN, Mark, 1926
FRAZER, Joe, 1895
FREEMAN, Jack, 1956
FREIBERT, Bob, 1966-68
FRITZ, Eddie, 1939-40
FROMM, Rick, 1972-74-75
FRY, Bob, 1950-51-52
FRYE, John, 1932-33
FUCCI, Dom, 1948-49-50
FULLER, Bruce, 1919-20-21-22
FULLER, Frank, 1950-51-52
FULLER, Ken, 1972

G

GAFFRON, Winston, 1971, Mgr.
GAIN, Bob, 1947-48-49-50
GAISER, Jake, 1909-10-11
GALLAGHER, Jack, 1957
GALLOWAY, Howard, 1906-11, Mgr.
GANN, Roger, 1967-68-69
GANUCHEAU, Eugene, 1972-73
GARDNER, John, 1893-94
GARLAND, Larry, 1936-37
GARRED, Ulysses, 1892-93
GARY, Bill, 1900
GASH, Dave, 1960-61-62
GAY, Augustus, 1916
GEMMILL, Pete, 1974-75-76
GENITO, Carl, 1946-48
GENITO, Ralph, 1947-48-49
GENTILE, Tony, 1930
GHOLSON, Ed, 1938
GIBSON, Frank, 1931-32
GILB, Elmer, 1926-27-28
GILBERT, John, 1900
GILTNER, Jim, 1910
GODWIN, Al, 1968-70
GOINS, Carl, 1958, Mgr.
GOINS, Homer, 1965-66
GOOCH, Tim, 1976-78
GOODE, Irvin, 1960-61
GOODWIN, William, 1903-04
GRABAN, Steve, 1941
GRABFELDER, Earl, 1915-16
GRADY, W. H., 1902-03-04
GRAHAM, J. H., 1898-99
GRANITZ, Hartford, 1945
GRANT, Jesse, 1962
GRANT, Jim, 1969-70-71
GRANT, Will, 1977
GRAY, Tony, 1973-74
GREEN, G. B. L., 1919
GREEN, Norm, 1978

GREER, Phil, 1967-68
GREER, Roger, 1969
GREGG, Turner, 1922-24
GRESHAM, Jim, 1966
GRIFFIN, Bill, 1942-46-47
GRIGGS, John, 1950-51-52
GRIGGS, Tom, 1978
GRUNER, Bunky, 1951
GULLION, Carroll, 1901-02
GUMBERT, George, 1914-15
GUNN, Thomas, 1893
GUSKY, Ed, 1972
GUYN, J. White, 1901-02-03-04-05
GUYN, Les, 1911

H

HAAS, Gene, 1944-45-46
HACKETT, Wilbur, 1968-69-70
HAGAN, Joe, 1936-37
HALCOMB, G. W., 1894
HALL, Bob, 1937
HALL, James, 1910
HAMBERG, Fred, 1971-73
HAMILTON, Allen, 1946-48-49-50
HAMILTON, Ed, 1949-50-51
HAMILTON, L. L., 1897
HAMMOND, Claude, 1941
HANLEY, Jack, 1952-53-54
HANSON, Dave, 1968-69-70
HARBOLD, Bill, 1924
HARDIN, Jim, 1938-39-40
HARDT, Dave, 1968-69-70
HARDY, Bob, 1953-54-55
HARPER, Tom, 1952-53
HARRINGTON, Roger, 1956
HARRIS, John, 1966
HARRIS, Wayne, 1945, Mgr.
HARRISON, W. C., 1910-11-12
HART, Rodger, 1966-67
HAWKINS, Robert, 1977-78
HAWTHORNE, Junior, 1960-61-62
HAY, Langan, 1934-35
HAYDEN, Charles, 1915-16
HAYDEN, Rick, 1976-77-78
HAYNES, Chastain, 1904
HAYNES, Terry, 1973-74
HEBER, John, 1916-17-18-19-20
HEDGES, Henry, 1912
HEDGES, Jimmy, 1913-14
HEICK, "Shorty", 1915-16
HEINZINGER, Ben, 1946
HELM, Foster, 1895
HENDRICKSON, George, 1907-08-09
HENNESSEY, Larry, 1951-52-53-54
HENSLEY, Dick, 1945-46-47
HERBERT, Bob, 1940-41-42
HERZOG, Woody, 1955-56-57
HESS, Jeff, 1975-77
HEWLING, Dick, 1936
HICKERSON, Broadus, 1916
HILL, Chris, 1976-77-78
HILL, Jim, 1960-61-62
HILLENMEYER, Walter, 1909
HINKEBEIN, Sherman, 1935-37-38
HITE, Cliff, 1975-76
HITE, Paul, 1912-13-14
HOBDY, William "Ed", 1892-93
HODGE, Lloyd, 1958-59-60
HODGE, Walter, 1936-37
HOGG, Houston, Jr., 1969-70
HOGG, Sam, 1897-98-99
HOLLAND, Don, 1967-68-69
HOLLIDAY, David, 1944, Mgr.
HOLLOWELL, Carney, 1922
HOLT, Bobby, 1953-55-56, Mgr.
HOLWAY, Dick, 1947-48-49
HOOPER, Hayden, 1952-54-55
HOOVER, Vin, 1975
HOPEWELL, Dave, 1976-77-78
HOPKINS, Elmer, 1916, Mgr.
HOSKINS, Calloway, 1930, Mgr.
HOVEY, Jim, 1971-72-73
HOWARD, Ledger, 1957-58-59
HOWE, Jim, 1944-48-49
HOYER, Eric, 1942
HUDDLESTON, Joe, 1934-35-36
HUGHES, Charles "Turkey", 1923-24
HUGHES, Delmar, 1953-54-55-56
HUGHES, Lowell, 1957-58-59
HUGHES, S. T., 1902-03
HUGHES, W. N., 1901
HULETTE, Sam, 1939-40-41
HUMPHREYS, Claude, 1897-98-99-1900
HUNDLEY, Tom, 1959-60
HUNT, Bob, 1958-59-60
HUNT, Herbie, 1951-52-53
HUNTER, David, 1968-69-70
HURST, John, 1942
HUTCHESON, F. M., 1900
HUTCHINSON, Tom, 1960-61-62

I

IGNARSKI, John, 1949-50-51
ILARI, John, 1955
ISHMAEL, Charles, 1938-39-40

J

JACKOWSKI, Ralph, 1937-38
JACKSON, Elmer, 1962
JACOBS, Bill, 1933
JACOBS, Chris, 1978
JACOBS, Ed, 1938-39-40
JACOBS, Joe, 1967-69
JAFFE, Richard, 1976-77-78
JAMERSON, Wilbur, 1947-48-49-50
JAMES, Pat, 1948-49-50
JANES, Ernest, 1932-33-34
JANSEN, Bill, 1966
JARDINE, Richard, 1975-77-78
JEAN, Jack, 1933
JENKINS, A. L., 1905
JENKINS, Bill, 1962-63-64
JENKINS, Paul, 1925-26-27
JETT, Charles, 1900-01
JIRSCHELE, Don, 1951
JOBE, Bill, 1933-34
JOHNS, Jimmy, 1957-58-59
JOHNSON, Bert, 1934-35-36
JOHNSON, Clyde, 1940-41-42
JOHNSON, Dick, 1892
JOHNSON, Ellis, 1930-31-32
JOHNSON, Harry, 1961
JOHNSON, J. E. C., 1904-10-11-12
JOHNSON, J. P., 1900
JOHNSON, Jack, 1897
JOHNSON, Marshall, 1962, Mgr.
JOHNSON, Marius, 1899, Mgr.
JOHNSON, Oliver "Ollie", 1928-29-30
JOHNSON, Percy "Duke", 1931, Mgr.
JOHNSTON, Wm. T., 1908-09
JOLLY, J. B., 1893-94
JONES, Bob, 1968-69-70
JONES, Charles "Junior", 1939-40-41
JONES, Chuck, 1976-78
JONES, Harry, 1950-51-52
JONES, Larry, 1950-51-52
JONES, Paul, 1949-51
JONES, Roscoe "Hut", 1942-46-47
JONES, Tom, 1899
JONES, Wallace "Wah Wah", 1945-46-47-48
JOYCE, Marty, 1967-68
JURGENS, Jon, 1960-61

K

KAREM, Paul, 1972
KARIBO, Lou, 1952-53
KATZENBACH, George, 1966-67-68
KEARNS, Tom, 1977-78
KEENE, Mark, 1977
KEHOE, John, 1898-99-1900-01
KELLY, E. E., 1915-18-19
KELLY, Henry, 1933
KELLY, John "Shipwreck", 1929-30-31
KELLY, Kevin, 1977-78
KELLY, Tom, 1895-96
KEMPER, Priest, 1903-04-05
KENNARD, Jim, 1946
KENT, George, 1944
KERCHEVAL, Ralph, 1931-32-33
KERRICK, Felix, 1895, Mgr.
KESTNER, Rick, 1963-64-65
KEYES, Howard, 1964-65
KIDD, A. S., 1896
KIEFER, Steve, 1954-55
KIMMEL, Charles, 1975, Trn.
KINCER, Bill, 1941
KING, Doyle, 1967-68-69
KING, Kenneth, 1921-24-25
KING, Kenny, 1970-71-72
KING, Lawson, 1955
KING, T. E., 1896
KING, Vic, 1967-68
KINNE, Howard, 1915-16
KIPPING, Bob, 1930-31
KIRCHBAUM, Kelly, 1975-76-77-78
KIRK, Harry, 1951-52-53-54
KIRK, Tom, 1971
KIRKENDALL, Jim, 1927
KIRN, Ted, 1951
KIRSCHNER, Frank, 1970-71
KIRWAN, Ab, 1923-24-25
KLEIN, Norman, 1944-46-47-48
KLEIN, Sam, 1944
KLINECT, Randy, 1977
KNUTSON, Gary, 1970-71-72
KOCH, Joe, 1952-53-54
KOMARA, Jim, 1962-63-65
KOON, Steve, 1967-68
KOSID, Bob, 1962-63
KOSTELNICK, Tom, 1975
KOTAR, Doug, 1971-72-73
KOVACH, Jim, 1974-75-76-78
KREUTER, Howard, 1931-32-33
KUHN, Charlie, 1941-42
KUHN, Dave, 1953-54-55-56
KUNKLE, Dennis, 1958
KURACHEK, Pete, 1937
KYPRISS, Mike, 1973

L

LAIR, Matt, 1946-47
LASSITER, W. A., 1895
LAUFER, Robert, Jr., 1928, Mgr.
LAVIN, Bobby, 1919-20-21
LAWSON, Cliff, 1949-50-51
LEE, Bobby, 1961
LeMASTER, Frank, 1971-72-73
LESKOVAR, Bill, 1949-50-51
LETT, Jim, 1970
LEWIS, Ernie, 1972-73-74
LEWIS, Jim, 1907
LIDVALL, Ned, 1972-73-74
LIGHTCAP, Jeff, 1974
LINDON, Bob, 1957-58
LINDON, Luke, 1937-39
LITTLE, Dwight, 1965-66-67
LITTLE, Jim, 1944
LITTLE, Tom, 1944
LIVINGS, Bill, 1956-57-58
LOGAN, Emmett, 1906
LOMBARD, Dick, 1958, Mgr.
LONG, Jim, 1934-35
LOONEY, Pat, 1966, Mgr.
LOPEZ, Luis, 1977
LOWRY, Neil, 1952-53-54
LOWRY, R. A., 1909, Mgr.
LUKAWSKI, Chet, 1950-51
LUTHER, Bill, 1931-32
LUTZ, Ken, 1955
LYLE, Ernest, 1898-99
LYLE, Joel, 1893-94, Mgr., 1895
LYONS, Dicky, 1966-67-68
LYONS, Les, 1970

M

MABRY, Dick, 1957
MACHEL, Rich, 1964-65-66
MacKENZIE, Jim, 1949-50-51
MADDOX, F. M., 1902-03
MADDOX, Roy, 1898
MAHAN, F. C., 1904-05
MAKIN, Raynard, 1968-69-70
MALONEY, William, 1925
MANZONELLI, Tony, 1964-65
MARGAVAGE, Dave, 1971-72-73
MARKEM, Dave, 1969
MARKS, Marty, 1972-73
MARRILLIA, Carl, 1977-78
MARTIN, Dick, 1947-48-49-50
MARTIN, Givens "Doc", 1922-23
MARTIN, Jack, 1957, Mgr.
MARTIN, John, 1959
MARTIN, L. Wynn, 1897-98-99-1900-01
MARTIN, Mike, 1975-76-77
MARTIN, Paul, 1968-69-70
MASON, Chester, 1938
MASON, Max, 1951
MATHERS, Albert, 1907
MATHEWS, Jack, 1968-69
MATTHEWS, A. M., 1907
MATTINGLY, R. E., 1912, Mgr.
MAYFIELD, Clarkie, 1960-61-62
MAYO, Jim, 1952
McCAULEY, Gates, 1935, Mgr.
McCLELLAN, George, 1967
McCLENDON, Charlie, 1949-50
McCLURE, Ulysses, A., 1901
McCLURG, Charles, 1934-35
McCOLLUM, Jim, 1971-72-73
McCOOL, Frank, 1934-35
McCORUM, Henry, 1934, Mgr.

McCRIMMON, Larry, 1978
McCUBBIN, Bill, 1937-38-39
McCUNE, Jesse, 1944
McDERMOTT, Lloyd, 1947-48-49
McDONALD, Louis, 1944-45
McELROY, Otho, 1929
McFARLAND, Bill, 1923
McGEE, Hilton, 1902-03
McGINNIS, Lawrence, 1930
McGRAW, Mike, 1964-65-66
McILVAINE, Ernest, 1915-16
McKAY, James, 1972
McKEE, N. T., 1901
McKINNEY, Walter, 1904-05-06
McLEAN, Grandison, 1924, Mgr.
McLEAN, Price, 1923
McMILLAN, Norris "Double O", 1933-34-35
MEADORS, Gilcin, 1911
MEAUX, Venus, 1978
MECK, Mike, 1970-71
MEEKS, Gene, 1942-46
MEGILL, Hilton, 1903, Mgr.
MEIHAUS, Johnny, 1948
MEILINGER, Steve, 1951-52-53
MENIFEE, John N., 1903
MEYER, Vernon "Bo", 1929-30-32
MICHAELS, Lou, 1955-56-57
MILBURN, Frank, 1899-1900
MILES, Jim, 1964-65
MILLER, J. F., III, 1957-58
MILLER, Jim, 1932
MILLER, Leonard, 1927
MILLS, Bradley, 1952-53-54-55
MINGUS, Jerry, 1952
MITCHELL, Bill, 1941
MITCHELL, Billy, 1954-55-56
MITCHELL, Dick, 1952-53-54
MITCHELL, Jim, 1968-69-70
MOFFETT, Tony, 1971
MOHNEY, Gayle, 1925-26-27
MOITIUS, Dave, 1975
MOLONEY, Dick, 1952-53-54-55
MONTGOMERY, Bob, 1931-32
MONTGOMERY, George, 1903-04-05
MONTGOMERY, Robert, 1924
MOORE, Don, 1957
MOORE, Roger, 1918
MORAJA, Joe, 1961
MORGAN, George, 1895, Mgr.
MORRIS, Tom, 1969-70-71
MORRIS, Waymond, 1957-58
MOSELEY, Bill, 1942-46-47
MOSELEY, Doug, 1949-50-51
MOTLEY, Greg, 1978
MUELLER, Dickie, 1958-59-60
MUENCH, Rick, 1969-70-71
MULLINS, Basil, 1963-65-66
MULLINS, Noah, 1940-41
MURGITA, Steve, 1972-73-74
MURPHREE, Eger V., 1916-17-18-19-20
MURPHY, Gerard, 1963-64-65
MURPHY, O. B., 1932-33
MURRAY, Robert, 1973-76-77
MUTCHLER, John, 1960-61
MUTH, Albert, 1919
MYERS, Art, 1972-73-74
MYERS, Gene, 1934-35-36

N

NEAL, Dan, 1971-72
NESBIT, J. C., 1904-05, Mgr.
NETOSKIE, Don, 1953-54-55-56
NETOSKIE, John, 1949-50-51
NEVERS, Stanley, 1934-35-36
NICHOLAS, Homer, 1936
NICHOLSON, John, 1971, Mgr.
NOCHTA, John, 1973-74-76
NORD, Greg, 1975-77
NORTON, Rick, 1963-64-65
NOWACK, Orval, 1928
NUERGE, Don, 1959-60
NUTTALL, John, 1894
NUZUM, Rick, 1972-73-74

O

O'BRIEN, Doug, 1961
ODLIVAK, Nick, 1947-48-49
OLAH, Arperd, 1933-35
O'LEARY, Ken, 1971-72
ORR, Joe, 1935
OTT, Isaac, 1926
OWEN, Oweney, 1969, Mgr.
OWENS, Dallas, 1974-75-76-77

P

PACK, Roger, 1954-55-56
PAGE, Greg, 1967
PALMER, Bob, 1938-39-40
PALMER, Dick, 1967-68-69
PAOLONE, Ralph, 1952-53
PARDA, Alex, 1937
PARILLI, Vito "Babe", 1949-50-51
PARK, Jim, 1911-13-14
PARK, Smith, 1919, Mgr.
PARKER, Sam, 1900
PARKER, Steve, 1972-73-74
PARKS, Frank, 1942, Mgr.
PARKS, Henry, 1978
PARR, Allen, 1940-41-42
PARRISH, Doug, 1932-33
PARRISH, Steve, 1969-70
PARROTT, Jim, 1944
PAUL, Henry, 1944-45
PAULLIN, Frank, 1905-06
PAVLOVICH, Bernie, 1945
PAYNE, J. Hamilton, 1907
PEAK, Bart, 1915
PENCE, Jim, 1925-26-27
PERKINS, W. H., 1900, Mgr.
PESUIT, Wally, 1973-74-75
PETERSEN, Scott, 1977
PETKOVSEK, Larry, 1976-77
PETRIE, Charles, 1914
PEURACH, Ted, 1978
PHANEUF, Al, 1966-67
PHELPS, Don, 1946-47-49
PHILLIPS, Bob, 1954-55
PHILLIPS, Hal, 1945
PHILLIPS, Randy, 1938
PHILLIPS, Steve, 1972
PHILPOT, O. E., 1954-55
PHIPPS, Frank, 1925-26-27
PHIPPS, Jack, 1929-30-31
PHIPPS, Tom, 1929-30
PICKETT, Phil, 1962
PIERCE, John, 1974-75-76
PLATT, Joe, 1952-53
PLUMMER, George, 1909
POPE, Bob, 1948-49-50
PORTER, Ray, 1947-48-49
PORTERFIELD, Don, 1968-69-70
PORTWOOD, Al, 1926-27-28
PORTWOOD, Bill, 1941
PORTWOOD, Henry, 1924-26
POST, Shelby, 1908
POSTEL, Chuck, 1978
POTTER, Derek, 1966-67
POTTER, Lexie, 1935-36
POTTER, Sam, 1934-35
POTTINGER, Sam, 1892, Mgr.
POWERS, Archie, 1955-56-57
POYNTER, Jimmy, 1959-60
PRESTON, Leonard, 1946-47
PRIBBLE, Birkett, 1919-20-21-22
PRIBBLE, Holton, 1932-34
PRIDE, J. T., 1902-03
PRITCHARD, Bob, 1933-34-36
PROFFITT, Jim, 1951-52-53
PUNTILLO, John, 1971
PURSELL, Dave, 1968-69-70

R

RAMEY, James, 1975-76-77-78
RAMPULLA, John, 1961
RAMSEY, Dell, 1920-21-22-23
RAMSEY, Derrick, 1975-76-77
RANIERI, Tom, 1972-74-75
RANSDELL, Bill, 1959-60-61
RATCLIFFE, Clark, 1952
RAY, Babe, 1945
RAYNOR, Keith, 1967
READER, Jim, 1959-60
REDMOND, Harry, 1893
REED, Jim, 1970-71-72
REED, Tom, 1972, Mgr.
REESE, A. S., 1896-97-98-99
REID, Walter, 1938-39-40
RELCHIE, Chester, 1939, Mgr.
REYES, Kent, 1973
RHODEMYRE, Jay, 1942-46-47
RHYNE, Dan, 1959, Mgr.
RICE, Chuck, 1920-22-23
RICE, Dennis, 1946
RICE, Guy, 1899
RICE, William H., 1922-24-25
RICHARDS, Dick, 1929-30-31
RICHARDSON, Clyde, 1962-63
RIDDLE, Ches, 1973-75-76
RIDDLE, Craig, 1917-18
RIDGE, Don, 1946-47
RIVEIRO, Dan, 1961
ROARK, Ken, 1978
ROBERTS, Craig, 1976-77-78
ROBERTS, Ronnie, 1965-66-67
ROBERTS, H. B., 1893
ROBERTSON, Kenny, 1955-56-57
ROBINSON, Tom, 1913, Mgr.
ROBINSON, Vincent "Dick", 1935-36-37
RODES, J. W., 1904-05
RODES, Pete, 1907-08
RODES, Wm. "Black Doc", 1915-16
RODES, Wm. "Red Doc", 1909-11-12
RODGERS, Tom, 1958-59-60
ROGERS, Harry, 1949-50
ROLLER, David, 1968-69-70
ROSE, Conrad, 1928-29-30
ROSS, John, 1925-26
ROTH, Abe, 1912-13-14
ROTUNNO, Tony, 1944
ROUTT, G. C., 1907-08-09
RUCKS, Frank, 1968-69
RUEFF, Gerald, 1968, Mgr.
RUPERT, Joe, 1932-33-34
RUSH, Leonard, 1966-68
RUSHING, Dick, 1952-53-54
RUSSELL, James, R., 1921-22-23

S

SADLER, Frank, 1946-47, Mgr.
SALSBERY, Harold, 1970, Mgr.
SANDERS, Curtis, 1921-22-23-24
SANDERS, Curtis, Jr., 1945, Mgr.
SAUER, Curtis, 1923-24
SAUERBRY, Bruce, 1970-71
SAUNDERS, Francis, 1944
SAUNDERS, Hugh, 1903
SAYLOR, Unis, 1948-49, Mgr.
SCHAFFNIT, Bill, 1948-49-50
SCHENK, Jim, 1952-53
SCHIFLER, Charles, 1941
SCHILLING, F. A., 1912
SCHLEGEL, George, 1941
SCHNELLENBERGER, Howie, 1952-53-54-55
SCHOENBAECHLER, Steve, 1972
SCHOLLETT, Frank, 1957-58-59
SCHOLTZ, Herman, 1898-1900-01-02
SCHORNICK, John, 1965
SCHRADER, C. C., 1912-13-14-15
SCHRECKER, Dennis, 1961
SCHRECKER, Ray, 1959
SCHU, Wilbur, 1944
SCHULTE, Ray, 1925-26
SCOTT, Bill, 1960
SCOTT, George, 1893
SCOTT, Herschel, 1912-13-14
SCOTT, John, 1893
SCOTT, Phil, 1938-39-40
SCOTT, Steve, 1969
SCOTT, Wellington, 1899-1900-01
SCOTT, William Paul, 1926
SCRUGGS, Bernie, 1969-70-71
SEALE, Frank, 1930-31-32
SEARCY, Tom, 1972
SEIPLE, Larry, 1964-65-66
SEMARY, Vince, 1962-63
SENGEL, George, 1942-46-47
SERINI, Wash, 1944-45-46-47
SERVER, Jim, 1915-19-20-21
SERVINO, Chuck, 1977
SETTLE, Ed, 1964
SETTLES, Barry, 1972, Mgr.
SETTLES, Pat, 1970, Mgr.
SEVERS, Roscoe, 1897-98
SEXTON, Doug, 1972
SHADOWEN, Leon, 1978
SHAHID, Cary, 1967-68-69
SHANKLIN, Arthur, 1917-18-19-20
SHANKLIN, Eugene, 1933
SHANKLIN, George, 1907-08-09-10
SHANNON, Hugh, 1944-45
SHATTO, Dick, 1953
SHAW, Fred, 1920, Mgr.
SHAW, Glenn, 1957-58-59
SHELBY, Joe, 1908-09
SHELDON, F. M., 1905
SHELTON, John, 1924
SHEPHERD, Joe, 1937-38-39
SHERMAN, Bob, 1937
SHIVELY, Doug, 1956-57-58

SHORT, J. Cleves, 1894-95
SHUTT, Mike, 1978
SIGANOS, Mike, 1974-75-76-77
SIMPSON, Clay, 1915-16
SIMPSON, Elmore, 1935-36-37
SIMPSON, Tommy, 1960-61-62
SINGELTON, Ed, 1973-74-75
SINOR, Don, 1958-59-60
SKAGGS, Wendell, 1935-36-37
SKINNER, George, 1930-31-32
SKUR, Rollie, 1976
SLADE, D. D., 1897
SLATES, Steve, 1975-76
SLATON, Paul, 1936, Mgr.
SLOAN, Paul, 1957
SMITH, Calvin, 1951
SMITH, Chuck, 1978
SMITH, D. P. 1892
SMITH, Ed, 1963
SMITH, Frank, 1924-25-26
SMITH, George, 1914
SMITH, Giles, 1964-65, Mgr.
SMITH, Jim, 1970-72, Mgr.
SMITH, Joe David, 1964-66
SMITH, S. J., 1898
SMOLDER, Ed, 1974-75-76
SMOTHERMAN, Frank, 1947
SPANISH, Dan, 1964-65-66
SPANTON, W. A., 1901-02
SPEARS, Howell, 1911
SPEARS, Larry, 1938-39-40
SPENCER, B. W., 1902-03
SPENCER, Howell, 1901-02
SPEYER, H. A., 1906
SPICER, Bill "Bud", 1958
SPICER, Carey, 1928-29-30
SPICKARD, Tom, 1938-39
SPONHEIMER, Paul, 1971-73-74
ST. JOHN, C. P., 1903
STACEY, Jim, 1899
STANKO, Ed, 1964-65
STECKLER, Dick, 1959, Mgr.
STEELE, Ron, 1973
STEELY, Sherman, 1893
STEPHAN, Joe, 1969-70-71
STEPHENS, David, 1975-77
STEPHENS, Elmore, 1971-73-74
STEPHENSON, E. A., 1923
STEWARD, Gary, 1960-61-62
STEWART, Rod, 1975-76-77
STILL, Art, 1974-75-76-77
STOFER, R. T., 1908
STOLL, Richard C., 1893-94
STONE, Earl, 1906
STONE, Neville, 1906-07
STOUT, B. E. W., 1908, Mgr.
STRANGE, Leo, 1953-54-55
STRAUS, Charles L., 1897-98
STROTHER, Jack, 1932, Mgr.
STUART, Joe, 1954
STURGEON, Charles, 1958-59-60
SUMMERS, George, 1927
SUMNER, G., 1906
SUTAK, John, 1944
SWART, Jim, 1964-65-66
SWINDLE, Earl, 1970-71-72
SWORD, Harvey, 1971-72-73
SYDNOR, Joe, 1937

T

TALAMINI, Bob, 1957-58-59
TATTERSON, John, 1972-73-74
TAYLOR, Harry, 1941-42
TAYLOR, Jim, 1941, Mgr.
TAYLOR, N. S., 1908
TERRILL, Flanery, 1928
THIESING, Bill, 1909
THOMAS, Ben, 1972-73-74
THOMAS, Hobart, 1944
THOMAS, Ron, 1978
THOMAS, Smith, 1903
THOMPSON, J. J., 1902
THOMPSON, Jim, 1913-14-15
THOMPSON, Joe, 1928-29
THOMPSON, Mark, 1961
THOMPSON, Phil, 1967-68-69
THOMPSON, W. T., 1919-20
THORNTON, David, 1920
THRELKELD, Polk, 1909-10
TICHENOR, Bill, 1933
TINGLE, Steve, 1969
TODD Talbott, 1963-64-65
TOLSTON, Bill, 1975-77-78
TOTH, Louis, 1928-29-30
TOWNES, Fay, 1915, Mgr.
TRACY, Bill, 1937
TRACY, Len, 1923-24-25
TRIBBLE, CLiff, 1956-57-58
TRIPLETT, Pete, 1942
TROSPER, Dave, 1975-76-77
TRUMAN, Lee, 1947-48-49
TUCCI, Rich, 1963-64-65
TUNSTILL, Jesse, 1942-45-46
TURNER, Herschel, 1961-62-63
TURNER, J. M., 1905
TURNER, James D., 1894-95-96
TUTTLE, William, 1911-12-13-14

U

ULINSKI, Harry, 1946-47-48-49
URBANIAK, Cecil, 1929-30-31
URBANIAK, Jim, 1955-56-57

V

VANCE, Wendell, 1949-50
VanMETER, Ben, 1893-94, Mgr.
VAN METER, Dave, 1969-70-71
VAN METER, Doug, 1965-66-67
VAN METER, Emanuel, 1924-26-27
VAN NOTE, Jeff, 1966-67-68
VANZANT, Russell, 1923, Mgr.
VAUGHN, Charles, 1959
VIRES, Pete, 1937-38
VOGT, John, 1899-1900-01-02

W

WADDELL, Beverly, 1926
WADLINGTON, Jim, 1935-37
WAGNER, Harry, 1932
WAGNER, Sheldon, 1933-34
WALKER, Bobby, 1954-55-56
WALKER, Charlie Bill, 1941-42-46
WALKER, H. L., 1907
WALKER, Harry, 1932-33-34
WALKER, W. G., 1917-19
WALTERS, Tom, 1927-28-29
WALZ, Roger, 1965-66
WANNAMAKER, Bill, 1948-49-50
WARD, A. F., 1896
WARD, Paul, 1896
WARRING, Leo, 1968-69, Mgr.
WATHEN, C., 1921
WATKINS, George C. "Possum", 1910-11
WATSON, Cova, 1921, Mgr.
WEAVER, Rufus, 1893
WEBB, Clayton, 1948-49-50
WEBB, Dick, 1907-09-10
WEINMAN, Al, 1950-51, Mgr.
WELCH, John T., 1897
WELD, David, 1967
WERT, Charles, 1925-26-27
WHAYNE, E. C., 1897-98
WHEELER, Bill, 1953-54-55
WHITTINGHILL, H. R., 1902, Mgr.
WHITTINGHILL, R. T., 1900
WILBURN, Bill, 1942
WILDER, Newell, 1931
WILEY, Ed, 1920
WILHELM, Jim, 1917-20
WILARD, Miles, 1951-53
WILLIAMS, Billy, 1977-78
WILLIAMS, Charles, 1940, Mgr.
WILLIAMS, Delon, 1911
WILLIAMS, Fred, 1974-75-77-78
WILLIAMS, Howard, 1928-29-30
WILLIAMS, James, 1929, Mgr.
WILLIAMS, John, 1898
WILLIAMS, Ken, 1953
WILLIM, W. C., 1898
WILLOUGHBY, Emmett, 1938-39-40
WILSON, Cullen, 1957-58-59
WILSON, Dick, 1898-1901, Mgr.
WILSON, Earl, 1977-78
WILSON, Felix, 1977-78
WILSON, James, M., 1906-07
WILSON, Murray, 1906
WILSON, S. E., 1896
WILSON, W. B., 1910
WINDSOR, Bob, 1965-66
WINKEL, Bob, 1974-75-76-78
WITHROW, Calvin, 1964-65-66
WIXSON, Bob, Jr., 1969-70-71
WODTKE, Bob, 1948
WOLF, Louis, 1966-67-68
WOLFE, Rod, 1969
WOOD, Clark, 1940-41-42
WOOD, Hugh, 1900-02-03-04
WOOD, Kenny, 1967
WOODCOCK, Jeff, 1971-72-73
WOODDELL, Harold, 1949-50
WOODS, Greg, 1973-74-75-76
WOODS, John, 1893-94-95
WOODSON, Harry, 1911-12-13
WOOLUM, Jerry, 1960-61-62
WRIGHT, Floyd, 1914
WRIGHT, Ralph, 1929-30-31
WRIGHT, Rich, 1957-58-59
WURTELE, Ed C., 1902

Y

YARUTIS, Leo, 1942-46-47
YATES, George, 1929-30-31
YOST, Roger, 1944-45
YOUNG, Walter, 1960, Mgr.
YOWARSKY, Walt, 1948-49-50

Z

ZAMPINO, Al, 1951-53-56
ZARANKA, Ben, 1947-48-49-50
ZERFOSS, George, 1919
ZERFOSS, Karl, 1913-14-15
ZERFOSS, Tom, 1913
ZINN, Tommy, 1941
ZOELLER, Dave, 1938-39-40

Louisiana State University

Location: Baton Rouge, Louisiana
Enrollment: 24,596
Nickname: Tigers or Fighting Tigers
Color: Purple and Gold
Stadium: Tiger (67,720)

Louisiana State University Head Coaching Records

COACH	YEAR	WON	LOST	TIED
C. E. Coates	1893	0	1	0
A. P. Simmons	1894-'95	5	1	0
A. W. Jeardeau	1896-'97	7	1	0
E. A. Chavanne	1898; 1900	3	2	0
J. P. Gregg	1899	1	4	0
W. S. Borland	1901-'03	15	7	0
D. A. Killian	1904-'06	8	6	2
Edgar R. Wingard	1907-'08	17	3	0
J. G. Pritchard	1909	3	1	0
J. W. Mayhew	1909-'10	4	6	0
J. K. Dwyer	1911-'13	16	7	2
E. T. McDonald	1914-'16	14	7	1
Dana X. Bible	1916	1	0	2
Irving R. Pray	1916; 1919; 1922	11	9	0
W. Sutton	1917	3	5	0
Branch Bocock	1920-'21	11	4	2
Mike Donahue	1923-'27	23	19	3
Russ Cohen	1928-'31	23	13	1
Lawrence M. "Biff" Jones	1932-'34	20	5	6
Bernie H. Moore	1935-'47	83	39	6
Gaynell "Gus" Tinsley	1948-'54	35	34	6
Paul Dietzel	1955-'61	46	24	3
Charles McClendon	1962-'78	128	56	7

Louisiana State University All-Time Scores

1893
0 Tulane 34

1894
36 Natchez AC 0
6 Ole Miss 26
30 Centenary 0
72 (2-1-0) 26

1895
8 Tulane 4
16 Centenary 6
12 Alabama 6
36 (3-0-0) 16

1896
46 Centenary 0
6 Tulane 0
12 Ole Miss 4
14 Texas 0
52 Miss. State 0
6 Southern AC 0
136 (6-0-0) 4

1897
28 Montgomery AC 6
0 Cincinnati 26
28 (1-1-0) 32

1898
37 Tulane 0

1899
0 Ole Miss 11
0 Sewanee 34
0 Texas 29
0 Texas A&M 52
38 Tulane 0
38 (1-4-0) 126

1900
70 Millsaps 0
0 Tulane 29
5 Millsaps 6
10 L.S.U. Alumni 0
85 (2-2-0) 35

1901
57 La. Tech 0
46 Ole Miss 0
11 Tulane 0
0 Auburn 28
38 YMCA (N.O.) 0
15 Arkansas 0
167 (5-1-0) 28

1902
42 SW Louisiana 0
5 Texas 0
5 Auburn 0
6 Ole Miss 0
5 Vanderbilt 27
6 Miss. State 0
11 Alabama 0
80 (6-1-0) 27

1903
16 L.S.U. Alumni 0
33 Eagles Club 0
16 La. Tech 0
5 Shreveport AC 0
0 Miss. State 11
0 Alabama 18
0 Auburn 12
0 Cumberland 41
0 Ole Miss 11
70 (4-5-0) 93

1904
17 La. Tech 0
0 Shreveport AC 16
0 La Tech 6
5 Ole Miss 0
16 Nashville 0
0 Tulane 5
0 Alabama 11
38 (3-4-0) 38

1905
16 La. Tech 0
5 Tulane 0
15 Miss. State 0
36 (3-0-0) 0

1906
5 Monroe AC 0
0 Ole Miss 9
0 Miss. State 0
17 La. Tech 0
12 Texas A&M 21
6 Arkansas 6
40 (2-2-2) 36

1907

28	La. Tech	0
5	Texas	12
5	Texas A&M	11
57	Howard	0
17	Arkansas	12
23	Miss. State	11
23	Ole Miss	0
4	Alabama	6
48	Baylor	0
56	Havana	0
266	(7-3-0)	52

1908

41	YMGC (N.D.)	0
81	Jksn. Barracks	5
26	Texas A&M	0
55	S'western	0
10	Auburn	2
50	Miss. State	0
89	Baylor	0
32	Haskell	0
22	La. Tech	0
36	Arkansas	4
442	(10-0-0)	11

1909

70	Jksn. Barracks	0
10	Ole Miss	0
15	Miss. State	0
6	Sewanee	15
23	La. Tech	0
0	Arkansas	16
52	Transylvania	0
12	Alabama	6
188	(6-2-0)	37

1910

40	Miss. College	0
0	Miss. State	3
5	Sewanee	31
0	Vanderbilt	22
0	Texas	12
0	Arkansas	51
45	(1-5-0)	119

1911

42	S.W. Louisiana	0
46	La. Normal	0
40	Miss. College	0
40	Meteor AC	0
6	Baylor	0
0	Miss. State	6
6	Southwestern	17
0	Arkansas	11
6	Tulane	0
186	(6-3-0)	34

1912

85	SW Louisiana	3
45	Miss. College	0
7	Ole Miss	10
0	Miss. State	7
0	Auburn	7
7	Arkansas	6
21	Tulane	3
165	(4-3-0)	36

1913

20	La. Tech	2
26	SW Louisiana	0
45	Jefferson	6
50	Baylor	0
0	Auburn	7
12	Arkansas	7
0	Miss. State	0
40	Tulane	0
7	Texas A&M	7
200	(6-1-2)	29

1914

54	SW Louisiana	0
60	La. Tech	0
14	Miss. College	0
0	Ole Miss	21
14	Jefferson	13
9	Texas A&M	63
12	Arkansas	20
0	Haskell	31
0	Tulane	0
163	(4-4-1)	148

1915

42	Jefferson	0
14	Miss. College	0
28	Ole Miss	0
7	Ga. Tech	36
10	Miss. State	0
13	Arkansas	7
0	Rice	6
12	Tulane	0
126	(6-2-0)	49

1916

24	SW Louisiana	0
59	Jefferson Col.	0
13	Texas A&M	0
50	Miss. College	7
0	Sewanee	7
17	Arkansas	7
13	Miss. State	3
41	Ole Miss	0
7	Rice	7
14	Tulane	14
238	(7-1-2)	45

1917

20	SW Louisiana	6
52	Ole Miss	7
0	Sewanee	3
0	Texas A&M	27
0	Arkansas	14
34	Miss. College	0
0	Miss. State	9
6	Tulane	28
112	(3-5-0)	94

1918—No Team

1919

39	SW Louisiana	0
38	Jefferson	0
13	Ole Miss	0
20	Arkansas	0
0	Miss. State	6
24	Miss. College	0
0	Alabama	23
27	Tulane	6
161	(6-2-0)	35

1920

81	Jefferson	0
34	La. Normal	0
40	Spring Hill	0
0	Texas A&M	0
7	Miss. State	12
41	Miss. College	9
3	Arkansas	0
0	Alabama	21
0	Tulane	21
206	(5-3-1)	63

1921

78	La. Normal	0
6	Texas A&M	0
41	Spring Hill	7
7	Alabama	7
10	Arkansas	7
21	Ole Miss	0
0	Tulane	21
17	Miss. State	14
180	(6-1-1)	56

1922

13	La. Normal	0
0	Loyola (N.O.)	7
0	S.M.U.	51
0	Texas A&M	47
6	Arkansas	40
25	Spring Hill	7
0	Rutgers	25
3	Alabama	47
0	Miss. State	7
25	Tulane	14
72	(3-7-0)	245

1923

40	La. Normal	0
7	SW Louisiana	3
33	Spring Hill	0
0	Texas A&M	28
13	Arkansas	26
0	Miss. College	0
3	Alabama	30
0	Tulane	20
7	Miss. State	14
103	(3-5-1)	121

1924

7	Spring Hill	6
31	SW Louisiana	7
20	Indiana	14
12	Rice	0
0	Auburn	3
7	Arkansas	10
7	Ga. Tech	28
40	La. Normal	0
0	Tulane	13
124	(5-4-0)	81

1925

27	La. Normal	0
38	SW Louisiana	0
0	Alabama	42
6	LSU Fresh.	0
0	Tennessee	0
0	Arkansas	12
6	Rice	0
13	Loyola	0
0	Tulane	16
90	(5-3-1)	70

1926

47	La. Normal	0
34	SW Louisiana	0
7	Tennessee	14
10	Auburn	0
6	Miss. State	7
0	Alabama	24
14	Arkansas	0
3	Ole Miss	0
7	Tulane	0
128	(6-3-0)	45

1927

45	La. Tech	0
52	SW Louisiana	0
0	Alabama	0
9	Auburn	0
9	Miss. State	7
0	Arkansas	28
7	Ole Miss	12
0	Ga. Tech	23
6	Tulane	13
128	(4-4-1)	83

1928

46	SW Louisiana	0
41	La. College	0
31	Miss. College	0
30	Spring Hill	7
0	Arkansas	7
19	Ole Miss	6
13	Georgia	12
0	Tulane	0
0	Alabama	13
180	(6-2-1)	45

1929

58	La. College	0
58	SW Louisiana	0
27	Sewanee	14
31	Miss. State	6
53	La. Tech	7
0	Arkansas	32
6	Duke	32
13	Ole Miss	6
0	Tulane	21
246	(6-3-0)	118

1930

76	SD Wesleyan	0
71	La. Tech	0
85	SW Louisiana	0
6	S. Carolina	7
6	Miss. State	8
12	Sewanee	0
27	Arkansas	12
6	Ole Miss	0
0	Alabama	33
7	Tulane	12
296	(6-4-0)	72

1931

0	T.C.U.	3
35	Spring Hill	0
19	S. Carolina	12
31	Miss. State	0
13	Arkansas	6
6	Sewanee	12
0	Army	20
26	Ole Miss	3
7	Tulane	34
137	(5-4-0)	90

1932

3	T.C.U.	3
8	Rice	10
80	Spring Hill	0
24	Miss. State	0
14	Arkansas	0
38	Sewanee	0
6	S. Carolina	0
0	Centenary	6
14	Tulane	0
0	Oregon	12
187	(6-3-1)	31

1933

13	Rice	0
40	Millsaps	0
0	Centenary	0
20	Arkansas	0
7	Vanderbilt	7
30	S. Carolina	7
31	Ole Miss	0
21	Miss. State	6
7	Tulane	7
7	Tennessee	0
176	(7-0-3)	27

1934

9	Rice	9
14	S.M.U.	14
20	Auburn	6
16	Arkansas	0
29	Vanderbilt	0
25	Miss. State	3
6	George Wash.	0
14	Ole Miss	0
12	Tulane	13
13	Tennessee	19
14	Oregon	13
172	(7-2-2)	77

1935

7	Rice	10
18	Texas	6
32	Manhattan	0
13	Arkansas	7
7	Vanderbilt	2
6	Auburn	0
28	Miss. State	13
13	Georgia	0
56	SW La.	0
41	Tulane	0
221	(9-1-0)	38

Sugar Bowl

2	T.C.U.	3

1936

20	Rice	7
6	Texas	6
47	Georgia	7
13	Ole Miss	0
19	Arkansas	7
19	Vanderbilt	0
12	Miss. State	0
19	Auburn	6
93	SW Louisiana	0
33	Tulane	0
281	(9-0-1)	33

Sugar Bowl

14	Santa Clara	21

1937

19	Florida	0
9	Texas	0
13	Rice	0
13	Ole Miss	0
6	Vanderbilt	7
52	Loyola	6
41	Miss. State	0
9	Auburn	7
57	La. Normal	0
20	Tulane	7
234	(9-1-0)	27

Sugar Bowl

0	Santa Clara	6

1938

7	Ole Miss	20
20	Texas	0
3	Rice	0
47	Loyola	6
7	Vanderbilt	0
6	Tennessee	14
32	Miss. State	7
6	Auburn	28
32	SW La	0
0	Tulane	14
160	(6-4-0)	89

1939

7	Ole Miss	14
26	Holy Cross	7
7	Rice	0
20	Loyola	0
12	Vanderbilt	6
0	Tennessee	20
12	Miss. State	15
7	Auburn	21
20	Tulane	33
111	(4-5-0)	116

1940

39	La. Tech	7
6	Ole Miss	19
25	Holy Cross	0
0	Rice	23
20	Mercer	0
7	Vanderbilt	0
0	Tennessee	28
7	Miss. State	22
21	Auburn	13
14	Tulane	0
139	(6-4-0)	112

1941
25 La. Tech 0
13 Holy Cross 19
0 Texas 34
0 Miss. State 0
27 Rice 0
10 Florida 7
6 Tennessee 13
12 Ole Miss 13
7 Auburn 7
19 Tulane 0
119 (4-4-2) 93

1942
40 La. Normal 0
16 Texas A&M 7
14 Rice 27
16 Miss. State 6
21 Ole Miss 7
34 Georgia Navy 0
0 Tennessee 26
26 Fordham 13
7 Auburn 25
18 Tulane 6
192 (7-3-0) 117

1943
34 Georgia 27
20 Rice 7
13 Texas A&M 28
28 La. Army STU 7
27 Georgia 6
14 T.C.U. 0
7 Ga. Tech 42
0 Tulane 27
143 (5-3-0) 144

Orange Bowl
19 Texas A&M 14

1944
27 Alabama 27
13 Rice 14
0 Texas A&M 7
6 Miss. State 13
15 Georgia 7
0 Tennessee 13
6 Ga. Tech 14
25 Tulane 6
92 (2-5-1) 101

1945
42 Rice 0
7 Alabama 26
31 Texas A&M 12
32 Georgia 0
39 Vanderbilt 7
32 Ole Miss 13
20 Miss. State 27
9 Ga. Tech 7
33 Tulane 0
245 (7-2-0) 92

1946
7 Rice 6
13 Miss. State 6
33 Texas A&M 9
7 Ga. Tech 26
14 Vanderbilt 0
34 Ole Miss 21
31 Alabama 21
20 Miami 7
40 Fordham 0
41 Tulane 27
240 (9-1-0) 123

Cotton Bowl
0 Arkansas 0

1947
21 Rice 14
19 Georgia 35
19 Texas A&M 13
14 Boston Col. 13
19 Vanderbilt 13
18 Ole Miss 20
21 Miss. State 6
12 Alabama 41
6 Tulane 6
149 (5-3-1) 161

1948
0 Texas 33
26 Rice 13
14 Texas A&M 13
0 Georgia 22
7 N. Carolina 34
19 Ole Miss 49
7 Vanderbilt 48
0 Miss. State 7
26 Alabama 6
0 Tulane 46
99 (3-7-0) 271

1949
0 Kentucky 19
14 Rice 7
34 Texas A&M 0
0 Georgia 7
13 N. Carolina 7
34 Ole Miss 7
33 Vanderbilt 13
34 Miss. State 7
48 SE Louisiana 7
21 Tulane 0
231 (8-2-0) 74

Sugar Bowl
0 Oklahoma 35

1950
0 Kentucky 14
19 Pacific 0
20 Rice 35
0 Ga. Tech 13
13 Georgia 13
40 Ole Miss 14
33 Vanderbilt 7
7 Miss. State 13
13 Villanova 7
14 Tulane 14
6 Texas 21
165 (4-5-2) 151

1951
13 Sou. Miss. 0
13 Alabama 7
7 Rice 6
7 Ga. Tech 25
7 Georgia 0
0 Maryland 27
6 Ole Miss 6
13 Vanderbilt 20
3 Miss. State 0
45 Villanova 7
14 Tulane 13
128 (7-3-1) 111

1952
14 Texas 35
20 Alabama 21
27 Rice 7
34 Kentucky 7
14 Georgia 27
6 Maryland 34
0 Ole Miss 28
3 Tennessee 22
14 Miss. State 33
16 Tulane 0
148 (3-7-0) 214

1953
20 Texas 7
7 Alabama 7
42 Boston College 6
6 Kentucky 6
14 Georgia 6
21 Florida 21
16 Ole Miss 27
14 Tennessee 32
13 Miss. State 26
9 Arkansas 8
32 Tulane 13
194 (5-3-3) 159

1954
6 Texas 20
0 Alabama 12
6 Kentucky 7
20 Ga. Tech 30
20 Texas Tech 13
20 Florida 7
6 Ole Miss 21
26 Chattanooga 19
0 Miss. State 25
7 Arkansas 6
14 Tulane 13
125 (5-6-0) 173

1955
19 Kentucky 7
0 Texas A&M 28
20 Rice 20
0 Ga. Tech 7
14 Florida 18
26 Ole Miss 29
0 Maryland 13
34 Miss. State 7
13 Arkansas 7
13 Tulane 13
139 (3-5-2) 149

1956
6 Texas A&M 9
14 Rice 23
7 Ga. Tech 39
0 Kentucky 14
6 Florida 21
17 Ole Miss 46
13 Okla. State 0
13 Miss. State 32
21 Arkansas 7
7 Tulane 6
104 (3-7-0) 197

1957
14 Rice 20
28 Alabama 0
19 Texas Tech 14
20 Ga. Tech 13
21 Kentucky 0
14 Florida 22
0 Vanderbilt 7
12 Ole Miss 14
6 Miss. State 14
25 Tulane 6
159 (5-5-0) 110

1958
26 Rice 6
13 Alabama 3
20 Hardin-Simmons 6
41 Miami 0
32 Kentucky 7
10 Florida 7
14 Ole Miss 0
50 Duke 18
7 Miss. State 6
62 Tulane 0
275 (10-0-0) 53

Sugar Bowl
7 Clemson 0

1959
26 Rice 3
10 T.C.U. 0
22 Baylor 0
27 Miami 3
9 Kentucky 0
9 Florida 0
7 Ole Miss 3
13 Tennessee 14
27 Miss. State 0
14 Tulane 6
164 (9-1-0) 29

Sugar Bowl
0 Ole Miss 21

1960
9 Texas A&M 0
3 Baylor 7
2 Ga. Tech 6
0 Kentucky 3
10 Florida 13
6 Ole Miss 6
35 S. Carolina 6
7 Miss. State 3
16 Wake Forest 0
17 Tulane 6
105 (5-4-1) 50

1961
3 Rice 16
16 Texas A&M 7
10 Ga. Tech 0
42 S. Carolina 0
24 Kentucky 14
23 Florida 0
10 Ole Miss 7
30 N. Carolina 0
14 Miss. State 6
62 Tulane 0
234 (9-1-0) 50

Orange Bowl
25 Colorado 7

1962
21 Texas A&M 0
6 Rice 6
10 Ga. Tech 7
17 Miami 3
7 Kentucky 0
23 Florida 0
7 Ole Miss 15
5 T.C.U. 0
28 Miss. State 0
38 Tulane 3
162 (8-1-1) 34

Cotton Bowl
13 Texas 0

1963
14 Texas A&M 6
12 Rice 21
7 Ga. Tech 6
3 Miami 0
28 Kentucky 7
14 Florida 0
3 Mississippi 37
28 T.C.U. 14
6 Miss. State 7
20 Tulane 0
135 (7-3-0) 98

Bluebonnet Bowl
7 Baylor 14

1964
9 Texas A&M 6
3 Rice 0
20 N. Carolina 3
27 Kentucky 7
3 Tennessee 3
11 Ole Miss 10
9 Alabama 17
14 Miss. State 10
13 Tulane 3
6 Florida 20
115 (7-2-1) 79

Sugar Bowl
13 Syracuse 10

1965
10 Texas A&M 0
42 Rice 14
7 Florida 14
34 Miami 27
31 Kentucky 21
21 S. Carolina 7
0 Ole Miss 23
7 Alabama 31
37 Miss. State 20
62 Tulane 0
251 (7-3-0) 157

Cotton Bowl
14 Arkansas 7

1966
28 S. Carolina 12
15 Rice 17
10 Miami 8
7 Texas A&M 7
30 Kentucky 0
7 Florida 28
0 Ole Miss 17
0 Alabama 21
17 Miss. State 7
21 Tulane 7
135 (5-4-1) 124

1967
20 Rice 14
17 Texas A&M 6
37 Florida 6
15 Miami 17
30 Kentucky 7
14 Tennessee 17
13 Ole Miss 13
6 Alabama 7
55 Miss. State 0
41 Tulane 27
248 (6-3-1) 114

Sugar Bowl
20 Wyoming 13

1968
13 Texas A&M 12
21 Rice 7
48 Baylor 16
0 Miami 30
13 Kentucky 3
10 T.C.U. 7
24 Ole Miss 27
7 Alabama 16
20 Miss. State 16
34 Tulane 10
190 (7-3-0) 144

Peach Bowl
31 Fla. State 27

1969
35 Texas A&M 6
42 Rice 0
63 Baylor 8
20 Miami 0
37 Kentucky 10
21 Auburn 20
23 Ole Miss 26
20 Alabama 15
61 Miss. State 6
27 Tulane 0
349 (9-1-0) 91

1970
18 Texas A&M 20
24 Rice 0
31 Baylor 10
34 Pacific 0

14	Kentucky	7
17	Auburn	9
14	Alabama	9
38	Miss. State	7
0	Notre Dame	3
26	Tulane	14
61	Ole Miss	17
277	(9-2-0)	96
	Orange Bowl	
12	Nebraska	17
	1971	
21	Colorado	31
37	Texas A&M	0
38	Wisconsin	28
38	Rice	3
48	Florida	7
17	Kentucky	13
22	Ole Miss	24
7	Alabama	14
28	Miss. State	3
28	Notre Dame	8
36	Tulane	7
277	(8-3-0)	96
	Sun Bowl	
33	Iowa State	15
	1972	
31	Pacific	13
42	Texas A&M	17
27	Wisconsin	7
12	Rice	6
35	Auburn	7
10	Kentucky	0
17	Ole Miss	16
21	Alabama	35
28	Miss. State	14
3	Florida	3
9	Tulane	3
235	(9-1-1)	121
	Bluebonnet Bowl	
17	Tennessee	24
	1973	
17	Colorado	6
28	Texas A&M	23
24	Rice	9
24	Florida	3
20	Auburn	6
28	Kentucky	21
33	S. Carolina	29
51	Ole Miss	14
26	Miss. State	7
7	Alabama	21
0	Tulane	14
258	(9-2-0)	153
	Orange Bowl	
9	Penn State	16
	1974	
42	Colorado	14
14	Texas A&M	21
10	Rice	10
14	Florida	24
20	Tennessee	10
13	Kentucky	20
24	Ole Miss	0
0	Alabama	30
6	Miss. State	7
24	Tulane	22
35	Utah	10
202	(5-5-1)	168
	1975	
7	Nebraska	10
8	Texas A&M	39
16	Rice	13
6	Florida	34
10	Tennessee	24
17	Kentucky	14
24	S. Carolina	6
13	Ole Miss	17
10	Alabama	23
*6	Miss. State	16
42	Tulane	6
159	(4-7-0)	202
*Won by forfeit		
	1976	
6	Nebraska	6
28	Oregon St.	11
31	Rice	0
23	Florida	28
33	Vanderbilt	20
7	Kentucky	21
45	Ole Miss	0
17	Alabama	28
*13	Miss. State	21
17	Tulane	7
35	Utah	7
255	(6-4-1)	149
*Won by forfeit		
	1977	
21	Indiana	24
77	Rice	0
36	Florida	14
28	Vanderbilt	15
13	Kentucky	33
56	Oregon	17
28	Ole Miss	21
3	Alabama	24
27	Miss. State	24
20	Tulane	17
66	Wyoming	7
375	(8-3-0)	196
	Sun Bowl	
14	Stanford	24
	1978	
24	Indiana	17
13	Wake Forest	11
37	Rice	0
34	Florida	21
17	Georgia	24
21	Kentucky	0
30	Mississippi	8
10	Alabama	31
14	Miss. State	16
40	Tulane	21
24	Wyoming	17
264	(8-3-0)	166
	Liberty Bowl	
15	Missouri	20

Louisana State University Lettermen—1893 to 1978

A

AARON, John, 1963-64-65
ABNEY, Wilbert, 1945
ABRAMSON, Louis J. "Luke", 1923
ABY, Hulette F. "Red", 1898-99
ADAMS, Jeff, 1946-47-48
ADAMS, John Aubrey, 1976-77-78
ADDISON, Don, 1968-69-70
ADDY, Ken, 1972-73
ADSIT, John R., Jr., 1943-44
ALBRIGHT, John G. "Jonnie", 1908-09
ALEXANDER, Arnold, 1954-55
ALEXANDER, Charles, 1975-76-77-78
ALEXANDER, Dan, 1974-75-76
ALEXANDER, Glenn, 1969-70
ALFORD, Andrew "Andy", 1952-53
ALLEN, Tommy "Trigger", 1966-67-68
ALLEN, W. D. "Bill", 1929-30-31
ALMOKARY, Joe, 1930-31-32
ALSTON, Francis H. "Frank", 1927-28
AMEDEE, Lynn, 1960-61-62
ANASTASIO, Charles, 1938-39-40
ANDERSON, Mike, 1968-69-70
ANDERSON, Roy Joe, 1937-38-39
ANDING, Aubrey, 1949
ANDREAS, Herman, 1930
ANDREWS, Charles P., 1893
ARRIGHI, J. H. "Hughes", 1894-95-96
ATIYEH, George, 1977-78
ATKINSON, James S., 1896
AUCOIN, Alvin, 1955-56-57

B

BABERS, Bertram "Bert", 1926-27
BAGGETT, Billy, 1948-49-50
BAILEY, Robert L. "Bunkie", 1926-27
BAIRD, Albert W. "Dub", 1916
BAIRD, Joe Garnett "Red", 1946-47-48-49
BALDWIN, Bob, 1955
BALDWIN, Harry, 1907
BALDWIN, Marvin, 1934-35-36
BALLARD, Shelton, 1946-47
BAME, Abie A., 1922
BANKER, Eddie, 1964-65-66
BANNISTER, Bobby, 1931-32
BARBER, Ronald J. "Ronnie", 1974-75-76
BARBIN, A. T., 1896
BARHAM, Garnett E. "Joe", 1925
BARNES, Walter "Piggy", 1940-46-47
BARNEY, Charles, 1943
BARRETT, Jack, 1940
BARRETT, W. Jeff, 1933-34-35
BARRETT, Woodrow, 1940
BARRILLEAUX, Jim, 1968
BARROW, Edward R., 1899
BARTON, James "Jim", 1949-50-51
BARTRAM, Dave, 1937-38-39
BASS, William "Bill", 1963-64-65
BATEMAN, Joel B., 1895, 1898
BATES, Oran P., 1903
BATES, William C., 1893
BAUER, Charles C., 1907
BAUR, F. Ogden, 1937-38-39
BEALE, L. S. "Rusty", 1919-21
BEARD, James, 1893-94
BENGLIS, Jim, 1970-71-72
BENNETT, Reldon, 1941
BENOIT, Robert L. "Rabbit", 1917-19-20
BENTLEY, Granville D., 1903
BERGERON, Carroll, 1958
BERNHARD, James, 1943-44-45
BERNSTEIN, Dave, 1939-40
BERNSTEIN, Joe, 1915-16-19
BERON, Phil, Jr., 1952-54
BERTUCCI, Gerald, 1944-45
BESSELMAN, Tom, 1970
BEVAN, George, 1966-67-69
BIENVENU, Greg, 1973-74-75
BIRD, Leo, 1939-40-41
BLACKETTER, Gary, 1975-76-77
BLAKEWOOD, Eldridge, G. "Blake", 1922-23
BLASS, Jay, 1977-78
BOFINGER, Bill, 1966-67
BOND, C. P., 1910
BOND, Jimmy, 1959
BOOTH, Barrett, 1936-37-38
BOOTH, Billy Joe, 1959-60-61
BORDELON, Kenny, 1972-73-74-75
BOUDREAUX, Wilfred, 1893
BOURGEOIS, Andy, 1958-59-60
BOURGEOIS, Louis C., Jr., 1921-22-23-24
BOURQUE, Hart, 1958-59-60
BOUTTE, Doug, 1973-74-75
BOWMAN, George, Jr., 1932-35
BOWMAN, Sidney S. "Stinkey", 1929-30-31
BOYD, Brad, 1972-73-74
BOZEMAN, Donnie, 1967-68-69
BRADLEY, John Edmund, Jr., 1976-77-78
BRADLEY, Richard "Dick", 1948-49
BRAINARD, Pete, 1931
BRANCATO, George, 1952-53
BRANCH, Mel, 1958-59
BRANNON, S. W. "Red", 1905-06-07-09
BRIAN, Alexis "Alex", 1893-94
BRITT, James, 1978
BRODNAX, J. W. "Red", 1956-57-58
BROGAN, John E., 1901
BROGAN, Lawrence E., 1904
BROHA, Max Kent, 1976-77-78
BROOKS, Richard "Bear", 1972-73-74
BROUSSARD, Billy, 1973-74
BROUSSARD, Ralph A., 1893-94
BROWN, A . D. "Andra", 1933-34-35
BROWN, Caswell, 1951
BROWN, E. A. "Fuzzy", 1929
BROWN, Gerald "Buster", 1964-65
BROWN, Harry, 1931-32
BROWN, Lobdell P. "Broncho", 1927-28-29-30
BROWN, R. Tommy, 1949-51
BROWN, Roland, 1932-34
BROWN, Rusty, 1977-78
BROWN, Samuel P., 1893
BRUE, Darryl, 1975
BRUNO, Phil, 1940
BRYAN, Jack, 1943-44
BUCK, Gordon "Charlie", 1906-07
BUCKLES, William, 1944
BULLIARD, Ed, 1950-51
BULLOCK, Farris, 1944
BULLOCK, Ray, 1946-47-48-49
BUNDY, Charles, 1965-66
BURAS, Leon "Buddy", 1973-74
BURGE, Pete, 1933
BURKETT, Jeff, 1941-42-46
BURNS, Craig, 1968-69-70
BURNS, Matthew, 1954-55-56
BURRELL, Clinton Blane, 1974-75-76-78
BYRAM, James E., 1900-01
BUSSE, Bert M., 1919-20-21
BUSSEY, Young, 1937-38-39
BUTAUD, Tommy, 1971-72
BUTLER, W. E. "Bill", 1929-30-31

C

CAIN, Clay, 1973-74
CAJOLEAS, Jimmy, 1937-38-39

CALHOUN, Shelby, 1934
CAMBON, F. Joseph, 1893
CAMP, Ivan, 1951-52-53-54
CAMPBELL, Cliff C. "Shorty", 1921-22-23-24
CAMPBELL, Edward (Bo), 1960-61-62
CAMPBELL, Eugene P., 1893
CAMPBELL, Irving, 1937-38-39
CANGELOSI, Dale, 1971-72-73
CANNON, Billy, 1957-58-59
CANTRELLE, Arthur, 1969-70-71
CAPONE, Warren, 1971-72-73
CARLIN, Kent, 1967
CARRIERE Oliver P. (Ike), 1923-24-25-26
CARROLL, Paul, 1935-36-37
CARSON, Carlos, 1977-78
CASANOVA, Jackie, 1975-76-77
CASANOVA, Tommy, 1969-70-71
CASCIO, Louis, 1969-70-71
CASON, Jim, 1944-45-46-47
CASSIDY, Ed, 1955-56-57
CASSIDY, Francis, 1940-41
CASSIDY, Steve, 1972-73-74-75
CAVIGGA, Al, 1940-41-44
CHADWICK, Gene, 1941
CHAMBERLIN, W. Benjamin (Ben), 1897-98-99
CHAMPAGNE, Ed, 1946
CHAMPAGNE, Gary, 1971-72-73
CHANDLER, Walter B. (Teeter), 1925-26
CHAVANNE, Edmund A. M., 1896-97-98-99
CHRISTIAN, Mickey, 1967-68
CLAITOR, Otto, 1915
CLARK, Blythe, 1937-38
CLRK, N. Jackson, 1976
CLRK, Samuel M. D., 1893-94
CLAUNCH, Ed, 1943-46-47-48
CLAY Jack T., 1924-25-29
CLEGG, Robert T. (Bobby), 1947-48
COATES, Ray, 1944-45-46-47
COCO, Walter A., 1898
COFFEE, Al, 1970-72-73
COFFEE, Pat, 1935-36
COLE, F. E. (Estes), 1929-30
COLE, John R. (Jack), 1948-49-50
COLEMAN, John J., 1899-1900-01-02-03
COLLE, Beau, 1963-64-65
COLINS, Albin Harrell (Rip), 1945-46-47-48
COLLINS, D. W. (Dan), 1917
COLLINS, Ray, 1947-48-49
CONN, Bobby, 1975-76-77
CONNELL, Allen P., 1924-24-26
CONNELL, George M., 1922-25
CONNELLY, Edwin M., 1904
CONNER, John C., 1894
CONWAY, Mike, 1975-76-77-78
COOK, Dave, 1973-74-75
COOK, Frederick W. (Freddie), 1901
COOPER, Philip (Chief), 1913-14-15-16
COPES, Charles, 1950
CORE, Harvey, 1944-45-46-47
CORGAN, Bill, 1943
CORMIER, Ken, 1963-64-65
CORMIER, Thomas (Skip), 1971-72
COX, Mickey, 1962-64
CYNE, Edward (Ed), 1949-50-51
CRANFORD, Charles, 1960-61-62
CRASS, Bill, 1935-36
CRAWFORD, John Egan, 1911-12-13
CUNNINGHAM, Ed, 1937
CUPIT, George D., 1976-77-78
CURTIS, Arthur M. (Jeff), 1921
CUSIMANO, Charles, 1945-48-49

D

DAILY, Ron, 1972-73-74
DAMPIER, Al, 1958
DANIEL, Loyd, 1970-71-72
DANIEL, Steve, 1966-67
DANTIN, Chris, 1970-71-72
DARK, Alvin, 1942
DASPIT, Armand P., 1895-96-97-98
DASPIT, Justin C., 1895-96-97-98
DAVIS, Arthur, 1944
DAVIS, Arthur, 1968-69-70
DAVIS, Brad, 1972-73-74
DAVIS, Grady, 1951-52
DAVIS, R. L. (Bebee), 1920-21
DAVIS, Tommy, 1953-58
DAYE, Donnie, 1958-59-60
DeCROSTA, Bob, 1956-57
deLAUNAY, Louis F. "Lou", 1976-77-78
DeLEE, Robert, 1977-78
DeMARIE, John, 1964-65-66
DeMARIE, Mike, 1969-70-71
DENNIS, Gordon A., 1893
DENNIS, Rand, 1972-73-74
DeRUTTE, Robert, 1978
DeSONIER, Richard, 1953
DESORMEAUX, Ronald Bill, Jr., 1976
DEUTSCHMANN, Lou, 1953-54
DIBETTA, Gawain, 1964-65-66
DICKINSON, Wayne, 1970
DIDIER, Melvin, 1944-45
DILDY, Gary, 1951-52-53-54
DIMMICK, Opie, 1924-25-26
DINKLE, Gary Mitchell "Mitch", 1974-75-76
DODSON, Adrian, 1940-41
DOGGETT, Al, 1951-52-53-54
DOMINGUE, Rusty, 1975-76
DONAHUE, Patrick Michael "Pat", 1974
DOUSAY, Jim, 1965-66-67
DOW, Robert, 1973-74-75-76
DOYLE, Mike, 1970
DREW, Harmon C., 1907-09
DRY, Ronald, 1950
DUGAS, Robert W., 1976-77-78
DUHE, A. J. Adam, 1973-74-75-76
DUHE, Butch, 1969
DUHE, Craig, 1975-76-77
DUHON, Mike, 1964-65-66
DUMAS, Bernie, 1935-36-37
DUNPHY, Robert Francis "Bo", 1973-74-75
DUPONT, John M., 1911-12-13-14
DUPONT, Lawrence H. "Dutch", 1910-11-12-13
DUPREE, Sam G., 1893-94
DURRETT, Bert E., 1925-26-27
DUTTON, John G. "Pete", 1917-19-21
DUTTON, Thomas W., 1912-13-19
Dyer, Jack, 1965-66-67

E

EARLEY, Jim, 1968-69-70
EASTMAN, Dan, 1939-40-41
EDMONDS, Walter R. "Ray", 1915-19
EDMONSON, Arthur T. "Shorty", 1921-22-23
EDWARDS, Bill, 1940-41-42
EDWARDS, Frank M. "Snake", 1903-04-05
EDWARDS, William E. Jr., 1976
EGAN, Raymond, 1934
ELKINS, Brent Louis, 1976-77-78
ELKINS, Jimmy, 1970-71-72
ELLEN, Don, 1963-64-65
ELLIS, Frank, 1927-28-29
ENSMINGER, Steven Craig, 1976-77-78
ERDMANN, Charles, 1938
ESTAY, Ronnie, 1969-70-71
ESTES, Don, 1960-61-62
ESTES, Stephen Clayton "Steve", 1974-75-76
ESTHAY, Terry, 1965-66-67
EVANS, Miller, 1941
EVANS, W. Morton, 1910-11-12-13
EWEN, Earl L. "Tubbo", 1920-21-22-23
EZELL, Billy, 1963-64-65

F

FAHEY, John K., 1903
FAKIER, Joe, 1971-72-73
FAMBROUGH, Larry, 1964-65
FARMER, Hermann "Red", 1936-37-38
FARRELL, William, 1978
FATHERREE, Jesse L., 1933-34-35
FAY, Theodore D. "Red", 1923-24-25
FENTON, G. E. "Doc", 1907-08-09
FERGUSON, Commodore, 1937
FERGUSON, O. K., 1955
FERGUSON, Pleasant L, 1907
FERRER, Steve, 1973-74-75
FIELD, Elmer "Bubba", 1949
FIELD, Jimmy, 1960-61-62
FIFE, Robert, 1938
FLANAGAN, H. F. "Mike", 1916
FLEMING, Walter "Goat", 1929-31-32
FLOOD, Martin T., 1925
FLOYD, J. C. "Red", 1915-16-19
FLUKER, H. V., 1913
FLURRY, Bob, 1960-61-62
FOGG, Ed, 1953-55
FOLEY, Art, 1931
FONTENOT, Ferdinand M., 1903
FORET, John, 1971-72
FORET, Lynn, 1970
FORGEY, Charles W. M., 1923
FORTIER, Bill, 1966-67-68
FOTI, Russ, 1947
FOURMY, James M., 1903-04
FOURNET, Emile, 1958-59
FOURNET, John B., 1917-19
FOURNET, Sidney, 1951-52-53-54
FRANCIS, Harrison, 1975-76
FRAYER, Jack, 1958-59
FREEMAN, G. A. "Nubs", 1927
FREEMAN, G. Chester, 1949-50-51
FREY, Ignatius, 1941
FRIEND, Ben, 1936-37-38
FRIZZELL, Tommy, 1978
FROECHTENICHT, W. H., 1939
FRYE, Barton, 1966-67-68
FRYE, Lloyd, 1969-70-71
FUCHS, George, 1899-1900-01
FUGLER, Max, 1957-58-59
FULKERSON, Jack, 1940-41-42
FUSSELL, Tommy, 1964-65-66

G

GAINEY, Jim, 1971-72
GAJAN, Hokie, 1977-78
GAMBLE, Harry P., 1894-95
GANDY, Marshall H. "Cap", 1906-07-08
GARDNER, Dennis, 1975-76
GARDNER, Jim W., 1956-57
GARLAND, Joseph M., 1900
GARLINGTON, John, 1965-66-67
GARY, Dexter, 1960-61
GATES, Jack, 1960-61-62
GATTO, Eddie, 1936-37-38
GAUBATZ, Dennis, 1960-61-62
GAUTREAUX, Russell, 1952-53
GAYDEN, George L. "Hack", 1926
GAYLE, Edwin F., 1893
GIACONE, Joe, 1941-42
GIANELLONI, Vivian J., 1939-40
GILBERT, Jimmy, 1967-68-69
GILL, Audis, 1945
GILL, Reuben O. "Rube", 1907-08-09
GIOVANNI, Charles "Tony", 1930-31
GLADDEN, Sterling "Buck" W., 1919
GLAMP, Joe, 1942
GODCHAUX, Frank A., 1897
GODFREY, Lola T. "Babe", 1925-26-27
GONZALES, Vincent "Vince", 1952-53-54-55
GOODE, Burton, 1943
GOREE, J. W., 1938-39-40
GORHAM, Edwin S., 1899-1900-01
GORINSKI, Walter, 1940-41-42
GORMLEY, Jack, 1936-37-38
GORMLEY, Richard, 1936-37-38
GOSSERAND, M. L. "Goose", 1910-11-12
GOURRIER, Samuel A., 1896
GRAHAM, Durwood, 1955-56
GRANIER, Richard, 1963-64
GRAVES, White, 1962-63-64
GRAY, Dale, 1946-47-48
GREEN, V. E. "Chick", 1914
GREEN, Winfred C. "Poss", 1913-14-15-16
GREENWOOD, Bobby, 1959
GREER, Ed, 1964
GREMILLION, F. V., 1899-1900
GREVEMBERG, Albert, 1927
GREVEMBERG, Joseph H., 1926-27
GREZAFFI, Sammy, 1965-66-67
GRIFFIN, Benny, 1965-66-67
GRIFFITH, Carroll, 1943-47-48-49
GRIFFITH, J. H. "John", 1905
GRIVOT, Maurice, 1894
GROS, Earl, 1959-60-61
GUENO, Albert J., 1901-02-03
GUGLIELMO, Al, 1951-52-53
GUIDRY, J. W., 1901-02-03
GUILLOT, Jerry, 1966-67-68
GUILLOT, Rodney, 1960-62
GUILLOT, Rodney "Monk", 1959-60-61

GUILLOT, Stephen Roch "Rocky", 1976-77-78
GUNNELS, Willie, 1978

H

HABERT, Ed, 1960-61-62
HAGUE, Perry G., 1919-20
HALEY, Otis, 1943
HALL, Fred "Skinny", 1941-42-46
HALL, J. O. "Doc", 1909-10-11-12
HAMIC, Garland "Buddy", 1961-62-63
HAMIC, Jimmy, 1965-66
HAMILTON, Andy, 1969-70-71
HAMILTON, W. J., 1907
HAMLETT, Bob, 1966-67-68
HAMMOND, W. M. "Bull", 1910
HANDY, Beverly B. "Spaghetti", 1907
HANLEY, William B. "Red", 1919
HARGETT, Dan, 1960-61
HARP, James F., 1896
HARRELL, Louis "Tee-Tee", 1929
HARRIS, Bill, 1953
HARRIS, Clinton "Bo", 1972-73-74
HARRIS, L. B., 1904
HARRIS, Sulcer, 1941-42
HARRIS, Wendell, 1959-60-61
HARRISON, Pollard E., 1913
HARTLEY, Joe, 1943
HARVEY, Hugh, 1906
HATCHER, George R., 1927
HAYNES, Everette H. "Hinkey", 1925-26-27
HAYNES, Fred, 1966-67-68
HAYNES, George, 1963-64-66
HEALD, Russell, 1971-72-73
HEARD, Holley, 1942-47
HEARD, T. J. "Fatty", 1904-05
HEDGES, Lee, 1949-50-51
HELM, Newton C. "Dirty", 1919-20-21-22
HELMS, Lee, 1926
HELSCHER, Harold, 1941
HELVESTON, Osborn "Butch", 1933-34-35
HEMPHILL, Don, 1945-46-47
HEMPHILL, Fred Bruce, 1974-75-76
HENDRICK, Bruce, 1938
HENDRIX, Billy, 1956-57-58
HENDRIX, John A. "Jonnie", 1928-29-30
HENDRIX, Sid W., 1922
HENRY, Thomas J., 1916
HENSLEY, James Craig, 1976-77-78
HERBERT, Arthur W. "Doc", 1916-17
HEREFORD, Robert M., 1920-21
HERGET, George C. "Warm-Up", 1925-26
HERNANDEZ, Jude, 1978
HEROMAN, Alfred, 1946-47-48
HERPIN, Joseph O., 1899-1901
HERRINGTON, James, 1944
HEWETT, Lem F., 1920
HIGHTOWER, Gerald, 1939-40-41
HILL, Jerry, 1978
HILL, Terry, 1973-74-75
HILLMAN, Mike, 1967-68-69
HILLMAN, William A., 1906-07-08-09
HIMES, Levi A. "Lee", 1906-07-08-09
HINTON, Lora, 1973-74-75
HODGE, Abner A., 1894
HODGES, Harry, 1954-55
HODGINS, Leo M., 1976
HODGINS, Norman, 1971-72-73
HOGAN, Bill, 1939-40-41
HOLDEN, T. D., 1929-30
HOLLAND, Pershing, 1941-42
HOLLAND, Woodrow, 1942
HORNE, Frank, 1952
HOVER, Allen, 1948-49-50
HOWELL, Robert C., 1903
HOWELL, Roland B. "Billiken", 1909-11
HOWELL, William C., 1897
HUBBELL, Mickey, 1978
HUCKLEBRIDGE, Robbi, 1961-62-63
HUEY, James M., 1893
HUFFMAN, Alva S. "Brute", 1926-27-28
HUGHES, Clyde B. "Red", 1921-23
HUMBLE, John, 1944
HUNSICKER, George R., 1905
HUNT, Ralph, 1943
HUNTER, Guy N., 1894
HUNTER, Louis T., 1894
HUNTER, Robert, 1950
HURD, Roy, 1967
HUYCK, Philip P., 1895-96-97-99

I

INDEST, Adalphe, 1944
IPPOLITO, Mark, 1978
IVES, Clarence A. "Fatty", 1917-19-20-21

J

JACKSON, Augustus W. "Gus", 1922-23-24
JACKSON, Dalton "Rusty", 1972-73-74
JACKSON, Steve Loran, 1974-75-76
JAMES, Albert, 1940-41
JANNECK, Carl, 1943-44
JAUBERT, Jack, 1969-70-71
JENKINS, Darryl, 1958-59-60
JENKINS, Harry, 1904
JENKINS, Marvin, 1939-40
JENNINGS, Joe Patrick, 1974-75-76
JETER, Ronald, 1965-66-67
JOFFRION, A. Bush, 1904-05
JOHNS, Levi "Chuck", 1953-54-55
JOHNSON, Charles, 1938-39-40
JOHNSON, Melvin F., 1912
JOHNSON, Phil, 1965-66
JOHNSON, Ray L., 1932
JOHNSON, William C., 1976-77-78
JOHNSTON, Jerry, 1956
JOHNSTON, Ronnie, 1956
JONES, Ben, 1972-73-74
JONES, Bert, 1970-71-72
JONES, Carroll, 1941
JONES, David, 1966-67
JONES, Keith E., 1915-16-17
JONES, Larry, 1953-54
JONES, LeRoid, 1977-78
JONES, LeRoyal, 1978
JONES, Mike, 1975
JONES, Norwood "Chubby", 1927-28-29
JONES, Richard, 1965-66
JOSEPH, Jerry, 1964-65-66

K

KAFFIE, Leopold, 1897-98
KAHLDEN, Larry, 1956-57-58
KAISER, Bradley, 1975
KALIL, Emile, 1952
KARAPHILLIS, John M., 1976
KAVANAUGH, Ken, Sr., 1937-38-39
KAVANAUGH, Ken, Jr., 1969-70-71
KEIGLEY, Gerald, 1970-71-72
KELLER, Joe L., 1930-31-32
KELLUM, Bill, 1945
KELLY, Angus H., 1906
KELLY, Charlie, 1951
KENDRICK, Herbert, 1939-40-41
KENDRICK, Robert "Bob", 1939
KENNEDY, Ralph M., 1901-02-03
KENNON, Robert F., 1924
KENT, Gerry, 1966-67-68
KENT, John, 1931-32-33
KHOURY, Ed "Big Ed", 1929-30-31
KILLEN, Logan, 1971-72-73
KIMBLE, Dennis, 1977-78
KINCHEN, Gary, 1960-61-62
KINCHEN, Gaynell, 1958-59-60
KING, Bobby Joe, 1968-69-70
KING, Larry, 1937
KING, Larry, 1955
KINGERY, Don, 1943
KINGERY, Wayne, 1945
KITTO, Armand, 1948-49-50
KIZER, Roland C. "Chesty", 1922
KLOCK, Arthur E., 1912-13-14-16
KLOCK E. L., 1902-03-04-05
KNEHT, Jas. Doyle, 1972-73-74
KNIGHT, Alex A. "Butch", 1974-75-76
KNIGHT, Gene "Red", 1943-44-45-46
KNIGHT, Roy, 1935
KOBER, Jerry, 1967-69
KONZ, Kenneth, 1948-49-50
KOSMAC, Andrew, 1942-45
KREMENTZ, F. B. "Freddy", 1915-16

L

LABAT, Leroy, 1951-52
LABRUZZO, Joe, 1963-64-65
LAFAUCI, Tyler, 1971-72-73
LaFLEUR, Greg, 1977
LALLY, Michael F., 1908-10
LAMBERT, James "Coot", 1967-68
LAMBERT, Sam, 1895-96
LAND, Fred N., 1944-45-46-47
LANDRY, Ben H., 1929
LANDRY, Henry E., 1899-1900-02
LANDRY, M. J., 1945
LANDRY, Walter M. "Bud", 1921-22
LANDRY, Willard, 1945-46
LANE, Clifton R. "Clif" 1976-77-78
LANGAN, John, 1957-58-59
LANGLEY, Leroy, 1932-33
LANGLEY, Willis, 1962-63
LANOUX, Paul R., III, 1974-75-76
LANSING, Bill, 1950-51-52
LaSUEUR, Leon J., 1902
LAVIN, Jim, 1956-57
LAWRASON, Charles M., 1899
LAWRENCE, Bob, 1951-52
LAWRIE, Joe, 1933-34-35
LAWTON, Jack E., Jr. "Jackie", 1976-77
LAY, Andrew, 1944
LEACH, Joe, 1946-47
LEAKE, Sam, 1953
LeBLANC, Allen, 1965-66-67
LeBLANC, Danny, 1962-63-65
LeBLANC, Lynn, 1957-58-59
LeBLANC, Maurice, 1966-67-68
LeBLEU, Claude A., 1929
LEDBETTER, Wiltz M., 1895-96
LeDOUX, Jimmy, 1970-71-72
LEE, David, 1973
LEE, Felix "Buddy", 1969-70
LEGGETT, Earl, 1955-56
LEISK, Wardell, 1935-36
LELEKACS, Steve, 1972-73-74
LEMAK, Charles, W., 1937
LEMOINE, Hampton T. "Tick", 1899
LEONARD, Michael B. "Mike", 1974-75-76
LEOPARD, Duane, 1957-58-59
LeSAGE, Joe, 1948
LESTER, Gordon, 1936-37
LeSUEUR, George B. "Heck", 1897-98-99
LEVY, Julius M., 1897
LEWIS, James, 1943-47-48
LEWIS, John W. "Johnnie", 1920-21
LEWIS, William J., 1894
LEWIS, William S. "Bill", 1915-16
LINDSEY, Clyde, 1944-45-46
LIPKIS, Bernie, 1939-40
LOBDELL, W. Y. "Bill", 1932-33
LOFLIN, Jim, 1946-47
LOFTIN, Billy, 1967-68
LONERGAN, Pat, 1978
LOTT, Bobby, 1956
LOTT, Tommy, 1957-58-59
LOUSTALOT, Albert L., 1903
LOUSTALOT, Matthew L. "Matt", 1923
LOUVIERE, William H. "Chick", 1914
LUKER J. B., 1928-29-30
LUMPKIN, Mark, 1967-68-69
LYLE, Jim "Egg", 1948-49-50
LYLE, Mel, 1946-47-48-49
LYLES, William M., "Buffalo", 1904-07
LYONS, Frederick G., 1893
LYONS, Pat, 1975-76-77
LYONS, Paul, 1970-71-72

M

MAGGIORE, Ernest, 1963-64-65
MAHTOOK, Robbie, 1978
MALONE, Jim, 1930-31-32
MAMOUDIS, Charles G. "Chuck", 1974-75
MANGHAM, Mickey, 1958-59-60
MANTON, Ronnie, 1965-66-67
MARCHAND, Jerry, 1952-53
MARTIN, C. Y., 1910
MARTIN, Curtis, 1969
MARTIN, G. H., 1914
MARTIN, Jackie, 1950
MARTIN, Steve, 1968-70
MARTIN, Wade O. "Skinny", 1902-03-04
MASON, C. C. "Charlie", 1926-27-28
MASTERS, Billy, 1964-65-66
MATHERNE, Durel, 1958-59
MATLOCK, Oscar, 1936
MATTE, Frank, 1966-67-68
MATTHEWS, Lawrence R. "Tubbo", 1922-23
MAY, Bill, 1934-35-36

MAY, Joe, 1954-55-56
MAY, Jon, 1977
McCAGE, Sam, 1977-78
McCALL, Henry L. "Mac", 1923-26
McCANN, John, 1968-69-70
McCANN, M. G. "Mickey", 1927
McCARSON, Paul, 1944
McCARTY, Dave, 1958-59
McCASKILL, Larry, 1967-68
McCLAIN, Jess, 1930-31
McCLAIN, Scotty, 1957-58-59
McCLELLAND, William, 1943-44-47-48
McCOLLAM, Andrew M., 1909
McCORMICK, Dave, 1963-64-65
McCREEDY, Ed, 1958-59-60
McDANIEL, Orlando, 1978
McDONALD, Robert, 1960
McDUFF, Charles, 1978
McFARLAND, Reggie, A., 1919-20-21-22
McFERRIN, Sherman S. "Mack", 1929
McHENRY, Barney G. "Mac", 1910-11
McINGVALE, Ralph, 1977-78
McKINNEY, Billy, 1939-41
McKINNEY, Jim, 1939
McLEOD, James, 1941-42-47
McLEOD, Ralph, 1950-51-52
McNAIR, Dan, 1973
McNEESE, Oswald W., 1900-01
McSHERRY, Robert, 1967-68
MENETRE, Ralph, 1945
MERCER, John, 1961-62
MESSA, Rene A., 1904-05
MESSINA, Jack, 1937-38-39
MESTAYER, Otto, 1914
MICHAELSON, Fred, 1967-68-69
MICHAELSON, Julius "Jay", 1969-70-71
MICIOTTO, Charles "Binks", 1971-72-73
MICKAL, Abe, 1933-34-35
MIHALICH, John "Mickey", 1934-35-36
MILEY, Mike, 1972-73
MILLER, Ben R., 1923-24-25
MILLER, Charles "Chip", 1972-73
MILLER, Dale, 1971
MILLER, Fred, 1960-61-62
MILLER, Herd, 1943-44-45-46
MILLER, Paul, 1950-52-53
MILLER, Willie, 1940-41-42
MILLET, Walter, 1973
MILLICAN, Samuel "Buddy", 1968-69-70
MILNER, Guy "Cotton", 1936-37-38
MINALDI, Thad, 1975-76-77-78
MISTRETTA, Albert, 1943
MITCHELL, George "Gee", 1932-33
MITCHELL, Jim, 1952-53-56
MIXON, Neil, 1931-32-33
MOBLEY, Larry, 1952-54
MOBLEY, T. R. "Ray", 1913-14
MODICUT, Joseph, 1951-52
MONGET, Gayle, 1937-38-39
MONSOUR, Eli "Mike", 1927
MONTGOMERY, William, 1942-43-45
MOORE, Charles, 1964-65
MOORE, Charles F. 1964-65
MOORE, D. Haywood, 1928-29-31
MOORE, Frank E. "Specks", 1932-33-34
MOREAU, Bobby, 1975-76-77
MOREAU, Doug, 1963-64-65
MOREL, Tommy, 1966-67-68
MORGAN, Mike, 1961-62-63
MORGAN, Paul C., 1927
MORGAN, Sam R., 1924-25-26
MORRIS, John E., 1895
MORTIMER, Eugene H., 1900
MORTON, Arthur "Slick", 1935-36-37
MOSES, Phil, 1972-73-74
MULLER, J. C., 1904-05
MULLINS, William B., 1894
MUNDINGER, Adam G. "Addie", 1900-01-02
MURPHREE, Jerry, 1977-78
MURPHY, Sammy, 1952-53-54
MURRAY, Phil, 1970-71-72
MYLES, Lonny, 1967-68
MYRICK, Basil, 1936

N

NAGATA, Joe, 1942-43
NAGLE, John, 1969-70-71
NEALY, Wrendall, 1951-52
NECK, Tommy, 1959-60-61
NELKEN, William, 1894
NELSON, Manson, 1958-59
NELSON, Robert J., 1894
NESOM, Guy W., 1926-27-28
NEUMANN, Danny, 1961-62-63
NEUMANN, Leonard, 1964-65-66
NEVILS, Ab, 1931-32-33
NEWELL, Edward T. J., 1894
NEWFIELD, Kenny, 1966-67-68
NICAR, Randy, 1971
NICHOLSON, Gordon B., 1894-95-96-97
NICOLO, Sal, 1952-54
NOBLET, Oren H. "Babe", 1904-05-07-08
NOONAN, James, 1976
NORSWORTHY, Bill, 1968-69-70
NORWOOD, Don, 1957-58-59
NUNNERY, R. B., 1954-55

O

OAKLEY, Charles, 1951-52-53
O'BRIEN, Robert "Bob", 1964-65-66
O'CALLAGHAN, Joe, 1952
ODOM, Sammy Joe, 1961
O'DONNELL, Joe, 1940
OGDEN, Don G., 1929-30
OLIVER, George, 1952
OLIVER, L. A., 1901
O'QUIN, Arthur "Mickey", 1914-15-16-17
O'QUIN, Leon, 1914
OUSTALET, Jimmy, 1972-73-75
OWENS, Richard "Ricki", 1967-68-69

P

PARDO, Diego, 1944
PARIS, Ted, 1954-55-56
PARKER, Enos, 1953-54-55-56
PARNHAM, Spencer, 1945
PEEBLES, Leo "Les", 1928-29
PEGUES, William T., 1900
PERCY, Chaille, 1968-69
PERE, Ralph, 1961-62-63
PERRY, Boyd, 1970-71
PEVEY, Charles, 1946-47-48-49
PHARIS, Mike, 1965-66
PHELPS, Joe R. "Polly", 1927
PHILLIPS, Ivan, 1977-78
PHILLIPS, Marty, 1973-74
PICKETT, Garland, 1933
PICOU, Richard, 1969-70-71
PIERCE, Spike, 1965
PIKE, Mike, 1973-74-75
PILLOW, Dudley, 1939-40
PILLOW, Walter, 1963-64-65
PITALO, Alex M., 1950
PITCHER, James E. "Jim", 1917
PITCHER, William, 1922-23-24
PITTMAN, Albert, 1944
PITTMAN, J. S. "Bit Pitt", 1914-15
PITTMAN, Paul, 1937
PLATOU, R., 1915
PLEASANT, Ruffin G., 1893
POLLOCK, William M. "Judge", 1908-09-10
POLOZOLA, Steve, 1967-68-69
PORTA, Ray "Coon", 1948
POTTER, Ray, 1949-50-51
POTTS, John H., 1910
POWELL, R. H. "Bob", 1929-30-31
POWELL, Tommy, 1963-64-65
PRATHER, Trey, 1966
PRATT, George K., 1899
PRATT, Joel M., 1893
PRESCOTT, Aaron, 1893
PRESCOTT, Dickie, 1951-52-54
PRESCOTT, Willis B., 1893-94
PRESSBURG, Joel W., 1929-30
PRICKETT, Greg, 1975-76
PRINCE, T. J., 1939
PRUDHOMME, Remi, 1962-63-64
PURVIS, Don "Scooter", 1957-58-59

Q

QUINN, Marcus, 1977-78
QUINTELA, Mike, 1975-76-77-78
QUIRK, Lewis A. W., 1894-95

R

RABB, Carlos C., 1966-67-68
RABB, Warren, 1957-58-59
RABENHORST, Oscar D. "Dudey", 1921-22
RACINE, Frank, 1971-72-73
RADECKER, Gary, 1975-76-77
RAIFORD, Albert "Rock", 1972-73-74-75
RAY, Eddie, 1967-68-69
REAGAN, C. R. "Jerry", 1915
REBSAMEN, Paul, 1955
REDHEAD, J. A., 1901
REDING, Joe, 1966-67-68
REED, J. T. "Rock", 1934-35-36
REEDY, Frank, 1929
REEVES, W. A. "Dobie", 1928-29-30
REID, Alfred J. "Alf", 1912-13-14-15
REID, Joseph "Joe", 1948-49-50
REILY, Charles S., 1910-11-12
RENFROE, John C. "Cherry", 1927-29-30
RENFROE, Olin, 1956
REYNOLDS, Gerald "Jerry", 1947-48
REYNOLDS, M. C., 1955-56
RHODES, H. J., 1900-01-02
RICE, George, 1963-64-65
RICE, R. E. "Red", 1915-16
RICE, Robert, 1962
RICH, Christopher J. "Chris", 1976-77-78
RICHARDS, Bobby, 1960-61
RICHARDSON, Lyman, 1940-41-42
RICHMOND, Dilton, 1941-42-46
RINAUDO, Martin, 1943
RIPPLE, Steve, 1975-76-77
RITTINER, Chris M., 1976
RIVERO, V. Victor, 1904
ROANE, James A., 1893
ROBERTS, Henry Lee, 1958
ROBERTSON, Archie Ed, 1896
ROBICHAUX, Al, 1951-52-53
ROBICHAUX, Mike, 1965-66
ROBINSON, Dwight, 1961-62-63
ROBINSON, Johnny, 1957-58-59
ROBISKIE, Terry, 1973-74-75-76
ROCA, Juan, 1972-73-74
RODRIGUE, J. C. "Friday", 1915-16
RODRIGUE, Ruffin, 1962-63-64
ROGER, Don, 1972-73-74
ROGERS, Steve, 1972-73-74
ROHM, Charles "Pinky", 1935-36-37
ROMAIN, Richard, 1973-74
ROSHTO, James "Jimmy", 1949-50-51
ROSS, George, 1975
ROUSSOS, George, 1949-50
ROWAN, Elwyn, 1944
RUKAS, Justin "Ruke", 1933-34-35
RUSSELL, Randy, 1971-72
RUSSELL, Tony, 1967-68-69
RUTLAND, James "Pepper", 1970-71-72
RUTLEDGE, D. H. "Don", 1917
RYAN, Mike, 1967
RYAN, Warren "Pat", 1908-09
RYDER, Robert "Red", 1968-69

S

SAGE, John, 1968-69-70
SAIA, S. J., 1975-76
ST. DIZIER, Roger V. "Blue", 1916-17
SALASSI, John R., 1894-95-96
SANCHEZ, A. C., 1914
SANDERS, Al "Apple", 1945-46
SANDERS, James W., 1895
SANDIFER, Dan, 1944-45-46-47
SANDRAS, Jules, 1956
SANFORD, James "Jim", 1951-52
SANFORD, Joseph H., 1901
SCHEXNAILDRE, Merie, 1958-59
SCHNEIDER, Edward D. "Pete", 1920
SCHNEIDER, F. H. "Teddy", 1929-30
SCHNEIDER, Frederick H., 1894-95-96
SCHOENBERGER, George C., 1893-96
SCHROLL, Bill, 1946-47-48
SCHROLL, Charles, 1946
SCHROLL, William, 1943
SCHURTZ, Hubert, 1946-47
SCHWAB, Don, 1963-64-65
SCHWALB, Gerald "Jerry", 1954-57
SCHWING, Ivan H., 1899-1900
SCOTT, E. E., 1893-94
SCOTT, Edwin A. "Ned", 1895-96-97
SCREEN, Pat, 1963-64-65
SCULLY, Don, 1955-56
SEAGO, Ernest "Son", 1933-34-35

SEBASTIAN, James A., 1901
SEIP, John J., 1907-08-09-10
SESSIONS, Wayne, 1965-66
SHARP, Linden E., 1902
SHAW, Elton, 1952
SHEEHY, Billy, 1956
SHERBURNE, Thomas L, 1897-98
SHIRER, Joe, 1950-51
SHOAF, James "Jim", 1948-49-50
SHOREY, Allen, 1969-70-71
SIBLEY, Llewellyn R. "Lew", 1974-75-76-77
SIGREST, Ed, 1944-45
SIMES, Ashford, 1938-39
SIMMONS, Charles, 1962-64
SIMMONS, Kelly, 1975-76-77
SIMMONS, Ray, 1952
SKIDMORE, Claude "Skid", 1931-32
SKIDMORE, Jim "Big Skid", 1930-31-32
SLAUGHTER, William S., 1894-95-96-97-98
SMEDES, William C., 1893-94
SMITH, Benny "Gunboat", 1919
SMITH, Billy, 1955-56-57
SMITH, Charlie, 1950-51
SMITH, Clarence I., 1905-06-08
SMITH, David C., 1976
SMITH, Glenn, 1967-68
SMITH, Guy, 1952
SMITH, John Hugh, 1936-37-38
SMITH, Rollis, 1944
SMITH, Spencer L., 1976-77-78
SMITH, Thielen, 1973-74-75
SMITH, Tom, 1929-30-31
SMITH, Tommy, 1970
SMITH, V. E. "Bob", 1905-08
SNYDER, John E. "Texas", 1894-95
SOEFKER, Buddy, 1961-62-63
SOILEAU, Danny, 1978
SOWELL, Claude, 1926
SPENCE, Ray, 1956-57
SPENCER, Curtis, 1925
SPENCER, Floyd W., 1912-13
SPENCER, Fritz L., 1919-20-21
SPENCER, George B., 1911-13-14
SPENCER, Hugh Frank, 1916-17
STAFFORD, David Grove, 1919
STAGG, Jack, 1943-44
STAGGS, John, 1970-71-72
STANFORD, John T., 1898-99
STANTON, Eddie, 1977-78
STAPLES, Duncan P., 1894-97
STAPLES, Jake, 1937-38-39
STAUDINGER, Louis P., 1904
STAYTON, William D. "Judge", 1903-04
STEELE, John E. "Pug", 1921-23-24-25
STELL, J. H. "Jabbo", 1937-38
STEPHENS, Harold, 1966-67-68
STEVENS, Ed, 1930-31
STEVENS, Norman, 1950-51-52
STEVENS, Norman G. "Steve", 1922-23-24-25
STEWART, Marvin "Moose", 1934-35-36
STINSON, Don, 1954-55
STOBER, Bill, 1967-68-69
STOKLEY, Nelson, 1965-66-67
STONECIPHER, Wade, 1939
STOVALL, Hefley H. "Hank", 1927-28
STOVALL, Jerry, 1960-61-62
STOVALL, Lloyd J., 1932-33-34
STOVALL, Robert L. "Strauss", 1906-07-08-09
STOVALL, Rowson F., 1907-08-09
STRANGE, Charles "Bo", 1958-59-60
STRANGE, Clarence "Pop", 1935-36
STRANGE, David, 1963-64-65
STREETE, Jon G., 1974-75-76
STREETE, Steve, 1971-72
STRICKLAND, Tom, 1972-73
STRINGFIELD, Cliff, 1951-52-53
STROTHER, Howard, 1945-48
STUART, Charles, 1969-70-71
STUART, Roy J., 1974-75-76
STUMPH, John C. "Shorty", 1926
STUPKA, Frank, 1934-35
STUPKA, Mike, 1958-59
SULLIVAN, Walter "Sully", 1932-33-34
SWANSON, A. E. "Nip", 1926-27-28
SWANSON, Arthur L. "Red", 1923-24-25
SYKES, Gene, 1960-61-62

T

TALBOT, Edward L., 1912
TALLEY, Jim, 1941-42
TARASOVIC, George, 1951
TAYLOR, Jimmy, 1956-57
TEAL, Willie, Jr., 1976-77-78
TEXADA, James C., 1906
THIBODEAUX, Benjy, 1977-78
THOMAS, Arthur J. "Tommy", 1908-09-10-11
THOMASON, Bill, 1967-68-69
THOMPSON, Leon, 1973
THOMPSON, Steve, 1956
THORNALL, Bill, 1942
THORNTON, Sam B., 1922-23
TILLY, L. R., 1909
TINSLEY, Gaynell "Gus", 1934-35-36
TINSLEY, Jess D., 1926-27-28
TISDALE, Charles H., 1893
TITLE, Billy, 1976, Mgr.
TITTLE, Y. A., 1944-45-46-47
TOCZYLOSKI, Edward, 1940
TOLER, Jack, 1943-44
TOMS, Randy, 1969-70
TORRANCE, Jack "Baby Jack", 1931-32-33
TOTH, Zollie, 1946-47-48-49
TRAPANI, Felix, 1943-45
TRICHE, Phil, 1975-76-77
TRICHEL, Walter S., 1893
TRIMBLE, Carl Otis, 1974-75-76
TROSCLAIR, Milton, 1962-63-64
TRUAX, Bill, 1961-62-63
TULLOS, Earl R., 1943-44-45-46
TUMINELLO, Joe, 1952-53-54-55
TURNER Jim, 1962-63
TURNER, Mike, 1978
TURNER, Win, 1953-54-56-57

V

VAIRIN, Kenny, 1963-64
VAN BUREN, Ebert, 1948-49-50
VAN BUREN, Steve, 1941-42-43
VENABLE, Jack, 1943
VENABLE, John, 1951
VERNON, Benton R., 1923-24-25
VINCENT, Mike, 1963-64-65
VINEYARD, Hershal "Sleepy", 1926-27
VIRGETS, Warren, 1950-51
VOSS, Harold, 1948-49-50

W

WADDILL, George D., 1894
WALDEN, Henry E., 1913-14
WALET, P. H., 1911
WALKER, Delmar "Del", 1969-70-71
WALKER, Jack, 1936
WALKER, R. F., "Foots", 1913-16
WALL, Benjamin B., 1898-99
WALLIS, Lionel, 1977-78
WALSH, Ewell, 1949-50
WALTON, R. H. "Tough", 1914-15
WARD, Steve, 1960-61-62
WARMBROD, James, 1936-37
WARNER, Ambrose D., 1922-23-25
WATSON, John, 1977-78
WEAVER, A. V. "Tubbo", 1924
WEAVER, Odell, 1940-41
WEAVER, Otto L., 1924-25
WEBB, Charles, 1943-44
WEBER, S. R. "Chink", 1924
WEBSTER, Rene J., 1894
WEIL, Edgar E., 1905-06
WEINSTEIN, John, 1970
WEST, Billy, 1949-50-51
WEST, Jim, 1967-68-69
WESTBROOK, John T., 1894-95-96-97
WHITE, Lyman, 1977-78
WHITFILL, Steve, 1973-74
WHITLATCH, Blake, 1975-76-77
WHITLEY John B. "Jay", 1976-77-78
WHITMAN, Ralph, 1938-39
WHYTE, Vernon, 1943
WILBANKS, T. E., 1917
WILKINS, Ray, 1960-61-62
WILLIAMS, Chris, 1977-78
WILLIAMS, Demetri, 1978
WILLIAMS, Henry L., 1906
WILLIAMS, Mike, 1972-73-74
WILLIAMSON, Charles "Chuck" 1971-72
WILSON, Barry, 1965-66-67
WILSON, N. A. "Fatz", 1926-27-28
WILSON, Roy, 1930-31-32
WIMBERLY, Abner, 1943-46-47-48
WINKLER, Joe, 1971-72-73
WINSTON, Roy "Moonie", 1959-60-61
WINTLE, James V. "Wee Willie" 1921-22
WOLF, Sidney K. "Izzy", 1920
WOOD, John, 1970-71-72
WOOD, John, 1954-55-56
WOODARD, Risdon E. "Red", 1919-20-22
WOODLEY, David, 1977-78
WORLEY, Mitch, 1966
WORLEY, Wren, 1946-47-48
WRIGHT, Mike, 1968-69-70

Y

YATES, Bertis "Bert", 1932-33-34
YATES, Jesse, 1949-50-51
YEAGER, Rudy, 1951
YOKUBAITIS, Mark, 1972
YOUNG, Charles G., 1893-94
YOUNG, Jerry, 1962-63
YOUNGBLOOD, Tommy, 1967-68

Z

ZAUNBRECHER, Godfrey, 1967-68-69
ZERINGUE, Brian, 1973
ZICK, Francis, 1941-42
ZIEGLER, Bob, 1956
ZIEGLER, Paul, 1954-55

University of Mississippi

Location: Oxford, Mississippi
Enrollment: 9,234
Nickname: Rebels
Colors: Cardinal Red and Navy Blue
Stadium: Hemingway (35,000)

University of Mississippi Head Coaching Records

COACH	YEAR	WON	LOST	TIED
Dr. A. L. Bondurant	1893	4	1	0
C. D. Clark	1894	6	1	0
H. L. Fairbanks	1895	2	1	0
J. W. Hollister	1896	1	2	0
T. G. Scarbrough	1898	1	1	0
W. H. Lyon	1899	3	4	0
Z. N. Estes, Jr.	1900	0	3	0
William Shibley, Daniel S. Martin	1901	2	4	0
Daniel S. Martin	1902	4	3	0
Mike Harvey	1903-'04	6	4	1
T. S. Hammond	1906	4	2	0
Frank Mason	1907	0	6	0
Frank Kyle	1908	3	5	0
Dr. N. P. Stauffer	1909-'11	17	7	2
Leo DeTray	1912	5	3	0
William Driver	1913-'14	11	7	2
Fred Robbins	1915-'16	5	12	0
C. R. (Dudy) Noble	1917-'18	2	7	1
R. L. Sullivan	1919-'21	11	13	0
R. A. Cowell	1922-'23	8	11	1
Chester Barnard	1924	4	5	0
Homer Hazel	1925-'29	21	22	3
Ed L. Walker	1930-'37	38	38	8
Harry J. Mehre	1938-'45	39	26	1
Harold (Red) Drew	1946	2	7	0
Billy R. Kinard	1971-'73	16	9	0
John H. Vaught	1947-'70; 1973	190	61	12
Ken Cooper	1974-'77	19	25	0
Steve Sloan	1978	5	6	0

University of Mississippi All-Time Scores

1893

56	SW Baptist	0
16	Memphis AC	0
36	SW Baptist	0
0	Southern AC	24
12	Tulane	4
120	(4-1-0)	28

1894

62	St. Thos. Hall	0
6	Alabama	0
0	Vanderbilt	40
12	Memphis AC	0
8	Tulane	2
6	Southern AC	0
26	L.S.U.	6
120	(6-1-0)	48

1895

18	St. Thos. Hall	0
2	Memphis AC	0
4	Tulane	28
24	(2-1-0)	28

1896

20	St. Thos. Hall	0
4	L.S.U.	12
0	Tulane	10
24	(1-2-0)	22

1897—No Team

1898

9	Tulane	14
9	St. Thos. Hall	2
18	(1-1-0)	16

1899

13	Central Univ.	6
0	Nash. Univ.	11
11	L.S.U.	0
0	Vanderbilt	11
0	Sewanee	12
5	Alabama	7
15	Tulane	0
44	(3-4-0)	47

1900

0	Vanderbilt	6
5	Alabama	12
0	Tulane	12
5	(0-3-0)	30

1901

6	Memp. U. Sch.	0
0	Alabama	41
0	Miss. State	17
17	SW Bapt.	0
0	L.S.U.	46
11	Tulane	25
34	(2-4-0)	129

1902

0	Vanderbilt	29
38	Cumberland	0
21	Miss. State	0
42	Mphs. U. Sch.	0
0	L.S.U.	6
10	Tennessee	1
10	Tulane	0
121	(4-3-0)	46

1903

0	Vanderbilt	33
17	Mphs. Medical	0
6	Miss. State	6
11	L.S.U.	0
34	(2-1-1)	39

1904

0	Vanderbilt	69

17 Miss. State 5
114 SW Bapt. 0
0 L.S.U. 5
42 Mphs. Medical 0
12 Nashville 5
0 Tulane 22
185 (4-3-0) 106

1905
0 Cumberland 18
0 Miss. State 11
0 (0-2-0) 29

1906
16 Maryville 6
0 Vanderbilt 29
9 L.S.U. 0
17 Tulane 0
0 Sewanee 24
29 Miss. State 5
71 (4-2-0) 64

1907
0 Alabama 20
6 Mo. Normal 12
0 Sewanee 65
0 Vanderbilt 60
0 L.S.U. 23
0 Miss. State 15
6 (0-6-0) 195

1908
30 Memp. U Sch. 0
0 Arkansas 33
17 Missouri Nor. 0
0 Vanderbilt 29
41 Miss. College 0
0 Tulane 10
5 Union 9
6 Miss. State 44
99 (3-5-0) 125

1909
18 Memp. U Sch. 0
15 Mphs. Medical 0
0 L.S.U. 10
0 Tulane 5
0 Alabama 0
0 Vanderbilt 17
12 Hendr.-Brown 12
45 Union 0
9 Miss. State 5
99 (4-3-2) 49

1910
10 Memphis HS 0
2 Mphs. Medical 0
16 Tulane 0
24 Miss. College 0
2 Vanderbilt 9
16 Alabama 0
44 Mphs. Medical 0
30 Miss. State 0
144 (7-1-0) 9

1911
42 Memphis HS 0
41 Southwestern 0
15 La. Industrial 0
24 Hendr.-Brown 11
0 Texas A&M 17
28 Miss. College 0
34 Mercer 0
0 Vanderbilt 21
0 Miss. State 6
184 (6-3-0) 55

1912
34 Memphis HS 0
* 1 Castle Hgts. 0
10 L.S.U. 7
0 Vanderbilt 24
12 Miss. College 0
9 Alabama 10
14 Texas 53
47 Mphs. Medical 6
127 (5-3-0) 100

1913
0 V.M.I. 14
14 Va. Tech 35
7 Va. Meds 6
46 Union 0
26 La. Ind. 0
6 Hendrix 8
21 Arkansas 10
7 Cumberland 0
13 Mo. Normal 7
0 Ouachita 0
140 (6-3-1) 80

1914
20 Ark. A&M 0
14 Southwestern 0
21 L.S.U. 0
7 Miss. College 7
0 Ouachita 7
21 Tulane 6
13 Arkansas 7
7 Texas 66
0 SW Texas 18
7 Texas A&M 14
110 (5-4-1) 125

1915
0 Ark. A&M 10
13 Southwestern 6
0 L.S.U. 28
0 Vanderbilt 91
32 Hendrix 7
0 Miss. State 65
6 Miss. College 74
0 Alabama 53
51 (2-6-0) 334

1916
30 Union 0
20 Ark. A&M 0
61 Hendrix 0
0 Vanderbilt 35
0 Alabama 27
0 Miss. State 36
3 Transylvania 13
0 L.S.U. 41
14 Miss. College 36
128 (3-6-0) 188

1917
0 Ark. A&M 0
7 L.S.U. 52
0 Alabama 54
14 Miss. State 41
7 Sewanee 69
21 Miss. College 0
49 (1-4-1) 216

1918
0 Payne Field 6
39 Union 0
0 Miss. State 34
0 Miss. State 13
39 (1-3-0) 53

1919
32 Ark. A&M 0
0 Alabama 49
0 L.S.U. 13
12 Tulane 27
25 Union 6
0 Miss. State 33
30 Southwestern 0
6 Miss. College 0
105 (4-4-0) 128

1920
33 Ark. A&M 0
54 Mo. Normal 0
6 B'ham-Sou. 27
0 Tulane 32
86 Union 0
0 Miss. State 20
38 S. W. Presby 6
217 (4-3-0) 85

1921
82 W. Tenn. 0
0 Tulane 26
49 Millsaps 0
35 Southwestern 0
0 Miss. State 21
7 Miss. College 27
0 L.S.U. 21
6 Tenn. Doctors 24
0 Havana 14
179 (3-6-0) 133

1922
0 Union 0
0 Centre 55
23 Southwestern 0
13 Miss. State 19
0 Tennessee 49
6 B'ham-Sou. 0
13 Hendrix 7
0 Tenn. Meds 32
13 Ft. Benning 14
19 Millsaps 7
87 (4-5-1) 183

1923
14 Bethel Col. 6
0 Alabama 56
33 Southwestern 0
6 Miss. State 13
3 St. Louis 28
6 B'ham-Sou. 0
0 Miss. College 6
0 Tulane 19
0 Tennessee 10
19 Ft. Benning 7
81 (4-6-0) 145

1924
10 Ark. A&M 7
7 Southwestern 0
0 Miss. State 20
0 Arkansas 20
0 Alabama 61
0 Sewanee 21
2 Furman 7
10 Miss. College 6
7 Millsaps 0
36 (4-5-0) 142

1925
53 Ark. A&M 0
0 Texas 25
7 Tulane 26
7 Union 6
0 Miss. State 6
0 Vanderbilt 7
9 Sewanee 10
19 Miss. College 7
31 Southwestern 0
21 Millsaps 0
147 (5-5-0) 87

1926
28 Ark. A&M 0
6 Arkansas 21
12 Florida 7
13 Loyola (Chi) 7
15 Drake 31
0 Tulane 6
32 Southwestern 27
0 L.S.U. 3
7 Miss. State 6
113 (5-4-0) 108

1927
58 Ozarks 0
7 Tulane 19
0 Hendrix 0
7 Tennessee 21
39 Southwestern 0
28 Sewanee 14
12 L.S.U. 7
6 Loyola (Chi) 7
20 Miss. State 12
177 (5-3-1) 80

1928
25 Arkansas 0
0 Alabama 27
12 Tennessee 13
19 Auburn 0
14 Loyola (N.O.) 34
26 Clemson 7
6 L. S. U. 19
34 Southwestern 2
20 Miss. State 19
156 (5-4-0) 121

1929
7 Vanderbilt 19
7 Alabama 22
7 Tennessee 52
26 Loyola (N.O.) 24
0 S. M. U. 52
6 Sewanee 6
7 Purdue 27
6 L.S.U. 13
7 Miss. State 7
73 (1-6-2) 222

1930
64 Union 0
0 Alabama 64
0 Tennessee 27
7 Sewanee 13
0 Chicago 0
0 Vanderbilt 24
0 L.S.U. 6
37 Southwestern 6
20 Miss. State 0
128 (3-5-1) 140

1931
13 Western Ky. 6
0 Tulane 31
6 Alabama 55
0 Tennessee 38
20 Southwestern 20
6 Marquette 13
0 Sewanee 7
3 L.S.U. 26
25 Miss. State 14
73 (2-6-1) 210

1932
49 Sou. Miss. 0
0 Tennessee 33
26 Howard 6
6 Centenary 13
13 Alabama 24
7 Auburn 14
0 Minnesota 26
27 Sewanee 6
7 Southwestern 0
13 Miss. State 0
0 Tulsa 26
146 (5-6-0) 148

1933
6 Southwestern 6
45 Sou. Miss. 0
0 Alabama 0
7 Marquette 0
41 Sewanee 0
13 Clemson 0
12 B'ham Sou. 0
6 Tennessee 35
0 L.S.U. 31
6 Centenary 7
31 Miss. State 0
167 (6-3-2) 79

1934
44 Memphis St. 0
19 Southwestern 0
0 Tennessee 27
6 Howard 7
19 Sewanee
0 Tulane
13 Florida
0 L.S.U.
6 Centenary
7 Miss. State
114 (4-5-1)

1935
20 Millsaps
92 Memphis St.
33 Southwestern
33 Sewanee
27 Florida
7 Marquette
21 St. Louis
13 Tennessee
26 Centre
6 Centenary
14 Miss. State
292 (9-2-0)

Orange Bowl
19 Catholic U.

1936
45 Union
6 Tulane
7 Temple
0 Geo. Wash.
0 L.S.U.
14 Catholic U.
24 Centenary
34 Loyola
0 Marquette
6 Miss. State
14 Miami
0 Tennessee
150 (5-5-2)

1937
13 La. Tech
0 Temple
21 St. Louis
0 L.S.U.
46 Ouachita
7 Tulane
27 Geo. Wash.
6 Arkansas
7 Miss. State
0 Tennessee
127 (4-5-1)

1938
20 L.S.U.
27 La. Tech
14 Sou. Miss.
7 Vanderbilt
47 Centenary
25 Geo. Wash.
14 St. Louis
39 Sewanee
20 Arkansas
19 Miss. State
0 Tennessee
232 (9-2-0)

1939
14 L.S.U.

41 Southwestern 0
34 Centenary 0
42 St. Louis 0
6 Tulane 18
14 Vanderbilt 7
27 Sou. Miss. 7
46 Memphis St. 7
6 Miss. State 18
30 (7-2-0) 64

1940

37 Union 0
19 L.S.U. 6
27 Southwestern 6
28 Georgia 14
14 Duquesne 6
20 Arkansas 21
13 Vanderbilt 7
34 Holy Cross 7
38 Memphis St. 7
0 Miss. State 19
21 Miami 7
51 (9-2-0) 100

1941

6 Georgetown 16
27 Southwestern 0
14 Georgia 14
21 Holy Cross 0
20 Tulane 13
12 Marquette 6
13 L.S.U. 12
18 Arkansas 0
0 Miss. State 6
31 (6-2-1) 67

1942

39 Western Ky. 6
6 Georgetown 14
13 Georgia 48
7 L.S.U. 21
6 Arkansas 7
48 Memphis St. 0
0 Vanderbilt 19
0 Tennessee 14
13 Miss. State 34
32 (2-7-0) 163

1943—No Team

1944

7 Kentucky 27
26 Florida 6
7 Tennessee 20
0 Tulsa 47
18 Arkansas 26
0 Jackson AAB 10
6 Alabama 34
13 Miss. State 8
77 (2-6-0) 178

1945

21 Kentucky 7
13 Florida 26
14 Vanderbilt 7
26 La. Tech 21
0 Arkansas 19
13 L.S.U. 32
0 Tennessee 34
7 Miss. State 6
6 Chattanooga 31
100 (4-5-0) 183

1946

6 Kentucky 20
13 Florida 7
0 Vanderbilt 7
7 Ga. Tech 24
6 La. Tech 7
9 Arkansas 7
21 L.S.U. 34
14 Tennessee 18
0 Miss. State 20
76 (2-7-0) 144

1947

14 Kentucky 7
14 Florida 6
33 S. Carolina 0
6 Vanderbilt 10
27 Tulane 14
14 Arkansas 19
20 L.S.U. 18
43 Tennessee 13
52 Chattanooga 0
33 Miss. State 14
256 (8-2-0) 101

Delta Bowl

13 T.C.U. 9

1948

14 Florida 0
20 Kentucky 7
20 Vanderbilt 7
7 Tulane 20
32 Boston Col. 13
49 L.S.U. 19
34 Chattanooga 7
16 Tennessee 13
34 Miss. State 7
226 (8-1-0) 93

1949

40 Memphis St. 7
40 Auburn 7
0 Kentucky 47
27 Vanderbilt 28
25 Boston Col. 25
27 T. C. U. 33
7 L.S.U. 34
47 Chattanooga 27
7 Tennessee 35
26 Miss. State 0
246 (4-5-1) 243

1950

39 Memphis St. 7
0 Kentucky 27
54 Boston Col. 0
14 Vanderbilt 20
20 Tulane 27
19 T.C.U. 7
14 L.S.U. 40
20 Chattanooga 0
0 Tennessee 35
27 Miss. State 20
207 (5-5-0) 183

1951

32 Memphis St. 0
21 Kentucky 17
34 Boston Col. 7
20 Vanderbilt 34
25 Tulane 6
7 Miami 20
6 L.S.U. 6
39 Auburn 14
21 Tennessee 46
49 Miss. State 7
254 (6-3-1) 157

1952

54 Memphis St. 6
13 Kentucky 13
20 Auburn 7
21 Vanderbilt 21
20 Tulane 14
34 Arkansas 7
28 L.S.U. 0
6 Houston 0
21 Maryland 14
20 Miss. State 14
237 (8-0-2) 96

Sugar Bowl

7 Ga. Tech 24

1953

39 Chattanooga 0
22 Kentucky 6
0 Auburn 13
28 Vanderbilt 6
45 Tulane 14
28 Arkansas 0
27 L.S.U. 16
40 N. Texas St. 7
0 Maryland 38
7 Miss. State 7
236 (7-2-1) 113

1954

35 N. Texas St. 12
28 Kentucky 9
52 Villanova 0
22 Vanderbilt 7
34 Tulane 7
0 Arkansas 6
21 L.S.U. 6
51 Memphis St. 0
26 Houston 0
14 Miss. State 0
283 (9-1-0) 47

Sugar Bowl

0 Navy 21

1955

26 Georgia 13
14 Kentucky 21
33 N. Texas St. 0
13 Vanderbilt 0
27 Tulane 13
17 Arkansas 7
29 L.S.U. 26
39 Memphis St. 6
27 Houston 11
26 Miss. State 0
251 (9-1-0) 97

Cotton Bowl

14 T.C.U. 13

1956

45 N. Texas St. 0
37 Kentucky 7
14 Houston 0
16 Vanderbilt 0
3 Tulane 10
0 Arkansas 14
46 L.S.U. 17
26 Memphis St. 0
7 Tennessee 27
13 Miss. State 7
207 (7-3-0) 82

1957

44 Trinity 0
15 Kentucky 0
34 Hardin Sim. 7
28 Vanderbilt 0
50 Tulane 0
6 Arkansas 12
20 Houston 7
14 L.S.U. 12
14 Tennessee 7
7 Miss. State 7
232 (8-1-1) 52

Sugar Bowl

39 Texas 7

1958

17 Memphis St. 0
27 Kentucky 6
21 Trinity 0
19 Tulane 8
24 Hardin-Sim. 0
14 Arkansas 12
0 L.S.U. 14
56 Houston 7
16 Tennessee 18
21 Miss. State 0
215 (8-2-0) 65

Gator Bowl

7 Florida 3

1959

16 Houston 0
16 Kentucky 0
43 Memphis St. 0
33 Vanderbilt 0
53 Tulane 7
28 Arkansas 0
3 L.S.U. 7
58 Chattanooga 0
37 Tennessee 7
42 Miss. State 0
329 (9-1-0) 21

Sugar Bowl

21 L.S.U. 0

1960

42 Houston 0
21 Kentucky 6
31 Memphis St. 20
26 Vanderbilt 0
26 Tulane 13
10 Arkansas 7
6 L.S.U. 6
45 Chattanooga 0
24 Tennessee 3
35 Miss. State 9
266 (9-0-1) 64

Sugar Bowl

14 Rice 6

1961

16 Arkansas 0
20 Kentucky 6
33 Fla. State 0
47 Houston 7
41 Tulane 0
47 Vanderbilt 0
7 L.S.U. 10
54 Chattanooga 0
24 Tennessee 10
37 Miss. State 7
326 (9-1-0) 40

Cotton Bowl

7 Texas 12

1962

21 Memphis St. 7
14 Kentucky 0
40 Houston 7
21 Tulane 0
35 Vanderbilt 0
15 L.S.U. 7
52 Chattanooga 7
19 Tennessee 6
13 Miss. State 6
230 (9-0-0) 40

Sugar Bowl

17 Arkansas 13

1963

0 Memphis St. 0
31 Kentucky 7
20 Houston 6
21 Tulane 0
27 Vanderbilt 7
37 L.S.U. 3
41 Tampa 0
20 Tennessee 0
10 Miss. State 10
207 (7-0-2) 33

Sugar Bowl

7 Alabama 12

1964

30 Memphis St. 0
21 Kentucky 27
31 Houston 9
14 Florida 30
14 Tulane 9
7 Vanderbilt 7
10 L.S.U. 11
36 Tampa 0
30 Tennessee 0
17 Miss. State 20
210 (5-4-1) 113

Bluebonnet Bowl

7 Tulsa 14

1965

34 Memphis St. 14
7 Kentucky 16
16 Alabama 17
0 Florida 17
24 Tulane 7
24 Vanderbilt 7
23 L.S.U. 0
3 Houston 17
14 Tennessee 13
21 Miss. State 0
166 (6-4-0) 108

Liberty Bowl

13 Auburn 7

1966

13 Memphis St. 0
17 Kentucky 0
7 Alabama 17
3 Georgia 9
14 Sou. Miss. 7
27 Houston 6
17 L.S.U. 0
14 Tennessee 7
34 Vanderbilt 0
24 Miss. State 0
170 (8-2-0) 46

Bluebonnet Bowl

0 Texas 19

1967

17 Memphis St. 27
26 Kentucky 13
7 Alabama 21
29 Georgia 20
23 Sou. Miss. 14
14 Houston 13
13 L.S.U. 13
7 Tennessee 20
28 Vanderbilt 7
10 Miss. State 3
174 (6-3-1) 151

Sun Bowl

7 Tex-El Paso 14

1968

21 Memphis St. 7
30 Kentucky 14
10 Alabama 8
7 Georgia 21
21 Sou. Miss. 13
7 Houston 29
27 L.S.U. 24
38 Chattanooga 16
0 Tennessee 31
17 Miss. State 17
178 (6-3-1) 180

Liberty Bowl

34 Va. Tech 17

1969

28 Memphis St. 3

9	Kentucky	10
32	Alabama	33
25	Georgia	17
69	Sou. Miss.	7
11	Houston	25
26	L.S.U.	23
21	Chattanooga	0
38	Tennessee	0
48	Miss. State	22
307	(7-3-0)	140

Sugar Bowl

27	Arkansas	22

1970

47	Memphis St.	13
20	Kentucky	17
48	Alabama	23
31	Georgia	21
14	Sou. Miss.	30
26	Vandy	16
24	Houston	13
44	UT-Chatt.	7
14	Miss. State	19
17	L.S.U.	61
285	(7-3-0)	220

Gator Bowl

28	Auburn	35

1971

19	Long Beach St.	13
49	Memphis St.	21
34	Kentucky	20
6	Alabama	40
7	Georgia	38
20	Sou. Miss.	6
28	Vanderbilt	7
24	L.S.U.	22
28	Tampa	27
48	UT-Chatt.	10
48	Miss. State	0
322	(9-2-0)	204

Peach Bowl

41	Ga. Tech	18

1972

34	Memphis St.	29
21	S. Carolina	0
13	Sou. Miss.	9
13	Auburn	19
13	Georgia	14
0	Florida	16
31	Vanderbilt	7
16	L.S.U.	17
0	Tennessee	17
51	Miss. State	14
192	(5-5-0)	142

1973

24	Villanova	6
0	Missouri	17
13	Memphis St.	17
41	Sou. Miss.	0
7	Auburn	14
0	Georgia	20
13	Florida	10
24	Vanderbilt	14
14	L.S.U.	51
28	Tennessee	18
38	Miss. State	10
202	(6-5-0)	177

1974

10	Missouri	0
7	Memphis St.	15
20	Sou. Miss.	14
21	Alabama	35
0	Georgia	49
7	S. Carolina	10
14	Vanderbilt	24
0	L.S.U.	24
17	Tennessee	29
13	Miss. State	31
26	Tulane	10
135	(3-8-0)	241

1975

10	Baylor	20
0	Texas A&M	7
3	Tulane	14
24	Sou. Miss.	8
6	Alabama	32
28	Georgia	13
29	S. Carolina	35
17	Vanderbilt	7
17	L.S.U.	13
23	Tennessee	6
13	Miss. State	7
170	(6-5-0)	162

1976

16	Memphis St.	1
10	Alabama	7
34	Tulane	7
28	Sou. Miss.	0
0	Auburn	10
21	Georgia	17
7	S. Carolina	10
20	Vanderbilt	3
0	LSU	45
6	Tennessee	32
*11	Miss. State	28
153	(5-6-0)	180

*Won by forfeit

1977

7	Memphis St.	3
13	Alabama	34
20	Notre Dame	13
19	Sou. Miss	27
15	Auburn	21
13	Georgia	1
17	S. Carolina	1
26	Vanderbilt	1
21	LSU	2
43	Tennessee	1
*14	Miss. State	1
208	(5-6-0)	19

*Won by forfeit

1978

14	Memphis State	
14	Missouri	4
16	Southern Miss	1
3	Georgia	4
17	Kentucky	2
17	S. Carolina	1
35	Vanderbilt	1
8	LSU	3
13	Tulane	
17	Tennessee	4
27	Miss. State	
181	(5-6-0)	24

University of Mississippi Lettermen—1893 to 1978

A

ABDO, Nicholas, 1927
ADAMS, Billy Ray, 1959-60-61
ADAMS, J. C., 1909-10-11-12
ADAMS, Robert O., "Tiger", 1952-53-54
ADAMS, Winfred C., 1908-09
AINSWORTH, Stephen Gregory, 1970-71-72
AKIN, Wm. E. "Dooley", 1921-22-23-24
ALDRIDGE, John B., 1968-69-70
ALDRIDGE, Walter P. "Bo", 1962-63-64
ALEXANDER, Charles H., Jr., 1972, Mgr.
ALEXANDER, George E., 1920-21
ALEXANDER, Raymond M., 1974
ALFORD, John Warner, 1958-59-60
ALLEN, Charles, B., 1923-24-25
ALLEN, Elmer Dale, 1969; 1970-71
ALLEN, Herman Eugene, 1971-72-73
ALLISTON, George B., 1966
ALLISTON, Vaughn S., Jr., "Buddy", 1953-54-55
AMES, Charles F., 1901-02
AMSLER, Guy, 1920
ANDERSON, Cephus, 1913-14; 1916
ANDERSON, James N., 1958-59-60
ANDERSON, Vernon, 1941, Mgr.
APPLEWHITE, Austin H., 1925-26-27
ARMSTRONG, Crowell H., 1969-70-71
ARMSTRONG, George W., 1923-24
ARNETTE, J. W., 1944
ARNOLD, John Wes, Jr., 1966, Mgr.
ARNOLD, Robert P., 1972; 1973-74
ASHFORD, Andre L., 1972, Trn.
ASTON, Vernon "Monk", 1935-36-37
AUSTIN, Oliver A., 1910, Mgr.
AUTREY, Winkey, 1937-38-39
AYERS, Richardson, 1908

B

BAGWELL, C. I., 1917-18
BAGWELL, Michael Wm., 1970
BAILESS, Robert R. "Bob", 1971-72-73
BAILEY, Jay Allen, 1978
BAILEY, Robert W., 1966-67-68
BAKER, Jerry E., 1954-55-56
BALL, John, 1914; 1916
BALL, Warren N. "Bo", 1958-59-60
BANE, Bob, 1977, Mgr.
BARBER, John T., 1954
BARBOUR, Calvin C., Jr., 1919-20-21-22
BARFIELD, Kenneth A., 1950-51
BARKER, Reuben A. "Rube", 1911-12
BARKLEY, William Donald, 1955; 1957
BARLOW, T. Michael, 1974
BARNES, Blake, 1977, Mgr.
BARNETT, Eddie Lee, 1967
BARRY, Wm. T. "Bill", 1971-72
BARTLING, McNeil "Doby", 1934-35
BASHAM, Wm. Earl, 1959-60-61
BASKIN, John Frank, 1969
BATES, G. C., 1905-06
BATTEN, H. C., 1926
BAUMSTEN, Herb, 1935-36-37
BEANLAND, Gayle C., 1898-99; 1902
BEATTY, Edwin M., 1951-52-53
BECK, John Robert, 1976-77
BECKETT, B. B., 1901
BECKETT, George B., 1900
BECKETT, Richard C., Jr., 1905
BEDDENFIELD, Marcus, 1934
BEDDINGFIELD, Wm. Ray, 1963-64-65
BELL, J. H., 1914
BENDER, Charles A., 1913-14
BENNETT, Gardner, 1937
BENNETT, Preston "Pep", 1940-41; 1946
BENTLEY, M. C., 1929
BENTON, Robert Hollis, 1958-59-60
BENVENUTTI, Joseph D., 1974
BERNARD, Dave, 1934-35-36
BERNOCCI, Robert, 1940-41-42
BERRY, O. L., 1925, Mgr.
BERRYHILL, Herman, 1934
BIDGOOD, Charles S., 1947-48
BIGGERS, Neal B., 1929-30-31
BIGHAM, C. S., 1908
BILBO, G. W., 1931-32-33
BILBO, J. P., 1935-36-37
BILES, George Lacey, 1924-25-26
BISBING, Willard, 1938
BISHOP, Clark D., 1949
BISHOP, Smith, 1913-14
BLACK, Willis W., 1954
BLACKWELL, Anse, 1938
BLACKWELL, Bernard, 1944-45-46-47
BLAIR, Earl E., 1952-53-54-55
BLAIR, George L., 1958-59-60
BLAIR, Wiley S., 1905
BLAKE, Walter G., 1893-94
BLALACK, Charley, 1956, Mgr.
BLALACK, John W., 1954-55-56
BLANKENBAKER, R. H., 1926-27-28
BLOUNT, Clayton, 1946
BLOUNT, Joseph L., 1967-68-69
BLOUNT, Kenneth Lloyd, 1970
BOGARD, Harold, 1935
BOGGAN, Rex Reed, 1949-50; 1954
BOLIN, Treva "Bookie", 1960-61
BOOKOUT, B. E., 1917
BOONE, James T. "Pete", 1970-71-7
BOOTH, Carl C., III, "Cliff", 1968
BOOTHE, R. V., 1893
BOUNDS, Wayne Stanley, 1973-197
BOURDEAUX, R. H., 1893
BOURNE, Robert, 1961
BOUTWELL, George, 1928-29-30
BOWEN, B. C., 1898
BOWEN, John H., Jr. "Buddy", 1946-47-48
BOWEN, John H., III "Bo", 1967-68-6
BOWEN, Mark Sutton, 1976
BOWERS, S. H., 1919
BOWLES, Wallace C., 1929-30-31
BOWMAN, Gayle, 1955
BOYCE, Boykin, 1944-45
BOYD, Lucas, 1953, Mgr.
BOYD, Robert C. "Bobby", 1962
BOYKIN, A. L. "Showboat", 1949-50-51
BRADLEY, Bruce B., 1949-50
BRADLEY, Kimble, 1936-37-38
BRADY, T. P., 1893
BRASHIER, Rodgers, 1952-53-54
BRELAND, Hugh Gregory, 1973-74
BRELAND, J. J., 1912-13
BRELAND, R. Q., 1923, Mgr.
BRENNER, George, 1950-51-52
BRENTS, Darrel, 1944
BRESSLER, Arthur, Jr. "Art", 1971-72-73
BREWER, Grady, 1945
BREWER, Jack, 1944
BREWER, John Lee, 1957; 1959-60
BREWER, William E., 1957-58-59
BREYER, Alex, 1934-35-36

RIDGERS, David I., 1946-47
RIDGERS, David, I., Jr., 1968-69-70
RIDGERS, Lloyd M., 1975, Mgr.
RIDGES, James T., 1951-52
RIDGES, Roy, 1917
RIGGS, Charles E., 1924, Mgr.
RISTER, Fred E., III, 1968-69-70
RISTER, Herndon, 1930
RISTER, Thomas S., 1916
RITT, Alvin, 1931-32-33
RITT, Oscar, 1940-41-42
ROUSSARD, Ken G., 1965
ROWN, Allen, 1962-63-64
ROWN, Alton L., 1971-72
ROWN, Carter, 1952
ROWN, Colon, 1929-30
ROWN, Ernest Herman, 1970-71
ROWN, Fred, 1946
ROWN, Jerry G., 1959-60-61
ROWN, Raymond L., 1955-56-57
ROWN, Wm. Van, 1967-68
RUCE, John, 1944-45
UCHANAN, John P., 1974
UCHANAN, Oscar, 1944
UCHANAN, Oscar W. "Red", 1946-47-48
UNTIN, R. R., 1915-16
URKE, Charles, G., Jr., 1955; 1957
URKE, Jack, 1931-32
URKE, Robert O., Jr., 1969-70-71
URKE, Webster W., 1924-25-26
URKHALTER, Charles Stephen "Steve", 1971-72-73
URLESON, Charles, 1952
URNETT, Harvey, 1930
URNETT, W. D. "Dump", 1927-28-29
URNS, Willie, 1977-78
USH, Alan L., 1965-66-67
UTLER, George H., 1900
UTLER, James, 1944
YRD, Ronard K. "Rocky", 1949-50-51

C

ACCAMO, Dan, 1977-78
AGE, Charlie Jr., 1976-77-78
AHALL, William C., 1911
AIN, George, 1977
AIRNES, George H., 1899-1900
ALDWELL, James T., 1950-51-52
ALDWELL, M. F., 1917
ALLAHAN, Lindy T., 1949-50-51
AMPBELL, Eugene P., 1898-99
AMPBELL, Henry A., 1948
AMPBELL, J. W., 1916
AMPBELL, William Mike, 1945
ANNON, Glenn D., 1967-68-69
ANTRELL, James Larry, 1975
APELLO, Harry, 1940
ARLISLE, Wm. Todd, 1968, Mgr.
ARLSON, Cully, 1935
ARNES, Robert Lee, 1916
ARNEY, A. B., 1918-19
ARPENTER, Charles W. "Chuck", 1971
ARPENTER, Preston Caswell, 1969-70-71
ARPENTER, Terry Carol, 1967
ARR, Oscar, 1914
ARRUTH, Lester, 1932-33-34
ARTER, Fred S., 1909-10-11
ARTER, Raymond, 1965
CARTER, Sam P., 1929-30
CARTER, W. Spinks, 1901
CASE, Harry, 1956
CASPER, Raymond, 1931-32-33
CASTLE, C. E., 1945
CASTLE, Lee, 1941
CASTLE, Richard, 1945
CASTON, Lester B. "Brent", 1964-65-66
CAUSEY, J. B., 1909-10-11
CAUSEY, Jimmy, 1971-72
CAVIN, Jack Ottis, 1958
CHAMBERLAIN, D. H., 1904
CHAMPION, James E., 1957-58-59
CHAMPION, Wm. L. "Billy", 1960-62
CHANDLER, John Caroll, 1970-71-72
CHANDLER, Kyle, 1899
CHEATHAM, Jack, 1945
CHILDRES, Robert D., 1952-53
CHISHOLM, Charles P., 1964
CHRISTIAN, Charles D., Jr., 1907
CHUMBLER, Brent S. "Shug", 1969-70-71
CHUNN, Clifton B., Jr., "Cliff", 1968
CHURCHWELL, Hanson "Bull", 1957-58
CLAPP, Robert P., 1899
CLARK, James H., 1944-47-48-49
CLARK, Marcus R. "Mark", 1976
CLAY, Wm. F. "Bill", 1963-64-65
CLIPPARD, Richard F., 1973-74-75
COATES, David Patrick, 1976-77
COHEN, Sollie, 1925-26-27
COHN, Abye A., 1901-03-04
COHN, Henry L., 1909-10-11-12
COKER, Wm. H. "Billy", 1968-69-70
COLE, Eddie Lee, 1975-76-77-78
COLEMAN, Dennis F. 1968-69-70
COLEMAN, Kem T., 1974-75-76-77
COLEMAN, Roy, 1977-78
COLLETTE, Allen, 1914-15
COLLIER, J. H., 1895
COLLIER, John Brooks, 1969
COLLIER, O. E., 1926
COLLIER, Terry Lee, 1967
COLLIER, William C., 1893
COLLINS, Dudley, 1931, Mgr.
COMMISKEY, Chuck, 1977
CONERLY, Cecil "Chip", 1977, Mgr.
CONERLY, Charles A., 1942; 1946-47
CONN, Abe H., 1898-1901
CONNER, Clyde R., 1902-06
CONNER, Edgar E., 1901
CONROY, James, 1944
COOK, Richard, 1925
COOK, William Henry, 1893-94
COOPER, Charles, 1945
COOPER, Harold, 1956-57-58
COOPER, Kyle M., 1907
CORRERO, Van Sam, 1973-74
COTHREN, Jennings Paige, 1954-55-56
COTTAM, Christopher C., 1978
COWAN, John Kuhl, 1893-94
COWAN, R. C., 1901
COWARD, Charles B., 1967
COWART, E. M., 1917-18-19
COX, Owen E., 1950
CRAIN, Milton, 1956-57-58
CRAIN, Sollie M., 1921-22-23-24
CRAWFORD, Edward S., III, 1954-55-56
CRAWFORD, James A., 1946-47-48-49
CRAWFORD, Othar A., Jr., 1947; 1949-50-51
CREEKMORE, Rufus H., 1918-19-20
CRESPINO, Robert, 1958-59-60
CRISMAN, William O., 1900-01-02
CRITZ, F. A., Jr., 1900; 1902
CROCKER, W. David, 1974
CROOK, G. W., 1920
CROOK, Jerry, 1945
CROSBY, William F. "Buddy", 1961-62
CROWDER, Talbert, 1937
CROWE, Dorman, 1938
CRULL, Luther P., Jr. "Putt", 1968
CUNNINGHAM, James W., 1905-06
CUNNINGHAM, Julian D. "Doug", 1964-65-66
CURD, H. P., 1919, Mgr.
CURLAND, Marvin, 1946
CURLEE, R. M., 1900
CURTIS, Chester, 1932-33-34
CURTIS, J. E., 1915

D

DABBS, Willis N. "Woody", 1960-61-62
DALE, Roland H., 1945-47-48-49
DALY, Jerome, 1942
DANIELS, Jerry S., 1958-59-60
DANTZLER, Larry D., 1974-75-76-77
DAVIDSON, J. W., 1939-40-41
DAVIDSON, P. G., 1919-20
DAVIS, Curtis Reed, 1961-62-63
DAVIS, Edwin D., 1929-30
DAVIS, Frank, 1945
DAVIS, Frank O., 1900
DAVIS, Harry, 1949-50
DAVIS, J. E., 1923-24
DAVIS, Paul, 1942; 1946
DAVIS, Robert, 1924-25-26
DAVIS, Shed H., 1921-22-23-24
DAVIS, Thomas D., 1899-1900
DAWSON, D. A., 1915
DAY, Charles, 1940
DAY, Herman "Eagle", 1953-54-55
DAY, William Glynn, 1976-77-78
DEAN, Guy D., 1901-02
DEAN, Wm. J. (Joe), 1962-63-64
DEAR, W. C., 1913; 1915
DEATON, Daniel B. "Penny", 1969
DENNIS, Walter M. "Mike", 1963-64-65
DENNY, Billy, 1977-78
DENT, Edward L., 1903
DICKENS, Luther "Curley", 1934-35-36
DICKERSON, Cecil R., 1946
DICKERSON, David L., 1952-53-54
DICKSON, Donald, 1960-61-62
DILL, John Reginald "Reggie", 1970-71-72
DILL, Kenneth D., 1961-62-63
DILLARD, Wilson, Jr., 1950-51-52
DILLINGHAM, Bruce, Jr., 1965-66-67
DODD, Allen P., 1902-03-04-05
DODSON, Leslie, 1938-39-40
DONGIEUX, Paul A., 1969-70-71
DORRAH, Clinton E., 1913
DOSSETT, Horace, 1938-39-40
DOTSON, Albert C., 1976-77
DOTTLEY, John, 1947-48-49-50
DOTY, Arthur W., 1960-61
DOWELL, Wade, 1977
DOWNING, H. M., 1903
DOYLE, L. A., 1918
DREWRY, Robet G., 1953-54-55
DUBUISSON, Gene H., 1953-54-55
DUCK, Charles E., 1955-56
DUKE, John Gayle, 1894
DUNAGIN, Charles Ado, 1937-38-39
DUNAWAY, James K., 1960-61-62
DUNN, Perry Lee, 1961-62-63
DUNN, Thomas, 1931
DURFEY, Allan P., 1918
DYKES, Jewell Kenny, Jr., 1968, Mgr.

E

EAST, F. J., 1915
EDWARDS, Arthur M., 1975, Trn.
ELLIS, Timothy L. "Tim", 1974-75-76-77
ELMER, Frederick W., 1900-01-02-03-04
ELMER, James C., 1906
ELMORE, J. W., 1924
ELMORE, James Douglas, 1959-60-61
ENOCH, Eugene S., 1900-01-02
ENOCHS, W. B., 1926-27
EPTING, John Booth, 1922
ERICKSON, W. C. "Bill", 1946-47
ERWIN, Clay, 1977
ESTES, Hermon Donald, 1964, Mgr.
ESTES, Terry, 1970, Mgr.
EUBANKS, Bill, 1940-41
EUBANKS, O. G., 1921
EVANS, Guy E. "Butch", 1974-75
EVANS, Harrison, 1916
EVANS, J. P. "Joe", 1912-13-14

F

FABRIS, Jon Michael, 1976-77-78
FABRIS, Robert S., 1975-76-77
FAGAN, Julian W., III, 1967-68-69
FAIR, Davis L., 1901
FAIR, Frank L., 1903
FAIR, Gene, 1937, Mgr.
FANT, Frank C., 1947-48-49
FARBER, Louis A. "Hap", 1967-68-69
FARISH, William S., 1899
FARMER, C. E., 1918-19
FARMER, Fred R., 1968-69-70
FARMER, James J., 1966-67
FARRAGUT, Kenneth D., 1947-48-49-50
FARRAR, Donald H. "Don", 1968-70
FARRIS, Wm. J. "Bill", 1973-74-75
FEDRIC, Jones, 1932, Mgr.
FEEMSTER, J. H., 1919-20-22
FELTS, Morris Leon, 1968-69-71
FERRILL, Charles, 1931
FERRILL, Charles B., 1960
FIELDS, Richard J., 1917
FINGER, William, 1915
FINLEY, J. A., 1904-05
FISCHER, David M. "Danny", 1976
FISHER, Bobby F., 1954-55
FLACK, Jackie, 1940-41
FLEMING, Gordon W., Jr. "Rocky", 1964-65-66
FLETCHER, Ralph E. 1912
FLETCHER, Robert J., 1947-48-49-50

FLOWERS, Charles, 1957-58-59
FLOWERS, Jesse, 1931-32-33
FOOSE, Sam, 1935
FORD, Cecil A., 1961-62-63
FORESTER, Michael W., 1974-75-76
FOSTER, John M., 1898-99-1900-01-02
FOSTER, Willie S., 1978
FOUNTAIN, Michael A., 1978
FOURCADE, John C., Jr., 1978
FOWLER, Ronald M. "Ronnie", 1964-65-66
FOXWORTH, T. J., 1893
FRAME, J. S. "Buntin", 1965
FRANKLIN, Bobby Ray, 1957-58-59
FRANKS, Floyd W., 1968-69-70
FRANKS, Michael Dwayne, 1970-71
FRASER, D. R., 1928, Mgr.
FRATESI, Michael L. "Mickey", 1971-72-73
FREIGHTMAN, Philip, 1978
FRISHMAN, Leon B., 1967, Mgr.
FRYE, J. P., 1940-41
FRYE, William, 1937
FUERST, Robert J., 1946-48-49
FUNDERBURK, Joe, 1915
FURLOW, Frank, 1940

G

GADDIS, J. T., 1913
GALEY, Charles D., 1945-46-47
GARDNER, Thomas, 1938, Mgr.
GARDNER, William P., 1919
GARDNER, Wm. Douglas, 1932
GARNER, Ernest L., Jr. "Lee", 1964-65-66
GARNER, John C., Jr., 1968
GARNER, Robert L. "Bobby", 1976-77-78
GARNET, O. L., 1895
GARRIGUES, Robert M., 1966-67-68
GARTRELL, J. E., 1900
GARY. Oscar Knox, Jr., 1951-52
GATES, Hunter, 1946
GAZELLE, J. J., 1922
GEORGE, Alonzo P., 1917-19-20
GERRARD, ALbert L., Jr. "Bud", 1945-49
GIBBS, Jerry D. "Jake", 1958-59-60
GIBSON, E. B., 1895
GILBERT, Kline, 1950-51-52
GILL, Virgil, 1932-33-34
GILLILAND, John L., 1968-69-70
GILRUTH, I. Newton, 1899-1900
GIPSON, Malvin, 1978
GLADDING, Charles, 1939
GLOVER, Will H., 1947
GOBER, Oscar, 1921
GOEHE, Richard, 1953-54-55
GOODWIN, Arthur, 1940
GORDON, J. O., 1919
GORDON, Roger, 1977
GRAHAM, Bonnie Lee, 1936-37-38
GRAHAM, Michael F. "Mike", 1965
GRANT, Roy Oliver, 1975-76
GRANTHAM, James Larry, 1957-58-59
GRAVES, Joe E. "Jody", 1965-66
GRAVES, Sam Ervin, III, 1966-67
GRAY, Dabney, 1969, Mgr.
GREEN, Allen L., 1958-59-60
GREEN, Norvin E., 1900
GREEN, Walker G., 1912
GREENICH, Harley, 1940-42
GREENLEE, Max H., 1964
GREENLEE, Phillip Murry, 1973
GREFSENG, Robert Leonard "Bob", 1976-77-78
GREGORY, George H., Jr., 1958
GREGORY, John Andrew, 1970-71-72
GRIFFIN, J. A., 1914-15
GRIFFIN, Wade H., 1974-75-76
GRIFFIN, William K., 1976
GRIFFING, Glynn, 1960-61-62
GUNN, Edgar Lindsey, 1972, Mgr.
GUNN, Lundy R., 1973-74
GUNTER, George, 1932-33-34
GUY, Louis B., 1960-61-62

H

HADDOCK, James W., 1965; 1967
HAIK, Joseph Michel "Mac", 1965-66-67
HALBERT, Frank R., 1960-61
HALL, Gary S., 1972-73-74
HALL, J. J., 1921
HALL, J. P., 1899
HALL, James S., 1957-58-59
HALL, Linus Parker, 1936-37-38
HALL, Wm. Whaley, 1961-62-63
HAMILTON, William F., 1976
HAMLEY, Douglas, 1946-47-48-49
HAMLEY, Stuart Douglas, Jr., 1973
HANNAH, Otis, 1928
HAPES, Clarence, 1934-35-36
HAPES, Merle, 1939-40-41
HAPES, Ray, 1935-36-37
HARALSON, M. FLint, 1912
HARBIN, Leon C., Jr. "Buddy", 1954-55-56
HARDEN, Edwin D., 1973, Mgr.
HARDY, Wm. H., Jr., 1903
HARPER, Everette L., 1945-46-47
HARRIS, Dan D., Jr. "Danny", 1971-73
HARRIS, George, 1952-53-54
HARRIS, I. H., 1912
HARRIS, J. Harley "Pop", 1913-14-15
HARRIS, James E., 1974-75
HARRIS, Luther C. "Luke", 1976
HARRIS, R. S., 1916, Mgr.
HARRIS, Wayne Stanley, 1964
HARRISON, Elvin Lee "Harry", 1971-72-73
HARRISON, Glenn D., 1968
HART, Frank E., 1936-37-38
HART, Granville W., 1950
HARTHCOCK, Billy Harold, 1966-67
HARTZOG, Hugh Miller, Jr., 1967-68-69
HARVEY, Addison, 1899
HARVEY, Fernando C., 1976-77-78
HARVEY, James B., 1963-64-65
HATCH, Johnny A., 1974
HATHORN, Samuel B. 1909-10
HAVARD, Gerald W. "Scooter", 1969-70
HAVARD, Richard J. "Rickey", 1969-70-71
HAWKINS, Jim, 1977-78
HAXTON, R. Kenneth, 1909-10-12
HAYNES, Kirk, 1930-31-32
HAZEL, Homer Lawrence, 1939-40-41
HAZEL, William, 1939-40-41
HEIDEL, Herlan Ray, 1968-69-70
HEIDEL, James B., 1963-64-65
HEIDEL, Roy E., 1963-64-65
HEMPHILL, Archie W., 1927-28
HEMPHILL, Robert E., 1948-49
HENDRIX, Robert E., Jr., 1965-66-67
HENRY, Patrick, Jr., 1898-99
HENRY, Robert B. 1975-76
HENSON, Erwin D., 1916
HERARD, Claude D., 1967-68-69
HERRINGTON, Bart, 1931-32-33
HERRINGTON, John C., 1903
HESTER, S. D., 1929
HEWES, Gaston, 1924
HICKERSON, Robert Gene, 1955-56-57
HICKERSON, Willie Wayne, 1957
HICKMAN, James E., 1973-74-75
HICKS, Rickye Allen, 1972-75-76
HIGHTOWER, C. C., 1905-06
HINDMAN, Stanley C., 1963-64-65
HINDMAN, Stephen H., 1966-67-68
HINTON, Benjamin E., 1975-76
HINTON, Charles R., 1964-65-66
HINTON, Cloyce M., 1969-70-71
HITT, Billy, 1951-52
HOFER, Paul D., 1972-73-74-75
HOFF, A. S., 1923-24
HOLDER, Owen H., 1968
HOLLOWAY, A. J., Jr., 1960-61-62
HOLLOWAY, Ernest D., 1913
HOLMAN, William O., 1900
HOLSTON, John C., 1958
HOOD, H. M., 1920
HOOKER, Clyde, 1944
HOOKER, Danny L., 1968-69-70
HOPKINS, O. S., 1901-02
HOPKINS, Thomas J., 1902-03
HORN, Jeffrey L., 1968-69-70
HORNE, James H., 1971-73
HOUCHINS, L. Larry, 1974, Mgr.
HOUSEHOLDER, Eddy, 1977-78
HOVATER, Nobel Owen, 1964
HOVIOUS, John A. "Junie", 1939-40-41
HOWELL, Earl O. "Dixie", 1947-48
HOWELL, J. M., 1920
HOWELL, L. F., 1918
HOWELL, Ray, Jr., 1950-51-52
HUBBARD, Ethelbert J., 1898
HUFF, Earl, 1955
HUFF, Kenneth A., 1973
HUGGINS, Cleveland P., 1904-05-06
HUGHES, David, 1927, Mgr.
HUMPHREY, William R., 1950
HURST, William Otis, 1955-56-57
HUTCHINSON, James W., 1898
HUTSON, Earl, 1932-33-34
HUTSON, Marvin L., 1934-35-36

I

INGRAM, James F., 1950-51-52
INZER, William H. 1929
IREYS, Junius Taylor, 1894
IRWIN, Billy Carl, 1962-63-64

J

JABOUR, Robert, 1948-49-50
JACKSON, Claude A. "Red", 1935-36
JAMES, Edward Thomas, Jr., 1965-66-67
JAMES, James Elwyn, 1969
JAMES, Jerome P., 1913
JAMES, Raymond L., 1952-53-54
JARMAN, Junius, 1924
JARVIS, Lewis Dewayne, 1973-74
JEANES, Kenneth L., 1974
JEFCOAT, H. Greggory, 1978
JENKINS, Eulas S. (Red), 1946-47-48-49
JENKINS, Robert L., 1954
JENKINS, Warren D., 1957-58
JENNINGS, David Sullivan, 1962-64
JENNINGS, Thomas Wood, 1975-76
JERNIGAN, Arthur F., Jr. "Skip", 1968-69-70
JERNIGAN, Frank D., 1951-52-53
JIGGITS, Louis M., 1917-19
JOHNSON, James L., 1901
JOHNSON, Joe C., 1944-47
JOHNSON, John, 1977-78
JOHNSON, Larry Leo, 1961-62-63
JOHNSON, Lawrence B., 1974-75-77-78
JOHNSTON, Hal G., 1907-08
JONES, Billy Ray, 1959-60-61
JONES, Garland, 1893
JONES, Gary M., 1975-76-77
JONES, George F. "Buddy", 1968-69-70
JONES, Hermit, 1942
JONES, Jerrell, 1941-42
JONES, Robert H., 1928-29-30
JONES, S. M., 1901
JONES, Walter M., III "Bill", 1967-68-69
JORDAN, James, 1976-78
JORDAN, Wm. Roberts "Bill", 1970-7
JUMPER, Zeke, 1927

K

KANUCH, Barry W., 1978
KATZENMEYER, Fritz A., 1972, Trn
KAUERZ, Don, 1945
KEATON, Grayson "Buster", 1921-22-23-24
KELLY, James A., 1951-52
KEMP, E. D., 1935, Mgr.
KEMPINSKA, Charles C., 1957-58-5
KENDALL, Sam, 1915
KENT, Robert W., 1972, Mgr.
KEYES, Jimmy Elton, 1965-66-67
KHAYAT, Robert C., 1957-58-59
KILLAM, John, 1944
KILPATRICK, Wendell Terry, 1972-7
KIMBRELL, Fred T., Jr., 1962
KIMBROUGH, Les, 1977-78
KIMBROUGH, Orman L., 1902-03-05
KIMBROUGH, Richard R. "Rick" 1973-74-75
KIMBROUGHT, Thomas C., 1893-94
KINARD, Billy R., 1952-53-54-55
KINARD, Frank M., 1935-36-37
KINARD, Frank M., Jr., 1962-63-64
KINARD, George, 1938-39-40
KINARD, Henry, 1938; 1940
KINCADE, Robert, 1935-36-37
KING, Kenneth A., 1973-74-75
KING, Michael L. "Mickey", 1969-70
KING, Perry Lee, 1968-69
KING, Stark H., 1966
KINNEBREW, Earl, 1909-10

KIRK, Dixon, 1918
KIRK, Ken H., 1957-58-59
KIRK, Robert D., 1976
KITCHENS, Donald Scott, 1976-77
KNAPP, C. E., 1927-28
KNELL, Doug, 1944
KNIGHT, Wm. R. (Bob), 1969-70-72
KNOX, Baxter N., 1908
KNOX, Ike C., 1907-08
KOTA, Charles U. (Chuck), 1975-76
KOZEL, Chester, 1939-40-41
KRAMER, Larry E., 1972-73-74
KRETSCHMAR, W. P., 1896
KYZER, Sam, 1929-30

L

LAIRD, Charles D., 1960
LAIRD, Dewitt, 1928
LAKE, R. H., 1918-19
LAMAR, Wayne Terry, 1959-60
LAMBERT, Franklin T. "Frank", 1962-63-64
LAMBERT, George R., 1946
LANGLEY, Carl Edward III "Hoppy", 1976-77-78
LANGSTON, Thomas E., 1950
LANTER, Lewis R., 1961-62
LAVINGHOUZE, Stephen M., 1972-73-74-75
LAWRENCE, Richard T. (Dick), 1973-74-75
LAWTON, Pat, 1929-30
LEAR, James H., 1950-51-52
LEAR, Jim, 1977
LEATHERS, Don Wayne, 1971-72
LEATHERS, W. S. "Dr.", 1902-03, Mgr.
LEAVELL, L. O., 1915
LEAVELL, Leonard, 1907-08
LeBLANC, Allen Michael, 1969-70-71
LEE, Alonzo Church, 1908-09-10
LEFTWICH, Frank M., 1921-22-23
LEFTWICH, George J., 1912
LENHARDT, John, 1937
LENTJES, Fred W., 1959-60-61
LEWIS, Robert Q. II, 1976-77
LEWIS, Wm. Irwin "Buddy", 1966
LILLIBRIDGE, David B., 1916
LILLY, Sale T., 1926-27
LILLY, T. J., 1926
LINTON, Henry, Jr., 1951-52-53
LITTLE, Jamie Ray, 1964
LLOYD, Donald J., 1978
LOCKHART, Walter W., 1893
LOFTON, Harol, 1951-52-53
LONGEST, Christopher C., 1898-99-1900
LOTT, Billy Rex, 1955-56-57
LOTTERHOS, George T., 1968-69-70
LOVELACE, Kent E., 1957-58
LUCAS, Thomas Edwin, 1962-64-65
LUKE, Tommy, 1964-65-66
LUMPKIN, John, 1916
LYELL, G. Garland, 1897, Mgr.
LYERLY, Frank G., 1921, Mgr.
LYLES, Sam, 1938-39
LYONS, Kenneth J., Jr., 1971-73-74

M

MABRY, Ed L., 1929
MacNEILL, John B., 1973-74-75
MADDOX, John Cullen, 1963-64-65
MADDOX, Milton Roland, 1959, Trn.
MADRE, John G., 1934-35-36
MAGEE, Robert M. "Mike", 1965-66-67
MAGEE, Wm. T. "Tommy", 1969-70
MAGRUDER, John M., 1901-02
MAJURE, Toby, 1946
MALOUF, Wm. A. "Bill", 1972-73-74
MANGUM, Ernest G. "Pete", 1951-52-53
MANN, B. F., 1946-47
MANN, William, 1937-38
MANNING, Elisha Archie, III, 1968-69-70
MANSHIP, Doug J., 1911
MARKOW, Gregory D., 1972-73-74
MARKOW, Peter J., Jr., 1972-73-74
MARSHALL, Wm. D. "Bill", 1973-74
MARTIN, Van, 1924-25
MASK, James E., 1950-51-52
MASON, James P., 1972-73-74
MASSENGALE, Kent, 1937-38
MASSENGALE, Marc B., 1978
MASSEY, Charles Patrick, 1949-51
MATTHEWS, E. William, Jr., "Bill", 1965-66-67
MATTHEWS, James R., 1952
MATTHEWS, William L., 1898
MATTINA, Rodney A., 1962-63-64
MAXWELL, Harold L., 1949-50-51
MAY, Arthur Wm. "Bill", 1972-73
MAY, Doug, 1970, Trn.
MAY, Jerry L., 1951-52
MAYFIELD, Charles R., 1917
McALPIN, Harry Keith, 1975-76
McALPIN, Rickey E., 1978
McCAIN, Robert, 1944-45
McCALL, D. A., 1915-16
McCALL, E. F., 1911-12-13
McCALL, J. W., 1908-09-10
McCAULLA, Michael E., 1976, Trn.
McCLARTY, W. H., 1918
McCLURE, Wayne L. "Mac", 1965-66-67
McCLURE, Worthy P., 1968-69-70
McCOOL, Robert A., 1952-53-54
McCRANEY, James, 1966
McDANIELS, Bennie O., 1918-19-20-21
McDONALD, Quentin, 1977-78
McDONALD, W. Percy, 1907; 1909
McDONNELL, Augustus H., 1906
McDOWELL, James R., 1898-99
McELROY, H. S., 1918
McFARLAND, Ben, 1898; 1900
McFERRIN, Charles P., 1894
McGRAW, Robert "Bob", 1977
McINTOSH, James T., 1899
McKASKEI, Jerry D., 1955
McKAY, Henry Earl, 1954-55-56
McKAY, Rush, 1960-61
McKELLAR, Frank Monroe, 1970; 1972
McKELLAR, George, 1958, Mgr.
McKELLAR, Lane, 1965, Mgr.
McKEY, Noel Keith, 1971-72
McKIBBENS, Thomas R., Jr., 1968
McKINNEY, Bob L., 1952-53-54
McKINZIE, Ralph Wm. "Mackey", 1972; 1974
McLEAN, George D., 1894-95-96
McLEOD, Larry Mikell, 1974
McLEOD, W. N., 1905-06-07
McNEAL, Theodis, 1976-77-78
McMURPHY, Fred H., 1899
McPHERREN, Charles A., 1894-95
McQUEEN, Marvin Earl, Jr., 1964-65-66
McWILLIAMS, Howard, 1934-35
McWRIGHT, Billy, 1945
MEADERS, E. L., 1906
MEEKS, Jessie E., 1975, Trn.
METZ, John Stephen, 1964
MIKUL, Daniel P., 1971-72-73
MILLER, James G., 1976-77-78
MILLER, Martin Van Buren, 1908, Mgr.
MILLER, Michael T.
MILLER, Vernon Terry, Jr., 1973
MILLETTE, T. J., 1950
MILLS, Ralph, 1913
MILLS, Wilmer R., 1964
MILNER, E. C., Jr., 1959, Mgr.
MILSTEAD, Don M. "Mike", 1968, Mgr.
MIMS, Crawford J., 1951-52-53
MIMS, Gerald C., 1978
MIMS, Marvin Taylor, 1964
MITCHELL, Adam H., Jr. "Buddy", 1968-69-70
MITCHELL, John I., Jr., 1959-61
MITCHELL, Lansing L., Jr., 1972, Mgr.
MITCHELL, R. P., 1909, Mgr.
MITCHELL, Steve F., 1909-10-11
MOLEY, Stanley Anthony, 1970-71-72
MONSOUR, Thomas Joseph, 1970-71
MONTGOMERY, Charles L., 1950-51-52
MONTGOMERY, John, 1920-21-22-23
MONTGOMERY, Lavelle, 1931-32-33
MOORE, Hugh W., 1907-08
MORELAND, Brian, 1977-78
MORGAN, Gerald, 1957
MORGANTI, Charles, 1951-52
MORPHIS, Rex, 1928-29
MORRIS, C. H. "Bill", 1927-28-29
MORRIS, Charles A., 1960-61-62
MORRIS, Herman, 1927
MORRIS, L B., 1918-19
MORROW, George C. "Buz", 1967-68-69
MOSBY, Herman Wm., 1969-70
MOSES, Ronald David, 1970-71
MOSES, Samuel S., Jr. "Rollo", 1963-64
MOSS, Charles E., Jr., 1974-75-76
MOSS, Edgar, 1903-04
MOUNGER, E. H., 1895
MUIRHEAD, Allen, 1951-52-53-54
MURFF, Dan E., 1973-74-75
MURPHY, C. E., 1914
MURPHY, Harvey A. "Ham", 1938-39
MURPHY, Thomas, 1937
MURRAY, Hugh, 1962, Mgr.
MUSE, Carl W., 1975
MUSTIN, John W., 1923-24-25
MUSTIN, Robert Wm. "Billy", 1946-47-48-49
MYERS, Charles William, 1964-65
MYERS, Dale, 1941-42
MYERS, L. D., 1911-12-14
MYERS, Riley D., 1968-69-71
MYERS, William D., 1899-1900

N

NASIF, George Milid, Jr., 1974-75-76
NEELY, Charles Wyck, 1968-69-70
NEELY, Paul, 1915-16
NELSON, Charles "Tex", 1933-34-35
NELSON, James Mitchell, 1963-64-65
NEWELL, Ronald Bruce, 1965-66-67
NICHOLS, Rodney J., 1974, Trn.
NIEBUHR, Robert Bryan, 1974-76-77-78
NORMAN, Charles R., "Chuck", 1965-66
NORTH, Roy, 1940
NORTHAM, Larry Ray, 1970-71-72

O

ODOM, Jack L., 1947-48
OLANDER, Carl John "Bubba", 1976-77
O'MARA, B. B., 1918-21
OSWALT, Robert J., 1946-47-48
OTT, Dennis H., 1952-53
OTT, Reggie, 1951-52
OTT, Timothy A., 1978
OWEN, Joe Sam, 1969
OWEN, Robert L., 1968
OWEN, Sam Walton, 1961-62
OWENS, Robert L., 1957-58-59

P

PAGE, W. Reginald "Reggie", 1974-75-76
PARHAM, David Howard, 1971-72-73
PARKER, Edd Tate, 1951-52-53
PARKER, Thomas, 1936-37-38
PARKES, James C., Jr., 1966-67-68
PARKES, Robert S., 1976
PARKES, Roger B., 1973
PARKS, Hugh Harold "Hank", 1970
PASLAY, Lee C., 1951-52-53-56
PATCH, Dan, 1944
PATRIDGE, C. K. "Dewey", 1957-58-59
PATTERSON, Jerome, 1915
PATTON, Elack Chastine, 1894
PATTON, Houston, 1953-54-55
PATTON, James R., Jr., 1952-53-54
PATTY, J. W., 1927-28-29
PAYNE, I. J., 1928-29-30
PEARCE, Rex, 1944
PEARSON, Thomas H. "Babe", 1947-48-49-50
PEEL, John, 1977-78
PEEPLES, Everett U., 1928-29-30
PEGRAM, James Allen, 1975
PENNINGTON, Gerard M. "Jerry", 1976
PERKINS, A. P., 1923-24
PERKINS, James B., Jr., 1905-06
PERKINS, P. A., 1904
PERRY, Leon, Jr., 1976-77-78
PETERS, Ned, 1934-35-36
PETTEY, Thomas J. "Joe", 1962-63-64
PETTIS, William S., Jr., 1900, Mgr.
PFEFFER, W. L., 1907
PHILLIPS, Hermon B., 1947
PIGFORD, W. L., 1917, Mgr.
PILKINTON, S. T., 1905-06-11
PITTMAN, James Bradley "Brad", 1974-75-76

PITTMAN, Thomas Michael "Mike", 1974-75-76
PIVARNIK, John, 1940
PLASKETES, George M., 1975-76-77
POOLE, Calvin Phillip, 1946-47-48
POOLE, George Barney, 1942-47-48
POOLE, Jack Lewyl, 1948-49
POOLE, James E. "Buster", 1934-35-36
POOLE, James E., Jr., 1969-70-71
POOLE, Oliver L., 1946
POOLE, Ray S., 1941-42-46
POOLE, Ray S., Jr., 1976
POPE, Carl Allen, 1965
POPP, Romeo, 1939-40
PORTER, James Edward, 1970-71-72
POSEY, H. H., 1895
POTTS, Ed, 1930
POWE, Alexander M., 1908
POWELL, Kenneth W., 1960
POWELL, Travis, 1962, Mgr.
POWERS, Jimmy T., 1954
PRICE, Charles, 1930
PRICE, James J., 1978
PRICE, James Richard, 1958-59-60
PRIESTLY, Harry D., Jr., 1897
PRINCE, T. J., 1925-26
PRUETT, Billy Riddell, 1955-56-57
PURYEAR, H. H., 1911-12

R

RADFORD, Jimmy W., 1973, Mgr.
RANATZA, Michael A., 1974
RANDALL, George M. "Buck", 1961-62-63
RANDOLPH, Vivian, 1911
RATCLIFF, Culley C., 1920
RATHER, Edward, 1939, Mgr.
RAY, E. H., 1917-18-19
RAY, S. T., 1974
RAYBORN, Jerry Joe, 1963
REDHEAD, John A., Jr., 1898-99-1900
REED, Garland R. "Randy", 1969-70-71
REED, James M., 1973-74-75
REED, John B. "Jack", 1951-52
REED, John E., 1907, Mgr.
REED, S. Leroy, Jr., 1955-56-57
REEDER, Herbert, 1931
REGAN, George Bernie, 1959
REID, Ed, 1924-25
REILEY, Marion W., 1903
RENSHAW, Paul, 1906-08-09
REYNOLDS, Robert R., 1916
RICE, Tommy, 1963, Mgr.
RICHARDS, Tyrone, 1976-78
RICHARDSON, Marion L., Jr. "Mel", 1972-73
RICHARDSON, John A, 1964-65
RICHARDSON, Jerry Dean, 1965-66-67
RICHARDSON, William, 1933-34-35
RICHMOND, W. M., 1895
RICKS, W. B., 1898, Mgr.
RIDDELL, T. H., 1919-20
ROANE, Ralph H., 1900
ROBBINS, Michael D. "Mike", 1966-67
ROBERSON, J. Lake, Jr., 1938-39-40
ROBERSON, Shed H., 1932-33-34
ROBERSON, Shed H., Jr., 1958-59
ROBERTS, Bobby David, 1969
ROBERTS, Fred F., Jr., 1961-62-63
ROBERTS, George, 1942
ROBERTS, James B., 1960-61-62
ROBERTS, Kelly, 1965
ROBERTS, Pinky, 1914
ROBERTSON, G. H., 1905-06
ROBERTSON, Joseph E., 1958-59-60
ROBERTSON, Reginald M., 1960
ROBERTSON, Steven B. "Chip", 1976, Mgr.
ROBERTSON, Will E. "Pete", 1973-74-75-76
ROBINSON, Bobby Dewitt, 1962-63-64
ROBINSON, George O., 1899
ROBINSON, Howard D., 1919-20-21
ROBINSON, John W., 1958-59-60
RODGERS, Paul C., 1950
RODGERS, Rab, 1933-34-35
ROGERS, Daniel B., 1974, Mgr.
ROSE, Henry, 1944
ROSS, L. A., 1929-30-31
ROSS, Richard D. 1960-61-62
ROUDEBUSH A. H., 1893
ROUNSAVILLE, C. L., 1932-33-34
ROWAN, Leon F., 1917
RUBY, Pete, 1931-32-33
RUCKER, Robert R. "Randy", 1976
RUSHING, Herbert "Doodle", 1928
RUSSELL, Jack, 1945
RUSSELL, Lucius Thompson, 1893
RUSSELL, Michael W., 1978
RUSSELL, Richard H. "Stump", 1972-73-74
RUTLEDGE, L. J., 1904

S

SALLEY, David W., 1950
SALLEY, James W., 1950
SALLOUM, Mitchell, 1923-25-26
SALMON, Farley, 1945-46-47-48
SAM, Billy, 1939-40-41
SAMUELS, E. S., 1912
SANDERS, Aubrey E., 1957-58
SANDERS, Donald Wayne, 1970, Mgr.
SANDERS, Wm. Ervin, 1938
SANDERS, William H., 1951, Mgr.
SARTIN, Daniel M. "Dan", 1965-66-67
SAUL, James K., 1965-66
SCALES, Ewell D., 1893-94-95
SCHNELLER, Bill, 1937-38-39
SCRUGGS, Arthur, 1921-22
SEARFOSS, Stephen A., 1978
SEARS, Billy, 1945
SEAWEIGHT, Norman H., 1978
SEAY, Clant J. M., 1934, Mgr.
SHANDS, Harley R., 1898
SHARMAN, J. R., 1915-16
SHARP, L. V., 1951
SHARPE, Elmer C., 1898; 1900
SHAW, Vernon, 1935
SHEFFIELD, Don W., 1961, Mgr.
SHELBY, John, 1942; 1948
SHEPHERD, Archie, 1952-53-54
SHIELDS, Frank L., 1910-11
SHIELDS, John R., 1905; 1909
SHINAULT, James Rushing, 1894
SHOEMAKER, Allen C., 1932-33-34
SHOEMAKER, James, 1915
SHOWS, Henry N. "Hank", 1966-67-68
SHOWS, James Larry, 1964-65-66
SHUMAKER, Leo, 1904
SHUMAKER, Michael E. "Mike", 1968
SIMMONS, Clyde D. "Doug", Jr., 1969
SIMMONS, Delmar, 1924
SIMMONS, L. G., 1917-18
SIMMONS, Wm. M. "Bill", 1972
SIMPSON, Glynne, 1959, Mgr.
SIMPSON, Jack M., 1955-56-57
SIMPSON, Jack R., 1972
SINQUEFIELD, Melvin H., 1950-51
SISLER, W. H., 1917
SLAY, James, 1950-51-52
SMALL, Wm. N. "Bill", 1973-74-75
SMITH, B. A., 1914
SMITH, Ben P., 1893-94
SMITH, Claude M. "Tad", 1926-27-28
SMITH, E. J. "Randolph", 1956-57-58
SMITH, Eric L., 1977-78
SMITH. H. A., 1942-46
SMITH, Howard E. "Bert", 1976
SMITH, Kenneth, O., 1963-64-65
SMITH, L. A., 1899
SMITH, L. Q., 1974-76-77
SMITH, Lee Joseph, 1940
SMITH, Marley, 1932
SMITH, Marvin G. "Erm", 1938-39
SMITH, O. R., 1922-24
SMITH, Ralph A., 1959-60-61
SMITH, Ralph Guy, 1963
SMITH, Richard Joel "Dicky", 1970
SMITH, Robert T., 1973
SMITH, Steven H., 1973-74
SMITH, Stewart, 1940
SMITH, Thomas Larry, 1961-62-63
SMITH, Timothy, 1971-72
SMITH, V. K., 1925-26-27
SMITH, Wayne B., 1921-22-23-24
SMITHSON, Claude T., 1921-22-23-24
SMYLIE, J. B., 1895
SMYTHE, Frank W., 1913-14
SNYDER, Michael E., 1974-75, Trn.
SOMERVILLE, Robert, Jr., 1903-04-05
SPEARS, James W., 1958
SPIERS, Tommy, 1952
SPIVEY, R. E., 1920
SPORE, Jerry P., 1978
STALLINGS, Danny Lee, 1970-71-73
STAGG, Leonard, 1942
STEELE, Wm. Scott, 1972-73-74-75
STENNIS, Dudley, 1894
STEPHENS, Hubert D., 1894-95
STEVENS, W. R. B., 1913, Mgr.
STEWART, H. F. "Chip", 1966-67
STEWART, Joel, 1977
STIGLER, Samuel James, 1958, Mgr.
STILL, Claude
STOLT, John J., 1955
STONE, Ed G., 1931-32-33
STONE, Henry Jerry, 1954-55-56
STOREY, James W., 1974-75-76-77
STOVALL, John A, 1922-23
STRAUGHN, Robert, 1951
STREET, Donald Earl, 1965-66-67
STRIBLING, James A. "Jack", 1946-47-48-49
STRIBLING, Majure B. "Bill", 1945-48-49-50
STRICKLAND, Randolph T., 1905
STRINGER, L. O., 1923
STUART, George E., 1974-75-76
STUART, James B., III, 1971-72-73
STUBBLEFIELD, Jerry, 1965
STUDDARD, Vernon Aaron, 1968-69-70
SULLIVAN, Charles J. "Jimmy", 1966-67
SULLIVAN, John, 1963, Mgr.
SULLIVAN, Louie Wesley, 1960-61
SULTAN, Dan I., 1902
SUMRALL, Wm. W. "Billy", 1962-63-64
SUMNERS, Chester L., 1917
SUTHERLAND, Leslie S., 1973-74
SWAYZE, Tom K., 1930-31-32
SWEET, Michael W., 1974-75-76
SWETLAND, Michael R. "Mike", 1965-66-67
SWINNEY, C. P., 1940-41
SWOR, Zollie Alton, 1931-32

T

TAYLOR, Charles "Chico", 1960-61
TAYLOR, Harry, 1948
TAYLOR, Leslie Edward, Jr., 1965-66-67
TAYLOR, Tommy F., 1956-57-58
TEMPFER, J. G. "Chuck", 1961
TEMPELTON, Billy, 1956-57-58
TERRACIN, Steve Wayne, 1964-65-66
TERRELL, Marvin, Jr., 1957-58-59
TERRELL, James M. "Mitch", 1962
TERRELL, Ray, 1941
TERRY, Decker L., 1957-58
THAMES, Mickey, 1977-78
THAXTON, James Cairy, 1964
THERREL, J. S., 1912
THOMAS, Dalton "Pepper", 1954
THOMAS, James Larry, 1968-69
THOMPSON, Robert, 1925
THOMPSON, Robert P., 1898
THOMPSON, Robert W., 1919
THORNTON, James Ray, 1951
THORNTON, Johnny H., 1978
THORSEY, Frank, 1940-41-42
TIBLIER, Jerome J., 1944-47-48
TILLERY, Douglas W., 1962
TILLMAN, James S., 1938-39-40
TILLMAN, Ronald, 1965
TIMMONS, Aaron, 1944
TIPTON, Julius R., 1893-94
TOLER, Kenneth P., 1978
TORGERSON, Larry Donald, 1968-69-70
TOTTEN, G. C., 1924
TOWNES, Clarence Henry, 1894
TOWNES, Jack A., 1964, Mgr.
TRANSOU, Lewis, 1940, Mgr.
TRAPP, Franklin Wm., 1966-67-68
TRAPP, Lee H. 1930-31-32
TRAUTH, Marvin H., 1950-51-52
TRAXLER, David, 1977-78
TRIMBLE, William, 1933
TROTTER, William C., 1907-08-09-1
TRUETT, George W., 1952
TUGGLE, Jimmy, 1952
TURNBOW, Guy, 1930-31-32
TURNER, Gary W., 1973-74-75-76
TURNER, John H., Jr., 1964
TURNER, Thomas N., 1929

U

UPCHURCH, Robert K., 1961-62-63
URBANEK, James Eugene, 1965-66-67

ZZLE, Robert H. "Bobo", 1966-67-68

V

ALVERDE, Charles V., 1907-08
anDEVENDER, Wm. J. "Billy", 1968-69-70
ANDEVERE, Wm. E., 1911-12
ANN, Thad "Pie", 1926-27-28
AUGHAN, Robert C., 1965-66-67
EAZEY, Burney S. "Butch", 1971-72-73

W

/ADE, Robert Myers "Bobby", 1965-66-67
'AINWRIGHT, Ralph, 1899
/AKEFIELD, Victor Reed, Jr., 1973-74
/ALKER, Donald, 1977, Trn.
'ALKER, Gerald H., 1928
/ALKER, Harrison Carroll, Jr., 1965-66
/ALKER, Harvey W., 1926-27-28
'ALKER, Paul L., 1973, Mgr.
'ALKER, Richard H., 1922-23
/ALKER, Terrence C., 1975-76-77
'ALLACE, James M., 1900
'ALLIS, James H. "Jimmy", 1967-68-69
'ALSH, Willie Henry, 1970-71-72
'ALTERS, James A., 1953-54
'ALTON, Byron S., 1910-11
'AMBLE, James E., 1976
'ANDER, Mose, 1933, Mgr.
'ARD, Jesse Davis, 1937-38
WARE, Harry, 1926, Mgr.
WARFIELD, Gerald Wayne, 1964-65-66
WARNER, Jack, 1945
WARREN, Homer E., 1916
WATKINS, Dennis Ray, 1976-78
WATKINS, Thomas B., 1900-01-03
WATSON, Bill E., 1949-50-51
WATSON, Henry D., Jr., 1907
WATSON, R. Virgil, 1914-16
WATSON, Thomas C., 1904
WEATHERLY, James D., 1962-63-64
WEATHERS, Curtis L., 1974-76-77-78
WEBB, Hunter, 1942
WEBB, Luther Wade, 1970-71
WEBB, Reed S., 1966-67
WEBSTER, Edgar, 1903-04-05
WEESE, Norris Lee, 1971-72-73
WEISS, Richard, 1952-53-54-55
WEISS, Richard, Jr., 1978
WELLS, David Kent, 1963-64-65
WELLS, Vernon, 1945
WEST, Carl E., 1950-51
WEST, John Wayne, 1955-56-57
WESTERMAN, Richard W., 1950-51-52
WETTLIN, D. G., 1906
WHITAKER, David, 1942
WHITAKER, Murray P., 1976-77-78
WHITE, Brad, 1931-32-33
WHITE, Bradford C., 1978
WHITE, Hugh L., 1898-99-1900
WHITE, James Thomas, 1960
WHITE, John U., Jr., 1974
WHITE, Lloyd, 1936-37
WHITE, Robert P. "Randy", 1975-76-77
WHITENER, Larry J., 1966-67
WHITESIDE, Paul L., 1951
WHITTEN, L. D., 1917
WHITTINGTON, John, 1938
WHITTINGTON, O., 1921
WILCOX, Reuben D., 1927-28-29
WILFORD, Dan S., 1961
WILFORD, Ned B., 1961
WILKINS, Ernest, 1905
WILKINS, Joseph Tyson, III, 1962-63-64
WILLIAMS, B. Frank, 1907
WILLIAMS, Bill, 1937
WILLIAMS, D. E., 1895
WILLIAMS, Don N., 1955-56-57
WILLIAMS, Freddie Lee, 1976-77-78
WILLIAMS, G. H., 1920
WILLIAMS, Gary Neil, 1971-72
WILLIAMS, J. M., 1921
WILLIAMS, John C., Jr., 1954-55
WILLIAMS, Murray L., Jr., 1968
WILLIAMS, Robert J. "Ben", 1972-73-74-75
WILLIAMSON, John D. "Hotshot", 1926
WILSON, Charles "Buddy", 1933-34
WILSON, David, 1934-35-36
WILSON, Robert, 1946-47-48-49
WINDHAM, John 1925-26
WINDHAM, Donald W., 1962-63-64
WINSTEAD, Bobby Ray, 1968
WINSTEAD, Jimmy Leroy, 1971-72-74
WINSTON, Lowell, 1957
WINTHER, Richard L. "Wimpy", 1969-70
WISE, William H., 1978
WISOZKI, Ray, 1941
WOHLGEMUTH, John Thomas, 1970-71
WOOD, Andrew, 1906-07
WOOD, Charles G. "Chuck", 1971-72-73
WOOD, Dan, 1941-42
WOOD, Meredith, 1930
WOODRUFF, James Lee "Cowboy", 1957-58-59
WOODRUFF, Lee T. "Cowboy", 1927-28-29
WOODWARD, H. G., 1923
WOODWARD, Ray, 1942
WORSHAM, Jerry Dean, 1963
WOULLARD, Reginald, 1975-76-78
WRENN, R. B., 1914-15
WYLLIE, Phillip, 1978

Y

YANDELL, Robert, 1941-42
YARBO, Welborn, 1916
YELVERTON, Billy G., 1952-54-55-56
YERGER, J. S., 1903
YERGER, Wm. G. 1903
YOUNG, Carl R., 1949-50
YOUNG, John Wm., Jr. "Bill", 1970-71

Z

ZANONE, Curtis J., 1974, Mgr.

Mississippi State University

Location: Starkville, Mississippi
Enrollment: 12,300
Nickname: Bulldogs
Colors: Maroon and White
Stadium: Scott Field (35,000)

Mississippi State Head Coaching Records

COACH	YEAR	WON	LOST	TIED
W. M. Matthews	1895	0	2	0
J. B. Hildebrand	1896	0	4	0
L. B. Harvey	1901	2	2	1
L. Gwinn	1902	1	4	1
Dan Martin	1903-'06	10	11	3
Fred J. Furman	1907-'08	9	7	0
W. D. Chadwick	1909-'13	29	12	2
E. C. Hayes	1914-'16	15	8	2
S. L. Robinson	1917-'19	15	5	0
F. J. Holtkamp	1920-'21	9	7	1
C. R. (Dudy) Noble	1922	3	4	2
E. C. Able	1923-'24	10	6	2
Bernie Bierman	1925-'26	8	8	1
J. W. Hancock	1927-'29	8	12	4
Chris Cagle	1930	2	7	0
Ray Dauber	1931-'32	5	11	0
Ross McKechnie	1933-'34	7	12	1
Ralph Sasse	1935-'37	20	10	2
Spike Nelson	1938	4	6	0
Allyn McKeen	1939-'48	65	19	3
Arthur (Slick) Morton	1949-'51	8	18	1
Murray Warmath	1952-'53	10	6	3
Darrell Royal	1954-'55	12	8	0
Wade Walker	1956-'61	22	32	2
Paul Davis	1962-'66	20	28	2
Charley Shira	1967-'72	16	45	2
Bob Tyler	1973-'78	39	25	3

Mississippi State University All-Time Scores

1895

0	Sou. Baptist	21
0	Memphis AC	16
0	(0-2-0)	37

1896

0	Union	8
0	Alabama	22
0	L.S.U.	52
0	N. Orleans AC	55
0	(0-4-0)	137

1901

0	C. B. C	0
17	Ole Miss	0
11	Meridian AC	5
6	Tulane	24
0	Alabama	45
34	(2-2-1)	74

1902

6	Cumberland	15
0	Ole Miss	21
11	Tulane	11
0	Alabama	27
26	Howard	0
0	L.S.U.	6
43	(1-4-1)	80

1903

11	Alabama	0
43	Meridian AC	0
11	L.S.U.	0
6	Ole Miss	6
0	Tulane	0
71	(3-0-2)	6

1904

0	Vanderbilt	61
0	Alabama	6
5	Ole Miss	17
0	Tulane	10
59	Tenn. Meds	0
5	Cumberland	27
32	La. Ind.	5
101	(2-5-0)	126

1905

0	Alabama	34
38	Marion	0
0	Auburn	18
44	Howard	0
5	Cumerland	27
11	Ole Miss	0
0	LSU	15
98	(3-4-0)	94

1906

30	Howard	0
62	Marion	0
0	L.S.U.	0
4	Alabama	16
5	Ole Miss	29
101	(2-2-1)	45

1907

7	Southwestern	0
0	Sewanee	38
12	Howard	5
80	Sou. Baptist	0
75	Mercer	0
6	Drury College	0
11	L.S.U.	23
4	Tennessee	11
15	Ole Miss	0
210	(6-3-0)	77

1908

47	La. Ind.	0
0	Ga. Tech	23
5	Sou. Polytechnic	6
12	Transylvania	5
0	L.S.U.	50
0	Tulane	23
44	Ole Miss	6
108	(3-4-0)	113

1909

21	B'ham-Sou.	0

34	Cumberland	6
0	L.S.U.	15
31	Southwestern	0
0	Tulane	2
25	Union	0
0	Howard	6
37	Chattanooga	6
5	Ole Miss	9
153	(5-4-0)	44

1910

24	Miss. College	0
0	Auburn	6
6	Memphis St.	0
3	L.S.U.	0
48	Sewanee	0
10	Tulane	0
46	B'ham-Sou.	0
82	Howard	0
0	Ole Miss	30
219	(7-2-0)	36

1911

27	Miss. College	6
30	Southwestern	0
48	Howard	0
6	Alabama	6
5	Auburn	11
62	B'ham-Sou.	0
6	L.S.U.	0
4	Tulane	5
6	Ole Miss	0
12	Havana AC	0
206	(7-2-1)	28

1912

19	Miss. College	0
38	Tenn. Meds.	0
7	Alabama	0
0	Auburn	7
7	L.S.U.	0
24	Tulane	27
7	Texas A&M	41
102	(4-3-0)	75

1913

66	Howard	0
* 1	Miss. College	0
31	Kentucky	0
0	Auburn	34
6	Texas A&M	0
32	Tulane	0
0	L.S.U.	0
7	Alabama	0
143	(6-1-1)	34

*Forfeit

1914

54	Marion	0
77	Cumberland	0
13	Kentucky	17
0	Auburn	19
9	Georgia	0
66	Mercer	0
61	Tulane	0
9	Alabama	0
289	(6-2-0)	36

1915

12	Miss College	0
0	Transylvania	0
12	Kentucky	0
0	Auburn	26
0	L.S.U.	10
65	Ole Miss	0
14	Tennessee	0
7	Texas A&M	0
100	(5-2-1)	36

1916

6	Miss. College	13
33	Chattanooga	0
13	Transylvania	0
3	Auburn	7
36	Ole Miss	0
3	L.S.U.	13
3	Kentucky	13
7	Maryville	7
20	Arkansas	7
124	(4-4-1)	60

1917

18	Marion	6
68	Miss. College	0
6	Auburn	13
41	Ole Miss	14
14	Ky. State	0
9	L.S.U.	0
7	Haskell	6
163	(6-1-0)	39

1918

6	Payne Field	7
12	Camp Shelby	0
0	Park Field	6
34	Ole Miss	0
13	Ole Miss	0
66	(3-2-0)	13

1919

12	Spring Hill	6
56	Miss. College	7
6	Tennessee	0
39	Howard	0
6	L.S.U.	0
33	Ole Miss	0
0	Auburn	7
6	Alabama	14
158	(6-2-0)	34

1920

27	Miss. College	0
0	Indiana	24
33	Southern MA	0
17	L.S.U.	7
13	Tennessee	7
10	Ole Miss	0
0	Tulane	6
7	Alabama	24
102	(5-3-0)	68

1921

20	B'ham-Sou.	7
21	Ouachita	6
14	Miss. College	13
0	Tulane	7
21	Mississippi	0
7	Tennessee	14
7	Texas	54
7	Alabama	7
14	L.S.U.	17
111	(4-4-1)	125

1922

14	B'ham Sou.	0
0	Howard	0
19	Ole Miss	13
0	Tulane	26
7	Ouachita	7
3	Tennessee	31
7	L.S.U.	0
6	Drake	48
0	Alabama	59
56	(3-4-2)	184

1923

28	Millsaps	6
6	Ouachita	0
13	Ole Miss	6
3	Tennessee	7
0	Vanderbilt	0
6	Union	0
0	Illinois	27
13	Florida	13
14	L.S.U.	7
83	(5-2-2)	66

1924

28	Millsaps	6
0	Ouachita	12
20	Ole Miss	0
7	Tennessee	2
14	Tulane	6
0	Vanderbilt	18
7	Miss. College	6
0	Florida	27
6	Wash. U.	12
82	(5-4-0)	89

1925

34	Millsaps	0
3	Ouachita	3
3	Tulane	25
6	Ole Miss	0
0	Alabama	6
46	Miss. College	0
9	Tennessee	14
0	Florida	12
101	(3-4-1)	60

1926

19	B'ham-Sou.	7
41	Miss. College	0
7	Alabama	26
34	Millsaps	0
7	L.S.U.	6
0	Tennessee	33
14	Tulane	0
6	Indiana	19
6	Ole Miss	7
134	(5-4-0)	98

1927

27	B'ham-Sou.	0
14	La. Polytechnic	0
13	Tulane	6
7	L.S.U.	9
7	Alabama	13
7	Auburn	0
6	Milsaps	0
12	Ole Miss	20
93	(5-3-0)	48

1928

20	Ouachita	6
6	Tulane	51
0	Alabama	46
0	L.S.U.	31
6	Michigan St.	6
6	Centenary	6
13	Auburn	0
19	Ole Miss	20
70	(2-4-2)	166

1929

0	Hendr.-Brown	7
13	Ga. Tech	27
0	Tulane	34
6	L.S.U.	31
6	Miss. College	0
19	Michigan St.	33
0	Millsaps	0
7	Ole Miss	7
51	(1-5-2)	139

1930

0	Southwestern	14
12	Miss. College	13
13	Millsaps	19
8	L.S.U.	6
0	N. C. State	14
0	Tulane	53
7	Henderson St.	25
7	Auburn	6
0	Ole Miss	20
47	(2-7-0)	170

1931

10	Millsaps	7
2	Miss. College	6
0	Alabama	53
0	L.S.U.	31
7	Tulane	59
0	N. C. State	6
14	Southwestern	0
14	Ole Miss	25
47	(2-6-0)	189

1932

0	Alabama	53
18	Miss. College	7
0	L.S.U.	24
9	Millsaps	8
0	Indiana	19
0	Tennessee	31
6	Southwestern	0
0	Ole Miss	13
33	(3-5-0)	155

1933

12	Millsaps	0
0	Tennessee	20
0	Alabama	18
7	Vanderbilt	7
0	Southwestern	6
18	Miss. College	0
0	Tulane	33
26	Sewanee	13
6	L.S.U.	21
0	Ole Miss	31
69	(3-6-1)	149

1934

13	Howard	7
0	Vanderbilt	7
6	Millsaps	7
0	Alabama	41
21	Southwestern	6
13	Miss. College	6
3	L.S.U.	25
0	Tennessee	14
20	Loyola	6
3	Ole Miss	7
79	(4-6-0)	126

1935

19	Howard	6
9	Vanderbilt	14
45	Millsaps	0
20	Alabama	7
6	Loyola	0
7	Xavier	0
13	Army	7
13	L.S.U.	28
27	Sou. Miss.	0
25	Sewanee	0
6	Ole Miss	14
190	(8-3-0)	76

1936

20	Millsaps	0
35	Howard	0
0	Alabama	7
32	Loyola	0
0	T.C.U.	0
68	Sewanee	0
0	L.S.U.	12
26	Ole Miss	6
32	Mercer	0
7	Florida	0
220	(7-2-1)	25

Orange Bowl

12	Duquesne	13

1937

39	Delta State	0
38	Howard	0
0	Texas A&M	14
7	Auburn	33
14	Florida	13
0	Centenary	0
0	L.S.U.	41
12	Sewanee	0
9	Ole Miss	7
0	Duquesne	9
119	(5-4-1)	117

1938

19	Howard	0
22	Florida	0
48	La. Tech	0
6	Auburn	20
12	Duquesne	7
0	Tulane	27
7	L.S.U.	32
0	Centenary	19
3	Southwestern	7
6	Ole Miss	19
123	(4-6-0)	131

1939

45	Howard	0
19	Arkansas	0
14	Florida	0
0	Auburn	7
37	Southwestern	0
0	Alabama	7
28	B'ham-Sou.	0
15	L.S.U.	12
40	Millsaps	0
18	Ole Miss	6
216	(8-2-0)	32

Orange Bowl

14	Georgetown	7

1940

27	Florida	7
20	SW Louisiana	0
7	Auburn	7
40	Howard	7
26	N. C. State	10
13	Southwestern	0
22	L.S.U.	7
46	Millsaps	13
19	Ole Miss	0
13	Alabama	0
213	(9-0-1)	51

1941

6	Florida	0
14	Alabama	0
0	L.S.U.	0
56	Union	7
20	Southwestern	6
14	Auburn	7
0	Duquesne	16
49	Millsaps	6
6	Ole Miss	0
26	San Francisco	13
191	(8-1-1)	55

1942

35	Union	2
6	Alabama	21
6	L.S.U.	16
33	Vanderbilt	0
26	Florida	12
6	Auburn	0
7	Tulane	0
28	Duquesne	6
34	Ole Miss	13
19	San Francisco	7
200	(8-2-0)	77

1943-No Team

1944

41	Jackson AFB	0
56	Millsaps	0

49 Ark. A&M 20
13 L.S.U. 6
26 Kentucky 0
26 Auburn 21
0 Alabama 19
8 Ole Miss 13

219 (6-2-0) 79

1945

31 SW Louisiana 0
20 Auburn 0
41 Detroit 6
16 Maxwell Field 6
13 Tulane 14
27 L.S.U. 20
54 NW Louisiana 0
6 Ole Miss 7
13 Alabama 55

221 (6-3-0) 108

1946

41 Chattanooga 7
6 L.S.U. 13
6 Michigan St. 0
48 San Francisco 20
14 Tulane 7
69 Murray St. 0
33 Auburn 0
27 NW La. 0
20 Ole Miss 0
7 Alabama 24

274 (8-2-0) 71

1947

19 Chattanooga 0
0 Michigan St. 7
21 San Francisco 14
34 Duquesne 0
27 Hardin-Sim. 7
20 Tulane 0
14 Auburn 0
6 L.S.U. 21
14 Miss. Sou. 7
14 Ole Miss 33

169 (7-3-0) 89

1948

21 Tennessee 6
7 Baylor 7
7 Clemson 21
27 Cincinnati 0
7 Alabama 10
0 Tulane 9
20 Auburn 0
7 L.S.U. 0
7 Ole Miss 34

103 (4-4-1) 87

1949

0 Tennessee 10
6 Baylor 14
7 Clemson 7
0 Cincinnati 19
6 Alabama 35
6 Tulane 54
6 Auburn 25
7 L.S.U. 34
0 Ole Miss 26

38 (0-8-1) 224

1950

67 Ark. State 0
7 Tennessee 0
7 Baylor 14
0 Georgia 27
7 Alabama 14
27 Auburn 0
21 Kentucky 48
13 L.S.U. 7
20 Ole Miss 27

169 (4-5-0) 137

1951

32 Ark. State 0
0 Tennessee 14
6 Georgia 0
0 Kentucky 27
0 Alabama 7
10 Tulane 7
27 Memphis St. 20
0 L.S.U. 3
7 Ole Miss 49

82 (4-5-0) 127

1952

7 Tennessee 14
41 Ark. State 14
14 N. Texas St. 0
27 Kentucky 14
19 Alabama 42
21 Tulane 34
49 Auburn 34
33 L.S.U. 14
14 Ole Miss 20

225 (5-4-0) 186

1953

34 Memphis St. 6
26 Tennessee 0
21 N. Texas St. 6
21 Auburn 21
13 Kentucky 32
7 Alabama 7
20 Texas Tech 27
21 Tulane 0
26 L.S.U. 13
7 Ole Miss 7

196 (5-2-3) 119

1954

27 Memphis St. 7
7 Tennessee 19
46 Ark. State 13
14 Tulane 0
13 Miami 27
12 Alabama 7
0 Florida 7
48 N. Texas St. 26
25 L.S.U. 0
0 Ole Miss 14

192 (6-4-0) 120

1955

14 Florida 20
13 Tennessee 7
33 Memphis St. 0
14 Tulane 0
20 Kentucky 14
26 Alabama 7
20 N. Texas St. 7
26 Auburn 27
7 L.S.U. 34
0 Ole Miss 26

173 (6-4-0) 142

1956

0 Florida 26
7 Houston 18
19 Georgia 7
18 Trinity 6
19 Ark. State 9
12 Alabama 13
14 Tulane 20
20 Auburn 27
32 L.S.U. 13
7 Ole Miss 13

148 (4-6-0) 152

1957

10 Memphis St. 6
9 Tennessee 14
47 Ark. State 13
29 Florida 20
25 Alabama 13
27 Tulane 6
7 Auburn 15
14 La. State 6
7 Ole Miss 7

175 (6-2-1) 100

1958

14 Florida 7
8 Tennessee 13
28 Memphis St. 6
38 Ark. State 0
7 Alabama 9
12 Kentucky 33
14 Auburn 33
6 L.S.U. 7
0 Ole Miss 21

127 (3-6-0) 129

1959

13 Florida 14
6 Tennessee 2
49 Ark. State 14
28 Memphis St. 23
0 Georgia 15
0 Alabama 10
0 Auburn 31
0 L.S.U. 27
0 Ole Miss 42

96 (2-7-0) 198

1960

10 Houston 14
0 Tennessee 0
29 Ark. State 9
17 Georgia 20
21 Memphis St. 0
0 Alabama 7
12 Auburn 27
3 L.S.U. 7
9 Ole Miss 35

101 (2-6-1) 119

1961

6 Texas Tech 0
10 Houston 7
3 Tennessee 17
38 Ark. State 0
7 Georgia 10
23 Memphis St. 16
0 Alabama 24
11 Auburn 10
6 L.S.U. 14
7 Ole Miss 37

111 (5-5-0) 135

1962

9 Florida 19
7 Tennessee 6
35 Tulane 6
9 Houston 3
7 Memphis St. 28
0 Alabama 20
3 Auburn 9
0 L.S.U. 28
6 Ole Miss 13

76 (3-6-0) 132

1963

43 Howard 0
9 Florida 9
7 Tennessee 0
31 Tulane 10
20 Houston 0
10 Memphis St. 17
19 Alabama 20
13 Auburn 10
7 L.S.U. 6
10 Ole Miss 10

169 (6-2-2) 82

Liberty Bowl

16 N. C. State 12

1964

7 Texas Tech 21
13 Florida 16
13 Tennessee 14
17 Tulane 6
48 Sou. Miss. 7
18 Houston 13
6 Alabama 23
3 Auburn 12
10 L.S.U. 14
20 Ole Miss 17

155 (4-6-0) 143

1965

36 Houston 0
18 Florida 13
48 Tampa 7
27 Sou. Miss. 9
13 Memphis St. 33
15 Tulane 17
7 Alabama 10
18 Auburn 25
20 L.S.U. 37
0 Ole Miss 21

202 (4-6-0) 172

1966

17 Georgia 20
7 Florida 28
20 Richmond 0
10 Sou. Miss. 9
0 Houston 28
0 Fla. State 10
14 Alabama 27
0 Auburn 13
7 L.S.U. 17
0 Ole Miss 24

75 (2-8-0) 176

1967

0 Georgia 30
7 Florida 24
7 Texas Tech 3
14 Sou. Miss. 21
6 Houston 43
12 Fla. State 24
0 Alabama 13
0 Auburn 36
0 L.S.U. 55
3 Ole Miss 10

49 (1-9-0) 259

1968

13 La. Tech 20
0 Auburn 26
14 Florida 31
14 Sou. Miss. 47
28 Texas Tech 28
17 Tampa 24
13 Alabama 20
14 Fla. State 27
16 L.S.U. 20
17 Ole Miss 17

146 (0-8-2) 260

1969

17 Richmond 14
35 Florida 47
0 Houston 74
34 Sou. Miss. 20
30 Texas Tech 26
17 Fla. State 20
19 Alabama 23
13 Auburn 52
6 L.S.U. 61
22 Ole Miss 48

193 (3-7-0) 385

1970

14 Okla. State 13
13 Florida 34
20 Vanderbilt 6
7 Georgia 6
14 Houston 31
20 Tex. Tech 16
51 Sou. Miss. 15
6 Alabama 35
0 Auburn 56
7 L.S.U. 38
19 Ole Miss 14

171 (6-5-0) 264

1971

7 Okla. State 26
13 Florida 10
19 Vanderbilt 49
7 Georgia 35
9 Fla. State 27
24 Lamar 7
7 Tennessee 10
10 Alabama 41
21 Auburn 30
3 L.S.U. 28
0 Ole Miss 48

120 (2-9-0) 311

1972

3 Auburn 14
42 N E Louisiana 7
10 Vanderbilt 6
13 Florida 28
13 Kentucky 17
21 Fla. State 25
26 Sou. Miss. 7
27 Houston 13
14 Alabama 58
14 L.S.U. 28
14 Ole Miss 51

197 (4-7-0) 254

1973

21 NE Louisiana 1
52 Vanderbilt 21
33 Florida 12
14 Kentucky 42
37 Fla. State 12
18 Louisville 7
10 Sou. Miss. 10
0 Alabama 35
17 Auburn 31
7 L.S.U. 26
10 Ole Miss 38

219 (4-5-2) 255

1974

49 Wm. & Mary 7
38 Georgia 14
13 Florida 29
21 Kansas St. 16
37 Lamar 21
29 Memphis St. 28
56 Louisville 7
0 Alabama 35
20 Auburn 24
7 L.S.U. 6
31 Ole Miss 13

301 (8-3-0) 200

Sun Bowl

26 N. Carolina 24

1975

17 Memphis St. 7
6 Georgia 28
10 Florida 27
* 7 Sou. Miss. 3
*28 Rice 14
15 N. Texas St. 12
*28 Louisville 14
10 Alabama 21
*21 Auburn 21
*16 LSU 6
7 Ole Miss 13

165 (6-4-1) 166

*Lost by forfeit, resulting from NCAA action

1976

*7	N. Texas St.	0
*30	Louisville	21
30	Florida	34
*38	Cal Poly-Pomona	0
*14	Kentucky	7
*42	Memphis St.	33
*14	Sou. Miss.	6
17	Alabama	34
*28	Auburn	19
*21	LSU	13
*28	Ole Miss	11
269	(9-2-0)	178

*Lost by forfeit, resulting from NCAA action

1977

*17	N. Texas State	15
*27	Washington	18
22	Florida	24
*24	Kansas State	21
7	Kentucky	23
13	Memphis State	21
7	Southern Miss	14
7	Alabama	37
*27	Auburn	13
24	LSU	27
*18	Mississippi	14
193	(5-6-0)	227

*Lost by forfeit, resulting from NCAA action

1978

28	W. Texas State	0
17	N. Texas State	5
44	Memphis State	14
0	Florida	34
17	Sou. Miss.	22
55	Florida State	27
34	Tennessee	21
14	Alabama	35
0	Auburn	6
16	LSU	14
7	Mississippi	27
232	(6-5-0)	205

Mississippi State University Lettermen—1895-1978

A

ABERNATHY, Tom, 1965
ADAMS, Hugh, 1966-67-68
ADDERHOLT, Oliver, 1965
ALDERMAN, Joe, 1971
ALEXANDER, Leon, 1973-74
ALEXANDER, Murry, 1946-47-48-49
ALEXANDER, V. B., 1905-06
ALFORD, G. H., 1895-96
ALFORD, John, 1938-39-40
ALFRED, Justin, 1968
ALLEN, A. H., 1910-11
ALLEN, E. R., 1927-28-29
ALLEN, Henry, 1917-18-19
ALLEN, Terry, 1971
AMOS, E. N., 1929
ANGER, Bob, 1970
ARMSTRONG, C. H., 1934-35-36
ARMSTRONG, Robby, 1970-71
ARNOLD, J. D., 1942-46
ARNOLD, Pat, 1947
ARNOLD, W. F., 1939-40-41
ARRINGTON, M. A., 1909-10
ASHCROFT, W. H., 1928-29
ASHLEY, Loren, 1950-51
ASKEW, J. W., 1918-19-20-21

B

BAGGETT, Greg, 1965
BAILEY, Jim, 1946-47-48
BAIN, Jim, 1955-56
BAKER, Billy, 1971-72
BAKER, H. G., 1912-13
BAKER, Johnny, 1960-61-62
BALL, Hilton, 1962-63-64
BALL, I. B., 1895
BALLARD, N. B., 1917
BANKS, J. H., 1928
BARKUM, Melvin, 1972-73-74
BARNETT, E. B., 1920-21-22-23
BARNETT, James, 1957
BARRON, George, 1965
BARRON, Jim, 1953-54-55
BASKIN, W. H., 1917-18
BASS, L. G., 1909-10-11
BATES, Bobby, 1958
BATTE, Jack, 1956-57-58
BAUGHMAN, J. C., 1950
BEACH, Jerry, 1966
BEACH, Wally, 1949-50-51
BEAN, David, 1976-78
BEENE, Charles, 1963
BELL, Bill, 1978
BELL, C. P., 1921
BELL, Frankie, 1964-65
BELL, Robert, 1970-71-72
BENEFIELD, Greg, 1978
BENGE, John, 1956-57
BENNETT, Ron, 1954-55-56
BENSON, Jack, 1956-57-58
BENTON, Howard, 1960-61-62
BETHUNE, Bobby, 1959-60
BETHUNE, J. F., 1942
BIGGERS, R. R., 1926
BILLINGSLEY, D. W., 1908-09
BILLINGSLEY, M. C., 1917-19-20
BISHOP, C. H., 1940-41-42
BLACK, J. T., 1940-41-42
BLACK, Stan, 1973-74
BLACKMORE, Richard, 1974-76-77-78
BLAIR, S. H., 1918-19-20-22
BLAKE, P. L., 1956-57-58
BLAND, Dan, 1963-64-65
BLEDSOE, Jim, 1947
BLOUNT, Jack, 1949-50-51
BLOUNT, Lamar, 1941-42
BOATNER, Buster, 1972
BOBO, W. H., 1915-16-17
BOISTURE, Tom, 1952-54
BOLTON, Grady, 1963-64
BOLTON, Ralph, 1953-54
BORDELON, Barry, 1967-68
BOWER, W. R., 1919
BOYD, Frank, 1959
BOZEMAN, Bob, 1972-73-74
BRABHAM, Joe, 1970-72-73
BRAMLETT, Graham, 1945-46-47
BRANAMAN, H. W., 1914
BRANCH, Frank, 1950-51
BRANTLEY, Allen, 1972-73
BRASWELL, Sandy, 1972-73-74
BREAZEALE, Mickey, 1965
BRETT, Homer, 1895
BRIDGES, E. A., 1928-30
BRISLIN, Andy, 1972
BRISLIN, Chuck, 1973-74
BROCK, E. N., 1933
BROOKS, E., 1929-30
BROOKS, H. H., 1895
BROOKS, J. H., 1927-28
BROOKS, Larry, 1974
BROOKS, Ned, 1957-58-59
BROOME, Art, 1950-51-52
BROWN, Dwayne, 1977-78
BROWN, G. L., 1903
BROWN, Louie, 1955
BROWN, Ralph, 1931
BROWN, Steve, 1969
BROYLES, E. N., 1902
BRUCE, Johnny, 1971-72-73
BRUCE, Sonny, 1938-40-41
BRUMFIELD, C. N., 1906-07
BRUNSON, Bill, 1925-26-27
BRUNSON, E., 1915-16
BRYANT, R. B., 1924
BUCKLEY, Bill, 1971-72-73
BUCKNER, Bill, 1965
BUFORD, Glenn, 1976-77-78
BUIE, Larry, 1973-74
BULLARD, P. E., 1933-34
BULLOCK, Rex, 1945-48-49-50
BUNCH, W. R., 1936-37
BUNTYN, J. R., 1932
BURCH, C. T., 1934
BURKES, H., 1928
BURKS, Sam, 1948
BURRELL, Don, 1978
BURRELL, Ode, 1962-63
BURRESS, Tom, 1944-45-47-48
BURTON, R. E., 1918
BUSH, C. L., 1901
BUSH, H. L., 1901
BUTTRAM, Jim, 1956-57
BYRNE, H. E., 1931

C

CADENHEAD, Bobby, 1945-47
CALDWELL, Dave, 1963-64-65
CALHOUN, John D., 1971-72
CALHOUN, Prentiss, 1965-66
CAMERON, C. B., 1921-22
CAMPBELL, Ed, 1948
CAMPBELL, Marvin, 1938-39-40
CANALE, Billy, 1966
CANALE, Conn, 1967-68-69
CANALE, Justin, 1963-64
CANNON, B. S., 1931
CAPERTON, F. M., 1930-31
CARLEY, G. L., 1928-29-30
CARMICAL, Ted, 1966-67-68
CARNELL, Roye, 1969
CAROLLO, Bobby, 1964-65
CARPENTER, Dickie, 1969
CARPENTER, H. H., 1914-15-16-17
CARPI, Sam, 1938
CARROLL, James, 1963-64-65
CARROLL, M. B., 1937
CARROLL, S. J., 1944-45
CARTER, G. W., 1937-38-39
CARTER, John, 1974
CARTWRIGHT, George, 1947-48
CASSANOVA, T., 1911-12
CASSELL, H. S., 1919-20
CASSIBRY, R. E., 1932-33-34
CASTLEBERRY, John, 1965-66
CAVALLARO, Sam, 1950-51
CAVEN, Charles, 1952-53-54
CAVETT, J. C., 1895
CHADWICK, A. R., 1912
CHADWICK, E. B., 1926-27
CHAMBERS, Frank, 1938-39
CHAMPION, Jim, 1947-48-49
CHAPMAN, Jackie, 1973
CHAPMAN, Mike, 1970
CHATMAN, Robert, 1975-76-77-78
CHEALANDER, Hal, 1971-72
CHRISTIAN, E. D., 1895
CHRISTIAN, Hugh, 1974
CHRISTOPHER, A. C., 1927-28
CIMINI, Joe, 1951-52
CLARK, S. J., 1924-25-26
CLARK, Steve, 1950-51-52
CLARK, W. F., 1919-21-22
CLARKE, J. S., 1895
CLAY, T. F., 1903
CLEMENT, Joel, 1966
CLEMENTS, E. C., 1930
CLOOS, W. D., 1907
COLE, George, 1910
COLEMAN, Jim, 1954
COLLINS, Bobby, 1951-52-53-54
COLLINS, Fred, 1977-78
COLLINS, Glen, 1978
COLLINS, Robert, 1957-58
COLSTON, Doug, 1944-47-48
COLTHARP, Will, 1974
CONKEL, Don, 1954-55-56
CONRAD, Jerry, 1969-70-71
COOK, A. L., 1929-30
COOK, Ashby, 1964-65
COOK, Billy, 1961-62
COOK, Kelly, 1957
COOK, Roger, 1971-72-73

COOKS, Johnie, 1977-78
COOLEY, Sims, 1949-50
COOPER, R. A., 1937
COOPER, S. F., 1911-12
COPELAND, Len, 1976-77-78
CORBELL, Dean, 1950-51
CORBETT, Tommy, 1965-67
CORHERN, W. H., 1938-39-40
CORLEY, Elbert, 1941-42-46
CORLEY, F. G., 1923-24
CORLEY, Fred, 1965-66
CORLEY, Pinson, 1949
CORNELIUS, Marvin, 1964-65
CORRERO, John, 1959-60-61
COSTICT, Ray, 1973-74
COTNEY, Barry, 1965
COURTNEY, Jim, 1965-67
COX, C. A., 1930
COX, Wally, 1973-74
CRAFT, T., 1926
CRAIG, Walter, 1940-41
CRICK, Bill, 1969
CROCKER, Jack, 1948
CROSS, Dennis, 1936
CRUMBLEY, Charles, 1948-49-50
CRUMPTON, F. B., 1902-03
CUEVAS, Ronnie, 1974
CULPEPPER, Joe, 1967
CULPEPPER, R. H., 1929-30
CULVER, H.F., 1901
CUTRER, H. H., 1904-05
CUTRER, W. D., 1905-06

D

DABBS, C. N., 1928
DALOHITE, J. H., 1896
DALY, John W., 1932
DALY, Rudy, 1947-48
DANIEL, Willie, 1957-58-59
DANIELS, Jimmy, 1957-58
DANNER, Hugh T., 1930
DANTONE, Sammy, 1960-61-62
D'AVIGNON, Dudley, 1968-69
DAVIS, Art, 1952-53-54-55
DAVIS, Billy, 1956
DAVIS, Fred, 1972
DAVIS, Harper, 1945-46-47-48
DAVIS, Jimmy, 1957-58
DAVIS, Kenneth, 1947-48-49
DAVIS, Kermit, 1941-42-46
DAVIS, N. P., 1920-21
DAVIS, R. T., 1918-20
DAVIS, Ralph K., 1946-47-48-49
DAVIS, William V., 1931
DAVISON, Henry, 1974-75-76-77
DAY, Stan B., 1934
DEARMAN, Tom, 1965
DeBAUM, E. D., 1902-05
DEDEAUX, Randy, 1966-67
DEE,T. H., 1905-06-07
DEES, Chuck, 1969-70-71
DEES, Wilbur, 1939-40-41
DeLOE, Ken, 1951-52
DENT, H. M., 1907
DICKERSON, A. R., 1928
DILLE, A. B., 1910
DIXON, Larry, 1975-76-77
DIXON, William, 1936-37
DODD, Jimmy, 1955-56-57
DOIRON, J. W., 1929
DOLLAR, Joe W., 1944-46-47
DOOLEY, Bill, 1954-55
DORROH, C. E., 1906-07-08
DORSEY, Danny, 1970
DOSS, James Otis, 1977-78
DOUGLAS, Sherman, 1963-64-65
DOWSING, Frank, 1970-71-72
DRAYTON, Wylie, 1956-57
DREHER, M. F., 1940
DREYSPRING, Fred, 1948-49-50
DUCKWORTH, Mike, 1964-65
DUDLEY, Don, 1968-69-70
DUGAN, Bob, 1962-63
DUNAWAY, David L., 1944
DUNAWAY, Rusty, 1968
DUNCAN, Speights, 1954-55
DUPLAIN, Norman, 1950-51-52

E

EAST, F. J., 1917-19
EASTERWOOD, Hal, 1952-53-54
EATON, Mike, 1969-70-71
EDWARDS, Don, 1963-64
EDWARDS, Don, 1977-78
EDWARDS, Joe, 1969-70-71
EDWARDS, L. D., 1936-37
EDWARDS, Matt, 1977-78
EDWARDS, Mike, 1976-77-78
EIDSON, Jim, 1974
ELLARD, J. A., 1910-11-12-14
ELLIS, Alton, 1966
ELLIS, David, 1977-78
ELLIS, Glenn, 1971-72
ELLIS, R. J., 1938
ELROD, Buddy, 1938-39-40
ENIS, Bill, 1972
EPPS, Tommy, 1965
EUSTIS, W. B., 1913
EVANS, Charles, 1953-54
EVANS, Ed, 1950-51
EVERETT, Ronnie, 1973-74

F

FAIRCHILD, Ollie, 1951-52
FAULKNER, Billy, 1957
FATHERREE, George W., 1933-34-35
FELKER, Rockey, 1972-73-74
FERGUSON, L. H., 1908
FESMIRE, Rob, 1978
FIEDOR, Rudy, 1950
FIKES, B. B., 1919
FISHER, Sonny, 1961-62-63
FITZGERALD, ROBERT, 1974
FLEMING, Bobby, 1959-60-61
FLEMING, Steve, 1976-78
FLETCHER, Jack H., 1938
FLOWERS, Walter, 1956-59-60
FLOYD, Douglas B., 1944-45
FOLLIARD, Tom, 1964
FORD, Robert B., 1940
FORD, W., 1918
FORTUNATO, Joe, 1950-51-52
FOUNTAIN, George A., 1944
FOUNTAIN, Greg, 1972-73
FOUNTAIN, J. B., 1926-27
FOX, Carl, 1895-96
FRANCE, Hal, 1944-45
FREEMAN, Steve, 1972-73-74
FRIDAY, Larry, 1978
FRIDRICH, Ray V., 1938
FROHM, Martin, 1941-42
FUGLER, C. S., 1903
FULTON, Billy, 1954-55-56
FULTON, G. R., 1923-24-25
FULTON, Tom, 1951-52-53
FURLOW, Charlie, 1960-61-62
FURLOW, W. L., 1934
FURMAN, H. B., 1907-08

G

GADDY, T. L., 1913-14-15-16
GALEY, Gene, 1949-50
GALLOWAY, Ernie, 1955-56
GARRETT, W. D., 1944-45-46-47
GARRISON, E., 1908
GARRISON, Ernie, 1955-56
GARRISON, Tommy, 1965-67
GARVIN, Bobby, 1960-61-62
GATCHELL, K. P., 1921-22-23-24
GATLIN, Tommy, 1972-73
GAULT, Bill, 1978
GAYDEN, W. P., 1895
GELATKA, Chuck, 1934-35-36
GEOGHEGAN, R. E., 1926-27-28
GIBBS, Gene, 1961-62
GILBERT, C. F., 1909
GILLARD, Larry, 1974-75-76-77
GILLELAND, R. V., 1911-12
GILLESPIE, J. F., 1906
GLASGOW, Bill, 1952-53-54
GOODE, Tom, 1958-59-60
GOOLSBY, Shag, 1937-38-39
GORKE, Bob, 1947
GOSSETT, Bobby, 1967-68-69
GOUGH, Byron, 1948
GOUSSETT, P. G., 1929-30-31
GRACE, J. R., 1901-02-03
GRACE, John, 1942-46-47
GRACE, Roman, 1978
GRAHAM, S. G., 1905-06
GRANGER, Hoyle, 1963-64-65
GRANT, R. P., 1907
GRAY, Malcolm, 1934-36
GRAY, Ronnie, 1967-69
GRAY, W. G., 1934-37-38
GREEN, Hal, 1960-61
GREEN, J. S., 1925
GREEN, N. E., 1901-02-03-04
GREENE, Lonnie, 1976-77-78
GREENLEE, Larry, 1971-72-73
GREGORY, Paul E., 1927
GRIFFIN, J. B., 1938-40
GRIFFIN, Randy, 1976-77
GROVE, Harold F., 1939-40-41
GRUBBS, Lewis, 1970-71-72
GUILLORY, Lloyd, 1974
GULLEY, P. L., 1904-05
GUYTON, T., 1910
GWIN, Jan Lee, 1970

H

HADLEY, F. A., 1910
HALBERT, Molloy, 1955-56-57
HALEY, J. L., 1932-33-34
HALL, Jack, 1970-71-72
HALLER, Bob, 1966
HAMILTON, J. R., 1915
HAMPTON, Bubba, 1964-65-66
HANDLEY, Jim, 1961
HARDISON, Bob, 1935-36-37
HARDWICH, Buddy, 1967-68-69
HARNESS, Jim, 1954-55
HARPER, Ronald, 1978
HARRIS, Amos, 1942-45-46
HARRIS, F. D., 1901-02
HARRIS, J. C., 1928-29
HARRIS, Jerry, 1971
HARRISON, Calvin, 1966-67-68
HARRISON, Granville, 1938-39-40
HARRISON, Ralph, 1938
HART, Joe, 1969-70
HARTLEIN, Alan, 1976-77-78
HARTNESS, R. A., 1925-26-27
HARVEY, L. B., 1901
HASTINGS, Gil, 1955
HATCHER, B. F., 1918
HAWKINS, C. W., 1935-36-37
HAYNES, M. W., 1933
HEARNE, Bun, 1908
HEFLIN, Duval, 1948-49-50
HEIDLEBERG, G. C., 1896
HENDERSON, N. C., 1925
HENLEY, R. N., 1917-18-19-21
HENSON, J. C., 1933-34-35
HERRING, Gay, 1947-48
HERRINGTON, Bob, 1930-31-33
HERRINGTON, Ken, 1962
HESTER, C. F., 1902–03
HIGGINS, Glenn, 1965-66
HIGHT, Fred, 1935-36-37
HILDEBRAND, Bill, 1944-45-46
HILL, Billy, 1959-60-61
HILL, Curtis, 1978
HINE, C. R., 1934
HITT, Mark, 1975-76-77
HODGES, Dave, 1958
HODGES, Price, 1963-64
HOELSCHER, Bob, 1954
HOGGATT, Eric, 1969-70-71
HOLDER, Barry, 1972
HOLLIMAN, Joel, 1969-70-71
HOLLINGSHEAD, Levaine, 1953-54-55
HOLLOWAY, W. A., 1895
HOLLY, Keith, 1972
HOLT, Bill, 1974
HOPPER, R. C., 1924-25
HOPPER, R. E., 1924-25
HORNE, Hillery, 1941-42-43
HORNE, Leslie, 1930-32
HORTON, G. C., 1917
HOUGH, P. M., 1918-19-20-21
HOUSTON, P. D., 1919
HOWARD, Anse, 1941-42-46
HOWARD, Billy, 1944-45
HOWARD, J. R., 1896
HOWELL, Stanley, 1976-77-78
HOWIE, R. M., 1901
HUBBARD, J. L., 1922-23
HUDGINS, Ed, 1965-66-67
HUFF, J. H., 1919-20
HUGHES, Jay, 1969-71
HUGHES, Jesse, 1941-42-46-47
HUGHES, John E., 1941-42
HUGHES, T. G., 1902
HUGHES, Vernon, 1944-46
HULL, Harvey, 1973-74
HULL, W. A., 1906
HUMPHRIES, C. D., 1905
HURST, F. J., 1913-14
HURST, J. I., 1917
HUTSON, Frank, 1960-61
HUTTO, Randy, 1960-61-62
HYMEL, Calvin, 1973-74

I

INMAN, Tommy, 1962-63-64
IRBY, Ken, 1957-58
IRBY, Peyton, 1966
IVY, Harry, 1967

J

JACKSON, A. C., 1937
JACKSON, Gerald, 1975-76-77-78
JACKSON, I. M., 1914-15
JACKSON, Jerry, 1966-67-68
JACKSON, Keith, 1977-78
JACKSON, Willie, 1977-78
JACOBS, E. H., 1921
JANOUS, Frank, 1960
JAYNE, J. M., 1895-96
JEFFERSON, W. C., 1938-39-40
JEFFREY, Bob, 1948-49-50
JEFFREY, R. H., 1945
JENKINS, Anthony, 1978
JENKINS, Jimmy, 1960-61-62
JENNINGS, Joe, 1967-68-69
JENNINGS, Morley, 1910-11
JOHNSON, Dennis, 1974-75-76-77
JOHNSON, Harvey, 1938-39-40
JOHNSON, Kenny, 1976-77-78
JOHNSON, M. E., 1946-47-48
JOHNSTON, Jerry, 1972
JONES, Bobby, 1963-64
JONES, E. B., 1925-26
JONES, E. R., 1909
JONES, H. T., 1914-15
JONES, H. W., 1939-40-41
JONES, I. L., 1901-02
JONES, James, 1976-77-78
JONES, L. I., 1922
JONES, Murphy, 1932-33-34
JONES, Ronny, 1970-71-72
JONES, W. W., 1946-47
JONES, Wayne, 1971-72-73
JORDAN, Chuck, 1969-70-71
JORDAN, Jack, 1973
JOSEPH, Donald, 1951-53
JOY, Buzz, 1969

K

KATUSA, John, 1951-52-53
KELLY, David, 1959-60-61
KELLY, M. E., 1917-18
KENNAN, Robert, 1934-35-36
KENNEDY, Buck, 1958-59-60
KERBY, E. M., 1944-45
KEY, Sidney, 1973-74
KEYS, Richard, 1973-74
KEYS, Tyrone, 1977-78
KIMBALL, Hunter, 1911-12-14
KIMBROUGH, Bob, 1970-71
KING, Billy, 1955-56
KING, Chick, 1970-71
KING, Donald Ray, 1978
KINGREY, Ken, 1974
KINNEY, H. C., 1913-14
KIRKLAND, Ronny, 1962-63
KISER, Bill, 1965-67
KIZER, J. G., 1917
KLICKER, Albert, 1948
KLINDWORTH, M. E., 1919-20
KNIGHT, Bobby, 1966
KNIGHT, C. A., 1908
KOTOWSKI, Tony, 1950-51
KOWALSKI, Anthony, 1941-42

L

LAIRD, R. F., 1924
LAMM, Art, 1976-78
LANCASTER, Bill, 1969-71
LANE, D. H., 1918-23
LANE, Jimbo, 1963-64-65
LARSEN, Bootsie, 1963-64
LATHAM, Sam, 1956-57
LATHRAM, M. W., 1936-37
LATTIMER, W. H., 1904
LAWRENCE, Mike, 1973-74
LEE, Bill, 1973-74-76-77
LEE, S. B., 1910
LENOIR, R. L., 1929-30
LEONARD, R. L., 1917
LEWIS, D. D., 1965-66-67
LEWIS, H. R., 1926-27-28
LEWIS, Howard, 1973-74
LEWIS, W. I., 1929
LEWY, H. E., 1913
LIGHTSEY, Jim, 1964-65
LILLY, C. E., 1902
LINVILLE, Billy, 1952
LITTLE, H. S., 1919-20-21
LLOYD, Curtis, 1959-60-61
LOCKHART, Otis, 1978
LOGAN, J. E., 1952-56-57-58
LOIACANO, J. E., 1962-63
LONG, R. I., 1918
LOTT, S. A., 1933-34-36
LOW, R. H., 1922-23-24
LOWE, Fred, 1944-45
LUCKETT, J. E., 1922-23-24
LUNDY, T. E., 1929-30-31
LYNCH, T. R., 1922
LYNCH, Thayer, 1937-38

M

MAGEE, Don, 1972
MAGEE, W. J., 1911-12
MAGILL, O. R., 1909-10
MAGRUDER, F. H., 1911
MAHONEY, J. C., 1901
MAIER, Chuck, 1976-77-78
MALE, John, 1971
MALLORY, R., 1918
MALONE, Danny, 1973-74
MANGUM, Wayne, 1956-57-58
MANLEY, Jack, 1951
MAPP, Marcus, 1937
MARBLE, John H., 1930
MARLER, Dave, 1977-78
MARSH, Tate, 1969-70
MARTIN, N. S., 1915-16
MARTIN, Rusty, 1977-78
MASSEY, Alan, 1977-78
MATTHEWS, Miller, 1928-29-30
MATTHEWS, W. M., 1895
MATULICH, Lawrence, 1942
MATULICH, Wallace, 1946
MAXEY, Bill, 1976-77-78
MAXWELL, Jesse, 1978
MAXWELL, William, 1930-31-32
MAY, George, 1977-78
MAYFIELD, George, 1948
McALPIN, Jim, 1969-70-71
McARTHUR, Harry, 1912-13-14
McARTHUR, R., 1915-16
McARTHUR, W. S., 1904
McBRIDE, B. A., 1917
McBRIDE, Jim, 1962

McCABE, J. H., 1927
McCAIN, W. C., 1942-46
McCLELLAND, S. F., 1895-96
McCLUER, Donald, 1913
McCOLLOUGH, Larry, 1972-73-74
McCORVEY, Jackie, 1977-78
McCOY, O. R., 1930-31
McCRACKEN, W. G., 1944
McCULLEN, I., 1916
McCULLOUGH, Jim, 1971
McDOLE, Mardye, 1977-78
McDOUGAL, Lloyd, 1945
McDOWELL, Guy, 1938-39-40
McELROY, Dick, 1970-71-72
McELROY, Tom, 1971
McELVEEN, M., 1927-28
McGEORGE, Hal, 1904-05-06-07
McGLASKER, Darryl, 1974-75-76-77
McGOWAN, W. G., 1920-21-22
McGRAW, Dick, 1965-67
McGRAW, F. A., 1901
McGUIRE, Bill, 1963-64
McINGVALE, George, 1942-45
McINNIS, D. C., 1920
McINNIS, E. C., 1905-06-07-08
McINTOSH, Mark, 1977-78
McINTOSH, P. K., 1905
McKAY, J. V., 1895
McKEE, John, 1952-53
McKENZIE, Duncan, 1974-75-76-77
McKINZIE, W. M., 1920-23
McKISSICK, Clovis, 1954
McMULLEN, A. H., 1923-24
McNAIR, E. H., 1918
McPHAIL, Bill, 1954
McPHERSON, H. A., 1911
McWILLIAMS, L. M., 1920
McWILLIAMS, Thomas, 1944-46-47-48
McWILLIAMS, W. K., 1916-17
MEEKS, J. H., 1924-25-26
MEIGS, Ralph, 1935-36-37
MIHALIC, Mike, 1941-42-46
MIKETINAS, Bobby, 1978
MILLER, Andy, 1974
MILLER, L. C., 1923-24
MILLER, Tom, 1956-57
MILLS, A. P., 1910-11
MILLS, E. E., 1902-03
MILNER, Sammy, 1968-69-70
MINOR, Longstreet, 1906
MINYARD, B. I., 1935
MINYARD, W. N., 1920-21
MITCHELL, David, 1976-77
MITCHELL, E. F., 1926
MITCHELL, T. A., 1895-96
MIZE, William, 1930
MOAK, Johnny, 1935-36-37
MOATES, W. J. B., 1941-42-46
MOHLER, Robert, 1950
MOLDEN, Bobby, 1975-76-77-78
MOLLERE, L. A., 1934-35-36
MONAGHAN, Mike, 1973
MONROE, Henry, 1976-77-78
MONTGOMERY, H. C., 1895
MONTGOMERY, J. F., 1906
MOODY, Jimmy, 1965
MOON, Bill, 1963
MOORE, Arnold, 1938-39-40
MOORE, Billy, 1964-65
MOORE, Duaine, 1965-66-67

MOORE, John O., 1944-47
MOORE, Ronnie, 1968-70
MORGAN, William E., 1955-56-57
MORGANTI, Fred, 1944-45-47
MORRELL, Al, 1967-68
MORRIS, Don, 1952-53-54
MORRIS, E. S., 1907-08
MORRIS, Tom, 1952-53
MORROW, Bill, 1950
MORROW, Grover, 1933
MOTT, J. C., 1921-22
MUNCHAUSEN, Louis, 1937
MUNSCH, Al, 1953
MURPHY, Billy Jack, 1941-42-46
MURRAY, Stan, 1972-73-74
MUSSELWHITE, W. B., 1936
MYERS, W. J., 1922
MYRICK, Bo, 1977-78
MYRICK, Gordon, 1955-56

N

NABERS, Jim, 1977-78
NANCE, Bill, 1960
NASH, Marshall, 1931
NATALE, Steve, 1971
NEAVES, Robert, 1958
NEILL, James, 1965
NELSON, Bill, 1966-67-68
NELSON, E. T., 1906
NELSON, G. B., 1907
NELSON, Jim, 1969-70-71
NeSMITH, Ed, 1956-57
NEVILLE, Tommy, 1962-63-64
NEWSOM, Buddy, 1968-69
NEWSOME, Frank, 1952-53
NEWTON, Leslie, 1964-65-66
NICKELS, Sam, 1973-74
NICKELS, Vic, 1973-74
NIX, Gordon, 1937
NIX, Jack, 1937-38-39
NOBLE, C. R., 1912-13-14-15
NOBLE, L. W., 1921-22-23
NOBLE, P. A., 1927
NOBLES, Bennie R., 1945
NUGENT, Dave, 1965-66

O

OAKES, N. C., 1917
O'CONNOR, CLIFF, 1948-49
ODEN, C. S., 1915
ODOM, Jerry, 1947
OGDEN, Charles, 1930-31-32
OSBOURNE, Ray, 1959-60-61
OSWALT, J. A., 1916
OVERSTREET, Hugh, 1903-04
OWENS, David, 1949-50

P

PACE, John, 1949-50-51
PACKER, Walter, 1973-74
PAGE, W. C., 1931-32-33
PAPA, Vic, 1947-48
PAPPENHEIMER, W. A., 1927-28-29
PARKER, Jackie, 1952-53
PARKS, W. J., 1944
PARVIN, David, 1959
PATRICK, J. W., 1939-40-41
PATRICK, Mike, 1972-73-74
PATRIDGE, Jim, 1969-71
PATTEN, T. W., 1915-16
PATTERSON, Bob, 1947-48

PATTERSON, R. B., 1940-42-46
PATTERSON, W. C., 1941-42-46
PATTY, R. P., 1924-25
PAUL, Albert, 1960-62
PAYNE, Jimmy, 1974
PAYNE, Preston, 1970-71
PEARSON, H. H., 1901
PEPPER, Fred, 1976-77-78
PERKINS, Fred, 1959-60-61
PERKINS, H. G., 1921-22-23
PERRERE, Clyde, 1955
PERRY, Frank, 1917-18-19
PETERSON, Gil, 1956-57-58
PETERSON, Glenn, 1971
PETRO, Emile, 1970-71-72
PEYTON, Raymond, 1975-76-77-78
PHARES, Bob, 1972
PHARES, Ken, 1970-71-72
PHARR, Tommy, 1967-68-69
PHILLIPS, F. M., 1929
PICKENS, W. H., 1926-27-28
PICKLE, Ike, 1934-35-36
PILLOW, George, 1932-33-34
PILLOW, Robert, 1942-46
PILLOW, W. N., 1895
PILLOW, Watson, 1971
PITTMAN, C., 1927-28-29
PITTMAN, C. F., 1949-51
PITTMAN, Hilton, 1966-67-68
PITTMAN, Jim, 1947-48-49
PITTMAN, Oren, 1935-36-37
POLK, S. T., 1909
POLLARD, H. T., 1907-08-09-10
POLOVINA, Pete, 1950-51
PORTER, Jerald, 1974-75-76-77
POTEETE, Jim, 1957-58
POTTER, F. E., 1912-13
POTTS, R. H., 1902
POWERS, Floyd, 1958-59-60
PREMONT, David, 1977-78
PRICE, Dave, 1935-36-37
PRICE, Jimmy, 1966
PRICE, Orlie, 1931-32
PRICE, R. N., 1938-39-40
PRIESTER, Bill, 1960-61
PURNELL, Hawes, 1932-33-34
PYRON, Billy, 1949-50-51

Q

QUILLIAN, Chris, 1976-77-78

R

RAINEY, E. R., 1912-13-14-15
RANAGER, Tommy, 1960-61-62
RAY, E. G., 1940-41
RAY, Pete, 1947-48
RAY, Raymond, 1940-41-42
REAGH, I. C., 1934-35-36
REDDOCH, J. N., 1934-35-36
REED, C. R., 1965-66
REED, Harland, 1964-65-66
REED, Joe, 1969-70
REED, Joseph R., 1964-65
REES, Gavin, 1974-75-76-77
REESE, R., 1916
REID, Bo, 1950-51-52
REID, W. D., 1905
REULE, P. A., 1912
RHEA, Rube, 1971
RHOADES, Andy, 1966-68
RHOADES, Stan, 1944-45
RHOADS, Glenn, 1965-66-67
RHODEN, Marcus, 1964-65-66
RHODES, Ray, 1948
RHODES, S. W., 1909-10-11
RICHMOND, W. L., 1932-33-34
RICKMAN, Jack, 1973-74
RICKS, J. R., 1901
RICKS, W. B., 1926
ROBBINS, F. W., 1917
ROBERSON, Murphy, 1951-52-53
ROBERTSON, Joe, 1952
ROBINSON, Don, 1945-48-49
RODRIGUEZ, Wallace, 1961-62
ROGERS, W. M., 1906
ROMANOFF, Alex, 1970
ROSE, C. M., 1908
ROSE, W. C., 1909
ROSENBERG, Dick, 1951
ROSETTI, Jerry, 1965-66
ROSS, Jim, 1954-55-56
ROYE, J. L., 1932
RUCKER, Bill, 1966
RUCKER, Jack, 1949-50
RUDD, E. I., 1909
RUFFIN, D. A., 1912-13
RUFFIN, Joe, 1937-38
RUFFIN, R., 1913
RUSCOE, Ben, 1949-50
RUSCOE, Herb, 1956-57
RUSHING, Dennis, 1971
RUSHING, J. B., 1958
RUSHING, Tom, 1950-51
RUSSELL, C. E., 1918-19
RUSSELL, Freddy, 1967-68-69
RUSSELL, J. G., 1904
RUTLEDGE, J. F., 1896

S

SAAB, Louis, 1973-74
SABBATINI, Frank, 1954-55-56
SADLER, Robert E., 1939
SAGET, Don, 1965-66-67
SAIA, Joseph C., 1944-45
SANDERS, Harold, 1934
SANDERS, R. D., 1917
SANFORD, Carl, 1963
SANTAGATA, Rich, 1966
SANTILLO, John, 1952-53
SAUNDERS, W. B., 1922
SAVELY, T. S., 1908-09
SAXTON, Curtis, 1942
SCALES, Walter W., 1930-31
SCHAFFHAUSER, Gary, 1977
SCHEER, Stu, 1966-67-68
SCHEIDER, Carl, 1948
SCHOENROCK, Bill, 1957-58-59
SCHWILL, Otto, 1915-16
SCOTT, D. M., 1915-16
SCOTT, Edward, 1937
SCOTT, Paul E., 1930
SEAL, Leo W., 1909-10
SEAL, Leo W., Jr., 1947-48
SHAMBURGER, Charles, 1939
SHAMBURGER, Sonny, 1967
SHANKS, Don, 1967-68
SHARPE, O. J., 1960
SHAW, M. J., 1913-14-15-16
SHAW, Robert, 1960-61
SHEFFIELD, Lanny, 1971
SHEPHERD, Billy, 1951-52-54
SHEPHERD, J. T., 1950-51
SHUFF, Ted, 1942-46
SHUTE, Pat, 1958-59-60
SIDORIK, Al, 1942-46
SIKES, Carl H., 1931-32-33
SILVERI, Joe, 1954
SIMMONS, Crosby, 1948
SIMMONS, M. L., 1913-14-15
SIMS, J. B., 1974
SISK, Bob, 1957-58
SISK, Dwight, 1967
SISTRUNK, R. L., 1929
SKIPPER, Frank, 1958-59
SLOAN, R. J., 1917
SMITH, B. W., 1918
SMITH, Charles H., 1934-35
SMITH, Charlie, 1961
SMITH, David, 1968-69-70
SMITH, Ed., 1957-58-59
SMITH, F. M., 1910
SMITH, James, 1973-74
SMITH, O. L., 1926-27-28
SMITH, Truett H., 1946-47-48
SMITH, William, 1932-33-34
SMITHART, Terry, 1968-69
SOILEAN, Joe, 1976-77-78
SOUTHWARD, Billy, 1970-71-72
SPARKS, J. C., 1903
SPARKS, John, 1962-63
SPURLOCK, K. L., 1913-14-15-16
STACY, Benny, 1959-60-61
STACY, Billy, 1956-57-58
STACY, Bobby, 1960-61
STAINBROOK, Max, 1947-48-49-50
STANLEY, Jack, 1948
STANSEL, H. S., 1913
STANTON, Bill, 1953-54-55
STEADMAN, C. W., 1935-36-37
STEPHENS, Durwood, 1968
STEPHENS, P. E., 1923-25
STEVENS, Bill, 1965
STEVENS, Lenny, 1967
STEWART, Bill, 1950-51
STEWART, Buck, 1950
STEWART, R. H., 1916
STONE, H. L., 1923-24-25
STONE, L. H., 1927-28-29
STONE, W. O., 1933-34-35
STOOTS, Steve, 1970
STRAHAN, Tommy, 1971-72-73
STREET, Mitchell, 1978
STRICKLIN, Basil, 1949-50-51
STUART, C. E., 1924-25
STUART, James, 1945-46-47-48
STUBBS, A. B., 1936
STUVER, Vic, 1952
SUBER, Scott, 1953-54-55
SUDA, George, 1953-54
SUDDUTH, W. P., 1923
SUGGS, Walter, 1958-59-60
SUMMEROUS, A. R., 1928-29
SUMMEROUS, John H., 1930-32
SWEARENGEN, Larry, 1962-63-64
SWILLY, Billy, 1938
SWILP, John, 1954-55

T

TAIT, Art, 1947-48-49-50
TAIT, Jim, 1955-56
TATE, H., 1904-05-06
TAYLOR, C. K., 1902
TAYLOR, J. A., 1920-21
TAYLOR, Jerry, 1948-49
TAYLOR, Leslie, 1931-32-35
TEMPLE, Keith, 1973-74
THAMES, G. T., 1959
THAMES, Robert W., 1935-36
THOMAS, Bill, 1966-68
THOMAS, E. F., 1937-38
THOMAS, Jack, 1968-69
THOMPSON, Eddie, 1929-30-31
THOMPSON, H. S., 1938
THOMPSON, L. R., 1925-26-27
THOMPSON, Larry, 1972-73-74
THOMPSON, W. L., 1896
THORNTON, Mack, 1971
THORPE, H. D., 1941-42
THREADGILL, Bruce, 1975-76-77
TOHILL, Billy, 1959-60
TOPP, J. S., 1937-39
TOUCHET, Jim, 1972-73-74
TRAMMELL, Bubber, 1956-57-58
TRIBBLE, Bobby, 1956-57-58
TRIPSON, John, 1938-39-40
TROGDON, Mark, 1975-76-77
TROTTER, H. M., 1902
TRUSS, F. W., 1916
TULLOH, John, 1950-51
TULLOS, Toxie, 1938-39-40
TURNER, John, 1937-38-39
TURNER, Tee, 1978
TURNIPSEED, Clint, 1978
TUTOR, Elmer, 1930-31-32
TYLER, Breck, 1977-78

U

UNGER, J. W., 1925

V

VALLAS, Ted, 1954
VANCE, W. B., 1916
VANDEVERE, D. C., 1928-29-30
VARNADO, George C., 1940-41-42
VARNER, F. W., 1937
VAUGHN, Oliver, 1948-49-50
VENIER, Lou, 1953-54-55
VERDERVER, Gil, 1951-52
VINCENT, Jim, 1954-56
VITRANO, Terry, 1974-75-76-77

W

WADE, Jerry, 1959-60
WADE, Mike, 1968-69
WAITS, Frank, 1932
WALDEN, Bobby, 1973
WALKER, Anthony, 1970-71-72
WALKER, Brownie, 1960-61-62
WALKER, Pete, 1948-49-50
WALL, I. B., 1895
WALLACE, Bobby, 1973-74
WALLACE, Ralph, 1954
WALTERS, Fred, 1934-35-36
WARD, Elwyn M., 1929-30-31
WARD, R. B., 1935-36-37
WARDLAW, Gene, 1971-72
WARLICK, Joe, 1941-42
WATSON, Pat, 1962-63-64
WATSON, W. A., 1907
WEATHERLY, Charles, 1957-58
WEAVER, Mackie, 1960-61-62
WEAVER, Richard, 1963-64-65
WEBB, A. B., 1920
WEBB, Hurst, 1933

WEBB, Jimmy, 1972-73-74
WEED, Oscar, 1936-37-38
WEEKS, L. R., 1916
WEEKS, Shed Hill, 1932-33
WEEMS, Joseph L., 1934
WEISSINGER, G. C., 1918-19
WELCH, Lee, 1959-60-61
WELLS, P. L., 1911-12-13-14
WELLS, W. C., 1927
WEST, Danny, 1971-72-73
WHALEY, Steve, 1969-70-71
WHEELER, James, 1944
WHITAKER, Joe, 1904-05-06
WHITE, Benton, 1956-57
WHITE, J. J., 1929
WHITE, James G., 1940-41-42
WHITE, Lavelle, 1957-58-59
WHITE, Mark, 1974-75-76-77
WHITE, Steve, 1975-76-77
WHITTINGTON, Garland, 1963
WHITTINGTON, W. L., 1960
WICHMAN, Marcus F., 1931-32-33
WIELGOSZ, S. F., 1934
WIER, J. M., 1927-28
WILBANKS, W. H., 1925
WILEY, Arthur, 1978
WILKERSON, Bill, 1972
WILLIAMS, Louis, 1945-47-48-49
WILLIAMS, Max, 1953-54-55
WILLIAMS, Ricky, 1976-77-78
WILLIAMS, Robert, 1945
WILLIAMS, W. J., 1909-10-11-12
WILLINGHAM, D. T., 1926
WILSON, R. S., 1901-02-03-04
WILSON, W. P., 1920
WILSON, Zerk, 1951-52-53
WINDHAM, Johnny, 1961-62-63
WINSTEAD, H. D., 1945
WISEMAN, R. C., 1927-28-29
WISHMAN, M. F., 1931-32-33
WOFFORD, W. J., 1901
WOHLERT, Steve, 1976-77-78
WOHNER, Collins, 1940-41
WOITT, John, 1965-67
WOLVERTON, M. L., 1944
WOOD, Gene, 1967-68-69
WOODWARD, J. W., 1908
WOOTEN, O. B., 1905-06-07
WORLEY, Lewis D., 1932-33
WRIGHT, Carroll B., 1930-31

Y

YANCEY, Charles, 1940-41-42
YARBROUGH, Butch, 1969-70-71
YARNICK, Ron, 1952-53
YERGER, J. L., 1904
YOUNG, Bob, 1969-70
YOUNG, J. C., 1923-24
YOUNGER, Mike, 1972-73
YOUNGER, Paul, 1948-49-50

Z

ZERINGUE, Lynn, 1968-69
ZIMMERMAN, Bill, 1952-53-54

University of Tennessee

Location: Knoxville, Tennessee
Enrollment: 30,468
Nickname: Volunteers or Vols
Colors: Orange and White
Stadium— Neyland (80,250)

University of Tennessee Head Coaching Records

COACH	YEARS	WON	LOST	TIED
(No Coach)	1891-93; 1896-97*	12	11	0
J. A. Pierce	1899-1900	8	4	1
George Kelley	1901	3	3	2
H. F. Fisher	1902-03	10	7	0
S. D. Crawford	1904	3	5	1
J. D. DePree	1905-06	4	10	2
George Levene	1907-09	15	10	3
Andrew A. (Alex) Stone	1910	3	5	1
Z. G. Clevenger	1911-15	26	15	2
John R. Bender	1916-20*	18	5	4
M. B. Banks	1921-25	27	15	3

COACH	YEARS	WON	LOST	TIED
Robert R. Neyland	1926-34; 1936-40; 1946-52	173	31	12
W. H. Britton	1935	4	5	0
John Barnhill	1941-45*	32	5	2
Harvey Robinson	1953-54	10	10	1
Bowden Wyatt	1955 62	49	29	4
Jim McDonald	1963	5	5	0
Doug Dickey	1964-69	46	15	4
Bill Battle	1970-76	59	22	2
Johnny Majors	1977-'78	9	12	1

*No teams in 1894, 1895, 1898, 1917, 1918 and 1943.

University of Tennessee All-Time Scores

1891
0 Sewanee 24

1892
25 Maryville 0
16 Chattanooga AC 6
0 Sewanee 54
0 Sewanee 10
4 Vanderbilt 22
0 Vanderbilt 12
6 Wake Forest 10

51 (2-5-0) 114

1893
32 Maryville 0
12 Asheville AC 6
0 Duke 70
0 N. Carolina 60
0 Kentucky 56
0 Wake Forest 64

44 (2-4-0) 256

1894
(No Team)

1895
(No Team)

1896
10 Williamsburg 6
4 Chattanooga AC 0
6 Va. Tech 4
30 Central College 0

50 (4-0-0) 10

1897
28 King College 0
6 Williamsburg 0
0 N. Carolina 16
18 Va. Tech 0
12 Bristol RC 0

64 (4-1-0) 16

1898
(No Team)

1899
11 King College 5
11 Wash. & Lee 0
41 Transylvania 0
0 Sewanee 51
12 Kentucky 0
0 Va. Tech 5
5 Georgia 0

80 (5-2-0) 61

1900
22 King College 0
0 Vanderbilt 0
5 N. Carolina 22
0 Auburn 23
12 Georgetown 6
28 Grant 0

67 (3-2-1) 51

1901
0 Transylvania 6
8 King College 0
6 Clemson 6
5 Nashville 16
0 Vanderbilt 22
12 Georgetown 0
5 Kentucky 0
6 Alabama 6

42 (3-3-2) 56

1902
12 King College 0
34 Maryville 0
5 Vanderbilt 12
6 Sewanee 0
10 Nashville Univ. 0
11 Mississippi 10
10 Ga. Tech 6
0 Clemson 11

88 (6-2-0) 39

1903
17 Maryville 0
38 Carson Newman 0
0 Vanderbilt 40
0 S. Carolina 24
10 Nashville Univ. 0
0 Georgia 5
0 Sewanee 17
11 Ga. Tech 0
0 Alabama 24

76 (4-5-0) 110

1904
17 Maryville 0
0 Nashville Univ. 0
0 Ga. Tech 2
0 Sewanee 12
0 Vanderbilt 22

0 Clemson 6
0 Cincinnati 35
23 Grant 0
5 Alabama 0

45 (3-5-1) 77

1905

16 School of Deaf 6
104 American Univ. 0
5 Clemson 5
0 Vanderbilt 45
6 Sewanee 11
0 Ga. Tech 45
31 Centre 5
0 Alabama 28
0 Grant 5

162 (3-5-1) 151

1906

0 Maryville 11
6 American Univ. 0
0 Sewanee 17
0 Kentucky 21
0 Clemson 16
0 Georgia 0
0 Alabama 51

6 (1-5-1) 116

1907

30 T.M.I. 0
15 Georgia 0
4 Ga. Tech 6
4 Clemson 0
34 Maryville 0
57 Chattanooga 0
0 Ky. State 0
11 Miss. State 4
14 Arkansas 2
0 Alabama 5

169 (7-2-1) 17

1908

12 N. Carolina 0
39 Maryville 5
7 Kentucky 0
10 Georgia 0
6 Ga. Tech 5
9 Vanderbilt 16
6 Clemson 5
35 Chattanooga 6
0 Alabama 4

124 (7-2-0) 41

1909

0 Centre 0
0 N. Carolina 3
0 Ky. State 17
0 Georgia 3
0 Ga. Tech 29
0 Vanderbilt 51
0 Alabama 10
0 Chattanooga 0
11 Transylvania 0

11 (1-6-2) 113

1910

2 Centre 17
7 Mooney School 0
0 Vanderbilt 18
5 Georgia 35
17 Howard 0
0 Miss. State 48
0 Kentucky 10
13 Maryville 0
6 Chattanooga 6

50 (3-5-1) 134

1911

27 Mooney School 0
0 Ga. Tech 24
22 Maryville 6
0 N. C. State 16
11 Va. Tech 35
0 Ky. Central 0
22 Southwestern 0
0 Tenn. Meds 0
0 Ky. State 12

82 (3-4-2) 93

1912

101 King College 0
38 Maryville 0
62 Tenn. Meds 0
6 Sewanee 33
67 Centre 0
14 Mercer 27
6 Ky. State 13
0 Alabama 7

294 (4-4-0) 80

1913

58 Carson-Newman 0
95 Athens 0
75 Maryville 0
6 Sewanee 17
9 Davidson 0
21 Chattanooga 0
6 Vanderbilt 7
0 Alabama 6
13 Ky. State 7

283 (6-3-0) 37

1914

89 Carson-Newman 0
55 King College 3
27 Clemson 0
66 Louisville 0
17 Alabama 7
67 Chattanooga 0
16 Vanderbilt 14
14 Sewanee 7
23 Ky. State 6

347 (9-0-0) 37

1915

101 Carson-Newman 0
21 Tusculum 0
0 Clemson 3
80 Ky. Central 0
101 Cumberland 0
0 Vanderbilt 35
0 Miss. State 14
0 Ky. State 6

303 (4-4-0) 58

1916

33 Tusculum 0
32 Maryville 6
14 Clemson 0
26 S. Carolina 0
24 Florida 0
12 Chattanooga 7
10 Vanderbilt 6
17 Sewanee 0
0 Ky. State 0

168 (8-0-1) 19

1917
(No Team)

1918
(No Team)

1919

29 Tusculum 6
32 Maryville 2
3 Vanderbilt 3
0 Miss. State 6
0 Clemson 14
0 N. Carolina 0
6 S. Carolina 6
33 Cincinnati 12
0 Kentucky 13

103 (3-3-3) 62

1920

45 Emory-Henry 0
47 Maryville 0
0 Vanderbilt 20
35 Chattanooga 0
7 Miss. State 14
49 Transylvania 0
20 Sewanee 0
14 Kentucky 7
26 Clemson 0

243 (7-2-0) 41

1921

7 Maryville 0
27 Emory-Henry 0
21 Chattanooga 0
3 Dartmouth 14
9 Florida 0
14 Miss. State 7
0 Vanderbilt 14
0 Kentucky 0
21 Sewanee 0

102 (6-2-1) 35

1922

50 Emory-Henry 0
32 Carson-Newman 7
21 Maryville 0
15 Camp Benning 0
3 Georgia 7
49 Ole Miss 0
6 Vanderbilt 14
31 Miss. State 3
14 Kentucky 7
18 Sewanee 7

239 (8-2-0) 45

1923

0 Army 41
14 Maryville 14
13 Georgetown 6
0 Georgia 17
7 Miss. State 3
13 Tulane 2
7 Vanderbilt 51
0 V. M. I. 33
10 Ole Miss 0
18 Kentucky 0

82 (5-4-1) 167

1924

27 Emory-Henry 0
28 Maryville 10
13 Carson-Newman 0
2 Miss. State 7
9 Georgia 33
7 Tulane 26
0 Centre 32
6 Kentucky 27

83 (3-5-0) 135

1925

51 Emory-Henry 0
13 Maryville 0
7 Vanderbilt 34
0 L.S.U. 0
12 Georgia 7
12 Centre 0
14 Miss. State 9
20 Kentucky 23

129 (5-2-1) 73

1926

13 Carson-Newman 0
34 N. Carolina 0
14 L.S.U. 7
6 Maryville 0
30 Centre 7
33 Miss. State 0
12 Sewanee 0
3 Vanderbilt 20
6 Kentucky 0

151 (8-1-0) 34

1927

33 Carson-Newman 0
26 N. Carolina 0
7 Maryville 0
21 Ole Miss 7
57 Transylvania 0
42 Virginia 0
32 Sewanee 12
7 Vanderbilt 7
20 Kentucky 0

245 (8-0-1) 26

1928

41 Maryville 0
41 Centre 7
13 Ole Miss 17
15 Alabama 13
26 Wash. & Lee 7
57 Carson-Newman 0
37 Sewanee 0
6 Vanderbilt 0
0 Kentucky 0
13 Florida 12

249 (9-0-1) 51

1929

40 Centre 0
20 Chattanooga 0
52 Ole Miss 7
6 Alabama 0
39 Wash. & Lee 0
27 Auburn 0
73 Carson-Newman 0
13 Vanderbilt 0
6 Kentucky 6
54 S. Carolina 0

330 (9-0-1) 13

1930

54 Maryville 0
18 Centre 0
27 Ole Miss 0
9 N. Carolina 7
27 Clemson 0
34 Carson-Newman 0
13 Vanderbilt 0
8 Kentucky 0
13 Florida 6

209 (9-1-0) 31

1931

33 Maryville 0
44 Clemson 0
38 Ole Miss 0
25 Alabama 0
7 N. Carolina 0
31 Carson-Newman 0
25 Duke 2
21 Vanderbilt 7
6 Kentucky 6
13 N.Y. Univ. 0

243 (9-0-1) 15

1932

13 Chattanooga 0
33 Ole Miss 0
20 N. Carolina 7
7 Alabama 3
60 Maryville 0
16 Duke 13
31 Miss. State 0
0 Vanderbilt 0
26 Kentucky 0
32 Florida 13

238 (9-0-1) 36

1933

27 Va. Tech 0
20 Miss. State 0
2 Duke 10
6 Alabama 12
13 Florida 6
13 Geo. Washington 0
35 Ole Miss 6
33 Vanderbilt 6
27 Kentucky 0
0 L.S.U. 7

176 (7-3-0) 47

1934

32 Centre 0
19 N. Carolina 7
27 Ole Miss 0
6 Alabama 13
14 Duke 6
12 Fordham 13
14 Miss. State 0
13 Vanderbilt 6
19 Kentucky 0
19 L.S.U. 13

175 (8-2-0) 58

1935

20 Southwestern 0
13 N. Carolina 38
13 Auburn 6
0 Alabama 25
25 Centre 14
6 Duke 19
14 Ole Miss 13
7 Vanderbilt 13
0 Kentucky 27

98 (4-5-0) 155

1936

13 Chattanooga 0
6 N. Carolina 4
0 Auburn 6
0 Alabama 0
15 Duke 13
46 Georgia 0
34 Maryville 0
26 Vanderbilt 13
7 Kentucky 6
0 Ole Miss 0

147 (6-2-2) 52

1937

32 Wake Forest 0
27 Va. Tech 0
0 Duke 0
7 Alabama 14
32 Georgia 0
7 Auburn 20
7 Vanderbilt 13
13 Kentucky 0
32 Ole Miss 0

189 (6-3-1) 47

1938

26 Sewanee 3
20 Clemson 7
7 Auburn 0
13 Alabama 0
44 Citadel 0
14 L.S.U. 6
45 Chattanooga 00
14 Vanderbilt 0
46 Kentucky 0
47 Ole Miss 0

276 (10-0-0) 16

Orange Bowl

17 Oklahoma 0

1939

13 N. C. State 0
40 Sewanee 0

28 Chattanooga 0
21 Alabama 0
17 Mercer 0
20 L.S.U. 0
34 Citadel 0
13 Vanderbilt 0
19 Kentucky 0
7 Auburn 0
212 (10-0-0) 0

Rose Bowl
0 Sou. Calif. 14

1940
49 Mercer 0
13 Duke 0
53 Chattanooga 0
27 Alabama 12
14 Florida 0
28 L.S.U. 0
41 Southwestern 0
41 Virginia 14
33 Kentucky 0
20 Vanderbilt 0
319 (10-0-0) 26

Sugar Bowl
13 Boston College 19

1941
32 Furman 6
0 Duke 19
26 Dayton 0
2 Alabama 9
21 Cincinnati 6
13 L.S.U. 6
28 Howard 6
14 Boston College 7
20 Kentucky 7
26 Vanderbilt 7
182 (8-2-0) 73

1942
0 S. Carolina 0
40 Fordham 14
34 Dayton 6
0 Alabama 8
52 Furman 7
26 L.S.U. 0
34 Cincinnati 12
14 Ole Miss 0
26 Kentucky 0
19 Vanderbilt 7
245 (8-1-1) 54

Sugar Bowl
14 Tulsa 7

1943-No Team

1944
26 Kentucky 13
20 Ole Miss 7
40 Florida 0
0 Alabama 0
26 Clemson 7
13 L.S.U. 0
27 Temple 14
21 Kentucky 7
173 (7-0-1) 48

Rose Bowl
0 Sou. Calif. 25

1945
7 Wake Forest 6
48 Wm. & Mary 13
30 Chattanooga 0
7 Alabama 25
33 Villanova 2
20 N. Carolina 6
34 Ole Miss 0
14 Kentucky 0
45 Vanderbilt 0
238 (8-1-0) 52

1946
13 Ga. Tech 9
12 Duke 7
47 Chattanooga 7
12 Alabama 0
6 Wake Forest 19
20 N. Carolina 14
33 Boston College 13
18 Ole Miss 14
7 Kentucky 0
7 Vanderbilt 6
175 (9-1-0) 89

Orange Bowl
0 Rice 8

1947
0 Ga. Tech 27
7 Duke 19
26 Chattanooga 7
0 Alabama 10
49 Tenn. Tech 0
6 N. Carolina 20
13 Ole Miss 43
38 Boston College 13
13 Kentucky 6
12 Vanderbilt 7
164 (5-5-0) 152

1948
6 Miss. State 21
7 Duke 7
26 Chattanooga 0
21 Alabama 6
41 Tenn. Tech 0
0 N. Carolina 14
13 Ga. Tech 6
13 Ole Miss 16
0 Kentucky 0
6 Vanderbilt 28
140 (4-4-2) 98

1949
10 Miss. State 0
7 Duke 21
39 Chattanooga 7
7 Alabama 7
36 Tenn. Tech 6
35 N. Carolina 6
13 Ga. Tech 30
35 Ole Miss 7
6 Kentucky 0
26 Vanderbilt 20
214 (7-2-1) 104

1950
56 Sou. Miss. 0
0 Miss. State 7
28 Duke 7
41 Chattanooga 0
14 Alabama 9
27 Wash. & Lee 20
16 N. Carolina 0
48 Tenn. Tech 14
35 Ole Miss 0
7 Kentucky 0
43 Vanderbilt 0
315 (10-1-0) 57

Cotton Bowl
20 Texas 14

1951
14 Miss. State 0
26 Duke 0
42 Chattanooga 13
27 Alabama 13
68 Tenn. Tech 0
27 N. Carolina 0
60 Wash. & Lee 14
46 Ole Miss 21
28 Kentucky 0
35 Vanderbilt 27
373 (10-0-0) 88

Sugar Bowl
13 maryland 28

1952
14 Miss. State 7
0 Duke 7
26 Chattanooga 6
20 Alabama 0
50 Wofford 0
41 N. Carolina 14
22 L.S.U. 3
26 Florida 12
14 Kentucky 14
46 Vanderbilt 0
259 (8-1-1) 63

Cotton Bowl
0 Texas 16

1953
0 Miss. State 26
7 Duke 21
40 Chattanooga 7
0 Alabama 0
59 Louisville 6
20 N. Carolina 6
32 L.S.U. 14
9 Florida 7
21 Kentucky 27
33 Vanderbilt 6
19 Houston 33
240 (6-4-1) 153

1954
19 Miss. State 7
6 Duke 7
20 Chattanooga 14
0 Alabama 27
14 Dayton 7
26 N. Carolina 20
7 Ga. Tech 28
0 Florida 14
13 Kentucky 14
0 Vanderbilt 26
105 (4-6-0) 164

1955
7 Miss. State 13
0 Duke 21
13 Chattanooga 0
20 Alabama 0
53 Dayton 7
48 N. Carolina 7
7 Ga. Tech 7
20 Florida 0
0 Kentucky 23
20 Vanderbilt 14
188 (6-3-1) 92

1956
35 Auburn 7
33 Duke 20
42 Chattanooga 20
24 Alabama 0
34 Maryland 7
20 N. Carolina 0
6 Ga. Tech 0
27 Ole Miss 7
20 Kentucky 7
27 Vanderbilt 7
268 (10-0-0) 75

Sugar Bowl
7 Baylor 13

1957
0 Auburn 7
14 Miss. State 9
28 Chattanooga 13
14 Alabama 0
16 Maryland 0
35 N. Carolina 0
21 Ga. Tech 6
7 Ole Miss 14
6 Kentucky 20
20 Vanderbilt 6
161 (7-3-0) 72

Gator Bowl
3 Texas A&M 0

1958
0 Auburn 13
13 Miss. State 8
7 Ga. Tech 21
14 Alabama 7
0 N. Carolina 21
6 Chattanooga 14
18 Ole Miss 16
2 Kentucky 6
10 Vanderbilt 6
77 (4-6-0) 122

1959
3 Auburn 0
22 Miss. State 6
7 Ga. Tech 14
7 Alabama 7
23 Chattanooga 0
29 N. Carolina 7
14 L.S.U. 13
7 Ole Miss 37
0 Kentucky 20
0 Vanderbilt 14
112 (5-4-1) 118

1960
10 Auburn 3
0 Miss. State 0
62 Tampa 7
20 Alabama 7
25 Chattanooga 0
27 N. Carolina 14
7 Ga. Tech 14
3 Ole Miss 24
10 Kentucky 10
35 Vanderbilt 0
209 (6-2-2) 79

1961
21 Auburn 24
17 Miss. State 3
52 Tulsa 6
3 Alabama 34
20 Chattanooga 7
21 N. Carolina 22
10 Ga. Tech 6
10 Ole Miss 24
26 Kentucky 16
41 Vanderbilt 7
221 (6-4-0) 149

1962
21 Auburn 22
6 Miss. State 7
0 Ga. Tech 17
7 Alabama 27
48 Chattanooga 14
23 Wake Forest 0
28 Tulane 16
6 Ole Miss 19
10 Kentucky 12
30 Vanderbilt 0
179 (4-6-0) 134

1963
34 Richmond 6
19 Auburn 23
0 Miss. State 7
7 Ga. Tech 23
0 Alabama 35
49 Chattanooga 7
26 Tulane 0
0 Ole Miss 20
19 Kentucky 0
14 Vanderbilt 0
168 (5-5-0) 121

1964
10 Chattanooga 6
0 Auburn 3
14 Miss. State 13
16 Boston College 14
8 Alabama 19
3 L.S.U. 3
22 Ga. Tech 14
0 Ole Miss 30
7 Kentucky 12
0 Vanderbilt 7
80 (4-5-1) 121

1965
21 Army 0
13 Auburn 13
24 S. Carolina 3
7 Alabama 7
17 Houston 8
21 Ga. Tech 7
13 Ole Miss 14
19 Kentucky 3
21 Vanderbilt 3
37 U.C.L.A. 34
193 (7-1-2) 88

Bluebonnet Bowl
27 Tulsa 6

1966
28 Auburn 0
23 Rice 3
3 Ga. Tech 6
10 Alabama 11
29 S. Carolina 17
38 Army 7
28 Chattanooga 10
7 Ole Miss 14
28 Kentucky 19
28 Vanderbilt 0
222 (7-3-0) 87

Gator Bowl
18 Syracuse 12

1967
16 U.C.L.A. 20
27 Auburn 13
24 Ga. Tech 13
24 Alabama 13
17 L.S.U. 14
38 Tampa 0
35 Tulane 14
20 Ole Miss 7
17 Kentucky 7
41 Vanderbilt 14
259 (9-1-0) 115

Orange Bowl
24 Oklahoma 26

1968
17 Georgia 17
24 Memphis State 17
57 Rice 0
24 Ga. Tech 7
10 Alabama 9
42 U.C.L.A. 18
14 Auburn 28
31 Ole Miss 0
24 Kentucky 7
10 Vanderbilt 7
248 (8-1-1) 110

Cotton Bowl
13 Texas 36

1969

31	Chattanooga	0
45	Auburn	19
55	Memphis State	16
26	Ga. Tech	8
41	Alabama	14
17	Georgia	3
29	S. Carolina	14
0	Ole Miss	38
31	Kentucky	26
40	Vanderbilt	27
315	(9-1-0)	165

Gator Bowl

13	Florida	14

1970

28	S.M.U.	3
23	Auburn	36
48	Army	3
17	Ga. Tech	6
24	Alabama	0
38	Florida	7
41	Wake Forest	7
20	S. Carolina	18
45	Kentucky	0
24	Vanderbilt	6
28	U.C.L.A.	17
336	(10-1-0)	103

Sugar Bowl

34	Air Force	13

1971

48	S. Barbara	6
9	Auburn	10
20	Florida	13
10	Ga. Tech	6
15	Alabama	32
10	Miss. State	7
38	Tulsa	3
35	S. Carolina	6
21	Kentucky	7
19	Vanderbilt	7
31	Penn State	11
256	(9-2-0)	98

Liberty Bowl

14	Arkansas	13

1972

34	Ga. Tech	3
28	Penn State	21
45	Wake Forest	6
6	Auburn	10
38	Memphis St.	7
10	Alabama	17
34	Hawaii	2
14	Georgia	0
17	Ole Miss	0
17	Kentucky	7
30	Vanderbilt	10
273	(9-2-0)	83

Bluebonnet Bowl

24	L.S.U.	17

1973

21	Duke	17
37	Army	18
21	Auburn	0
28	Kansas	27
20	Ga. Tech	14
21	Alabama	42
39	T.C.U.	7
31	Georgia	35
18	Ole Miss	28
16	Kentucky	14
20	Vanderbilt	17
272		219

Gator Bowl

19	Texas Tech	28

1974

17	U.C.L.A.	17
17	Kansas	3
0	Auburn	21
17	Tulsa	10
10	L.S.U.	20
6	Alabama	28
29	Clemson	28
34	Memphis St.	6
29	Ole Miss	17
24	Kentucky	7
21	Vanderbilt	21
204	(6-3-2)	178

Liberty Bowl

7	Maryland	3

1975

26	Maryland	8
28	UCLA	34
21	Auburn	17
24	LSU	10
7	Alabama	30
14	N. Texas St	21
28	Colo. State	7
40	Utah	7
6	Ole Miss	23
17	Kentucky	13
14	Vanderbilt	17
18	Hawaii	6
253	(7-5-0)	193

1976

18	Duke	21
31	T.C.U.	0
28	Auburn	38
21	Clemson	19
42	Ga. Tech	7
13	Alabama	20
18	Florida	20
21	Memphis St.	14
32	Ole Miss	6
0	Kentucky	7
13	Vanderbilt	10
237	(6-5-0)	162

1977

17	California	27
24	Boston College	18
12	Auburn	14
41	Oregon State	10
8	Ga. Tech	24
10	Alabama	24
17	Florida	27
27	Memphis State	14
14	Mississippi	43
17	Kentucky	21
42	Vanderbilt	7
229	(4-7-0)	229

1978

0	UCLA	13
13	Oregon State	13
10	Auburn	29
31	Army	13
17	Alabama	30
21	Miss. State	34
34	Duke	0
14	Notre Dame	31
41	Mississippi	17
29	Kentucky	14
41	Vanderbilt	15
251	(5-5-1)	209

University of Tennessee Lettermen—1891-1978

A

ABERNATHY, George "Owl" T., 1926-27
ACKERMANN, Norbert J., Jr., 1963-64
ACKERMANN, Norbert J., Sr., 1939-40
ADAMS, Ralph, 1952
ADKINS, Stockton, 1955-56-57
AGUILLARD, Kyle, 1977-78
AITKEN, Malcolm, 1930-31-32
ALEXANDER, Frank, 1950-51-52
ALEXANDER, W. C., 1900
ALLEN, David C., 1970-71-72
ALLEN, Jimmy, 1970
ALLEN, John H., 1929-30-31
ALLEY, E. H. "Herc", 1927-28
ANDERSON, Bill, 1955-56-57
ANDERSON, Charles, 1974-75-76
ANDERSON, Malcolm S., 1932-33-34
ANDES, Julian, 1942-44, Mgr.
ANDRIDGE, Bob "Breezer", 1938-39-40
APPLEWHITE, J. M., 1911
ARBO, Billy, 1975-76-77-78
ARCHIBALD, Doug, 1964-65-66
ARMSTRONG, Jack, 1946-47-48
ARMSTRONG, Murray, 1956-57-58
ASBURY, E. J., 1944-45
ATKINS, Doug, 1950-51-52
ATTKISSON, Eugene R., 1896-97, Mgr.
AUGUSTINE, Pat, 1959-61-62
AUSTELLE, Alfred, 1934
AUTRY, Keith, 1974
AYMETT, Julian, 1902-03

B

BACON, J. B., 1899
BACON, Pryor E., 1938-39
BAILEY, Howard H., 1932-33-34
BAILEY, John "Skeeter" W., 1938
BAIRD, James A., 1896-97
BAIRD, Robert R., 1896-97
BAKER, Bill, 1966-67-68
BAKER, Charles B., 1960
BAKER, Charles F., 1947-48-49
BAKER, Tommy, 1967-68-69-70, Mgr.
BAKER, W. G., 1906-07-08
BALDINI, Ralph, 1961
BALITSARIS, George, 1946-47-48
BALITSARIS, Mike, 1939-40-41
BALTHIS, R. F., 1901
BALTHROP, Joe, 1969-70-71
BANDEMIER, Bill, 1973
BARACCA, Marty, 1960-61
BARBISH, Bill "Moose", 1951-52-53
BARKSDALE, Val, 1977-78
BARNES, W. O., 1896
BARNES, William "Billy", 1937-38-39
BARNHILL, John H., 1925-26-27
BARRON, David, 1974-75-76-77
BARTHOLOMEW, Sam, 1937-38-39
BASS, Ben, 1969
BATES, Jim, 1966-67
BATES, William M., 1892
BATEY, Jack S., 1924
BAUCOM, Tom, 1967-68-69
BAUGH, William M., 1893
BAYER, J. T., 1909
BAYER, S. D., 1913-14-15
BAYLESS, John D., 1931-32-33
BEARD, Ed, 1961
BECKER, Hubert, 1947
BECKLER, David, 1970
BEENE, F. R., 1906
BEENE, Jones C. Jr., 1901-02-03-04-05
BEENE, L. Phillip, 1928-29-30
BEENE, Patton, 1901-02
BEHRENS, John, 1975-76
BELL, C. A., 1897
BELL, J. D., 1897
BELL, L. L., 1896
BELLIS, Leonard, 1945
BELLMONT, L. T., 1940
BENDER, Joe, 1949, Mgr.
BENNETT, Andy, 1969-71
BENNETT, William R. "Bill", 1956-57
BENNETT, Tom L., 1969-70-71
BENTON, Steve, 1975, Mgr.
BERGMIER, Ron, 1947-48-49
BERKHAM, Rick, 1977
BERNARD, George R., 1893
BERRY, James, 1978
BEUTEL, Jim, 1954-55
BEVANS, Mike, 1968-69-70
BEVIS, William "Billy", 1942-44-45
BIBEE, M. Bert, 1932-33
BIBLE, Alvah, 1970
BIRD, Terry, 1964-65-66
BLACKSTOCK, William "Bill", 1951
BLAIR, Hal Edward, 1919-20-21
BLAIR, Reuben Moore, 1919
BLAKE, Tom, 1945
BLANKENSHIP, Warren, 1959-60-61
BLESSING, Hugh, 1944
BOLTON, Chris, 1977-78
BOND, Robert U., 1924
BONE, William "Bill", 1923-24
BORDINGER, Don, 1951
BORING, Frank "Boomer", 1949-50-51
BOURCHES, Joe E., 1893
BOURKARD, Harrison O., 1934-35
BOURNE, T. P., 1900
BOWMAN, Larry, 1974
BOYD, Samuel B., 1893
BOYNTON, John, 1965-66-67
BRACKETT, H. B. "Deke", 1931-32-33
BRADFORD, Jim B., 1919-20
BRADY, David, 1973-74-75-76
BRANCH, Rufus C., 1910-11-12
BRANDAU, Arthur A., 1942
BRANDT, Frederic "Fritz" P., 1928-29-30
BRANN, Ray O., 1958
BREEDING, Ken, 1960-61
BRENGLE, Bobby, 1952-53-54
BRIDGES, Hal, 1956
BRIDGES, Jesse, 1977
BRIXEY, Tom, 1948-49
BRONSON, Tommy E., 1955-56-57
BROOKS, Albert O., 1932, Mgr.
BROOME, W. Lloyd, 1938-40
BROUG, J. L., 1900-01
BROWN, Bob G., 1960
BROWN, C. D., 1892
BROWN, Earle W., 1939-45
BROWN, Eddie, 1971-72-73
BROWN, Fred "Bo", 1923-24-25
BROWN, Herbert T., 1928-29-30
BROWN, James P., 1892-93
BROWN, Kenny, 1960-61-62
BROWN, W. C., 1906
BROWN, W. P., 1908
BROWNE, David, 1968-69-70
BROZOWSKI, John, 1969
BRYAN, C. L., 1899
BRYSON, G. G., 1899
BRYSON, William J., 1940

BUCKINGHAM, H. L., 1910
BUCKINGHAM, T. N. "Nash", 1901-02
BULLARD, Ralph, 1974-75-76-77
BURDETTE, A. M., 1906-07
BURDETTE, George M., 1923-24-25
BURGESS, Robert E., 1927
BURKLOW, Sammy, 1956-57-58
BURNETT, Jon, 1973
BURNHAM, Bruce, 1954-55-56
BURTON, Lee Otis, 1978
BUSH, Wayne, 1962-63
BUTCHER, Elvin, 1925-26-27
BUTLER, Dan, 1951-53
BUTLER, Johnny W., 1939-40-41
BYBEE, Joe T., 1927
BYRD, Ray I., 1951-52

C

CAFEGO, George, 1937-38-39
CALDWELL, Chan, 1945-46-47
CALDWELL, J. A., 1902-03-04-05
CALDWELL, J. H., Jr., 1903-04-05
CALDWELL, Lamar, 1970-71-72
CALDWELL, Mike, 1972-73-74
CALLAHAN, P. H., 1914
CALLAWAY, Richard, 1967-68-69
CAMERON, A. D. "Scotty", 1912-14-15
CAMERON, Bill, 1963-64-65
CAMPBELL, David, 1971-72-73
CAMPBELL, Earl, 1950-51-52
CAMPBELL, L. Roe, 1920-21-22-24
CAMPBELL, M. R., 1896-99
CANALE, Frank, 1962
CANALE, George, 1960-61-62
CANALE, Whit, 1962-64
CANINI, Pat, 1963
CANNON, Gary, 1960-61
CANNON, R. L., 1892
CANTRELL, Edd M., 1953-54-55-56
CARETHERS, Paul, 1972-73-74
CARMICHAEL, Nick, 1971-72-73
CARPENTER, Don, 1969-70
CARR, Hilrey, 1966
CARROLL, Alonzo M. Jr. "Goat", 1911-12-13-14
CARROLL, Steve, 1967-68-69
CARTER, Al, 1955-56-67
CARTER, George, 1950
CARTER, Howard, 1976
CARTER, J. W., 1959-60-61
CARTWRIGHT, Jim, 1958-59-60
CATES, Clifton B., 1914-15
CHADNOCK, John, 1944-45
CHADWELL, James J., 1942
CHADWICK, Dennis, 1970-71-72
CHADWICK, Walter, 1965-66-67
CHAMBERS, Harold, 1960
CHANCEY, Ralph E., 1946-47-48-49
CHANCEY, Steve, 1971-72-73
CHANDLER, Allen E., 1942
CHANDLER, H. C. 1913
CHAPMAN, D. C., 1896
CHAPMAN, Ray M., 1953
CHAVIS, Johnny, 1977-78
CHILDERS, Ray, 1960, Mgr.
CHRISTIAN, Bill, 1977
CHRISTMAS, E. K., 1924
CIFERS, Ed, 1938-39-49
CIFERS, Robert G. 1941-42
CISSELL, Don, 1959-60
CLABO, Neil, 1972-73-74
CLABO, Phil, 1973-74-75
CLAXTON, J. O. "Jim", 1932-33-34
CLAY, Boyd, 1937-38-39
CLAYTON, Rufus, 1922
CLEMENTS, H. H., 1930, Mgr.
CLEMMENS, Bob B., 1921
CLEMMER, James H., 1930-31
CLONINGER, Bob O., 1952-53
COCHRAN, E. R., 1906
CODY, J. R., 1907
COFFEY, Charles, 1953-54-55
COFFMAN, Leonard, 1937-38-39
COGGINS, Roger, 1948-49
COLE, Bill, 1973-74-75
COLE, Harry A., 1910
COLEMAN, James "Jimmy" L., 1938-39-40
COLEMAN, Lee, 1969
COLEMAN, Wayne A., 1960-61-62
COLHOUN, Adams, 1897
COLLIER, Harris T., 1893
COLQUITT, Craig, 1975-76-77
CONE, Steve, 1973-74
CONNELLY, Robert C., 1941
COOPER, J. S., 1901-03, Mgr.
COOPER, W. C., 1948-49-50
CORNICK, T. R., 1899
COSTELLO, Mike, 1959
COTTON, Jackie, 1963-64-65
COTTRELL, C. B., 1907
COVINGTON, C. L., 1903
COX, J. T., 1901-02
COX, John B., 1891-92
COX, William G., 1929-31
CRADDOCK, Charles E., 1911, Mgr.
CRAIG, George P., 1933-34-35
CRAIG, T. E., 1899
CRAWFORD, Denver, 1942-46-47
CRAWFORD, Edwin S., 1934-35
CRAWFORD, Frank J., 1935-36-37
CRAWFORD, S. D., 1901-02
CREASEY, George, 1945, Mgr.
CROSS, Roy L., 1942-45
CROWSON, Larry, 1951
CRUZE, Kyle "Buddy", 1955-56
CUMMINGS, Charles L., Jr., 1949
CUMMINGS, Charles L., Sr., 1919-21
CUNNINGHAM, Mike, 1976
CVETNICK, John, 1954

D

DAFFER, Ted, 1949-50-51
DALTON, Benny, 1968-69
DALTON, Bob, 1961-62-63
DALTON, Ray, 1962
DALTON, Terry, 1966-67-68
DANYCHUK, Bill, 1964
DARTY, Landon, 1955-56-57
DAVIS, Bob, 1949-50-51
DAVIS, John "Tex", 1951-52
DAVIS, Kevin, 1974-75-76
DAVIS, Steve, 1977-78
DAVIS, Willie, 1941, Mgr.
DAWSON, D. A, 1912-13
DEAVER, Everett E. H., 1924
DECKER, James Quinn, 1928-29-30
DeFILLIPPO, Joe, 1975
DeHART, Dick, 1966
DeLONG, Ken, 1967-68-69
DeLONG, Steve, 1962-63-64
DeLUCCA, Jerry, 1954-55
DEMASTUS, Mike, 1974-75
DeMELFI, Joe, 1962
DENBO, Don, 1968-69-70
DENLINGER, H. K., 1891
DENNEY, Austin, 1965-66
DERRYBERRY, F. Woodrow, 1935-36
DERRYBERRY, O. Merton, 1930-31
DERRYBERRY, W. Everett, 1925-27
DERWIN, Jim, 1963
DICKENS, Phil W., 1934-35-36
DIETZEN, Walter N., 1919-20-21
DINGES, D. C., 1907
DINGUS, Vic, 1967-68-69
DISNEY, Theodore E. "Ty.", 1929-30-31
DISSPAYNE, Elmer, 1939
DITMORE, Frank M., 1934-35
DITMORE, J. M., 1958
DOAK, Alf, 1920
DOBELSTEIN, Robert, 1942-44-45
DOBELSTEIN, Russ, 1944-45-48
DOCKERY, Rex, 1963
DODD, Robert Lee "Bobby", 1928-29-30
DODSON, Richard B., 1925-26-27
DONAHUE, Ken, 1949-50
DONALDSON, R. C., 1896
DONALDSON, W. J., 1906
DONELSON, A. J., Jr., 1911-12
DOOLIN, Phil, 1973
DORSEY, Albert, 1965-67
DORSEY, Richard T., 1932-33-34
DOUGHERTY, Joe Q., 1933-35-36
DOUGHERTY, Nathan W., 1906-07-08-09
DOUGLAS, A. H., 1901-02
DOWLING, Clark, 1932-33, Mgr.
DOWNEY, Pat, 1962-63
DROST, Ray, 1942-46-47
DRUMMOND, Keith, 1954-55
DRUMMONDS, Ronnie, 1968-69-70
DUDLEY, Bubba, 1969
DUNCAN, Alan, 1978
DUNCAN, Clark, 1977-78
DUNCAN, Edwin Cheek, 1936-37-38
DUVALL, Jim, 1975-76

E

EARL, Richard, 1970-71-72
EBLEN, R. Hooper, 1935
EDMISTON, Don "Speedy", 1939-40-41
EDMONDS, H. M., 1896-97-1900
EDMONDS, Oscar, 1944
EDWARDS, Anthony, 1969-70-71
EDWARDS, Skip, 1964-66
ELDRED, Ralph E., 1936-37-38
ELDRIDGE, Robert "Dink", 1939-40, Mgr.
ELKAS, Ray, 1948-49
ELKINS, L. E., 1910
ELLIOTT, Frank S., 1925-27
ELLIS, Carl, 1963-64
ELLIS, Dick, 1967
ELLIS, J. B., 1931-32-33
ELLSPERMANN, Steve, 1966
ELMORE, James W., 1925-26-27
EMANUEL, Frank, 1963-64-65
EMBRY, Jim, 1974
EMENDORFER, Bill, 1970-71-72
EMMONS, Bobby, 1976-77-78
EMORY, Bill, 1915-16
EMORY, David, 1957
ENSLEY, Jerry, 1960-61-62
EPPERSON, Harry G., 1935-36
ERNSBERGER, Dick, 1949-50-51
ETTER, Gene, 1958-59-60
EVANS, Joe, 1919-20
EVEY, Dick, 1961-62-63

F

FAIR, Dale, 1974
FAIRCLOTH, Mallon, 1961-62-63
FAIRFIELD, C. D., 1897
FALCO, Joe, 1963-64
FARRAR, Scot, 1976-77
FAUST, Hugh D., 1930
FEATHERS, Beattie, 1931-32-33
FELTY, Gene, 1949-50
FENDER, M. W., 1912
FERRIS, Charles E., 1892
FIELDEN, Alan, 1946-47-48-49
FILSON, Dave, 1968-69
FINCH, H. B., 1902, Mgr.
FINCH, Kelsey, 1976-77-78
FINNEY, James I., 1928-29
FISHER, Bob, 1951-52-53
FISHER, Buddy, 1961-62-63
FISHER, James C., 1892-93
FISHER, Jody, 1941-42
FISHER, Tom, 1964-65
FITCHPATRICK, Tim, 1973-74-75
FLENNIKEN, Hector, 1933, Mgr.
FLORA, Charles, 1949-50
FLOWERS, George, 1924
FLOWERS, Richmond, 1966-67-68
FONDE, C. H., 1910-11-12
FORD, Howard, 1931, Mgr.
FOURMAN, Nate, 1950, Mgr.
FOWLER, Harley, 1908, Mgr.
FOWLER, W. S. "Monk", 1947
FOX, D. N., 1904
FOX, R. E., 1904
FOXALL, Joe, 1960-61-62
FOXX, Bob, 1938-39-40
FOXX, Frank, 1976-77-78
FRANCIS, Hugh, 1919
FRANCIS, J. H., 1910
FRANCIS, John, 1941-46-47
FRANK, Milton, 1931-32-33
FRANK, Richard, 1936, Mgr.
FRANKLIN, Coy, 1958
FRANKLIN, John, 1930-31-32
FRANKLIN, L. D., 1908-09
FRANKLIN, Mack, 1951-52-53
FRANKLIN, Robbie, 1964-65-66
FRAZIER, Bobby, 1963-64-65
FRENCH, F. D., 1900
FRERE, Rob, 1970-71-72
FRERE, Ron, 1972
FROST, Ken, 1959-60
FUGATE, Stanley, 1964-65-66, Mgr.
FULLER, Ben F., 1927-28-29
FULLER, C. J., 1902-03
FULMER, Phillip, 1969-70-71
FULTON, Charles, 1965-66-67
FULTON, Robert W., 1935-36
FUSON, Clyde, 1942

G

GAFFNEY, James T., 1941-42
GAINES, Greg, 1978

GALBREATH, John, 1926, Mgr.
GALIFFA, Art, 1964-66
GALLAGHER, Joe, 1973-74-75-76
GAMBLE, A. M., 1899
GAMBLE, R. M., 1901-02
GAMMAGE, Elliott, 1965-66-67
GANN, GENE, 1960-61
GARNER, Hugh, 1952-53-54
GAUT, David, 1907, Mgr.
GAUZE, J. W., 1911
GAYLES, Mike, 1974-75-76
GAYLOR, Jim, 1975-76-77
GEARING, Paul, 1946-47-48-49
GEBHARDT, W. T., 1892
GEISLER, J. V., 1911-12
GENTRY, Mack, 1964-65-66
GETAZ, David, 1916, Mgr.
GETTEYS, P. E., 1902
GETTYS, R. E, 1899
GIDDENS, Clarence E., 1934-35
GLASCOTT, Bob, 1956
GLASS, Glenn, 1959-60-61
GLEAVES, Bob, 1956
GLOVER, Jimmy, 1965-66-67
GODZAK, Ed, 1952
GOLD, Bill, 1941-42-46
GONCE, J. W., 1903
GOOCH, Mike, 1965-67-68
GOODRICH, Guinn B., 1932-33
GORDON, Bobby, 1955-56-57
GORDY, John, 1954-55-56
GOWDY, Jerry, 1962-63
GRAHAM, Conrad, 1970-71-72
GRAHAM, J. H., 1910
GRAHAM, Joe, 1964-67
GRANT, H. P., 1905, Mgr.
GRANT, Stan, 1976
GRATZ, Bobby, 1963-64-65
GRAVES, Samuel Ray, 1940-41
GRAVITT, Mitchell, 1973
GRAY, Glenn, 1963-64-65
GREEN, Louis A., 1926
GREEN, T. B. 1900-01-02-03
GREENWOOD, B. J., 1912
GREER, R. A., 1899
GRIESBACH, Bob, 1952
GRIFFITH, Dave, 1952-53
GRIM, Joe, 1901-02-03
GRIM, W. H., 1904
GRIZZARD, Kenneth, 1921-22
GRUBB, Jim, 1956-57
GRUBB, Wayne, 1958-59-60
GRUBLE, John, 1947-48-49-50
GUDALIS, Bill, 1958
GUDGER, V. L., 1902-03
GUNTHER, J. A., 1906
GUST, RON, 1952-53-54

H

HACKMAN, J. S. "Buddy", 1928-29-30
HAGY, Everett, 1896
HAHN, Jimmy C., 1966-67-68
HAHN, Jimmy R., 1949-50-51
HAIR, Sammy, 1972-73-74
HAMBAUGH, P. C, 1915-16
HAMILTON, H. T., 1900
HAMMOND, Bill, 1962-63
HANCOCK, Anthony, 1978
HANNAH, Carl, 1956
HARGISS, Joseph E., 1893
HARKLEROAD, Rod, 1966
HARKNESS, W. S. "Bill", 1923-24-25-26
HARP, Thomas "Red", 1935-36-37
HARPER, Reggie, 1977-78
HARRIS, Jack, 1935, Mgr.
HARRISON, W. R., 1899, Mgr.
HASLAM, Jim, 1950-51-52
HATCHER, Adolphus H. "Buck", 1915-16-19-20
HATCHER, Bill, 1923
HATCHER, O. C., 1916
HATLEY, Ralph L., 1932-33-34
HAVELY, Casco, 1961-62-63, Mgr.
HAYES, Joe Black, 1935-36-37
HAYLEY, Samuel B., 1911-12-13
HAYNES, Samuel H., 1893
HAYS, Robert L., 1891
HAZEN, T. Flem, 1914, Mgr.
HEATH, Ricky, 1973
HEDGECOCK, Leland, 1922, Mgr.
HELTON, L. T., 1960-62
HENDERSON, Joseph Ray "Possum", 1916-19
HENDRICKS, Gerald S., 1936-37-38
HENSLEY, Tom, 1952-53
HERNDON, L. Houston, 1928-29
HERRING, Melvin G., 1936-37
HERRMANN, Gary, 1951
HERZBRUN, Lon, 1955-56-57
HEYDRICK, Paul D., 1929
HIBBARD, Bob, 1954-55-56
HICKMAN, Herman, 1929-30-31
HICKS, Bob, 1947
HIDINGER, Lee, 1973-74-75
HIGGINBOTHAM, Roger, 1974
HILL, Claude, 1946-47-48
HILL, Gaylon, 1970-71-72
HILL, Jimmy, 1948-49-50
HILLMAN, Bill, 1942-46
HITE-SMITH, Van O., 1896
HODGE, Bonnie, 1937
HOLLOPETER, C. E., 1899-1900-01
HOLLOWAY, Condredge, 1972-73-74
HOLLOWAY, Jerry, 1967-68
HOLOHAN, Francis, 1950-51-52
HOLSCLAW, Claude, 1944
HOLT, Laird, 1929-30-31
HOLT, Lemonte, 1978
HOLT, Robert "Tarzan", 1920-21-22-23
HONEA, Ken, 1961-62-63
HOOD, Merlyn, 1970-71
HOOSER, P. Hobart "Hobe", 1927
HORNER, Amos J., 1927-28
HOUGH, Joe, 1976-77
HOWARD, Chip, 1971-72-73
HOWARD, Ermal, 1946-47-48
HOWE, Bubba, 1954-55-56
HOWELL, Frank, 1970-71
HUBBARD, Bill, 1953-54
HUBBARD, Hal, 1951-52-53
HUBBELL, Franklin S. "Bud", 1941-42-46
HUBBELL, Webster E., 1941
HUBBUCK, Carl, 1937
HUDDLESTON, Ben, 1946-47
HUDSON, John Bill, 1960-61-62
HUESER, Vernon, 1946-47-48
HUFFMAN, Dick, 1942-46
HUG, Paul N., 1928-29-30
HUMPHREYS, Cecil C. "Sonny", 1933-34-35
HUNDLEY, Elmo E., 1927
HUNEYCUTT, Ralph, 1947-48-49
HUNT, George, 1969-70-71
HUNT, Walter, 1935, Mgr.
HUNTER, George L., 1936-37-38
HURLEY, Leonard F., 1920-21-22
HUSBAND, Tom, 1958-60
HUST, Al, 1940-41-42
HUST, Emil R., 1939-41
HUTCHINSON, Byron, 1942
HYDE, Jerry, 1951-52-53

I

IJAMS, Howard A., 1891-92-93
INGLETT, Paul, 1959-60
INGRAM, Brian, 1977-78
INGRAM, Phil, 1978
IRWIN, Tim, 1978

J

JACKSON, Howard, 1956-57-58
JAMES, Roland, 1976-77-78
JANES, Palmer, 1919-20-21
JARED, W. Bennett, 1915
JARNAGIN, F. W., 1899-1900-01
JARVIS, Ron, 1965-66-67
JASPER, Bill, 1949-50-51
JEFFRIES, Danny, 1970-71-72
JELLICORSE, Reggie, 1964-65
JENKINS, Danny "Pert", 1975-76-77
JERNIGAN, Tom, 1967-68
JESTER, Mike, 1978
JOHNSON, Bill, 1955-56-57
JOHNSON, Bob, 1965-66-67
JOHNSON, Carl, 1970-71-72
JOHNSON, Frank, 1905
JOHNSON, Harold, 1950
JOHNSON, Howard, 1926-27-29
JOHNSON, L. B. "Farmer", 1926-27-28
JOHNSON, Paul, 1973-74-75
JOHNSON, Stewart, 1946, Mgr.
JOHNSON, Tom, 1963
JOHNSON, Tom D., 1970-71-72
JOHNSON, W. C., 1906-07-08-09-10
JOHNSTON, James G., 1928-29
JONES, Frank D., 1926
JONES, Greg, 1974-75-76-77
JONES, Kenny, 1978
JONES, Mike E., 1967-68-69
JONES, Mike S., 1971
JONES, Philip E., 1924
JONES, Richard H., 1923
JONES, Sam W., 1923-24-26
JONES, Wilbert, 1978
JORDAN, Dick, 1942-46
JUMPER, Tommy, 1950

K

KASETA, Vince, 1949-50-51
KEENER, Samuel, 1906
KEEVER, Wade, 1934
KEFAUVER, Estes, 1922-23
KELL, Chip, 1968-69-70
KELLER, John, 1968-69-70
KELLY, Farmer, 1911-12-13-14
KELLY, Van W., 1936-37
KEMP, C. M., 1915
KENNEDY, Edwin M., 1919
KENNERLY, Robert, 1927, Mgr.
KERN, R. A., 1905
KERR, R. V., 1911-12-13-14
KESTERTON, T. O., 1909
KILE, Jack, 1959
KILLIAN, Gene, 1971-72-73
KINCAID, Bill, 1956
KINER, Steve, 1967-68-69
KING, Harry F., 1922-23-24
KING, William, B., 1941
KINGMAN, Dan, 1901, Mgr.
KIPP, S. S., 1909
KLARER, Rudolph "Rudy", 1941-42
KNAPPE, E. C., 1900
KOHLHASE, Charles E, 1929-30-31
KOLEAS, George L., 1935-36
KOLENIK, Vic, 1951-52
KOLINSKY, Frank, 1955-56-57
KOZAR, Andy, 1950-51-52
KRAUSE, Dick, 1958
KREIS, Gary, 1967-68-69
KREMSER, Karl, 1967-68
KROUSE, Henry W., 1932-34-35

L

LABACH, Joe E., 1893
LACORE, John O., 1893
LaCOSTE, Kelley, 1967
LAMBERT, Ken, 1971-72
LANE, Hunter, 1919-20-21-22
LANTER, Bill, 1956-57
LaSORSA, Mike, 1958-59-60
LASSITER, Robert, 1970-72-73
LATHAM, F. S., Jr., 1909-10
LATHROP, Herbert A., 1891
LAURICELLA, Hank, 1949-50-51
LAVIN, Robert, 1924
LAW, Allen, 1944
LAWDER, Rynd, Jr., 1893
LEACH, J. Walker, 1905-06-07-08
LEACH, Sonny, 1970-71-72
LEACHMAN, Lamar, 1952-53-55
LEAKE, David, 1963-64-65
LEAKE, Don, 1958-59-60
LEDFORD, Dennis Marshall, 1941
LEE, Alan, 1974
LEFFLER, Willie T., 1936-37
LETNER, Cotton, 1958-59-60
LEVINE, Sam, 1936-37
LINDSAY, Charles, 1919-21
LINDSAY, Robert M. "Rus", 1911-12-13-14
LINEBARIER, Chip, 1976-77-78
LIPPE, William T., 1934-35
LIPSCOMB, Paul, 1942
LIS, Stan, 1952
LITTLE, Joseph P. "Joe", 1936-37-38
LITTLEFORD, Hal, 1947-48-49
LLOYD, Owen C., 1941-42
LOCKETT, W. E., 1911
LOGAN, J. G., 1899-1900
LOGAN, Kim, 1975-76-77
LOGAN, Nicholas E., 1893
LONG, R. A., 1942-45-46
LONGMIRE, Wayne, 1900-01
LOTHROP, D. B., 1915
LOUCKS, J. C., 1906-07-08
LOVE, Emmon, 1971-72-73
LOVINGOOD, Frank, 1934
LOWE, Andy, 1916-21
LOWE, J. G., 1922-23-24-25
LOWE, Jim, 1963-65

LOWE, Theodore, 1927
LOWE, W. O. "Chink", 1914-15-16-19
LUCCI, Mike, 1960-61
LUCK, James K., 1915-16
LUKOWSKI, Joe, 1957-58-59
LUND, Bob, 1945-46-47-48
LUTTRELL, Bill, 1938-39-40
LYMAN, Elbert J., 1896-1900
LYONS, Vernon, 1950-51

M

MADDEN, L. J., 1911
MAIURE, Joe, 1950-51-52
MAJOR, Mark, 1944-45-46-47
MAJORS, Bill, 1958-59-60
MAJORS, Bobby, 1969-70-71
MAJORS, John, 1954-55-56
MALONE, Robert, 1976-78
MALONEY, Frank, 1896-97
MANKIN, Carr, 1892
MANNING, John, 1944-45
MAPLES, Talmadge R. (Sheriff), 1931-32-33
MARFIELD, George R., 1892
MARINO, Rick, 1966-67-68
MARK, Alton S., 1931-32-33
MARKLOFF, Dave, 1949
MARKS, Arthur, 1952, Mgr.
MARQUART, Cliff, 1959-60-61
MARREN, Bill, 1977-78
MARSH, Pat, 1971, Mgr.
MARTIN, Fred, 1963-64
MARTIN, Ray, 1951-52
MARVIN, Mickey, 1973-74-75-76
MASSEY, R. H., 1910
MATTOX, Bruce, 1961-62
MAUCK, Mike, 1974-75-76
MAURIELLO, Bob, 1966
MAXWELL, Jim, 1970-71
MAY, W. E. "Bill", 1913-14-15
MAYER, Eugene S., 1930-31
MAYES, J. C., 1908
MAYES, Vin, 1966
MAYOCK, Dick, 1952
McALLESTER, Sam J., 1903-04
McALLISTER, W. L., 1909
McARTHUR, Dave E., 1925-26-27
McCABE, Willis, 1919
McCARREN, William, 1936-37-38
McCARTNEY, Ronnie, 1973-74-75
McCLAIN, Hubert, 1961
McCLAIN, Lester, 1968-69-70
McCLELLAN, Bob "Skeet", 1928, Mgr.
McCLENEGHAN, Frank, 1921, Mgr.
McCLOUD, Ted, 1959-62
McCLUNG, C. J., 1904, Mgr.
McCLURE, Robert L., 1929, Mgr.
McCLURE, W. K. "Bill", 1912-13-15
McCOLLUM, Clarence H., 1907-08
McCONNELL, E. M., 1900
McCORD, Darris, 1952-53-54
McCROSKEY, Frank, 1952-53
McDONALD, Jim, 1966-67-68
McDOUGAL, Ed, 1974
McEVER, Gene, 1928-29-31
McFADDEN, Bud, 1955
McGEEHAN, Chick, 1968
McGLOTHIN, Bill, 1970-71-72
McGUIRE, R. L., 1910-11-12
McKEEN, E. Allyn, 1925-26-27
McKELVY, Jerry, 1965
McLEAN, Evan A., 1912-13-14-15
McLEARY, Don, 1968-69-70
McMEANS, Neal, 1966-67-68
McNAMARA, Jim, 1966
McPHERSON, C. L., 1932
McQUADY, Claude, 1954
McREE, Kenny, 1945
McSPADDEN, Malcolm, 1914
McWILLIAMS, John, 1954
MEEK, Bill, 1940-41-42
MELAS, Alex, 1966
MELTON, Gary, 1966-67
MENESES, Oscar, 1944
MERRITT, J. B., 1968
MESEROLL, Norman, 1946-47-48-49
MEYER, Charles, 1951
MICHELS, John, 1950-51-52
MIDDLETON, Albert, 1932
MILAM, Kevin, 1970
MILCHIN, Jerry, 1961-62-63
MILLER, Ben, 1944-45
MILLS, Joe, 1973-74
MILLS, Johnny, 1964-65-66
MILNER, Orvis, 1946-47
MINER, Jim, 1947-48-49
MINNICK, Hagen, 1948, Mgr.
MITCHELL, Charles T., 1941-42-46
MITCHELL, D. K., 1931
MITCHELL, Stan, 1963-64-65
MITCHELL, Steve, 1971-72-73
MIXON, Manley, 1968-69-70
MOELLER, Gene, 1951-52
MOLASKEY, Ron, 1965
MOLCK, Ricky, 1971-72
MOHRMAN, Mike, 1972-73-74
MOLINSKI, Ed, 1938-39-40
MONDELLI, Jim, 1967-68
MOOERS, Charles A., 1891
MOORE, Charles C., Jr., 1891-92
MOORE, Gary, 1977-78
MOORE, Jeff, 1975-76-77-78
MOORE, Owen Bud, 1920
MOORE, Terry, 1972-73-74-75
MORAN, Charley B., 1897
MOREL, Bobby, 1964-65-66
MORGAN, Ed, 1950-51-52
MORGAN, Stanley, 1973-74-75-76
MORRIS, B. Y., 1922-23
MORRIS, W. W., 1915-16
MORROW, Russ, 1944-45
MORTON, Bobby, 1962-63
MORTON, Robert, 1975
MOSES, Fred J., 1933-34-35
MOSS, Ray, 1956-57-59
MULLINIKS, Jack, 1955, Mgr.
MULLOY, Richard, 1939-40-41
MUNRO, Colin, 1951-53
MURDIC, Jon, 1972-73-74
MURPHY, David, 1966-67
MURPHY, John, 1975-76-77-78
MURRELL, W. J., 1911
MURRELL, William, 1936
MURRIEL, Martin, 1977-78
MUTTER, Mitch, 1967
MYERS, Andy, 1950-51-52
MYERS, James, A. "Jim", 1941-42-46

N

NAUMOFF, Paul, 1964-65-66
NEAL, G. F., 1896
NEAL, Ray, 1947, Mgr.
NEEDHAM, Kenneth L. "Shorty" 1933-34-35
NEFF, Herbert Artie, 1922-23-24-25
NETTLES, Ray, 1969-70-71
NEWMAN, Fred, 1939-40
NEWMAN, W. M., 1896-99-1900
NEWTON, H. R., 1909, Mgr.
NEYLAND, Bob, Jr., 1952-53
NICHOLS, Jack, 1960-61
NICHOLSON, Jacob H. "Jake", 1920-21
NICKLA, Ed, 1951-52
NICKLIN, Strang, 1896-97
NOEL, Henry W., 1940-41
NOONAN, Jim, 1976-77-78
NORTH, Lee, 1978
NOWLING, William E., 1940-41-42

O

OLDHAM, Donnie, 1977
OLEKSIAK, Pat, 1952-54
OLMSTEAD, H. S., 1899
O'NEAL, Art, 1963
ORR, Bunny, 1959-60-61
OVERBY, Glenn, 1920
OVERHOLT, Bobby, 1957
OVERTON, Mike, 1973-74-75-76

P

PAFFORD, R. W., 1904-05
PAGE, David, 1973-74-75
PAIDOUSIS, Mike, 1944-45-46
PALMER, Edwin C. 1933-34-35
PARKER, S. Y., 1903-04-05
PARMAN, D. C., 1910
PARSONS, David, 1974-75-76
PARSONS, Newt, 1957-58, Mgr.
PARTIN, Maxwell R., 1941-45-46
PATTERSON, Bobby, 1967-68
PATTERSON, Don, 1958-59-60
PATTERSON, Jack, 1963-64-65
PATY, John M., 1962-63-64
PATY, John W., 1934-35
PAYNE, Harold "Herky", 1949-50-51
PEARCE, Lanny, 1968
PEARMAN, Bill, 1947-49-50-51
PEAY, Johnny, 1956, Mgr.
PEDERSEN, Arnold, 1962-63
PEEL, Ike, 1939-40-41
PEERY, Arnall, 1906-07-08-09
PENLAND, J. D., 1910
PERKINS, Marion, 1936-37
PERSINGER, Tim, 1969
PETRELLA, Bob, 1963-64-65
PETRUZZI, Leo, 1932-33
PETTWAY, William D., 1925, Mgr.
PHILLIPS, Ed, 1963
PHILLIPS, Frederick H., 1893
PHILLIPS, Greg, 1975-76
PHILLIPS, Jimmie R., 1920-22
PHILLIPS, Marvin, 1958-59-69
PHIPPS, F. L., 1910, Mgr.
PICK, Jack M., 1934-35
PICKENS, Richard, 1966-67-68
PIERCE, Phil, 1969-70-71
PIERCE, W. W., 1899
PIKE, Patrick "Buddy", 1944-45-46
POLEY, David, 1973-74
POLOFSKY, Gordon, 1949-50-51
POOLE, Steve, 1973-74-75
POPE, Jackie, 1960
PORTER, James W., 1934-36
PORTER, Steve, 1976-77-78
POTTS, Tommy, 1956-57-58
POUNDERS, Louis E., 1932-33-34
POWELL, Don, 1923
POWELL, Jim, 1942-46-47-48
POWELL, John, 1951-52-53
POWERS, Eddy, 1975-76-77
POWERS, Rick, 1976-77
POWERS, William K., 1919
PRATER, Tracy, 1938, Mgr.
PRICE, Mike, 1966-67-68
PRICE, Royal, 1942-46-47
PRIEST, Tim, 1968-69-70
PRIEST, Tom, 1953-55
PRITCHARD, Ken, 1962-63
PROCTOR, E. B., 1904-05-06
PROCTOR, J. B., 1946-47-48
PRUETT, Kenneth, 1949-50
PUKI, Craig, 1975-76-78
PULLIAM, Robert, 1972-73-74

Q

QUILLEN, Ford, 1958

R

RABENSTEIN, Russ, 1973-74-75
RADER, Charles, 1954-55-56
RAGSDALE, T. M., 1905-06
RAINEY, Horace "Red", 1913-14
RAMSEY, Allen C., 1936-37
RAMSEY, R. W., 1909
RAULSTON, C. S., 1909
RAYBURN, Virgil H., 1930-31-32
RECHICHAR, Bert, 1949-50-51
REDDING, Jack, 1944
REED, C. H., 1892
REEDER, Claude S., 1906
REGEN, Dick, 1944
REGISTER, Arch, 1921
REID, Junior, 1977-78
REINEKE, Charles W., 1928-29-30
REVIERE, Dee, 1976-77-78
REYNOLDS, Art, 1971-72-73
REYNOLDS, Jack, 1967-68-69
REYNOLDS, Mike, 1964
RHEA, Charles McClung, 1891
RICE, Alvin, 1937
RICE, Charles, P., 1925-26
RICE, E. B., 1909
RICE, J. C., 1897
RICHARDS, Larry, 1960-61-62
RICHARDSON, Jim, 1973-74
RICHARDSON, W. A., 1903-04
RIKE, Jim, 1938-39
RING, J. J., 1906-09
RING, N. S. "Ned", 1915-16
RITCHEY, Jim, 1954
ROACH, Gary, 1975
ROBERTS, Louis T., 1928-29-30
ROBERTSON, Sam, 1963-64-65
ROBINSON, Charles, 1956
ROBINSON, Dick, 1953-54, Mgr.
ROBINSON, Edwin G., 1893
ROBINSON, Fred, 1923-24
ROBINSON, Harvey L., 1931-32
ROBINSON, Steve, 1968-69-70
ROBINSON, Tom, 1923-24-25
ROBISON, Charles W., 1916-19-20
ROE, Joe, 1957
ROGAN, C. B., 1896-97

ROGERS, E. N., 1908-09
ROMINE, Dave, 1940
ROSE, Roy Eugene, 1933-34-35
ROSENFELDER, Charles, 1966-67-68
ROSS, G. W., 1897
ROTELLA, Al, 1942-46-47
ROTELLA, Jamie, 1970-71-72
ROTROFF, Roger, 1951-52-53
ROWAN, Bill Joe, 1946-47
ROWE, Gary, 1974-75-76
ROWSEY, Thomas, 1975-76
RUBIN, W. P., 1911
RUDDER, Bill, 1971-72-73
RUDDER, David, 1978
RUSHIN, Don, 1954
RUSSAS, Al, 1946-47-48
RUSSELL, Don, 1919
RYAN, Pat, 1977

S

SABATO, Al, 1942
SADLER, Ken, 1958-59
SANDERS, William, 1937
SANDERSON, Glenn, 1934, Mgr.
SANDERSON, Ken, 1976
SANDLIN, Bobby, 1956-57-58
SATTERFIELD, Larry, 1972-73-74
SAUNDERS, W. Raymond, 1929-30-31
SAXTON, N. L., 1907-08
SCHAFFER, Joe, 1957-58-59
SCHENK, C. G., 1900
SCHLEIDEN, Roy, 1944
SCHNEITMAN, Dale, 1978
SCHOLES, Charles, 1954
SCHUBERT, H. A., 1920, Mgr.
SCHULTZ, Don, 1958
SCHWANGER, Ted, 1952-53
SCHWARTZINGER, Jimmy, 1940-41
SCOTT, Bob, 1953-54-55
SCOTT, Bobby, 1968-69-70
SEIVERS, Larry, 1974-75-76
SEKANOVICH, Dan, 1951-52-53
SELLERS, Larry, 1972, Mgr.
SEVERANCE, Charles, 1959-60
SHAFER, Bo, 1956-57-58
SHAFFER, David, 1971-72-73
SHANNON, H. I., 1908-09
SHARP, Sam J., 1935
SHARPE, W. P., 1900
SHAW, Robert, 1975-76-77-78
SHAW, William H., 1904-05
SHELBY, A. G., 1916
SHERRILL, J. W., 1948-49-50
SHERROD, Horace "Bud", 1947-48-49-50
SHIELDS, David, 1961
SHIELDS, Lebron, 1958-59
SHIRES, Marshall "Abe", 1938-39-40
SHIRES, Pat, 1950-52-53
SHOFNER, Austin C., 1936
SHOULDERS, William, 1915-16
SHOWALTER, Nick, 1966-67-68
SHUFORD, George, 1962
SHULL, F. E., 1930-31-32
SILBERMAN, Doe, 1934-35
SILCOX, J. H., 1902
SILVEY, George, 1968-70-71
SIMERLY, A. E., 1902
SIMMONDS, R. M., 1915
SIMONETTI, Leonard, 1940-41
SIMONTON, Claud, 1970-71-72
SIMPSON, Hubert, 1976
SIMPSON, T. N. 1919, Mgr.
SIMS, Burt L., 1892
SIVERT, Jim, 1949
SIZEMORE, Bernie, 1949-50
SLACK, Tom, 1948
SLATER, Walter, 1941-42-46
SLOAN, Ira, 1920-21
SMARTT, Leon, 1958-59-60
SMELCHER, Jim, 1955-56-57
SMITH, Alfred E., 1892
SMITH, Billy, 1961
SMITH, Boyd M., 1932
SMITH, C. H., 1899
SMITH, Carl E., 1956-57-58
SMITH, Gordon E., 1931-32-33
SMITH, H. W., 1896-97
SMITH, Jerry, 1964-65-66
SMITH, Jimmie F., 1920-21-22-23
SMITH, Mike, 1973-75
SMITH, Roy "Looney", 1947-48-49-50
SMITH, Thomas, 1938-39
SMITH, Wayne, 1968-69
SMITH, Wiley Corry, 1924, Mgr.
SMITHERS, Bob, 1956
SNEED, Robert, 1936-37-38
SNEED, W. Bush, 1923
SNIPES, Herman, 1931
SNOWDEN, Robert B., 1919
SOLLEE, Neyle, 1958-59
SORRELLS, Frank G., 1913-14-15
SPAIN, Wayne, 1969-70
SPENCE, J. W., 1906
SPENCE, Shirley E., 1891
SPIVA, Andy, 1973-74-75-76
SPOONE, Bill, 1953
SPRADLING, Danny, 1977-78
STANBACK, Haskel, 1971-72-73
STANCELL, Harold, 1964-65-66
STANSELL, Ken, 1972
STAPLETON, Clayton, 1941-46-47
STARLING, Marcus, 1977-78
STARR, Lee, 1951, Mgr.
STEFFY, Joe, 1944
STEINER, Max, 1938-39-40
STEPHENS, Buster, 1944-45
STEPHENS, Don, 1958
STEPHENSON, Casey, 1944-45
STEPHENSON, Dave, 1946
STEPHENSON, Guy, 1922
STEWART, Bo, 1944
STEWART, Clifton, 1967-68
STEWART, Howard L., 1931-32-33
STEWART, Lyonel, 1975
STILL, J. Ralph, 1930-31
STOKES, Charles, 1950-51
STOTTLEMYER, Dave,1955-56-57
STOWERS, Donnie, 1977
STRATTON, Mike, 1959-60-61
STREATER, Jimmy, 1977-78
STRIEGEL, Roy B. "Pap", 1919-20-21-22
STROUD, Jack, 1947-48-49-50
STUART, Mark, 1910
STUPAR, Francis, 1949
SUFFRIDGE, Robert "Bob", 1938-39-40
SULLIVAN, Jimmy, 1962-64
SULLIVAN, Ned, 1961-62-63
SUMMERS, T. P., 1906, Mgr.
SUMPTER, Nate, 1977
SUTTON, Phil, 1978
SWAFFORD, J. H., 1908
SWEENEY, Terry, 1953
SZAWARA, Al, 1976

T

TADE, Herbert, 1935
TALBOT, Joe, 1923
TANARA, Al, 1962-63-64
TANNER, Don, 1947
TANNER, Larry, 1939
TANSIL, Vernon G., 1934-35
TARWATER, A. B., 1897
TAYLOR, R. L. "Bob", 1912-13-14-15
TAYLOR, W. H., 1901
TEDFORD, Gene, 1963
TEMPLETON, Conrad C., 1929-30
TERRY, William L., 1899
THAYER, Harry J. "Hobo", 1928-29-30
THEILER, Gary, 1969-70-71
THOMAS, Alfred, 1937-38-39
THOMAS, Bobby, 1971
THOMAS, Jimmy, 1967-68-69
THOMASON, R. F. "Tommy", 1912-13-14-15
THOMPSON, Joe, 1969-70-71
THOMPSON, Johnny, 1970-72
THOMPSON, Van, 1939-40
THORNTON, D. B., 1903-04-05
TIDWELL, Blane, 1976
TILSON, Paul, 1959-61-62
TOMLINSON, Billy, 1963-64-65
TOMPKINS, F. M., 1910-11
TOWNES, Tim, 1970-71-72
TOWNSEND, Ricky, 1972-73-74
TRACY, Tom, 1953-54
TRIPP, Arthur M., 1926-27-28
TROTT, Stan, 1970-71-72
TUCKER, Glenn, 1976-77
TUCKER, Willis, 1940
TUDOR, D. Vincent, 1927-28
TUNNELL, S. M., 1915, Mgr.
TURNAGE, Gordon, 1969-71-72
TURNBOW, Jesse, 1975-77
TWILFOLD, H. H., 1916

U

URBANO, Bobby, 1956-57-58
URBANO, Roger, 1954-55-56
URUBEK, Steve, 1971-72-73
USSERY, Bob, 1952-53

V

VALBUENA, Gary, 1972-73
VAUGHAN, Charles W. "Pug", 1932-33-34
VENABLE, Sam A., 1932
VERNER, Randy, 1974-75
VEST, Roger, 1951-52
VICK, Warren, 1941
VITUCCIO, Gary, 1965
VOWELL, J. Graham, 1914-15-16-21
VOWELL, Morris A., 1913-14-15-16
VOWELL, Ritchie, 1924
VUGRIN, James, 1946-47-48-49

W

WADDELL, Ken, 1959-60
WADE, Jimmy, 1951-52-53-54
WAFF, Wayne, 1962
WAGSTER, John, 1970-71-72
WALKER, Jackie, 1969-70-71
WALKER, Jeff, 1975
WALLACE, Randy, 1974-75-76
WALLEN, Joe, 1936-38-39
WALTER, Hank, 1972-73-74
WALTERS, John M., 1906-07-08-09
WANTLAND, Hal, 1963-64-65
WARD, Ernie, 1973-74-75
WARMATH, Murray, 1932-33-34
WARNER, E. T., 1896
WARREN, Buist, 1938-39-40
WARREN, Dewey, 1965-66-67
WARREN, Phil, 1905
WASHINGTON, Anthony, 1976
WATKINS, Arthur B., 1897
WATKINS, T. R., 1903-04
WATSON, Bob, 1923, Mgr.
WATSON, Brent, 1974-75-76-77
WATSON, Curt, 1969-70-71
WATTS, Brad, 1976
WATTS, Jim, 1972-73-74
WATTS, Johnny, 1977-78
WEATHERFORD, Derrick, 1965-66-67
WEATHERFORD, Jim, 1966-67-68
WEAVER, DeWitt T., 1934-35-36
WEAVER, Herman, 1967-68-69
WEBB, Charlton, 1975-77-78
WEBB, Danny, 1958
WEBER, Nick, 1939-40
WEBSTER, Chris, 1977
WEGENER, Albert B., 1892–93
WEISENBERG, Andrew, 1908-09
WELCH, F. W., 1915
WEMLINGER, Gary, 1969
WERT, Lee K., 1907
WERT, R. Y., 1900-01
WERTS, Edwin S., 1891-92
WEST, Hodges "Burr", 1938-39-40
WEST, Tom, 1973-74-75
WHEELER, Ronnie, 1973-74-75
WHITAKER, James A., 1929
WHITAKER, Walter C., 1913, Mgr.
WHITE, Brad, 1978
WHITE, H. Benton, 1907-08
WHITE, Lynn T., 1892-93
WHITE, Steve, 1975
WHITE, W. C., 1921
WHITTLE, Matt, 1905
WIDBY, Ron, 1964-65-66
WILDMAN, Charles, 1944-45-46-47
WILLIAMS, Bob, 1954-55
WILLIAMS, Cliff, 1956
WILLIAMS, Dick, 1966-67-68
WILLIAMS, Jay, 1977-78
WILLIAMS, Russ, 1974-75-76-77
WILLIAMS, Tom, 1960-61-62
WILSON, Eddie, 1971-72-73
WILSON, Rollin, 1922-24
WINSTEAD, Jid, 1956
WINSTON, D. B., 1937, Mgr.
WITHERINGTON, Sid, 1973
WITHERSPOON, Carl, 1971-72
WITT, Roy E., 1926-27-28
WOLD, Steve, 1968-69-70
WOLFE, Dennis, 1976-77-78
WOLFE, Lloyd S., 1914-15-16
WOOD, Carl, 1945
WOOD, James R., 1891
WOOD, Walter "Babe", 1936-37-38
WOODALL, David, 1973-74-76, Mgr.

WOODRUFF, George R. "Bob", 1936-37-38
WOODS, Gerald, 1963-64-65
WOODY, James, 1968-69-70
WOOFTER, Jim, 1974-75-76
WORD, Roscoe, 1902-03-04-05-07
WORTHAM, C. L., 1900
WRIGHT, Gary, 1966-67
WRIGHT, George, 1957-58
WRIGHTMAN, A. L., 1901
WYATT, Bowden, 1936-37-38
WYCHE, Bubba, 1967-68
WYNN, Herman D. "Breezy", 1931-32-33
WYRICK, Charles, 1960-61

Y

YANOSSY, Frank, 1967-68-69
YARBROUGH, John, 1973-74-75
YOUNG, Bill, 1966-68-69
YOUNG, Carroll, 1956-57
YOUNG, Ed B., 1925-26
YOUNG, Eddie, 1955
YOUNG, J. R., 1910
YOUNG, Jimmy, 1970-71-72

Z

ZONTINI, Lawrence, 1942
ZVOLERIN, Bob, 1963

Vanderbilt University

Location: Nashville, Tennessee
Enrollment: 7,000
Nickname: Commodores
Colors: Old Gold and Black
Stadium: Dudley Field (34,000)

Vanderbilt University Head Coaching Records

COACH	YEAR	WON	LOST	TIED
Elliott H. Jones	1890-'92	8	5	0
W. J. Keller	1893	6	1	0
Henry Thornton	1894	7	1	0
C. L. Upton	1895	5	3	1
R. G. Acton	1896-'98	10	7	3
J. L. Crane	1899-1900	11	6	1
W. H. Watkins	1901-'02	14	2	1
J. H. Henry	1903	6	1	1
Dan McGugin	1904-'17; 1919-'34	197	55	19
Ray Morrison	1918; 1935-'39	29	22	2
Red Sanders	1940-'48	36	22	2
E. H. Alley	1943	5	0	0
Doby Bartling	1944-'45	6	6	1
Bill Edwards	1949-'52	21	19	2
Art Guepe	1953-'62	39	54	7
Jack Green	1963-'66	7	29	4
Bill Pace	1967-'72	22	38	3
Steve Sloan	1973-'74	12	9	2
Fred Pancoast	1975-'78	13	31	0

Vanderbilt University All-Time Scores

1890

40	Nashville Univ.	0

1891

22	Sewanee	0
6	Wash. Univ.	24
26	Sewanee	4
4	Wash. Univ.	0
58	(3-1-0)	28

1892

4	Sewanee	22
22	Tennessee	4
40	Nashville	4
4	Wash. Univ.	14
14	Sewanee	28
10	Tennessee	0
20	Ga. Tech	10
0	N. Carolina	24
114	(4-4-0)	106

1893

68	Memphis AC	0
10	Sewanee	8
10	Auburn	30
35	Georgia	0
36	Louisville AC	12
10	Sewanee	0
12	Ky. Central	0
181	(6-1-0)	50

1894

64	Memphis AC	0
6	Centre	0
8	Louisville AC	10
20	Auburn	4
40	Ole Miss	0
34	Ky. Central	6
62	Cumberland	0
12	Sewanee	0
246	(7-1-0)	20

1895

0	Missouri	16
10	Ky. Central	0
0	N. Carolina	12
0	Centre	0
9	Auburn	6
20	Nashville AC	4
4	Virginia	6
6	Georgia	0
18	Sewanee	6
67	(5-3-1)	50

1896

6	Kentucky	0
0	Centre	46
0	Ky. Central	0
6	Missouri	26
36	Southwestern	0
0	Nashville	0
10	Sewanee	4
58	(3-2-2)	76

1897

24	Ky. College	0
14	Ky. Central	0
12	V.M.I.	0
50	Kentucky	0
31	N. Carolina	0
10	Sewanee	0
0	Virginia	0
141	(6-0-1)	0

1898

0	Cincinnati	10
0	Georgia	4
5	Nashville	0
0	Virginia	18
0	Ky. Central	10
4	Sewanee	19
9	(1-5-0)	61

1899

32	Cumberland	0
12	Miami (O.)	0
0	Cincinnati	6
0	Indiana	20
0	Ole Miss	0
22	Bethel	0
6	Texas	0
21	Ky. Central	16
5	Nashville	0
156	(7-2-0)	46

1900

6	Ole Miss	0
0	Texas	22
0	Tennessee	0
0	Centre	11
0	N. Carolina	48
27	Ky. Central	0
10	Sewanee	11
29	Bethel	0
18	Nashville Univ.	0
90	(4-4-1)	92

1901

22	Kentucky	0
25	Ky. Central	0
47	Georgia	0
44	Auburn	0
11	Wash. Univ.	12
22	Tennessee	0

0	Sewanee	0
10	Nashville	0
181	(6-1-1)	12

1902

45	Cumberland	0
29	Ole Miss	0
24	Ky. Central	17
12	Tennessee	5
33	Wash. Univ.	12
16	Kentucky	5
23	Tulane	5
27	L.S.U.	5
5	Sewanee	11
214	(8-1-0)	60

1903

0	Cumberland	6
30	Alabama	0
40	Tennessee	0
33	Ole Miss	0
33	Georgia	0
5	Texas	5
41	Wash. Univ.	0
10	Sewanee	5
192	(6-1-1)	16

1904

61	Miss. State	0
66	Georgetown	0
69	Ole Miss	0
29	Missouri Mines	4
97	Ky. Central	0
22	Centre	0
22	Tennessee	0
81	Nash. Univ.	0
27	Sewanee	0
474	(9-0-0)	4

1905

97	Maryville	0
34	Alabama	0
0	Michigan	18
45	Tennessee	0
33	Texas	0
54	Auburn	0
41	Clemson	0
68	Sewanee	4
372	(7-1-0)	22

1906

28	Kentucky	0
29	Ole Miss	0
78	Alabama	0
45	Texas	0
4	Michigan	10
33	Rose Polytech	0
37	Ga. Tech	6
4	Carlisle	0
20	Sewanee	0
278	(8-1-0)	16

1907

40	Kentucky	0
6	Navy	6
65	Rose Polytech	10
0	Michigan	8
60	Ole Miss	0
54	Ga. Tech	0
17	Sewanee	12
242	(5-1-1)	36

1908

11	Southwestern	5
32	Maryville	0
32	Rose Polytech	0
41	Clemson	0
29	Ole Miss	0
6	Michigan	24
16	Tennessee	9
6	Ohio State	17
28	Wash. Univ.	0
6	Sewanee	6
207	(7-2-1)	61

1909

52	Southwestern	0
28	Mercer	5
28	Rose Polytech	3
0	Alumni	3
17	Auburn	0
17	Ole Miss	0
51	Tennessee	0
0	Ohio State	5
12	Wash. Univ.	0
5	Sewanee	16
210	(7-3-0)	32

1910

34	Mooney School	0
23	Rose Polytech	0
14	Castle Hgts.	0
18	Tennessee	0
0	Yale	0
9	Ole Miss	2
22	L.S.U.	0
23	Ga. Tech	0
23	Sewanee	6
166	(8-0-1)	8

1911

40	B'ham Sou.	0
46	Maryville	0
33	Rose Polytech	0
45	Ky. Central	0
8	Michigan	9
17	Georgia	0
18	Kentucky	0
21	Ole Miss	0
31	Sewanee	0
259	(8-1-0)	9

1912

105	Bethel	0
100	Maryville	3
54	Rose Polytech	0
46	Georgia	0
24	Ole Miss	0
13	Virginia	0
3	Harvard	9
23	Ky. Central	0
7	Auburn	7
16	Sewanee	0
391	(8-1-1)	19

1913

59	Maryville	0
48	Ky. Central	0
33	Hendr.-Brown	0
0	Virginia	34
2	Michigan	33
7	Tennessee	6
6	Auburn	14
63	Sewanee	13
218	(5-3-0)	100

1914

42	Hendr.-Brown	6
3	Michigan	23
59	Ky. Central	0
9	N. Carolina	10
7	Virginia	20
14	Tennessee	16
0	Auburn	6
13	Sewanee	14
147	(2-6-0)	95

1915

51	Middle Tenn.	0
47	Southwestern	0
75	Georgetown	0
60	Cumberland	0
100	Hendr.-Brown	0
91	Ole Miss	0
35	Tennessee	0
10	Virginia	35
17	Auburn	0
28	Sewanee	3
514	(9-1-0)	38

1916

86	Southwestern	0
42	Transylvania	0
45	Kentucky	0
35	Ole Miss	0
27	Virginia	6
67	Rose Polytech	0
20	Auburn	9
6	Tennessee	10
0	Sewanee	0
328	(7-1-1)	25

1917

41	Transylvania	0
0	Chicago	48
5	Kentucky	0
69	Howard	0
0	Ga. Tech	83
7	Alabama	2
7	Auburn	31
13	Sewanee	6
142	(5-3-0)	170

1918

0	Cp. Greenleaf	6
6	Cp. Hancock	25
33	Kentucky	0
76	Tennessee	0
21	Auburn	0
40	Sewanee	0
176	(4-2-0)	31

1919

41	Union	0
3	Tennessee	3
0	Ga. Tech	20
7	Auburn	6
0	Kentucky	0
16	Alabama	12
10	Virginia	6
33	Sewanee	21
110	(5-1-2)	68

1920

54	B'ham Sou.	0
20	Tennessee	0
0	Ga. Tech	44
6	Auburn	56
20	Kentucky	0
7	Alabama	14
34	Middle Tenn.	0
7	Virginia	7
21	Sewanee	3
169	(5-3-1)	124

1921

34	Middle Tenn.	0
42	Mercer	0
21	Kentucky	14
20	Texas	0
14	Tennessee	0
14	Alabama	0
7	Georgia	7
9	Sewanee	0
161	(7-0-1)	21

1922

38	Middle Tenn.	0
33	Hendr.-Brown	0
0	Michigan	0
20	Texas	10
25	Mercer	0
14	Tennessee	6
9	Kentucky	0
12	Georgia	0
26	Sewanee	0
177	(8-0-1)	16

1923

27	Howard	0
0	Michigan	3
0	Texas	16
17	Tulane	0
0	Miss. State	0
51	Tennessee	7
35	Georgia	7
7	Sewanee	0
137	(5-2-1)	33

1924

13	Hendr.-Brown	0
61	B'ham-Sou.	0
13	Quantico Mar.	13
13	Tulane	21
0	Georgia	3
13	Auburn	0
18	Miss. State	0
3	Ga. Tech	0
16	Minnesota	0
0	Sewanee	16
150	(6-3-1)	53

1925

27	Middle Tenn.	0
41	Hendr.-Brown	0
14	Texas	6
34	Tennessee	7
7	Georgia	26
7	Ole Miss	0
0	Ga. Tech	7
9	Auburn	10
19	Sewanee	7
158	(6-3-0)	63

1926

69	Middle Tenn.	0
7	Alabama	19
48	Bryson	0
7	Texas	0
14	Georgia	13
50	Southwestern	0
13	Ga. Tech	7
20	Tennessee	3
13	Sewanee	0
241	(8-1-0)	42

1927

45	Chattanooga	18
39	Ouachita	10
53	Centre	6
6	Texas	13
32	Tulane	0
34	Kentucky	6
0	Ga. Tech	0
7	Tennessee	7
39	Maryland	20
26	Sewanee	6
14	Alabama	7
295	(8-1-2)	93

1928

20	Chattanooga	0
12	Colgate	7
13	Texas	12
13	Tulane	6
34	Virginia	0
14	Kentucky	7
7	Ga. Tech	19
0	Tennessee	6
26	Centre	0
13	Sewanee	0
152	(8-2-0)	57

1929

19	Ole Miss	7
26	Ouachita	6
6	Minnesota	15
41	Auburn	2
33	Maryville	0
13	Alabama	0
23	Ga. Tech	7
0	Tennessee	13
26	Sewanee	6
187	(7-2-0)	56

1930

39	Chattanooga	0
33	Minnesota	7
40	Va. Tech	0
27	Spring Hill	6
7	Alabama	12
24	Ole Miss	0
6	Ga. Tech	0
0	Tennessee	13
27	Auburn	0
22	Maryland	7
225	(8-2-0)	45

1931

52	Western Ky.	6
13	N. Carolina	0
26	Ohio State	21
0	Tulane	19
0	Georgia	9
49	Ga. Tech	7
39	Maryland	12
7	Tennessee	21
6	Alabama	14
192	(5-4-0)	109

1932

20	Mercer	7
39	N. Carolina	7
26	Western Ky.	0
6	Tulane	6
12	Georgia	6
12	Ga. Tech	0
13	Maryland	0
0	Tennessee	0
0	Alabama	20
128	(6-1-2)	46

1933

50	Cumberland	0
0	Oklahoma	0
20	N. Carolina	13
0	Ohio State	20
7	Miss. State	7
7	L.S.U.	7
9	Ga. Tech	6
27	Sewanee	14
6	Tennessee	33
0	Alabama	7
126	(4-3-3)	107

1934

7	Miss. State	0
27	Ga. Tech	12
32	Cincinnati	0
7	Auburn	6
0	L.S.U.	29
7	Geo. Wash.	6
19	Sewanee	0
6	Tennessee	13
0	Alabama	34
105	(6-3-0)	100

1935

34	Union	0
14	Miss. State	9
32	Cumberland	7
3	Temple	6
7	Fordham	13
2	L.S.U.	7
14	Ga. Tech	13
46	Sewanee	0
13	Tennessee	7
14	Alabama	6
179	(7-3-0)	68

1936

45 Middle Tenn. 0
37 Chicago 0
0 Southwestern 12
0 S.M.U. 16
0 Ga. Tech 0
0 L.S.U. 19
14 Sewanee 0
13 Tennessee 26
6 Alabama 14

115 (3-5-1) 87

1937

12 Kentucky 0
18 Chicago 0
17 Southwestern 6
6 S.M.U. 0
7 L.S.U. 6
0 Ga. Tech 14
41 Sewanee 0
13 Tennessee 7
7 Alabama 9

121 (7-2-0) 42

1938

20 Wash. Univ. 0
12 Western Ky. 0
14 Kentucky 7
13 Ole Miss 7
0 L.S.U. 7
13 Ga. Tech 7
14 Sewanee 0
0 Tennessee 14
0 Alabama 7

86 (7-3-0) 49

1939

13 Tenn. Tech 13
13 Rice 12
13 Kentucky 21
13 V.M.I. 20
6 Ga. Tech 14
6 L.S.U. 12
7 Ole Miss 14
25 Sewanee 7
0 Tennessee 11
0 Alabama 39

96 (2-7-1) 165

1940

19 Wash. & Lee 0
6 Princeton 7
7 Kentucky 7
0 Ga. Tech 19
0 L.S.U. 7
7 Ole Miss 13
20 Sewanee 0
21 Tenn. Tech 0
21 Alabama 25
0 Tennessee 20

101 (3-6-1) 98

1941

3 Purdue 0
42 Tenn. Tech 0
39 Kentucky 15
14 Ga. Tech 7
46 Princeton 7
14 Tulane 34
20 Sewanee 0
68 Louisville 0
7 Alabama 0
7 Tennessee 26

260 (8-2-0) 89

1942

52 Tenn. Tech 0
26 Purdue 0
7 Kentucky 6
0 Miss. State 33
66 Centre 0
21 Tulane 28
19 Ole Miss 0
27 Union 0
7 Alabama 27
7 Tennessee 19

232 (6-4-0) 113

1943

20 Tenn. Tech 0
40 Cp. Campbell 14
26 Milligan 6
12 Carson-Newman 6
47 Tenn. Tech 7

145 (5-0-0) 33

1944

0 Sewanee 0
19 Tenn. Tech 7
20 Tenn. Tech 9
28 Sewanee 7

67 (3-0-1) 23

1945

12 Tenn. Tech 0
7 Mississippi 14
7 Florida 0
19 Kentucky 6
7 L.S.U. 39
13 V.M.I. 27
6 Chattanooga 13
0 Alabama 71
0 Tennessee 45

71 (3-6-0) 215

1946

35 Tenn. Tech 0
7 Ole Miss 0
20 Florida 0
7 Kentucky 10
0 L.S.U. 14
19 Auburn 0
7 N. C. State 0
7 Alabama 12
6 Tennessee 7

108 (5-4-0) 43

1947

3 Northwestern 0
14 Alabama 7
10 Ole Miss 6
0 Kentucky 14
13 L.S.U. 19
28 Auburn 0
68 Tenn. Tech 0
33 Miami 7
6 Maryland 20
7 Tennessee 12

182 (6-4-0) 85

1948

0 Ga. Tech 13
14 Alabama 14
7 Ole Miss 20
26 Kentucky 7
35 Yale 0
47 Auburn 0
48 L.S.U. 7
56 Marshall 0
34 Maryland 0
28 Tennessee 6
33 Miami 6

328 (8-2-1) 72

1949

7 Ga. Tech 12
14 Alabama 7
28 Ole Miss 27
22 Florida 17
6 Arkansas 7
26 Auburn 7
13 L.S.U. 33
14 Tulane 41
27 Marshall 6
20 Tennessee 26

177 (5-5-0) 183

1950

47 Middle Tenn. 0
41 Auburn 0
27 Alabama 22
20 Ole Miss 14
27 Florida 31
14 Arkansas 13
34 Chattanooga 12
7 L.S.U. 33
29 Memphis State 13
6 Tulane 35
0 Tennessee 43

252 (7-4-0) 236

1951

22 Middle Tenn. 7
14 Auburn 24
22 Alabama 20
34 Ole Miss 20
13 Florida 33
7 Ga. Tech 8
19 Chattanooga 14
20 L.S.U. 13
10 Tulane 11
13 Memphis State 7
27 Tennessee 35

201 (6-5-0) 195

1952

7 Georgia 19
0 Virginia 27
20 Northwestern 20
21 Ole Miss 21
20 Florida 13
0 Ga. Tech 30
67 Wash. & Lee 7
9 Miami 0
7 Tulane 16
0 Tennessee 46

151 (3-5-2) 199

1953

7 Pennsylvania 13
12 Alabama 21
6 Ole Miss 28
6 Baylor 47
28 Virginia 13
0 Ga. Tech 43
14 Kentucky 40
21 Tulane 7
31 Middle Tenn. 13
6 Tennessee 33

131 (3-7-0) 258

1954

19 Baylor 25
14 Alabama 28
7 Ole Miss 22
14 Georgia 16
13 Rice 34
7 Kentucky 19
0 Tulane 6
34 Villanova 19
26 Tennessee 0

134 (2-7-0) 169

1955

13 Georgia 14
21 Alabama 6
0 Ole Miss 13
12 Chattanooga 0
46 Middle Tenn. 0
34 Virginia 7
34 Kentucky 0
20 Tulane 7
21 Florida 6
14 Tennessee 20

215 (7-3-0) 73

Gator Bowl

25 Auburn 13

1956

14 Georgia 0
46 Chattanooga 7
32 Alabama 7
0 Ole Miss 16
7 Florida 21
23 Middle Tenn. 13
6 Virginia 2
6 Kentucky 7
6 Tulane 13
7 Tennessee 27

147 (5-5-0) 113

1957

7 Missouri 7
9 Georgia 6
6 Alabama 6
0 Ole Miss 28
32 Penn State 20
7 L.S.U. 0
12 Kentucky 7
7 Florida 14
27 Citadel 0
6 Tennessee 20

113 (5-3-2) 118

1958

12 Missouri 8
21 Georgia 14
0 Alabama 0
7 Clemson 12
6 Florida 6
39 Virginia 6
28 Miami 15
0 Kentucky 0
12 Tulane 0
6 Tennessee 10

131 (5-2-3) 71

1959

6 Georgia 21
7 Alabama 7
0 Ole Miss 33
13 Florida 6
33 Virginia 0
6 Minnesota 20
11 Kentucky 6
6 Tulane 6
42 Florence St 7
14 Tennessee 0

138 (5-3-2) 106

1960

7 Georgia 18
0 Alabama 21
0 Ole Miss 26
0 Florida 12
23 Marquette 6
27 Clemson 20
0 Kentucky 27
22 Wm. & Mary 8
0 Tulane 20
0 Tennessee 35

74 (3-7-0) 193

1961

16 W. Virginia 6
21 Georgia 0
6 Alabama 35
21 U.C.L.A. 28
0 Florida 7
0 Ole Miss 47
3 Kentucky 16
14 Tulane 17
7 S. Carolina 23
7 Tennessee 41

95 (2-8-0) 220

1962

0 W. Virginia 26
0 Georgia 10
7 Alabama 17
6 Citadel 21
7 Florida 42
0 Ole Miss 35
22 Boston College 27
0 Kentucky 7
20 Tulane 0
0 Tennessee 30

62 (1-9-0) 215

1963

13 Furman 14
0 Georgia 20
6 Alabama 21
0 Florida 21
7 Ole Miss 27
6 Boston College 19
0 Kentucky 0
10 Tulane 10
31 Geo. Wash. 0
0 Tennessee 14

73 (1-7-2) 146

1964

2 Ga. Tech 14
0 Georgia 7
0 Alabama 24
9 Wake Forest 6
14 Geo. Wash. 0
7 Ole Miss 7
21 Kentucky 22
2 Tulane 7
17 Miami 35
7 Tennessee 0

79 (3-6-1) 122

1965

10 Ga. Tech 10
0 Georgia 24
0 Wake Forest 7
7 Alabama 22
21 Va. Tech 10
7 Ole Miss 24
13 Tulane 0
0 Kentucky 34
14 Miami 28
3 Tennessee 21

85 (2-7-1) 180

1966

24 Citadel 0
0 Ga. Tech 42
0 Florida 13
6 Va. Tech 21
6 Alabama 42
12 Tulane 13
10 Kentucky 14
14 Navy 30
0 Ole Miss 34
0 Tennessee 28

72 (1-9-0) 237

1967

10 Ga. Tech 17
14 Wm & Mary 12
12 N. Carolina 7
21 Alabama 35
22 Florida 27
14 Tulane 27
7 Kentucky 12
35 Navy 35
7 Ole Miss 28
14 Tennessee 41

165 (2-7-1) 241

1968

25 V.M.I. 12
17 Army 13
7 N. Carolina 8
7 Alabama 31
6 Georgia 32
14 Florida 14
21 Tulane 7
6 Kentucky 0
53 Davidson 20

7	Tennessee	10
163	(5-4-1)	147

1969

14	Michigan	42
6	Army	16
22	N. Carolina	38
14	Alabama	10
8	Georgia	40
20	Florida	41
26	Tulane	23
42	Kentucky	6
63	Davidson	8
27	Tennessee	40
242	(4-6-0)	264

1970

39	UT-Chattanooga	6
52	Citadel	0
6	Miss. State	20
7	N. Carolina	10
11	Alabama	35
3	Georgia	37
16	Ole Miss	26
7	Tulane	10
18	Kentucky	17
36	Tampa	28
6	Tennessee	24
201	(4-7-0)	213

1971

20	UT-Chattanooga	19
0	Louisville	0
49	Miss. State	19
23	Virginia	27
0	Alabama	42
0	Georgia	24
7	Ole Miss	28
13	Tulane	9
7	Kentucky	14
10	Tampa	7
7	Tennessee	19
136	(4-6-1)	208

1972

24	UT-Chattanooga	7
6	Miss. State	10
21	Alabama	48
10	Virginia	7
21	Wm. & Mary	17
3	Georgia	28
7	Ole Miss	31
13	Kentucky	14
7	Tulane	21
7	Tampa	30
10	Tennessee	30
129	(3-8-0)	243

1973

14	UT Chattanooga	12
21	Miss. State	52
0	Alabama	44
39	Virginia	22
20	Wm. & Mary	7
18	Georgia	14
14	Ole Miss.	24
17	Kentucky	27
3	Tulane	24
18	Tampa	16
17	Tennessee	20
181	(5-6-0)	262

1974

28	UT-Chatt.	6
45	V.M.I.	7
10	Alabama	23
24	Florida	10
31	Georgia	38
24	Ole Miss	14
38	Army	14
12	Kentucky	38
30	Tulane	22
44	Louisville	0
21	Tennessee	21
307	(7-3-1)	193

Peach Bowl

6	Texas Tech	6

1975

17	UT-Chatt.	7
9	Rice	6
7	Alabama	40
6	Tulane	3
0	Florida	35
3	Georgia	47
7	Ole Miss	17
17	Virginia	14
13	Kentucky	3
23	Army	14
17	Tennessee	14
113	(7-4-0)	200

1976

3	Oklahoma	24
27	Wake Forest	24
14	Alabama	42
13	Tulane	24
20	LSU	33
0	Georgia	45
3	Ole Miss	20
0	Kentucky	14
34	Air Force	10
7	Cincinnati	33
10	Tennessee	13
131	(2-9-0)	282

1977

23	Oklahoma	25
3	Wake Forest	0
12	Alabama	24
7	Tulane	36
15	LSU	28
13	Georgia	24
14	Mississipi	26
6	Kentucky	28
28	Air Force	34
13	Cincinnati	9
7	Tennessee	42
141	(2-9-0)	276

1978

17	Arkansas	48
17	Furman	10
28	Alabama	51
3	Tulane	38
7	Auburn	49
10	Georgia	31
10	Mississippi	35
14	Memphis State	35
2	Kentucky	53
41	Air Force	27
15	Tennessee	41
164	(2-9-0)	418

Vanderbilt University Lettermen—1890 to 1978

A

ABERNATHY, George, 1970-71-72
ABERNATHY, James, 1940
ABERNATHY, Richard, 1927-28-29
ADAMS, Alfred T. "Alf", 1914-15-16-17-19
ADAMS, Mark, 1973-74-75
ADAMS, Morton B., 1909
ADAMS, Ralph, 1927-28
AGEE, Joe, 1936-37-38
AGEE, Sam, 1935-36
AHRENS, William Norman, 1954-55
AKER, John, 1943
AKIN, Lewis Edmond, 1958-59
ALLEN, Alex, 1890
ALLEN, Carl, 1978
ALLEN, Howard, 1891
ALLEN, James W., Jr., 1945-46-47
ALLEN, Richard M., "Rip", 1890-91-92
ALLEN, Rives Calvin, 1950-51-52
ALSUP, Roger Wendell, 1975-76-77-78
ALSUP, Walter David, 1972-73-74
AMES, W. G., 1895
ANDERSON, Blake, 1972
ANDERSON, Charles, 1936-37
ANDERSON, J. M. "Tubby", 1909-10
ANDERSON, Joe, 1937-39-40
ANDERSON, John Neil V., 1947-48
ANDERSON, Walton H., 1914
ANDRUS, Raymond, 1937-38-39
ANGLIN, Leonard, 1937-38-39
ANTHONY, Wayne Lamar, 1961-62-63
ARCHBOLD, Carl Thomas, 1959
ARMISTEAD, James C., 1926-27-28
ARMSTRONG, Homer, 1929-31
ASHER, Robert Dabney "Bob", 1967-68-69
ASKEW, Burgess, 1931-32
ASKEW, John C., Jr., 1928-29-30
ASKEW, Pierce "Yank", 1931
ASKEW, Wesley L., 1913
ATKINSON, Eddie, 1941-42
ATKINSON, Fitzgerald, 1914
ATKINSON, James Edwin, 1946
ATKINSON, Joe, 1939-40-41
AUSTIN, Lee, 1943-44
AVERY, James, 1970-71-72

B

BAGLEY, Sandy, 1973
BAILEY, Donald Wycoff, 1953
BAILEY, Kenneth K. "Red", 1925
BAILEY, Lucien L. "Fats", 1917-19-20-21
BAIRD, Calvin, 1942
BAIRD, Renfro "Sonny", 1941-42
BAKER, Issac B., "Ike", 1918-20
BALDRIDGE, Duke, 1925-27
BALDWIN, Bennett Midgley, 1962-63-64
BALLMAN, Thomas William, 1973-74-75-76
BANKS, Larry Sangster, 1962
BARBEE, John F. H., 1898-99-1900
BARNES, Nolan T., 1924
BARR, Richard A., 1891-92
BARRETT, Timothy Craig, 1976-77-78
BARRETT, Virgil Caldwell, Jr., 1961-62
BARRON, Billy, 1942
BARTON, Bryan, 1936
BASKERVILLE, Charles R., 1890-92-93
BATES, Joseph Norman, 1957-58-59
BATES, William "Billy", 1943
BAUGHN, James Harrison, 1946-47
BAYLESS, Robert, 1970
BEANE, Von Rhea, 1937
BEARD, Bruce, 1911
BEARD, Byron, 1935
BEARD, William E. "Billy", 1892
BEASLEY, James, 1930-31-32
BEASLEY, Thomas O. "Bunt", 1916-18
BECK, Eugene, 1932-33-34
BECKLEHEIMER, Herman, 1914
BELL, Alvin "Pep", 1920-21-22-23
BELL, Charles "Jelly", 1909-10
BELL, Robert H., Jr., 1938-39
BEMIS, H. E., 1890
BENNETT, Steve, 1973
BENSON, Steve "Reno", 1972-75, Mgr.
BERNHARDT, Thomas Edward "Tom", 1969-70-71
BERRY, Allen, 1930
BERRY, Julius, 1907
BERRY, Robert Leo, 1946-47-48-49
BERRY, William Irvin, 1947-49-50
BERRYHILL, Grailey L., 1916-18-19-20
BERSON, Clarence, 1930-31
BERSON, Robert, 1931-32-33
BIGELOW, Steven Herbert, 1968
BIGHAM, David Michael, 1969-70-71, Mgr.
BIGHAM, William Dean, 1977, Mgr.
BILES, Shelton, 1942-43
BILLINGS, Paul Barrett, 1950-51-52
BILLS, Sam Crutcher, 1958
BINKLEY, Charles Cody, 1959-60-61
BIRDSONG, John Michael, 1975-76-77
BLACK, Benson H., 1895
BLACK, Terry Rawls, 1960
BLACKMAN, Ed, 1924, Mgr.
BLAIR, Dwight, 1970-71
BLAIR, Frank "Count", 1915-16
BLAIR, James William, 1974
BLAKE, Daniel B., 1902-03-04-05-06
BLAKE, J. Vaughn Weldon, 1903-06-07-08
BLAKE, R. E. "Bob", 1903-04-05-06-07
BLAKE, Vaughn, 1925-26-27
BLAND, S. K., 1892, Mgr.
BLANE, Robert H., 1918
BOENSCH, Hord, 1911-13
BOHNER, Richard Hugh, 1962-63
BOLDT, John Wesley, 1949-50
BOLLES, W. E., 1891
BOMAR, Lynn, 1921-22-23-24
BOMER, J. O. "Mike", 1912, Mgr.
BONNER, M. H., 1899
BOOGHER, Howard M., 1894-95-96-97
BOONE, Luther Erskine, III, 1958-59-61
BOOTH, Powers, 1937
BOOTH, Vaughn, 1925
BOOTH, William M., 1899-1900-01
BOSTICK, Dick, 1943-44-45
BOWEN, Gary, 1943
BOYD, Charles Ray "Chuck", 1965-66-68
BOYD, Terry Joe, 1977-78
BOYER, Dale Eugene, 1948-49
BOYTE, R., 1895
BRADFORD, C. R. "Tex", 1921-22
BRADFORD, Mark, 1905, Mgr.
BRADFORD, Mark, Jr., 1927-28
BRANSFORD, John, 1926-27
BRIGHTWELL, Irvin, 1941-42
BRISTOW, Alex, 1928
BROADBEAR, Michael Webster, 1962

BROCK, Jack, 1943-44
BROGDON, Paul Gilliam, 1972-73-74-75
BROGDON, Preston, 1975
BROOKS, Phillip Wayne, 1963-64-65
BROTHERS, Claud Harold, 1952-56
BROWN, Allen, 1909-10
BROWN, Calvin Smith, 1891
BROWN, Charles H., 1910-11-14-15
BROWN, Claud Harold, 1952-56
BROWN, Enoch "Nuck", 1910-11-12-13
BROWN, Innis, 1903-04-05
BROWN, J. Hamilton "Bull", 1897-98-1903-04
BROWN, John Neil "Bull", 1926-28-29
BROWN, Lester Watson, 1969-70-72
BROWN, Mack, 1970
BROWN, Malvern, 1936
BROWN, Morton Lindon, Jr., 1966-67
BROWN, Preston Melville, 1976-77-78
BROWN, Robert Lee, 1891
BROWN, Robert R., 1910
BROWN, Sam, 1933-34-35
BROWN, Sperry, 1927
BROWN, Tom, 1910-11-12-13
BROWN, Van Thompson, 1946-47-48-49
BROWN, W. C. Foskett, 1916, Mgr.
BROWNING, Manning, 1922-23
BRUCE, William Billington, 1963-64-65, Mgr.
BRUNO, John, 1966
BRYAN, Claiborne N. "Ick", 1901-02-03
BRYAN, Kenneth M. 1923-24-25
BRYAN, W. J. "Bill", 1922-23
BRYNGELSON, Bill, 1943
BUCK, Howard Lee, 1973-74
BUCKLEY, Ray, 1902, Mgr.
BUCKNER, Allen M., 1919-20
BUCKNER, Matthew G., 1893
BUGGS, Marmon Charles, 1978
BULKELEY, Richard Chase, 1959
BURCH, Lucius E., 1892-93-94-95
BURCH, Lucius E., Jr., 1931
BURGE, Len, 1937
BURGER, Steve, 1970-71-72
BURKE, Orvill G., 1898-99
BURKE, Vance, 1936-38-39
BURNS, John, 1941
BURNS, John Olen, 1967-68-70
BURNS, Red, 1942
BURTON, Barry Ferguson, 1973-74-75
BURTON, James Boyd, 1959
BURTON, Larry, 1932
BURTON, Nelson Lynch, 1949-50
BUSHMIAER, Binks Addams, 1940-41-46
BUTCHER, Wade Elvin, Jr., 1960-61
BYRD, Eugene Leon, Jr., 1973-74
BYRN, Charlie, 1942

C

CAGE, John Bright, 1972-73-74, Trn.
CAINE, Winston Paulding, Jr., 1958
CALDWELL, William T., 1948
CALHOUN, Bedford L., 1946-47, Mgr.
CALHOUN, Donald John, 1967
CALHOUN, James Richard, 1947-48-49
CALVIN, Reginald Lydell, 1974-75-76-77
CAMPBELL, Vincent A. "Demon", 1907
CANINGTON, Larkin Lee, 1976
CANTRELL, Hubert Randolph, 1976
CANTRELL, Wayne Edward, 1946-47-48
CANTWELL, Frank Pierce, Jr., 1965-66
CAPPELLETTI, Robert Anthony, 1952-53-54
CARGILE, Neil, 1924-25-26
CARLEN, Bill, 1940
CARLOSS, Matt, 1933-34
CARMAN, Charles "Chili", 1913-14-16
CARMAN, George, 1917
CARMICHAEL, Dave, 1971
CARNEY, John Wesley, 1969-70-71
CARSON, James "Kit", 1935-36
CARTER, David Kelly, 1977
CARTWRIGHT, John, 1925
CASELLA, Joseph Francis, 1978
CATE, Billy, 1943
CECIL, Ernest Bernard, 1975-76-77-78
CECIL, Hugh, 1925-26-27
CHALFANT, Bertram "Trinny", 1928
CHANDLER, John Wilson, 1976-77
CHAPMAN, John B., 1927
CHEADLE, John Roaten, 1950-51-52
CHENAULT, Frank, 1938
CHERRY, L. W. "Wink", 1936
CHESHIRE, J. Ross, 1909, Mgr.
CHESLEY, Curtis Lee, 1968-69-70
CHESLEY, Gary William, 1969-71-72
CHESLEY, Jay Emory, 1972-74-75
CHESTER, Martin S. "Yunk", 1912-13-14-15
CHESTER, Sam, 1915
CHILTON, Bobby, 1943
CHORN, Walker K., 1906
CLAFFEY, Harold "Hal", 1933-34-35
CLAIBORNE, Daniel W., 1903
CLANCY, William Francis, 1952
CLARK, Allen B., Jr., 1910
CLARK, Cory, 1972
CLARK, John Henry, 1942-46-47-48
CLARK, Thomas Barron, 1963
CLARY, Ronald Perry, 1950
CLERE, Raymond, 1936
CLEVELAND, Hal, 1914, Mgr.
CLEVELAND, Jon Raymond, 1962-63
CLINARD, Zack Norman, 1947-48
CLINTON, Richard Dean, 1976
CLOSE, Vernon, 1931-32-33
CLUNAN, Charles William, 1949
COBB, David George, 1953, Mgr.
COBB, Rodney Allen, 1958-60
CODY, Josh, 1914-15-16-19
COFFEY, John W., 1891
COHEN, H. Russell, 1913-14-15-16
COLE, Kenneth Bridges, Jr., 1978
COLEMAN, Andrew, Frank, 1978
COLEMAN, Stephen Albert, 1968-69
COLES, Zach A., 1924-25-26
COLLIER, Harris 1938
COLLINS, Christopher Alan, 1964-65-67
COLLINS, Wilson, 1911-12
COMBS, James Lee, 1968-69
CONNELL, Allen, 1909
CONNELL, W., 1892-93-94-95-96-97
CONYERS, Percy, 1920-21-22
COOK, Joe, 1970-71-72
COOK, Sylbert Malcolm, 1950-51-52
COOKE, John, 1943
COOPER, Kenneth Rousseau, 1942-46-47-48
COPP, Carl Andrew, Jr., 1946-47-48-49
CORBIN, William Fizer, 1959-60-61
CORCORAN, Ollie Anthony, 1941-46-47
CORLETTE, Marvin, 1898
CORLETTE, Marvin, Jr., 1927
CORNELIUS, William R., 1900
COSTEN, Sam, 1904-06-07
COUNCIL, Francis E., 1923
COVERDALE, Jonas, 1923
COVINGTON, Cecil B., 1908-09-10
COVINGTON, Joel B., 1908-11-12
COVINGTON, Leslie, 1907-09
COVINGTON, William T., Jr., 1915
COX, Allen, 1908, Mgr.
COX, E. A., 1897-98
COX, James Martin, 1975-76-77-78
CRAGWALL, A. O., 1898-99
CRAIG, John L. "Honus", 1904-05-06-07
CRAIG, Wesley W., 1890-91-92-94
CRAWFORD, Guy, 1905-06-08
CRAWFORD, James Allen, 1941-42-46
CRAWFORD, John K. "Jack", 1934-35
CRAWFORD, William Harris, 1960-61-62
CREAGH, Charles Edward, Jr., 1959-60-61
CREIGHTON, Dudley, 1931
CRESON, Larry "Kitty", 1925-26-27
CRESON, Robert Paul, 1920
CRICHLOW, Collier, 1944
CRIDDLE, Edward S. "Chug", 1918
CRIMM, Lloyd "Cremo", 1931
CROCKER, Julian Doss "Jule", Jr., 1960-61-62
CROPP, John Williamson, 1959-60-61
CROWNOVER, Arthur, Jr., 1927-28-29-30
CRUTCHFIELD, Wallace M "Baby", 1896-97-98-99-1901
CULLEY, David Wayne, 1973-75-76-77
CULPEPPER, Clifford Lee, 1972-74-75
CUMMINGS, Bob, 1942
CUMMINGS, Joe, 1937, Mgr.
CUNDIFF, Dan Bradley, 1966-67
CUNNINGHAM, Alex, 1906
CUNNINGHAM, James Frank, Jr., 1953-54-55
CUNNINGHAM, James Warren, Jr., 1968-69-70
CURLEY, Pete, 1933-34-35
CURLIN, Zach, 1911-12-13
CURNUTTE, Stephen Bryant, 1973-74-75
CURRY, Irby Rice "Rabbit", 1913-14-15-16
CURTIN, Francis William, Jr., 1965-66-67
CURTIS, Allen B., 1898
CURTIS, Arnold E., 1947-48-49
CURTIS, Ernest Jackson "Bucky", 1947-48-49-50

D

DABNEY, John, 1902
DANIELS, Bert, 1936
DANIELS, Bill, 1927
DARNELL, Alex Whitefield, 1948-50-51
DARNELL, Jesse Cloyce, 1965-66
DARNELL, Leonard, 1910
DAVES, Herman, 1912-17-18
DAVID, Gary Michael, 1966-67
DAVIDSON, Simpson Dean, 1947-48-49-50
DAVIE, Edgar Byron, 1956
DAVIN, Charles C., 1915
DAVIS, Abe, 1928
DAVIS, Cato, 1897
DAVIS, Charlton, 1939-40
DAVIS, Daniel Muncaster, 1958
DAVIS, H. A., 1892
DAVIS, H. W. "Huldy", 1899-1900-01-02
DAVIS, Herbert W. "Peaches", 1929-31
DAVIS, J. T., 1925
DAVIS, Jefferson, Jr., 1956
DAVIS, Simeon Benton, III, 1963
DAVIS, Thomas Larkin, 1968
DAVIS, Thomas W., 1894-95-96-98
DAVIS, Thomas W., Jr., 1933
DAWSON, Michael Howard, 1965-66
DAY, Frank L., 1892
DEAN, Richard Darrell, 1977-78
DEAN, Richard Nils, 1974
DEIDERICH, George Ronald, 1956-57-58
DeMAIN, James Henry, 1951-53
DEMMAS, Arthur George "Art", 1952-53-55-56
DEMMAS, Constantine George, 1953
DEVANE, John Thomas, 1968
DICKERSON, George Washington, 1977
DICKERSON, Gordon, 1925
DICKINSON, Joe, 1936
DICKINSON, Overton, 1931
DICKISON, Leo, 1932-33-34
DIEHL, Willie, 1970-71
DIETRICH, Mark William, 1972-73-74
DIFFEE, Jimmy, 1944
DIXON, Paul Randall "Rand", 1933-34-35
DOAK, E. L., 1895
DODD, Thomas Speer, 1951-53
DONAHOO, Duane, 1970
DONALDSON, Sammy Lanier, 1956
DONNELL, Ben Clay, 1957-58
DORTCH, Fred W., 1891-93-94-95
DOSS, Aubrey K., 1896
DOTY, Burnett J., 1920
DOUGHTERTY, Lew W., 1911
DOWNS, Bobby, 1971
DOZIER, Steven, 1976-77-78, Mgr.
DRAKE, Bill, 1931
DRAKE, John Allen, Jr., 1969-70-71
DUBOIS, Charles, 1933-34
DUDLEY, Edward Gordon, 1957-58
DUDLEY, Guilford, Jr., 1927-28
DUFFEY, Mack, 1970
DUNCAN, Roy Lester, 1950-52

DUNCAN, William Erastus, Jr., 1952
DUNGAN, William Jeff, 1977
DUNKERLEY, Herbert, 1938-39
DUNN, Robert E., Jr., 1927-28
DUNSTER, Michael Edward, 1978
DURAND, Harry "Happy", 1930-31
DUVAL, Robert Edward, III, 1969-70-71
DYE, John S., 1895-96-98
DYE, Terrell Eugen, 1960-61-62

E

EARL, Carl, 1933-34
EARLY, James, 1917-19-20
EDGERTON, John E., 1898-99-1900-02
EDMONDSON, Brandon Lee, 1978
EDWARDS, Austin "Peggy", 1929
EDWARDS, Charles Leon, 1977-78
ELAM, Frank "Pos", 1921
ELDER, Rick, 1971
ELLINGTON, Edward Perry, 1946-47-48
ELLIOTT, Floyd Strother, Jr., 1976, Mgr.
ELLIOTT, W. Y., Jr., 1893-94-95
ELLIS, John, 1938-39-40
ELROD, Parker, 1938
ENGLISH, Timothy Joseph, 1975-76-77-78
ERNST, Steven Earl, 1967-68
ERVIN, Andy Lee, 1978
ERVIN, Norwood Martin, 1977-78
ESTES, Pat M., 1890
EVANS, David Mulbern, 1961
EVELAND, William Greg, 1975-76-77-78
EVINS, Joe, 1932
EWERS, William "Bill", 1944-45

F

FAILS, Terence Neil, 1950-54
FAIRCLOTH, Bryan, 1926
FANT, Lester G., 1897-98
FARRELL, Louis "Tab", 1896-97
FARRIS, Robert Gordon, 1951
FAULKINBERRY, Russell Miller, 1947-48-49-50
FERNANDEZ, Medina Anibal, 1955, Mgr.
FINNERN, Mike, 1970
FISHER, Frederick Morrell, 1972-73-74-75
FITZGERALD, William S., 1893-94-95-96
FLANIGAN, Mickey, 1939-40
FLEMING, Partee, 1936-37
FLETCHER, F. M., 1892
FLOYD, John Franklin, 1975
FLOYD, John "Red", 1915-16-19-20
FLYNN, Barry Burgin, 1978
FOLMAR, Jimmy, 1941
FORD, Turney, 1936-37-38
FORTUNE, Selman "Chuggy", 1930-31-32
FOSTER, Julian, 1930-31-32
FOSTER, Ray, 1923
FOSTER, Richard Henry, 1950-51-52
FOTTRELL, Harold, 1928
FOUST, Buryl, 1929-31
FRANCIS, Clyde Milton, III, 1976-77-78, Trn.
FRANCIS, Raymond, 1937-38
FRANK, Laurence Milton, 1952-53-54-55
FRANKLIN, Marvin "Preacher", Jr., 1936-37-38
FRANKLIN, Tom, 1928
FREELAND, Ewing "Big 'Un", 1908-09-10-11
FRIEL, Gaylord N. "Billy", 1915
FRIERSON, Greer, 1944
FRITTS, Steven Bradford, 1968-69-70
FRITZ, Gregory William, 1972-74
FRITZ, Emile, 1941
FUGE, Linc, 1971-72-73
FUGLER, Clarence, 1905
FULGER, Pearly M., 1900
FUNK, Charles Barrett, 1959-60
FUNK, David Franklin, 1978
FUQUA, John Herman, 1968
FUQUA, Lindsay Wilford, 1962-63-64
FUQUA, William George, 1945-46-48

G

GAINES, Charles L., 1894
GAINES, Robert F., 1961-62, Mgr.
GAIBIERZ, Thomas Richard, 1972-73-74-75
GALLALEE, William "Bill", 1944
GARCIA, Martin Anthony, 1972-73-74
GARDEN, Thomas Proctor, Jr., 1959-60-61
GARDENHIRE, F. M., 1891
GARRISON, Frank M., 1975
GAUDET, Thomas Andrew, 1962
GAULDEN, Charles, 1938-39
GENY, Charles Francis "Willie", 1933-34
GERST, Gerald Garrett, 1964
GIBSON, Everett, 1923-25
GIBSON, Geoffory Jay, 1969-70
GIBSON, Roy M., 1926-28-29
GILLESPIE, Paul Trowbridge, 1966-67-68
GILLILAND, Frank, 1911, Mgr.
GILTNER, Michael Eugene, 1966-67-68
GILTNER, Robin Lynn, 1976-77-78
GLASGOW, McPheeters "Mack", 1935-36
GLEISNER, Donald Allen, 1950-52
GOAD, Paul Ellis, 1952
GOAR, Frank, 1916-17-18-19-20
GODCHAUX, Frank A., 1899-1900
GODCHAUX, Frank A., Jr., 1920-21
GOLDEN, Hawkins, 1972-73
GOLDEN, Winfred Lewis, 1950-51
GOODALL, Robert Harden, 1952-53-54
GOODGAME, John, 1943
GOODRIDGE, Robert Wayne, 1966-67
GOODSON, Joe A., 1893-97-98
GORRELL, Frank Cheatham, 1945-46-47
GOSSAGE, Matthew Edward, 1973-74-75
GOTHARD, Dennis Michael, 1975-76-77-78
GRACEY, Clarence "Pete", 1930-31-32
GRAHAM, Joe Harold, 1962-63-64
GRAHAM, Thomas B. "Irish", 1902-03-04
GRASTY, Felix K., 1923, Mgr.
GRAVES, Joe, 1943-44-45
GRAVES, Junius Greenwood, 1948-50
GRAY, Tommy, 1945
GREEN, Charles C. "Willie", 1904, Mgr.
GREER, George J., 1916
GRIFFEN, Malvern U., 1908-09
GRIMMETT, Hill, Jr., 1936
GROVER, Billy Dwain, 1956-57-58
GROVES, Adolph Milton, Jr., 1974-75-76
GRUBER, Wayne Edward, 1952
GUDE, Bob, 1939-40-41
GUEPE, Arthur Albert, 1961-62-63
GUFFEE, Paul Owen, 1962-63-64
GULLETT, James B., 1929
GURLEY, Rodney Steven, 1978
GWYNEE, Walter E., 1901

H

HAGER, R. B. "Dick", 1908
HAGER, Samuel E., 1892
HAGEWOOD, Jack Douglas, 1958-59
HAGGARD, Wallace C., 1919-20
HAIL, Conway, 1939, Mgr.
HALE, David Lebron, 1974-75-76
HALE, R. E., 1892
HALE, Ronald Corey, 1976-78
HALEY, Parnell, 1936
HALFORD, Jack, 1948
HALL, Glenn A. "Spick", 1906-07
HALL, John Richard, 1951-52-53-54
HALL, Millard Wayne, 1960-61
HALL, Robert Hall, 1935-36
HALL, Scott Richard, 1965-66-67
HALLIBURTON, Ben, 1917
HALLMAN, David Alton, 1959
HAMBRICK, Thomas C., 1931
HAMILTON, Bob, 1942-43
HAMILTON, C. M. "Big Six", 1915-16
HAMILTON, Ed J., 1902-03-04-05
HAMILTON, Fred Samuel, 1941-42-46
HAMILTON, Fred Samuel "Buzz", Jr., 1969-70-71
HAMILTON, James "Bones", 1943-45
HAMMER, Bruce Wesley, 1960-61
HAMMERSCHMIDT, John Howard, Jr., 1964-65-66
HAMMERSCHMIDT, Michael Lawrence, 1969-70
HAMMOND, Harry Ken, 1978
HAMPTON, Jerry Randall, 1976-77
HAMPTON, Wade, 1933-34
HANNA, Ross, 1937-38-39
HANNER, J. P., 1892-93
HARBER, David Mark, 1974-75
HARDAGE, Lewis, 1911-12
HARDEN, James, 1939
HARDEN, W. Holmes, 1890-91-92
HARDY, Arnold Rance, 1945-48-49
HARDY, Edward D., 1916
HARDY, J. C., 1899
HARDY, Lamar, 1899
HARKINS, Thomas Vincent, 1954-55
HARLOW, Gene, 1939-40
HARRIS, Charles Edward, 1978
HARRISON, Claude, 1942
HARRISON, Dennis, 1974-75-76-77
HARRISON, Durwood, 1971-72-73, Mgr.
HART, Gary Curtis, 1962-63-64
HART, W. B., 1909
HART, William, 1977
HARWELL, W. S., 1900
HASSETT, Charles R., 1896-97
HASSLOCK, Lewis W. "Red", 1907-08
HAUCK, Walter Christie, 1967-68-69
HAUN, David, 1970-71
HAURY, Karl Edward "Sandy", Jr. 1969-70-71
HAUSE, Francis, 1937-38
HAWKINS, Charles, 1926-27-28
HAWKINS, Charles Winstead, III 1951-52-53
HAYES, Frank M. "Squint", 1914-15-16
HAYES, Larry Gene, 1954-55
HAYES, Larry Wayne, 1969-70-71
HAYGOOD, Jimmy "Shag", 1904-05
HAYS, Sammy, 1939
HAYS, William, 1935-36-37
HEALY, William Raymond "Chip", Jr. 1966-67-68
HEBBERGER, Arthur Francis, 1950
HEFLIN, Terence Van, 1977-78
HEISTAND, Ed, 1938-39-40
HELLER, Frank R., "Hank", 1920
HENDERSON, Thomas, 1930-31-32
HENDERSON, Woodrow "Tomcat", 1937-38
HENDRICK, Harvey "Gink", 1917-19-20
HENDRIX, W. R. "Bill", 1924-25-26
HENLEY, Guy, 1944
HENLEY, William Roger, 1952
HENRY, Douglas "Duck", 1910-13
HERBERT, John, 1927-28
HERBERT, Robert, Jr., 1928
HERNDON, Don Wayne, 1961
HEWITT, Buddy, 1945
HEYWOOD, Humphrey Barrett, III, 1953-54-55
HICKS, Henry Joe, 1947-48-49
HIGGINS, Gene, 1939-40
HILDEBRAND, James, B., 1892-93-94-95
HILL, Horace G., Jr., 1918–19-20
HILL, Merlin Michael, 1977
HILL, Page, 1936, Mgr.
HILLEY, Rayford Carrol, 1957-58-59
HINKLE, Carl Columbus, Jr., 1935-36-37
HINKLE, Carl Columbus "Chris", III, 1967
HINTON, Ralph, 1937-38-39
HIRSCH, Edward M., 1974-76
HOATS, Joseph Miranda, 1968
HOBBS, Maurice "Preacher", 1930
HOBBS, S. F. "Fatty", 1905
HOLBY, William Arthur, 1974-75
HOLDER, Fred 1940-41-42
HOLDGRAF, Maurice "Tiny", 1938-39-40
HOLLAND, Al, 1937
HOLLINS, Lunsford, 1936-37-38
HOLMES, Andrew, 1926, Mgr.
HOLMES, Billy Hamlin, 1952-53-55
HOLMES, Francis "Ducky", 1917-19-20-21

HOLT, Carleton "Pete', 1948-49-50
HOLT, Charles Everette, 1941-42-46
HOOD, Lamar, Eddie, 1977-78
HOOVER, Charles Ellis, 1952-53-54-55
HOOVER, Charles Marcus, 1942-46
HOOVER, John, 1970-71
HORTON, Charles, 1952-53-54-55
HOSKINS, Leon, 1931, Mgr.
HOUSMAN, Hardy, 1937-38-39
HOUSTON, Frank K., 1900-01-02
HOUSTON, George, 1931, Mgr.
HOWARD, Matthew Thomas, 1961
HOWE, John B. A., 1895-96
HOWELL, Clark, 1892-95
HOWELL, Joseph T., 1901-02-03
HUDGINS, Loie Malcolm, 1978
HUDGINS, Ward, 1930-31
HUDSON, Gary Richard, 1960-61-62
HUDSON, Gerald Jack, 1954-55-56
HUFFMAN, Chester C., 1911-12-13-14
HUGGINS, James, 1935-36-37-38
HUGGINS, Roy, 1939-40
HUGHES, Charles, 1929-30-31
HUGHES, Floyd Ray, 1977
HUGHES, Robert Littleton, 1958
HUGHES, Thack, 1931
HUGHES, Thomas W. "Tootie", 1923
HUGHES, Travis Hubert, 1957-58-59
HUGHES, William Wightman, 1893-94-95-96-99-1900-01
HUGHES, William Wightman, Jr., 1927
HUMBLE, John Randolph, 1963-64-65
HUME, Fred, 1901
HUMPHREY, Howard, 1938-39
HUMPHREYS, William Douglas, 1974-75-76-77
HUNT, Donald Austin, 1953-54-55
HUNTER, Pat, 1973
HURLEY, James, 1970
HURST, Dunlap, 1959
HURT, Sidney, 1896
HUSBAND, Phillip Daniel, 1968
HUTTO, James Albert, 1947-48-49
HUTTON, W. G., 1897

I

ILGENFRITZ, Mark, 1971-72-73
ILGENFRITZ, Scott Carter, 1976-77-78
INGRAM, John Thomas, 1967-68-69
IRBY, Jack, 1938-39
IVEY, Robert Barnes, 1966-67
IZLAR, Paul Roberts Poinsett, 1975
IZZAGUIRRE, Carlos, 1943

J

JABALEY, Michael Ellis, 1954
JACKSON, Felix, 1938
JACKSON, Granbery, 1894-95, Mgr.
JACKSON, John, 1936-37
JACKSON, N. Baker, 1910, Mgr.
JACKSON, Robert F., 1915-17
JACOBS, Michael W., 1973-74-75
JACOBS, Wayne, 1971-72
JACOWAY, Boyd Gaines, 1948-49
JALUFKA, Earl Davis, 1953-54-55
JAMES, Jesse Ray, 1925-26-27
JAMES, William, 1970
JARRETT, John "Straighty", 1914-15
JENKINS, Jack, 1940-41-42
JENKINS, William O., 1900
JOHNSON, Barney Paul, 1976
JOHNSON, David Eugene, 1973-74-75-76
JOHNSON, Eugene, 1931
JOHNSON, James Bishop, 1959-60-61
JOHNSON, Ralph Lamar, 1977
JOHNSON, Smith Alexander "Babe", 1900
JOHNSON, Walter Dillon, 1959
JOHNSON, Warren Murphy, Jr., 1976-77
JOHNSTON, Donald McDonald "Duck", 1968-69-70
JOHNSTON, Fred "Froggy", 1929-30-31
JONES, Billy Mac, 1948-49
JONES, Daniel Morgan, 1958
JONES, Elliott H., 1890-91-92
JONES, Erwin Arthur Jr., 1952-53
JONES, Grinnell, 1901-03
JONES, Herbert, 1910
JONES, Madison, 1944
JONES, Ogle "Cowboy", 1926
JONES, Robert Knapp, Jr., 1975-76
JORDAN, Nancy "River", 1931-32-33
JORDAN, Walter Arnell, 1975-76-77-78
JOSEPH, Anthony A., 1972-74
JUDAY, William Robert, 1962-63-64
JUMPER, James Calhoun, Jr., 1976

K

KAELIN, Richard Bruce, 1966
KALEY, Jack, 1943-45
KATZENTINE, Frank, 1920
KEATHLEY, Royalyn, 1952-53
KEENE, Arthur, 1936-37-38
KEENE, Buford C. "Pete", 1933
KEENE, Jesse, 1924-25-26
KEESE, Virden Lamar, 1949-51
KELLER, William J., 1893-94
KELLEY, Chester, III, 1976
KELLY, Everett E. "Tuck", 1922-23-24
KELLY, Fred, 1926-27-28
KELLY, Harry, 1942
KELLY, J. C., 1938
KELLY, William Brown, 1965-66-67, Mgr.
KEMP, William Harold, Jr., 1975-76-77-78
KEMPLE, Bernard James, 1965-66-67
KENNEDY, Edward F., 1895
KENNEDY, Lyndal Ray, 1968
KENNY, Thomas Francis, 1961-62-63
KERR, Robert William, 1964-65
KILLEBREW, Joe, 1922, Mgr.
KILLEBREW, William, 1928, Mgr.
KILPATRICK, Lyle Reed, 1977-78
KILZER, Walter, 1942
KING, Clarence "Clancy", 1931-32
KING, John J., 1906-07
KING, Philip Edgar, 1955-56-57
KIRK, Michael, 1970-71-72
KIRKES, Leonard, 1923
KIRKLAND, Joseph Theodore, Jr., 1949-50
KIRWAN, Pat, 1929-30-31
KISER, Samuel Hugh, III, 1969-70-71
KISS, Stephen Michael, 1964-65-66
KITTRELL, Thomas G., 1891-92-93-94-95
KLAASS, Reinhard Manfred, 1966-67
KNAPP, Bradford, 1890-91
KOMISAR, Sol, 1938-39
KRIETEMEYER, William Ernest, 1952-53
KUGLER, Doyle Edward, 1950
KUHN, Oliver W. "Doc", 1920-21-22-23
KYLE, Charles, 1925
KYLE, Frank "Stitch", 1901-02-03-04-05

L

LACY, Chancellor, 1933-34
LAINHART, Stephen P., 1972-74
LAKOS, T. M. "Mickey", 1950-51-52
LAMBERSON, Lambert George, 1952-54-55
LANCASTER, James, 1924-25-26
LANGHORST, Henry F., 1896-97-98
LASSITER, R. L. "Big Un", 1917
LATHAM, Robert, 1970-71-72
LATHAM, Swayne, 1919-20
LATIMER, Robert W., 1974-75
LAWRENCE, Robert L., III, 1943-46-47-48
LAWRENCE, Robert L. "Fatty", 1921-22-23-24
LAWS, Robert Chesley, 1955-56-57
LAWSON, Ronnie, 1972
LEA, Percy, 1930, Mgr.
LEAK, William, 1928
LEDYARD, Q. R. "Bob", 1924-25-26
LEE, Bill David, 1972-73-74
LEE, Charles, 1931
LEFFERS, David, 1970-71-72
LEHARD, Jack, 1942
LEMAY, Richard Ervin, 1964-65
LEONARD, Amos "Mouse", 1929-30-31
LESESNE, Henry Roby, 1960-61-62
LEVINE, Alfred T., 1935, Mgr.
LEYENDECKER, Charles "Tex", 1930-31-32
LILLY, Mitchell Keith, 1975-76-77
LINDSAY, Paul, 1922-23-24
LINDSAY, Dick J. R., 1931
LINDSEY, Edwin W., 1899
LINDSEY, Robert, 1933, Mgr.
LINVILLE, James Harrison, 1956-57
LIPE, J. T., 1927-28
LIPPERMAN, Daniel Douglas, 1967-69
LIPSCOMB, David "Rusty", 1926-27
LIPSCOMB, Tom, 1914-15-16-19
LITTLE, Joe, 1937
LLEWELLYN, Mark B., 1972-73-74
LOCKETT, Robert L. "Big Bob", 1930
LOCKETT, Robert W. "Little Bob", 1930
LOCKHARD, James E. "Fatty", 1906
LOCKMAN, Paul "Tex", 1918-19
LOGAN, Terrance Michael, 1976
LOKEY, Warren, 1928-29
LONG, William Royston, 1967-68
LONGLEY, David Bennett, 1962
LOONEY, James Francis, 1953-54
LO PARO, Joe, 1936
LOVE, William S., 1902
LOVELACE, Carl, 1899
LOVELACE, James Robert, 1952
LOWE, R. E., 1912-13-14
LUCAS, James, 1933-34-35
LUCK, Malcolm, 1912
LUCKEY, Joseph Frank, 1957, Mgr.
LUSK, Curtis Eugene, 1976-78
LUSKY, Lehman "Pluto", 1926-27-28
LYLE, Leslie Neil, 1967-68-69
LYNCH, Charles D., 1895
LYON, John Hill, 1969

M

MACK, Lester Frank, 1978
MacKENZIE, Charles, F., 1891
MacLEAN, Alexander Wallace, IV, 1966
MADDUX, David Douglas, 1964-65-66
MADDUX, James Edward, 1946-47
MADISON, Charles Scott, 1978
MAHAFFEY, Dan, 1972
MAHAN, James, 1970-71-72
MAJORS, Charles, 1938, Mgr.
MALLORY, C. Buford, 1898
MALONE, David Julian, 1962-63-64
MALONE, W. Battle, 1893-94-95
MALSBERGER, Douglas Robert, 1945-48-49
MANIER, J. Owsley, 1904-05-06
MANIER, Miller, 1917, Mgr.
MANSFIELD, Vaughn, 1930
MAPLE, Ralph Earl, 1957
MAPLES, Gilbert "Firpo", 1927
MARCHETTI, Gino, 1970-71
MARGO, Dee, 1973
MARLIN, George, 1939-40-41
MARSH, Earl, 1931
MARSHALL, Bert, 1937-38
MARSHALL, George G., 1901, Mgr.
MARTIN, Carl "Zeke", 1909-10-11
MARTIN, Charles P., 1898-99-1902
MARTIN, Douglas H., 1972-73-74
MARTIN, Gregory Allan, 1975-76-77
MARTIN, James D., 1948, Mgr.
MARTIN, Thomas Floyd, 1962-63
MASON, John, 1925
MASSEY, Felix M., 1899-1902
MATHERS, Jesse Lee, Jr., 1973-74-75
MATHEWS, William Douglas, 1968-69
MATLOCK, Mark Daniel, 1977-78
MAUERMAN, George Schmid, 1958
MAY, Daryle Cline, 1946-47-48-49
MAY, Roger Tyler, 1966-67
MAYES, Cannon Roberts, 1949
MAZAR, Dennis, 1971
McALESTER, J. B., 1897
McARTHUR, Gene, 1943
McCAIN, John Michael, 1977-78
McCALL, Danny Campbell, 1956-57
McCARLEY, Trimmier, 1939, Mgr.
McCARTER, Gordon William, 1950
McCASKELL, Dave, 1971
McCLAIN, Sidney, 1938
McCLELLAN, Charles "Jack", 1931
McCLURE, James, 1898
McCOWN, Jim Elvin, 1949
McCULLERS, David Wayne, 1978
McCULLOUGH, C. R. "Tot", 1920-21-22
McDONALD, Jim, 1943
McDONALD, Kenneth, 1899-1900
McDONALD, William Howell, 1967-68-69
McELREATH, W. A. "Dutch", 1937-38-40

McFARLAND, James K., 1900
McGAUGHY, Paul, 1926-28-29
McGEHEE, Bruce R., 1907-08-09
McGILL, Ralph Emerson, 1917-19
McGUGIN, Dan, Jr., 1929-31
McGUGIN, George Bew, 1960-61
McILWAIN, Eugene "Nig", 1927-28-29
McKEE, James Edward, 1958-59
McKENZIE, K. W., 1921, Mgr.
McKIBBON, Fred Cox, 1924-25-26
McKINNEY, Raymond Carl, Jr., 1953, Mgr.
McKINNON, Thomas Benson, 1952-53-54
McLAIN, W. Tyler "Fatty", 1905-06-07-08
McLEAN, George D., 1899-1900-01
McLEMORE, Morris, 1936-37-38
McNAMARA, Martin, 1928-29-30
McNAMARA, Robert John, 1974-75-76-77
McNEVIN, Bill, 1930-31
McNUTT, William "Billy", 1943
McQUEEN, Ernest D., 1913
McWHIRTER, Terrell, 1941
MEIERS, John F. "Freddie", 1921-22-23
MERCER, James Andrew, 1977-78, Mgr.
MERCER, John Patrick, 1977-78, Mgr.
MERIWETHER, Thomas Nelson, 1967
MERLIN, Ed, 1935-37
METZGER, W. E. "Frog", 1908-09-10-11
MEYER, Kelly Hugh, 1966-68
MILHOLLAND, W. G. "Whitey", 1912-13
MILLER, Brevard, 1925, Mgr.
MILLER, George Daniel "Danny", 1968-69-70
MILLER, John Stevens, 1968-69-70
MILLER, Ronald Vincent, 1957-58-59
MILLS, Daryl Steven, 1973-75-76
MILLS, William, 1941, Mgr.
MINNICK, Norman, 1917-19
MIRON, John Paul, 1952
MITCHELL, Michael W., 1976-78
MITCHELL, R. H., 1890
MIXON, Hugh C., 1920-21-22
MONK, Alonza, Jr., 1903, Mgr.
MONTGOMERY, John, 1944
MOONEY, James C., 1919
MOORE, Barry Timothy, 1978
MOORE, Coke, 1930-31
MOORE, Douglas "Red", 1917
MOORE, Jerry Porter, 1941-42-46
MOORE, Thomas Marshall "Tom", 1957-58-59
MORDICA, Frank Lucious, 1976-77-78
MOREHEAD, William G., 1929-30-31
MORGAN, Albert Johnson, 1898-1902
MORGAN, Hugh "Buddy", 1910-11-12-13
MORRIS, Nathan E., 1892-93
MORRIS, Russell Franklin, Jr., 1958-59-60
MORRISON, Dwight W., 1907
MORRISON, Kent, 1910-11-14-15
MORRISON, Ray, 1908-09-10-11
MORROW, Garland "Gus", 1919-20-22
MORTON, David H., 1907-08
MOSHIER, Eugene, 1972-73-74
MOSS, W. P. "Bill", 1917-19-20
MULLEN, Robert Waynick, 1959-60
MULLIN, William H., Jr., 1933
MURDOCK, John Bush, 1951, Mgr.
MURRAH, Wilson F. "Babe", 1910-11
MURRAY, Jerry David, 1959-60
MURRAY, Tom "Buck", 1913
MYERS, Joe, 1930-31-32
MYRICK, Ronnie, 1976-77-78

N

NALLEY, Lee N., Jr., 1947-48-49
NAREWSKI, Edward, 1970
NAY, Bobby Earl, 1959-60
NEELY, Jesse Claiborne, 1920-21-22
NEELY, W. D. "Bill", 1908-09-10
NEIL, John, 1923
NEILL, Frank K. "Scotty", 1919-20-22
NEILL, Sam, 1922-23
NETTLES, Doug, 1971-72-73
NEUHOFF, John, 1931
NEWMAN, Charles Bradley, 1951-52-53
NEWTON, Harry, 1931
NICHOLS, John, 1900
NICHOLS, William Ronald, 1973-74
NICKSON, Rodrick Matthew, 1976
NILAN, George, 1926
NOEL, Edwin, 1906
NOEL, Hayes, 1935-36
NOEL, Lee Francis, 1967-68
NOEL, Oscar F. "Hoss", 1905-06-10
NOEL , Oscar F., III, 1933-34
NOLEN, Beverly T., 1902
NORFLEET, Vance, 1925
NORMAN, Newton L., 1916
NORMAN, Robert S., 1947-48, Mgr.
NORRED, Van, 1925-26-27
NORTH, Donald Christopher, III, 1966-68
NORTH, John Puckett, 1942-46-47
NORTHCUTT, H. B. "Cutter", 1914-15
NORVELL, Spencer, 1916
NOVAK, Andrew Michael, 1951-52-53

O

OAKS, Ralph Edward, 1973-74-75
O'CONNOR, Myles P., 1895-96-98
OETTER, Robert Leighton, 1975, Mgr.
OLIVER, Bobby, 1933-34-35
OLIVER, James "Country", 1926-27-28
OLSEN, Julian, 1940-41-42
O'NEAL, Gregory Merle "Greg", 1969-70-71
O'NEAL, John Elvin, 1975-76
O'NEAL, Robert, 1971-72
ORDUNG, John, 1971
ORMAN, John, 1934, Mgr.
O'ROURKE, James P., 1971-73-74
ORR, Donald Cooper, 1954-55-56
ORR, Perry, 1922-23
ORR, Rufus W. "Dub", 1924
ORTH, Charles William, 1964-65-66
OUSLEY, Charles Rogers, 1964-65-66
OVERALL, P. V. "Putty", 1921
OVERLEY, Glenn, 1933-34-35
OVERTON, John, 1900
OVERTON, Walter J., 1971-72-74
OWEN, Ralph "Peck", 1925-26-27
OWEN, Thomas Braden "Big Tom", 1941-43-45-46
OWEN, Thomas "Lil Tom", 1942

P

PAGE, Thomas Everette, 1946-48-49
PAGE, Walter Robert, 1947-48
PAINTER, Dennis Sherman, 1969-70-71
PALMER, Abe, 1938
PALMER, Ed, 1907, Mgr.
PALUMBO, Paul Louis, 1976
PAPUCHIS, Jason Avery, 1952-54
PARKER, Benny, 1929-30
PARKER, Chester Leon, Jr., 1964-65
PARKER, George Phillip, 1964-66
PARKER, Harold, 1915
PARKER, William Lafayette, 1956
PARR, Travis, 1973
PARRISH, Charles, 1970-71-72
PARRISH, Edward, II, 1974-75-76-77
PATRICK, Jim, 1945
PATTERSON, David, 1938
PATTERSON, Michael Curtis, 1967-68-69
PATTERSON, Robert C. "Emma", 1900-03-04-05
PATTERSON, Thomas Keys, 1946-47-48-49
PATTON, Bo, 1971-72-73
PATY, Ben, 1972
PAUL, Bill, 1925
PEACOCK, A. F., 1895
PEAY, Charles, 1917
PEEBLES, Arnold "Nollie", 1933-34
PEEBLES, Jeff, 1970-71-72
PEEBLES, Mac, 1939-40-41
PEEBLES, William, 1936
PEGG, Robert Lamoine, Jr., 1966-67-68
PEOPLES, Joe, 1927
PEPOY, Steve Joseph, 1954–55
PEREZ, Ernest Joseph, 1969
PERRY, Alex, 1901-02-03
PERRY, Carlton, 1937-38
PETRONE, Emile, Jr., 1938-39-40
PETRONE, Joseph Anthony, 1977-78, Trn.
PHELPS, Carlyle, 1933
PHILLIPP, Louis S. "Dutch", 1914-15
PHILLIPS, Williar Keith, 1978
PHILLIPS, Y. Y., Jr., 1948-49-50
PHILPOT, Richard Horace, 1949-50-51
PICKETT, James "Iron Man", 1929-31
PIERCE, George, 1933
PILCHER, Campbell, 1900
PITMAN, J. B., 1890
PITTMAN, Allen, 1907
PITTMAN, Kenneth M., 1972-74-75
PLASMAN, Herbert G. "Dick", 1934-35-36
PLUNKETT, Junius "Doc", 1937-38-39
POINTER, John Leslie, 1976-77-78
POLYTINSKY, Eugene B., 1920
POOL, Yelton, 1947-49
PORTER, P. H., 1890
PORTER, S. T., 1921-22-23
PORTER, W. E. "Slim", 1921-22-23-25
POST, Orville, 1941
POTTER, James Terry, 1977-78
POTTS, Hugh F. "Rabbit", 1907
POWELL, Andrew J., 1907-08
POWELL, Hagan, 1931-32-33
POWELL, Will Ed, 1941-42
POWELL, William Eugene "Bill", 1947-48-49
POWER, Daniel Edward, III, 1964
POWERS, T. W., 1898
PRESTON, Morgan "Bo", 1913
PRESZNICK, Joe, 1936
PRICE, Charlie, 1914-16
PRICHARD, Joe "Beersheba", 1903-04-05-06
PUTNAM, Emmett P., 1913-14-15
PYATT, Frank, 1895

Q

QUINN, Whayne, 1928-29

R

RAGLAND, Charles S. "Hoss", 1915
RAGSDALE, Earl, 1941
RAINES, James Rex, 1965-67-68
RAINEY, Horace, Jr., 1938-39
RALSTON, Michael Anthony, 1976-77-78
RAMSEY, William, 1930
RANSOM, Robert Sidney, Jr., 1965-66-67
RAY, Buford "Baby", 1935-36-37
RAY, David Preston, Jr., 1957-58
RAY, Henry K. "Dough", 1915-16
RAY, William Jennings, Jr., 1951-52-56-57
RAYBURN, Charlie R. "Oklahoma", 1920
REAMS, Boudinot, 1897
REAMS, Glen H., 1912-13-14
REBROVICH, Art, 1940-41-42
REDMOND, Thomas Benjamin, Jr., 1958
REED, James, 1918
REED, Mark, 1970-71
REESE, Gil, 1922-23-24-25
REESE, Michael Gilbert, 1960-61-62
REEVES, John Murphy, 1918-19
REEVES, Terry Cameron, 1968-70
REGAS, Chris, 1971
REGEN, Joel Damon, 1973-74-75
REGEN, W. D., 1938
REID, Rayford S. "Griper", 1924-25
REILLY, Edward Joseph, 1975
REINSCHMIDT, Clarence "Dutch", 1936-37-38
REMMERS, John, 1971-72
RETTIG, Terrance Michael, 1968-69-70
REYER, George "Pud", 1912-13-14-15
REYNOLDS, Joseph F., 1972-73-74-75
RICE, Grantland, "Granny", 1895
RICE, William Russell, Jr., 1965-66
RICE, Zelotes "Country", 1933
RICH, David Tate, 1972-73-74-75
RICH, Herbert Richard "Herb", 1946-47-48-49
RICH, John, 1945
RICHARD, Amon Jackson, 1946
RICHARDS, Jack, 1941-42
RICHARDSON, Charles, 1919, Mgr.

RICHARDSON, Charles B., 1914-15-16
RICHARDSON, Doyle Ernest, 1955-56-57
RICHARDSON, Mark S., "Top", 1916-17-19
RICHEY, Robert C., 1900
RICHTER, Harry, 1940-41-42
RICKETSON, Greer, 1936-37
RIDGEWAY, Frank, 1910
RIDLEY, Tom, 1915
RIGGS, Frederick Martin, 1958-59-60
RILEY, Timothy L., 1974-75-76
RITTER, Gerald, F., 1948
RIVES, Bob, 1923-24-25
ROACH, Joe, 1915-16
ROBBINS, Charles "Splitter", 1935-36
ROBBINS, Fred "Rabbi", 1909-10-11-12
ROBERTS, Albert, 1923
ROBERTS, Claude, 1932
ROBERTS, Clyde "Dixie", 1930-31
ROBERTS, Jerry Lee, 1976-77-78
ROBERTS, John, 1901
ROBERTS, Kenneth Lewis, 1951-52
ROBERTSON, William Alexander "Tex", Jr., 1941-46-47
ROBINSON, Charles Stanley, 1976
ROBINSON, Garner Een, 1957
ROBINSON, Harry Thomas, 1943-46
ROBINSON, John Ray, 1968-69-70
ROBINSON, Mac Edward, 1947-48-49-50
ROBINSON, Thomas Michael, 1950-51-52
RODEFFER, Henry DeWitt, 1976
RODERICK, Benjamin Aaron, 1950-51-52
ROGERS, Britt, 1930, Mgr.
ROHLING, Bernard Joseph, 1941-42-47
ROLFE, John McKain, 1958-59
ROONEY, E. F. "Mike", 1920, Mgr.
ROSENBLATT, W. F., Jr., 1927-28-29
ROSS, E. B. "Ted", 1908-09-10
ROUNTREE, Walter, 1921-22-23
ROWELL, Hendrix, 1928, Mgr.
ROWLAND, J. H. "Bo", 1923-24
RUCKER, Granville, 1926-27
RUE, Harrison, 1940-41
RUHM, Herman D., 1890
RUSHING, John Bryan, 1969-70
RUTLEDGE, Andrew Richard, 1976-77
RYAN, Graham, 1925-26
RYAN, Tom, 1920-21-23-24

S

SADLER, Lonnie R., 1972-73-74-75
SADLER, Robert "Bobby", 1944
SANDERS, Bennett A., 1891
SANDERS, Dan, 1936
SANDERS, Henry R. "Red", 1924-25-26
SATTERFIELD, Alfred Neal, 1941-42-46
SAYLES, Richard, 1970
SCALES, Joseph Hugh, 1955-56
SCARBROUGH, A. L., 1900
SCARRITT, Charles W., 1891
SCHAFFLER, John, 1971-72-73
SCHAFFLER, Thomas F., 1973-74
SCHEFFER, Charles, 1928-29-30
SCHEFFER, Joe, 1928-29-30
SCHELLENBERG, James B., 1973-74-75
SCHLANT, Bob, 1945
SCHWARTZ, William R., 1928-29-30
SCHWILL, Herman, 1917
SCOGGINS, James, 1933-34
SEEGER, William F., 1915
SEMLOW, David Nicholson, 1966
SEWELL, Isaac, 1898-99
SHACKLEFORD, Burton, 1930-31-32-33
SHANKLIN, J. Gordon, 1930-31
SHAPIRO, John, 1936
SHARP, Alfred D. "Alf", 1919-20-21-22-23
SHARP, Dan, 1929-30-31
SHARP, John Bradley, 1977-78
SHARP, Thomas Hilliard, Jr., 1953, Mgr.
SHARP, Vernon, Jr., 1925-26-27
SHARPE, James C., 1926
SHAVER, Isaac Darrel, 1948-49
SHAW, William Steven, 1961-62-63
SHEA, Tom P., 1912
SHELTON, Howard W., 1948
SHERMAN, James Richard, 1976-78
SHERMAN, N. W. "Dooch", 1917-18-19
SHERRELL, Horace E., 1905-06-07
SHIPP, Cleveland C., 1912
SHIVERS, Ernest E., 1900
SHUFORD, Jerry Franklin, 1963-64-65
SHUGHART, John Albert, Jr., 1966-68
SIBLEY, Jesse, 1902-04
SIKES, Ammie, 1911-12-13-14
SIMMONS, Robert Dean, 1959
SIMMONS, Walter, 1942
SIMMONS, Walter H., 1897-98-99-1900-01
SIMPKINS, Douglas, 1933-34-35
SIMS, Robert J., 1927-28
SINQUEFIELD, J. L., 1931
SITTASON, Randall Gray, 1975-76-77-78
SKAGGS, Cessna Lynn, 1957
SKINNER, David Godfrey, 1978
SKUPAS, John Steven, 1964-65-66
SMART, Richard, 1898-99
SMARTT, Felix, 1939
SMITH, Baxter, 1932
SMITH, DeWitt, 1936-37-38
SMITH, Elmer R., 1895-96-97
SMITH, Flavious Joseph, Jr., 1976-78
SMITH, Frank B., III, 1973-74-75
SMITH, Gary Fred, 1961
SMITH, George Stewart, 1960-61
SMITH, Henry Edward, IV, 1975-76-77-78
SMITH, Howell Stennis, 1958, Mgr.
SMITH, Neal, 1967-68-69
SMITH, Robert Glenn, 1918
SMITH, Rupert, 1921
SMITH, Steven Leslie, 1968-69-70
SMITH, Steven Val, 1963-64-65
SMITH, Viston R., 1929
SMITH, William Boyce, Jr., 1956-57-58
SMITH, William C. "Dub", 1933-34-35
SOBEL, Richard Allen, Jr., 1958-59, Mgr.
SOESBE, Eric Lee, 1956-57
SOUTHALL, L. T., 1971-72-73
SPAIK, Nickolas John, 1962-63
SPALDING, Alanson Reed, III, 1964
SPEAR, Allan Ward, III, 1968-69-70
SPEARS, Bill, 1925-26-27
SPICKARD, Anderson, 1925
SPIER, Charles Allen, 1947-48-49
SPRAGGINS, Thomas Lamar, 1927
SPRINGFIELD, Charles William, 1967-68-69
ST. CHARLES, William Latham, 1975, Trn.
STACK, Bill, 1923
STACK, Jeffrey H., Trn.
STACK, William Edward, 1952-53-55
STAHL, Noel Francis, 1967-68-69
STAHLMAN, James G., 1915, Mgr.
STARLING, Marion Jefferson, 1960-61-62
STEAGALL, George W. "Babe", 1909-10
STEBER, John, 1942
STENDER, Richard Bendict, 1968
STEPHENS, W. R., 1895
STEPHENSON, Joseph Edmond, 1953-54-55
STEPHENSON, Sonny, 1971-72-73, Mgr.
STEVENS, Edward Clarence, 1957
STEVENSON, John Torrey, 1957
STEVEN, L. H., 1901
STEWART, Willis "Slick", 1908-09-10
STEWMAN, Stephen K., 1972-73-74
STOKES, Taylor, 1971
STONE, J. N. "Stein", 1904-05-06-07
STONE, Kenneth, 1970-71-72
STONE, Lawrence Anderson, 1951-52-53
STONE, Pete, 1971-72, Mgr.
STOVER, Earl Bishop, 1947-48-49-50
STRAYHORN, Eugene, 1933-34
STRINGER, Kenneth, 1931
STRINGFIELD, Thomas, 1897
STRONG, David Caldwell, 1967-68-69
STUART, James, 1934
STUMB, Paul, Jr., 1921
STURM, Gerald Wilson, Jr., 1956
SUHRHEINRICH, William, 1932-33
SULLINS, Don, 1944
SULLINS, Robert Milton, 1961-62-64
SULLINS, Samuel Luttrell, III, 1961-62-63
SUTTON, Barrett, 1970-71-72
SWAN, Robert Patterson, Jr., 1955-56-57
SWEENEY, James, 1936-37
SWINDOLL, Phillip Lamar, 1978

T

TABOR, James Carter, 1947-48-49-50
TALLENT, Guy Stanfield, 1960
TALLEY, Marion, 1930-31-32
TATE, Ben, 1908
TAYLOR, Ford, 1893
TAYLOR, Hillsman "Red", 1904-05
TAYLOR, J. R., 1927
TAYLOR, Landon Carter, 1950-51
TAYLOR, Robert Campbell, 1951-52
TAYLOR, Robert Downing, III, 1956-57
TEAGUE, John K., 1915-16
TEAS, Floyd Parson, 1953
TEASLEY, Amos, 1935-36
TEATS, Richard Lee, 1961-62
THIGPEN, Zealand B., 1947-48
THOMAS, James Anthony, 1963-64-66
THOMAS, Jesse, 1929-30-31
THOMAS, John, 1922
THOMAS, Julian, 1919-20
THOMAS, William Madison, 1959-60-61
THOMASON, O. B., 1945
THOMPSON, Benjamin Way, Jr., 1958
THOMPSON, Davison Wheeler, 1960-61
THOMPSON, DeWitt Clinton, IV, 1966-67
THOMPSON, Ed, 1906, Mgr.
THOMPSON, Richard Arland, 1957
THOMPSON, William Eugene, Jr., 1964
THREALKILL, James Ronald, 1977-78
THRO, Linn A., 1917
THROGMORTON, Rannie, 1933-34-35
THRONE, Binford, 1891-92
THURMOND, James C. "Doc", 1929
THURMOND, Paul E., 1961
TIGERT, John J., 1901-02-03
TIGERT, McTyiere, 1915
TIPTON, R. R., 1941
TIPTON, Waymon Reuben, 1976
TKAC, Peter James, 1955-56
TOMLIN, H. B., 1940, Mgr.
TOMLINSON, George, 1970-71-72
TOMPKINS, Tommy, 1971-72-73
TOOMAY, Patrick Jay, 1967-68-69
TOPMILLER, William J., 1972-74
TOUPS, Carroll Marx, 1952-55
TRABUE, Charles Clay, III, 1962-63-64
TRAVIS, James Kerlin, 1957
TRUITT, Alex, 1934-35-36
TRUNDLE, Winfield Scott, 1960
TUNE, Bill, 1945
TURNER, Lester, 1945, Mgr.
TURNER, Phil, 1931
TURNER, Robert, 1913-14-15
TURNER, Vance, 1913
TURNER, W. H. "Peck", 1911-12-13
TUTTLE, R. G., 1894
TYLER, Henry Brown, 1954-55-56
TYREE, Billy, 1945

U

UFFELMAN, Tommy, 1933-34-35
UNDERWOOD, Marvin, 1896
UTLEY, Larry Glenn, 1975-76

V

VALPUT, John William, 1967-68-69
VAUGHAN, William Campbell, 1950, Mgr.
VAUGHN, Harry S., 1892

W

WADDEY, Walter Orum, 1952
WADE, Charles Donelson, 1950-51-52
WADE, David Reynolds, III, 1949, Mgr.
WADE, Grady Lamar, 1960-61-62
WADE, James Paquin "Jamie", 1946-47-48-49
WADE, Joseph Bruce, 1902

WADE, Wheless, Jr., 1938
WADE, William E., 1948, Mgr.
WADE, William J. "Pink", 1919-20-21
WADE, William James "Bill", Jr., 1949-50-51
WAGNER, Larry Eugene, 1958-59
WAKEFIELD, Henry S. "Hek", 1921-22-23-24
WALDRUP, William C., Jr., 1961-62-63
WALKER, James L., 1922-23-24
WALKER, W. T., 1891-92
WALL, John C., 1890
WALL, Mal Loveless, Jr., 1967-69-70
WALLER, David Hager, 1963-64-65
WALLER, E. M. "Nig", 1924-25-26
WALLER, George, 1921-22-23-24-25
WALSH, Bob, 1972-73
WALTON, Dan, 1939-40-41
WALTON, James Richard, 1950
WARD, George William, 1958
WARD, James E. "Mutt", 1927, Mgr.
WARNER, Howell, Jr., 1927-28-29
WARREN, H. F. "Doc", 1913-14
WARWICK, Bill, 1928-29-30
WATKINS, Ernest M. "Buck", 1930-31-32
WATSON, Francis, 1931
WATSON, Herman Austin, Jr., 1952-53-54
WATSON, Wesley, 1935-36
WEAVER, Kimmie Dwight, 1974-75-76-77
WEBB, James Arrington, Jr., 1941-42-46
WEBB, Thomas I., 1900
WEINER, L. D., 1944
WEISS, Karl Robert, 1968-69-70
WELLS, Charles Hilliary, 1961
WELLS, Wallace, 1907
WERCKLE, Robert, 1947-49-50-51
WEST, Bob, 1927-28
WESTGATE, Frank N. "Punky", 1919
WHITE, David Joyce, 1959
WHITE, Gus Barrett "Bart", 1977
WHITE, Hal, 1935-36
WHITE, Tom, 1913
WHITEAKER, Raymond C., 1949, Mgr.
WHITEHEAD, James Tillotson, 1957
WHITESIDE, James Hayes, 1965-66-67
WHITFIELD, Joe, 1931
WHITMAN, Frank L., 1897-98
WHITMAN, W. C., 1896
WHITNEL, Charles Winfred, 1923-24
WHITNELL, W. M., 1913, Mgr.
WHITSITT, Tom, 1931
WHITT, Cody Christopher, 1977
WHORLEY, John H., 1922
WIGGS, Hubert, 1915-19
WILBOURN, David Michael, 1974
WILDMAN, Ronald Joseph, 1958-59-60
WILHITE, Sam, 1915-16-17
WILLET, Kerry Shane, 1976
WILLIAMS, Arthur "Monk", 1936
WILLIAMS, Charles D. "Red", 1921
WILLIAMS, Ernest B. "Freshman", 1919-20
WILLIAMS, Greg, 1972-73
WILLIAMS, Henry "Bo", 1907-08-09-10
WILLIAMS, Pete Turney, 1952-53-54
WILLIAMS, Pryor "Pig Iron", 1915-16
WILLIAMS, Ray Clark, 1962
WILLIAMS, Roy Lee, 1977-78
WILLIAMSON, Charles, 1901
WILLIAMSON, Ford Jay Montague, 1956-57
WILLIAMSON, James, R., 1900-01-02-03
WILSON, Brenard Kenric, 1975-76-77
WILSON, Mizell, 1920-21
WILSON, Thomason Henry, 1965
WILSON, Virgil, 1927-28-29
WILSON, William Whiteford, 1978
WILT, Toby Stack, 1963-64-65
WINGFIELD, Thomas Scott, 1973-74
WODKA, Mario Chester, 1955-56-57
WOLBE, Lane Edward, 1963-64-65
WOMACK, Frank, 1937
WOOD, Joseph Alexander, 1969-70-71
WOODROOF, Thomas Schram, 1954-55
WOODROOF, Thomas Schram, Jr., 1976-77-78
WOODSON, B. Palmer, 1920
WOODWARD, Michael Lee, 1978
WOOLRIDGE, W. Birch, 1896
WOOTEN, John David, 1975-76-77-7
WORDEN, Richard Lewis, 1966, Mg
WORLEY, Jack, 1936
WORLEY, Tully, 1898
WRIGHT, Michael Jay, 1975-76-77
WRIGHT, Robert Lee, 1967
WROTEN, Charles Langdon "Lang" 1933-34
WYATT, James Malcom, 1963-64-65
WYNNE, Frank O., 1906
WYRICK, Steve, 1970

Y

YEARWOOD, Jack, 1924
YEISER, Robert J., 1968
YOUNG, B., 1929, Mgr.
YOUNG, Beverly, 1931
YOUNG, Claude, 1891
YOUNG, Hoyle, 1924-25
YOUNG, William Alton, 1969-70-71
YUSK, John Francis, 1961-62

Z

ZABOROWSKI, Edward John, 1977
ZEHNDER, Charles "Buddy", 1931
ZERFOSS, Thomas B. "Tommy" 1915-16-19

THE UNIVERSITY OF ALABAMA
1831
ALABAMA

ALABAMA POLYTECHNIC INSTITUTE
RESEARCH
INSTRUCTION
EXTENSION
1872
AUBURN

University of Florida
CIVIUM IN MORIBUS REI PUBLICAE SALUS
1853
FLORIDA

UNIVERSITAS GEORGIAE
1785
GEORGIA

UNIVERSITY OF KENTUCKY
UNITED WE STAND - DIVIDED WE FALL
MDCCCLXVI
KENTUCKY